Tricia —

See you in Space!

Fred Mull
Artist
3/25/95

LIFTOFF!

An Astronaut's Dream

★ ★ ★ ★ ★ ★

Astronaut R. Mike Mullane

SILVER BURDETT PRESS

Parsippany, New Jersey

To mom and dad, who gave me wings to fly.

Published by Silver Burdett Press,
A Paramount Communications Company
299 Jefferson Road, Parsippany, NJ 07054

Designed by Marie Fitzgerald

Manufactured in Mexico

10 9 8 7 6 5 4 3 2

Library of Congress Cataloging-in-Publication Data
Mullane, R. Mike.
Liftoff!: an astronaut's dream / by R. Mike Mullane;
illustrated by Mike Wimmer. p. cm.
1. Space flight—Juvenile literature. 2. Atlantis (Space
shuttle)—Juvenile literature. 3. Mullane, R. Mike.
4. Astronauts—United States—Biography. [1. Space
flight. 2. Astronautics. 3. Mullane, R. Mike.
4. Astronauts.] I. Wimmer, Mike, ill. II. Title.
TL793.M79 1995 629.45′4—dc20
94-18122 CIP AC

ISBN 0-382-24663-2

ISBN 0-382-24664-0 (pbk.)

"*Atlantis*, the weather plane is making one last check of some clouds, and as soon as the pilot gives us a clearance, we'll continue the countdown."

The commander answers the launch director's call. "Roger. We're ready."

I hear the announcement through my "Snoopy" cap headset and think, *Please, let the weather be okay and let us launch.*

I'm mission specialist 1, seated right behind the pilot, in the cockpit of the space shuttle *Atlantis*. I'm ready for my second ride into space. I'm also miserable. I wiggle in my seat to try to get comfortable, but it's impossible. I have eighty-five pounds of equipment wrapped around my body: long underwear, pressure suit, boots, helmet, gloves, parachute, oxygen bottles, life raft, and survival harness. There are straps coming over my shoulders, between my legs, and around my waist, all holding me tightly to the steel chair. The space shuttle seats are not couches like the ones they had in the old days of the space program. Then, there were just a few astronauts. Now, there are many, and it would be too expensive to build separate couches for all their different sizes. So the seats are all the same, just flat plates of heavy steel with thin cushions covering them. They're torture to lie in and I've been lying in mine for the past four hours waiting for the weather to clear. Try tilting your chair on the floor and then lying in it for a couple of hours on your back. You'll have a sense of what an astronaut feels like waiting for launch.

And the diaper I'm wearing is soaked. Yes! A diaper! Astronauts wear diapers during launch. When you're in a spacesuit and strapped on your back to a seat, you can't get up and use the shuttle toilet. A diaper is the only solution. Actually, there are three times when an astronaut has to wear a diaper: during launch, during reentry, and during a space walk. During each of those times, it's impossible to get to the toilet. So, I'm lying in a very wet diaper, knowing why babies cry when they have wet diapers. It's gross!

I try to gain some relief from the pain by inflating my pressure suit. It expands like a big, orange balloon and gives me a little room to wiggle. Actually, it *is* a balloon. It's a balloon in the shape of a suit. We wear them during launch and reentry in case a window should break or air should leak out of the cockpit for any reason. If that ever happened, and we weren't wearing pressure suits, our blood would boil inside our skin and we would die. The suit has nothing to do with the g-force pressure of the rocket

4

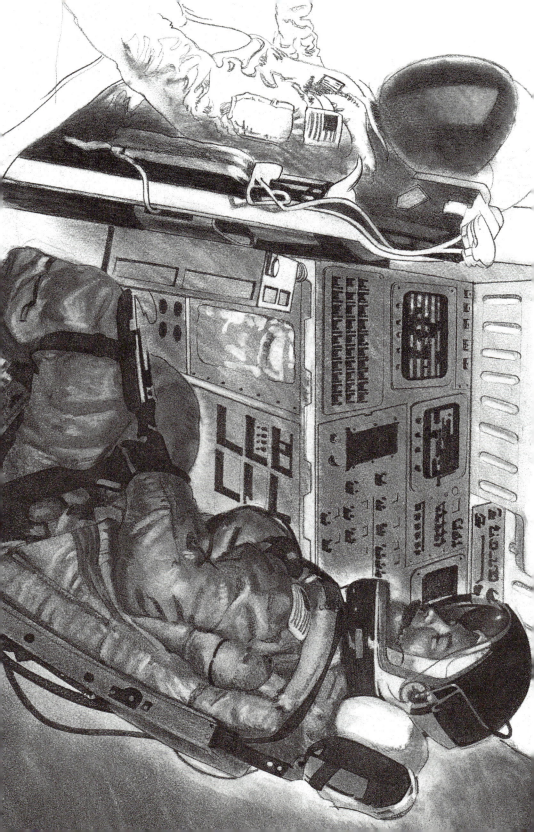

pushing us. Rather, the word *pressure* refers to the need to keep air pressure on our skin so our blood doesn't boil.

"*Atlantis*, the weather pilot just reported that the clouds are no longer a problem. We'll be coming out of the hold in five seconds . . . four . . . three . . . two . . . one . . . T-minus nine minutes and counting."

"Roger, we see the clock running."

I silently shout for joy, *Finally, we're counting down to launch!* Each of the three computer screens has a digital countdown clock flickering toward zero.

Humming, whirring, flashing electronic boxes are now checking everything about the shuttle and sending the information, the *data*, to the Mission Control team. The thought of that wonderful team of men and women watching over us erases a little of the fear that we feel.

Astronauts get the "glory" part of a space mission. You see them floating around the cockpit and doing space walks. You see their pictures in the newspapers and the president shaking their hands. But have you ever thought about the rest of the NASA team? It takes thousands of people working together as a team to accomplish a space mission. Nobody can do it alone. It's just like a football or soccer team. The person who scores the winning goal is the one who gets the cheers. But did he or she win the game alone? No. Somebody else passed the ball. Somebody else blocked. Nobody wins the game and nobody flies into space without a lot of help. It's a team effort. Everybody depends on everybody else.

"Okay, review your emergency escape procedures."

The order is from the commander. He wants us to look over the procedures we would have to follow in case there is an emergency before launch. Remember, we are sitting on top of four million pounds of dangerous fuel. If something went wrong and there was a fire before liftoff, we would want to shut off the engines and get away as quickly as possible.

I look at the checklist of emergency procedures that is stuck with Velcro on the back of the pilot's seat. It tells me the steps I would need to follow to release my seat belts, oxygen hoses, and communications cords. Then, it says I should crawl from the cockpit, run across the launch pad platform (called the *gantry*), and jump into a basket hanging two hundred feet above the ground. As I read the steps, I think, *I hope I never have to do this!* It would be an awesome ride, like something out of an Indiana Jones movie, but it would also be very scary.

Just imagine for a moment that it's happening to you. . . .

"*Atlantis!* We see a fuel leak! Get out! Mode 1 egress! Mode 1 egress!" *Egress* means "exit." The launch team has detected an emergency that might cause the shuttle to explode, and they want you to escape using the basket.

Because you've just reviewed your emergency procedures, it takes you only a moment to release all the connections that hold you to the seat. Next, you roll off your seat and crash onto the back instrument panel. Remember, the shuttle is standing on its tail, so the back wall of the cockpit is the "floor."

There's no room to stand, so you crawl to the side hatch.

In ten seconds you have it open and crawl out onto the gantry. Water is everywhere! What's going on? Then you remember. The launch team has turned on the water sprinklers to help protect you from any fire.

After making certain that the rest of the crew is out of the shuttle, you run through the water spray and jump into an escape basket. The ground is two hundred feet straight down and the basket swings and bounces. You think, *This is the scariest thing I've ever done.*

BAM! You smash your fist onto a paddle that cuts a cord and releases the basket. This begins your escape from the launch pad. You can't go down the stairs or the elevator. It would take too long. Besides, if there were a fire at the bottom of the gantry, running down the stairs or taking an elevator would put you right in the middle of it. The escape basket takes you to the ground while moving you *away* from the rocket. It slides on a steel cable that stretches sideways a thousand feet from the launch pad.

What a ride! A loud hiss comes from the cable as the basket accelerates. The ground rushes toward you. If you crash into it, you'll be killed. What's going to stop you?

WHAM! Just before the basket reaches the ground, it slaps into a net hung between two poles. The net drags your basket to a stop.

But you're still not safe. Even though you're a thousand feet from the launch pad, a big explosion could kill you. Get going!

You jump from the basket and run into a nearby underground bunker. Or maybe you decide the danger is so great that even the bunker wouldn't protect you. So you get in an old Armored Personnel Carrier (called an APC for short, it looks something like a tank), and drive away. NASA parks an APC near the bunker for that purpose.

Good job! It took you only four minutes and thirty-five seconds to unstrap from your seat, get out of the shuttle, run to the basket, and slide down the cable.

My countdown continues. The clock shows T-minus six minutes.

I check that all of my straps are tight. There will be a lot of vibration during launch. I double-check that my parachute is attached. After the solid-fueled boosters burn out and the liquid-fueled engines stop, the space shuttle is a glider. In a launch emergency, there's always the possibility that we might not be able to glide to a runway for landing. In that case we would bail out, using the parachutes attached to our backs. After floating into the ocean, we would get in small life rafts that are also folded up and clipped to our backs. We hope we could stay alive long enough for a helicopter to reach us.

"*Atlantis*, start the APUs."

The call comes from the launch director. The countdown has reached T-minus five minutes, and it's time to start the hydraulic motors that will steer the three giant rocket engines. APUs stands for Auxiliary Power Units. Calling every piece of equipment by its complete name would be tongue twisting, so astronauts and the rest of the NASA team use abbreviations like APU, IMU, EPS, MPS, MECO, and MLS. We learn hundreds of them during our training.

The APU switches are on the pilot's side, so I watch him follow the checklist. Everything an astronaut does is written on a checklist. The walls, ceiling, and instrument panel are papered with them. Why do we use checklists? You never see anybody on *Star Trek* using a checklist. But *Star Trek* is make-believe. Nobody on Captain Picard's *Enterprise* is really going to die if he or she makes a mistake. But in the real world, a mistake could threaten an astronaut's life. There are nearly two thousand switches and controls in the shuttle cockpit, so a mistake is certainly possible. Even though we practice the mission until we know what every one of those switches does, we never trust our memories. We always do things by following our checklists.

The APU motors are at the back of the shuttle, but as they start I can feel their vibrations in the cockpit. For the first time, I get the sensation that the machine is alive. It's like some giant beast stirring from its sleep.

No longer do I think about my backache and wet diaper. Now, I'm scared. In just a few minutes *Atlantis* will lift off in a thunderous cloud of fire and smoke. With such enormous power, there is a lot that can go wrong and put us in danger. The rocket has many parts. It's a very complicated machine. So, in these last few minutes before launch, I'm scared. My heart pounds inside my chest. I can feel it in my throat . . . THUD . . . THUD . . . THUD . . . like I've just run a race. I try to swallow, but my mouth is dry. Fear does that to you. It makes your heart pound and your mouth feel like it's full of cotton.

"*Atlantis*, close visors."

"Roger. Closing visors."

The countdown has reached T-minus two minutes, and the checklist says to close our helmet visors. These are the clear plastic coverings on the faces of the helmets. Before I close mine, I pull a drink container from a Velcro patch on the wall and suck down a few swallows of water through a plastic straw. The container has the same design as the ones we use during orbit, a foil pouch with a straw at the end. I clip the straw closed, reattach the container to the Velcro, and lock my visor down. A cool flow of oxygen swirls around my face. If a window should break during launch, now I'm completely protected.

The beast awakens some more. I can feel it shaking. The computers are making a final check of the steering controls, causing the rocket to sway back and forth. The bottoms of the two solid-fueled rocket motors are held to the launch pad by eight giant threaded nuts, so I know we can't fall over. Still, the shaking is another indication that the shuttle is readying itself to fly. My fear increases and my breathing becomes faster. I can hear it inside the sealed helmet . . . SSSSSSSSSS . . . SSSSSSSSSS . . . SSSSSSSSSS . . . as air is inhaled and exhaled.

The movies always make it look like astronauts are never afraid. But that's not true. We know flying into space is dangerous and there's a chance we could be killed. So we're scared. At the same time, though, our hearts are ready to explode with happiness. Many of us have dreamed all our lives of flying into space. Now, that dream is about to come true, so we're joyous. In a small way, getting on a roller coaster gives you the same feeling. You're afraid, but you're happy, too.

"One minute."

The instruments begin to change as the engine system prepares to start. Green, glowing digits on the computers flicker with new data. Meters move. The beast is more alive than ever, and my heart pounds deeper and faster.

I think of my family, of my wife and my three teenage children. They are three miles away on the roof of the LCC, the Launch Control Center. I know they are more scared than any of us inside the rocket. It may be *Atlantis* standing on the launch pad, but in their minds they can only see *Challenger*. That was the space shuttle that blew up in 1986 and killed its crew. I know my family fears the same thing will happen to me.

It's always much harder to watch somebody you love do something dangerous than it is to be the one in danger. Can you remember when you were learning to ride a bike? I'll bet you were very scared the first time you wobbled along without training wheels. But I know your parents were more scared because they were afraid you would get hurt. In this final minute before the engines start, I know it's that way with my wife and children. I know they are clutching each other and praying for my safety. I love them even more for their courage to stand on that roof and watch *Atlantis* take me to my dream.

"T-minus ten seconds. Go for main engine start."

Atlantis's computers are ready to start the engines.

There's nothing to do now but watch the instruments. Astronauts don't really fly the shuttle into orbit. Things happen too fast for an astronaut to control, so we have to depend on the computers. We watch the instruments while they steer us into orbit. Only if something went terribly wrong would we try to fly the shuttle the way a pilot flies an airplane.

"T-minus nine . . . eight . . ."

"Seven . . . six . . . main engine start."

The three liquid-fueled engines ignite, and there is a deafening noise in the cockpit. A growling, wrenching vibration shakes us. I have to force myself to keep watching the instruments. It's like trying to read a book on a theme park ride. The noise and vibration and the thrill and fear make it impossible to concentrate.

"Five . . . four . . . three . . . "

The countdown continues while *Atlantis's* computers check that the liquid-fueled engines are working okay. The three liquid-fueled engines are started early because they can be turned off if something is wrong, just as a car engine can be turned off. But the solid-fueled boosters on the sides of the shuttle are like bottle rockets on the Fourth of July. Once they're started, they cannot be turned off. Only at the very last moment, when the countdown reaches zero, will they be ignited.

"Two . . . one . . . liftoff!"

The solid-fueled rocket boosters ignite, the threaded nuts holding them to the pad explode into pieces, and the giant machine blasts from the launch pad. The noise is incredible! Only because I'm wearing a helmet can I hear Mission Control talking to us. The engines are so powerful that I'm shoved backwards into my seat by a force one-and-a-half times as strong as gravity. It makes my body and everything I'm wearing seem to weigh an extra hundred pounds.

"Roll program!" the commander shouts into his microphone. *Atlantis* is rolling to the right to aim its trajectory over the ocean.

"Throttle down!" The commander sees that our engines are automatically reducing power. *Atlantis* is accelerating too fast and there is a danger that the thick atmosphere will tear it apart. The computers prevent this from happening by commanding the engines to pull back their power.

Shock waves form on the nose and wings and add to the shaking. *Atlantis* is going through the sound barrier. In just forty seconds the huge engines and solid-fueled rocket boosters have pushed a four-and-a-half-*million*-pound machine straight up to the speed of sound! Just imagine the incredible power needed to do that. The rushing sound of supersonic air howls around the machine. It's louder than any airplane you've ever heard. The vibrations increase. My eyes skip from instrument to instrument. Is everything still okay? Will all this shaking damage something? Will our air leak out? Will the engines quit? Will they explode? I

worry about everything. But the instruments tell me that *Atlantis* is *nominal*, that everything is okay.

A cloud zooms into our windshield and disappears behind us. Once again, I can feel my body being squeezed backwards. It's happening because the engines are returning to full power. We're above the thick atmosphere and don't have to worry anymore about the air pressure tearing *Atlantis* apart. The ride is smoothing out.

There is no line that you pass where all the air is below and space is above. The atmosphere just keeps getting thinner and thinner, and as it does, the sky changes from blue to black. It becomes as black as night. Sirius, the brightest star, appears. It's so strange to see a black sky and a bright star while sunlight is filling the cockpit, but that's what I see from the shuttle windows.

"PC less than fifty!" The numbers are flashing on our computer, and the commander calls them to Mission Control. The pressure inside the solid-fueled rocket motors has decreased to fifty pounds per square inch. That means the boosters are nearly out of fuel.

BANG! WHOOSH!

A loud bang shakes the cockpit, and a flash of yellow fire covers the windshield.

Has something exploded? Is there an emergency?

No. The noise and fire are from the release of the giant boosters. They have burned out, and small rockets on their noses and tails have blown them away from the shuttle. Parachutes will lower them into the ocean where tugboats will pick them up so they can be used over again.

As the boosters fall away, total silence comes to the cockpit. It's a silence as empty as the sky in our windows. We are so high now that the air is too thin for sound to be able to travel. We can't hear any noise from our three liquid-fueled engines or hear any air rushing by the cockpit. The ride becomes as smooth as glass. The only feeling we have of being thrust into space is an increasing force on our bodies. As the engines draw the liquid fuel out of the big orange belly tank and burn it, the rocket gets lighter and lighter. It goes faster and faster, and we get squeezed backwards into our seats. Imagine being in a dark, quiet room with an invisible hand pushing on your chest. That's what it feels like.

"*Atlantis*, you're two-engine TAL."

"Roger, Houston."

The call from Mission Control means that we are now high enough and going fast enough that if one of our engines quits, we could fly across the Atlantic Ocean and make an emergency landing in Europe. If that happened, it would be a thirty-five-minute flight. It takes an airplane seven hours, but in a space shuttle you fly across the ocean in just thirty-five minutes!

"*Atlantis*, you're negative return."

"Roger, Houston. Negative return."

We always repeat to Mission Control what they tell us, so they know we've heard them correctly. This latest call, "negative return," means that we're now too far away and going too fast to be able to make an emergency landing back at the Kennedy Space Center. Now, if anything goes wrong and we can't reach orbit, we have to fly straight ahead to an emergency field in Africa or Europe.

One of the crew members is a rookie, and he lets out a cheer. It seems strange, doesn't it, that an astronaut would cheer while this dangerous ride is still going on? But he has good reason to celebrate. *Atlantis* has just passed fifty miles altitude. What's so special about that? The official definition of an astronaut is anybody who has traveled at least fifty miles above the earth. The man cheering is a rookie, so this is the first time he's ever gotten high enough to be an "official" astronaut.

"*Atlantis,* you're press to MECO."

"Roger, Houston. Press to MECO."

Now the space shuttle is going so fast and is so high that if one of its engines quits, we could still make it to MECO, Main Engine Cut-Off. We could limp into orbit on two engines.

Higher! Higher and faster! The velocity meter shows our incredible speeds . . . thirteen . . . fifteen . . . seventeen . . . twenty times the speed of sound!

Atlantis is leveling its nose, silently tearing into the black of space. Throughout the entire flight, it slowly has gone from pointing straight up to being nearly level with the earth.

Twenty-one . . . twenty-two . . . twenty-three times the speed of sound!

My heart is thumping wildly. But it's not from fear. Now, it's from the thrill of the adventure. Once again, I'm going into space! Once again, the joy of having a dream come true is sweeping over me! I want to scream my happiness! I want to shout for all the world to hear! I'm going into space! I'm an astronaut!

3

I can still see myself as a small child, dreaming about flying. It was almost as if I was born with that dream. Perhaps it was the influence of my father, who had flown on bombers during World War II and who was flying on Air Force transport planes as I was growing up. He often took my brothers and sister and me to see airplanes. He would take us into the cockpit and let us sit in the pilot's seat and touch the controls. I would grab the steering wheel (it's called the *yoke*) and for a few moments pretend I was flying. Was it this early fun with airplanes that gave me the dream of flight? Of course I can never know for sure, but in my dimmest, most distant memories, my dream was to fly. I was in love with the sky and everything in it.

Before I could read, I drew pictures of swirling, diving airplanes with dashed pencil lines coming from their noses and wings. The dashes were the machine-gun fire. In my imagination, I was in the cockpit of that fighter, shooting an enemy plane from the sky. My childhood was a time when there was great fear in the world. World War II had ended, but the Cold War had replaced it. Everybody was afraid that Russian bombers would drop atomic bombs on American cities. In school we practiced air raid drills and hid under our desks. I imagined that someday I would be in a fighter jet and would shoot down Russian bombers. I thought it would be fun to be in combat. Many years later, in the skies over Vietnam, I would learn a much different reality.

But as a child, when I went to bed on Christmas Eve, the only reality was toys. I prayed that Santa would bring me models of the fastest jet fighter planes. Even their names made my imagination fly at light speed: *Starfighter, Super Sabre, Shooting Star, Thunder Chief, Delta Dagger.*

For my birthdays, I wanted balsa wood gliders and airplane coloring books. I made Tinker-Toy airplanes and Erector-Set airplanes and paper airplanes and would run around the house holding them in my hand and making roaring sounds like a dive bomber. I used cloth and thread from my mother's sewing cabinet to make parachutes for my little plastic pilots.

As I grew older, my interest in flying and the sky intensified. I began to design my own gliders powered by rubber bands. Some flew magnificently, soaring silently across the nearby New Mexican desert. I would chase my creation and try to grab it before it ran out of power and crashed into a tumbleweed. Other designs crashed as soon as I released them. Hours of work would end up in a pile of splintered balsa wood and fabric covering. Back in my room, I would make a change and try again. I didn't realize it then, but I was already learning something very important to a scientist and engineer. I was learning how to experiment. I was learning how to ask a question and then design a test to find the answer.

Some experiments were pretty dumb. One day, I decided to make my own parachute by just holding a sheet over my head and jumping off a high pillar on my grandmother's porch. Needless to say, the experiment failed. I ended up with a broken leg. Dumb! Dumb! Dumb! Don't ever do experiments that put your health and life at risk.

School brightened my dream of flight. I didn't like everything about school. I hated tests and homework and counted the days to summer vacation. But there was a lot that I did like about the classroom. I loved learning about the sky. I loved learning about the weather, about the clouds and lightning, why it rained and why the wind blew. I built my own weather station. Paper cups on a twisted piece of coat hanger wire served as an anemometer (a wind speed instrument). To measure humidity I used a hair from my mom's hairbrush. Did you know that human hair grows and shrinks as the humidity changes? I put a thermometer outside and built a rain gauge. I learned to recognize the different types of clouds: cirrus, cumulus, stratus, and nimbus. I would spend hours watching thunderstorms form over the Albuquerque mountains. What magnificent creations of Nature! Their tops would be churned into giant, white cauliflowers by the summer heat. Skirts of purple rain would gather at their base. Jagged, blue-white forks of lightning would crackle through them and send booms of thunder sweeping across the desert. I loved the sound of that thunder. It was the voice of the sky, calling to me.

Weather fascinated me, but astronomy stole my soul. My most vivid grade-school memory is the day I was first told about our solar system. There were other worlds out there! My imagination bubbled like a volcano! What would it be like to be on another planet? What was Venus like? Mars? Could there be other beings out there? I wanted to know everything about the solar system and the rest of the universe. Before the day was out I had memorized the names of all the planets. I took my science book home and read and reread everything in it about astronomy.

I began my astronomy experiments. First, I decided that I would map the universe. I would plot where every star was located. I took a tablet and a pencil and sat in my front yard and put a dot on the tablet to mark each star I could see. When I got inside and looked at my tablet it was just a crazy bunch of dots. It didn't look anything like the real sky.

Then, I tried to build a telescope by taping a magnifying glass to the end of a toilet paper tube. It didn't work. It made everything look farther away and upside down. But the important thing was that I tried. I experimented. I wanted to know.

Some experiments did work. After learning in class that the earth rotates about an axis that points at the North

Star, I wanted to see for myself. I used my dad's camera to make a time exposure of the northern sky at night. The photos showed a bunch of circles. Those were the streaks of starlight the camera had recorded as the earth turned. It was proof! I felt like Galileo!

Other incredible stories of the heavens came from my teacher and my science books. The starlight that I could see was thousands and thousands of years old. I was looking at a time machine. Cave men were hurling rocks at woolly mammoths when some of the starlight reaching my dad's camera had first left its source. Incredible! What would it have been like to have ridden that beam of light? What would it have been like to have streaked through trillions and trillions of miles of black space? Imagine the sights you would have seen! Imagine the swirling galaxies and planets and moons and asteroids you would have passed. I wanted to take that trip! And I did, time and time again in my dream of flight.

What I wanted most for my eleventh Christmas was a telescope. I imagined myself seeing the things in my science book, the cloud of space dust shaped like a horse's head, and remote galaxies glowing like giant pinwheels. With a telescope I would have a machine that could fly me deeper into space.

Every night for two months leading up to Christmas 1956, I grabbed the Sears catalog and dreamed of its riches. In the past it had been the pages of bicycles and BB guns that I had drooled over. But not this year. Now, it was the pages of telescopes. Sleek beauties with white barrels and mahogany tripods captured my eye. I can see them now as if the pages were in front of me. They were awesome time machines fueled by nothing but light.

On Christmas morning, my wish came true. Standing next to the tree was a telescope with my name on it! I didn't want to look at any other presents. For the first time in my life, I wanted Christmas day to end . . . immediately! I wanted the sun to set and the stars to rise. But the earth's rotation seemed to stop. Time crawled. I busied myself by shining the barrel of the scope. It was brand new and didn't have a speck of dirt on it, but I polished and polished until the white was as gleaming as the stars it would reveal.

Finally, the sun disappeared below the western horizon and . . . a STAR! The evening star had come out! In seconds I had focused my telescope on the tiny point of light. It looked like a small half-moon. Then I remembered: The evening star isn't a star at all. It's a planet. It's Venus. I was seeing Venus! I stared at it and let my imagination fly through the lens, out the tube, and into orbit around the planet. What would the thick clouds look like? Would there be breaks in them so you could see the ground? What would Venus's surface look like? Would there be strange plants or other creatures on it?

A half-moon rose above the mountains. I turned my telescope to it and gasped. It wasn't smooth, the way it looks to the naked eye. Now, hundreds of rugged craters and mountains were visible. The peaks cast razor-sharp shadows and seemed close enough to touch. I had seen many science-fiction movies where men and women had

gone to the moon. That night, with my eye to the telescope, it was easy for me to believe somebody, someday would get there. I wanted it to be me.

Other bright "stars" caught my attention, and I discovered Jupiter and its necklace of moons. I could only see the five or six brightest moons, but it was enough to make me think that we earthlings had been cheated. How come we ended up with only one moon? Wouldn't our sky be much more fun with five moons, or ten, or fifteen?

The rings of Saturn sent my heart into a new flutter of excitement. It was just like the picture in my science book, with a tilted halo surrounding a yellowish ball. Another glorious string of moons laced it.

As the night wore on, I swung my telescope to look at star after star, hoping to find one that was really a distant galaxy. Nothing ever looked like a glowing pinwheel. The telescope was too weak to see any detail across those vast distances. Still, I wasn't disappointed. I felt closer to everything I looked at, including those tiny points of light. Were there planets in orbit about those suns? Was there life out there? Was there some alien child standing in his or her front yard looking at our sun through a telescope and wondering the same thing?

After many hours, I finally folded my treasure and put it in its box. Then, with the cold night air biting at my fingers and ears, I stood for a moment and stared at the dome of the heavens. Venus had set. Saturn and Jupiter and the moon would be up for many more hours. Shooting stars streaked to their deaths in glowing trails of white and orange. I watched and I wished. I wished as only an eleven-year-old can wish. I wished I could fly into space.

"*Atlantis*, you're single-engine press to MECO."

The call from Mission Control means that we are now traveling so fast and are so high that even if two of our engines failed, we could still make it into orbit on the last engine.

We're upside down and, for the first time, Earth appears in our windows. It's an ocean-blue world sprinkled with dazzling white clouds. A border of black space makes the blue and white colors even more intense. It's more beautiful than anything I have ever seen on Earth. It's more beautiful than desert thunderstorms and new-fallen snow and rainbows and waterfalls and everything else I have ever called beautiful.

But we don't see the earth as a ball. Only the astronauts who traveled to the moon have been far enough away to see planet Earth as a ball. For shuttle astronauts the earth is hugely close, like an enormous blue balloon put right up to your face. From our orbit altitude of about two hundred and seventy miles, we can see that the horizon is curved, but we don't see a complete circle.

We're in the final minute of powered flight. Most of our fuel is gone, and *Atlantis's* acceleration crushes us into our seats. We hit two times the force of gravity. Then two and a half. Then three g's. With all the equipment on my body, I now weigh seven hundred and twenty pounds! The air is being squeezed from my lungs, and I struggle to breathe. Talking is done in short grunts. It reminds me of the times when I was a kid wrestling with my brothers and one of them ended up sitting on my chest. I could hardly breathe, just like now. But the force isn't as bad as you see in the science-fiction movies, where it looks like the astronauts' skin is being peeled off their faces.

"The engines are throttling."

The pilot grunts the observation. Though you would think the space shuttle could withstand anything, it really is a fragile machine. It can't take more than three times the force of gravity, or it would tear itself apart. So the engines automatically begin to reduce their power to keep us at three-g's.

On the computer screen I can see the numbers counting down to engine stop . . . three . . . two . . . one . . . zero! The crushing force on my chest is instantly gone. The engines are off. They have pushed *Atlantis* to twenty-five times the speed of sound, or 17,500 miles per hour!

I'm weightless! My arms float up. My body floats underneath the seat belt. Tethered checklists float on the ends of cords like snakes rising to a charmer's flute. The drink container that I used earlier has shaken loose during launch, and now it floats in front of my face. I grab it and stick it to the wall. Then, my eye is caught by something moving, and I turn to see the most amazing sight. A mosquito! It must have flown aboard when the hatch was open. It looks hilarious trying to fly in weightlessness. It's upside down and then right-side up and then turning in a loop.

Here we are just ten seconds in orbit, and we already have an emergency. A loose mosquito is definitely an emergency! I laugh to myself. We've trained for hundreds of hours in simulators to be ready for every possible event. We have stacks of checklists and boxes of tools to get us out of any kind of trouble. But we don't have a can of bug spray! I try to whack our stowaway with my hand, but it flies away.

For a moment, the cockpit is very still and quiet. Then . . . BOOM! BOOM! BOOM! *Atlantis* shivers and shakes. The empty fuel tank is jettisoned, and the commander fires the shuttle's small maneuvering rockets to move us away from the giant container. The tank will burn up in the atmosphere like a meteor.

The shuttle itself would follow the same trajectory and end up in the Indian Ocean if we didn't do something. We're not quite in orbit yet. We need just a little more speed. So the commander fires our OMS (Orbital Maneuvering System) engines to make the final push into orbit. For a minute, we are all shoved back into our seats with a small g-force. Then the two OMS engines shut down and weightlessness returns for good. We're in orbit.

I unsnap my seat belt and remember to use my fingers to propel myself. Fingers allow for better control than legs do. Most of the time legs are in the way in space. They were designed for walking, which is impossible in weightlessness. About the only thing we use legs for is to hold ourselves steady when we want to work on something. We have canvas loops taped to the floor. By sliding our feet under these loops we can have both hands free. So legs aren't really important. In fact, someday I'm sure people who have lost the use of their legs from injury or disease will live and work in space like anybody else. There will be no wheelchairs in space.

Our first real problem develops. A crew member pulls a plastic bag from his pocket and vomits. Nobody understands why, but many astronauts get sick in weightlessness. Even astronauts who have never had motion sickness on Earth have gotten sick in space. And others who do suffer motion sickness on Earth have never been sick in space. It's a big mystery. But those who are bothered by the sickness are usually over it in one or two days.

As you might imagine, throwing up in space is messy. But it's also dangerous. If you are sick enough to throw up, you are also sick enough to make a mistake. And if you were doing a space walk, vomiting could even kill you. You wouldn't be able to get the fluid away from your face, and you could choke to death. Or it could plug up the oxygen circulation system, and you could suffocate. That's one reason why NASA never plans a space walk before the third day in orbit. That way astronauts have time to get over any sickness they might have.

For the next several hours everybody follows the check-list to get the shuttle ready for orbit operations. The commander programs the computers. The pilot shuts off the APUs. The mission specialists open the cargo bay doors and turn on the toilet. Finally, we can change our clothes and take off our diapers. Because of the long, long delay before launch, I notice that I have diaper rash!

After going to the bathroom, I float upstairs to check out the shuttle's robot arm. This is a military mission, and my job will be to use the arm to pick up a giant, secret satellite and release it into space. To do this, I will use two hand controls that look like the joysticks on video games. With these, I will be able to "fly" the arm almost like a pilot flies an airplane. I will steer the end of the arm over a spike on the satellite and squeeze a trigger that wraps a cable around the spike. Then, I will be able to lift the satellite up. But that's on tomorrow's checklist. For now, I just use the two joysticks to lift the robot arm from its cradle. Then I float downstairs to help with the experiments.

Many of the experiments are designed to help scientists better understand how the human body adjusts to weight-lessness. We check our vision by looking into a box that has an eye test. We chew on cotton balls and put them in test tubes so that doctors can later analyze our saliva. We take measurements of our calves and thighs and find that we have lost several inches. It isn't because we have lost weight, though. It's because the extra body fluid that used to be held in our legs by gravity is now equally spread through our bodies. Our legs have gotten skinnier, but our chests and faces have gotten fatter. That's where the fluid has gone.

We also measure our height. Would you believe that we are almost two inches taller than we were on Earth? What's happening? The reason we've grown taller is that the vertebrae in our spines are no longer crunched together by gravity. They have spread apart, lengthened our spines, and made us taller.

Another experiment involves testing how much space radiation astronauts are exposed to. This experiment includes a human skull! The person it belonged to willed his body to science. Doctors took the skull and put a device that measures radiation inside it. Then they covered the bone with a plastic face. With it, they are able to tell how much space radiation penetrates a live astronaut's skull and reaches the brain. Using this data doctors can design radiation shields to protect astronauts who are in space for long periods of time. Too much radiation could cause sickness or even death.

Another mission specialist and I decide to "borrow" the skull for a minute to have some fun. I get in one of our sleeping bags and pull my head below the opening. The other mission specialist then tapes the skull to the top of the bag so that it looks like the head of whoever is in the bag. The disguise is really scary. The face of the skull has evil-looking eyes, and there are two bolts sticking up from the back of the head that look like horns. Even Captain

Kirk would have run if he had seen this thing floating around his spaceship!

Ever so quietly, my accomplice floats me to the upper deck where the rest of the crew are working. I have my arms through the armholes in the sides of the sleeping bag. Carefully, I push myself to float to the back of an unsuspecting crew member. Hovering behind him, I breathe loudly and slowly, making a deep, raspy, evil sound. The victim turns to investigate and . . . aieeeeeeeeeeeeeeeeeeeeee! He screams as I grab him! It's the attack of the horned alien from Planet X!

Later, we stuff the sleeping bag with clothes and buckle our alien onto the toilet seat to surprise another crew member. As you can see, astronauts like to joke around, too.

After many hours of conducting experiments, Mission Control tells us that we can go to sleep. Most of the crew tie their sleeping bags downstairs to get away from the sunlight. There are no windows in the lower deck, so we can sleep in the dark. Upstairs, the sun will be rising and setting every forty-five minutes, making it hard to sleep. I want to stay awake awhile longer, so I tie my sleeping bag under the windows that are on top of the aft cockpit. Then I unpack my portable tape player and put on headphones to listen to music. NASA provides the tape player and we are each allowed to bring six music tapes. Some astronauts bring country or rock or easy listening music, but my choice is music by classical composers like Beethoven, Pachelbel, and Bach. I like the slow majesty of their music. To me, it better fits the silent flight of an Earth-orbiting space shuttle and the grand sights passing below.

With these soothing melodies in my ear, I get in my sleeping bag and watch our beautiful world slowly glide by. The shuttle is flying upside down, so the windows on top of the cockpit are facing the earth. It's like being in a hammock with the world in your face.

The other crew members are asleep, and Mission Control is watching the shuttle data to make certain nothing goes wrong. Gravity is holding us in orbit so nobody needs to "steer" the shuttle.

The only sound in the cockpit is the soft whoosh of the fans that cool the electronic equipment. My mind struggles with the strange reality. It's so different from anything I've ever known on Earth. I'm traveling almost five miles each second! At that speed I could fly from Los Angeles to New York in just ten minutes! Yet our motion makes no sound. Always in the past, when I've been traveling fast on a bicycle or in a car or on a train or plane, the faster it went, the louder the noise. Sometimes—like in a fighter airplane, for instance—there was lots of noise. But now, there's no noise. Nothing. No air rushes by the cabin. No engines roar. Nothing!

Adding to the strangeness of the situation is that I'm floating inside my sleeping bag with no force on my body. You don't need a bed or a floor to sleep in weightlessness. The air is your mattress. In fact, the only reason we use bags is so we don't float around and bang into something. You could actually sleep by clipping a tether to your belt loop, hooking it someplace, and just floating on the end of the line like a kite. Some astronauts have done that.

But I'm in my sleeping bag, listening to Beethoven's violins, floating in an absolute stillness, watching the beautiful Earth. The sight is the very definition of the word *beautiful*.

Many kids ask me if astronauts watch television on the space shuttle. No, we don't. We don't receive ground television. But even if we did, we would never watch it. For entertainment everyone does exactly what I'm doing. They watch Earth. If you were up there, you would do the same thing, too.

I feast my eyes on the glory of Earth. The primary color is blue, for we live on a water planet. What would aliens from a strange desert world who have never seen water think of ours? Would they assume that any intelligent earth life must live in all that "blue stuff"? Would they land their flying saucer in the ocean? Maybe at the bottom of the oceans there are flying saucers with drowned aliens inside.

The clouds thrill me as much as they did when I watched them as a kid. In some places they are scattered across the ocean like little puffs of popcorn. In other places they completely cover the earth. There are great milky swirls of low pressure areas, like the swirls you see going down the bathtub drain. Feathery mare's-tails (cirrus clouds) look like they are painted on the blue sea. Thunderstorms are another joy. Even from my great height, it's obvious they rule the sky. Sometimes there are lines of them, standing shoulder to shoulder like warrior chiefs

wearing great feathered headdresses. At other times they are just scattered across the ocean. But always their tops are smeared into long, pointed anvils by invisible jet streams.

I turn my attention to the sky. It is absolutely, totally black. And the sun is absolutely, totally white. You can't look directly at the sun, but in your side vision you can see its brilliant white rays. Unlike sunlight seen from Earth, it has no yellow in it.

There's also a quarter-moon looking very lonely in the huge blackness. It doesn't appear any bigger than it does when you see it from Earth. Remember, the moon is 240,000 miles away. We're only three hundred miles closer! That's like being on one side of the classroom looking at a globe on the far side, and then taking a one-inch step toward the globe. It doesn't look any bigger. You can think of an orbiting space shuttle as having taken just a tiny, tiny step toward the moon.

The brightest planets are also visible from the cockpit windows. Even though I'm still on the day side of Earth, I can see Jupiter and Saturn. If Venus were up, I would be able to see it also. But the planets look no different than they look from Earth. They appear as bright stars. They are tens of *millions* of miles away, so being three hundred miles closer doesn't make any difference.

Sirius, the brightest star, is also visible. It's just a steady point of light. There's no twinkle to it as you see on Earth. That's because its light has reached me without going through air. It's the atmosphere that causes stars to twinkle.

But Sirius is the only star I can see. Why? Where are the others? I don't see them because there is too much sunlight reflecting off Earth and the shuttle. That causes the pupils of my eyes to close and cuts off the dim light that is coming from the other stars. They're out there, but I can't see them in daylight. It's just like trying to see stars from the middle of a city. You can't. You have to go into the country away from lights so the pupils of your eyes will open wide and take in the dim starlight. So now you can laugh when you see science-fiction TV programs, like *Star Trek*, showing stars out the windows during daylight.

Silently, *Atlantis* glides eastward and the sun sinks behind it. Below, the tallest thunderstorms cast shadows that are hundreds of miles long. Now comes the most beautiful sight of all. As the sun sets, the earth's atmosphere acts like a prism and splits the light into its individual colors. For a moment, after the sun is completely down, the horizon is outlined with a brilliant rainbow of colors: red, orange, yellow, turquoise, blue, and purple. The colors get dimmer and dimmer as we fly farther and farther to the east. Finally they blink out. Then, there's no trace of the earth. We're swallowed by the black. It's as if we've flown into a deep, deep cave.

I remove my headphones, yawn, and close my eyes. It's time to go to sleep. But it's hard to turn off my brain. I'm worried about tomorrow. The team is depending on me. I will have to use the robot arm to grab our secret payload and lift it from the shuttle's cargo bay. What if I'm not good enough? What if I make a mistake? What if I can't do it? Back in Houston, I practiced a thousand times in a simulator that looked like a video game. I also practiced lifting giant helium balloons out of a simulated shuttle cargo bay with a simulated mechanical arm. The helium made the balloons weightless, as our cargo will be. But practicing with video games and balloons is one thing. Working with a real arm and a real cargo is something else. One mistake, and I could ruin the mission. I feel like the field goal kicker who is warming up on the sidelines of a football game. The team has gotten the ball within range of the goal. They've done all they can do. Time is running out. The kicker will have just one chance to win the game.

I'm like that kicker. The members of my team, the NASA team, have done all they can. They have put me in position. Tomorrow, I'm going to have one chance to win. With that thought comes a nibble of fear. I don't want to let the team down. I don't want to let the nation down. Everyone is counting on me.

But in the end my exhaustion overcomes the worry, and I fall asleep.

I awaken early for the big day and sail headfirst to the lower deck. The rest of the crew are still asleep. What a strange sight that is! Like bats, some of them are on the wall floating upside down in their sleeping bags. One is asleep on the ceiling. And all of them have their arms floating outward from their chests. That's what happens when you fall asleep in weightlessness. Your arms float in front of you. It looks weird, as if the crew is in suspended animation.

It's time to use the bathroom, so I slip behind a curtain and face the monstrosity that is our toilet. Except for the seat, it doesn't look anything like your toilet at home. For one thing, it has no water in it. In weightlessness, water wouldn't flush, so you need something else to carry the waste away. Our toilet uses airflow.

There are several switches and valves on its front, and on each side are things that look like handles. These are really "thigh-holders," bars to twist over your legs to keep you from floating off the toilet seat. You don't want that to happen! Then, there's a long, flexible hose coming up from the front of the toilet. That's the urinal. In the shuttle, liquid and solid waste go into different places. The solid waste goes into an opening on the top of the toilet, while urine goes into the hose. There is even a separate container for toilet paper. You can't put paper down our toilet. And there are several checklists on the bathroom wall to remind you how to operate everything.

After turning on a couple of switches, I urinate into the hose. How do women do that in space? They put a curved piece of plastic on the hose and hold it against their bodies. For men and women, though, the hose works the same way. It's like a vacuum cleaner, and the urine is sucked away. On a trip to Mars, that urine would be recycled into drinking water, but on the space shuttle, we dump our urine overboard. Don't worry, though. That doesn't mean it's raining down on Earth. The sun will dissolve the urine.

Airflow is also used for solid waste collection, but that process is a little more complicated. You sit on the toilet, clamp your legs with the thigh-holders, and open a valve. The valve turns on a ring of air jets that encircle the inside opening of the toilet seat. Those jets shoot air toward your rear end. As it bounces off your body, it carries the waste away from you and into a big tank. After you're done, you close a valve that traps the waste. It isn't dumped in space. It's brought back to Earth.

Suddenly, rock music blares from our speakers. Mission

Control is waking us up. "Good morning, *Atlantis!*"

"Good morning, Houston!" the commander answers the call. It's not really morning where we are. We're over the deserts of Australia, and it's late afternoon. But we ignore earth time when we're in a shuttle. We're spinning around the world every ninety minutes, crossing another time zone every four minutes. It would be crazy to try to set our watches every four minutes! So we ignore earth time and do everything according to a clock that started at liftoff. It's called the MET (Mission Elapsed Time) clock. Right now, that clock says it's morning, so everybody says, "Good morning."

The crew member who was sick yesterday still doesn't feel well and asks for a shot of medicine from our medical kit. Our crew "doctor" prepares a hypodermic needle with an injection that will stop the vomiting. The doctor is really just a Marine astronaut who was given a little medical training back in Houston. This will be the first shot he's ever given! Would you like to get a shot from a Marine? No way!

The injection goes okay, but as the "doctor" withdraws the needle, the patient moves. That tears a tiny hole in his skin, and he starts to bleed. It's nothing serious, but it gives us a chance to watch bleeding in weightlessness. The blood doesn't "run" or drip as it does on Earth. It's weightless, like everything else in the cockpit. So it just bubbles on the skin. It grows bigger and bigger until it's a red marble. I watch one of these spheres come loose and float in the center of the cockpit like a ruby planet. What strange things you see in weightlessness! Finally, we stop the bleeding with a bandage and return to work.

"*Atlantis*, you have a GO to grapple the payload."

The moment has finally arrived. My hands are sweaty with excitement, and I wipe them on my shirt. I slip my feet under the canvas loops on the floor and grab the two joysticks. On my right side is a television screen. A TV camera at the end of the mechanical arm sends pictures to this screen. By looking at those pictures, I can pretend I'm riding on the tip of the arm. The two joysticks allow me to "fly" it wherever I want. It's just like a jet fighter video game at an arcade.

I twist and turn the joysticks and watch from the windows as the arm bends and moves like a human arm. In fact, it's modeled after a human arm. It has a shoulder joint that connects it to the shuttle, an elbow joint that bends just like your elbow, and a wrist joint that moves like your wrist.

On the television, I see the secret satellite come into view. Then, I see the foot-long spike sticking out of it. That's what I'm after. Slowly, I move the joysticks to bring the end of the arm over the spike. In the TV screen, the spike gets bigger and bigger and bigger, until it finally disappears inside a "can" on the end of the arm. I squeeze a joystick trigger, and some cables twist around the spike. The arm is now firmly attached to the satellite.

That was the easy part. Lifting the giant machine without damaging it will be the tough part. There's very little

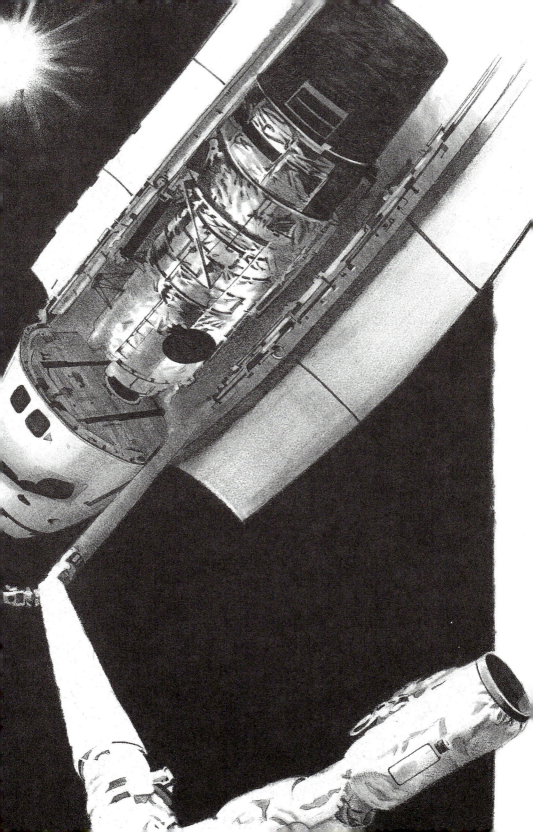

Liftoff! An Astronaut's Dream

room. If I bang it into the side of the shuttle, some dangerous things could happen. A fuel tank might be ripped open and cause an explosion. I might damage the shuttle's cargo bay doors so they wouldn't close. If that happened, we couldn't return to Earth. We'd be stranded in orbit, slowly dying as our oxygen was used up. So any mistake could ruin the mission and might even threaten our lives. It's a huge responsibility. I'm scared, but I have confidence in myself and the way the team trained me.

Another mission specialist flips the switches to release the latches that are holding the satellite in the cargo bay. It's finally free to pull upward. Very, very carefully, as if I'm taking apart a bomb, I use the joysticks to bring it higher. I keep looking back and forth from the window to the television screen. My concentration is intense. My heart is pounding. I'm holding my breath. Weightless drops of sweat ooze from my pores and tickle my face. I duck my head into my shirt sleeve to wipe the sweat away.

One foot, two feet, three feet. Higher and higher I bring the machine. Other crew members help me by watching out the window and using other TV cameras.

"Stop!" somebody yells. I release the controls. "You're getting too close to the back wall."

I look at the television and make a correction with the joysticks.

Five feet, six feet. Higher and higher I lift. Ten feet, twelve feet. I start to breathe again. It's finally clear of the space shuttle. I've done it! The monster satellite is floating on the end of the arm, out of danger.

48

The rest is easy. The commander floats to my side and grabs the joysticks that control the space shuttle. After I release the machine, he will fire the shuttle's maneuvering rockets to move us away from it.

"I'm ready when you are, Mike."

"Let's do it."

I squeeze a trigger, and the cables unwind from around the spike. Then I pull back the arm, and the satellite is free. The shuttle vibrates with rocket firings as the commander flies us away.

Against the black of deep space, the secret satellite is left gleaming in the sun. The red, white, and blue of an American flag proudly shines from its side. It's a wonderful moment in my life. Thousands of hours of training have paid off. I did my part for the team. I kicked the field goal. I've put a satellite in orbit that will help guard our country and keep us free.

That evening I'm relaxed enough to want a big supper. I float to the kitchen. It's called the *galley*. It's just a small part of the downstairs shuttle cockpit, right next to the toilet. In fact, our bathroom, kitchen, gym, bedroom, living room, and experiment laboratory all share the same tiny area.

I select my supper from a locker: a hamburger patty, mashed potatoes, mixed vegetables, and strawberries for dessert. It sounds great, until you realize it's all dehydrated. The water has been taken out of a lot of our food to make it more compact and save storage space. Our drinks are the same way. They're powdered: milk, coffee, cocoa, tea, orange juice, and so on. We don't carry any soft drinks because carbonated drinks don't work very well in weightlessness.

Each food item is in a separate dish sealed in plastic. I put them in the galley's rehydration station, where a machine adds water. A water-gun needle pierces the plastic, and water squirts into the dish. Using my fingers, I squeeze down on the plastic covering and stir the water into the food. Then I put it in the oven. It's not a microwave. Microwave energy could interfere with the shuttle's electronics. So our oven just has hot air blowing around inside it to heat the food.

When it's ready, I cut the plastic top open with some scissors and eat with a fork and spoon just like I would on Earth. Sometimes the food gets loose and you have to catch it. I've seen astronauts swimming around in weightlessness snapping at loose food like sharks chasing fish.

I've got tea to drink, but it's not in a glass. If I tried to drink from a glass in weightlessness, what would happen? Nothing. If I tilted the glass to my mouth, the tea would stay in the bottom. So we have to drink with straws. We have aluminum pouches with various flavored powders inside. At the rehydration station, we push the water-gun needle into the end of the pouch and add water. After we pull out the needle, we push in a straw and use it to suck out the drink.

"Hey, guys, check it out!" One of the crew has squeezed some orange juice from his drink pouch, and it's floating in midair. In weightlessness, all fluids float as balls. So a perfect sphere of orange juice floats in the middle of the cockpit!

"Let's make a solar system!"

I take peanut M&M candies and place them around the orange juice, like planets around the sun. Mercury is a red

M&M. I use a yellow one for Venus. Earth is green. I continue until I have nine M&Ms floating around our orange juice sun. It looks like a scene from a *Star Trek* movie where strange planets circle around a strange star!

Then I attack my creation, gobbling down the candy planets. Finally, I take a straw, touch it to our "sun," and slurp it away. I've eaten our entire solar system!

Another crew member suggests a game of baseball. The commander pitches peanut M&Ms to a mission specialist who uses a pencil to hit the candy to the rest of us. We chase after "pop flies" with our mouths. The games are a fun way to end a very busy and exhausting day.

Bedtime arrives. Mission Control says good night, and the rest of the crew climb into their sleeping bags. As I did last night, I stay awake at the windows and watch the world spin by.

It's dark now. We're on the midnight side of the earth. I float around the cockpit and turn off all the lights. With no reflections on the windows I can see outside. The view takes my breath away!

The Milky Way looks like its name, like milk. It's a white fog of stars. It seems as if I can see trillions of them! Below me, meteors crash into the atmosphere as shooting stars. They make long streaks of fiery orange and white. Sometimes they explode into pieces when they hit the deep part of the atmosphere.

Lightning illuminates the tops of thunderstorms like sputtering light bulbs. Over the warm parts of the earth, where there are lots of thunderstorms, I can see hundreds of flashes a minute. But can I hear the thunder? No. Sound needs something to move through, like air. The space shuttle orbits in space, which is a vacuum. There is no air, so there can't be any sound. In fact, somebody could set off an atomic bomb right outside the window and I wouldn't hear it. *Atlantis* couldn't be rattled by the shock wave of an outside explosion, either. Shock waves can't travel in a vacuum. The next time you watch *Star Trek*, ask your mom and dad if they think the *Enterprise* crew would get thrown around by a "near-miss" explosion. You'll surprise them by knowing more than the producers of the show. If there's no air, there can be no sound or shock waves or vibrations.

A really special treat comes into view. It's an aurora! You've probably heard of the aurora borealis or the northern lights. At the north pole the earth acts like a giant magnet and sucks electrically charged particles from space towards the ground. As those particles strike the atmosphere, they glow. That causes the northern lights. The same thing happens near the south pole. I'm seeing the southern lights. They're spectacular, like enormous green snakes slithering over the antarctic ice!

We float over Australia, and I see city lights. Cities look like glowing yellow spiders because of the roads that come out from their centers. The city of Sydney, Australia, has some clouds covering it, but the lights are so bright they shine through.

Seeing these lights reminds me of another bet you could win with your parents. Ask, "Is it true the only object built by people that an astronaut can see from space is the Great Wall of China?" Almost all adults believe this. Even the TV quiz program *Jeopardy* gave that as the correct answer to a question. But it's the wrong answer! From orbit you can see such things as city lights, vapor trails of airplanes, large smoke trails from factories, long stretches of straight roads, very large buildings, and airport runways.

What's that? I see something moving! A bright point of light is slowly gliding through space! Could it be a UFO? I grab the binoculars and look, but it's too far away. Then, it starts flashing! Are alien creatures trying to signal me?

It's impossible to know for sure, but I have a hunch what the light is. It's not an alien spaceship. It's just another satellite. There are nearly ten thousand pieces of junk floating around the earth. One of those pieces was probably far enough away that the sun was shining on it. I was seeing sunlight reflecting from a piece of junk. It was probably tumbling, and that's what made it appear to flash. See how your eye can be tricked?

But what about UFOs? Are we alone in the universe? Have other creatures flown to Earth to examine us? There's no way to know for sure. Many people have reported seeing strange things. Some people have even claimed to have been aboard UFOs. But scientists have never found any real proof. What do I believe? Looking from *Atlantis's* windows I see a universe filled with stars. There are so many that it's easy for me to think some have planets circling them. I also think some of those planets might have life. So, I believe there is other life in our universe. But I don't think any creatures in flying saucers have visited us, yet. That's what I believe. What do you believe?

A brilliant rainbow appears on Earth's eastern horizon. Sunrise! Our forty-five minute night is over, and another forty-five minute day is about to start. But the earth below us is still pitch black. It's like being on top of a mountain three hundred miles high. The sun always shines on mountaintops before it shines in valleys. So we have sunlight shining on us in orbit while it's dark on Earth below. Can you think what this means to people who might be watching the sky from the ground? It means they could see us! Just as I saw light reflected from the space junk, they would be looking into a dark sky and *Atlantis* would be reflecting the sunlight! So you can see satellites from Earth. Just go outside about an hour before sunrise or an hour after sunset and stare at the sky. Within a few minutes you will probably see a moving point of light. It won't be an airplane. It won't have any red, green, or flashing lights on it. It will be a satellite!

Atlantis streaks farther eastward, and the sun rises high enough to flood the earth with light. A new day comes to the Pacific Ocean. I see rings of coral islands that look like floating necklaces. On a large island, smoke drifts away from an active volcano. The long white vapor trail of a jet crossing the sea is also visible. It's probably an airliner going from Australia to Los Angeles. It will take those people thirteen hours to get across the Pacific Ocean. *Atlantis* will make the same flight in about thirty minutes!

The Hawaiian Islands come into view. Clouds cover the

tops of the volcanoes like ice cream on a cone. Many more jet vapor trails appear in the sky. Some of them crisscross each other like a giant game of tick-tack-toe.

For a moment I hear the whirr of the toilet fan. The last crew member is getting ready for bed. Then *Atlantis* becomes as still as a sleeping house. I'm very tired, too, and I know I should get some rest, but my brain begs me to stay awake a little while longer.

Far to the east, I see a change. Brown appears on the horizon. It's California. *Atlantis* is approaching the western coast of America. Los Angeles appears as a gray smudge. Smog covers it. Inland, I see snowcapped mountains and huge deserts. Edwards Air Force Base, where we will land in a few days, is easy to see because it's built next to a giant dry lake.

The Colorado River cuts through the desert like a twisting, black vein in the earth's body. I can see the large lakes that it fills: Lake Powell, Lake Mead, and Lake Havasu. Las Vegas, Nevada, glistens in the sun.

A beautiful mixture of red and tan colors passes underneath. It's the Grand Canyon! I'm right over it! The sight makes me think of Nature's patience and power. It took millions of years for water to carve through thousands of feet of earth to make the canyon.

I look south and see a giant hole in the ground. What is it? Then, I remember. It's a meteor crater. Forty-nine thousand years ago a meteor crashed into the earth near present-day Winslow, Arizona, and left the hole. Can you

imagine what that must have been like? A black rock the size of a small house had been tumbling through empty space for billions of years. Maybe, at one time, it had almost collided with another planet in another galaxy. Maybe it had just missed getting sucked into a black hole. Maybe some alien spacecraft had to put up its deflector shields to keep from being hit by it. But on its intergalactic journey it missed everything until it passed too close to our earth. Then, our gravity grabbed it and pulled it down.

There were probably no humans living in North America when it crashed, so the only witnesses would have been prehistoric animals. What would they have seen? Let your imagination take you to that moment. . . .

A plain of amber grasses stretches to a distant, smoking volcano. A small herd of woolly mammoths slowly walks toward a stream. Near them, a saber-toothed tiger eats a bison he recently killed. In the sky, giant condors wheel in circles waiting for the leftovers. It's a clear and quiet summer day in prehistoric Arizona.

The tiger is the first to see the meteor. He glances upward from his meal and watches the strange appearance. The huge object is still fifty miles overhead, but air friction has already heated it to thousands of degrees. It glows brighter than the sun and leaves a long trail of white smoke behind it.

The other animals also begin to notice that something is different. A cluster of bison stare at the meteor while continuing to chew the grass and swish their tails. A mother mammoth senses danger and bellows for her calf to come closer. The tiger also feels uneasy and gives up on his meal. He bounds away toward his cave.

Then the panic starts. The fiery object grows huge. It fills the sky above the animals. There's still no sound because it's traveling at 45,000 miles per hour, many times faster than the speed of sound. But just the brightness is enough to stampede the animals. They run in all directions, stirring up clouds of dust in the process.

But there's no escape. The meteor slams into the earth with an explosive force that is equal to fifteen million tons of dynamite. Everything within miles of the impact is instantly killed. Even far away, animals are killed by the rain of dirt and boulders that the impact throws into the air. Hot pieces of rock fall in forests and start raging fires. The sonic boom of the meteor finally reaches Earth and cracks across the plain, but there's nothing alive to hear it. Where all the animals were is now nothing but a smoking hole four thousand feet wide and six hundred feet deep.

Can you see it? As I glide over the crater, I can see the story as clearly as a movie.

Another river appears. It's the Rio Grande. A dark patch spreads from its eastern shore. It's Albuquerque, New Mexico! It's my home!

The sight chokes me with tears. They flood my eyes and cling in weightless drops to my eyelids. I blot them away, but more follow. I'm not ashamed. I'm not embarrassed. I'm overcome with happiness. From three hundred miles high, I'm watching my dream come true. I want to shout my joy for all the world to hear!

More memories of the dream flash in my mind's eye like photographs from a picture album. One shows me sitting in the cockpit of my dad's plane, pretending to be a pilot. Another captures my balsa wood glider soaring through the crystal-blue New Mexican sky. I can see my airplane coloring books and Tinker-Toy planes and my telescope. I can see myself watching the stars from my front yard, from the very place now passing three hundred miles beneath me! I can see everything about my dream. Everything . . .

RUSSIAN SPUTNIK CIRCLING EARTH!

That was the newspaper headline on October 4, 1957. I was twelve years old.

That night I stood in my front yard. My brothers and sister and parents were with me. Up and down the block, other families were also in their yards. It was like Halloween. Everybody was out. Everybody was talking. Everybody was excited. Some people had brought radios into their yards, and the voices coming from the radios were excited, too. The entire neighborhood, the entire city, in fact people across the entire country were standing outside watching the birth of the space age. The Russian *Sputnik*, the first satellite, was flying over, and we were all outside to watch it.

In Albuquerque it was cold and clear, with the cream of the Milky Way spilling across the sky. Shooting stars occasionally streaked through the black and brought "oooohs" and "ahhhhs" from the crowd.

Then, just as the newspaper had predicted, a tiny light appeared on the southwestern horizon and slowly, silently glided over our heads. Voices were hushed by the sight. People stood in awe. Some cried. Some were frightened. The Russians were our bitter Cold War enemy, and *Sputnik* proved they were better than we were. If they had missiles that could put satellites in orbit, it was feared they could also hurl hydrogen bombs to America. But I was too young to be afraid. I was excited. I wanted to fly where *Sputnik* was flying!

A month later *Sputnik II* carried a dog into orbit. Then, in January 1958, America launched its first satellite. The country was wild with space fever! Everybody was infected: newspeople, politicians, teachers, scientists, moms and dads. Walt Disney produced TV programs about space travel. Songs were written about satellites. The Boy Scouts started a space merit badge. Toy companies started selling model kits of satellites and rockets. Schools had space days. Students went on space field trips to planetariums and museums. "Moon Watch" clubs were formed to observe the new satellites. I joined one of these clubs and spent hundreds of hours staring into space watching Sputniks, Explorers, Vanguards, Echoes, and Telstars. Those were just some of the satellite names.

It was during these exciting days that my imagination was captured by rocketry. I would stay glued to the TV, watching launch after launch. In these early days, many rockets only went a few feet before blowing up in clouds of orange flame. But some worked beautifully, rising into the Florida sky on thunderous columns of fire.

I wanted to know everything about rockets. I went to the library and read about them. I bought books about them. In fact, I still have my favorite childhood rocket book: *The Conquest of Space* by Willy Ley. More than any other book, I loved this one. It did much more than merely explain how rockets work. It had beautiful paintings that showed what it would be like in space and on other planets. At night I would fall asleep reading it and dream of being on the moon or Mars. In the morning I would risk being late for school by trying to read just a few more pages. *The Conquest of Space* taught me the power of books and the power of reading. No television, movie, or video can ever fill the imagination like a book.

Besides reading about rockets and space travel, I also wrote to NASA for information. They sent me photos and fact sheets. I looked at these and then sent them my suggestions on how they could make their rockets better. I even told them they could use my designs for free! I laugh, now, to think I told NASA I had better designs than they did. But I was so caught up in my dream of space flight I really believed I could do anything. I really believed I could design a better rocket than NASA. That's the great part of a dream. Dreams let you believe in yourself. Dreams let you do anything. Dreams let you be anything.

By the age of thirteen, I was a space geek. My classmates were in love with rock stars and cars. They had posters on their bedroom walls of Corvettes and T-Birds, of Elvis

Presley and the Beatles. But on my walls were posters of rockets: Atlases, Jupiters, and Titans. I couldn't tell the difference between a Ford and a Chevy. I didn't know any pop songs. But I could tell you everything about NASA's rockets and satellites.

At this time in my youth there were no toy rockets like the ones you can now buy in hobby stores. If you wanted to experiment, you had to build your own. Rocket clubs were organized for that purpose. Every school had one, and I joined ours. Under the supervision of teachers, rocket designs and rocket fuel formulas were explained. Homemade rockets were soon being built and launched by kids all over the country. There were reports in the newspapers of some of these reaching altitudes of 30,000 feet! Some kids even talked about trying to orbit their own satellites!

Initially, I had adult supervision for my experiments. Then, like many kids, I learned how to get the chemicals to make rocket fuel by myself. I stopped going to the rocket club meetings and started doing my own experiments. Now, I can see how dangerous that was. My rockets got bigger and bigger, until they were taller than I was. Instead of a few ounces of fuel they soon required ten or fifteen pounds of it. I would take them into the desert, light a fuse, and run for cover. Sometimes they blew up and sent steel pieces flying over my head, just like a bomb. Other times they disappeared in the sky, and I never found them again. Only a miracle saved me from serious injury. My dream could have ended in blindness or burns or even death. As it was, many other children were injured, and some were killed, by their rocket experiments. Am I making this up? No. In fact, while I was an astronaut, I met a man who was blind and missing some fingers. He told me that when he was a child, one of his homemade rockets blew up in his face and caused the injuries. Always remember: Never risk your health or life in an experiment of any kind! Injury and death will end your dream!

On April 12, 1961, another headline rocked America: RUSSIANS ORBIT MAN! His name was Yuri Gagarin, and he became the first human to go into space.

America had already selected its first astronauts. They were called the "Mercury Seven" because there were seven of them and they would fly in the Mercury capsule. But none had yet flown in space when Gagarin was launched. America's rockets seemed to blow up every time they were launched, so they were still being tested. Also, they were less powerful than the Russian rockets and couldn't carry much weight into space.

I was fifteen years old then, and because of America's puny rockets I dreamed that I would be the first American in space! That's crazy, isn't it? But I really did dream that NASA would find its Mercury astronauts were too heavy for the rockets to lift, so they would have to pick some skinny kid to go instead. I dreamed they would pick me! I even stopped drinking milkshakes to stay light.

Of course, nobody from NASA ever knocked on my door and said, "Your rocket is ready, Mike." It was still a wonderful dream. You should never be ashamed or afraid to dream of being anything. Dreams do come true.

The older I got, the more determined I became to be a pilot. I washed cars and mowed lawns to make money for flying lessons. After some instruction, at age seventeen I had my first solo airplane flight. It's another memory of my dream that's as clear as a photograph.

When I lined up the plane on the runway, my heart was thumping in my chest like a big drum. I pushed the throttle forward, and the engine roared until the spinning propeller was invisible. Then, I released the brakes and watched the airspeed increase. Twenty knots, thirty, fifty, seventy knots. I gently pulled the yoke backwards, and the ground seemed to fall away from the plane. I was flying! For the first time in my life I was actually flying! I was a pilot! On that day, and many that followed, I flew over the New Mexican deserts and mountains and dreamed of the day I would be a jet fighter pilot doing the same thing.

In 1963, after graduating from high school, I went to West Point, the U.S. Military Academy. West Point is a very strict school that trained me to be a military officer. It also challenged me to be the best that I could be. At first, that was very scary. Nobody had ever done that before. In grade school and high school nobody had really challenged me to do my absolute best. But West Point did. Bellowing seniors would tell me to run up a mountain or swim across a lake holding a rifle in my hands. In class I was given very difficult tests in every subject, every day. Many, many times, I thought, *I can't do this. I'm not good enough. I'm not smart enough. I'm not strong enough.* But I discovered the most amazing thing. I could!

West Point dared me to be my best. It challenged me mentally and physically. At the time, I had no idea how important that was. But for a dream to come true, you have to know how good you are. Most young people never know, because nobody challenges them. Young people say to themselves, "I can't be a doctor or lawyer or teacher or astronaut. I can't go to college. I'm not smart enough." But you are! You really are much smarter and stronger than you think. To find out, dare yourself. Dare yourself to do better. Dare yourself to read more books, learn more words, do more math, do more than your teacher or parents ask of you. Dare yourself to follow a dream!

As my West Point graduation approached, I was very excited. I was going into the Air Force. Soon, I thought, I would be in pilot training. I would learn to fly supersonic jets! The sky wouldn't even be able to hold me. I would take my jet higher and faster than anyone had ever been before. My sonic booms would rattle windows as I climbed and dived all over the sky. Nobody would ever beat me when we practiced dogfighting. I would go to test pilot school and learn to fly the fastest jets, the way Chuck Yeager did. I'd be a top gun. Finally, after many years of training, I would be ready to be an astronaut. What a wonderful, beautiful dream it was. I had my life planned. I knew exactly what I wanted.

Then something terrible happened. A few days before graduation, my commander called me into his office. "Mike," he said. "I have the results of your physical exam for pilot training. You failed the vision test. The doctor says you need eyeglasses."

He didn't have to say anything else. I knew the rules. The Air Force would not let anybody be a pilot without perfect eyesight. I needed glasses, so I could never be a jet fighter pilot. It was the end of the world for me. I went to my room and cried. My dream was over.

Imagine wanting something very, very much. Maybe it's a new bicycle or a baseball glove. Maybe it's a position on the school cheerleading squad or the lead role in the school play. Whatever it is, it's all you can think about. Night and day you dream about having it. Maybe you work very hard to get it. Maybe you spend hours every day shooting baskets or practicing gymnastics to get on a team. You practice and work and study. It seems as if your whole life is at stake. Then, at the last minute, you're told that you can never have it. Maybe you're told that somebody better than you got the position. Maybe you're told you can't be something because of a problem with your health. But, whatever the reason, you're told that your dream is over.

That's what it was like for me when I was told I could not be a pilot. There would be no jet fighters, no test pilot school, no top gun, no astronaut job. It seemed as if somebody had cut out my heart. I cried.

Now, though, I can see the important lesson this experience taught me. I learned you cannot always have what you want. Sometimes things happen that you cannot control. I had no control over my eyesight, so I couldn't be a pilot. I had to find another dream and follow it.

I couldn't be a jet fighter pilot, but I could still fly in jets that had two seats. So that became my new dream. I would be the best fighter "backseater" in the Air Force. I trained to operate the radar and radios and electronic equipment in the rear cockpit of Air Force fighters. It wasn't the "star" position. The pilot had that. But it was still a very important job, and I dared myself to do my best at it.

When I was twenty-five, I went to Vietnam. I had to leave my wife and two babies and go to fight in a terrible war. There, we flew very low and fast over the enemy and took pictures of their airfields and bridges so the bombers could attack them. Red tracers of machine-gun fire and exploding shells streaked by my cockpit. When we flew at night the enemy couldn't see us, but it was even more dangerous. We had to fly in deep valleys at six hundred miles per hour and depend on our instruments and radar to keep from crashing into the mountains.

I was very scared in Vietnam, and I learned another lesson. When I was a little boy, I used to play "war" with my friends and think it would be a lot of fun to shoot guns and drop bombs. But real wars are not fun. They're not like the ones you see in the movies and on TV. Young people get killed in real wars and never return to see their families and children or their mothers and fathers. Many of my West Point classmates were killed or seriously injured. They lost legs and arms or were horribly burned or disfigured.

Something very important in space happened when I was in Vietnam. On July 20, 1969, Neil Armstrong became the first person to walk on the moon! I listened to him say, "That's one small step for a man . . . one giant leap for mankind." I watched the movies of him skipping in the moon dust, and I wanted so badly to be an astronaut. But I knew that dream was dead. NASA would only select people who were test pilots, and I could never be one of those because I wore glasses.

After Vietnam, the Air Force sent me to England for four years. This was during the Cold War, when Russia was our enemy. We trained in our jets in case a real war should start. That never happened, but the training was dangerous and more people died. It was another lesson that wars are very sad.

In 1974 I returned to America and went back to college to become an aeronautical engineer. If I couldn't be a pilot or an astronaut, I could still help to design and test the planes and rockets that the pilots and astronauts would fly. At this school, I once again dared myself to do my best. I graduated with honors.

Next, I went to Edwards Air Force Base in California for another special school that taught me how to test airplanes. You would love to go to this school! Imagine getting in the back seat of a supersonic jet and taking measurements while the pilot flies it as fast as it can go. It was awesome! And because of another self-dare, I again graduated from this school with honors.

One day, as I was getting out of my jet, a friend rushed up to tell me some incredible news. NASA had just announced they were going to select new astronauts for their latest rocket, the space shuttle. Some of these astronauts would be called *mission specialists*. They would do experiments and space walks and release satellites. What was so incredible about this? Mission specialists didn't have to be pilots! They could wear glasses! Imagine my joy at this news! Ten years earlier I had been told I could *never* be an astronaut because of my eyesight. Now, the dream was back! I had a chance!

But was I good enough to be an astronaut? Weren't astronauts like supermen? When they were kids, didn't they all get straight-A's in school and graduate number one in their college classes? Weren't they the smartest and bravest people on Earth? The newspapers and magazines said they were.

I knew I wasn't the smartest or bravest person on Earth. I didn't get straight-A's on my report cards. And I had been scared many times when I was flying. But I had always dared myself to do my best. Now, because of those dares, I had a very good record to mail to NASA.

But just think what *could* have happened. I could have given up ten years earlier. Remember? I had been curled on my bed, crying, thinking my life was over. I could have quit daring myself. For ten years, I could have done just enough to squeak by. But if I had, I would have lost this one chance to be an astronaut. You can never go wrong by doing your best.

I had a chance, but it seemed a very slim one. NASA was expecting over ten thousand applications for only thirty-five astronaut positions! How could I possibly be picked? There were just too many people.

Many months later I was amazed to be called to NASA for an interview. I sat at the end of a long table, and astronauts who had walked on the moon asked me questions. Did they ask me about math and science and aeronautical engineering? Did they ask me to name all the planets or explain how a rocket works? No. They wanted to know about me as a person. They wanted to know about my dream!

"Mr. Mullane," they said, "tell us about your childhood. How long have you wanted to be an astronaut?"

I told them the story of my dream, of wanting to be a pilot, of building rockets.

They also wanted to know if I could get along with other people. NASA is a giant team made up of men and women of all races and religions. NASA wanted men and women who could be part of a team.

The interview lasted two hours. Next, I was sent to doctors for a physical examination. NASA will only pick people as astronauts who are in good physical condition. Since I had never used tobacco or drugs or abused alcohol, my lungs and heart and the rest of my body were in perfect shape.

I went home to wait for NASA to call with a decision. It was November 1977. Would I be selected as an astronaut? Would my dream come true? One week went by without a call. Two weeks. A month. It was torture.

The Air Force moved me to Idaho and I waited for the

call there. December passed, and I was sure that NASA had not picked me.

Then, one cold January morning the phone rang. It was NASA. I had been selected as one of the first mission specialist astronauts!

I cheered! I screamed my head off! I skipped around the room! It was like hitting a home run to win the World Series! It was like catching a touchdown pass in the Super Bowl! It was wonderful! Incredible! I WAS GOING TO BE AN ASTRONAUT!

That night I walked into the Idaho desert and looked at the sky. It was cold and bright with stars. Satellites drifted silently over my head as dim specks of light. *Someday soon*, I thought, *I will be up there with them.*

It's our third morning in space, and Mission Control wakes us with more rock music. Everyone feels great. The one crew member who had been vomiting is now completely well. One of the crew floats me a foil pouch of coffee, and I sip it while watching the giant satellite I released yesterday. It's many miles away, but the reflecting sunlight has turned it into a morning star brighter than Venus.

Yes, it's a great day.

Then a call comes from Mission Control that changes our mood.

"*Atlantis?* Houston. We were wondering if you saw anything break off the top of the right booster during ascent?"

The commander grabs the microphone. "Negative, Houston. Ascent looked nominal. What's up?"

"In a review of the ground films of your launch, engineers thought they saw something come off the tip of the booster."

I get a sinking feeling in my stomach. If something broke off, it could have hit the belly of the shuttle. The belly is covered with thousands of very fragile heat tiles. They are made out of silica, the same stuff that's in sand, and they could be destroyed by an impact. That doesn't affect us while we're in space. But on reentry, the friction of the atmosphere could turn *Atlantis* and everything in it into ash. The heat tiles are the only things that keep us from burning up.

But what can we do? How can we look at the belly of the shuttle to find out if it's damaged? The NASA team has the answer.

"*Atlantis*, we want Mike to use the robot arm to look at the belly. We're transmitting some instructions on how to do that."

Once again the team is depending on me. But now I'll be doing something that I haven't practiced. They want me to bend the robot arm around the side of the shuttle and look underneath. The TV camera on the end of the arm will transmit pictures of what the belly looks like.

I'll have to be extra careful. The arm will be bent at a crazy angle. It will be very close to the shuttle. One mistake and I could damage the tiles for sure.

As I grab the joysticks and begin the maneuver, I'm scared at the thought of what I might see. Suppose there is a lot of damage? There's no way we could repair it. There's no way to space walk to the belly of the shuttle, and even if we could, we wouldn't have any tools to make such a repair.

I shiver with fear as I imagine what would happen to *Atlantis* if there is major damage. On reentry, fire would melt a hole in the belly and then start burning through wires and equipment. Alarms would sound in the cockpit as hydraulic pumps, electrical generators, computers, and other equipment began to fail. The fire alarm would go off as the heat started a fire in the cockpit. The other mission specialists and I would leave our seats to fight the blaze. But the reentry g-forces would make me weigh three-hundred and sixty pounds. My legs would buckle, and I would crash to the floor and have to crawl to the fire. Air would start leaking out, and a shrieking hiss would be added to all the other alarms. To keep us alive, our pressure suits would automatically inflate, making the arms and legs as hard as an inflated tire. We would be like the Tin Man in *The Wizard of Oz*, barely able to move.

Meanwhile, the commander and pilot would be doing everything possible to keep the shuttle flying straight. They would be madly flipping through checklists and shouting emergency procedures to each other. But in the end, atmospheric friction would win the battle. The shuttle would start groaning and vibrating as pieces of the wings burned off. The last hydraulic pump would explode, and the shuttle would slowly spin out of control. From the ground it would look like a giant shooting star, scattering flaming pieces of aluminum across the sky. I would be dead.

That's what I'm thinking as I carefully twist the robot arm under the fuselage.

Finally, the belly heat tiles come into view on the television screen. We gasp. Hundreds of tiles are scraped and gouged! At least one tile is completely missing. What's going to happen to us on reentry?

"*Atlantis*, this is Mission Control. You have a GO for the deorbit burn."

"Roger, Houston. Go for the burn. We're coming home."

For the past two days, Mission Control has reviewed the TV images of the belly. They think *Atlantis* will survive reentry. They can't be certain, but they believe the damage to most of the tiles is minor. Even the missing tile should be no problem since the shuttle was designed to withstand reentry with a few gaps in the tiles.

But the TV image from the robot arm camera was not very good, and we couldn't see the entire belly. What if there are huge areas of missing tile that were hidden from the camera?

Five . . . four . . . three . . . two . . . one . . . BOOM!

The OMS engines fire. *Atlantis* is pointing backwards in orbit, so the engines are now slowing us down. The shuttle is doing the same thing that you do when you try to stop yourself on a water slide or a snowy sled ride. You use your hands and feet to try and push yourself back up the hill. Usually you don't stop. You just slow down a little. When a shuttle comes out of orbit, it does the same thing. Its OMS engines try to thrust it backwards. That doesn't stop the shuttle, but it slows it down enough so its orbit altitude decreases. It decreases enough so that *Atlantis* falls into the atmosphere. Atmospheric friction then slows it down for landing.

After about two minutes, the engines shut down and the commander turns *Atlantis* around and pulls the nose up. We want the belly to hit the atmosphere first.

From this point on, *Atlantis* is a glider. For the next hour it will slowly fall earthward toward the dry-lake runway of Edwards Air Force Base. It will glide across the Indian Ocean, Australia, and the Pacific Ocean. It will glide for 12,000 miles! The OMS engines can't be used in the atmosphere, so there's no way to fly around and look for a runway. If there's an error in our computer navigation, we could fall too fast and crash into the Pacific Ocean. Or, we could come in too slowly. Then we would be too high to land at Edwards, and we would crash in the deserts of Arizona or New Mexico. We must rely on *Atlantis's* computers to steer us correctly.

For the first half of reentry, it's very quiet in the cockpit. We don't have much to do except watch the instruments, the way we did during launch. Out the windows I see nothing but black. We're on the night side of the earth.

The instruments show us getting steadily closer to

California. Our altitude meter shows a slow descent. We're gliding at almost 18,000 miles per hour, but we don't hear noise or feel vibrations. The earth's air doesn't really get thick enough to affect the shuttle until about fifty miles from the ground. Since we started at three hundred miles, we fall in silence for about two hundred fifty miles.

I see something falling from the ceiling. It's an M&M candy! We must have lost it playing M&M baseball. While we were in orbit, things floated everywhere. The M&M I'm watching must have floated into a corner. Now, as we pass through the top of the atmosphere, the shuttle is slowing down. Everything in the cockpit that isn't put away slowly falls toward the floor. We're no longer weightless. The falling M&M is an indication that we are experiencing the very beginning of reentry g-forces. Other "lost" things begin to experience the same force. A piece of plastic, a small screwdriver, a tiny battery, and a bit of granola bar all join the M&M in a slow drift to the floor. It's "raining" lost garbage.

The g-forces also affect my body. My arms feel heavy. It's hard to hold up my head. Even the small g-forces feel huge because my body is used to being weightless.

We fall farther and farther. The atmosphere gets thicker and thicker. The g-forces slowly increase to one-quarter the force of gravity . . . one half . . . then normal gravity. My body is at its usual weight, but it seems to weigh a ton. I'm crushed into my seat.

When I see the fire, fear makes me forget about the invisible elephant on my shoulders. It's still night outside, but the windows are now covered with an orange glow. The shuttle has struck the thick atmosphere, and friction is heating its belly to thousands of degrees. The glow is the hot air. Or is it? Maybe it's the shuttle's aluminum skin melting. Maybe the tile damage is so severe that we're burning up like a shooting star. Everybody stares at the instruments. If we were melting, the instruments would show various emergencies. So far, though, everything is nominal.

The orange glow brightens. It turns pink and then white hot. Brilliant flashes come through the upper windows. The super-hot air is flowing around the shuttle and forming a wake behind us, like the one behind a boat. It flashes through the top windows like lightning. I try to look up through those windows. If the shuttle is burning, I'll see flaming pieces of it flying off. But the g-forces have paralyzed me in my seat. I can't move enough to see from the windows. All I can do is watch the instruments and pray that the tiles are holding up.

The sun rises in our faces and reveals the Pacific Ocean. Through the fire on the window, I can see a lace of clouds covering it. It's a beautiful day.

We enter radio blackout. The air surrounding *Atlantis* is now so hot that it blocks all radio signals. Mission Control is blind. They have no data to see what's going on. *This is it*, I think. This is the hottest the shuttle will get. In some places it's three thousand degrees! I'm sitting in the middle of a fireball. The windows are white with the heat. If we can only get through this, we'll be safe. A call from

Mission Control will mean the blackout is over and the damaged tiles have protected us.

The seconds on the clock seem to drag. Ten, eleven, twelve, thirteen. Fear fills the cockpit. Will we make it? Will the tiles hold out?

Twenty-one, twenty-two, twenty-three seconds.

The commander's hand hovers over the control stick. If something goes wrong, he's ready to take control from *Atlantis's* computers.

Thirty-eight, thirty-nine, forty, forty-one seconds.

My eyes are like pinballs. They bounce from instrument to instrument. The navigation display shows a flashing green "bug"—the shuttle—moving precisely along the planned trajectory. Meters, dials, and flickering numbers show everything is nominal.

Forty-seven, forty-eight, forty-nine, fifty seconds.

What's keeping Mission Control?

A "bump" ripples through the cockpit. My heart leaps into my throat. The commander's hand jerks closer to the control stick. What was it? Did something finally burn off the shuttle? All eyes sweep across the instruments. But everything is still okay. We decide it must have been a tiny change in the density of the upper atmosphere.

The seconds seem to move like hours.

Then . . .

"*Atlantis*, Houston is back with you. Your energy and ground track look nominal."

"Roger, Houston. We read you loud and clear."

I can almost hear everybody sigh. We're breathing again. We're through the worst heat and still alive! We're going to make it!

Now the vibrations begin. We're passing thirty miles altitude, and the air is really thick. At least it feels thick to a huge glider that's traveling through it at ten thousand miles per hour! It howls around the cockpit and shakes us like a roller coaster. It's also rapidly slowing us down and putting us in danger.

Danger? What danger?

We're in danger of fainting. The same g-force that pulled the loose M&M to the floor is now pulling blood from our heads. I get tunnel vision. There's not enough blood reaching the part of the brain that allows me to see. My side vision slowly gets blacker and blacker until I feel like I'm looking through a tunnel. I'm in danger of complete blackout, of fainting.

I have a way to fight the g's. Underneath my pressure suit, I'm wearing an anti-g suit. It's a rubber bladder that goes around my stomach and legs. I twist a control knob on the leg of my suit, and air rushes into the bladder. It squeezes my stomach and legs very hard. My belly button feels like it's being crushed into my backbone, the squeeze is so tight. It hurts. But I don't care. The terrible squeeze of the suit cuts down the blood flow to my legs and allows my heart to send it to my brain. It's keeping me from fainting. But the stomach squeeze makes it difficult to talk. We grunt like weight lifters.

The shuttle continues to fall, gliding closer and closer to the earth.

Land ho! The coast of California comes into view. Los Angeles sparkles in hazy sunlight. In a minute, the city will be hit with our shock wave. It will rattle windows with a BOOM-BOOM. Edwards Air Force Base appears. There isn't a cloud in the sky. It's perfect landing weather.

Things begin to happen quickly now. The shuttle is plunging earthward with all the grace of a brick. The commander will have only one chance for a landing. To help him, a steady stream of information comes from Mission Control. The radios are filled with a babble of technical talk.

"TACANs look good."

"Roger."

"Air data probes are out."

"Roger, incorporate air data."

"Good MLS lock."

"I'm going CSS."

"Winds are two-five-zero at five knots."

"Energy is nominal."

"I'm on the HAC."

The desert grows bigger and bigger in the windows. *Atlantis* is in a diving turn for the runway.

"Radar altimeter is in . . . three hundred knots . . . looking good . . . four thousand feet . . . two hundred ninety knots . . . three thousand . . . two thousand . . . pre-flare."

The commander raises *Atlantis's* nose. We're only a minute from landing, and the wheels are still up. Why do we wait so long? It's because *Atlantis* is a glider. If we lower the wheels early, the extra air-drag confuses the computers. So we wait until the last second. Many people worry about this and say, "But what happens if the wheels don't come down?" It doesn't matter if the wheels don't come down at fifty thousand feet or one thousand feet. We'll still crash-land. You can't keep a glider in the air to try some type of emergency wheel lowering. So, you might as well wait until the last second and let the shuttle fly for as long as possible as a streamlined glider.

"Gear!" The commander finally orders the wheels to be lowered. The pilot presses two buttons and the landing gear begins to unfold.

"Three hundred feet . . . two hundred . . . one hundred . . . two hundred five knots . . . fifty feet . . . two hundred two knots . . . "

The pilot keeps up a steady call of our altitude and air-speed so the commander can concentrate on the runway.

"Twenty feet . . . ten . . . five . . . touchdown." The shuttle shakes and rattles over the dry lake desert. The nose comes down in a puff of dust.

We're safely on the ground. The mission is over. In the cockpit we all cheer and shake hands. But my heart is a little sad. I wish I could still be in space, living my dream. What a glorious, wonderful, magnificent dream it's been!

But it's somebody else's turn now. Somewhere a girl or boy is watching on TV as *Atlantis* rolls to a stop. Model airplanes and rockets and *Star Trek* posters decorate this dreamer's bedroom. Books about rockets and astronauts fill the bookshelves.

Is it you? Do you have the dream of being an astronaut? Or do you dream of being a teacher, lawyer, doctor, nurse, scientist, engineer, or anything else? How do you make that dream come true? Or do dreams only come true for a few very smart, special kids?

I wasn't particularly smart. I had to work very hard to get good grades. In high school I was a B+ student. And I certainly wasn't special. I didn't come from a famous family. We weren't rich, and we weren't poor. I had four brothers and a sister. I was the second child. When I was nine years old, my father caught polio, and he lived the rest of his life in a wheelchair. Except for that, my family was an ordinary one.

So my dream didn't come true because I was different from all the other boys and girls my age. I played with trucks and frogs. I played Little League baseball. I was in the Cub Scouts and the Boy Scouts. Sometimes I got in trouble at school or with my parents and was punished for it. One time I was even arrested by the police for throwing a water balloon at some other teenagers. There was nothing special about me.

Why, then, did my dream of being an astronaut come true? How can you turn a dream into reality?

First, you must believe in yourself. You must believe that you can be anything, do anything. Remember . . . dare yourself! There's another boy or girl inside you who wants to prove how smart he or she really is. Give that part of you a chance. Offer yourself a dare. Dare yourself to dream BIG! Dare yourself to believe you can be anything!

Does that mean it will automatically happen? Just because you believe you can be a doctor or nurse or teacher or scientist or astronaut, will it happen? No. Just believing won't make a dream come true. Michael Jordan would never have become a great basketball player by just sitting around dreaming about it. He worked very hard to develop the tools needed to be a star. He worked to develop his endurance and speed and agility. People always need tools to turn their dreams into reality. What tools do you need?

You need an education. Without an education dreams shrivel up and die. You can wish all you want. You can believe in yourself. But without an education, you will never see your dream come true. Stay in school! Study!

What's the most important subject to study? That's an

easy one. Reading. If you can't read, your education stops. You can't study math, history, science, or anything else. You must be a good reader for a dream to come true!

What else do you need?

You need your health. You can have everything I've talked about. You can believe in yourself. You can be a straight-A student. You can be the best reader in the world. But if you have damaged your health with drugs, alcohol, or tobacco, will your dream come true? No. These are poisons that will take your dream and your life. Take care of your body. It's the only one you'll ever have, and you're the only person who can guard it from danger.

Respect for others is another key to making dreams come true. You can't dream of being a pilot and hate to work with people of the opposite sex. The person who will guard your tail in a dogfight may be a woman. You can't be an astronaut and hate people whose backgrounds differ from yours, or who have a different skin color. Your commander, the person who holds your life in his or her hands, could be black, white, Asian, Hispanic, in other words, anyone.

For a dream to come true, you must be a team player. You must respect everybody regardless of gender or race or religion. Remember my astronaut interview? Did NASA ask me to do a calculus problem? No. They wanted to know if I could work well with other people. They wanted to know if I was a team player. Are you? Could you be on a team with somebody who is a different color or believes in a religion different from yours?

In your dream quest, you must also be prepared to face things that you cannot control. Remember my story. I had believed in myself. I had worked hard in school. I had taken care of my body and learned to respect other people. But I had no control over my eyesight. When that weakened, my dream of being a fighter pilot and test pilot and top gun and astronaut came to a screeching stop. But if something you cannot control interferes with your dream, what do you do? Do you give up? Or do you dare yourself to follow another dream? That's what I did. I dared myself to be the best backseater in Air Force fighters. I dared myself to be the best aeronautical engineer. I didn't know it at the time, but those dares kept my dream of being an astronaut alive for ten years! Don't ever give up. When things you can't control get in the way, then dare yourself into another dream. Who knows, maybe the second or third dream will make the first one come true. It did for me.

Atlantis is stopped now. A convoy of support trucks is speeding toward us. In the upper cockpit we follow checklists to power down the shuttle. We unbuckle our safety belts, climb down the ladder to the lower cockpit, and duck through the hatch. Stairs have been driven up to the side of the shuttle. For a moment, we all stand on the top platform breathing deeply of the wonderful scent of desert sagebrush. The commander, pilot, and other mission specialists file down the stairs. I follow them, holding on to the rail in case my wobbly legs should collapse. When a TV

camera momentarily focuses on me, I smile and wave. Though they don't know it, I'm waving at all the dreamers who are watching. I'm waving at the kids who someday will feel the roar of mighty engines at their backs and the crush of g-forces on their chests and see the black of space racing into their faces.

Author's Notes

What did we find when we looked at *Atlantis*'s belly? More than seven hundred heat tiles had been damaged so badly that they would later have to be replaced. Only one tile was completely missing, but the others around it had kept *Atlantis*'s aluminum skin from melting. We had been very lucky.

What had caused all this damage? In the factory, the very tip of the right-side rocket booster had been made too weak. The wind pressure during launch had broken it off, and it had hit the belly. To make certain it would not happen on another mission, NASA changed the way the boosters were built to make them stronger.

On Being an Astronaut

There are two types of NASA astronauts: pilot astronauts and mission specialist astronauts. Pilot astronauts sit in the front seats and have the controls and instruments to fly the shuttle during launch and landing. The pilot astronaut who sits in the front left seat is also called the **commander**. He or she is the overall boss. The pilot astronaut who sits in the front right seat is called the **pilot** and helps the commander fly the spaceship. He or she is really like a copilot in a regular airplane. **Mission specialists** are the crew members (usually three) who do most of the work once the shuttle reaches orbit. They operate the robot arm, do experiments, go on space walks, and release satellites.

What kind of an education do you need if you want to be an astronaut? NASA requires all astronauts to have a college degree in math, science, or engineering. You can't be an astronaut if you get a degree in English, history, music, law, or other non-science fields. NASA says you only need a bachelor's degree to be eligible for an astronaut job, but almost everybody chosen so far has at least a master's degree. Ask your teacher to explain bachelor, master's, and doctorate degrees.

Do you have to be a pilot or be in the military to be an astronaut? No. About one-third of the astronauts are civilians who are not pilots. But if you're not a pilot you can only apply to be a mission specialist astronaut.

To be a pilot astronaut, NASA requires that you have at least one thousand hours of jet flying time. For this reason all pilot astronauts are military flyers. You should plan on being a military test pilot if you want to be a pilot astronaut.

The Space Transportation System (STS)

The mission of the space shuttle, or STS as NASA calls it, is to carry satellites and experiments into orbits about one hundred fifty to three hundred fifty miles above the earth. While it can't fly to the moon (that's about 240,000 miles away), the shuttle can do something no rocket before it could ever do. It can be recycled. Before the shuttle, all of our rockets, including the moon rockets, were "throwaway" rockets. In other words, during their missions all of their parts were jettisoned to fall into the water or burn up in the atmosphere. The only thing that ever came back was the capsule with the astronauts in it. Even the capsule was never used again. It was sent to a museum. But almost all of the STS can be reused, which saves money.

There are three parts to the STS:

The **orbiter** is the winged vehicle that carries the astronauts. Six orbiters have been built: *Enterprise, Columbia, Challenger, Discovery, Atlantis*, and *Endeavour*. The orbiter *Challenger* was destroyed and its astronauts were killed on January 28, 1986, when a hole burned through the side of one of the solid-fueled rocket boosters.

The **external tank** (ET) is the giant orange fuel tank that is attached to the belly of the orbiter. The ET is the only part of the STS that is not reused. It is jettisoned into the atmosphere.

The **solid-fueled rocket boosters** (SRBs) are the giant white booster rockets that are attached to each side of the ET. When they burn out, they are jettisoned and parachute into the ocean. Tugboats pick them up and tow them to shore so they can be cleaned, refilled with solid fuel, and used over again.

The Future

The shuttle is not the end of America's space program. It's just a step, like the Mercury, Gemini, Apollo, and Skylab space projects before it. Soon, if our Congress gives NASA the money, the next step will be taken. We will work with the Russians, Japanese, Canadians, and Europeans to assemble a space station in orbit about three hundred miles above Earth. We need such a station so astronauts can live and work in space for very long periods. While the shuttle may be recyclable, it can only stay in orbit for about two weeks before it runs out of electricity. That's not enough time to complete many experiments. If we could stay in orbit for years on a space station, we might be able to make new medicines, metals, computer chips, and many other things that will help us have better lives on Earth.

After the space station, NASA plans to return to the moon. Astronauts would build a permanent moon base with telescopes and other instruments to help us better understand our universe.

Then, NASA wants to send people to the planet Mars. Who will be the first human to set foot on the red planet? Could it be you? A mission to Mars could begin in as little as thirty years. The astronauts who take that trip will be about forty to forty-five years old. That means they are now students between ten and fifteen years old. That's your age! That means YOU could be the first Martian! Imagine that incredible journey. . . .

After blasting away from earth orbit at a speed of twenty-five thousand miles per hour, you would begin a long silent drift into deep space. Earth would shrink to a ball and then to a marble, and finally it would appear as just a bright star. You and your crew members, men and women from several nations, would now depend on each other more than ever.

Then, as the months passed, Mars would grow bigger and bigger. Its polar ice caps and two small moons, Deimos and Phobos, would become visible. Olympus Mons, a volcano three times taller than the tallest mountain on Earth, would appear. You would see the great Valles Marineris, a canyon so long and so deep it makes our Grand Canyon look puny.

Finally, with the red planet looking huge in your window, you would fire your braking rockets. The first firing would stabilize you in Martian orbit. A second firing, weeks later, would start you to the surface. Clouds of reddish dust would swirl around your windows and block your view, but your instruments would help guide you. A warning light and a thump would indicate landing. You would open the hatch and back down the ladder. For a moment you would hesitate, trying to control your excitement. Slowly you would open your hands and let the weak Martian gravity pull you the last few inches to the ground. Then, you would raise your boot. Through tears of joy, you would look at the first human footprint on another planet . . . *your* footprint.

The Chief

Or
of
nu
Fo
ed
Ro
As

The Chief

Douglas Haig and the British Army

Gary Sheffield

Foreword by Saul David

For John Bourne and Peter Simkins
with thanks for friendship, support and inspiration

First published 2011 by
Aurum Press Limited
7 Greenland Street
London NW1 0ND
www.aurumpress.co.uk

This paperback edition first published in 2012 by Aurum Press Ltd.

A catalogue record for this book is available from the British Library.

ISBN 978 1 84513 769 4

10 9 8 7 6 5 4 3 2 1
2016 2015 2014 2013 2012

Typeset in Dante by SX Composing DTP, Rayleigh, Essex

Printed and bound by CPI Group (UK) Ltd, Croydon, CR0 4YY

Contents

Foreword by Saul David

Having written a life of Lord Cardigan of Balaklava fame, I am no stranger to controversial generals. But surely none is more controversial than Douglas Haig. While Cardigan is remembered for the destruction of the Light Brigade of 670 men, the carnage of the Somme and Passchendaele is laid at Haig's door. Conversely, Haig's vital contribution to the great victories of 1918 that won the First World War has been largely forgotten. Haig has attracted historians and biographers like moths to a candle, and there is little in the way of consensus. His detractors have essentially updated Alan Clark's 'Lions led by Donkeys' school of thought of the 1960s with an impressive array of footnotes to sustain their case; his supporters follow in the footsteps of the late John Terraine, who saw Haig as one of the 'Great Captains' of history. So much has been written about Haig, particularly over the last few years, that one might imagine the debate at an impasse.

But, as Gary Sheffield shows in this masterly new biography, there is much left to say. For the first time we are presented with a portrait of Haig 'in the round'. High command involves much more than generalship on the battlefield, and by highlighting the sheer variety of Haig's activities (involvement with training and logistics, writing doctrine, dealing with allies and politicians) Professor Sheffield makes a compelling case that Haig should be judged on more than just his record as a commander in battle, important as that undoubtedly was. Not that he ignores the battlefield. His account of the Battle of the Somme, for example, is particularly original in that it demonstrates there was a real chance of success on 1 July 1916. It was thrown away not on account of

Haig's inadequacies but rather because of those of his principal subordinate, General Rawlinson, who subverted his chief's plan of operations. Perhaps the most surprising aspect of the book is that Sheffield refurbishes Haig's reputation as a cavalry general. Haig never lost his faith in horsemen as an arm of mobility, and Gary Sheffield shows that in the context of the Western Front this might have proved critical.

A fine piece of work, *The Chief* is even-handed in its treatment of Haig, based on a formidable array of sources, and pulls off the difficult trick of being both scholarly but also highly accessible. Gary Sheffield has established himself as one of the foremost authorities on the British Army of the First World War, and this book will add to his reputation. No book is ever truly definitive, but *The Chief* represents the fairest and most insightful life of Haig thus far.

Preface

This book represents the culmination of a decade of research and writing on Douglas Haig. In many ways it is the companion piece to my *Forgotten Victory: The First World War – Myths and Realities*, published in 2001, but reflects the evolution of my thinking since then. Haig has emerged as a more impressive figure than I then thought, and people who have read my earlier work will be able to detect the ways in which my thinking has moved on.

A word about the title: Haig had three nicknames. The least respectful was 'Duggie', used by the mass of the army. Some in the higher echelons used his initials, DH. But to many, from the Prince of Wales downwards, he was simply The Chief.[1]

The book is founded on Haig's writings, and the papers of various contemporaries scattered in a number of archives. Three different Haig diaries are quoted in this book. Before the First World War he often kept a brief diary, referred to in the footnotes as 'DHD'. During the war he wrote a much longer manuscript diary ('DHMsD'), which was later typed up ('DHTsD'). The latter includes some additions and corrections, but not major deletions.[2] Where I have used the typed version, Haig's additions to the manuscript are indicated by square brackets plus a note in the footnotes. Capitalisation has generally been standardised; '&' replaced by 'and'; and the numbers of exclamation marks reduced. Surnames, except in the case of Kitchener (Lord K) and Lloyd George (LG), have been given in full.

Acknowledgements

I would like to the thank Lord and Lady Haig, and the rest of the Haig family, especially Monica Scott and the late Douglas Scott. I would also like to put on record my gratitude to Dawyck, Second Earl Haig.

Quotations from material held in the Royal Archives appear by gracious permission of Her Majesty Queen Elizabeth II. Crown copyright material appears by kind permission of The National Archives and Commonwealth copyright material by kind permission of the Australian War Memorial.

I would like to thank the following for permission to quote from material for which they hold the copyright:

Lord Haig (Haig papers)
The Trustees of the National Library of Scotland (Haig papers)
Lord Kitchener (Kitchener papers)
Liverpool Record Office, Liverpool Libraries (17th Earl of Derby papers)
The Trustees of the Royal Green Jackets Museum (Fuller papers)
The *Spectator* (Strachey papers)
The Master, Fellows and Scholars of Churchill College Cambridge
    (Hankey Papers)
Andrew Rawlinson (Rawlinson papers)
Parliamentary Archives (Lloyd George papers)
Bodleian Library (Asquith papers)
Bovington Tank Museum (Lindsay papers)
The Syndics of Cambridge University Library (University Archives)
The Trustees of the Imperial War Museum (Wilson papers)

National Army Museum (Ellison papers)
Professor Eugene Ryan (Ryan papers)
Joint Services Command and Staff College (various papers and
    Montgomery-Massingberd papers)
New College Oxford (Milner papers)
The Trustees of the Liddell Hart Centre for Military Archives
    (Clive papers, Grant papers, Howell papers, Kiggell papers,
    Maurice papers)
Lord Cholmondeley (Sassoon papers)
Mrs Joanna Butler (Butler papers)
Lord Esher (Esher Papers, copyright administered by Churchill
    College Cambridge)

Every effort has been made to trace the copyright holders in the Price-Davies, Boraston, Hedley, and Thompson papers held in the Imperial War Museum. Both the author and the Museum would be grateful for any information as to the current copyright holders. To anyone whose copyright I have unwittingly infringed I offer my apologies and will seek to rectify the matter in later editions of this book.

One of the last, but most rewarding parts of writing a book is to complete the acknowledgements. It is a genuine pleasure to mention those people and institutions that have supported me in writing this book. Some gave me specific help, and others have contributed to the development of my understanding of the British army in the First World War, and the role of Douglas Haig, over many years. Yet others have simply been kind to me while I was writing the book. If I named them all the list would be vast, so I hope any not mentioned here will forgive me.

At the head of the list are Peter Simkins and John Bourne. I have dedicated *The Chief* to them as a small tribute to all they have achieved as historians, and in recognition of everything they have done for me – not least in discussing my ideas and reading drafts of this book. Stephen Badsey has been kindness itself, sharing unpublished work with me, reading drafts and being a sounding board for ideas. Naturally none of this distinguished trio bears any responsibility for remaining imperfections in the finished product. Saul David very kindly wrote a flattering preface and has been hugely supportive of the project; as a fellow Arsenal fan we have been suffering together in recent seasons. My colleague in the University of Birmingham War Studies project Peter Gray has been a tower of strength. Thanks are also due to Niall Barr, Jim Beach, Jonathan Boff, Brian Bond, Bob Bushaway, Jeremy Crang, Bob Foley, David French, Bryn Hammond, Simon Higgens, John Lee, Elspeth Johnstone, Spencer Jones, David Jordan, Chris McCarthy, Helen McCartney, Stuart Mitchell, Michael Orr, Bill Philpott, Andy Simpson, Michael Snape, Carolyn Sweet, William Spencer, Kathy Stevenson, the late John Terraine, Rob Thompson, Dan Todman, Ion Trewin, Tony Vines and Jamie Wilson. Two doctoral candidates at Birmingham, Ross Mahoney and Michael LoCicero, were exceptionally generous with their time in helping me with this book, both indirectly and directly.

I have learned a huge amount from my students over the years. I would especially like to thank my military students (and colleagues) on the Higher Command and Staff Course; the students on the MA in British First World Studies at the University of Birmingham; and my research students. I have benefited greatly from the knowledge and insights of members of Birmingham War Studies Seminar, the Western Front Association, of which I am proud to be a Vice-President, and the British Commission for Military History. I would also like to thank General Sir Nick Parker for inviting me to become Regimental Historian of The Rifles, and the members of the regimental family for their inspiration at many levels.

It has been a pleasure to be reminded of the worldwide community of scholars working on the British army of the First World War. The Australian team of Robin Prior and Trevor Wilson has set the agenda to a very large extent. In this book I have disagreed with some of their arguments, (and elsewhere they have disagreed with some of mine) but our disputes are always conducted with respect and affection. Also in Australia Roger Lee deserves particular thanks, not least for his excellent hospitality, along with Jeffery Grey and Peter Stanley. Thanks are also due to Steve Gower, Ashley Ekins, Craig Tibbitts and the staff at the Australian War Memorial, one of the world's great museums and archives. I have benefited greatly from the wisdom of New Zealand historian, Chris Pugsley, currently based in the UK; and Canadian historian Tim Cook. In the USA, Jay Winter has been extremely supportive. As the book neared completion I was invited to lecture at the University of Southern Mississippi, and was able to benefit from the input of Andy Wiest, a friend for nineteen years and counting, and author of the best short biography of Haig. Andy and Jill, thank you for your hospitality.

While putting the last touches to the book I heard the sad news of the death of Richard Holmes. A very kind man, Richard had a huge and positive impact on my career, and was a fine historian of the Great War. Military history, and the lives of us who knew him, are poorer for his passing.

Of the many archivists, librarians and museum people who have helped me, I would especially like to thank Alison Metcalfe (National Library of Scotland); Pamela Clark and Allison Derrett (Royal Archives); Chris Hobson and his staff (library of Joint Services Command and Staff College); Andrew Orgill and his staff (library of Royal Military Academy Sandhurst); Simon Robbins and Rod Suddaby (Imperial War Museum); Lianne Smith (Liddell Hart Centre for Military Archives); Helen Langley (Bodleian Library); Allen Packwood and the staff of the Churchill Archives Centre; William Spencer (National Archives); and Richard Smith and his staff (Bovington Tank Museum).

The publication of this book was delayed by about a year through two factors beyond my control. One was illness, and the other one wasn't. Since 2009 I have seen publishers at their best and worst. I will draw a veil over the latter, and instead I'll confine my comments to thanking the folk at Aurum Press: it has been a pleasure to work with Graham Coster, Stuart Cooper and Barbara Phelan. Barbara Taylor produced the excellent maps. As ever, thanks are due to my literary agent, Simon Trewin, and his assistant at United Agents, Ariella Feiner. Many thanks to my research assistant, Pam Cooper.

It is no exaggeration to say that this book would not have been completed without the loving and long-suffering support of my family: my wife, Viv, to whom I owe more than I can say; my daughter and son, Jennie and James, both now young adults; my parents; and all the members of the Sheffield and Davis clans, far too numerous to mention individually. In addition I owe so much to our church family at Grove Parish Church and at the Cornerstone cafe for their support, and also to Alan and Mandy Bird, who are everything that true friends should be.

Abbreviations

appx.	appendix
AQ	*Army Quarterly*
BAR	*British Army Review*
BP	Boraston papers
BTM	Bovington Tank Museum
CCC	Churchill College Cambridge
CCS	Casualty Clearing Station
C-in-C	Commander-in-Chief
CoS	Chief of Staff
CSO	Chief Staff Officer
DAN	Détachement de l'Armee du Nord
DCP	Duff Cooper Papers
DGMS	Director General of Medical Services
DGT	Director General of Training
DH	Douglas Haig
DHD	Haig's pre-1914 diary
DHMsD	Douglas Haig's Manuscript Diary
DHTsD	Douglas Haig's Typescript Diary
DMT	Director of Military Training
DSD	Director of Staff Duties
DCRO	Durham County Record Office
ed./eds	editor/s
edn	edition
EHR	*English Historical Review*
EP	Esher papers

FP	French papers
GAF	Groupe d'Armées des Flandres
GHQ	General Headquarters
GQG	Grand Quartier Géneral
H.C. Deb	House of Commons Debates
HMSO	Her/His Majesty's Stationery Office
HP	Haig Papers
HyP	Hankey papers
HQ	Headquarters
IWM	Imperial War Museum
JCFWWS	*Journal of the Centre for First World War Studies*, University of Birmingham
JMilH	*Journal of Military History*
JRUSI	*Journal of the Royal United Services Institution*
JSAHR	*Journal Society for Army Historical Research*
JSCSCL	Joint Services Command and Staff College Library
JSS	*Journal of Strategic Studies*
KP	Kiggell Papers
LG	Lloyd George
LGP	Lloyd George papers
LHCMA	Liddell Hart Centre for Military Archives
Lt Col	Lieutenant-Colonel
MI	Mounted Infantry
Ms	Manuscript
MMP	Montgomery-Massingberd papers
NAM	National Army Museum
n.d.	not dated
NLS	National Library of Scotland
ODNB	Oxford Dictionary of National Biography
OH	Official History
OHL	Oberste Heeresleitung
Pte	Private
RD	Rawlinson diary, Churchill College Cambridge
RFC	Royal Flying Corps
RP	Ryan Papers
RwP	Rawlinson papers, Churchill College Cambridge
SP	Sassoon Papers

ST!	*Stand To!*
SWC	Supreme War Council
TF	Territorial Force
TNA	The National Archives
TP	Thompson papers
Ts	Typescript
UP	University Press
W&S	*War and Society*
WiH	*War in History*
WO	War Office
WP	Wilson papers
WPC	War Policy Committee

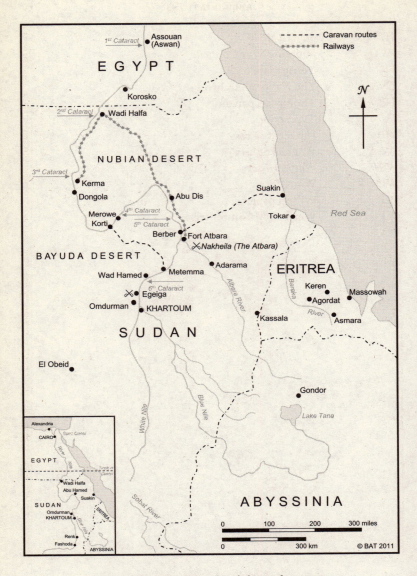

The River War: Egypt and the Sudan, 1898

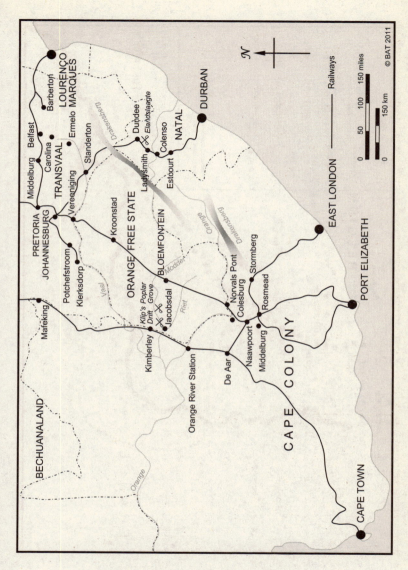

South Africa: Theatre of Operations, 1899–1902

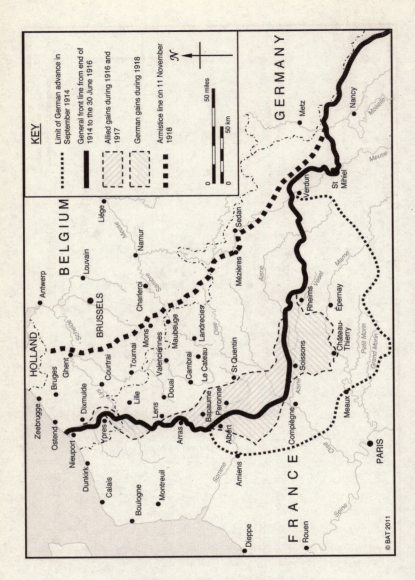

The Western Front, 1914–1918

Introduction

Douglas Haig: Incompetent General or National Hero?

Once, Douglas Haig was a British national hero. When they arrived at a ceremony at the University of Edinburgh in May 1919

> Sir Douglas and Lady Haig were given a reception, the tumultuous warmth of which visibly embarrassed them. Following prolonged cheering, the whole audience . . . joined in singing 'For he's a jolly good fellow'.

The formal presentation of Haig for an honorary degree of Doctor of Laws was interrupted by students chanting 'We want Duggy! – We want Duggy!' In his speech, the Dean referred to Haig in the most glowing of terms. The degree was being conferred

> in recognition of the peerless services he has rendered to the country, the Empire, and to civilisation itself in the supreme crisis of our national history . . . We are honoured by the presence of the gallant soldier who has trained and commanded, with consummate military skill, the greatest armies the Empire has ever sent into the field, and has led them to decisive victory over the most formidable forces ever arrayed for the enslavement of Europe.

'In Roman fashion', the Dean continued,

we may well salute him as the modern Germanicus, who has baulked the
Prussian eagle of its destined prey, tamed its haughty spirit, clipped its
wings, and cut its cruel claws.[1]

For anyone who is only aware of Haig through popular history, war
poetry and *Blackadder*, this hero-worship may seem unbelievable. Yet the
reaction of this audience was typical of the way that Haig was treated
across Britain and the Empire following his victorious return from the
Western Front. Remarkably, his prestige and popularity actually
increased in the nine years of life left to him.

From late 1915 onwards Douglas Haig commanded the largest British
army in history. His British Expeditionary Force (BEF) dwarfed the army
commanded by Wellington a century earlier or Montgomery a generation
later. Haig's army won in 1918 a series of victories that, judged by their
scale, were the greatest in British history. The vast majority of the British
people firmly believed that the war, however dreadful, had to be fought
and won against a dangerous and cruel enemy. As recently as April 1918
Britain had seemed on the verge of defeat. In the immediate aftermath of
victory Haig was seen as the instrument of a wonderful deliverance.

When he returned home, everything Haig did was news. In what
must rate high on the list of great non-stories of the twentieth century,
a newspaper solemnly informed its readers that 'Sir Douglas Haig, who
became indisposed . . . was much better last night'.[2] Retiring from the
army, instead of resting on his laurels Haig assumed a demanding role as
the champion of the ex-serviceman adrift in a country whose politicians
had forgotten the promises of 'a land fit for heroes'. This role fuelled his
popularity, but also aroused suspicion. To some it seemed that Haig had
political ambitions and would try to gain power by riding the wave of ex-
service discontent. Some believed Haig was a potential British Mussolini.

Haig's death in 1928 triggered national mourning on a vast scale. Yet
within a few years Haig's reputation lay in ruins. Coincidentally, in 1928
a wave of revulsion against the First World War set in. Works such as
Sassoon's *Memoirs of an Infantry Officer*, the poems of Wilfred Owen, and
Sherriff's play *Journey's End* questioned the purpose of the mass killing.
Although by no means everyone shared in the view, the war seemed to
be a bloody exercise in futility that had meant nothing and had solved
nothing. The ordinary soldiers were depicted as 'lions led by donkeys'.

Haig's reputation, which had risen so high, had the furthest to fall.

David Lloyd George, Prime Minister from 1916 to 1922, came off second best in his wartime clashes with Haig, but his belated revenge did more than anything else to push his enemy's reputation into the gutter. Suffering from guilt – after all he, as Prime Minister, bore his share of responsibility for the great battles of 1917–18 – and with Haig safely in his grave, Lloyd George carried out a sustained and vitriolic assault in his best-selling multi-volume war memoirs (1933–36). Haig was depicted as the arch-donkey responsible for the deaths of hundreds of thousands of British and Empire troops because of his incompetence. The index gives a flavour of Lloyd George's style. Under 'Haig, Field-Marshal Earl' we find entries for 'his limited vision'; 'unreliability of his judgments'; 'obsessed with Passchendaele', and so on. Lloyd George helped deflect some of the criticism that by right belonged to him and his fellow politicians onto the dead Field Marshal. Another key figure in the decline of Haig's reputation was the military writer and polemicist Basil Liddell Hart, who assisted Lloyd George with his memoirs. In his own writings Liddell Hart painted a fundamentally damning portrait of Haig that helped to establish the parameters of the debate. Historians have yet to break entirely free of the prison that Liddell Hart constructed.[3]

Not everyone turned against Haig's memory – the British Legion stayed loyal, and some writers continued to take a more or less positive view of his generalship – but this unflattering picture of Haig became the dominant one which has been adopted by generations of popular writers and on stage and screen, from Alan Clark's *The Donkeys* and the play and film *Oh! What a Lovely War* in the 1960s to the present day. Haig appears as a fool with a bushy moustache, callously indifferent to the sufferings of his men, convinced that he had God on his side, and criminally inept in his generalship. In popular imagination Haig has the status of a pantomime villain, divorced from the real man and general. The First World War came to be seen as an unredeemed national disaster for a variety of reasons, but at the core lay revulsion at the unprecedented numbers of war dead: one million fatalities among the forces of the British Empire. Haig, as the man in command on the Western Front during the bloodiest British battles of the war, naturally became the focus of the blame and came to embody everything that was seen as wrong about the war.

Even at the height of Haig's popularity, questions about his generalship rumbled away in the background. Although it was seen as unpatriotic to criticise British generalship in public while the war was going on, behind closed doors and occasionally in public there was considerable disquiet from the likes of Lloyd George, Winston Churchill and the journalist Lovat Fraser. In the 1920s criticism remained fairly muted, although Haig was active behind the scenes in defending his reputation. Given Haig's huge popularity in the 1920s, many critics publicly held their peace. Obituaries of Haig tended to skirt around questions of generalship.

The historical tide was running strongly against Haig after interest in the Great War revived in the mid-1950s. But one writer set out on a lonely, and some thought Quixotic, defence of Haig against what he angrily dismissed as 'instant history'. In books, articles and lectures from the 1950s to the 1990s, John Terraine argued that there was no short cut to victory on the Western Front, that the way was always going to be hard and bloody, but that under Douglas Haig the BEF wore down the German army in a series of attritional battles before delivering the *coup de grâce* in 1918. Haig was, in Terraine's view, a 'Great Captain', fit to stand alongside Marlborough and Wellington.

Terraine's was an uncomfortable, deeply unfashionable thesis, and in the 1960s provoked an extremely hostile response. But forty and more years later it is in surprisingly good shape. His 1963 biography *Douglas Haig: The Educated Soldier* remains indispensable, in spite of its age. The core of its argument about the nature of the fighting and the role of the BEF has never been successfully rebutted, and Terraine is acknowledged by the revisionist school of historians of the BEF that came into being in the 1980s and 1990s as a sort of spiritual godfather. But in acclaiming Haig as a 'Great Captain', Terraine claimed too much. Still, discounting his more extravagant claims still leaves a powerful and convincing picture of a general who was very different from the incompetent buffoon of caricature. The impact of Terraine's writings on the rehabilitation of Haig's reputation was profound.[4]

Among academic historians who have worked in the original records, much of the sound and fury surrounding the history of the British army in the First World War has died down in recent years. A rough consensus has emerged that the army eventually adapted well to the new conditions of warfare on the Western Front, and by 1918 it had emerged as a highly effective fighting force. There is no such consensus about Haig. Historians such as Tim Travers, Ian Beckett, Paul Harris, and the team of Robin Prior and Trevor Wilson, take a generally dim view of his generalship. Other historians, such as Stephen Badsey, Andrew Wiest, Brian Bond, John Bourne and Peter Simkins, although far from uncritical, regard Haig in a more positive light.

We are not short of books on Haig; I deliberately refrained from reading the most recent – by Paul Harris, published in 2008 – until the first draft of this manuscript was completed. The obvious question is, why write yet another biography of Haig? The first answer is that there are still some important things to say about Haig the man. In 2005 I co-edited with John Bourne a scholarly edition of Haig's wartime diaries and letters, the first for over fifty years. However much I thought I knew about the subject at the beginning of the process, I knew much more by the end. Haig emerged as a more complex, and certainly more interesting, figure than I had anticipated. This book is intended as a combination of a conventional biography with an examination of Haig's role in the context of the performance of the British army as a whole. Haig's personality has, I think, often been misunderstood, and this book offers some insights into his motivations, character, upbringing, and relationships with his family, friends and colleagues. I have deliberately cast my net wide in my research, and this book includes some evidence that, to my knowledge, has not been used before.

The second answer is that the debate on Haig has far from run its course. Editing his papers raised questions that had not, to my mind, been answered adequately. To take one example, most historians agree about the scale of the achievement in transforming the British army from the flat-footed amateur force that began the battle of the Somme in 1916 to the war-winner of 1918. But how much credit did the man at the top, Douglas Haig, deserve for this change? Did he, as the Dean at Edinburgh asserted in 1919, train as well as lead his army? Was Haig a passive spectator of the process of transformation? An active participant? Or something in between? Haig's tenure as Commander-in-Chief must be judged in the round. It is not enough to assess him on just one of his many roles, even one as important as his battlefield generalship.

Another fact that intrigued me is the number of apparently incomprehensible decisions that historians have attributed to Haig. This has contributed to the view held by many, including some reputable writers, that the Commander-in-Chief of the BEF was several rounds short of a .303 Lee Enfield magazine. But there is plenty of evidence that Haig was not stupid. For one thing he worked closely with Richard Burdon Haldane in reforming the army before the First World War. Haldane, one of the greatest Secretaries of State for War Britain has ever had, possessed a formidable intellect – and yet admired Haig. So how can this pre-war Haig be reconciled with the Western Front Haig who some think left his brains behind in Aldershot – but somehow went on to command the BEF during the great victories of 1918?

The simple fact is that, given careful study of the documents and understanding of the context, many of Haig's apparently 'inexplicable' decisions and views lose their mystery. That is not to say that Haig was invariably right, but that his decision-making was not as irrational as it sometimes appears. A supposed mystery about Haig's command on the first day on the Somme put forward by one writer disappeared when in the course of my research I realised that he had misread the date on a document that actually dealt with a completely different battle, fought two weeks later.[5]

Biographies are invariably tinted by whether or not the author has come to like or dislike the individual they are writing about. It is of course nonsense to say that a biographer must be in sympathy with their subject to produce a good book – decent biographies of Hitler and Stalin would be thin on the ground if that were the case – and most serious historians strive for objectivity. But, consciously or not, some writers on Haig seem to have started from the assumption that he was incompetent or even stupid and then interpreted the evidence in that light.

It is easy to understand why modern audiences find it hard to warm to Douglas Haig. He was a late Victorian, his public persona rigid and austere, and many of his attitudes – whether his enthusiasm for the British Empire or his belief in military executions for the sake of example – the product of a long-gone era. Above all, he appears out of touch with the realities of modern war. The title of a piece on Haig by a modern historian included the phrase 'Educated Soldier or Cavalry Officer': the implication being that he couldn't be both.[6] When writing about the Great War it is impossible to escape from the shadow of the appallingly long casualty lists, and Haig was the man ultimately, and in some cases directly, responsible for the 'butcher's bill'. Haig was the product of an era very different from our own, but, because he died within living memory, it is easier judge him by the standards of our own day than it would be for, say, Henry VIII.

If Haig was miraculously resurrected today and was interviewed on television, there is little doubt what questions he would be asked: 'How do you feel about the casualties?' and 'Will you say sorry?' 'We live in a confessional culture', a leading Haig expert has written. Haig's virtues of 'Strength, reticence, privacy, religious faith, devotion to duty are no longer much admired. Our society admires the ability to confess weakness and to be seen to be struggling to overcome it'.[7] Ironically, Haig did have some things in his background that might be used to construct a classic twenty-first-century 'through adversity to success' story. His father was an alcoholic, and the young Douglas overcame ill-health and as an adult battled throughout to control his asthma. But his early life produced a strong silent man who would not have dreamed of laying bare his soul in public. In the Second World War 'People's Generals' such as Bernard Montgomery and Bill Slim redefined the image of the senior British military leader – media-savvy popularists, matey with their troops and the people at home. Their successors are today's generals who, equipped with media training, appear confident and articulate on our television screens. Such modern commanders have built a barrier between us and Haig, the tongue-tied, starchy Victorian. Like the Duke of Wellington, Haig's lodestar was a sense of duty. Both men appear as relics of a remote past.

And yet, unlike Wellington's era, Haig's time was not really that long ago. Some who were children when Haig was in command on the Western Front are still alive today. Many of the challenges with which he had to grapple – coalition warfare, the impact of casualties on the home front, adjusting strategy and tactics to take account of advanced technology – have a very contemporary ring. We have a paradox. Haig was the product of a world very different from ours, but he was a recognisably modern commander.

In examining the documentary evidence I have worked from the assumption that Haig was a rational and competent soldier, and have tried to judge him by the standards of his own time, not ours. As a result, the picture that has emerged is rather different from the traditional image of Haig as a serial blunderer who learned nothing from his errors. This book does not argue that Haig was always right, or that he was a military genius. On the contrary, he made some serious mistakes that had bloody consequences, and I have not hesitated to criticise him. I was gratified to be described by Jay Winter, one of the world's leading historians of the Great War, as 'neither an apologist for Haig, nor one of his many scathing detractors'.[8] But what has emerged from my research is, I think, a more nuanced picture of Haig the man and Haig the general. He was a flesh-and-blood human being, not an ogre. For all his faults he made substantial contributions to turning the BEF into a battle-winning force, and his generalship was a significant factor in determining the outcome of the war.

The story does not stop in 1918. In the last decade of his life Haig emerged as the *de facto* leader of British ex-servicemen, as President of a voluntary organisation of veterans, the British Legion. In a time of economic hardship Haig threw his energies and immense prestige into improving the lives of former soldiers, sailors and airmen struggling in an uncaring, pre-welfare-state world. Now, in another era of hard times, with public services in retreat and an officially sponsored return to the values of voluntarism in vogue, Haig's role deserves a fresh look. In some ways, like it or not, our society is beginning to resemble interwar Britain, but the Haig of the 1920s has no equivalent today.

If we do not understand our past, we impede our understanding of who we are and where we are today. History, in short, provides essential context for the present. The dreadful human tragedy of the First World War, more than any other single event, shaped the world in which we live. We owe it to ourselves to escape from the bad habit of viewing this cataclysmic event, and its leading actors, through a mist of myths or half-truths. This book is an attempt to present a portrait of the single most important British soldier of that war that differs radically from the Douglas Haig caricature of *Oh! What a Lovely War* and *Blackadder Goes Forth*. In spite of the best efforts of many historians, this mythical version remains the way that Haig is seen by most people in the English-speaking world. I make no claim that this book is definitive – as they say, 'other views of Haig are also available' – but I offer this contribution to a debate that shows no sign of ending any time soon.

I

Apprenticeship

At the end of October 1918, as the British Expeditionary Force prepared to launch its final victorious battle on the Western Front, a letter appeared in *The Scotsman* about the ancestors of the Commander-in-Chief, Field Marshal Sir Douglas Haig. The Haigs, it said,

> have always been a martial family . . . One fought with Wallace at the battle of Stirling Bridge. One fought in Bruce's army at Bannockburn, and afterwards at Halidonhill, where he fell . . . [Another] was in the army of the Regent Arran which defeated the English invaders at Ancrum in 1544, and had the honour of capturing Lord Evers, one of the English Generals . . . This is indeed a warlike record . . .

Douglas Haig was 'a worthy and able successor of his warrior ancestors'.[1]

He was born on 19 June 1861 in a house on Charlotte Square, Edinburgh, the eleventh and last child of John and Rachel Haig.[2] The baby was born into a life of wealth and privilege. A Norman knight, Petrus de Haga (the Latin version of Pierre de la Hague) had come to Scotland from Normandy in the mid-twelfth century and settled in the Borders near Bemersyde. The Haig family, as they became known, quickly cemented a place in Scottish society. The thirteenth-century bard Thomas the Rhymer had prophesied:

> Tyde what may, what'er betide
> Haig will be Haig of Bemersyde.

'Tyde What May' appears on the Haig family crest, and Bemersyde has remained in the family to the present day. Field Marshal Earl Haig became the 29th Laird of Bemersyde when he took in possession of the estate in 1923.

By the early nineteenth century the social standing of the Haigs had slipped. John Haig, Douglas's father, was remembered as a rough old man with a thick Scottish brogue.[3] What he lacked in social polish he more than made up for in money. John Haig was a wealthy whisky distiller, laying the foundations for a company that became a household name in Britain. In 1839 he made a shrewd marriage to Rachel Veitch, who was from another Border family of distinctly higher social standing than his branch of the Haigs. Victorian Britain was class-ridden and class-conscious, but it was a society in which families with 'new' money from 'trade' could make their way into high society, particularly if a judicious match raised their social profile. Social barriers could be porous. 'Who can say', asked a contemporary commentator, 'where the upper class ends or the middle class begins'?[4] John's money and Rachel's family helped their children ease into the social elite. Douglas, by being sent to a public school, attending Oxford and being commissioned into a smart regiment, took three important steps to consolidating his and his family's place in the upper classes, although fellow officers could occasionally be snobbish about Haig's origins in 'trade', even when he was a field marshal. In 1918 Major-General Pinney referred to him as 'the opulent whiskey distiller'.[5]

John Haig is a rather shadowy figure. He was 59 at the time of his youngest son's birth, and suffered from ill health that was exacerbated by heavy drinking. A letter of 1877 from Rachel to the 16-year-old Douglas speaks volumes. His father had 'for the first time . . . done without Brandy, Whisky or Kirsche before breakfast'. John died, according to his death certificate probably of cirrhosis of the liver, in 1878.[6] John Haig's foul temper did not always make for a happy relationship with his children. It is always risky to argue from silence, but Douglas's later reticence about his father probably reflects the emotional space between the two. But John Haig should not be written off simply as a stereotypical drunken, abusive Victorian father. His namesake, Douglas's elder brother, remembered their father, for all his faults, with fondness.[7] For all that, John Haig's strongest influence on his youngest son was perhaps a negative one. Later in life, Haig was notably abstemious and health-conscious – although he seems to have lived the good life to the full as an undergraduate at Oxford – and it is tempting to read this as a reaction against his father's excesses.

'Willie' Haig, the eldest of the brood, was a full two decades older than Douglas, and even before John Haig's death he seems to have acted as something of a stand-in father for the youngest children.[8] By far the greatest influence on the young Douglas, though, was his mother. Rachel had been just 19 when she married her 37-year-old husband. She was, remembered her daughter Janet, 'a capable, sensible, clearheaded woman, absolutely unworldly, and with a deep and reverent sense of Duty'. Rachel was '[s]elflessly devoted to her children', but 'she loved her youngest above them all'.[9] Douglas's Christian faith, instilled as a child, owed much to her. His mother had grown more pious with age: 'I desire', she wrote to her son John, 'to acknowledge His loving Hand *in this as in every other event*'.[10] Likewise, at the time of the greatest crisis of his life, the First World War, Douglas Haig found solace in a deepened relationship with God and affection for his Church. Haig revered his mother's memory to the end of his days. She was, as his adoring wife Doris wrote, 'perhaps the most abiding and powerful influence on his whole life'.[11]

Rachel's affection for her youngest may have been linked to the fact that Douglas was a sickly child, an asthmatic. A visitor wrote of young Douglas 'sitting up in bed with a shawl around his shoulders fighting for breath'.[12] Self-control, especially in exercising regularly and keeping a close watch on diet, is the key to maintaining health for asthmatics. Later in life, Haig went out of his way to avoid anything, especially food, which might trigger a fresh attack. Memories of childhood asthma, added to a desire to avoid his father's unfortunate example, offers a partial explanation of the adult Douglas Haig's 'cool', restrained, personality.

The general who mastered the 'mask of command' – keeping his feelings to himself, no matter how severe the crisis – was certainly very different from the spoiled small boy who was subject to temper tantrums. One of those moments was frozen in time in a photograph that captures an extraordinarily grumpy-looking three-year-old Douglas glaring at the camera. The normal process of growing up, and the battle to maintain his health, gradually saw Douglas's temperament move onto a more even keel. At fourteen he wrote a polite letter to his brother John. This was obviously out of a sense of duty; he wrote about a cat show before finishing, 'as I have no more news'.[13]

Schoolboy and Undergraduate

After attending Edinburgh Collegiate, a day school, from 1869, Douglas was sent to Orwell Preparatory School in 1871. He did not shine at his lessons. Ill-health and not beginning formal education until the age of eight could not have helped. To Rachel's disappointment, Douglas was not thought up to the academic standards demanded for Rugby. Instead, in 1875 he went to Clifton College, a relatively new public (i.e. socially exclusive, fee-paying) school near Bristol. There too he initially struggled with his studies, although he improved over time. The scholastic high point was coming first in Latin in his last term, and overall he finished a respectable seventh in his form. Douglas seems to have had few close friends at Clifton.[14]

A public-school education in the Victorian and Edwardian period was about far more than just academic subjects. Attending a 'good' school was almost a rite of passage into the top layers of the army, the civil service, and the church. It was partly a matter of meeting the right people, of being an initiate in an experience shared by a privileged few. It was also about absorbing the virtues of muscular Christianity, chivalry and, not least, the classics. Public schools aimed to mould 'character'. Sport was especially prized. Although he does not seem to have shone at sport at Clifton, Haig in 1919 enthused that team games required 'decision and character on the part of the leaders, discipline and unselfishness among the led, and initiative and self-sacrifice on the part of all'. Moreover, the 'inspiration' of games 'has brought us through this war, as it has carried us through the battles of the past'.[15]

Douglas Haig's character was moulded by a series of identities that spread out like ripples from a stone thrown into a pond. He was proud of the city of his birth. He was a Lowland Scot, but he was also British, a member of the United Kingdom's upper classes and was to end his days as a member of the nobility. By religion he was a Presbyterian, a member of the Church of Scotland, a fact that undoubtedly influenced his suspicion of Roman Catholicism that broke the surface at various times. A convinced Imperialist, Haig (like many Scots) was to make his name in the far reaches of the Empire. Moreover, he grew up with a sense of what it was to be a gentleman. Gentlemen had a sense of duty; had 'character'; held values founded on Christian and chivalric principles; behaved in a certain way in social situations; and had a set of attitudes about what was, and was not, right and acceptable. Thus gentlemanliness could lead to snobbery and prejudice, such as anti-Semitism.

Douglas Haig grew up at a time when the image of 'heroic masculinity' had set up the soldier of Empire as a role model for the young male. The frontier soldier embodied 'the virtues of manhood', and saw 'war as [the] ultimate test and opportunity. A "real man" . . . was prepared to fight (and if necessary, to sacrifice his life) for Queen, Country and Empire'.[16] Among the qualities of heroic masculinity were physical health, self-restraint and devotion to duty.[17] All three were central to Haig's persona. His personality was inclined to self-control, and, consciously or unconsciously, he became the heroically masculine Imperial Soldier incarnate. Some historians have seen the sublimation of sexual urges as a motivation in the drive to acquire the Empire. Perhaps; but sexual licence was also a notable characteristic of the British imperial military experience.[18]

England and Scotland had shared a monarch since 1603, but political union did not follow for another 104 years. In the course of the eighteenth century English and Scots cautiously edged closer together. A new sense of Protestant British nationalism emerged, forged by wars against a common enemy, Catholic France, and facilitated by trade and the common endeavour of building an overseas empire. British nationalism did not entirely replace older loyalties or institutions, but as a commentator wrote in 1887, 'An Englishman has but one patriotism, because England and the United Kingdom are to him practically the same thing. A Scotchman [sic] has two but he is sensible of no opposition between them.'[19]

Douglas Haig never lost his sense of Scottishness and, like the vast majority of his compatriots, had no problems in reconciling it with a British identity. He often used England as a synonym for 'Great Britain' (i.e. England, Wales and Scotland) or the 'United Kingdom' (which included Ireland), or even 'the British Empire'. Today no self-respecting Scot would do so, but many did then.

By Victoria's reign the separate aristocracies of England, Wales,

Scotland and Ireland had melded into a new British upper-class which provided leadership for the British state in the army and navy and in government. This gave the social elite of all four countries a stake in the new nation-state.[20] Douglas Haig's career demonstrates this process in action. The army was a primary vehicle for forging a 'UK' identity, even though it consisted of a number of regiments and corps, many of which had a strong national and local identity. Haig did not join the sole Scottish cavalry regiment, the Scots Greys, but rather the 7th Hussars, which had at least been raised in Scotland in the seventeenth century; he later commanded another English regiment, the 17th Lancers. As a high commander he was a member of an elite drawn from all parts of the United Kingdom, and, although he had patronage to bestow, he showed no particular preference for Scots.

Like wider British society, the elites and masses in the Victorian and Edwardian army were divided by a huge social and economic chasm. Edinburgh in the year of Haig's birth presented the visitor with a picture of 'antique grandeur', but alongside its 'extraordinary beauty' was poverty and 'unspeakable filth'. About a third of Scottish dwellings consisted of just one room, and in 1861 the average size of such a 'house' was 14 feet by 11½ feet.[21] The upper classes had an uneasy suspicion of 'the mob' – especially, in the Scottish context, if it was of Irish Catholic origin. But the products of urban and rural slums from all over the British Isles provided the vast majority of the army's ordinary soldiers ('Other Ranks'). In his socially-insulated childhood and youth Douglas Haig would not have come across many members of the working classes, and only then in the form of servants, grooms, bootblacks and the like. That was to change dramatically once he joined his regiment.

In a stratified society where social snobbery was rife, having origins in 'trade' could be a severe handicap for the wealthy young man seeking to make his way in the world. One of the ways in which Haig overcame this was by going up to Brasenose College, Oxford, in October 1880.[22] This was at his mother's prompting. She had a very clear idea of the steps that her children needed to take to establish themselves in the top social bracket: an Oxbridge man '*is of a higher stamp*' than those who are not', she wrote to her son John, concerning Douglas, not least because it would bring him into contact with the future 'great men of the day . . . and the training makes a gentleman.'[23]

Rachel died in 1879. Haig's childless sister Henrietta, ten years older than him and married to Willie Jameson, of another whisky dynasty, became his primary confidante and supporter, and was only eventually supplanted in this role by Haig's wife Doris.[24] At Oxford, Haig developed from a boy to a man, growing in confidence and coming to realise that he could be popular with his peers, but also that he had the ability to make a success of his life.[25]

At some point in his time as an undergraduate, Haig made up his mind to have a career in the army and to take his calling seriously. 'It all depends on a man himself how he gets on in any profession. If I went into the Church I'd be a Bishop', he informed a fellow student.[26] In recent years his had not been a military family. Why, and when, he decided on the army is unclear. In hindsight, contemporaries detected stirrings of interest in a military career as far back as Clifton,[27] but it seems certain that he did not make a definite decision until Oxford. Possibly it was connected with his love of horses, and his discovery that he was a talented polo player.

The picture that emerges from Haig's diary is of an idyllic, idle rich sort of life, a precursor to the Oxford of Evelyn Waugh's *Brideshead Revisited*. There was riding and polo, lunches and dinners. He was a member of several fashionable clubs, including the Bullingdon, later described as 'the acme of exclusiveness at Oxford; it is the club of sons of the nobility, the sons of great wealth'.[28] To pick entries at random, Haig recorded a 'very good champagne lunch' on 18 January 1883, and on the following day he 'hunted with the Bicester'.[29]

He also became involved in the politics of college and club, and took part in long, alcohol-fuelled discussions. As a handsome and popular, if rather quiet, young man 'with a pushed-out chin and marked jaw', Haig fitted in well with a socially elite crowd that included Edward Grey, a future Liberal Home Secretary, and Lord Henry Bentinck, another future MP. If there had ever been any doubt about Douglas Haig's social status, his Oxford days removed it.[30]

Although Haig's undergraduate career seems to have been characterised by the advice given to undergraduates by Dr Craddock, the College Principal – 'Drink plenty of port' and 'Ride, sir, ride. I like to see the gentlemen of Brasenose in top boots' – there was an underlying note of earnestness.[31] Certainly not a swot, Haig was reasonably diligent in his studies, although Brasenose was a 'hearty' rather than an intellectual college, and the Pass degree for which Haig was studying was not particularly academically demanding. In the event he left without a degree, having missed a term's residence because of illness and decided against coming back for the additional term which would allow the degree to be awarded. Time was getting short if he was to enter Sandhurst – he was already nearly 23 – and in any case possession of a degree would bring him no benefit in the army of the time.

Douglas Haig enjoyed Oxford and remembered it fondly in later years,[32] but it is not clear from his undergraduate diaries whether he had any sort of emotional or sex life. There is no indication in his diaries or letters of any emotional attachments or sexual activity. Did he have homosexual inclinations? The evidence for this is non-existent, despite the insinuation that 'there was a *frisson* of homosexuality attaching to [Haig's] patrons'. His patron Sir Evelyn Wood was not, as has been suggested, gay.[33] If he was not homosexual, some have argued that Douglas Haig's woman-free world is explained by misogyny. This seems to rest on a few throwaway comments and is counterbalanced by several pieces of evidence from Haig's time as a junior officer. 'Sly rascal', a brother officer wrote to Haig, probably in the late 1880s, 'I knew you could not keep off the females . . .' And his diary contains unexplained excisions, for which the finger of suspicion points at Haig's wife, Doris, perhaps seeking to destroy evidence of his youthful dalliances.[34]

Haig was, of course, inarticulate and shy, particularly in female company. When Major Haig served on the staff of the Aldershot Cavalry Brigade in 1899 the son of his brigade commander, Major-General John French, recalled that he [Haig]

> was a man of few words, especially in the presence of women, and we were always much amused at the stock remarks which he invariably produced on these occasions.
>
> One, addressed to my sister Essex, was: 'Very nice tea to-day, Essex,' and the other to the old dog, gazing up at him with hungry eyes, was: 'Daphne, poor dog'. These, practically speaking, were the beginning and end of his observations, until the rest of us had gone off and left him with my father. They would then have long talks on the possibility of war [in South Africa] . . .

Perhaps Haig's shyness was mistaken for misogyny. At Oxford, like many other undergraduates, Haig seems to have been content with all-male company. His near-contemporary Leo Amery lived an 'almost monastic' life at Oxford but then went on to marry and have children. Haig's views on gender, like those on race and class, were very much of his time.[35]

The Young Officer

He arrived at the Royal Military College Sandhurst on 12 February 1884, after attending a 'crammer' to bring himself up to speed for the examination. He did well, passing out in December 1884 first of 129 Gentleman Cadets. In his examinations he earned 2,557 out of a possible 3,350 marks. It seems that the marks were fairly tightly bunched: Walter Congreve, who was to command XIII Corps on the Somme, came fifth with 2,486 marks, and another future subordinate, Sydney Lawford, commander of 41st Division on the Western Front, was, appropriately, 41st, with 2,153 marks.[36] A cadet's performance at Sandhurst was not necessarily an accurate predictor of future achievements. Charles Monro, who was to command First Army under Haig, finished 120th in 1879, and his Sandhurst report described him as 'rather below the average of the cadet of his time'.[37]

Haig reaped the rewards of success. He was awarded the Anson Memorial Sword, and appointed Under Officer. An instructor at the RMC is also said to have commented that 'A Scottish lad, Douglas Haig, is top in everything, books, drill, riding and sports. He is to go into the cavalry, and before he is finished he will be top of the Army', but there seems to be no contemporary source for this; it first seems to have appeared in print in Lady Haig's biography of her husband.[38] However, it is possible that someone said something like this about Haig at Sandhurst. He was, after all, the outstanding student of his year and this anecdote – whether accurate in detail or not – seems to reflect that.

The picture emerges of a driven man, determined to succeed, and at Sandhurst Haig's social life took second place to sheer hard work. Congreve commented, with some awe, that he copied out his lecture notes – something no cadet had ever done before or since.[39] A more typical cadet, Haig's future protégé Hubert Gough, enjoyed the lessons, but the bulk of his recollections of Sandhurst were given over to reminiscences of fox-hunting.[40]

At Sandhurst, Haig was admired rather than liked. His age may have contributed to this. He was a relatively sophisticated young man with three years of Oxford under his belt. So, given his 'reserved nature and industrious habits', it is not surprising that he 'kept very much to himself' when plunged into the company of 17- and 18-year-olds. A fellow Old Cliftonian and future Army commander, William Birdwood, who overlapped with Haig at Sandhurst, wrote that he was 'four years my senior in age, and consequently seemed to belong almost to another generation'.[41]

As an Under Officer, Haig in effect had the responsibilities of an NCO in a regular army unit (including punishing fellow cadets). This time-consuming role placed him in a position of leadership among his peers in a hierarchical society. As a result of reforms in the 1870s, Sandhurst was intended to give future officers a basic military education, together with an introduction to discipline, seen as the cornerstone of army life, inculcated via the parade square. One cadet who attended Sandhurst before the First World War said that it was famous for 'turning out a very good private soldier'.[42] The quality of the course has been questioned, although it was probably more demanding than Haig's Oxford career. There was ample opportunity for officer-like activities, and, in spite of his self-imposed regime of hard work, he found time to ride and play polo.

In February 1885 Douglas Haig joined the 7th Hussars. In November 1886 the regiment departed for India, remaining there for a decade. It soon settled into a rhythm: 'each year was spent in somehow getting through the hot season, safeguarding the well-being of horses, families and men, and in the cold weather working up to the winter exercises, inspections and annual manoeuvres'.[43] Haig himself suffered from typhoid in 1887. Within three years, Lieutenant Haig had been appointed as Adjutant, a significant position, responsible for day-to-day adminis-tration of the regiment. Promoted to captain in January 1891, he gave up the position of Adjutant in July of the following year. He had several staff jobs in India in 1892–3, and then returned to the 7th Hussars briefly, before setting out for Europe in April 1894.

'The life of the regimental officer in time of peace', wrote one of Haig's contemporaries, 'is not sufficiently interesting to dwell upon at any great length, and soldering in the eighties of [sic] last century was not so strenuous as it became a few years later'. Officers 'danced, hunted, shot, fished, played polo, raced and enjoyed [them]selves tremendously'. The writer was Haig's *bête noir* Charles à Court Repington, late Rifle Brigade. Perhaps one can detect a damning comment on Haig in another of Repington's sentences: '[w]e all thought that we received half a day's pay for half a day's work, and all but a few *enthusiasts* acted upon this principle'.[44]

Douglas Haig was that rare thing, a subaltern (junior officer) who took peacetime soldiering seriously. While he too played polo, hunted and generally enjoyed himself, a stripe of seriousness ran through Haig that set him aside from most of his fellow officers. His regimental nickname was 'Doctor', because of his university career, and probably because he was a thinking soldier.[45] His nature included a mixture of a sense of duty and burning ambition that made him an excellent regimental officer.

There is a fascination in reading in his letters and diaries of the inconsequential details of his life in India: parades on the dusty *maidan*, tiger shoots and polo matches.[46] Yet in seeking to understand Haig the commander, there are some important pointers to the future here. The first concerns his relationship with his men; the second, his development as a professional in an officer corps dominated by amateurs.

Haig's views on the ordinary soldier were very much those of his late-Victorian peers. The second half of the nineteenth century saw the emergence of the ideal of the British officer as a Christian gentleman. '*Noblesse oblige*', the idea that privilege carried with it the burdens of responsibility, was translated into practical, paternalistic concern for the well-being of the Other Ranks, bridging the vast social gulf between the officers' mess and the barrack room; looking after the men became a central part of the officer's code. Relations between the ranks were far from close, but they were often characterised by mutual respect and even affection, and common soldiers admired brave, paternal and competent officers.[47] As a young officer, Haig imbibed a full measure of this paternal ethos, and it shaped his behaviour throughout his life.

Glimpses of his relations with his men emerge from the written record. His regimental colleague (and future general) John Vaughan recalled spending time with Haig going around an English town to buy fish and chips for the men. Ex-Sergeant Griffiths recalled many years later that as Adjutant Haig would visit the hospital to 'talk to the

serious cases'. He would 'ask if he could do anything for you, he would
write to your friends in England if you was [sic] not well enough, he
was most kind to me'.[48] In 1903 Reginald Teale wrote to Haig to thank
him for his influence in helping him fifteen years before to break from
'bad companions' who were leading him astray: 'the thought struck
me "what would Captain Haig think of me if he saw me now" and I put
down the glass and said "I have done with drink" . . . [I]t is through my
deep respect for you that I have been enabled to raise myself to my
present position'.[49] In 1903 Teale was Regimental Quartermaster
Sergeant, a highly responsible post that would have been envied by
many other soldiers.

Another tribute came from the 7th Hussars' senior NCO, Regimental
Sergeant Major Humphries. Haig noted, with evident pleasure, that on
leaving the regiment in 1892 'Humphries wrung my hand and said I was
"the best sort he had ever had to do with"'. As Adjutant, Haig would have
had frequent dealings with the RSM, a powerful and influential figure, and
in its way, this was among the greatest compliments Haig ever received:
Vaughan recalled that Humphries would 'buck' up young officers on
sword drill by saying 'Captain Haig is coming off leave next week'.[50]

It is clear that Haig was a first-class Adjutant. To be a success in such
a post an officer needed exacting standards. But he also needed a mixture
of efficiency and compassion, to know when to offer helpful advice and
when to wave the stick, when to turn a blind eye and when not, and,
above all, to keep his finger on the pulse of the regiment. Naturally, an
effective Adjutant was not going to please everyone, and there is little
doubt that Haig came down hard on soldiers he did not consider up to
the mark. At least one ex-soldier, who felt himself hard done by, had
mixed feelings about Haig at this period, but he still wrote to Haig's
widow in laudatory terms about 'the finest Soldier in the world . . . an
English [sic] Gentleman'.[51] One suspects that many former 7th Hussars
would have echoed CQMS Teale's comment that he had 'watched your
splendid career throughout the last Soudan [sic] and African wars with so
much interest and delight . . .'[52]

As Repington noted, there was an 'undercurrent of seriousness'
beneath the frivolity of the army of the 1880s. The late Victorian army
was constantly on operations. The record was not unblemished, as
defeats by the Zulus in 1879 and the Boers in 1881 and 1899 testified, but

nonetheless there was an impressive level of success. Such success owed a great deal to high levels of competence among the officers. There were those that did take peacetime soldiering seriously: at any time they could be called to active service. On campaign in India or Africa, officers developed battlecraft, flexibility of mind, the ability to improvise, understanding of logistics and staff work, the power of command, the ability to lead in battle. Generals such as Lords Roberts, Wolseley and Kitchener proved highly effective commanders. Further down the command chain many junior officers also proved very competent.

One was Douglas Haig. Even before he had seen any campaign service, senior officers were taking note of the determined young Scot. In 1891 General Sir George Luck, the Inspector General of Cavalry in India, chose him as Brigade Major (chief of staff), and Haig was tasked to prepare a report on the January 1892 cavalry manoeuvres. In 1892 he joined the staff of Lieutenant-General Sir George Greaves, Commander-in-Chief, Bombay; the irascible Greaves thought highly of Haig, recommending him for the Staff College. Much later Haig paid tribute to his old boss, hinting at the scars borne by his staff officers – Greaves had 'a personality we were not . . . likely to forget' but generously asserting that he could not 'name any other general from whom I learned more practical soldiering'.[53]

This is not to suggest that Haig had an outstanding intellect. An uncharitable critic might argue that he only stood out because of the low standard of his peers in the army. He had some important assets as an officer: a sharp, if not outstanding, mind; capacity for hard work; willingness to learn; and an excellent grasp of the essentials of soldiering. One commanding officer neatly summed up Haig's attributes: 'whatever he undertakes he puts his whole heart and soul into it, and always, you may be sure, he makes things a success'.[54]

Climbing the Ladder

An ambitious officer with an aptitude for staff work, and prepared to do jobs uncongenial to many regimental officers, Haig was also keen to become a student at the Staff College in Camberley[55] – at that time still regarded with suspicion by old-school officers. A very professional soldier, he took his own arm of service extremely seriously, and within a few years he had become one of the leading figures in the cavalry, both as a theorist and a practitioner. What is more, he achieved his reputation as a 'coming man' without alienating his brother officers. When Haig finally left the 7th Hussars, Lieutenant-Colonel Hamish Reid alluded to the fact that, having failed to get into Staff College at first attempt (a bad setback to his career), he had been forced to return to the regiment to play 'second fiddle' as a squadron second-in-command. 'Instead of making a grievance of it all, I know what a lot of pains you have taken and how much the improvement in that Squadron has been owing to you'. Presciently, Reid said Haig was 'bound to succeed because you mean to'.[56]

For an officer who had started his military career late, attending Camberley offered a good way to catch up with contemporaries. In 1893, after visiting Germany to improve his grasp of the language, and attending a 'crammer', Haig sat the exam for the Staff College. He failed it, despite scoring higher marks than the lowest-ranking successful candidate; he had failed to achieve 50 per cent in the mathematics paper, and thus was ruled out. (The formulaic questions of previous years had, without warning, been made more difficult, which caught out nearly a third of the candidates. The abrupt change led to questions in parliament and a statement from the Secretary of State for War that unsuccessful candidates had a 'very substantial grievance'.) Worse, he was told by Sir Redvers Buller, the Adjutant General, that colour-blindness precluded any further work on the staff. This double blow could have ended Haig's upward trajectory there and then, and it is difficult to imagine him plodding along for the rest of his career as a regimental officer. However, he knuckled down and in 1895 achieved one of nine nominations from the Commander-in-Chief, thanks to the influence of Generals Fraser and Wood.[57]

Before returning to India and the 7th Hussars, Haig attended French cavalry exercises and wrote a thoughtful 40-page report.[58] This may have helped to ensure that his stay with his old regiment was brief, because in the autumn of 1894 he became aide de camp to General Sir Keith Fraser, the Inspector General of Cavalry. To become an ADC, a junior personal assistant to a senior officer, was only a modest advancement, but this particular one was especially useful to Haig, given his professional interests. At the IGC's side, he was at the centre of developments in the cavalry. He seems to have revelled in the opportunity: for instance, visiting a trial mobilisation of a French cavalry regiment in October 1894, the subsequent report being published.

When Keith Fraser moved on from the post of Inspector General in early 1895, Haig took a period of leave before setting out in late April on a journey to study the Imperial German army, and especially the cavalry. As a result of its crushing victories over the French in 1870–71, the German army had the reputation as the finest in Europe. During his two months in Germany Haig's studies were aided and abetted by his hosts, who were models of kindness, and he underwent a range of experiences, including informal discussions with cavalry officers, attendance at manoeuvres and dinner with Kaiser Wilhelm II.

He was impressed by what he saw, and produced another authoritative report. The German method of devolving command to allow subordinates to use their initiative (a system today known as mission command) struck him as superior to the British model of 'top-down' command. Twenty-one years later, as Commander-in-Chief on the Western Front during the Somme, Haig's command style was heavily influenced by this German approach – with decidedly mixed results, as will be seen. Haig's German trip thus assumes in retrospect a greater significance than could possibly have been evident at the time.[59]

One of the leading figures in the British cavalry at this time was Colonel John French, late 19th Hussars. French had first met Haig in India in 1891. It is a mark of the latter's burgeoning reputation in cavalry circles that four years later French, commanding a cavalry force in a 'Staff Tour' [i.e. an exercise without troops] in June 1895 invited Haig to act as his staff officer. For Haig, there was the added advantage that he met Sir Evelyn Wood, the Quartermaster General, who was to prove a powerful patron. Wood wrote to Haig in terms that promised well for the future. He had, Wood wrote, known 'you pretty well on paper before' – an indication that Haig's reports and memoranda had made a favourable impression in high places – and paid the younger man a graceful compliment by commenting on 'the pleasure you gave me by your conversation'. Wood asked questions about the German cavalry, to which Haig gave detailed answers. Haig was understandably elated by the encounter. 'Sir E.W. is a capital fellow to have upon one's side,' he wrote to Henrietta, 'as he always gets his way!'[60]

The patronage system of the late Victorian and Edwardian army has come under searching examination from historians. The two leading generals of the late nineteenth century, Sir Garnet Wolseley and Sir Frederick Roberts both gathered around them a 'ring', or coterie of officers, whose careers they promoted. One influential author refers to the 'strangely personalized' pre-1914 army 'and its undeclared system of operating in the areas of promotions, dismissals and cover-ups'.[61] While there is much to recommend this line of argument, at its most extreme it can lead to the belief that Haig's excellent contacts enabled a duffer to reach senior rank.

There is no doubt that Haig did indeed benefit from patronage, but his career was promoted by Wood, French *et al.* precisely because they recognised him as an outstanding officer with huge potential – that is why, for instance, Haig a mere captain, was given a major role in the revision of the Cavalry Drill Book that appeared in 1896.[62] Contemporaries drew a distinction between up-and-coming men being given a helping hand by senior officers, and the undeserving being advanced beyond their capabilities. Haig was far from being the only beneficiary of the system. Herbert Plumer (York and Lancaster Regiment) had an impressive Boer War. 'We must push Plumer,' Roberts told Kitchener in 1901. 'He is evidently a good man.' Henry Rawlinson (60th Rifles and later Coldstream Guards) had a less distinguished path to the top, but he clearly had potential, and his father had been a friend of Roberts's; he served as an ADC first to Roberts, and then to Kitchener.[63] By contrast, Haig was a Wood protégé, and Rawlinson was a member of the Wolseley Ring. This factionalism was almost certainly a factor in the initially difficult relationships that Haig had with Plumer and Rawlinson as commanders of Second and Fourth Armies respectively during the First World War.

Second, influential backers only advanced Haig so far through the formal promotion route in time of peace. His career did not really take off until he had proved his competence as a staff officer and commander on active service in South Africa in 1899–1902. (He was still a major in 1899, but by 1903 had risen to major general.) Finally, the British army of the late Victorian period was not unique in operating a system that relied, in part at least, on relationships between patrons and protégés. As one historian commented, 'how else do they think organisations work'?[64]

Staff College

When Douglas Haig took up his place as a student at the Staff College in January 1896 it marked an important stage of his career. Staff College graduates did not have a monopoly on senior posts, but having the coveted letters *psc* – passed staff college – after an officer's name in the Army List was still extremely helpful for the ambitious. The course was fairly small, which allowed high-flyers to get to know each other. Other students on Haig's course included Edmund Allenby of 6th Inniskilling Dragoons, who served as Third Army commander under Haig in 1916–17; James Edmonds of the Royal Engineers, the future Official Historian; George Macdonogh, another sapper, who was to hold key intelligence posts during the First World War; one future Western Front corps commander and two divisional commanders.[65] In the intake above Haig was Herbert Lawrence of the 17th Lancers, the Master of the Staff College Drag Hunt, who was to be his Chief of Staff in 1918.

At Camberley Haig seems to have behaved very much as he had when a cadet a mile up the road at Sandhurst 12 years earlier. But we should be careful before writing him off as a pariah. One of Haig's closest friends in the army, Arthur Blair of the King's Own Scottish Borderers, was in the same intake, and the famous story that Haig's peers deliberately avoided him in the mess at lunch is almost certainly exaggerated. Such stories were related long after the events by two men who came to nurse resentment against Haig: Edmonds and George Barrow. One of the stories often told to demonstrate his unpopularity is that the students voted for Allenby, rather than Haig, as Master of the Drag Hunt, although Haig was the better horseman. Allenby and Haig were cavalry contemporaries and rivals, and were to have a difficult, although on both sides correct, relationship, which came to a head in 1917.[66] At least as valid as evidence is a contemporary report of a point-to-point race won by Haig on 20 March 1896. 'In this race the best horse won, and we congratulate the Oyster upon having so good a man up.'[67]

As at Sandhurst, Haig was an outstanding student. Colonel G.F.R Henderson, Professor of Military Art and History and the dominating figure at Camberley, viewed Haig as the 'coming man in the army', 'a future Commander-in-Chief'.[68] Henderson repeated this to Edmonds in 1903, who passed on the news to Haig. In 1911 Edmonds reminded the newly appointed GOC Aldershot Command of the prophecy. Haig's reaction was an embarrassed 'I think dear old Henderson was talking through his hat'.[69]

The Staff College, as its title indicates, was primarily intended to train officers in staff work. However, under the influence of Henderson, students were also taught the constituents of command through the study of military history, with an emphasis on the operational level (referred to as 'grand tactics' at the time). There was a stress on the Napoleonic Wars, as well as more recent campaigns such as the American Civil War, on which Henderson was a renowned expert.[70] Haig's time at Camberley has been seen by many historians as a critical phase in his professional development. At Staff College, it has been claimed, he was taught that 'war was mobile, structured, and decisive'. The general's task was to defeat 'the main enemy army. Battles were inevitably fought in three stages: preparation and the wearing out of enemy reserves; a rapid decisive offensive; and cavalry exploitation.' These phases would swiftly follow on from each other, 'and since both sides were technically much the same, the decisive elements were morale, determination, and the will of the commander'. The C-in-C's role was 'to set strategy' and then let his subordinates carry out the job 'with minimal interference'. It is said that this teaching, absorbed at Camberley twenty years before, underpinned Haig's thinking as C-in-C on the Western Front. The notion of a 'structured battle' has been seen as particularly damaging as 'it may help explain why it was difficult for Haig to change strategy (or battle tactics) during the First World War'.[71] Moreover, Haig commanded 'in nineteenth-century style' which was not the best way of conducting operations in the First World War.[72]

The army's command philosophy was not dissimilar in principle to the 'directive command' practices of their German opponents. This called for the higher commander to make clear his 'intent', and for subordinates to devise and execute plans within the overall structure. This devolution of command authority allowed the 'man on the spot', who probably had a better idea of local conditions, to exercise his initiative, to take advantage of opportunities on the battlefield without slowing down the decision-making process by constantly referring matters to a superior officer. In theory, this is very close to what today is considered best practice, but there was a flaw. Superiors were often unwilling to intervene decisively when things went awry, a practice that has been described as 'umpiring'.[73]

The Staff College syllabus can fairly be criticised in a number of ways, but too much has been made of its influence on Haig. The very idea that his views on command and strategy in the First World War can be deduced from student essays and lecture notes from twenty years before has been questioned.[74] For instance, the notes that Haig took on the 'authority of the C in C' – that it was 'impaired by permitting subordinates to advance their own ideas' – flies in the face of Haig's consultative methods of command on the Somme and during Third Ypres.[75] At least in later life, Haig was sceptical about Henderson's twisting of history to prove a point.[76] Clearly, though, Camberley did have some effect. Much of the teaching at Staff College was unexceptionable and sensible, being drawn from study of military history from the Napoleonic Wars onward. Although technology has changed the conduct of war radically over the years, the human element and certain principles have not altered: military operations in different eras of history have more in common with each other than with any other human activity, in spite of vast dissimilarities in terms of weapons and tactics. That is why twenty-first-century militaries study the campaigns of Napoleon – and Haig.

The structured battle was not self-evidently silly as a guideline, any more than the current military mantra of 'find, fix, strike, pursue'. Napoleon's victory over Prussia in 1806 was an example of the model working well at the operational/strategic level, and it was a favourite for study before 1914.[77] Field Marshal Bill Slim, widely seen as the greatest British commander of the Second World War, described the 1944 Imphal-Kohima campaign in terms very similar to the derided structured battle.[78]

Staff College teaching can fairly be described as leading to a 'Napoleonic' approach, but that is not the same as saying that it was an archaic, obsolete one. Rather, it is a recognition that the underpinning principles demonstrated in the Napoleonic period were not unique to this time, and late nineteenth-century officers could not afford to ignore them. Moreover, rather than a rigid, doctrinaire method, Haig learned at Camberley – or more likely had confirmed – an adaptable, empirical, pragmatic approach to war. This gave him an overall framework within which he could work out his ideas. Haig's time at Camberley badly needs a thorough reassessment, but suffice it to say that the idea that the problems of 1916 and 1917 were caused by his rigidly sticking to faulty Staff College doctrines looks increasingly threadbare.

For decades, late nineteenth- and early twentieth-century cavalry was seen by historians (reputable and otherwise) as obsolescent, an anachronism on battlefields dominated by high explosive and machine-gun bullets. Recently careful scholarship has substantially revised this damning picture. Cavalry developments across Europe from 1871 to 1914 were 'less about preserving the charge than increasing the firepower and flexibility of the horse soldier so that he could adapt to new battlefield conditions'.[79] Cavalry even had a role, under some circumstances, among the trenches and barbed wire of the Western Front. All this has a major bearing on Douglas Haig's reputation. Far from being a reactionary technophobe wedded to an antediluvian way of fighting, he was a moderately progressive reformer in an arm evolving to meet the challenges of modern war.

Active Service in the Sudan

Shortly after he left Camberley, Haig finally had the opportunity for active service. A conflict broke out in the Sudan, and he and two other recent Camberley graduates, Capper and Blair, were recommended by Wood, the Adjutant General, to accompany Major-General Sir Herbert Kitchener's expeditionary force down the Nile. Wood's recommendation came with a sting in its tail. Haig was expected to write privately to him to give his views on the campaign, which would inevitably involve commenting on Kitchener's generalship. Such private 'back-channel' reporting was by no means unheard of, and it is difficult to believe that Kitchener would have been unaware of the possibility of junior officers reporting back to senior patrons. Wood was not the only man interested in Haig's views. He stayed with the Prince of Wales shortly before he left for Egypt – interestingly, Wood was also present – and noted that 'HRH desires me to "write regularly"' while on campaign.[80]

The roots of the 1898 campaign lay in the revolt of the religious leader Muhammad Ahmad, who had proclaimed himself the 'Mahdi', or Expected One, and by 1885 had captured most of the Sudan. In the process the Mahdists had destroyed an Egyptian force led by a British officer in 1883 and besieged and captured Khartoum, the Sudanese capital, in 1885. A relief expedition arrived too late to save the garrison, and a national hero, General Charles Gordon, was killed. After more than a decade of non-engagement, in 1896 an Anglo-Egyptian army returned to the Sudan. At first the strategy was strictly limited, but soon 'mission creep' set in. The campaign became one to destroy the Mahdists, now ruled by Khalifa Abdallahi.[81]

Haig joined the Anglo-Egyptian-Sudanese force at Wadi Halfa, just on the Sudanese side of the border, in February 1898. Although he was given a 'cordial' reception by Kitchener, initially he had little to do apart from prepare for the rigours of campaigning. His entourage included two camels 'to carry my plates, cooking pots and supplies', a cook, 'the black fellow Suleiman' who was his 'body servant', and servants to tend his horses and camels.[82] Sent further south into the war zone, Haig arrived at Berber on 28 February, where he was attached to an Egyptian cavalry squadron, with which he carried out some patrols.

A clash with a Dervish force that was marching north seemed imminent. Kitchener sent a brigade of British troops on a punishing march across the desert to reinforce those at Berber. In a letter to Wood, Haig was sharply critical, as the march had exhausted many troops, and he wondered if these men would have been in much of a state to fight, had a battle with the Dervishes actually materialised.[83]

Haig was also unimpressed by Kitchener's command methods. 'He is a man that does every thing [sic] himself and in fact has no H[ead]d Q[uarte]r staff at all!' he wrote to his sister. Kitchener 'is most silent and no one has ever had the slightest notion what is going to be done until he gives his orders!'[84] Kitchener's ADC Henry Rawlinson also thought it was 'too much of a one-man show'.[85] When Haig led the BEF, with Rawlinson as one of his Army commanders, Haig had very different methods of command; Kitchener's example was undoubtedly an influence on the development of Haig's ideas.

While there was some validity in Haig's criticisms of Kitchener and high command, there was something of the arrogance of youth about them. The high-flying Staff College graduate with time on his hands had mental horizons wider than that of the average regimental officer. He looked at what was being done and believed he could do better. Haig's view of Kitchener was tainted by frustration that he had yet to be assigned a formal role, and annoyance that he had been promised command of an Egyptian squadron, only to be told that the 'Sirdar' (Kitchener's formal title as commander of the Egyptian army) opposed command changes while battle threatened.[86] Haig's criticisms were, in hindsight, very significant in retrospect, as we know that 18 years later, as Commander-in-Chief of the British Expeditionary Force, he was to work with Field Marshal Earl Kitchener of Khartoum, Secretary of State for War and lynchpin of the British war effort – and whose tendency to behave as a one-man band was still all too evident.

Kitchener was in fact a painstaking commander, thoroughly conversant with logistics and an excellent strategic planner. He built the Sudan Military Railway, described by a contemporary war correspondent as 'the deadliest weapon' wielded against the Dervishes. An electric telegraph was laid alongside the railway. It was a bold move to construct the railway across unknown, waterless terrain with an enemy force within striking distance. Kitchener took a calculated risk, based on largely accurate intelligence on the Dervish forces.[87]

Douglas Haig, his eyes and ears wide open on his first campaign, was clearly impressed by the railway. 'It is wonderful the way the railway is put down,' he wrote to Henrietta, before launching into a detailed description of the laying of track.[88] As Commander-in-Chief on the Western Front, his diary was littered with descriptions of visits to road-stone quarries and the like. Haig may have been right to criticise some aspects of Kitchener's command, but his first campaign gave him, or reinforced, a very strong sense of the importance of logistics.

In late March 1898 Kitchener's army advanced towards the Atbara river. Among the troops that pushed ahead to reconnoitre was Douglas Haig, still attached to a squadron of Egyptian cavalry 'as a sort of odd man'. On 21 March 1898 he had his first experience of combat. A patrol was surprised by a Dervish group, who lured a cavalry squadron into a trap where it was faced by fifty or so mounted opponents. The patrol was forced to pull back, and, although the enemy eventually retreated, they got the better of the skirmish, having lost six or seven men, while the patrol had ten men wounded and eight killed.

The First Taste of Battle

No soldier can know how he will react to his first taste of battle. From the tone of Haig's description of this small skirmish, he had a sense of quiet exhilaration, perhaps underpinned by relief that he had passed a test and, he would certainly have thought, proved his manhood.[89] But he also sat down and, ever the professional soldier, analysed the action, sending Sir Evelyn Wood his thoughts. Haig was critical of some aspects of the work of the Egyptian troops in the skirmish but, in keeping with his view that with good leadership (unlike the 'duffers' of Egyptian cavalry officers) they could be effective troops, he concluded 'The pluck of the Egyptian cavalryman is right enough in my opinion'.[90]

Haig's final lesson from the action concerned weapons:

> The Horse Artillery against enemy of this sort and in scrub is no use. We felt the want of machine-guns when working along outside of scrub for searching some of the tracks.[91]

Much nonsense has been written about Haig's supposed antipathy to technology, and particularly machine-guns. In reality, just before he left for Egypt, Haig had taken the trouble to visit the Royal Ordnance Factory specifically to 'learn mechanism of Maxim [machine] gun'.[92] Haig's comment gives a further insight into his military thought. He was not thinking in terms of pure cavalry action, but of a combined-arms battle. This was not in the least original, though, and the point would not have been worth stressing, were it not for frequent caricaturing of Haig as a technophobe addicted to cavalry charges.

On 25 March Haig was finally given a proper job, when he was appointed Chief Staff Officer to the Cavalry Brigade. He promptly busied himself with arranging supplies, but also seems to have continued to go on patrol, 'get[ting] plenty of fun chasing the dervish horsemen who won't face us at all in the open now, but make off at once into the bush and scrub near the river'.[93] Kitchener's forces advanced towards the enemy army. Commanded by Mahmud Ahmed, a cousin of the Khalifa, it set up a defensive position near the River Atbara. The Mahdist army dug trenches and set up a 'zariba', a barricade of thorns.

On 5 April a strong force with the Cavalry Brigade at its core, pushed on to reconnoitre the Dervish 'dem' or camp. Haig wrote a lengthy description in his diary. The arrival of the force stirred up a hornet's nest. Having located the enemy's right flank, 'Brigade then fell back North

Eastwards with object of seeing the enemy's left clearly'. As they pulled back, the Dervish cavalry and infantry attacked. It was a dangerous moment. The Egyptian cavalry's discipline wavered, and there was a real danger that it would run away. Haig was in the midst of the action. He played a critical role in organising the response, at one stage giving direct orders to the Maxim machine-guns

> . . . to come into action at once, and that I would bring cavalry back towards their flanks so as not to mask their fire. The gunner officers . . . responded nobly, and I galloped towards Enemy, met [Lieutenant-Colonel R.A.] Broadwood [the brigade commander] on way, who approved of what I had done and led the squadrons as I had suggested. All this time the Dervish Infantry were putting in a hot fire and their Cavalry had quite cut off our line of retreat.

A combination of machine-gun fire and a flank attack by the cavalry stabilised the situation.[94]

It is clear Douglas Haig acquitted himself exceptionally well in this action, even allowing for gilding of the lily in his diary and letters home. Broadwood and Kitchener were both impressed with Haig, who was rewarded with promotion to brevet major. He had kept cool under fire, taken some critical command decisions, and in one incident had demonstrated two of the cardinal virtues of the late Victorian officer, courage and concern for his men. He wrote to Henrietta how, as the cavalry had fallen back,

> I was able to pick up a poor devil of an Egyptian who was wounded in the shoulder, and had given himself up for lost, and put him in the front of my saddle and carried him to the guns . . . This is quite the 'gymkhana' style of things which you used to see in India!

In spite of Haig's protestations that it was the sort of thing that happened during equestrian training, this act of courage might, had the rescued soldier been British, have earned Haig the Victoria Cross. As it was, he earned the approbation of peers in the 7th Hussars, who presented Haig with a painting of the incident.[95]

Kitchener launched a full-scale, frontal assault on the Mahdist positions on 7 April. Haig and the cavalry played a relatively small role in the Battle of the Atbara: they 'did all that the Sirdar would allow us to do, quite early; namely, we drove the Enemy's cavalry across the river and halted on the bank'.[96] Atbara was won by the Anglo-Egyptians but at the price of 568 casualties. Dervish losses amounted to over 2,500, and Mahmud was taken prisoner. Haig sent a thoughtful critique to General Wood, arguing that, given dependable troops, Kitchener could have been more adventurous in combining infantry, artillery, cavalry and machine-guns in an attack which might have brought about the annihilation of Mahmud's army. This was a perfectly valid point; but he gave Kitchener credit for understanding the frailties of his 'black' troops and not overreaching himself by asking them to do too much.[97] Ironically, a valid criticism of Haig's generalship at the beginning of the Battle of the Somme 18 years later is that he failed to recognise what it was reasonable to ask raw troops to do.

Haig was unimpressed with the Sirdar's extravagant entry into the village of Berber on a white horse, parading a bound Mahmud. Kitchener's objective was to overawe the local population and make a political statement about the impending end of Mahdism, but such show was never to Haig's taste. Neither did he like the way that the press treated the Battle of Atbara. He particularly disliked that 'loathsome creature' Burleigh Bennett of the *Daily Telegraph*. Twenty days after their publication in London, Haig was able to read press accounts of Atbara. 'What rubbish the British Public likes to read,' he thundered. 'The headlines of the "DT" are so overdrawn that instinctively one says "Waterloo Eclipsed". But the story of Mahmoud [sic] the C-in-C being taken "under his bed" rather gives the show away'![98] Journalists were, in Haig's view, ungentlemanly liars.

But war correspondents had been significant actors on British campaigns for some forty years, ever since William Howard Russell had shaken up the military and political establishment with his reports from the Crimea. One of the journalists present in the Sudan, G.W. Steevens, played a major role in turning Kitchener into 'a household name, the focus of hero-worship and the pride of the empire' through his highly-coloured reports in the *Daily Mail* and the best-selling book *With Kitchener to Khartoum*.[99] Haig had attitudes to the press that even in 1898 were starting to look old-fashioned.

Although a Mahdist army had been defeated, the war was not yet over. Kitchener waited for the railway to be extended and for more supplies and reinforcements to arrive. Above all, he waited for the Nile to rise, so he could send his gunboats south towards Omdurman, the Khalifa's capital. During this four-month lull Haig was busy. At last he commanded a squadron, and he filled his days with training and leisure activities such as polo. In July Kitchener asked if he would like a young 4th Hussars officer to be attached to his squadron. Haig declined, and so Winston Churchill was eventually found a niche with the 21st Lancers.[100]

Omdurman

The Anglo-Egyptian army, some 20,000 strong, began their advance on 24 August, screened by cavalry, including Haig's squadron. By the end of the month it was obvious that battle was near. On 1 September the cavalry pushed ahead on a reconnaissance. Haig, leading his squadron, noted disapprovingly that the inexperienced 21st Lancers went ahead 'rather somewhat recklessly' (he had learned respect for the 'fox-like enemy'). Standing on a ridge, Haig wrote, 'Omdurman was visible some 5or 6 miles off, with the Mahdi's tomb standing high above every other building'. Continuing the advance, the cavalry reached a 'round topped hill' where

> A most wonderful sight presented itself to us. A huge force of men with flags, drums and bugles was being assembled to the west of the city. The troops formed up on a front some 3 miles long . . . There were about 30,000 men extending across the plain, and all in movement before we left the round hill.

There followed a tricky manoeuvre as the Anglo-Egyptian force tried to extract itself and reach safety before being attacked by the Dervishes. Haig's squadron 'acted as rearguard . . . to 5 companies of camel corps and 2 machine-guns'. It was a difficult and dangerous task. At one stage, receiving an erroneous report that one of his men had been unhorsed and chased by Dervishes, Haig led a troop to 'within 250 yards or less of the Enemy's advancing line. They commenced firing briskly, but, as usual, high.' Falling back to a hill, Haig ordered some of his men to dismount and open fire, joining in the firing line, armed with a carbine. This helped buy time for the party to escape.[101]

The climactic battle of the campaign took place on 2 September 1898. The Mahdist army attacked Kitchener's forces and was defeated comprehensively, so much so that in 1991 a commentator reached for Omdurman as an appropriate historical analogy for another one-sided conflict: the First Gulf War. A combination of crude Dervish tactics and modern firepower cost the Mahdist forces some 10,800 killed and perhaps 16,000 wounded. The Anglo-Egyptians suffered 48 dead and 382 wounded.[102]

Haig's squadron was deployed to screen the front of the infantry on the Sirdar's right flank. He was ordered to pull back as the Dervishes advanced, and ended up behind the guns. The enemy closed in and, Haig noted, 'poured in a very hot fire' and forced the cavalry to retire once again behind the artillery.

I said I thought the position unsuitable for us: I had scarcely made the remark, before my trumpeter was shot above the right temple . . . My leading troop leader standing next was hit, and the guide behind him was hit in the thigh . . . all in less time than it takes to write.[103]

Rawlinson was sent with a message to the cavalry:

we could see our contact squadrons under Douglas Haig gradually withdrawing as the Dervishes advanced . . . When I reached him he was within about six hundred yards of the enemy's long line, and I noticed that his confident bearing seemed to have inspired his *fellaheen* [i.e. the Egyptian soldiers], who were watching the Dervish advance quite calmly.[104]

Haig's impressions of the Dervish assaults have a note of admiration:

The Enemy seemed to me to come on in countless numbers and in rank after rank. Their order and manoeuvring power was wonderful . . . The dervishes rushed on heedless of the hail of bullets.

With the Mahdist attacks broken, the cavalry were sent to pursue the enemy and occupy Omdurman.

Many wounded men still rose up and fired at us as we approached . . .
many little groups dropped on their knees in submission, though some
firmly resisted till killed by our lances.

Resistance stiffened as the cavalry pushed on. The advance was
becoming ragged, so Haig's squadron halted to allow others to catch up
and, dismounted, fired volleys at the enemy. When the advance resumed
the cavalry found the going very difficult. They were plunging into the
midst of armed Dervishes, which caught the cavalry in 'cross fire from all
directions'.[105]

Worse was to come. Having reached Omdurman, they were ordered,
at dusk, to pursue the Khalifa, who had just escaped from the city; a
fruitless trek ensued, which resulted in tired, hungry men and horses.
Haig's men did not return to Omdurman until 4 September. As he told
Henrietta wryly, the city was 'well looted' before his arrival. His
squadron had been reduced from 140 men at the beginning of the battle
to just 40, but of these only five had been killed.[106]

As was now customary, Haig analysed the battle. He saw the Khalifa
as having thrown away possible advantages by failing to occupy key
ground, and criticised Kitchener for apparently having no other plan than
letting the Mahdists attack and use superior firepower to smash up the
enemy army. Up to a point, Haig was correct. The Mahdists could have
complicated Kitchener's task by holding the high ground of the Jebel
Surkham, and Haig's plan for the use of manoeuvre to defeat the Mahdist
forces was perfectly sound. However, Kitchener *had* originally planned
to take the offensive.

More to the point was Haig's analysis of the charge of the 21st Lancers,
which, with Lieutenant Churchill attached, was sent to harry the
retreating Dervishes. It was lured towards a force of some 2,000 Mahdist
spearmen concealed in a shallow valley. In two minutes of intense
fighting, for which three VCs were awarded, the Lancers lost heavily.
Clearing the valley, the men of the 21st dismounted and opened fire,
breaking up the enemy force.

Haig was incensed. Lieutenant-Colonel R.H. Martin, he wrote to
Henrietta, 'should be strongly reprimanded for what he did: there was no
object in his charging, while the casualties were enormous considering
the numbers engaged – 21 killed and 45 or more wounded and 120

horses! *Result* absolutely Nil'. Before Omdurman the 21st Lancers, raised in 1858, had failed to win a single battle honour (the joke in the army was that the regimental motto was 'Thou shalt not kill'). The regiment was determined 'to charge something before the show was over', Haig believed. 'I trust for the sake of the British Cavalry', he wrote to Wood, 'that more tactical knowledge exists in the higher ranks of the average regiment than we have seen displayed in this one.' This was what happened when the powers that be 'put duffers in command of regiments'.[107]

This was outspoken stuff. As a thinking soldier dedicated to his arm, Haig's professionalism was offended by Martin's slapdash approach – he had failed to put out scouts, Haig noted – and his glory-hunting. Under certain conditions the mounted charge was a valid tactic – and remained so throughout Haig's military career – but simply blundering towards the enemy was gross negligence. Haig's own performance as a junior cavalry commander in the Sudan demonstrates that he used dismounted fire action as well as the *arme blanche* ('white arm', that is, cold steel) – in short, he was an up-to-date officer, thoroughly conversant with the most effective cavalry tactics. The suggestions that the real lesson of the 21st Lancers' action was the effectiveness of firepower against cavalry meant that the cavalry charge was obsolete, and that Haig failed to realise this, are very wide of the mark.[108]

Haig's time in the Sudan was nearly spent. Sir Evelyn Wood advised him to return home, holding out the prospect of a job at the Horse Guards. Haig resigned from Egyptian service, and was home in early October 1898. The Horse Guards post did not materialise, and Haig returned to regimental service with the 7th Hussars before moving to be French's right-hand man at the Aldershot Cavalry Brigade.

Douglas Haig emerged from the River War with considerable credit. He now had combat experience, having done well both as a staff officer and as a squadron commander. He had demonstrated his courage and his proficiency at modern tactics, showing a lively understanding of the importance of firepower and combined-arms methods. He had received favourable attention from Kitchener, and seen a master organiser at work. Haig's actions and his writings reveal a man with plenty of self-confidence, a man with the streak of ruthlessness essential in successful commanders. He was very ambitious, and his outspoken criticisms of his seniors, including Kitchener, to Wood, the Adjutant General, reveal an unattractive side to his character. Indeed, writing in the 1930s, Haig's official biographer felt the need to excuse his behaviour.[109] Haig was a coming man, determined to use his connections for his advancement. But, unlike Colonel Martin, he was no duffer. With the Sudan experience behind him, he had every reason to feel optimistic about the future.

Rising Star

Haig's time at the Aldershot Cavalry Brigade was to be short. Over the summer of 1899 tension grew between Britain and the two Boer Republics in South Africa: the Transvaal and Orange Free State. There had already been a brief war between Britain and the Transvaal in 1880–81, ending in a humiliating British defeat. While the headline issue in 1899 was the treatment of *Uitlanders,* foreigners attracted to the Boer states by gold, the underlying cause was the desire of some influential figures in Britain and South Africa to bring the entire region under British rule. Backed into a corner, the Boers lashed out, declaring war, in October 1899, and *commandos* (militia-type forces on horseback) attacked Natal, hoping to stir up insurrection in British territory and deter the British by quick victories. London's response was to rush troops to South Africa. Faced by the might of the British Empire, in the long run the Boers stood no chance.

The Second Boer War – On the Defensive

As part of the British build-up of troops, French was ordered to take command of the cavalry in Natal, and Major Haig accompanied him as his Chief Staff Officer. That French was available to be appointed to the position owed much to Haig: earlier that year Haig had lent French £2,500 to prevent him being bankrupted and having to leave the army. Haig was undoubtedly sincere when he wrote that he acted because French was an asset to the army, but he also acknowledged the importance of the act to his own career. This loan was ethically questionable, as in theory it rendered French beholden to Haig –

although, in truth, French needed no persuading of the younger man's talents.[1]

The two men arrived in Durban on 19 October and almost immediately left for Ladysmith, close to the border with the Orange Free State, which was coming under pressure from Boer forces. (There was some concern about the enemy sabotaging the tracks, but Haig laconically recorded that he 'slept soundly' on the journey, arriving at 5.40 a.m. on 20 October.[2]) While dining at 9 p.m. on the 20th Haig received orders for an operation against Elandslaagte on the following morning. He had a busy night ahead of him issuing orders.[3]

French's small force won the battle, and as the Boers began to fall back cavalry squadrons charged through and over the beaten enemy. Boer prisoners were 'wild at the way the fugitives were killed with the lance!' Haig reported. 'They say it is butchery not war.' Haig's day did not end until he had finished 'preparing for the return of the troops and wounded to Ladysmith'.[4] Elandslaagte was the one bright spot in a gloomy outlook for the British in Natal. Defeats and retreats led to a concentration of troops at Ladysmith, with Mafeking and Kimberley coming under siege, and a Boer force apparently poised to invade Cape Colony. By early November Ladysmith was in danger of encirclement. The cavalry saw plenty of service during this phase, with good reason. When an infantry detachment was forced to surrender on 30 October, Haig noted that the force had lacked cavalry: 'As well let out a blind man without his dog, as Infantry without some horseman to attend and reconnoitre for it!'[5] French's cavalry attacked a Boer *laager* on 2 November. 'The Boers seemed to be at breakfast . . . At the first burst of the shells there was a regular stampede.' Returning to Ladysmith, French was handed a telegram from General Sir Redvers Buller. It was an order, dressed up as a request from Buller, for French to assume command of the Cavalry Division that was *en route* from Britain, and Haig was to go with him.[6]

Within two hours French and Haig were on a train, just ahead of the Boers who were surrounding Ladysmith. The train had been shot at by the Boers earlier that day, and Haig noted 'the railway authorities doubted our getting through'. That they might have been right seemed a distinct possibility thirty minutes into the journey, when 'the train came under a heavy fire from both sides of the railway. We heard shells bursting and bullets hit the carriages. We all lay down on the seats and floor'! A truck was hit by a shell 'Had the shell hit the engine or a wheel', Haig recorded, 'we should have been on our way to Pretoria [the capital of the Transvaal] instead of to Durban'![7]

Haig went from Durban to Cape Town, where he was needed for staff work, and compiled a private *aide memoire* on recent operations. He was surprised to find that 'the effect of Artillery fire is chiefly moral' and drew the conclusion that the effectiveness of shrapnel fire had been overrated. This was fair comment on the experience of the war so far. The performance of artillery had been disappointing; not until the introduction of indirect suppressing fire on the battlefield at Tugela Heights in February 1900 did it begin to improve.[8]

His review of the cavalry highlighted 'the greatly increased power of action possessed by Cavalry, now that is armed with a good carbine'. Success or failure was clearly going to turn on mobility, and horsemen were the only way of achieving this. Haig's comments included best practice learned from the Boers, and reflected his keen awareness that cavalry should be flexible. Dismounted cavalry firepower was important, as was the combination of mounted action with other arms. Implicit in his comments was the superiority of conventional cavalry over Mounted Infantry (MI). The Imperial Light Horse, a locally recruited regiment trained and organised as cavalry, came in for praise.[9]

Haig was more explicit in his letters of this time to Henrietta. MI, he told her, 'are not intended to reconnoitre and are not trained for it'. Several weeks later, he was even more forthright. 'The one thing required here is "Cavalry"! . . . This Mounted Infantry craze is now I trust exploded. So far, they have proved useless and are not likely to be of use *until they learn to ride!*'[10]

At a distance of more than 110 years the debate over different types of horsed soldier may seem impossibly arcane but at the time it had very practical consequences.[11] The Mounted Infantry concept, whose supporters, as Haig well knew, included Evelyn Wood, was an attempt to increase mobility by training infantry to ride horses. MI might be improvised in the field, combining the primary role of fighting on foot with 'outpost, advance guard and rearguard duties'. An improved version, sometimes referred to as 'mounted riflemen', were better trained and could carry out the duties of standard cavalry, except for the *arme blanche* charge.[12]

Haig's objection was that Mounted Infantry were not very good at their job. Their poor horsemanship (which could lead to their mounts becoming worn out – a significant matter in a war in which horses died in droves), combined with inefficiency and the inability to undertake the full range of cavalry duties led Haig to believe that MI were not worth their rations.[13] His answer was a 'hybrid' cavalryman who was also capable of being an effective infantryman. The events of the next two decades were to show him as precisely right on this issue.

In the meantime, French and Haig had to work with the material to hand. A newly arrived regiment of Australian volunteers, the New South Wales Lancers, 'can scarcely be called *efficient* cavalry,' Haig thought, although it seems that inexperience was their main fault. He was more complimentary about a New Zealand unit, 'a sensible lot of men dressed like Boers'. However they were deficient in one respect: they were armed with carbines, but not swords. Their lack of cold steel was overcome by an improvisation ordered by French; the New Zealanders fixed their bayonets to their firearms, thus creating a makeshift lance, and began training with it.[14] This was not a piece of reactionary nonsense but rather a pragmatic move – the mounted charge was to continue to prove useful throughout the Boer War and beyond.

The initial Boer advance had damaged the British but failed in its objective of bringing their enemy to terms. Instead, reinforcements headed for South Africa from all over the Empire. Militarily, the situation was difficult for the British at the end of 1899. Three widely separated forces were concentrating to take the offensive, but a Boer attack from the Colesberg area into Cape Colony threw British plans into disarray. French was sent to the region by Buller with orders to 'maintain an active defence' and tie down the enemy. He did so with great success at a time when elsewhere in South Africa there was a grim litany of retreat and defeat for the British army. In 'Black Week' in December 1899 the Boers inflicted three sharp defeats, and the new year brought more setbacks. These defeats shocked the Empire. Not since the rebellious American colonists had 'turned the world upside down' at Yorktown some 120 years earlier had there been such a humiliation. Arthur Balfour, a senior Cabinet minister and future Prime Minister wrote of 'blunders . . . of the most serious kind', pointing the finger at 'our Generals in the field'.[15]

Against a background of such unremittingly grim news, French's operations around Colesberg, carried out over three months, offered a glimmer of hope. The name of John French was alone 'associated with victory', and the British 'army knew that Haig was at French's elbow'. If there is any point at which we can say that Haig's wider reputation took root, this was it. French was generous in his praise of his Chief Staff Officer, praising his 'zeal, untiring energy and consummate ability' in his despatch of 2 February 1900.[16] Haig's name gradually became familiar to the public. A journalist, J.G. Maydon, wrote of accompanying French's force at this time and finding 'in Major (now Colonel) Haig a chief of staff of no small ability, and of a singular grasp of the special qualities needful of subduing the wily Boer . . . one does not hesitate to predict a very distinguished career [for him]'.[17]

Some sense of the 'active defence' in the Colesberg sector can be gained from Haig's diary and letters. There were 4,000–5,000 Boers on French's front, Haig believed, and the 'task was to bluff them with the few Cavalry we have'. The method was to raid, march and counter-march. A typical operation took place on 11 December when a small force of cavalry with two guns was sent to an area threatened by the Boers. After the bombardment of a farm the enemy 'fell back in great hurry leaving ammunition'. These operations placed a premium on good staff work, and it seems that Haig took some command decisions when French was absent. Anyway, French and Haig worked closely together, carrying out a daily joint reconnaissance at 4.30 a.m. accompanied by an escort of 12 or so men.[18]

On to the Offensive

By the end of January 1900 French was ready to pass over to the offensive. The British had a new command team in South Africa – Lord Roberts had arrived to take overall command, with Kitchener as his Chief of Staff – and the main effort was to be a drive towards Kimberley, currently under siege, with the Cavalry Division playing a major role. French had moved on to take command of the Division in mid-January, taking Haig with him – though not as Chief of Staff. Roberts had insisted that a more senior officer, Colonel the Earl of Errol, be appointed. French protested vociferously – Haig's 'services have been invaluable', he telegraphed Kitchener – but it was no use. Haig, who had previously benefitted from patronage, now experienced the downside and was demoted to Deputy Assistant Adjutant General (DAAG). Haig was irritated by this episode, but philosophical about it, as he 'kept the strings of his work between his fingers'. Maydon claimed that Errol 'conniv[ed] with the fiction of a change'.[19]

The relief of Kimberley proved to be a cavalry epic. Roberts carried out a wide outflanking movement seeking to surprise General Piet Cronje, whose main force was south of Kimberley. Kitchener laid out 'the importance of our mission' in stark terms, Haig reported; if it failed, no one could tell what the result on the 'Empire' might be. It 'all depended on "surprise"', and so on 12 February French's horsemen set out.[20]

They travelled light and fast, and on 13 February arrived at Klip Drift, within striking distance of Kimberley. In Haig's words: 'The 12th Lancers attacked Klip Drift, dismounted and pushed across and held the kopjes [hills] beyond . . . The Boers were completely surprised'. This was followed by an operational pause, 'for we had no supplies except what we carried in our wallets'. Renewing the advance on the 15th, within three miles of Klip Drift the cavalry came under Boer fire. It seemed that there were two separate Boer forces opposing the cavalry, but 'an open plain' between the two. Although the nature of the terrain was unclear – wire fences could play havoc with cavalry – there seemed to be few Boers about.

> There seemed only one thing to be done if we were to get to Kimberley before the Boers barred our path, namely charge through the gap between the 2 positions. Half our guns were ordered to keep down the fire from the kopjes in our front (which would be on the right flank of the charging cavalry) and half engaged the enemy's guns. The 9th and 12th Lancers were then ordered to charge, followed by Broadwood's Brigade in support. For a minute it looked in the dust as if some of our men were coming back, but they were only extended towards a flank. Porter's Brigade followed with the M.I. and brought on the guns. Our lancers caught several Boers and rode down many others in the open plain, and really suffered very little from the very hot rifle fire – about 20 casualties I fancy, and we passed within 1,000 yards of the Boer position! We got to Kimberley about 6 p.m. The garrison made not the slightest attempt

to assist us. Alone we cleared all the Boers investing positions in the south
and took 2 laagers.[21]

The Cavalry Division's relief of Kimberley was a stunning affirmation of
the continuing utility of horsed cavalry on the battlefield, using mobility
to match strength against weakness, and employing speed and shock
action to devastating effect. For Haig, Kimberley was a vindication of
what properly trained 'hybrid' cavalry could do. What is more, it further
added to Haig's reputation as a highly competent Chief of Staff.[22]

The cavalry were soon in action again, pursuing Cronje. The best part
of two brigades caught up with his force at Koedoesrand Drift on 17
February. In the battle that ensued, 'All day and all night we held on'
until the infantry caught up on the 18th. But Haig was not impressed
with the Battle of Paardeberg that followed. Kitchener launched 'Piece
meal and frontal-attacks . . .: each one beaten back in turn without
inflicting on Cronje any real damage'.[23] Roberts arrived on 19 February
and invested the position, and on the 27th Cronje surrendered.

Haig's personal stock continued to rise. On 21 February, he was
appointed lieutenant colonel and given command of 3 Cavalry Brigade.
As he told Henrietta, this was 'a great piece of good luck' because there
were 'any number of old fossils about – full Colonels etc.'. Through
French's efforts Haig had been promoted over their heads. Events moved
rapidly. Errol was moved sideways, and on 22 February Haig was
appointed French's Assistant Adjutant General – effectively, his Chief of
Staff: 'This,' Haig wrote, 'will suit me very well'.[24]

Haig was becoming very disenchanted with the 'old fossils', and
indeed the state of the army and British strategy in general. He was
unfairly scathing about the infantry.[25] Haig's criticism of poor staff work
and confusion at Roberts's HQ echoed his criticisms of Kitchener's set up
in the Sudan.[26] Several months later he was appalled that the citizens of
one town had surrendered their weapons to the British and taken an oath
not to take up arms again, and, when British troops then withdrew,
hostile Boers returned and burned down the farms. 'Such conduct
merely brings us into contempt, although Roberts no doubt expected to
gain popularity with the British Public by being generous and merciful
to the conquered!' He particularly resented Roberts's perceived lack of
sympathy for the cavalry and his bad temper. 'I am afraid,' he wrote in

May 1900, 'that he is a silly old man scarcely fit to be C in C of this show'.[27]

By late February 1900 the strategic initiative in South Africa had passed to the British. Ladysmith was relieved on 29 February, and Roberts drove on the Orange Free State's capital, Bloemfontein. The road to the city was blocked by a strong Boer force at Poplar Grove. Roberts ordered French's horseman to carry out a 17-mile flank march. On 7 March the Cavalry Division, reinforced by two MI brigades, attempted to cut the Boers' line of communications to Bloemfontein. The defenders fell back and made a stand, inflicting losses on the British horsemen, mainly in the course of dismounted action (although, as Haig took pains to point out, an infantry assault would have been even more costly). In the confusion, Kruger and Steyn, the Presidents of the two Boer Republics, and a senior commander, Christiaan de Wet slipped out of the trap.

Poplar Grove was regarded by some, certainly by Lord Roberts, as a great missed opportunity for ending the Boer War with a decisive coup. This is highly doubtful. Even if the two Boer leaders had been taken prisoner it is all too likely that guerrilla warfare would have simmered on. In any case Roberts's plan was flawed. French seems to have believed that 'his task was impossible', not least because of the poor state of the horses.[28] 'I have never seen horses so beat as ours on this day', Haig wrote. They 'practically have been starving since we left Modder River' on February 11th. The problem was exacerbated by the large number of 'Colonial Skallywag Corps' that had been formed, which meant that fodder was dangerously short. If that wasn't bad enough, these irregular units and the MI were, in Haig's blunt assessment, 'quite useless'.[29] There is an element of special pleading here, as Haig was obviously disappointed at the failure of the cavalry to deliver victory. Yet his analysis (which implicitly reflected poorly on Roberts's decision-making) was essentially sound.[30] Modern historians have indentified misman-agement of horseflesh as a critical factor in the patchy performance of British cavalry in the Boer War, and indeed as more important than the traditional idea that cavalry was unable to prevail against firepower.[31] Poplar Grove would cast a long shadow over debates on cavalry doctrine after the Boer War.

Bloemfontein, abandoned by the Boers, was occupied by the British on 13 March. There Roberts paused before renewing the advance in mid-

April. In the meantime, the cavalry were kept busy, although not always usefully. Roberts seemed to Haig to order the cavalry to respond to any 'alarm', which wore out the horses. Even 'the most ignorant', Haig wrote a little later, 'must have foreseen that horses which are worked in an almost waterless country . . . will soon give out'.[32] Logistics, not the Boers, seemed to be the British army's greatest enemy.

Johannesburg fell on 31 May, Pretoria on 5 June. To many, including Haig, it seemed that the war was almost over. A year earlier Haig had judged that an attack on Pretoria would be decisive, as the Boers had to defend the city, and once this army was defeated, 'the country is at our mercy'.[33] Now Haig wrote from Pretoria, 'quite a nice town with plenty of trees and running water', 'I fancy that if Buller would only come on, and if an able man was sent to sweep up the N.E. corner of the Free State the war would soon be finished'.[34]

Fighting the Guerrillas

Such optimism was badly misplaced. In July 1900 Haig was surprised that '[Christiaan] de Wet is still able to defy some 70000 odd British troops with barely 2000 men at most'.[35] This was an ominous sign. In spite of war-weariness among much of the Boer population, a hard core of 'bitter-enders' fought on, and the conventional war gradually meta-morphosed into a guerrilla conflict that lasted until May 1902. The British army learned a type of conflict that had much in common with modern counterinsurgency. In the process Douglas Haig emerged as a ruthless practitioner of a brutal form of warfare.

For the rest of 1900 Haig remained with Johnnie French, who was understandably keen to hang on to his CoS; Haig affected not to mind. British strategy moved increasingly towards pursuit of elusive guerrillas, as well as dealing with formed Boer forces still in the field. The Cavalry Division continued to see much action, notably at Diamond Hill (11–12 June 1900) against Louis Botha, whose forces appeared to offer a threat to Pretoria. At Barberton, a key Boer supply depot attacked on 13 September, French executed a bold plan to surprise the enemy. Haig had a narrow escape during the advance, when he and John Vaughan encountered a group of Boers and had to gallop to safety. Like soldiers down the ages, he tried to assure the folks at home (who had heard about the incident from another source) that it was 'not so terrifying as you imagine'.[36] The final approach to Barberton was very difficult. 'We could bring no guns or vehicles of any kind, but crossed the mountains by a bad footpath. We had to walk most of the way on foot in single file'. The Boers were taken by surprise, and the British captured a considerable amount of equipment.[37]

Much of the responsibility for the effectiveness of the Division's operations rested with Haig as CoS. His orderly mind and grasp of detail – the mark of the good staff officer – is shown in orders such as this one:

> To General Dickson C.B. Com[mande]r. at Middelburg, 30.vii.00 – 6 p.m.
> A convoy of about 100 empty ox wagons will leave here about 3 p.m.
> tomorrow for the Oliphants river *Bridges*. Please detail about 25 mounted
> men to escort them, to the high ground about 7 miles S.W. of this which
> overlooks the river.

> By order D. Haig Lt Col, C.S.O.[38]

Someone who came across him at this time was impressed that, despite his many duties, Haig set 'everything else on one side in order to give full attention, at a moment's notice, to the requests of a young chaplain'. Haig gave him 'every facility and every support' in aiding 'spiritual welfare of both troops and [local] people'.[39]

In December Roberts returned home, leaving Kitchener to tie up the loose ends of the campaign. To many the victory at Barberton appear to mark the end of major combat operations, leaving only what Haig referred to as 'a lot of bands of marauders' that needed to be dealt with. French's Cavalry Division was split up in November. Haig approved of this. Cavalry was needed in 'detachments' to protect lines of supply, leaving mobile columns to chase guerrillas unencumbered by wagons.[40] Under Kitchener, the veldt was divided up by miles of wire with blockhouses, manned by small garrisons, at intervals, making it ever more difficult for the guerrillas to operate.

In an attempt to undermine support for the guerrillas, the British rounded up Boer civilians and put them in concentration camps (the name describing their purpose precisely). The death rate was high, although caused by administrative incompetence and neglect rather than deliberate cruelty. Kitchener's soldiers applied a scorched-earth policy, which had begun under Roberts, that included the burning of farms to deny food to the insurgents and to damage their morale. Boers who surrendered, and stayed loyal to their oaths, were dealt with relatively leniently. Others were treated with extreme harshness. Haig had long been sceptical about the value of compassion. In July 1900 he had complained that surrendered Boers 'go out on commando again' as soon as they could.[41] Recent historians have stressed the importance of colonial warfare in the development of total war – no-holds-barred conflict, with all that term implies – in the twentieth century.[42] Haig believed that harsh policies were the surest way to breaking enemy morale and forcing surrender.

Independent Command

In September 1900 French finally recommended Haig for an independent command, but this did not materialise for another five months. So Haig briefly remained with French when he took over in the Johannesburg area, but in January 1901 he was at last given the command he craved, with the job of clearing north-west Cape Colony of insurgents. The core of Haig's formation, of roughly brigade strength, was three mobile columns, but this was a flexible 'force package' that grew to as many as seven columns for specific tasks.[43] An unsuccessful hunt for De Wet in December convinced Haig, who seems to have been mentally preparing to go home, that the end was not nigh.[44] But there were certainly compensations for an ambitious officer. It was 'a nice change to have a show of one's own', especially as he had more actual independence than if he had commanded a conventional cavalry brigade. 'I can get no orders from anyone', he wrote, so he exercised his initiative in hunting guerrillas.[45]

One word sums up the feelings of the British military leadership in early 1901: frustration. They were simply unable to translate military victory into a political settlement. Kitchener, Haig thought,

> occasionally gets alarmed without real cause and hurries troops to this or
> that point, with out [sic] sufficiently considering what the effect must be
> . . . So one is forced to conclude that the Sirdar is not that large minded
> man capable of taking a broad view of the *whole* situation which the

papers would have us believe he is. At the same time there is no doubt
that he has great energy and power of organizing: so let us hope that the
present state of this country will soon improve.[46]

Haig's letters home showed his frustration: at failing to destroy De Wet's
force in March; and at what he thought was the undue leniency of the
civil authorities in failing to hang captured rebels ('There is too much
"*law*" not enough of the rough and ready justice in this land').[47]

In March, Haig was moved to the renamed Orange River Colony. His
task involved 'clearing the country (which is unpleasant work)', pursuing
Boers and blocking enemy forces from entering Cape Colony. The
'unpleasant work' included seizing 120,000 head of cattle in a week. By
early April Haig estimated that another eight weeks of his scorched-earth
policy would leave the Boers without 'much to live on in the district'.[48]
In mid-April he was back in Cape Colony, having been ordered by
Kitchener to 'take command of all columns now operating in the
midland area of Cape Colony' and 'Act vigorously with the object of
clearing Cape Colony of the enemy as soon as possible'. It is a tribute to
Haig's growing reputation for competence that Kitchener selected him
to inject dynamic leadership into a failing situation. It is worth
remembering that only three years earlier Haig had been a mere
squadron commander serving under Kitchener in the Sudan. Not
surprisingly, Haig thought it 'very satisfactory to be again chosen for this
job when things have got into a mess'.[49]

Technically, the people of Cape Colony were subjects of the King, and
so those who fought against Crown forces were therefore rebels. British
commanders, Haig included, believed that they should be punished
severely. It was difficult operating against guerrillas in Cape Colony
'where all farmers are secretly their friends,' Haig wrote: at least in the
Transvaal everyone could be 'treat[ed] as an enemy'.[50] Haig explained his
internal security methods to Henrietta.

[The people] of each farm house [are] registered and a ticket posted on the
front door giving a description of each man. Then our patrols pay surprise
visits at night and arrest any one [sic] not on the list, and note the
absentees as rebels.

No house was 'to have more than a month's supply of food for its inmates, calculated at the rates allowed in the refugee camps. This will cut the supplies of the commandos'.[51]

Such measures went hand in hand with military operations. A three-week effort in August 1901 had as its aim 'to get all the troops we could to the south of the Boer commandos and then drive them North against a line of blockhouses which had recently been made along the Durban–Stormberg Railway'. Haig controlled operations in the east, by a good deal of hard riding, while French oversaw activities in the west. Haig 'had a line of "stops"' spread across some 200 miles. Kritzinger attempted to break through but Haig herded the forces to the north. On 9 August Haig lamented 'I really had Kritzinger and his men surrounded, but somehow he managed to slip through'. Haig ordered a column commander to 'kill every horse if necessary' in the pursuit. The chase achieved some success, but other Boers escaped to fight again.[52] This was all too typical of British drives against the Boers.

In September 1901 Jan Christian Smuts led an invasion of Cape Colony. Smuts never had more than 3,000 men, the vast majority Cape rebels. In a classic guerrilla campaign, he forced much larger British forces to dance to his tune. 'In spite of all that French's and Haig's energy could do', Smuts sustained a nine month campaign in the Cape that lasted until the end of the war, but he failed in his objective, to generate a rising in Cape Colony.[53] One of Smuts's early victories was hugely embarrassing for Haig, who in 1901 had been appointed to command the 17th Lancers, a post he held concurrently with his brigade command. On 17 September this regiment's C Squadron was ambushed by some Boers, who were allowed to approach too close because they were wearing khaki; 85 out of 140 Lancers became casualties. Haig deserved at least part of the blame for an injudicious positioning of the regiment. Belying his later image of indifference to suffering, he was clearly upset at the deaths of 'so many poor fellows'.[54]

That said, Haig could be ruthless in his dealings with the enemy. In September 1901 he wrote of some enemy combatants taken prisoner. 'Those taken in khakee [sic] we shot at once. One man was taken actually riding with our scouts and wearing the uniform of Nesbitt's Horse . . . Finally he confessed that he was a Boer and was promptly shot'.[55] Anger at Boer subterfuges, such as that blamed by Haig for the disaster to the

17th Lancers, played a part in such drastic summary executions, but it was also part of a wider pattern of brutalisation of the conflict.

Some comments to Henrietta in March 1902 show that, on the surface, the situation had changed little in six months. 'We go slowly forward with the blockhouse line . . . and my columns hunt back strong parties of Boers'. In fact, the cumulative impact of the British measures had eroded the willingness of the Boers to continue the struggle. After a series of negotiations, within the Boer hierarchy and with the British, the Boer leadership accepted peace terms on 31 May 1902, and the war came to an end. Haig was unrepentantly hardline in his attitudes, in April writing privately that 'It would be much better to go on fighting for 10 years than give way in anything to them.' At the end, he was content with the final terms, although he was aware that loyalist South Africans were not.[56]

Haig and his regiment sailed for home on 23 September 1902. Unofficially he had heard that he was in line for a major post in India, but first he wanted to go on leave. 'For 3 years straight away on active service against a well armed and active enemy like the Boers [brings] . . . much anxiety at times upon those responsible for giving and transmitting orders'.[57] The strain of command had begun to tell on Haig.

Haig's reputation was riding high at the end of the Boer War. Lieutenant-General Ian Hamilton, Kitchener's CoS, wrote confidentially to Roberts that Haig was 'one of the most thoughtful, educated, and large-minded of our staff officers'.[58] Haig was now a colonel with an impressive CV that included successfully carrying out the role of chief of staff to a major formation on campaign; command of a smart cavalry regiment; and exercising both political and military authority as a *de facto* brigade commander. The highest positions within the army were now within his grasp. No matter how well-thought of officers are in peacetime, the challenges of active service can make or break reputations. Haig's rise in the army was not inevitable. A poor performance in South Africa – even a slice of bad luck – could have had damaging consequences.

South Africa was significant for Haig's career in other ways. The role of the cavalry during the war prompted a fierce debate that would absorb much of Haig's professional energies in the decade to come. He had honed his skills as a staff officer and learned those of a higher commander. And he had forged, or developed, relationships with many of the men with whom he would work in the First World War, Kitchener and French among them. Also among the men who served with him were Horne, Lawrence, Gorringe, Lukin, Byng and Greenly – all of whom commanded at least a division under Haig on the Western Front. And, as later on the Western Front, in South Africa Haig worked with civilians in uniform from Britain and the Empire. Perhaps most significant, in retrospect, is that Haig had developed the ruthless mentality of a total warrior. The Douglas Haig of the Somme owed much to the Douglas Haig of Cape Colony.

Regimental Commander

For some officers command of a regiment or battalion is the summit of their military career. For Haig, on his return from South Africa, it was a pleasant way of marking time before being propelled up the military hierarchy. French was keen that he should take over the Aldershot Cavalry Brigade, Kitchener that he become Inspector General of Cavalry in India. In the end Roberts decided that Haig was to head for India.

Douglas Haig brought the 17th Lancers home from South Africa in October 1902, and the regiment was sent to Scotland, so he was based in his home city. There was a touch of controversy about Haig's appointment to command this smart outfit. Herbert Lawrence, who had served with Haig in South Africa,[59] was a 17th Lancer who expected to command his regiment. According to an officer of the 17th, when Haig was brought in from outside, Bertie Lawrence resigned from the army 'at once in high dudgeon', and this is the line that most historians have followed.[60] In fact, Lawrence delayed his departure for ten months after Haig's appointment. They were never soul mates, but Lawrence seems to have maintained at least superficially cordial relations with the man who had supplanted him.[61] This became of some consequence some fifteen years later when, after making a great deal of money in the City and returning to the Colours at the outbreak of the war, in early 1918 Lawrence became Haig's Chief of Staff at GHQ.

During his stint as a peacetime regimental commander Haig worked hard, worked his men hard, and successfully strove for efficiency; but he could also be fiercely protective of his own. A 17th Lancers officer left an account of how Haig went into battle on his behalf against the bureaucracy of the War Office.[62] One incident shows a side of Haig very different from his public image. Some regimental officers had played a practical joke on the Lord Provost of Glasgow, a teetotaller, by affecting to believe he was a waiter and ordering 'three whiskies and sodas'. The affronted local dignitary complained to Haig, who summoned the miscreants to see him. The result was 'an abject apology', but the 17th's officers 'enjoyed the joke for a long time, and no one more than Colonel Haig'.[63]

Haig's finest hour as colonel of the 17th Lancers came on the polo field. He was determined to win the Inter-Regimental Polo Tournament, but refused the captaincy, telling Tilney, the existing captain, 'If you think I am good enough to play, I will. You are responsible for winning the tournament and don't hesitate to curse me'. The regimental team consisted of W.A. 'Pongo' Tilney; R.W.J. Cardin (a skilled 'pig-sticker' who in 1916 was to be killed commanding an infantry battalion on the Somme); Alan Fletcher (later Haig's ADC in France), and Haig. In the semi-final in July 1903 the Lancers were lagging badly behind the Rifle Brigade. Haig's enigmatic order was 'Pray as hard as you can and we will win!' – and, amazingly, they did, going on to beat the Royal Horse Guards in the final. (The future Mrs Haig, the Hon. Dorothy Vivian, watched the game, but the two of them were not introduced). Haig had already been on the winning side for the 7th Hussars three times.[64] It seemed that everything he touched turned to gold.

Cavalry Reformer

Horsed soldiers had been invaluable in the open spaces of the South African veldt. For the most part, horses had been used to convey from place to place soldiers who then dismounted to fight. Anti-guerrilla activities had been added to the traditional cavalry duties, such as scouting, raiding and pursuit. However, the mounted *arme blanche* charge remained a valuable tactic, and Klip's Drift and other actions demonstrated that not even infantry dug in and armed with modern rifles could be guaranteed to resist it; a charging horse was a surprisingly difficult thing to kill.[65] Leading British cavalrymen, with Haig at the helm, were fully aware of the strengths and weaknesses of cavalry. It is strange indeed that the next decade should see a protracted and often acrimonious debate on cavalry doctrine between progressives such as

Haig and others who sought to deny the lessons of the Boer War – and stranger still that some historians have labelled Haig as a reactionary on the subject.

Haig's views were clear. As early as July 1900 he had outlined his ideas: 'Cavalry as now arrived is a new factor in tactics'. He saw the hybrid cavalryman as hugely versatile, a great improvement on traditional horsed soldiers, and optimistically wanted up to a quarter of the army to consist of what he saw as a new troop type.[66] In his post-war evidence to the Royal Commission on the War in South Africa Haig reiterated his view that 'the ideal cavalry . . . can fight on foot and attack on horseback'. Both rifle *and* sword or lance were essential. Mounted Infantry or Mounted Rifles were no substitute because they were incapable of shock action that could break enemy morale.[67]

Lord Roberts, the Commander-in Chief, had very different opinions. Not realising that Haig did not share them, in 1902 Roberts gave him the job of writing the new manual on cavalry training. (Realising his mistake, Roberts subsequently had much of it rewritten.) Haig was in India by the time the 1904 *Cavalry Training* Manual appeared, which insisted that cavalry's main weapon was the rifle.[68] As part of a wider programme of army reform, Roberts abolished the lance and downgraded the importance of the sword. His motives probably owed more to personalities and his lingering anger at Poplar Grove than genuine tactical analysis. In 1910, when out of office, 'Bobs' also supported the bizarre but inexplicably influential ideas of Erskine Childers, who wanted to do away with the sword and teach cavalry to 'make genuinely destructive assaults upon riflemen and guns' by firing from the saddle, an immensely difficult and generally unrewarding tactic.[69]

The lasting testimony to Haig's thought on his arm of service is the 1907 book *Cavalry Studies*, based on staff rides he had run in India, which demonstrated cavalry's place on the modern battlefield. In it he argued that 'the rôle of Cavalry on the battlefield will always go on increasing'.[70] This passage, wrenched from its historical context, has become another weapon with which to attack Haig's reputation, but if the words 'mobile troops' were to be substituted for 'cavalry', it appears as 'a reasonable prediction of future war' – and cavalry were the only available mobile troops in 1907.[71]

In 1907 Haig (as Director of Military Training) and French were in positions that allowed them to replace the 1904 manual. Their 1907 edition directed that the cavalryman should combine traditional cavalry roles, including shock action, with dismounted firepower. This balance of fire and the sword produced the type of cavalrymen, equally at home on horseback and on foot, that proved such a vital part of the BEF in 1914–15. One over-enthusiastic sentence, which claimed that cavalry charges were 'irresistible' and has been used by critics from Childers onwards to rubbish cavalry thinking, quite overshadowed a realistic and sensible doctrine.[72]

In India Haig, who arrived there in October 1903, devoted his time to reforming the cavalry regiments, both British and Indian, to ensure that they were abreast of the latest developments. The wider context was Kitchener's determination to fit the army in India for fighting a war overseas, Haig's and Kitchener's views on cavalry largely coinciding.[73] Haig was his usual tireless self, visiting regiments, conducting exercises and Staff Rides. 'Want of co-operation with other arms,' ran a typical critique of one exercise.[74] Haig kept in touch with developments at home. He was in regular contact with Robert Baden-Powell, Inspector-General of Cavalry in Britain, to whom he gave 'much far-seeing and practical advice'. George Barrow, no uncritical admirer of Haig, wrote that 'His instruction was more practical and realistic than anything the cavalry in India had known previously . . . We who were fortunate to attend the "rides" learnt a tremendous lot under Haig'.[75]

At that time there was a power struggle going on between Kitchener, as C-in-C India, and Lord Curzon, the Viceroy. Although egos were involved, the point at issue, as Haig put it, was that Kitchener 'has really little power'. Vital logistic matters were the responsibility of the Military Member of Council, who answered to the Viceroy. 'Such a system is obviously ridiculous'.[76] Kitchener was the eventual winner of the contest. Haig's support for Kitchener marked a significant step in their relationship.

Marriage and Army Reformer

In 1905 Haig returned to England on leave and, to everyone's surprise, including probably his own, got married. Like almost everything else about Haig, his courtship and marriage to the Hon. Dorothy Maud Vivian was controversial. Haig met Miss Vivian in June 1905 at Windsor

Castle, where he was staying for the Ascot races. Introduced on the Thursday, they played golf on the Friday, and he proposed on Saturday morning; they were married in the chapel of Buckingham Palace barely a month later, on 11 July 1905.[77]

Some have seen this as a cynical act by a 44-year-old bachelor to acquire a younger wife to improve his career prospects, not least because Doris (as she was known) was a Maid of Honour to Queen Alexandra. Actually, it was common for army officers of Haig's generation to marry in their thirties or forties; and Haig's hasty marriage did not gain him 'Royal favour', as Philpott claims[78] – he already had it. Haig had been on good terms with the Prince of Wales (who became King Edward VII in 1901) since the 1890s, having been admitted to his circle through Willie, Henrietta's husband. King Edward made Haig an ADC in 1902 and the following year he awarded Haig the CVO as 'a mark of HM's personal esteem', and asked him to write from India on the condition of the cavalry. The simplest explanation for the rapid courtship is also the most likely: it was a case of love at first sight. Douglas and Doris had a very happy marriage. Their first daughter, Alexandra, was born in 1907, and her sister, Victoria, in 1908. Doris displaced Henrietta as Haig's confidante and primary source of emotional support, although it is clear that he did not immediately shed the habit of writing long and detailed letters to his sister.[79] James Edmonds, who delighted in gossip, claimed many years after the event that Haig committed adultery, but there is no credible evidence of this.[80] Haig's private life was as blameless as Johnnie French's was colourful.

From India, Haig kept a keen eye on military developments at home.[81] The initial failures of the army in South Africa had humiliated Britain in the eyes of the world, leading to calls to reform the army. In early 1904 a committee chaired by Lord Esher proposed far-reaching reforms. The post of Commander-in-Chief of the Army was to go, to be replaced by an Inspector-General of the Forces. A General Staff, with a Chief of the General Staff, was to be created along continental lines, and the existing Committee of Imperial Defence was to be enhanced.

Esher and Haig were by this stage friends and allies. 'Now, thanks to your energy, things seem on the right road for efficiency,' Haig wrote, congratulating Esher on his activities.[82] Reginald Brett, the second Viscount Esher, was a man of great influence on defence matters who preferred to stay behind the scenes. Esher was on good terms with the King, and he played an important role in accelerating Haig's career. Haig, Esher thought, was 'a very fine type of officer, practical, firm and thoughtful, thoroughly experienced not only in war, but in military history'.[83] Having identified Haig's qualities, Esher intrigued mercilessly to get his protégé into the centre of the reform process.

In February 1904 the 'clean sweep' of senior figures at the War Office took place, but in-fighting and incompetence among the 'new gang' hampered further movement. Bringing in the up-and-coming men such as French, Haig, Rawlinson, Henry Wilson and James Grierson was an obvious step, but in 1905 even Esher's formidable Machiavellian skills initially failed to land Haig the key post of Director of Staff Duties (DSD).[84] Haig eventually left India for Britain in May 1906, some months before his term as IGC was due to expire, to become Director of Military Training (DMT). By this time there was a new man in the War Office. Richard Burdon Haldane, Secretary of State for War in the new Liberal government, was to prove one of the greatest reformers in British military history. Esher had high hopes of a Haldane–Haig partnership. He gave Haldane highly favourable reports on Haig, as did French and Gerald Ellison, a soldier who was Haldane's Principal Private Secretary, and Esher wrote to Haig in India 'cracking up' Haldane 'like anything', not forgetting to square Kitchener on Haig's move back to Britain.[85] Esher's faith was not misplaced.

Preparing for war

Details of military reform do not set the pulse racing. But it is essential to look at Haig's pre-war activities because they represent one of his major successes as a soldier, perhaps even his main achievement. He had a clear vision of updating and standardising organisation and doctrine across the army. This vision was set against a fear, which grew almost to a certainty, that Germany would pose a military threat to the British Empire sooner rather than latter. By 1909 he was writing about 'meeting "the storm" which we all foresee' – Grierson and Robertson, among others, shared these fears. The war would be lengthy and '[we] will win by wearing the enemy out, if we are only allowed 3 more years to prepare and organise the Empire'. Three year earlier he had presciently predicted that it would be 'a great war requiring the whole resources of

the Nation to bring it to a successful end'.[86] Before he took over the
Aldershot Command in 1912 he told his protégé Captain John Charteris
that war was highly likely 'within three or four years'.[87] Haig was
determined to make the most of this period of grace.

The effectiveness of the Haldane reforms, and of Haig's part in them,
should not be exaggerated, but neither should they be minimised. On
the eve of war in August 1914 the army was in an incomparably better
shape than at the beginning of the Boer War. Haig's work prefigures his
administrative and organisational labours on the Western Front, the
importance of which historians are realising.

As Director of Military Training, Haig 'sought to inculcate the
precepts of uniformity, efficiency, and preparedness by organising staff
tours, formulating mobilization plans, devising training schemes, and
testing embarkation and disembarkation procedures'. This was
demanding, unglamorous work, involving long hours and hard graft,
and he made an immediate impact. 'Douglas Haig has impressed me
greatly by the change for the better initiated even in the first fortnight,'
wrote Haldane in September 1906. A number of officers made significant
contributions to the reform process, including Wilson and Grierson, but
increasingly Haldane leaned on Haig. As a bonus, Haig helped smooth
the way for Royal approval of Haldane's schemes.[88]

At first sight, it was not obvious that a close partnership should
develop between the cavalryman and a philosophically trained barrister
turned Liberal cabinet minister. In fact, both men had close connections
with Edinburgh and shared a passionate desire to reform the army. Haig,
although undoubtedly politically and socially conservative, was
pragmatic when it came to party politics. On hearing of Haldane's
appointment he commented that he 'cannot be worse than Arnold-
Forster' (his Unionist, i.e. Conservative, predecessor), and later even
forgave Haldane's association with 'the pack of rascals' such as Lloyd
George who were 'ruining the country'.[89] The relationship was not
always smooth, but for the most part, the two men had a harmonious
and productive relationship. Haig did not much care for politicians as a
class but came to have a huge admiration for Haldane, whom he rightly
saw as instrumental in preparing the army for war in 1914.[90] Haldane's
respect for Haig is the strongest possible counter to the calumny that
Haig was stupid. A man with such a brilliant mind would not be

impressed by a well-connected duffer. Ellison, who worked closely with both men on the reforms, described Haig's role as 'quite invaluable'.[91]

Haig finally became Director of Staff Duties in 1907, taking part of his previous duties with him. In his new post Haig's main role was to oversee the writing of *Field Service Regulations Part II (FSR II)*. This was an organisational and administrative manual for the army in the field that also served as a rudimentary doctrine, covering things such as the man-on-the-spot command doctrine, the need to establish fire superiority and the importance of the decisive battle. To impose a doctrine on the British army was no easy task. British military culture, rooted in attitudes in wider society, laid much emphasis on individualism and 'character', which resulted in a cult of pragmatism, flexibility and an empirical approach relying on experience, not theory. The consequence was a 'muddle-through' mentality resistant to prescriptive doctrine. Haig was not immune from this influence. *FSR* was not prescriptive, laying stress on the principles of war, which he saw as broad precepts rather than bullet points in the modern sense, but it gave a sound basis for problem-solving in which Regular officers could bring their experience to bear. *FSR* encountered some opposition from traditionalists, but Haig eventually won the day.[92]

Haig's other major contribution to the Haldane reforms was in the reorganisation of auxiliary forces. The ambition was to bring the Militia, Yeomanry and Volunteers into a proper relationship with the Regulars, but this meant breaking down a great deal of entrenched opposition. Haig was one of the few senior soldiers to throw his weight behind Haldane's concept of a volunteer part-time force. In 1906 Haig had sketched out a concept of a 'National Army', an 'Imperial Militia', based on compulsory training, but was well aware it was more than the political market would bear, and eventually settled for a voluntary body considerably smaller than his original concept. He had hoped for 900,000 men, but the new Territorial Force, which came into being in 1908, never numbered more than 270,000 in peacetime. However the TF, hugely expanded after the outbreak of war, was to be one of the mainstays of Haig's army on the Western Front.[93]

In 1909 Haig returned to India as Chief of Staff to the C-in-C, General Sir O'Moore Creagh. Initially reluctant to take on the role, he changed his mind when he saw the importance of developing the general staff in

India; Creagh was a lightweight in comparison to his predecessor, Kitchener (his nickname was 'No More K').[94] Lieutenant-General Sir Douglas Haig, as he now was, brought his War Office experience to bear on the situation in India, modernising the army and preparing it for war, spreading the gospel of *FSR*.[95] Again the reformers faced vested interests, but Creagh and Haig did manage to bring the 'higher military organisation' much more in line with that in Britain. The big failure was to prepare the Indian army for major operations outside India, where Haig was unable to make much headway. Forbidden by the Viceroy to produce plans, Haig used the subterfuge of paper exercises, which in 1914 were used to organise expeditionary forces to France and the Middle East, but this was no substitute for thorough preparation.[96] Indian and British troops, sent on improvised and sometimes disastrous expeditions during the Great War, paid the price.

Aldershot Command

After eight years of demanding staff jobs, in March 1912 Haig once again took command of soldiers. He was given a plum post: the Aldershot Command, consisting of 1st and 2nd Division and 1 Cavalry Brigade. Haig's arrival from India accompanied by some of his own staff, such as Captain John Charteris, was regarded by some with suspicion as a 'Hindoo Invasion'. He made an immediate impact. As one officer noted, 'the training of both officers and soldiers became much more strenuous'.[97] Much of Haig's work involved mundane but essential preparation of his troops for war. He earned such a reputation for attention to the detail of logistics that he was even consulted by Captain Robert Falcon Scott RN on logistic preparations for his ill-fated expedition to the South Pole.[98]

Over the next two years Haig imposed his personality on his command, entertaining at his home and letting his guests see an informal side to his character. This was a crucial period in forging team spirit. Many of the officers who served under Haig at Aldershot were to be part of the I Corps team that went to France in August 1914. Another, Colonel H.S. Horne, was to rise to command First Army under Haig.

One event that occurred at Aldershot has entered the Haig legend. Supposedly, in the 1912 manoeuvres Haig neglected the importance of using aeroplanes in reconnaissance and was thus outgeneralled by

Grierson, who did use aircraft in this role. This has been seen as symptomatic of the army's neglect of the potential of airpower and general technophobia, with Haig one of the worst culprits. '[F]lying can never be of any use to the army,' Haig allegedly said in 1911, while in July 1914 he supposedly denounced as 'foolish' the idea that 'aeroplanes will be able to be usefully employed for reconnaissance purposes in war. There is only one way for a commander to get information . . . and that is by the use of cavalry.' These quotations, which appear in the memoirs of Frederick Sykes, written many years after the First World War, are distinctly dubious. Sykes seems to have disliked Haig because of his support for his RFC rival, Trenchard.[99]

These supposed comments read oddly when juxtaposed to the contemporary record. As early as 1911 Haig commented very favourably on the experimental use of aircraft in exercises in India. While at Aldershot, Haig showed interest in the pioneering airman Samuel Cody.[100] At the notorious 1912 manoeuvres Haig's defeat was caused not by ignoring aerial reconnaissance but by placing too much emphasis on it. He used aircraft and cavalry for scouting, but both failed to locate the presence of an 'enemy' force on Grierson's flank.[101] Expecting too much of prototype technology was a mistake that Haig was to repeat during the First World War,[102] but the idea that Haig disdained the military use of aircraft before the First World War is simply untrue.

The Curragh Incident

In March 1914 Haig was involved in a crisis that threatened to destroy the army he loved. After the second general election of 1910 Asquith's Liberals were reliant on Irish Nationalist votes to stay in office. Their price was a bill on a limited degree of Home Rule for Ireland, but Protestant Ulster, supported by the Unionist opposition at Westminster, recoiled from the prospect of 'Rome rule' from Dublin. A paramilitary body, the Ulster Volunteer Force, was recruited to resist Home Rule. By 1914 it numbered around 100,000; civil war in Ireland was a real possibility.

If the army were to be ordered to coerce Ulster, it would place many officers, especially those of Anglo-Irish origin, on the horns of a particularly difficult dilemma. Should they obey their orders or their consciences? If the latter, what would be the consequences? For the first time since the Glorious Revolution of 1688 there was a serious question-mark over the willingness of the leadership of the British army to obey their Sovereign's government.

On 18 and 19 March, as political tensions heightened, General Sir Arthur Paget, GOC Ireland, attended meetings in London with 'Jack' Seely, the Secretary of State for War, and others to discuss precautionary measures to be taken in Ireland. Back in Ireland on 20 March, he held a meeting with senior officers. He implied that military operations against Ulster were imminent, and, while officers with homes in Ulster need not participate, the choice for others was stark. Hubert Gough, commander of 3 Cavalry Brigade at the Curragh, near Dublin, telegraphed his brother Johnnie, Haigh's CoS, at Aldershot: 'Have been offered dismissal service or undertake operations against Ulster. Two hours to decide.' Paget's stance was a disastrous miscalculation, a wholly unnecessary escalation of the crisis. He made things worse by addressing Gough's brigade on 21 March, which prompted 60 of the 72 officers to offer to resign.[103] The 'Curragh Incident' was under way.

As far back as September 1913 Johnnie Gough had attempted to raise his worries, but Haig seemed 'anxious to avoid discussing the subject and not to realise that Ulster was in earnest'.[104] He played his cards so close to his chest that when the crisis broke no one was sure what his position would be. Haig was inevitably drawn in as a senior commander, with the added complication that the Gough brothers, both strong Unionists, emerged as leading actors in the drama. Haig's position was difficult. Even if civil war was avoided, the potential for damage to the army was enormous at a time of increasing German threat; on 25 March Haig warned his senior commanders about the 'danger of Disruption in Army to Empire'. However Haig recoiled from 'coercing our fellow citizens who have done no wrong'. Therefore Haig opted for conciliation by steering a middle course.[105]

Johnnie Gough wrote to Haig (who was on leave) on 20 March that 'my views [on Ulster] . . . mean everything to me' and he was on the verge of resigning. Haig's response was to try to calm him down, replying that 'I feel equally strongly on subject as you. There is no question of Army fighting against Protestants or against Catholics. Our duty is to keep the peace between them'. Haig on 23 March visited London, where he bluntly informed Sir John French, the CIGS, that if

Hubert Gough were removed from command 'all the officers of the Aldershot Command would resign'. This news came as an unpleasant shock to French.[106]

Having tried to prevent the army authorities from exacerbating the problem, Haig worked with Haldane, by now the Lord Chancellor, to come up with a public form of words to which all could agree. They were unsuccessful, but at a separate meeting on 23 March, in which Haig was not involved, a public statement was agreed. The Goughs were satisfied, but the incident claimed the scalps of French, Sir J.S. Ewart (the Adjutant General) and Seely, who were judged by Asquith to have exceeded their authority in brokering the deal.[107]

Haig did not play a major role in ending the crisis but his interventions were nonetheless significant, especially in conveying to French the extent of support for the Gough brothers at Aldershot. His principal concern was to avoid 'the terrible results of disintegration in the Army', the imperilment of 'our status as a Great Power' and he tried to influence the officers under his command 'to keep aloof from politics'. Haig was apparently unconscious of the irony that he was arguing that soldiers should *have nothing to do with politics*', while engaging in politics at a high level. He viewed politics narrowly, as being about parliamentary parties, and it is instructive that he wishes a 'plague on both their houses', resenting the use of the army as 'a political tool by each party in turn'.[108]

The Curragh did not have the damaging effects that Haig had feared, not least because the outbreak of the First World War four months later concentrated minds. March 1914 did irreparable damage to some relationships: Major-General Henry Wilson and the Gough brothers fell out spectacularly. Haig's careful stance meant that he kept on good terms with, for instance, the Goughs, but also Philip Howell, second-in-command of the 4th Hussars, who was in the opposite camp. By avoiding making enemies over the Curragh, Haig made it easier for himself to impose his authority in future commands.

One consequence of the Curragh was that Haig's opinion of French, which had been in decline for some time, dropped to a new low. As far back as 1909 he had disapproved of the way that French's views on cavalry had apparently evolved, and Haig had not been impressed by French's performance at the 1913 manoeuvres.[109] This eroding of a previously strong friendship was a sad spectacle. Neither man was wholly blameless, but there is something distasteful about the way Haig distanced himself from the man who had done so much to further his career. In the end Haig's professionalism took precedence. He felt that French 'was out of touch with the Army', had mishandled the affair and deserved to go. Two years later, when their relationship was in ribbons, Haig wrote that French had 'sacrificed the whole Army during the Irish crisis before the war'.[110]

Haig on the Eve of War

There is no doubt that Haig was a driven man – a professional in a rapidly transforming army; highly ambitious, dedicated to his vocation. But becoming a husband and father rounded out his personality. John Charteris, his Assistant Military Secretary at Aldershot, said that marriage ended Haig's 'aloneness'. He was able to compartmentalise his life, and took care not to neglect spending time with his family, which was an oasis in a busy life. With a home in Farnborough, a wife and reunited with the small children upon whom he doted (they had been left behind in Britain while he and Doris went to India in 1909) Haig's personality thawed. Haig was noticeably more sociable at Aldershot than he had been as CO of the 17th Lancers. For exercise he played golf or tennis, or went riding, often mischievously evading his companions by suddenly galloping off and greeting them, when they finally caught up, with 'Did you not see the way I went?' One facet that was later very marked, his Christian faith, was not much in evidence at this stage. Indeed, under his sister's influence he briefly flirted with the fashionable fad of spiritualism, largely, it seems, to please her.[111]

Ill health as a child, overcome in part by self-control, seems to have influenced two of Haig's character traits. The first was a highly structured approach to life. In India and in Britain, during a typical day time was set aside for office work, for visiting units, for exercise, for meals, for relaxation. The other was a concern for his health that bordered on hypochondria. He tried various faddish diets, such as 'sour milk' and 'Sanatogen'.[112] It was while he was at Aldershot that he first met Colonel Eugene 'Mickey' Ryan RAMC, who was to become his trusted doctor and friend.

Haig's manner could be abrasive, and that, allied to his lack of small talk and inarticulacy (punctuated by thunderous silences), could alienate people. But people who worked closely with him could become fiercely loyal to 'the Chief'. George MacMunn, a gunner who worked for Haig in India, wrote that 'if he liked a man he was the most loveable of masters' with the 'greatest personal charm that ever opened a junior's heart.' But Haig had a 'supreme disability when called upon to talk', that MacMunn put down to shyness.[113]

MacMunn was right: Haig's lack of verbal fluency was a distinct handicap. Some of the stories probably grew in the telling, but there are plenty of anecdotes, such as one of an attempted impromptu speech at a military conference that went disastrously wrong, or of Haig saying at a cross-country race 'You have run very well. I hope you will run as well in the presence of the enemy'.[114] Lloyd George later affected to see Haig's verbal inarticulacy as evidence of stupidity, but a glance at his carefully argued staff papers suggests otherwise. Haig was not an intellectual, but he was well read and thoughtful. Military histories were his staples – allegedly he never read novels – and he had good French and could get by in German. A French report from 1911 on the army of their future ally stated that Haig 'is considered one of the best British generals. He has a good eye and wide command experience'.[115]

Some historians have depicted the pre-war army's command structure as being rigidly hierarchical, riven by clashes between powerful personalities, anti-intellectual and wedded to outdated doctrine that favoured throwing soldiers against barbed wire rather than seeking a technological solution: 'the British Army as a whole was . . . its own worst enemy'.[116] It is difficult to square this portrait with the performance of the British army on the Western Front in adapting to the new conditions and mastering a new way of warfare, and the argument that these improvements occurred in spite of Haig and the army hierarchy simply will not do.[117] The army had transformed itself since the Boer War, and was to do so again on the Western Front. Haig deserved a sizeable share of the credit for the pre-war reforms.

Now, having reformed the army, he was fated to take it to war.

Corps Commander

August 1914 seems a thing apart from the rest of the First World War, a strange blend of old and new. On the 22nd British troops advanced past a memorial erected to commemorate the battle of Malplaquet in 1709. The uniforms were very different, but the war up to that point had been one of open warfare that the Duke of Marlborough himself would have recognised. The men were on the way to Mons, where the BEF had a brutal introduction to modern battle just 24 hours later. By November manoeuvre had vanished, its place taken by trench warfare. The men who survived 1914 had even worse experiences ahead of them, as the conduct of warfare underwent profound changes. For Lieutenant-General Sir Douglas Haig, General Officer Commanding I Corps, the 1914 campaign was the time he emerged as a figure of national significance.

Haig was involved in the formulation of strategy from the very beginning of the war.[1] Joining other senior military and naval and political figures at a council of war on 5 August 1914, he argued that it might be prudent to hold the BEF back from France for up to three months, building a mass army on the cadre and mobilising the resources of the Empire. This was in line with his long-held conviction that the war would be long, and Britain would need a mass 'National Army' to fight 'in great offensive operations with hope of decisive success *before we are financially* exhausted'.[2] Strategic realities rendered this plan redundant. Franco-British staff talks had been going on since 1912, French plans had been made on the basis of British support, and the disciplines of coalition warfare meant that Britain did not have a free hand. Many men went to France and were killed in the early battles who would have been invaluable in training the mass citizen army that was authorised within a week of this session. By the end of the meeting, at which Haig asked 'certain fundamental questions' which helped focus the rather haphazard debate, he came to support the need to send the BEF to France without delay. Although Haig had had some idea of the staff talks since November 1912, apparently he only became fully aware of the strategic picture at a preliminary meeting with Henry Wilson.

To France

Haig crossed to France on 15 August 1914. To command troops in war is the height of most soldiers' ambitions, and Haig approached the task with a mixture of pride and a keen sense of the awesome responsibility that was now his. He was happy with his 'first rate Staff' and his subordinates, but Haig had a low opinion of Sir John French and his CoS, Archie Murray – 'In my own heart, I know that French is quite unfit for this great Command at a time of crisis in our Nation's History'. When the King had visited Aldershot on 11 August 1914 Haig passed on a modified version of these thoughts to George V.[3] This mistrust underpinned some of the key decisions Haig made in August–September 1914.

While he was travelling to Amiens on a train on 17 August Haig was informed that Jimmy Grierson, his fellow Corps commander, had died of a heart attack in another carriage. Haig grieved for his friend but gave instructions for the train to continue; nothing would be gained by halting.[4] He correctly deduced from the scanty intelligence available and from his study of German doctrine and military history that the Germans were seeking to turn the left flank of the French army. On 20 August, sensing battle was near, he held a conference of his senior officers. At this time he was still anticipating taking the offensive, and was 'particularly emphatic that all German teaching, strategy and tactics aim at envelopment'. Fearing that the Germans might encourage the British to advance while slipping around the attacker's flanks, he was determined to 'retain the possibility of breaking off the attack at any moment if required'.[5]

During the course of the encounter battle that unfolded on 23 August 1914, it was the Germans, not the British, who did the attacking. Having advanced to the area of Mons, Sir John French grew perturbed at the news reaching him of the strength of German forces in the area. On the evening of 22 August French cancelled the British offensive and ordered the BEF to hold in place for 24 hours. Most of II Corps (under Smith-Dorrien, who had replaced Grierson) faced north, deployed along the Mons-Condé canal. However the British positions bulged out around the village of Obourg, before turning to form a dogleg, I Corps extending the British position to the south-east. 2nd Division began to move at 3 a.m. on 23 August, reaching its positions between 11 a.m. and 12.30 p.m. By that time, the battle was under way.[6]

From around 9 a.m. the Germans launched a series of attacks on II Corps. For the most part, they were contained, except in the Obourg salient. Here German artillery fire and infantry attacks in the afternoon forced the defenders to withdraw. By nightfall, there was a more general retirement from the line of the canal to another position in the rear. II Corps had achieved a clear tactical defensive victory. I Corps' role had been distinctly secondary, suffering a mere 40 casualties throughout 23 August.[7] Until 2 p.m. when German guns began shelling there was little action on I Corps front. At about 2.30 p.m. the German cavalry passed across I Corps' front heading north-west. Haig's troops did not face a serious infantry attack all day.

In his diary Haig wished that he could have actively supported II Corps. He was certainly asked to do so, but ultimately did very little. Lack of accurate information, fear of encirclement and mistrust of French's judgement induced a degree of caution in Haig's decision-making that seems wildly at odds with the optimism for which he is famous. His reaction to being instructed, late on 22 August, to move to support II Corps was that this was 'an ill-considered order in view of the condition of the reservists in the ranks, because it meant a forced march by night . . .'.[8]

French, Haig, Smith-Dorrien and Allenby (GOC Cavalry Division) conferred at II Corps HQ at 5.30 a.m. on 23 August. Haig reacted unfavourably to French's apparently casual treatment of the intelligence gathered by aerial reconnaissance that 'at least 3 [German] corps [were] suitably placed for an attack on Mons and neighbourhood'.[9] Haig later stressed French's mental divorce from the intelligence picture, describing a conversation with Lieutenant-Colonel G.M.W. Macdonogh, French's Intelligence chief, after the conference (which Macdonogh did not

attend) in which the latter said 'that aeroplanes reported all the roads
running west from Brussels to Ath and Tournai were thickly covered
with masses of German troops of all arms marching very rapidly
westwards'. Haig, possibly charitably, concluded that Macdonogh and
French had not discussed the matter. Although retrospective, this
evidence is consistent with other sources. Macdonogh and Lieutenant
E.L. Spiers (liaison officer with French Fifth Army) separately warned
French on 22 August of German attempts to envelop the Allies. French
however had ordered the BEF to continue to advance, even though this
risked walking into the enemy trap.[10] By the end of the day wiser
counsels had prevailed. With the conclusion of the early-morning
conference on 23 August, the C-in-C headed for Valenciennes. He took
no part in the coming battle.

All this reinforced Haig's anxiety about German intentions. He was
'gravely concerned' that the threat to the BEF's flank posed by superior
numbers of enemy troops was not being taken seriously by GHQ. Haig
was well versed in German military doctrine, and knew the stress they
laid on encirclement of the enemy. The absence of a major attack on I
Corps, in Charteris's words, 'increased rather than diminished his
anxiety'. If indeed the Germans were attempting to envelop the BEF, as
in fact they were, 'they would not attack the inner flank in force'.[11] The
German bombardment of I Corps – rated by Haig as 'very heavy' (it was
not, in comparison to shelling later in the war) – might have been
intended to pin I Corps in place. Haig was given an additional reason to
fear for his right flank when at 3 p.m. cavalry reported that units of
Lanrezac's French Fifth Army had been pushed back.[12] Haig was
fundamentally correct. On bumping into the BEF, German intelligence
on the BEF's whereabouts was poor, the commander of German First
Army, Kluck's instinct was to get around the flank.[13]

All these factors influenced Haig's decision, taken at about 3 p.m., to
turn down a request from Major-General Hubert Hamilton, GOC 3rd
Division, for support. Haig was aware that 3rd Division was coming
under heavy pressure, but at an earlier meeting with Hamilton he
thought him 'quite worn out with fatigue', and probably queried
Hamilton's judgement. As Haig's 'right was still being attacked' (this may
refer to the shelling, or may indicate that Haig believed German troops
were in contact with his forces),

I therefore ordered the 4th Guards Brigade to Hartweg with instructions
to detach 2 Battalions to hill 93 . . . so as to relieve two battalions of 3rd
Division now on it. I also had Haking's Brigade and the bulk of the
artillery of 2nd Division in readiness near the X roads north east of
Bougnies to support in case of necessity.[14]

Haig sent a letter to Smith-Dorrien at 5.30 p.m. informing him of his
actions. A sentence refers to an earlier time when 'our line east of Givry
was being attacked from the direction of Binche'; this implies that that
the crisis had passed, or at least that Haig had gained more confidence,
and helps to explain why Haig was responsive to Smith-Dorrien's later
request for help. He had decided that the potential threat to I Corps was
more serious than the actual threat to 3rd Division. If I Corps had
become heavily committed in the fighting in the salient, and he had then
faced a crisis at the other end of his line, it could have been disastrous.
Haig's letter to Smith-Dorrien of 5.30 p.m. suggests that by this stage he
was less worried about the threat of envelopment:

Let me know your views for tomorrow as soon as darkness sets in. If all
goes well on my right I should like to support Hamilton in driving enemy
back into Mons while to reduce the gap between your 3rd and 5th
Divisions would it not be possible to attack from your left?
    Shall I come over and see you about 8 p.m.? Unless you and I meet, co-
ordination between our two corps will be difficult.[15]

The last sentence highlights a major command-and-control problem:
in the absence of the Commander-in-Chief, two commanders of equal
status were attempting to co-ordinate operations. The pre-war
conception of a corps essentially as a post-box through which the C-in-
C could deliver orders to divisions[16] broke down as both Smith-Dorrien
and Haig were forced, whether they liked it or not, to act as independent
commanders. There was no higher 'command' at Mons, no one
individual able to stand back and take an overall view of the situation,
allocate reserves and resources, assert his authority and issue orders to
both Corps. French's absence was a major error that casts doubt on his
judgement as a commander – and supports Haig's unflattering views of
the capability of his boss. At approximately 5 p.m. French 'received a

most unexpected message from General [Joseph] Joffre [French C-in-C]
. . . telling me that at least three German corps . . . were moving on my
position in front'. Clearly there was little if any attempt on the part of
either corps commander to keep the Commander-in-Chief informed.[17]

Later, at about 6.30 p.m., Haig responded more positively to a request
for support delivered in person by Smith-Dorrien and his chief of staff
Brigadier-General G.T. Forestier Walker. The latter said 'The battle is
won if you will only send us a battalion or two'. Haig sent three
battalions, to little effect.[18]

For most of 23 August Haig was at his command post at Le Bonnet.
When in the early afternoon he received Hamilton's plea for support he
was driven 'to X roads about 3 miles north of Le Bonnet' where he could
personally observe the scene.[19] According to Sergeant T. Secrett, his
soldier valet, Haig crawled on his stomach to the crest of a hill. Secrett
'heard his exclamation to the general beside him and the next minute
the appalling panorama was laid out before my eyes'. They saw '[d]ense
– inconceivably dense – masses of grey-clad figures advancing', with
many more moving up to the battle . . ., with British troops 'literally
mowing them down'. Further away they could see German cavalry and
artillery 'moving into action' and columns of infantry marching along a
road. 'Haig just looked at the other general [Johnnie Gough] without a
word, and then moved back'. If Secrett's recollections are broadly
accurate, this is further evidence of the fear of being overwhelmed that
influenced Haig during the Battle of Mons.[20]

That night Johnnie Gough was summoned to a conference at Le
Cateau, which eventually began at about 1 a.m. on the 24th. Sir John
French had reluctantly decided to retreat, having discovered that
Lanrezac, commander of the French Fifth Army, was falling back.
Murray passed on French's orders: the BEF was fall back some eight
miles to the south and 'the corps were to retire in mutual co-operation,
the actual order of retirement to be settled by the two corps commanders
in consultation'. Given the poor communications between the corps,
this arrangement, by which Murray devolved to subordinates
responsibility that was properly his, was highly unsatisfactory. At this
point II Corps HQ could not be reached by either telephone or telegraph.
Forestier-Walker, II Corps CoS, had to deliver the message in person,
arriving at 3 a.m. on the 24th. Smith-Dorrien and Haig only met to

confirm the arrangement at midday on 24 August, when the II Corps commander arrived at I Corps headquarters at Le Bonnet.[21]

I Corps was more fortunate. At about 2 a.m. on 24 August Haig was woken and given a telegram sent by Gough from GHQ.[22] It ordered

> retreat at once on Bavai where a defensive position would be taken up. 1st Corps to cover retirement of 2nd Corps!. . . [sic] This seemed impossible, as I was much further to East, and not being allowed to pass through Maubeuge had to make a flank march in the face of the enemy!

These orders aroused Haig's worst nightmare of envelopment. There were only two hours of darkness left, and Haig feared that I Corps would be attacked at dawn strung out on the line of march. Instead, he formed a rearguard and marched the rest of I Corps south. Charteris commented that Haig had 'a clear conception' of the challenge, which was similar to problems posed in Staff Rides in India. Haig had likewise commented before the war to J.F.N. 'Curly' Birch (a trusted friend who acted as his senior artillery adviser from May 1916 onwards) that the 'manoeuvre of retreat' might be of the greatest importance in the coming war. He had witnessed it during the 1913 French army manoeuvres and rehearsed retreating at Aldershot. Haig firmly believed that the BEF had to avoid battle, to outmarch their pursuers to give themselves a chance of regrouping and striking back, and to remain in contact with the French. To be forced into fighting a battle while on the retreat was to have failed.[23]

Haig's reaction shows him at his best as a staff officer. In the absence of Gough he did the work himself, sending Charteris to liaise with II Corps; briefing Jeudwine and Malcolm, (senior staff officers of I Corps) and then motoring to the headquarters of 1st and 2nd Divisions and issuing orders. Haig even 'marked [Monro's] map, as he and his Staff Officer (Colonel Gordon) were very sleepy'.[24] After the war Major-General Sir Frederick Maurice suggested that Haig had some advance warning on the 23rd that French Fifth Army had retreated and had therefore 'made his plans for the withdrawal, which he saw to be inevitable'. The evidence for this is ambiguous, but Smith-Dorrien's suggestion seems plausible:

[I]t was Sir Douglas Haig's own foresight which had enabled him to
appreciate on the 23rd that a retirement would be probable, for he was in
touch with the general situation which I . . . was not.[25]

French was remarkably sanguine about Haig's defiance of his orders,
apparently deferring to the 'man on the spot' as recommended by
contemporary doctrine.[26] The C-in-C arrived at Le Bonnet in the
morning of 24 August. Haig thought he was 'evidently v[ery] anxious'
but by French's own account the sight of the methodical withdrawal of
I Corps gave him confidence.[27] French even paid tribute to I Corps'
'excellent stand to cover the retirement' of II Corps on the morning of
24 August, which suggests a rationalisation of the fact that his orders
were disregarded as being unworkable as well as the desire to denigrate
Smith-Dorrien, whom the C-in-C hated. The calmness of Haig and his
troops had a steadying effect on his boss.[28]

The withdrawal of I Corps was generally smooth, except that Haig's
driver took a wrong turning and continued for a short distance along the
road towards the Germans before the mistake was realised. Had the car
continued on its way, the history of the British army in the First World
War might have been very different.

Haig regarded the ease of I Corps' retreat as suspicious. As he pointed
out to Sir John French when they met at Bavai at 4 p.m. on 24 August,
it might simply have indicated that the BEF was being encircled further
to the west.[29] Haig had reconnoitred the Bavai position and was
unimpressed. What happened at this Bavai meeting with French, and its
outcome, is controversial. 'All seemed much excited', Haig wrote in his
diary, 'but with no very clear plan beyond holding this wretched Bavai
position. I pointed out strongly to Sir John that if we halted for a day at
Bavai the whole force would be surrounded by superior numbers.'
According to an account of the conference Haig wrote in 1919, 'The Field
Marshal replied that "Smith-Dorrien had just stated that his troops could
march no further, that they could not march on the following day but
must halt for rest".' Smith-Dorrien vehemently denied that he had passed
any such message on to GHQ.[30] According to Haig's contemporary
diary, French accepted Haig's assessment of the danger and 'ordered the
[British Expeditionary] Force to continue its retreat. By Murray's request
I arrange roads for retirement of my Corps on Landrecies, *giving the direct*

route to Le Cateau to the II Corps . . .'[31] Haig's opinion was not the only factor in French's decision to retreat. In the afternoon GHQ was informed that French Third, Fourth and Fifth Armies were continuing to fall back, and reports from air reconnaissance were disquieting. To march the entire BEF to either the east or west of the Forest of Mormal was extremely inadvisable for practical reasons. French therefore reluctantly decided to divide his force, sending II Corps to the east and I Corps to the west of the Forest. Haig was consulted and, over tea provided at a 'charming house' in Bavai, wrote a note signifying his consent.

French was tempted to order the BEF to retire into the fortress of Maubeuge. Charteris credits Haig with successfully arguing against this by stressing the importance of out-marching the Germans, and the dangers of fighting on the retreat.[32]

At the end of a long day Haig retired to bed in a farm that was 'filthy and full of flies'. He was taken ill with diarrhoea. Secrett defied orders that he was not to be disturbed and woke Charteris, who fetched Colonel Ryan, I Corps' Medical Officer. 'D.H. was at his worst', Charteris reported, 'very rude but eventually did see Ryan who dosed him with what must have been something designed for elephants, for the result was immediate and volcanic!' It was actually sodium bicarbonate solution. It did help Haig to get to sleep after two hours, but in the morning he was 'ghastly to look at'. Ryan insisted that he travel by car rather than ride.[33] At this time Haig was put under stress by a number of factors: inadequate command arrangements, climatic conditions (it was very hot around the time of Mons); heavy workload; lack of sleep, physical danger; difficult interpersonal relations. Up to the night of 24 August he had managed to cope and not allow these to affect his decision-making, but a sudden bout of illness – perhaps more difficult to cope with as he generally enjoyed good health – helps to explain his behaviour on the following day.

On 25 August the retreat continued. By the late afternoon Haig's I Corps headquarters, along with 4 (Guards) Brigade, was in Landrecies at the southern tip of the Forest of Mormal, which covers a bridge crossing the River Sambre. 6 Brigade was at the village of Maroilles, near where a second bridge spanned the river. At 3 p.m. Haig received a message from GHQ, asking whether I Corps would be able to come into the line on the flank of II Corps in the Le Cateau position. Haig was aware of the gravity of the situation, having received at midday reports from aerial reconnaissance that German troops were marching on Bavai. Orders were issued for I Corps to march to take its place on the flank of II Corps in the Le Cateau area, but they were later amended after the receipt – at 7.30 p.m. – of orders from GHQ to retire to Busigny, about seven miles south-west of Le Cateau. Sir John French had decided, learning of the further retirement of Lanrezac's forces and getting some alarming reports of the size of the German forces opposing him, that it would be too dangerous to stand and fight at Le Cateau. This conviction was to colour French's attitudes to the very different decisions of his two Corps Commanders over the next 24 hours.

A German advance guard, initially unaware of the presence of I Corps, moved into the area. As rumours of an impending battle spread, 4 (Guards) Brigade prepared to fight. Given the presence of Haig and the staff of I Corps, Landrecies has been aptly compared to 'a small frigate with an admiral on the bridge'. Charteris recorded how Haig 'was quite jolted out of his usual placidity. He said, "If we are caught, by God, we'll sell our lives dearly".' (Ryan however, said nothing of this, and remarked on Haig's calmness over the next couple of days. Did Charteris exaggerate?) That night at Landrecies, Haig strode around personally organising the defence. He seems to have been glad to focus on something practical and familiar, to revert to doing the job of a regimental officer. In the early hours, faced with the possibility of staying in Landrecies and being captured, Haig and Charteris had a hair-raising drive in the dark in a car with no lights along unfamiliar roads and, of course, involving the constant possibility of running into German troops and being killed or taken prisoner.[34]

At 12.30 Haig issued orders that set I Corps on the road.[35] He abandoned the idea of marching to take position on the flank of II Corps, and instead decided to fall back on Guise. For the second time in three days, Haig exercised his initiative by ignoring GHQ's orders. Lacking accurate intelligence, he seems to have feared that he was about to be overwhelmed, an assumption that in the circumstances was wholly reasonable.[36] Landrecies offered more evidence, if any were needed, to reinforce Haig's conviction that the only way to safety lay through retreating out of the grasp of a German pincer movement. On 27 August, when informed that a French formation was demanding use of the main road to Guise, Haig anxiously noted that 'If I allowed them to use this road it would be impossible for my Corps to escape'. Therefore he 'was prepared to fight them' for it.[37]

Haig phoned GHQ at 1.35 a.m. on 26 August claiming to be under 'heavy attack', and the situation was 'very critical'.[38] Sir John French was awoken 25 minutes later by Henry Wilson, Sub-Chief of the General Staff, who gave him an inevitably garbled version of the fighting at Landrecies, adding his view that the Germans could well succeed in slipping between I and II Corps. French reacted with alarm. At 3.50 a.m. he signalled to II Corps, asking Smith-Dorrien, to move to support Haig (Haig had requested reinforcements at 10 p.m. the previous day), but Smith-Dorrien declined. Smith-Dorrien's refusal to co-operate was sensible, but it gave French further ammunition to use against him. Later Haig returned the compliment by refusing a request from French for I Corps to go to the help of Smith-Dorrien.[39] At 6 a.m. Major G.P. Dawnay arrived at 3 Brigade's HQ at La Grand Fayt, where he found Haig. Dawnay passed on orders from GHQ that I Corps was to 'fall back southeast with the French and rejoin later by rail, or move on St Quentin'. Having already set in motion a retreat south to Guise, Haig decided to let his orders stand. Later he reflected that they were within the 'spirit' of French's instructions. Whichever instructions had been followed, French's or Haig's, they had the same effect of dividing the BEF and ensuring that the two corps would be operating as independent commands. As Haig noted in his diary on 26 August, 'GHQ had evidently given my corps up as lost from their control!'[40]

In fact, the German attack at Landrecies was beaten off fairly easily. The initial estimate of 800 German dead proved to be far too high – the British Official History gives a figure of 52 killed – and perhaps as a consequence Landrecies has tended to be downplayed. But it could easily have developed into a serious action, and if I Corps HQ had been overrun it would have been a severe blow to the cohesion of the BEF.[41] At the time Landrecies was believed to have been a major action, which posed a serious threat to I Corps.[42]

Actually, I Corps spent 26 August marching south without being unduly molested.[43] The one exception was the 2nd Connaught Rangers, involved in a sharp action at Le Grand Fay; Haig blamed this on Monro's misunderstanding of the verbal orders he had earlier received in Landrecies. Given Haig's lack of verbal facility, one wonders if the fault was all on one side.[44] French acquiesced in Haig's decision. He seems to have been relieved that I Corps had escaped from potential disaster at Landrecies. 'No sooner had anxiety on Haig's account ceased', he wrote in his diary for 26 August, 'than trouble arose with Smith-Dorrien'.[45] That 'trouble' was II Corps' desperate fight at Le Cateau.

During the night of 25–26 August Smith-Dorrien had taken the difficult decision that it would be less hazardous to fight on the Le Cateau position than attempt to retreat. Like Haig, he worked on the principle that as the man on the spot he was in a better position to judge what his force was capable of achieving than was GHQ, and took the decision to ignore French's orders to continue to retreat. Smith-Dorrien's intention was to deliver 'a stopping blow, under cover of which we could retire'.[46] Sir John French was desperately anxious about this. GHQ gave reluctant sanction to Smith-Dorrien's decision, but made it clear that it wanted him to continue to retreat as soon as he could.[47] The resulting battle achieved this aim, buying II Corps a breathing space to retreat, but only at the cost of casualties that by the standards of the BEF in August 1914 were very high: some 7,800.[48]

One of the factors in Smith-Dorrien's original decision to fight at Le Cateau was his belief that Haig's Corps would support him on his flank, although it became clear during the night that this was unlikely to happen.[49] I Corps' failure to support Smith-Dorrien resulted in II Corps having an open right flank that the Germans proceeded to turn. On 26 August Haig was aware of gunfire from the direction of II Corps. But having ordered his Corps to retreat, he exercised his judgement by choosing not to march towards the sound of the guns. The two Corps were physically separated by the Forest of Mormal, and in a classic example of the 'fog of war' Haig was forced to make a decision based on fragmentary and incorrect information derived from rudimentary communications. To play the game of 'what if?': if he had obeyed GHQ's original orders, it would have brought I Corps squarely into the battle, but the subsequent orders (to retire on Busigny) would have carried I Corps beyond immediate support of Smith-Dorrien. Haig would then have faced the dilemma of whether to order his formations to retrace their steps and head north towards the battlefield, all the while fearing that I Corps was marching into a trap which would result in its encirclement and destruction.

To return to the actual events, Haig was out of direct contact with II Corps on 26 August. He telegraphed to GHQ twice (the second time to Smith-Dorrien via GHQ) offering help, but very late in the day; the first message, sent at 8.30 p.m., read 'No news of II Corps except sound of guns from direction of Le Cateau and Beaumont. Can I Corps be of any assistance'.[50] Haig received a reply to neither message. It seems that, having eluded the Germans on that day[51] and achieved his primary aim of avoided disaster to I Corps, Haig believed he was in a position to offer support to Smith-Dorrien. However the tone of Haig's second telegram, sent at 11 p.m. – 'we could hear the sound of your battle, but could get no information as to its progress, and could form no idea of how we could assist you' – lends itself to a less charitable interpretation.[52] John Terraine argues that Haig's oft-stated conviction that Smith-Dorrien was wrong to fight at Le Cateau suggests that the I Corps commander 'was conscious of having fallen below his own standards'.[53] Alternatively, Haig genuinely continued to believe that on 26 August Smith-Dorrien took an unwarranted gamble. In the aftermath of Le Cateau French, Wilson and Murray at General Headquarters (GHQ), and Joffre at GQG (the French version of GHQ) all assumed that II Corps had been effectively removed from the BEF's order of battle.[54] Over the coming days and weeks it became clear that this was not so, and French praised Smith-Dorrien in his dispatch of 7 September. But French's hatred of Smith-Dorrien continued to fester. In his post-war memoir, French attacked Smith-Dorrien's decision to fight at Le Cateau. This initiated a bitter public dispute between the two men, in which Smith-Dorrien was vindicated, and French's reputation was holed beneath the waterline.

Haig has been accused of allowing rivalry and 'professional jealousy' toward Smith-Dorrien to distort his decision-making.[55] This is based in part on a suspect source, consisting of information passed on to Basil Liddell Hart long after the war was over. His informant was Sir James Edmonds, the British official historian. Edmonds was a fount of gossip that was sometimes unreliable and malicious. Moreover, as far as Haig was concerned, both Edmonds and Liddell Hart had axes to grind. This is not to deny that Haig was ambitious, or even that he saw Smith-Dorrien, who was senior to him, as a rival. However, it is surely incredible that Haig – who, as we have seen, was acutely conscious of his responsibility as a commander – would risk the destruction of half of the

BEF in pursuit of a personal ambition. Haig's decisions in August 1914 are not above criticism, but they are perfectly explicable without recourse to conspiracy theories. They were decisions taken by a 53-year-old man, short of sleep, undergoing the privations of life on a mobile campaign, groping around in the fog of war: a man above all aware that if he made a mistake it could have catastrophic consequences.

I Corps was to retreat until 5 September. A corps of two divisions was a small enough formation for Haig to dominate with his personality, and he led by example, riding whenever possible rather than going by car (on 29 August Mickey Ryan noted he had ridden for 45 miles with Haig 'all around his army'). It was a difficult time. 'The men were not in condition', Haig wrote, 'their feet got sore from marching, and the heat was very great so it was most difficult to get them along. Nobody likes retreating'.[56]

On the evening of 28 August Lanrezac asked Haig to support him in an attack that French Fifth Army was mounting on the following day. He agreed, and asked GHQ for permission, only to be turned down; offensive operations at this stage simply did not fit in with the pessimistic mental picture of the campaign held by French, Murray and Wilson. Lanrezac had already determined to attack, having been ordered to do so by Joffre.[57] Haig phoned him personally in the early hours of 29 August to explain, and Lanrezac was understandably livid.[58] Haig then received a sharp telegram from GHQ, demanding to know why he had agreed to an 'official exchange of ideas' without consulting GHQ.[59] Haig's reply turned the tables by explicitly commenting upon GHQ's failures and the resulting 'false position' in which he had been placed. GHQ's petulant telegram bore traces of the pre-war conception of a corps as a mere post-box, which was not supposed to undertake independent operations.[60] However Haig's reply was firmly founded on the reality that circumstances had placed him in the *de facto* position of an independent command, in which was not possible to refer every decision up to GHQ. He had sought French's approval before definitely agreeing to the Guise offensive, and, given the time pressure and the difficulties of communication between GHQ and I Corps, a conditional commitment seems an eminently suitable arrangement. According to Haig, French apologised to him at a meeting at GHQ on the following day.[61]

Perhaps Haig was being disingenuous. There is some evidence that Haig did indeed initiate 'an official exchange of ideas'. According to a French officer, Captain Jacques Helbronner, on 28 August he met a 'very animated' Haig being briefed by a British airman who had seen German troops moving south-west of Saint-Quentin. Haig told him to go to Lanrezac and tell him 'The enemy is exposing his flank as he advances. Let him act. I am anxious to co-operate with him in his attack.[62] There is some difficulty in reconciling this story with other evidence.[63] For all that, it is likely that something like it occurred, and Haig had decided that having outmarched the enemy it was now time to seize the initiative, even if only to buy time for a further retreat. Perhaps one might speculate that Haig, excited by an opportunity to take the offensive and frustrated at what he saw as the dead hand of GHQ, made a verbal commitment to Lanrezac via Helbronner and only later attempted have it confirmed by Sir John French; if so, it seems that the French were not aware of the conditional nature of Haig's offer.[64] Haig's decision to support Lanrezac was the right one:[65] the battle of Guise was a success, but the French attack was checked in the sector where Haig's Corps would have fought. As it was, the battle forced von Bülow's German Second Army to pause for two days, thus buying time for the Allies. It also caused Kluck to swing from the south-west, where he threatened to encircle the BEF, to the south-east. Ultimately, by forcing Kluck to abandon the idea of marching around Paris, it paved the way for the battle of the Marne a week later. French, weary, faced with a crushing burden of responsibility, desperately worried by the state of his army, especially II Corps, took the wrong decision. Haig's military instinct was correct. Outwardly, the incident did not damage his relationship with the C-in-C, as French's opinion of Haig remained high. Privately, it can only have reinforced Haig's view of the Field-Marshal's unfitness for high command.

With the successful withdrawal from the Landrecies area, the worst of the crisis was over. But there was still plenty of danger. Haig was incensed on 27 August to discover that the rearguard battalion, 2nd Munsters, had been destroyed at Etreux, and he later blamed Brigadier-General F.I Maxse for not pulling them out in time.[66] Several days later, on 1 September, there was another sharp rearguard action at Villers-Cotterets. British casualties amounted to some 460, the heaviest losses sustained by I Corps since the campaign began. On the same day contact with II Corps was resumed. The retreat continued until 5 September, when orders arrived from GHQ to advance. I Corps was to play its part in the allied offensive that is known to history as the Battle of the Marne.

Haig's reaction to the news was sceptical. He pointed out two 'ifs' to Murray, who visited I Corps on 5 September: 'if the French advance, and if the Germans don't attack before the French organise their forces for an attack, then the situation seems very favourable for us'.[67]

The Battle of the Marne

The Allied offensive of early September 1914, the Battle of the Marne, was one of the decisive phases of the First World War. Although overshadowed by what came later, Haig's command of I Corps in the battle is controversial: was he too cautious in the advance? Did his timidity play a role in the Allies failing to inflict a decisive defeat on the Germans in September 1914?

Haig displayed considerable wariness on the first day of the attack: on 6 September his anxiety about the possibility of German forces striking his flank caused him to cautiously feel his way forward.[68] Similarly, I Corps' advance was limited on the following day. Haig had to wait until noon for his orders from GHQ. In anticipation, he sent out aircraft, and by mid-morning he had enough information on the enemy to order an advance. When French's orders did arrive, they called for an unrealistic advance of 14 miles – which, as Haig pointed out to Murray, could not be accomplished by midnight, and the CGS agreed to a halt at 6.30 p.m. Haig was well aware of the importance of driving forward, as the enemy was in retreat; he motored to see both his divisional commanders to 'impress on them [the] necessity for quick and immediate action'. In order to retain contact with the French on his flank, Haig pushed forward five miles beyond the line eventually ordered by GHQ, closing up to the southern bank of the Grande Morin watercourse.[69]

The Germans chose not to defend the Grand Morin in any strength, but they did make a stand on 8 September on the Petit Morin, the last serious obstacle before the River Marne itself. There was nothing of chateau generalship about Haig's activities that day. At one point, hearing that Monro was at Boitron, Haig discovered a party of Irish Guards sheltering behind the church, with an artillery battery firing at

German positions under half a mile away. I Corps was across the Petit Morin by about 3 p.m. The advance continued for another three or so hours, until torrential rain forced a halt. The River Marne lay ahead, and there was every indication that this would be heavily defended.[70]

The Germans did not elect to make a stand on the Marne. The Allied advance triggered a retirement that signalled passing of the strategic initiative to the French and British. As I Corps pushed forward, the troops found that the Germans had left a bridge intact. Two conflicting emotions seem to have been jostling in Haig's mind. He was keenly aware of the need to drive on, to capitalise on the evident disarray of an enemy in retreat, but still full of respect for the German army and unwilling to take unnecessary risks. So when, late on the 9th, he found 5 Cavalry Brigade 'moving at a walk and delay[ing] the advance of our infantry', he urged the brigade commander forward, for 'a little effort now might mean the conclusion of the war'.[71]

From Haig, who knew perfectly well that cavalry horses need to be walked sometimes to keep them fresh, this was a significant comment. But at about noon on 9 September, with I Corps on the far bank of the Marne, Haig received information from aerial reconnaissance of a large German force to his front, and he ordered a halt. News also arrived that caused him to suspect (erroneously) that the French had suffered a heavy defeat. Given the information he had, far from being 'inexplicable',[72] Haig's decision to order a halt was perfectly understandable. When he later received further reports from his airmen that the Germans were in fact retreating, he ordered the advance to resume. When he discovered that 2nd Division had interpreted his halt order as meaning that troops should pull back across the river, and he personally intervened to stop them, Haig used some unfair language about Monro in his diary. He was weary and under great strain.[73]

By 12 September the BEF was closing up to the River Aisne. The combination of a wide and deep river and high ground on the north bank meant that the Aisne was an obvious place for the Germans to turn and make a stand. Therefore it was imperative for the British to cross the Aisne and seize the heights as soon as possible. Was the German army in such a state of chaos that the Allied forces should configure themselves as if pursuing a beaten enemy? If they advanced like that, only to discover that the German army was still intact, the Allies would risk defeat by attacking in an uncoordinated and unprepared fashion. With little hard information to work on, indications of German forces ahead, and his men struggling through roads made muddy by heavy rain, Haig chose to ignore GHQ's orders to seize the crossings of the River Aisne and occupy the high ground. Instead, he ordered I Corps to halt short of the river.[74] This was the wrong call. If Haig and the rest of the BEF had pushed further on 12 September there was at least a chance that they would have won the race to occupy the Aisne heights. By daylight on the 13th the German defences had been strengthened, as retreating troops halted and regrouped and reserves were rushed to the Aisne.

In his orders for the 13th, Haig, unsure if the Germans would put up much resistance, took a cautious approach. During the day he was frequently on the move. Motoring along the towpath of the river, he came under shellfire and was persuaded to move his HQ further back from the line because of the danger. By the end of the day I Corps, on the right of the BEF, was across the Aisne in two places. The recently-formed III Corps on the left also got across, but in the centre II Corps had less success. 'The German position on the Aisne was good', reported the commander of 2nd Royal Irish Rifles.

> Their artillery commanded the flat marshy valley, all bridges were broken so that our guns could not cross and, as a result, when our infantry occupied the southern edges of the bluffs on the north of the valley, they found themselves without artillery support, close to entrenched infantry who could not be reached by our guns, and exposed to the full force of artillery fire.[75]

Haig still believed I Corps was faced only by a screen of cavalry, and he hoped to bounce forward 'without making a formal attack'. But the Germans did just enough, just in time to hold the Allied advance. At the end of 13 September the BEF had three widely dispersed bridgeheads on frontage of all three corps, with Haig's the furthest forward.

On the following day Haig threw his battalions into an attack on the Chemin des Dames ('the ladies' road', named after daughters of King Louis XV, who had ridden there), which he described as

> a considerable ridge (some 400 feet or more above the river) . . . It seemed

to me very necessary to have a foothold on the ridge before putting our transport north of the river.[76]

He was correct in his assessment of the tactical significance of the ridge, which was to see some of the bitterest battles of the war. The attack of I Corps and French XVIII Corps was a confusing battle in which higher commanders had little influence. Attacking uphill, in what served as a taster for so much of the experience of the British infantry on the Western Front over the next four years, in rain and fog, the men of 1st and 2nd Divisions inched forward in the face of German counterattacks and heavy artillery.

Haig spent the day moving around I Corps, visiting his commanders. He faced a crisis thanks to the failure of II Corps to get further forward, leaving a two-mile gap on the left of I Corps. More problems followed. At 2 p.m. he was informed that 3rd Division had been pushed back, and he realised that this posed a serious threat to the left flank of 2nd Division. There were no reserves at corps or divisional level but he managed to scrape together two cavalry brigades (each with the dismounted strength of perhaps an infantry battalion) which were sent to the left flank. Haig's intervention was potentially decisive, for if the Germans had mounted a major attack it might have had catastrophic consequences.

By about 4 p.m. Haig was receiving more encouraging reports from various parts of I Corps front, and it seemed that 'this was the moment for a general offensive all along my front'. In spite of the men's exhaustion, they 'answered readily to my demand'. Unfortunately I Corps did not get very far forward.[77]

Lomax, commander of 1st Division, reported the dire state of his division to Haig. If the Germans were able to commit reserves, it would imperil the British line. Haig told Lomax 'to dig in, and hold on' until the rest of the BEF and the French took the offensive on the following day. The BEF had failed to break through the German positions, although the day's efforts had prevented a major German attack that could have pushed the Allies back across the river. At 11 p.m. Sir John French ordered the BEF to entrench. Although no one could know it, this marked the end of genuinely open warfare for the British army on the Western Front. The stalemate would last until March 1918.

Haig was pleased with the performance of his troops in the Aisne campaign. He told Doris

> My Army Corps . . . is having a very hard time and is holding the position
> which we won after hard fighting. The last 4 or 5 days have been very
> wet, and the men in the trenches have suffered a great deal. But they are
> very cheery and have fought wonderfully . . .[78]

In the official history there is some veiled criticism of Haig (as well as some praise), but Edmonds principally blamed GHQ for the failure to push on, and indeed, reading the GHQ diary, one gains little sense of urgency.[79] Haig undoubtedly made mistakes, and could have pushed his men harder, but overall his generalship during the advance to the Aisne was prudent and sound.

The Beginning of Trench Warfare

The fighting on the Aisne marked the beginning of a new phase in operations. Up to that point, the BEF's campaign had been traditional, in the sense that battles had been brief and sandwiched between considerable periods of marching. On the Aisne the situation was very different. As the two sides dug in within a matter of yards of each other, the difference between being in and out of battle vanished. Combat had become a continuous process. The only ways for the front-line soldier to escape from battle were by being relieved from trench duty, wounding or death.

In his orders of 16 September, in the same sentence that ordered the BEF to entrench, French stated that 'it was his intention to assume a general offensive at the first opportunity'. Warfare had frequently featured periods of deadlock, eventually mobile warfare had always resumed. This at least appeared to be the lessons of recent major conflicts, such as the fighting in Manchuria during the Russo-Japanese war (1904–5).[80] There was no reason to suppose that this period of trench warfare would be anything other than a temporary phase.

Initially, Haig shared this view. On 16 September he contemplated taking the offensive in co-operation with the French: 'Altogether the situation is very uncertain'.[81] But during September his views began to change. By 20 September he was pressing for his troops to be relieved from the front line, which suggests that he realised that the chance of an imminent breakthrough had disappeared. So does his eager acceptance on 23 September of eight 6-inch 'siege howitzers', which he claimed had been spurned by the other corps commanders because of their lack of mobility.[82] During the rest of September Haig never quite abandoned hope that the Germans could be dislodged from their positions on the Aisne, especially if the French made a significant advance,[83] but by 4 October Haig had accepted that 'we are carrying on a kind of siege warfare'.[84]

The Tactics of Trench Warfare

Traditional siege warfare was above all a sappers' and gunners' affair, with artillery being used to batter a breach in a fortress through which the infantry would storm. The years 1914 to 1918 demonstrated that success in trench warfare likewise depended heavily on artillery: to suppress the enemy's guns, keep down the heads of the hostile infantry and to help the assaulting foot soldiers onto the defender's entrenchments. As early as 16 September Haig was alarmed by reports of superiority of German artillery, and he rapidly grasped the advantages to be gained from marrying the aircraft to the gun battery. On 14 September he noted on a report of the success of the French in using aircraft spotting for artillery, 'G.H.Q. must . . . give Corps Commanders an adequate number of machines to be permanently attached to us and we'll do the rest'. Within a fortnight I Corps had evolved a procedure by which aircraft went searching for enemy batteries and passed on the information, flew over the targets, observed the fall of shot and signalled 'any necessary corrections' using wireless. Johnnie Gough wrote a memorandum, which reflected Haig's views, that stated that the Germans were 'superior to us both in ingenuity and in science. We must learn from their methods'. This was a *leitmotif* of I Corps and, indeed, the BEF as a whole: rapid adjustment to a new situation and the learning of lessons was essential to the way it did business. The edge the Germans had in machine-guns and heavy artillery was deeply worrying. A I Corps report of late September gave sensible advice on the situation of battery positions and trenches (on a reverse slope, thus sacrificing a wide field of fire in favour of greater protection from enemy shelling). Ominously, the report said that a lesson of the Boer War needed to be relearned: that attacks by 'thick, regular, rigid lines of infantry' simply gave the enemy excellent targets, and should be replaced by 'loose and irregular elastic formations'. In September 1914 the BEF still consisted of well-trained and disciplined Regular troops. A terrible combination of under-estimating the tactical proficiency of wartime volunteers and overestimating the power of British artillery led to disaster on the first day on the Somme using inappropriate tactics.[85]

Haig was acutely aware of the strain that the campaign was placing on individuals, and hence the threat to the morale, discipline and cohesion of his force. He reacted to this with a mixture of harshness and sympathy. Brigadier-General R.H. Davies, a New Zealander commanding 6th Infantry Brigade, did not bear up well under the stress of field command. Haig sent him back to England: he was an officer who needed preserving for the good of the Empire, so he decided it was wise to request that Davies was granted a change of scene before he collapsed altogether.[86]

There was a rather different reaction to the case of Lieutenant-Colonel F.W. Towsey. His battalion, 1st West Yorks on 20 September suffered a 'disaster' when the Germans got round its flank and forced much of it to surrender. Haig found it

> difficult to write in temperate language regarding the very unsoldierlike behaviour of the W. Yorks on the 20th inst. Apparently they fled from their trenches on the appearance of some 150 Germans. This is the worst incident of which I have heard during this campaign. I do not know Lt. Col Towsey but in view of the high character which he holds it may be well to give him another chance, but I recommend that he and his Battalion be strongly rebuked and that they be told that it rests with them to regain the good name and reputation which our infantry holds, and which they have by their conduct on the 20th forfeited.[87]

Haig's use of language is interesting. He condemned the 'unsoldier-like' behaviour of the Yorkshiremen that had besmirched their 'good name and reputation' and implicitly questioned their manliness. In short, he appealed to honour as warriors, hoping to shame them into improvement rather than simply punish them. Before the war what has been dubbed the 'moral battlefield' increasingly concerned senior officers in European armies. The perceived lessons of recent wars suggested that, while firepower was dominant, soldiers with high morale and staying power could prevail on the battlefield. There was a degree of concern about the resilience of working-class morale in wartime.[88] Haig's reaction to the performance of the West Yorkshires undoubtedly reflected his fear that the extreme stress of combat would eat away at discipline and cohesion, the very things that separate an army from an armed mob. Simple punishment was not enough. The West Yorkshires had to be given a chance to rejoin the brotherhood of arms.

La Bassée and Ypres

British troops were not destined to remain for long on the Aisne battlefield. In October the BEF was sent north into Flanders. If the Aisne has largely vanished from the popular memory of the First World War, it is surely in part because within weeks of leaving the area British soldiers were engaged in desperate combat around what became one of the most notorious places on the Western Front: Ypres. Between October 1914 and September 1918 British forces fought five major battles around 'Wipers', in addition to a myriad of smaller actions in defence of 'the Immortal Salient'. It became, and remains, a place of evil renown. All of that was in the future in mid-October 1914 when I Corps left the Aisne.

To send the BEF northwards made much sense, as it brought it into a traditional area of British interest, one that was closer to the coast and hence to its supply ports. Joffre took a little persuading, perhaps reflecting a well-founded suspicion that British armies operating on the Continent like to have the Royal Navy near at hand 'just in case'. The BEF's move was part of the series of operations known as the 'Race to the Sea', as, faced with trenches and barbed wire, the opposing armies sought to outflank each other. The term was a misnomer. Once the armies had reached the Channel, their strategic gambits had failed.

Haig finally left the Aisne on 16 October. He arrived at St Omer at about 5.30 p.m., to find Sir John French 'quite satisfied with the general situation and said that enemy was falling back and that we "would soon be in a position to round them up." '[89] French was far too sanguine. In reality, the advancing BEF soon encountered the Germans intent on coming the other way. A period of confused and bloody semi-open warfare ensued, and the names of places like Messines and Armentières started to take on a dreadful significance. On 19 October 1914 French gave Haig ambitious orders to attack what he believed were weak German forces north of Ypres, push on to take Bruges and then advance to Ghent. The reality was different. Haig was wary of French's optimism,[90] and, sure enough, I Corps soon found itself in a classic encounter battle. 2nd Division, on reaching an obscure village on a ridge some seven miles from Ypres, clashed with advancing German forces and became involved in severe fighting 'that came,' Haig recorded, 'to bayonet work'.[91] This was the British army's introduction to Passchendaele, and the combat that seemed fierce in October 1914 was little more than a skirmish by the standards of the battles fought over the same ground three years later. Coming under strain from enemy attacks, and uncertain if he would be supported by French forces on his flank, on 21 October Haig wisely ordered his troops to go on to the defensive. This recognition that the initiative had tilted to the Germans was the death-knell of the BEF's attempts to break through in Flanders. What historians call the Battle of La Bassée, the attempted Allied advance, was over.

In the next phase it was the Germans who took the offensive. Reinforced by troops released by the surrender of Antwerp on 10 October and some newly raised divisions, the German army attempted to smash through the Allied positions in a series of attacks from Béthune to the coast that became known as the First Battle of Ypres.

Such artificial divisions were, of course, meaningless to the men of the BEF. All they were aware of was confused fighting as units had to be sent in piecemeal to shore up the line against heavy German attacks. As a result of French's abortive advance, Haig's I Corps was now in position at the point of greatest danger, around Ypres. This beautiful medieval city was a major communications centre, through which passed roads, a railway and a canal. For the Germans the capture of Ypres offered the enticing prospect of blasting open the Allied positions in Flanders and reopening mobile warfare, with the Channel ports within easy reach. In late autumn 1914 there was no more vital piece of ground on the Western Front.

Writing in a private letter after the war, James Edmonds said First Ypres was the making of Douglas Haig's reputation. In contrast to earlier in the campaign, when French was bustling about and interfering, at Ypres the C-in-C stayed clear and thus allowed Haig to show his mettle.[92]

This book has shown that, on the contrary, Haig enjoyed a great deal of autonomy of command in August and September – but otherwise Edmonds was right. At Mons and Le Cateau Haig and I Corps had played a lesser role than Smith-Dorrien and II Corps. The savage fighting around Ypres thrust the burden of 'saving the BEF' on to Haig. His calm and resilient generalship greatly enhanced his standing as a commander.

For the BEF the first crisis began on 29 October, building to a crescendo of danger two days later. Von Falkenhayn, who had replaced von Moltke as overall German commander, assembled an Army Group under General von Fabeck, reinforced with sufficient divisions and guns to give it a 2:1 advantage at the point of attack. Army Group Fabeck's assault brought it against Haig's I Corps and Allenby's dismounted cavalrymen further south. The main focus of I Corps was the vital major road running from Ypres south-east towards the town of Menin. The German attacks of 29 October captured the crossroads at Gheluvelt, about 4½ miles from Ypres. Gheluvelt village stands on a small bump in the ground, but in a war dominated by guns, a few feet of additional height could prove critical for artillery observation. By 'puttying up', shoving troops into the line to stave off short-term crises, Haig and his commanders limited the damage to the British position, and Gheluvelt village remained in British hands on the 29th, although a counterattack by Bulfin's 2 Brigade to retake the crossroads at Gheluvelt crossroads was only partly successful. A basic tenet of military command is to always keep a reserve in hand, but Haig was desperately short of reserve units, and those he had were already tired and understrength.[93] The fact that Haig did not act to prevent six battalions of 1st and 2nd Divisions from occupying trenches on a forward slope, i.e. in view of the enemy, only added to I Corps's difficulties. Curiously, he had earlier been critical of 7th Division for exactly this.[94]

Just how difficult the situation was on the ground had passed Sir John French by. Late on 29 October, he ordered the BEF to attack on the next day, hoping for 'a decisive result'. Haig was much more realistic, instructing his corps to dig in. This prudent ignoring of unrealistic orders may 'have saved the day on the 30th'.[95]

30 October saw more puttying, using units that should have been used to carry the fight to the enemy to shore up the line, which was bending ominously under the weight of German attacks. Passively awaiting the

next attack is never appealing, and on 30 October Haig began to think of a limited attack to retake positions lost that day. While the idea was sound in principle, it was based on an underestimate of German strength and the formidable firepower at their disposal.[96] It was probably just as well that the attack was overtaken by events.

On Saturday, 31 October 1914 the German army came closer to defeating the BEF than at any time in the war. The British official histories generally used bloodless, measured prose, but not when describing the state of the BEF on that day:

> A decisive [German] victory seemed assured: for everything pointed to the British being completely exhausted. And they may well have appeared so to the enemy. The line that stood between the British Empire and ruin was composed of tired, haggard and unshaven men, unwashed, plastered with mud, many in little more than rags.[97]

The first act of Halloween was a German assault in the Gheluvelt area shortly after 6 a.m. On this occasion 1st Division succeeded in repulsing most of the attackers, but the attacks were to grow in strength and fury throughout the day. Further south, the Cavalry Corps defending the Messines–Wytschaete area came under intense pressure. The previous day, Haig had sent the 1/14 Londons (London Scottish) from I Corps reserve to the Cavalry Corps. Committed to battle on 31 October, the London Scottish became the first Territorial infantry unit to see action, their ranks containing two men then unknown but who were to find fame in Hollywood after the war – Ronald Coleman and Basil Rathbone.[98] In spite of the heroics of the defenders (which included Indian troops as well as cavalrymen), the Germans seized control of Messines Ridge. It was not to return to British control until June 1917.

The crisis at Gheluvelt was even more serious.[99] After the early morning push, for about two hours from 8 a.m. the British infantry of 1st Division were pounded by German artillery. Even by the undemanding standards of 1914, their trenches were rudimentary, and the subsequent German infantry attack rapidly pushed back the defenders. By 11.30 a.m. fighting was taking place in Gheluvelt village, which was in German hands in its entirety by 1 p.m. The loss of Gheluvelt signified far more than just a terrain feature changing possession. It signalled the collapse of British defences on the main axis of the German advance and of the reserves that would normally have been thrown in to stabilise the position. Lomax of 1st Division faced up to reality at 12.45 p.m. when he stated, 'My line is broken'.[100] If the situation appeared black, it was about to get worse. On 29 October Haig had vacated Hooge Chateau to allow 1st Division HQ to move out of a small cottage. Moving into such a large and obvious target for German artillery was a mistake, especially as Lomax's staff was now co-located with Monro's 2nd Division HQ. At 1.15 the inevitable happened: Hooge Chateau was hit by German shells. Monro, who was much shaken up, was revived at Haig's headquarters by a rest and a drink from Haig's brandy flask,[101] but Lomax was fatally wounded (eventually dying in April 1915). A key link in the command chain had been destroyed at a critical time.

In his HQ at the White Chateau, some four miles behind the frontline, Haig was suffering the typical frustration of a First World War senior commander. He was receiving only fragmentary snippets of information and could do little to influence the fight. He recalled that when Johnnie Gough arrived to tell him of the fate of 1st Division 'it was rather a shock'. This is confirmed by French, who related to Kitchener that Haig was rather alarmed when he informed the C-in-C Monro's division had given way.[102] Anxious as he was – and had every right to be, as historian John Hussey has emphasised in his careful study of the events of 31 October – Haig remained calm throughout. There was no repetition of the supposed loss of nerve at Landrecies in August. Indeed, Monro recalled that the only outward sign of the stress that Haig was undoubtedly feeling was that he incessantly tugged at his moustache.[103] Years after the war Edmonds alleged in a conversation with Liddell Hart that Haig had panicked, that he had issued orders for I Corps to carry out a general retreat, and this embarrassing episode had subsequently been hushed up.[104] Hussey's work demonstrates conclusively that there is no evidence to substantiate this.

The truth was rather more mundane. Haig had prudently (and entirely properly) taken some preliminary steps in planning to extricate his Corps in the event of a major setback. On 29 October, he had sent his Commander Royal Engineers, Brigadier-General Rice, with two staff officers to examine routes across the canal that ran near Ypres. Rice had identified two possible defensive positions closer to Ypres.[105] At 7 a.m. on

31 October, Haig had consulted with General d'Urbal, commanding French troops in Belgium, on arrangements should a retreat become necessary. When it became clear that 1st Division's front had given way, Haig opted to fall back to the first of Rice's alternative positions, and orders went out at about 1.30 p.m.[106] This was a dangerous manoeuvre, which could have led to the complete disintegration of 1st Division. Often in military history there has proved to be a fine line between a withdrawal under difficult conditions and a rout. Haig presumably took the judgment that the alternative, ordering the troops to stay put and fight it out, was even less appealing, and he trusted the discipline of his troops.

Field-Marshal French turned up at I Corps HQ at about 2 p.m., but he could offer nothing more than moral support and sympathy, for which Haig was genuinely grateful. French then left, shortly before Rice arrived, red-faced and puffing, with the dramatic news that an attack by the 2nd Worcesters had retaken Gheluvelt and restored the situation – at least for the moment. Haig was characteristically sceptical. Charteris recorded that, after another tug at his moustache, Haig said he 'hoped it was not another false report' and decided to continue with a ride to the front line.[107]

Haig's ride has been the stuff of controversy among historians, with disputes about its timing, whether it was undertaken as a PR stunt after 'its purpose had evaporated', or, bizarrely, whether it ever happened in the first place. A rather more sensible question is whether Haig, as a Corps commander, was wise to leave his HQ at this critical time.[108] In the First World War, lacking effective voice communications, the closer an officer got to the front line the fewer troops he could actually command. In an echo of Edmonds's idea that Haig panicked, it has been argued that 'anxiety certainly clouded his [Haig's] judgment'.[109] This is dubious.

In his diary Haig gave a straightforward and entirely believable motive for his ride: 'I got on my horse and rode forward to see if I could do anything to organise stragglers and push them forward to check enemy'; this was the instinct of an old regimental officer to go forward and lead.[110] But there was more to it than that. Shortly after the war, Rice referred to Haig and his staff going forward beyond Hooge Chateau 'where we established a sort of advanced HQ'.[111] This makes perfect sense. Haig did not undertake a joyride, nor did he go towards the front line just to stiffen the morale of whatever soldiers happened to see him. The commander of I Corps went forward to assess the situation for himself, to speak to commanders on the spot: Capper (7th Division); Byng (3rd Cavalry Division); Landon (now commanding 1st Division); FitzClarence (1 (Guards) Brigade),[112] Monro (2nd Division). Later he rode on to speak to the French commander on his flank, General Moussy. As a result of these consultations, Haig ordered some redeployment of troops, in part to create a reserve, and gained a clear picture of the state of his forces. It was not reassuring:

> Troops very exhausted and 2 Brigadiers assure me that if the enemy makes a push at any point, they doubt our men being able to hold on. Fighting by day and digging to strengthen their trenches by night has thoroughly tired them out.

Yet the British line held. The Germans failed to deliver an attack that seriously threatened to break through. Haig ordered a withdrawal of some 600 yards – which left Gheluvelt to the enemy – to establish a more defensible line. Bulfin, reinforced by 6th Cavalry Brigade dispatched by Haig, mounted an attack and pushed the Germans back. Haig, mislead by Bulfin's success ordered that it should continue, but Bulfin persuaded Johnnie Gough to cancel the order.[113]

At 8 a.m. on 1 November Landon reported to Haig that his 1st Division was 'so disorganised that no organised attack could really be withstood. Rifles jammed owing to mud and soil and no opportunity for cleaning and oiling'. In spite of fears that another German attack would smash through the British lines, the immediate crisis passed, as the Germans did not make another push until 11 November.[114] This, like the Halloween offensive, came perilously close to success. The situation was saved by a counterattack in which the 2nd Oxfordshire and Buckinghamshire Light Infantry played the primary role.[115] In a battle of this type the influence of the Corps commander was inevitably limited, and Haig was in the position of a facilitator rather than a commander. He spent the day doing what he could: organising reserves, sometimes by withdrawing soldiers from the firing line, to meet possible eventualities; keeping subordinate commanders in touch with the situation on other parts of the Ypres front; impressing on Sir John French (via Colonel G.M. Harper of GHQ staff) of the gravity of the position; and preparing to pull back to a new defensive line should it prove impossible to dislodge the Germans from their gains. As on 31 October, Haig had no direct input into the decision to counterattack; it was taken at a local level by a subordinate commander. Haig's response to the news of the German attack was to find out what FitzClarence of 1 Brigade and Monro of 2nd Division proposed to do.[116]

The attacks of 11 November proved to be the German army's last major throw in the First Battle of Ypres.

Conclusion

Douglas Haig emerged from the fighting of 1914 with an immensely enhanced reputation. He had been overshadowed by Horace Smith-Dorrien in the earlier stages of the campaign, but Kitchener's private secretary believed the actions on the Aisne 'made Haig's reputation as a Corps Commander'.[117] 'The action of the First Corps . . . [on 14 September] under the direction and command of Sir Douglas Haig was of so skilful, bold and decisive a character', wrote Sir John French his official dispatch, 'that he gained positions which alone have enabled me to maintain my position for more than three weeks of very severe fighting on the north bank of the river.'[118]

This was for publication, but French was similarly complimentary about Haig in private correspondence with Kitchener, on 15 September contrasting Haig's aggressive push on the previous day with the more modest achievements of II and III Corps.[119] Haig's reputation was consolidated by his generalship at Ypres and clearly marked him out as a rival to Smith-Dorrien for the top command should Sir John French fall under the proverbial omnibus. Ironically, French's praise was a significant factor in building Haig up as a rival who, in a little over a year's time, would replace him as Commander-in-Chief.

Haig's contacts with figures such as the King, who was highly complimentary when he received Haig at Buckingham Palace in late November, and the creator of Sherlock Holmes, Sir Arthur Conan Doyle, who was lent suitably edited copies of Haig's diaries as a source for a book on 1914, did his reputation no harm.[120] But the importance of Haig's generalship, especially in the critical days at Ypres, was widely recognised throughout the army. Major 'Sally' Home, on the staff of the Cavalry Division wrote admiringly in his diary of Haig's 'iron resolution and . . . great personality' which was 'required to not only give the orders but to inspire the confidence required by the men to fight like they have'.[121] A modern historian has concluded that, whatever Haig's later failings on the offensive, with his combination of a 'cool head', 'moral courage' and skill in 'higher tactics', the army has rarely produced such a fine 'defensive general'.[122] In the eyes of some contemporaries Haig's performance at the defensive battle of Ypres seems to have eclipsed his role in the offensive battle of the Aisne. As late as 5 July 1916 a hostile witness, Henry Wilson, described Haig as a 'good stout hearted *defensive* soldier', going on to imply that success in the defence required little but tenacity: '[Haig had] *no* imagination, and very little brains and very little sympathy'.[123] The remark must of course be placed in the context of the recent attack on the Somme. But at the end of 1914, Haig had proved his worth on the defence at First Ypres and in attack on the Aisne.

Haig was fortunate in his unit commanders: subordinates like Brigadier-Generals FitzClarence and Lord Cavan (4 (Guards) Brigade), and Lieutenant-Colonel H.R. Davies, CO of 2nd Oxf and Bucks. Cavan, at a critical moment in the early afternoon of 31 October sent a message that 'Sir D. Haig relied on us to save the First Corps and possibly the Army', a message that clearly made an impression on the Guards officers who heard it. Haig later made a point of visiting Cavan, a gesture that the brigade commander obviously appreciated.[124] Above all, Haig owed his success to the regimental officers, NCOs and ordinary soldiers. He did not wear his heart on his sleeve about this any more than he did for anything else, but in his private correspondence one can see the respect of the typical paternalistic Edwardian officer. To Sir Evelyn Wood he wrote 'Our troops have had and are having terribly hard times', while he told Doris that 'My 1st Corps have fought splendidly but our losses have been very great. I hope soon my men will be relieved'.[125] Of the sufferings of the front-line soldiers, one example must stand for all. 'On the 11th November, 1914,' wrote an officer of the 1st Northamptonshire Regiment, in Haig's I Corps, the Battalion 'as constituted at the outbreak of war, ceased to exist . . . So ended the old 48th, holding the line doggedly, notwithstanding terrific casualties against appalling odds.'[126]

What had Haig learned from the campaigns of 1914? Apart from reinforcing his healthy respect for the German army, and for the skill and resilience of his own men, several things stand out. The first is encapsulated in a letter of early October:

> There seems to me nothing new to be learnt, only pay attention to old principles. Don't advance in *rigid* lines but throw forward clouds of skirmishers (5 or 6 lines apart) according to the ground and available cover.[127]

Throughout the war Haig held to the belief that the British army's doctrine, founded on experience rather than theory, was basically sound, and simply needed to be adapted to the new circumstances.

Second, Haig was keenly aware how narrow the margin between survival and defeat had been at First Ypres. Had the Germans pressed their attacks, especially on 31 October and 11 November, the BEF would probably have been defeated. This fed into his belief, encapsulated in the 1909 *Field Service Regulations* (written, of course, under Haig's guidance), that 'decisive success in battle can be gained only by a vigorous offensive'.[128] As we will see, memories of the fighting at Ypres in 1914 undoubtedly influenced his strategy and conduct of operations in the years to come. On one occasion, in the Third Battle of Ypres, he cited the German failure of 31 October 1914 to take advantage of British weakness to warn his Army commander not to fall into the same trap.[129] At First Ypres, Haig's 'bloody-minded obstinacy' served the army well.[130] That was not always to be the case.

Finally, Haig's opinion of Sir John French had not improved. Haig's copy of French's dispatch of 7 September is punctuated by question marks and comments such as 'not true'. 'A most misleading document!' was Haig's conclusion, scrawled in pencil and initialled.[131] By contrast, French's esteem for Haig was at its peak. At lunch with Sir John French on Christmas Day 1914 Haig received gratifying news: 'We were ordered to form Armies tomorrow. I am to command the First: Smith-Dorrien the Second.'[132]

He had already been promoted to full general in the aftermath of First Ypres. The year ahead promised new challenges as an Army commander.

4

Grappling with Trench Warfare

The year 1915 marks the beginning of the period by which Haig's modern reputation stands or falls. Had he remained at Hooge Chateau on 31 October 1914 and been killed during the shelling, he would probably be remembered by a few military historians as a man of much promise tragically killed before fulfilling his potential. The public would remember him not at all. Instead, it was Haig's fate to survive into 1915 and command First Army in the first full year of trench warfare. He was the principal operational commander in the BEF's first major offensives under the new conditions, and when Sir John French self-destructed during 1915 Haig succeeded him as Commander-in-Chief, widely acknowledged as the best man for the job. And yet the best that can be said for Haig's record in 1915 is that it was a sequence of near misses and 'might have beens', the worst that it was a series of outright defeats. All were very costly in human life. While one of the most influential indictments of Haig's generalship in 1915 – Alan Clark's *The Donkeys* (1961) – is poor history, the most recent scholarship on Haig's generalship in 1915 has painted an unflattering picture of over-optimism, inflexibility, dogmatism, and faulty decision-making.[1] An obvious explanation is that Haig was stupid. Some reputable historians have put forward much more sophisticated analyses that nonetheless, in effect, charge Haig with serial bungling. Whatever else might be said about Haig, though, he was not dim-witted. And yet he persevered with a course that brought about heavy casualties but not the success he sought. An examination of First Army's battles in 1915 reveals that the path Haig chose, although unsuccessful, was not the product of irrationality or stupidity.

The Challenges

Long before the first shots were fired on the Western Front, it was clear to military men that the emergence of new and ever more powerful weapons was complicating the fighting of battles. Breech-loading rifles, machine-guns, and artillery pieces made the battlefield a more lethal place than ever before. Soldiers did not ignore the implications of this new technology, but the lessons of conflicts such as the Second Boer War and the Russo-Japanese War seemed to point to the ability of attackers to prevail on the battlefield, albeit at heavy cost, given two things: sufficient firepower to overcome enemy positions; and determined infantry imbued with high morale. Unfortunately, in France and Belgium circumstances were different. Here, there were very large numbers of troops with powerful weapons crammed into a confined battlefield hemmed in by sea to the north and mountains to the south. There were no weak spots to be exploited or flanks to turn. Every attack had to be a frontal one, and it soon became clear that well-armed defenders backed up by artillery and protected by entrenchments had built-in advantages over the attacker.

A comment by Lieutenant-General Sir James Willcocks, commander of the Indian Corps, encapsulates much of the frustration of the high commander under these new conditions. On 10 March 1915, 'As I stood . . . expectantly by the telephone, awaiting the first news of the attack, it seemed as if ages were rolling by . . .'[2] Without robust communications, commanders could do little to influence the course of a battle. Armies were simply too big and too dispersed to be commanded in person as generals had done in the past, and would be able to do again in the future, thanks to radio. The commanders of 1914–18 were instead reliant instead on 'runners' (soldiers physically carrying messages), signal flags, carrier pigeons and the like; only gradually did 'wireless' (radio) make a, distinctly limited, impact. The fog of war meant that commanders' main way of influencing a battle became extremely haphazard. Reserves were committed too late, or in the wrong place, or not at all. Defending commanders often had the advantage of intact telephone wires, but, stuck on the far side of No Man's Land and with a telephone system that ended in the front-line trench, their opposite numbers experienced a dark age of command.

Although the instincts of many generals were to be as far forward as possible, it soon became clear that if a higher commander was to have any effect on a major battle he needed to have access to the telephone that allowed him to receive reports and intelligence and to give orders. That usually meant being based in a large building, often a chateau, connected to the telephone network. When a general went up among the fighting troops he effectively demoted himself to a platoon commander, only able to direct soldiers within shouting distance. The death of three divisional commanders at Loos prompted GHQ to remind generals not to push too far forward: 'These are losses that the Army can ill-afford'.[3]

The major tactical problem lay not in 'breaking-in' to an enemy position, but in exploiting the initial advantage. First World War armies lacked a useable 'instrument of exploitation' – fast-moving troops able to harry a retiring enemy. Cavalry could not regularly be used for this role, and tanks, only introduced in 1916, were unreliable and slow. Deadlock was eventually overcome by a combination of methods. Using artillery to suppress enemy fire was to be critical, by knocking out artillery and machine-guns, often by killing or disabling the crews, or simply forcing them away from their weapons. To do this, gunners had to be able to accurately locate and hit targets on a regular basis, and in 1915 the means of doing so were very primitive. It would take some major advances in gunnery technique, particularly the use of aircraft for spotting fall of shot, to improve matters. The changes in the conduct of war amounted to a 'Revolution in Military Affairs'.

Infantry tactics were also revolutionised, the introduction of the light machine-gun being critical. In 1915 the British infantryman was only armed with a rifle and bayonet and perhaps some primitive and unreliable grenades (or 'bombs'). And the 'weapons system' that in 1918 blended together the crucial elements – infantry, artillery, airpower, and tanks into a synergistic whole – barely existed in 1915. Before the war, the meat and drink of the British army had been 'small wars' and colonial policing, which was very different from the high-intensity conflict against a first-class enemy on the Western Front. In time, as the British economy geared up for total war, the British army fought a rich man's war. In 1915 the BEF fought a pauper's war, short of guns, grenades and nearly everything else. Worse, the heavy casualties meant that the army was deskilled at the very time it was undergoing massive and unprecedented expansion, as Lord Kitchener's mass volunteer force took shape. The BEF was literally holding the line until the New Army and Territorial divisions arrived.[4] Across No Man's Land was the German army, and the battles of 1915 were defined by a race to learn and apply lessons. The British were to learn the hard way that generally the German army was able to improve its defences faster than they were able to improve their assault techniques.

Army Commander

There were no precedents for Haig's situation in early 1915, as an Army level of command had not been envisaged before the war, and certainly not under these circumstances. He carved out a role for himself, visiting units and rear areas, and meeting key personnel. As commander of First Army, Haig behaved like a good Managing Director, becoming familiar with all parts of the organisation. He was keenly aware of the importance of unglamorous matters such as sanitation, inspecting baths where soldiers had their clothes disinfected, and also was a regular visitor to Casualty Clearing Stations. In December 1915, while preparing to take over as Commander-in-Chief, he made time to visit the CCS run by his old friend Mickey Ryan, paying careful attention to the unit's preparations for winter. In fact, Haig took a particular interest in all matters medical. He established good relations with senior medical men such as Sir Anthony Bowlby, a civilian consulting surgeon to the BEF, and Sir Arthur Sloggett, Director General of Medical Services, BEF (and the fact that Haig was on good terms with the civilian specialist and the Regular RAMC officer may have helped smooth over problems between the two men).[5] This wide-ranging grasp of all aspects of his command, and a willingness to back 'subject-matter experts' was typical of him.

This readiness to lean on experts was one of the keys to Haig's ability to pace himself. 'D.H. is a wonder', wrote an officer on his staff, Major Gerry Thompson of the 17th Lancers, 'always working and always well: he makes a point of always going for a ride in the afternoon: it's a pity other generals don't do likewise'.[6] It helped him to deal with the hundred-and-one things that every day demanded his attention. One was a tricky situation in his old regiment. The 17th Lancers was commanded by Lieutenant-Colonel 'Pongo' Tilney, his polo teammate of 1903. Tilney had been seriously ill with malaria and sunstroke, and his problems recurred in the trenches at Festubert in January 1915. Sent on leave to England, his brigade commander tried to prevent Tilney from returning. Tilney complained to Haig, who rode over to the regiment to consult with the officers. Major Ronnie Carden, another member of the victorious polo team, was in temporary command, and he thought Tilney 'was madder now than when he had sunstroke'. Haig seems to have handled the matter sensitively, continuing to write friendly letters to Tilney throughout the war, and Tilney maintained his high opinion of Haig.[7]

February 1915 brought a major change to Haig's staff when Johnnie Gough was selected to command a new division at home. To Haig's sorrow, he was fatally wounded while saying goodbye to his old battalion in the trenches. Haig and Richard Butler, Gough's replacement, were soon planning for a major attack.

Breakthrough or Attrition?

Writing to Sir John French early in 1915, Kitchener argued that if a breakthrough on the Western Front did not occur

> then the German lines in France may be looked upon as a fortress that
> cannot be carried by assault and also cannot be completely invested, with
> the result that the lines can only be held by an investing force while
> operations proceed elsewhere.[8]

Future events, such as the BEF's failure at Aubers Ridge despite superior numbers, only served to reinforce Kitchener's belief that victory in France was unlikely.[9] He warned French at the end of March that he had only a month or so to demonstrate that 'substantial advances' were possible, or it would be 'essential' for the government to switch its attention to another theatre.[10] (Naval operations were already under way at the Dardanelles). Attempting to juggle the demands of his own strategy – which called for the New Armies to be trained and withheld from France until an appropriate time, when Britain could intervene decisively and dictate the peace – and the strident calls from the French for ever larger numbers of British troops to be sent to the Western Front, Kitchener opted for a strategy of attrition. In this context that meant limited operations to grind down enemy strength or to repel German offensives.[11]

Haig and French had a rather different vision. In January Haig told the Military Correspondent of *The Times,* Colonel Repington,

> that as soon as we were supplied with ample Artillery ammunition of high explosive, I thought we could walk through the German lines at several places. In my opinion the reason we were here was primarily due to want of Artillery ammunition and then to our small numbers last November.[12]

The Origins of Neuve Chapelle

Sir John French selected First Army to carry out the first major British offensive of the trench war. The capture of the low Aubers Ridge would give tactical benefits to Haig's forces, not least in gaining observation for artillery fire, but it also appeared to offer the possibility of capturing the key city of Lille in co-operation with the French. Moreover, British commanders were aware that German forces in the Neuve Chapelle area were fairly weak. Above all, as Lieutenant-General Sir William Robertson (now French's Chief of Staff) put it, the 'French don't believe we mean business', so the BEF had to attack 'on a big scale'.[13]

The ruined village of Neuve Chapelle lay just behind the German line, and behind it were meadows crossed by drainage ditches. Beyond that was a battered wood, the Bois du Biez. The country was flat and rather depressing, with water so close to the surface that breastworks had to be built to supplement the shallow trenches.[14] Haig's initial orders of 6 February 1915 had the modest aim of capturing the village and thus carrying out some 'line straightening', but he always had something more ambitious in mind.[15]

Two days later, the opportunity arose to expand the aims of the attack when French called upon his two Army commanders to submit plans for an offensive. Haig proposed to GHQ that the eventual objectives should be on Aubers Ridge, six miles away. From there, La Bassée could be threatened, and even the enemy positions near Lille, some seven miles off, would be in reach.[16] While undoubtedly ambitious, from the perspective of late February 1915 the plan was not wholly unrealistic.

By the end of the month Haig was aware that the French would not be attacking alongside First Army. A planning document of 28 February struck a note of realism: First Army was planning for a breakthrough, but, given the limited ammunition and troops available, the advance would have to halt after a maximum of three days. Haig therefore discussed whether it was feasible to halt in front of the German defences near Lille.[17] Whether even this modest aim was actually achievable is debatable. Charteris on 3 March commented that the BEF's size meant that it could not do more than 'make a small gap' and could not cause 'a big break'.[18] Although there were to be post-battle recriminations about spurning an opportunity for a major advance, Haig had entered the battle aware that at best it would lead to a three-day advance before the line once again congealed.

Haig called upon his Corps commander to put forward plans for the offensive.[19] Rawlinson seemed to be dragging his feet, delegating planning to subordinate commanders. Haig was deeply unimpressed.[20] Worse, he thought IV Corps' plan was too complex and lacked detail and ambition: Rawlinson and his staff did little more than nod in the direction of a major advance towards Lille following the capture of Neuve Chapelle. At a meeting on 5 March, Haig left Willcocks, the Indian Corps commander, with the impression 'that the Hun was on the eve of receiving a blow so severe that it would be with difficulty he could recover'.[21] In spite of Haig's prodding, Rawlinson remained lukewarm about anything but a limited attack; he waited until four days before the battle before asking his divisional commanders for their views on exploitation after the capture of the village, and even then he gave them 24 hours to respond.[22]

The planning of Neuve Chapelle reveals things about the state of command in the BEF in early 1915. Haig had a clear concept of his role as a commander – to set broad objectives, call for plans from subordinates, and to modify these plans until they were fit for purpose – to his satisfaction at least. Rawlinson saw his role as a 'post-box' in passing on plans from Army to divisional level, but Haig, perhaps reflecting his own proactive role as a corps commander in 1914, was not satisfied with this approach. We also see signs of Haig's optimism. His setting on 6 February of a mere 10-day deadline for the planning and preparation demonstrates his own naivety at this stage – Rawlinson rightly commented on the need for the ground to dry.[23] Similarly, the clash between Rawlinson's conception of a limited, 'step-by-step' approach to operations and Haig's more expansive ideas were also there to see, as was the uneasy process of negotiation between the two men and their staffs that was to continue up to and including the Somme offensive, more than a year later.

That Haig truly believed that a major success was possible is not in doubt. His eve of battle message to the troops read

> At no time in this war has there been a more favourable moment for us, and I feel confident of success. The extent of that success must depend on the rapidity and determination with which we advance . . . To ensure success, each one of us must play our part, and fight like men for the Honour of Old England.[24]

This remarkable message was an attempt to convey to the lowliest private the need for celerity in the advance. In many ways it was an admirable effort to put across the commander's intent, but, as a regimental officer noted shortly after the battle, 'The communication, although confident of our superiority in numbers, was without doubt too keen to underrate [the difficulties]' of battle.[25]

First Army carried out extensive preparations before the battle: moving guns into place; stockpiling ammunition; training for the attack. The Royal Flying Corps, having proved invaluable in providing reconnaissance in the mobile battles of 1914, was now to be no less useful in trench warfare by, for the first time, systematically photographing the enemy positions. By poring over aerial photographs the intelligence section were able to build up a detailed picture of the far side of No Man's Land. The commander of the RFC Wing supporting First Army was Brigadier-General Hugh Trenchard, who was apprehensive about meeting Haig, having heard rumours that he was 'Reserved, austere and . . . did not believe a great deal in the air'. Trenchard found that the rumours lied, at least about the last bit. He related how, faced with opposition from some gunner officers dubious about the usefulness of aircraft, Haig gave the RFC robust support. He would not stand for 'early Victorian methods'. Haig made clear that 'he was going to use the air', and they were to do likewise.[26] It was the beginning of an important relationship between the two men, of enormous consequence for the development of air power on the Western Front.

Haig personally briefed a divisional commander on the importance of careful preparation, making sure every single man knew of his part in the overall plan: 'Thanks to our excellent photos, this can all be planned out beforehand'.[27] Only during the battle itself did it become clear that the British had missed a line of obstacles. These were to have a disastrous effect on the attackers on the day of battle.

The Battle of Neuve Chapelle

The early morning of 10 March was overcast and cloudy, creating 'conditions adverse to aerial observation of artillery fire and reconnaissance'. Faced with improving conditions, at 6.45 a.m. Haig decided to proceed with the attack: a graphic illustration of the importance that he already attached to the air at this early stage in the war.[28] Thanks to the 35-minute bombardment by the Royal Artillery, the opening of the battle was highly successful. In spite of some setbacks, First Army that morning captured Neuve Chapelle village and advanced up to 1100 yards. Although defenders held out on either flank, the stage appeared to be set for the next stage of Haig's ambitious plan.[29]

Instead, Haig could only sit frustrated as delay after delay occurred. The assault brigades were ordered to consolidate their gains while reserve formations moved forward. These were intended to leapfrog through the first wave and push forward. But Rawlinson refused to continue the advance until 1.15 p.m. when he was sure that his front was clear. Only then, despite the entreaties of the aggressive Major-General Capper of 7th Division, eager to exploit the opportunity he could see on his front, would he sanction an advance. Willcox too refused to move until he was sure that IV Corps was in position, with the result that a general advance was only ordered at about 2.50 p.m. – and the problems of co-ordination and issuing orders meant that it was not until 5.30 or even 6.00 p.m. when the battalions of the two corps finally got under way. The better part of a day had been frittered away. German reserves had arrived, the light was fading, artillery support was poor, and it should have surprised no one that the attack became bogged down. In retrospect it is clear that the fleeting opportunity for a substantial advance had already vanished when IV and Indian Corps renewed the attack.

This was not clear to Haig, and at 7 a.m. on 11 March a fresh attack began. Without the advantages that had given the British the edge on 10 March, the results were catastrophic. There was no surprise. Worse, the

Germans had dug new trenches overnight, and there had been no opportunity for guns to register on the new targets; in any case, it was difficult to get precise information about the location and extent of these new defences back to the artillery.[30] The artillerymen's dilemma was captured in a subsequent report, which said that with 'communications . . . cut, the heavy Batteries and Howitzers resorted largely to shooting by the map. They had to choose between this method and remaining silent'. Doing this simply wasted precious ammunition, though. With developments in artillery technique, in years to come 'shooting by the map' – i.e. without preregistering the guns – was to become a highly effective method,[31] but in March 1915 it amounted to little more than firing blindly, hoping to hit an enemy position.

Deprived of effective artillery support, the infantry stood no chance in the face of enemy machine-guns and artillery fire. By the afternoon First Army's offensive capability had been wrecked; artillery was unable to hit the targets that were doing damage to the attackers; infantry had taken heavy casualties; and commanders at all levels from Haig downwards, deprived of timely and accurate information, were unable to perform their primary role of directing their forces. The one thing that could be done was to order the artillery to bombard the new German front line, and when Haig visited the front line on the evening of the 11th, he ordered that artillery be moved forward and fire concentrated on the strongpoints holding up the attackers prior to a fresh effort on the following day.[32]

8th Division's attack failed, but two battalions of 7th Division made some progress, creeping close to the enemy position under the cover of artillery fire, and when the guns lifted rushing the trenches. A captured German 'complained bitterly that the bombardment wasn't war "it was carnage"'.[33] These actions seemed to show that even on the third day of the offensive, when the initial impetus had vanished, effective use of artillery could bring about success, which perhaps helps to explain Haig's continued optimism. Capper, misled as to the extent of the success, ordered an attack as if a substantial breakthrough had occurred. It foundered against a cobbled-together defence.[34]

Haig was equally bamboozled by the situation. At his HQ he received a stream of encouraging but usually misleading information, It appeared to him that, after two days of attrition, the German defences in the northern part of the Neuve Chapelle battlefield were collapsing. The arrival at 1.58 p.m. of a report from IV Corps seemed to confirm that the crisis of the battle had arrived: the wearing-out fight was over, and the moment of rupturing of the enemy front was now here. Only the pursuit remained.

Shortly after 3.06 p.m. the telegraphs clattered as Haig's order came down the wires:

> Information indicates that enemy on our front are much demoralized. Indian Corps and IV Corps will push through the barrage of fire regardless of loss, using reserves if required.[35]

Haig ordered up cavalry for the pursuit phase, and ordered I Corps, which was not involved in the main battle, to be ready to co-operate with the Indian Corps. As late as 6.20 p.m. he asked for the support of troops from GHQ reserve.[36]

He did not get his breakthrough. The German line was intact, and the assaults of the late afternoon and early evening were a sorry tale of confusion and failure. Haig arrived at Willcocks's HQ at about 5 p.m. convinced that victory was his for the taking. Actually, Indian Corps' chain of command was almost at breaking point. A brigade commander postponed the attack, then Willcocks cancelled it altogether. IV Corps attacks failed. Both decisions were entirely justified. The true state of affairs gradually became known at First Army HQ in the course of the evening. After telephoning Indian and IV Corps HQs at 10.40 p.m. Haig ordered the attacks to cease. The battle of Neuve Chapelle was over.

Neuve Chapelle was a significant action for a range of reasons. It was the BEF's first major offensive under trench-warfare conditions. The battle demonstrated to both the French and Germans that the British army, although small, was prepared to take serious offensive action. Most importantly, Neuve Chapelle offered tantalising evidence of near-success. Many of the factors that had brought this about – such as the achievement of surprise aided by a short 'hurricane' artillery bombardment, and infantry moving across No Man's Land under the cover of artillery fire to rush enemy positions – were to be part of the winning formula that in 1918 would help win the war. As one French critic was to write, Neuve Chapelle 'influenced subsequent operations to a degree . . . [that] greatly exceeded the lessons the battle had actually to teach'.[37]

After the battle, Haig stated in his official report that, in effect, Rawlinson had sacrificed an opportunity for a substantial advance. Privately, he was scathing about the IV Corps commander: 'if Rawlinson had only carried out his orders and pushed on from the village at once, we would have had quite a big success'.[38] The relationship between the two men was further complicated when Rawlinson attempted to scapegoat Major-General F.J. Davies of 8th Division for the failure on 10 March. Davies fought back. Rawlinson confessed to Haig, and French and Haig decided, on balance, not to send Rawlinson home. Over the next three years Rawlinson became one of Haig's most important lieutenants, with the Davies affair silently in the background.[39]

Rawlinson seized on 'the great point' from the battle, 'that we have now proved that a line of trenches can be broken with suitable artillery preparation combined with secrecy', although his thinking then went off in a rather different direction from Haig's.[40] Most importantly, a GHQ memorandum asserted 'that in spite of wire and trenches we can break the enemy's line, given adequate numbers and preparation'.[41] This belief, that the stalemate could be broken relatively easily, propelled the BEF into its next battle on a wave of optimism.

This is not to say that the problems encountered in the battle were ignored. Before the end of March Major-General Du Cane produced a thoughtful report which concluded that after the capture of Neuve Chapelle village First Army's command-and-control began to fracture, and on the second day of the battle it disintegrated. Du Cane concluded that Haig made intent crystal clear, but his subordinates failed to understand the 'spirit' of his battle plan. Although Du Cane was to become an advocate of a 'step-by-step' approach to battle (see below), in this report he refers to Haig's attempt to achieve a breakthrough as 'a good plan which failed' because 'subordinate commanders' failed to 'push on rapidly from one point to the next'.[42] It is possible that Du Cane refrained from being too critical of a senior officer, but up to a point his comments made a great deal of sense. There was a reluctance to push forward on the part of Rawlinson and Willcocks. Willcocks later commented in what reads as an implicit rebuttal of Du Cane's criticisms:

The orders of the First Army were always clear and distinct, and I never experienced any difficulty in thoroughly recognising their object. [But] We had not got the munitions . . . and hence any advance up to or beyond the Aubers Ridge would have resulted in a Pyrrhic victory.[43]

These failures of individual commanders disguised the wider implications of the experience of First Army at Neuve Chapelle. There was a failure to recognise the sheer difficulty of communications on the battlefield, and thus of commanders exercising any sort of control once the infantry had gone 'over the top'. In the initial stages of battle, if things went well it was possible to make a substantial advance: it was in the subsequent phases that major problems occurred. Haig was justified in blaming his corps commanders for failing to push on in accordance with his orders, but, even if they had done so, the chaos of the battlefield would almost certainly have prevented First Army from achieving the deep advances he sought.

In the wider context of the war what mattered was that Haig and others were convinced that a major success had been thrown away through human error. If things were managed a little differently, with one more heave, the BEF would be able to win a major victory. This assumption underpinned Haig's conduct of operations for the rest of 1915.

Operations Elsewhere

While preparing for Neuve Chapelle, Haig was brought the unwelcome news that 23 Indian soldiers had deserted to the Germans. On 19 February an Allied fleet had bombarded Turkish positions on the Gallipoli peninsula as a preliminary to an attempt by warships to force the Dardanelles, the strategically vital straits that allowed access to the Black Sea from the Mediterranean. This attack on a Muslim power, originally the brainchild of Winston Churchill, First Lord of the Admiralty, was thought to have triggered the desertions.[44] After Neuve Chapelle it soon became apparent that this new Eastern campaign was limiting the flow of ammunition to the Western Front and thus hampering the BEF's operations. Haig was bemused by why the Fleet started shelling the Turks before land forces had arrived 'to reap the fruits of the bombardment'. There was, Haig mused, 'some Winstonian subtlety in the plan which has not appeared yet!'[45] When British, French and Anzac troops did land on 25 April, they were pinned into their beachheads. The Gallipoli campaign bogged down, replicating the conditions of the Western Front under a burning Mediterranean sun. Haig's opinion of the operation did not improve over time. He pointed out an obvious flaw in the plan: even if the Allies did capture the Peninsula, the Turkish guns on the opposite shore would still dominate the Straits.[46]

The Dardanelles fiasco reinforced Haig's conviction that the maximum concentration of troops and materiel should be in the decisive theatre, the Western Front. He worried that the French would think that the British were not taking the war seriously by sending scarce resources to Gallipoli, which would encourage the 'peace party' in Paris.[47] As an Army Commander in 1915 his strategic opinions were of little consequence. After he became C-in-C they mattered a great deal, particularly when faced with a Prime Minister determined to pursue an 'Easterner' agenda.

Smith-Dorrien's Second Army was not idle in spring 1915. Using a new weapon, chlorine gas, the Germans attacked around Ypres on 22 April. By limiting their efforts to pinching out the Ypres salient, they failed to capitalise on the initial surprise and achieve a major break-through. Nonetheless, after weeks of vicious fighting, the Allies were driven back, with the front line resting only two miles from Ypres. Second Ypres had an immediate knock-on effect on Haig's army. In the medium term Second Ypres was highly significant for Haig, as it resulted in the sacking of Horace Smith-Dorrien from the command of Second Army. This could not have come as much of a surprise to Haig, as the C-in-C had been dripping poison into his ear about his fellow Army commander for some time. At the end of April French told him that Smith-Dorrien 'was quite unfit to hold the Command of an Army'. Smith-Dorrien's treatment was vindictive and unjustified, but it was French's doing, not Haig's. French was a good hater and had feuded with Smith-Dorrien for years. Haig certainly believed, quite mistakenly, that Smith-Dorrien had been wrong to fight at Le Cateau in August 1914. The argument that Haig used his diary to undermine Smith-Dorrien's position with the King is unconvincing, not least because of the friendship between George V and Smith-Dorrien (Haig was not the only general with strong Royal connections). Unwittingly, French had removed Haig's major rival for his own post.[48]

Aubers Ridge

Haig was careful to incorporate the lessons of Neuve Chapelle into his plan for his next major offensive.[49] These improvements and the fact there was to be a simultaneous major French offensive push allowed both Sir John French and Haig to contemplate a major success. Clearly intending to avoid the situation that had occurred on 10 March, of subordinates failing to press on, Haig stressed the objective of the battle was 'to deploy the entire force at our disposal and fight a decisive battle'.[50] A two-pronged attack, I and Indian Corps on the right and IV Corps on the left, would advance about 3,000 yards to Aubers Ridge, and then there would be 'a general advance through Illies and Herlies upon Don'.[51] Haig told his senior commanders on 27 April that

> All plans are to be made with the object of getting right on and continuing the advance . . . Fresh troops are always to be at hand to fill up gaps and to push on the forward movement when troops in front are fatigued or held up.[52]

Drawing on the lessons of Neuve Chapelle, reserves were to be husbanded carefully – for the battle, Haig was to control one brigade from each corps as an Army Reserve.[53] Fresh troops were to be used to leapfrog the troops that carried out the initial assault who, it was recognised, would be exhausted by their efforts.

Subjecting the plans of his subordinates to detailed scrutiny – so much so that Rawlinson sourly commented that it 'does not leave much room for me'[54] – Haig was anxious to achieve surprise, suggesting some rudimentary deception measures. He was also concerned that careful attention should be paid to overcoming obstacles such as the Bois de Biez.[55] The advance would not be slowed by using the assault troops to fortify and defend captured positions; rather troops from the rear would be dedicated to this task. Some artillery pieces were to be ready to move forward to keep in range as the successful infantry went forward, and machine-guns, mortars and guns were to be pushed up in direct support of the attacking troops to help them deal with buildings and similar strongpoints.[56]

The command challenges were recognised as critical. 'In order that the offensive may be continued without interruption and be suited to the changing conditions of the fight', a First Army memorandum instructed that commanders and staff officers were to be well forward, and the communications were planned to ensure a constant flow of information, with signal flags and lamps being used when telephone wires were severed.[57] This was very much on the right lines, and foreshadowed developments in communications over the next few years on the Western Front.

French too sought a breakthrough and substantial advance, maintaining under GHQ's control a reserve of two cavalry corps and three infantry divisions for exploitation.[58] GHQ had slightly different views on cavalry to First Army, which assigned divisional cavalry an important role in facilitating the breakthrough, and 2nd Cavalry Division in exploiting success.[59] A memorandum, written by Robertson but reflecting French's views, drew attention to the difficulties of using cavalry under conditions of deep defences covered by artillery fire; only once the trench lines were broken could cavalry assume their traditional role.[60]

Intriguingly, Haig told French that

in my opinion we had not enough troops to *sustain* our forward movement and reap decisive results . . . more good [infantry] divisions are required in addition to my eight Divisions in a position to *sustain* our attack and prevent us from being held up after we have really broken the line . . .[61]

Haig's analysis was sensible enough. Perhaps this was a case of his being overcome by doubts about his plan, a streak of realism tempering his habitual optimism. More likely, Haig was attempting to pressurise on French to build up more reserves, and indeed three divisions were added to GHQ's operational reserve. With the tactical lessons of the previous offensive absorbed and applied, plans carefully laid, and commanders thoroughly briefed, it seemed that First Army was on the eve of a major success. Even Rawlinson, who had thought that his Corps had a 'tough job', believed that there was a 'very reasonable prospect of success'.[62]

It was not to be. Aubers Ridge, 9 May 1915, most closely matches the stereotype of the First World War battle: soldiers advancing across No Man's Land only to be cut down by machine-gun fire; generals frustrated by the lack of progress ordering further fruitless attacks; minimal gains for huge losses: an appallingly high 10,000 casualties.[63]

A.W. Pagan, CO of 1st Glosters, argued that the Germans too, had learned lessons from Neuve Chapelle. The methods used by the British on 10 March had lost their novelty, and the Germans had considerably strengthened their defences. The British artillery bombardment was simply inadequate to suppress German fire. The most basic infantry tactics of 'fire and movement' were neglected, with the advancing infantry lacking 'covering rifle or machine-gun fire', and co-operation between arms was poor. Pagan stressed the success of methods that developed over the course of the war. But at Aubers Ridge, British fighting methods were at an extremely rudimentary stage.[64]

The first indications of failure reached Haig at his HQ at about 8 a.m. As ever, the situation was cloudy, and the scale and causes of the failure were not yet apparent. Haig therefore ordered that I Corps and Indian Corps should mount another attack at noon. He then visited Indian Corps HQ, where the gravity of the failure began to become more apparent, and the zero hour was delayed until 3.20 p.m. for the artillery, and 4 p.m. for the infantry assault.[65] Haig continued to have faith in the artillery's ability to achieve fire superiority. The preliminary bombardment had failed to suppress the forward machine-guns. For the new attack Haig ordered that the fire of the 18-pdrs and 6-in howitzers be concentrated on the parapets. This was undoubtedly the correct response, but, although to Haig the fresh bombardment appeared 'terrific, and [it] seemed as if nothing could withstand it', the gunners were simply incapable of delivering either the weight or accuracy of fire needed to neutralise these machine-guns. The infantry attack was stopped by enfilade machine-gun fire, leaving No Man's Land freshly carpeted with the dead, dying and wounded.[66]

Coming under pressure from GHQ to renew the offensive to support the French, who were achieving some success in their operations, Haig ordered a fresh bombardment followed by an attack at 8 p.m. Finally, faced with the evidence that it simply was not possible to launch the attack in time, Haig sensibly postponed it.[67] Even at this stage, the full extent of First Army's defeat was not clear to its commanders. A conference with all three of his corps commanders discussed whether to push on during the night or to delay until dawn. The night attack would have been made 'with the bayonet' and without a preliminary bombardment. It was agreed to opt for a dawn assault with artillery preparation to attempt to eliminate the all-important German machine-guns.[68] This too was cancelled as the scale of the British casualties, the shortage of ammunition and the poor state of the artillery became clear. Haig's summary of the situation at dawn makes depressing reading. It indicated a sense of realism about the limitation of the forces at his disposal, and the need to undertake 'more deliberate and methodical artillery preparation' than were needed against 'the field entrenchments hitherto encountered'.[69]

Festubert

The profound sense of failure felt by high command is evident from the documents that passed between GHQ and First Army. French made a half-hearted effort to talk up Aubers Ridge in a special order in which he wrote of the importance of the battle in aiding the successful attacks of the French.[70] Otherwise the tone was of bleak realism, and a consensus emerged in favour of abandoning brief artillery for 'a steady and delib-erate bombardment'. On 14 May French called for a 'deliberate and persistent attack', which would give the enemy no rest until its position collapsed.[71]

Despite the gloom, senior British soldiers shared a feeling that, having driven into a blind alley, it was only a matter of reversing out and taking a different road. 'I think you have a better chance this time,' Robertson told Haig. 'I believe what is needed is deliberate, observed and controlled fire'. There was no thought of abandoning the offensive. Second Army was still engaged in the Second Battle of Ypres, where the Germans had attacked on 22 April, and it was hoped that further attacks by Haig's Army would reduce strain on its sister formation. The French, of course, demanded that the BEF take action. As Robertson told Haig, if First Army did not take the offensive, 'we ought to relieve more French divisions and let them attack. This was Joffre's natural proposal at a rather stormy meeting today . . .'.[72] Joffre was particularly grumpy because on 12 May German reserves moved from the British to the French front.[73] First Army's next battle was largely to satisfy the French that the BEF was pulling its weight. Freed from expectations of a major advance, First Army used more limited methods and achieved a modest level of success as a consequence.

Gunnery was the key. Commanders were consulted as to whether they believed that shelling had caused sufficient damage to the enemy trenches to allow the infantry attack to succeed.[74] This was a reversion to siege warfare methods of old, when the fortress would not be stormed until the breach in its walls was judged practicable. On 14 May Haig requested permission to postpone the attack for 24 hours. GHQ agreed, although the tone of the reply, which referred to delays as being 'prejudicial to the success of the Allied operations', gives some sense of the extent to which Joffre was putting French under pressure.[75]

No one would suggest that the Battle of Festubert (15 to 27 May 1915) was a new Waterloo. It was, however, enough of a success to convince High Command that it was back on the right track. Some 10,000 infantry carried out the first British night attack of the war at 11.30 p.m. on 15 May. A second phase, a renewed effort by 2nd and Meerut Divisions at 3.15 a.m. to coincide with 7th Division's attack to the south, was stillborn thanks to the carnage and confusion in the northern sector. Haig at his HQ was, as ever, receiving confused reports, but by 5.40 a.m. the situation was clearer, and he ordered that the troops in this sector should go onto the defensive.[76]

Hubert Gough's 7th Division also had some initial success. On the afternoon of 16 May, Haig visited the headquarters of Indian and I Corps, and 2nd and 7th Divisions. It was apparent that the best opportunity for further progress was in Gough's sector. Haig therefore decided to shift the weight of First Army's attack to the right flank and to attempt to close the gap between 2nd and 7th Divisions. When the Quadrilateral strongpoint was captured by 21 Brigade at about 10.15 a.m. Haig began to sense that the crisis of the battle had arrived. At 11.30 a.m. he informed I Corps HQ: 'There are signs of the enemy's resistance breaking down' and urged the brigadiers on the spot to 'take the opportunity of pressing on', but to local objectives, not the distant ones of the 9 May battle. Haig then visited HQs of I Corps and

2nd and 7th Divisions to stress the importance of consolidation before pushing on.[77]

On the morning of 17 May the German defenders were under severe stress. They could not mount major counterattacks to retake the lost positions, as reinforcements had to be pushed into the line merely to hold on to existing trenches. A new line was established in the rear of the original positions, and troops fell back to it during the night, often in some disorder. First Army was unable to capitalise on its initial success. Attempts to advance in the afternoon of the 17th were met by fire from the new German position – which had not yet been identified. 'Friendly fire' from British artillery halted the advance of one battalion. The sheer difficulty of organising and co-ordinating a major attack proved to be beyond the capabilities of First Army, and the day petered out in a series of small-scale, largely unsuccessful efforts.[78] Although the battle still had some distance to run until it ended on 27 May, the opportunity for a further substantial advance had passed.

In the topsy-turvy world of the Western Front, Festubert was judged a success because of its attritional effect on the enemy and because it pinned the Germans to the British front and forced them to divert reserves, which benefited the French. It also appeared to show that the new artillery tactics worked. Some thought that the battle had been 'tantalising': the Germans had been forced back to a new, hastily constructed line, and could have been pushed out if attacked immediately.[79] French sent Kitchener an oblique reply to his warning that his strategy was 'on trial':

> our experiences at Neuve Chapelle and again this week and that of the French near Arras show clearly that it is possible to break through the enemy's defences, provided sufficient artillery ammunition of the proper nature is available and sufficient troops are resolutely employed.

French went on to say that to capitalise on early successes, recent events showed that a continual flow of reinforcements was needed to engage in long-drawn-out and wearing combat.[80]

An Alternative to Breakthrough?

Was there a viable alternative to attempts to achieve a breakthrough? It has been argued that the so-called 'step-by-step' or 'bite-and-hold' approach was proposed at GHQ 'as early as February 1915 and repeatedly endorsed by some senior officers thereafter' but was ignored by Haig with disastrous results.[81] Although superficially attractive, this analysis presents serious problems.[82]

Rawlinson was one of the primary proponents of this fundamentally attritional method. After Neuve Chapelle he wrote:

> What we want to do now is what I call, 'bite and hold'. Bite off a piece of the enemy's line . . . and hold it against counter-attack. The bite can be made without much loss, and, if we choose the right place and make every preparation to put it quickly into a state of defence there ought to be no difficulty in holding it against the enemy's counter attacks and in inflicting on him at least twice the loss that we have suffered in making the bite.[83]

This key was massing sufficient artillery firepower, in accordance with pre-war doctrine, to overwhelm the opposition and sending the infantry forward to seize ground. What this method did not seek to do was achieve an immediate breakthrough.

During the First World War, the BEF developed bite-and-hold operations to be an extremely effective operational method, as witnessed by battles such as Messines and Menin Road in 1917. But this does not mean that Haig earlier, wrongheadedly, refused to abandon attempts at breakthroughs in favour of a more limited approach.

For all the Cabinet's dislike of costly offensives,[84] the limited method, which was not cheap in attackers' lives, offered the prospect of heavy casualties in endless fighting, with no end in sight, and victory to be delivered – if at all – at some time in the remote future. The prospect of generals convincing politicians to support a seemingly indefinite war, or of politicians selling the idea to the civilians on the home front, was remote. It would in all likelihood have strengthened the hands of those politicians such as McKenna and Runciman who favoured a truly radical approach to strategy, of foregoing a large British army on the Western Front, instead relying on the 'British Way of Warfare' of financial muscle and seapower.[85] In the real world it took the deployment of a mass British army to France to first help stave off defeat, and then bring about victory.

A radical reorientation of British strategy towards step-by-step could only have been undertaken in co-ordination with the French. Since they wanted to remove the enemy from their territory as speedily as possible, a flat refusal was the most likely outcome of such a request; and if the British had persisted, the coalition would have been plunged into crisis. In any case, the choice between the two methods was not clear-cut. Rawlinson, was in fact inconsistent (or, put more positively, flexible) in his approach, trimming his methods to suit the circumstances.[86] It was by no means obvious in 1915 that 'one more heave' would not work: each battle appeared to offer evidence that, with a little modification of methods, the next effort would be crowned with substantial success. Moreover, the limits of Haig's power as an Army Commander or even as Commander-in Chief were such that it is simply not the case that he could decide upon a strategy and it would be automatically translated into reality. In 1915 he was trammelled by having to refer up to GHQ; at all times he had to take account of the views of his subordinate commanders and staffs, and a host of other factors.

Limited operations brought limited success, at least in terms of ground gained. At best they led to salients, surrounded by the enemy on three sides. Bitter experience showed that a law of diminishing returns rapidly set in, as the ground became so cratered by artillery, it became ever more difficult to move men, supplies, and crucially, guns forward to begin the next step.[87] And, as Haig repeatedly argued, it was essential to keep up the pressure on the enemy – to maintain operational tempo – by rapidly following up an attack with another one. Therefore, to capitalise on a step-by-step approach it was necessary rapidly to switch forces from place to place to renew the attack, or have sufficient forces (and, above all, guns) to attack on a wide front. Neither option was logistically feasible until 1918; nor were guns and shells available in requisite numbers. In short, using the step-by-step approach as the precursor to a break-out made good sense; as an end in itself, it was a strategic *cul de sac*.

The battles of 1915–17 presented several occasions on which the intelligent use of a small mobile force might have led to substantial gains. And Haig never lost sight of the importance of manoeuvre, nor, unlike some other cavalrymen, did he lose faith in the usefulness of mounted troops. '[W]e cannot hope to reap the fruits of victory', he told two cavalry officers in April 1915, 'without a large force of mounted men'.[88]

The likelihood of the German defences caving in, allowing a mass of cavalry held in reserve to be unleashed in a major charge was fairly remote – although French and Haig, entirely properly, continued to plan for the possibility.

Using cavalry as part of a small all-arms team that also included infantry, machine-guns, armoured cars and bicycle-mounted troops – as advocated by Haig in particular – was a rather different matter. The planning for Loos in September 1915 had cavalry held ready for use at various levels to exploit success. Four cavalry divisions were under GHQ's control, to be used in conjunction with motorised infantry (in buses); First Army had two cavalry brigades: and 1st and 9th Divisions each had a mounted squadron to be used in conjunction with cyclists and motor machine-guns.[89] In short, from mid-1915, 'the doctrine was beginning to develop of cavalry fighting their way forward to create or widen a gap in conjunction with the infantry, rather than waiting for a perfect gap to be cleared'. This approach 'was not the opposite of "step-by-step" but a way of making it more effective'.[90]

By the summer of 1915, as a result of analysing the sobering experience of the spring battles, Haig's operational thinking had evolved. In a letter to the Prime Minister in June he argued that hitherto attacks had been launched on too narrow a front, which gave Germans dense targets that could be enfiladed by machine-guns on the flanks. 'With such changed conditions,' Haig continued, 'it might be thought that the old principles of war had also changed. But I do not think that is so'. They simply needed to be adapted to new circumstances. This meant an attack on a front of some 25 miles, heavily supported by artillery, to wear down the Germans, implicitly by sucking the enemy reserves into the fight. This was the 'bataille d'usure' of Napoleon', but modernised and on a greater scale, although Haig still grossly underestimated the time necessary for the 'wearing-out fight' to take effect. A large reserve was to be held back 'at a central position', to be conveyed by railway and motor transport and committed, at the appropriate moment, where the enemy was at his weakest. A little later Haig began thinking on an even grander scale, of an offensive on a 100-mile front.[91]

In summer 1915, as Haig well knew, these offensives were impossible, but in time an operation on these lines would become feasible as the Allies grew stronger. (His letter to Asquith must be seen in the context of wanting resources to be sent to the Western Front rather than Gallipoli). Three years later, in 1918, the Allies were able to keep up relentless pressure on a 100-plus mile front, grinding down the defenders. Even in autumn 1918 the tactical situation did not allow the deep penetration and exploitation that Haig craved. It is Haig's failure to come to terms with the tactical conundrum, rather than his operational concepts, that deserve criticism. This was strange. From the beginning of trench warfare, Haig had taken an active interest in minor tactics and weaponry, championing trench mortars and light machine-guns and discussing the use of hand grenades,[92] but in 1915 he failed to grasp the tactical difficulties of creating the conditions in which his operational ideas could become realities.

The Road to Loos

The failures of the spring offensives had important political ramifications. Repington published an article in *The Times* on 14 May blaming Kitchener for the shell shortage that supposedly hampered military operations. It caused outrage, worsened by the *Daily Mail's* attack on Kitchener a week later. The 'shell scandal' contributed to the extinguishing of Britain's last ever purely Liberal government, which was replaced by a coalition under Asquith. In feeding information to Repington, Sir John French and members of his staff had stepped well beyond the behaviour usual for soldiers in a democracy.[93] It was one of the most serious cases of military intervention in politics since the seventeenth century. Haig was not involved, and when Clive Wigram, the King's assistant private secretary, wrote to him about the plot he replied that '*The Times* sh[oul]d be suppressed, and Northcliffe [the owner of the newspaper] locked up'. Haig took the opportunity to undermine French, in the sure knowledge his views would get back to the King: 'The fact is that Sir J. is of a jealous disposition, and is at the same time not quite sure *in his own mind* as to his fitness for his present position!'. By mid-July the King was telling Haig that he had lost confidence in French. Haig's opinions were a factor in this, but hardly the only one. Both Kitchener and the King told Haig to keep Kitchener informed.

> The King quite realised the nature of such conduct on my part, because he told me he had said to Lord Kitchener with reference to it 'If anyone

acted like that, and told tales out of school, he would at school be called a "sneak"'. Kitchener's reply was that we are beyond the schoolboy's age![94]

That was not the only subject on which Haig wrote to the Palace. Smith-Dorrien's replacement by Plumer left Haig as the most important commander in the BEF barring only French. One of Haig's liaison officers worried that his boss deserved a rest: 'unfortunately he is the only really good Englishman [sic] in high command, so they won't spare him'. Eager to preserve his position, in June Haig wrote to Wigram questioning the rumoured appointment of Paget to the shortly-to-be-created Third Army. Paget, the villain of the Curragh incident, would have been a very divisive choice – Robertson also cautioned the King against it – but Haig's self-interest was also at stake.[95]

Under Joffre's prodding, French planned for First Army to attack on the Lens–La Bassée front around 10 July. Haig carried out a reconnaissance and discussed the situation with key subordinate commanders. This was Haig the staff officer at his best. In a sombre report to GHQ Haig gave his suggestions as to where, if necessary, the attack should occur; but pointed out the problems of lack of heavy artillery, shortage of ammunition and that the intended battlefield was 'not favourable for attack'. He did not want to fight over this flat and exposed area punctuated by miners' cottages, slagheaps (or *crassiers*) and winding gear. German observers could call down fire on attackers, while machine-guns threatened to do terrible damage to infantry that attempted to advance over such exposed ground. Evidently Haig saw the Loos–Lens front as a very different proposition from the Festubert area, and believed it could only be tackled by 'siege methods . . . using bombs, and by hand to hand fighting in the trenches'.[96]

Although Haig's gloom extended to the immediate prospects of his allies, overall his strategic views had not changed. 'I still think that it is *fatal* to pour more troops and ammunition down the Dardanelles sink!' he wrote to Wigram.

Our diplomatists ought to have bribed Bulgaria long ago to join us. In my opinion it is the only way to ensure the capture of Constantinople . . . Fundamental principles of strategy seem daily to be ignored. This is the decisive point: bring all the strength of the Empire to this point and beat the Enemy. Then all else will be ours for the picking up![97]

Haig's uncharacteristic pessimism in summer 1915 perhaps helps to explain why he seized upon an apparent technological solution to the deadlock when it became available.

Already digesting the unwelcome news from the Boulogne munitions conference that troops and guns sufficient for a breakthrough would not be available until 1916, Haig's blunt report forced French to think again.[98] Joffre determined on a major push on the Champagne front with a secondary attack in Artois. To Sir John French's annoyance, the BEF's offensive would be subsidiary to this one.[99] Haig was asked whether he stood by his negative assessment. The answer could not have improved the C-in-C's mood. Instead, Haig recommended another attempt to get onto Aubers Ridge.[100]

The French remained obdurate: the BEF must attack around Loos. At a meeting on 27 July French and General Ferdinand Foch, Commander French Northern Army Group, experienced a particularly spectacular non-meeting of minds, while on 5 August Joffre told French that 'no more favourable ground than that which extends north of Angres to the canal de La Bassée can be found'.[101] Perhaps this was his idea of a joke.[102] Trying to balance his obligations to an ally with his concern to preserve his army from inevitable heavy casualties, Sir John offered to support the French by committing the BEF's artillery, but not infantry, to battle around Loos. Haig understood his part of this plan involved using his heavy guns on counterbattery work 'so as to prevent them [the German guns] from interfering with the French attacks on our right', and to pin 'the hostile infantry on my front'. First Army's infantry would not carry out major operations.[103]

To Joffre, who wanted the British to carry out a 'large and powerful attack' with a minimum of 10 divisions, this was unacceptably half-hearted stuff. In the summer of 1915 Lord Kitchener became convinced, partly by Esher, that defeatist sentiment was so widespread in France that, if it appeared as if Britain was not pulling its weight, this might lead to the 'pro-German sympathiser' Joseph Caillaux gaining power. Although exaggerated and alarmist, this advice had an impact on Kitchener. Kitchener also saw an offensive as necessary to aid the Russians. 'K's' mind was made up, Haig gathered after talking to him, that 'we "must act with all our energy, and do our utmost to help the French, even though, by doing so, we suffered very heavy losses indeed"'.[104]

In mid-August Kitchener visited French to order him to mount a major offensive. Haig was told however that this pledge would not 'interfere with you proceeding deliberately and progressively as you think advisable'. The artillery plan, as a further instruction explicitly stated, was dead. [105] Even before this point Haig had begun to plan for an infantry advance to seize any opportunities presented by French success to the south.[106] Haig's new plans, outlined at a conference on 6 September, aimed at nothing less than a rupture of the enemy front and the resumption of open warfare. First Army would capture the line Loos–Hulluch, extending to Hill 70 and the Haute Deule canal. In language reminiscent of Neuve Chapelle, Haig stated he was seeking more than a mere 'tactical success. The direction of our advance must be such as will bring us upon the enemy's rear so that we will cut his communications and force him to retreat.'[107] The factor that had converted him from his pessimistic views of earlier that year was the emergence of chlorine gas as a potentially decisive weapon.

Gas has a reputation as a particularly dreadful method of warfare, even by the standards of the Western Front. In reality only 4.3% of British fatalities were caused by gas, as opposed to 24% of non-chemical casualties that resulted in death. Chlorine gas was inefficient in comparison to chemical weapons developed later on. That is not to minimise the psychological effect of gas, or its ability to incapacitate soldiers, or the fact that solders forced to wear their respirators were far less efficient and became exhausted more quickly, which sapped morale. By the end of the war gas was firmly integrated into the weapons systems of the armies, but it was emphatically not a war-winner, nor even decisive in any battle.[108]

But in summer 1915 chlorine gas did appear to have huge potential. Haig was intrigued by the German gas attack at Ypres. As early as the second day of the battle, he recorded in his diary lengthy details of the mechanics of the attack gleaned from a prisoner. Initially, he was sceptical, although he recommended anti-gas measures for First Army's front. Haig was still eager to gain knowledge of gas, dispatching his ADC to Hill 60 on 2 May to report back on a German chemical attack.[109]

Gradually Haig became convinced of the utility of gas as a weapon, and came to believe that on 22 April the Germans had thrown away a major opportunity, failing to capitalise on the rout of the French by digging in after an advance of a few hundred yards rather than driving into the Allied rear.[110] The level of panic that occurred among the Algerians and French Territorials at Second Ypres suggested gas offered a short cut to victory that would allow the British to overcome enemy firepower, break through the German trenches, and reopen mobile warfare. This analysis was reinforced by the surprise 'liquid fire' (i.e. flamethrower) attack on 30 July 1915 near Ypres. A British battalion was overwhelmed, some falling back in disorder. Haig took careful note of this incident, noting that the ability of liquid fire to make men panic was greater than the physical damage it caused. By July 1915 Haig was contemplating using gas in an attack on Aubers Ridge. He seems to have seen surprise as a force multiplier, as the German defenders could not be relied upon to panic as easily as the French at Second Ypres. Intelligence was also suggesting that German anti-gas equipment and training was deficient, which added to the sense that it would be possible to catch the enemy by surprise; the experience of the Battle of Loos was to show there was some truth in this.[111]

Haig was far from alone misinterpreting the evidence. A consulting physician to the BEF reported in May that 'The enemy have it in their power to take any position they like whenever the wind is favourable'.[112] Initial qualms about indulging in an ungentlemanly form of warfare were rapidly thrust aside, perhaps helped by some with a vested interest in putting the best possible gloss on the potential of gas. Lieutenant-Colonel C.H. Foulkes, who was commander of the Special Companies (gas services), gave a highly encouraging report on a test release of chlorine gas in England. By the time of Loos in September, there was something of a consensus among British high command on the importance of gas as a weapon.[113]

In practice, chlorine gas was a difficult weapon to use, not least because it was dependent on the wind blowing in the right direction to carry it towards its target. Too little wind, and it merely hung around; wind in the wrong direction could blow it back into friendly trenches. Haig certainly recognised that wind speed and direction were critical and wanted GHQ to assess day-by-day whether to launch an attack, but this would have posed major difficulties in co-ordinating with the French. As a standby he planned limited attacks if gas could not be used.[114] Second Ypres had shown that chlorine clouds diluted as they wafted over the British trenches, so even the rudimentary pads placed over the nose and mouth could be useful, but these limitations on the usefulness of gas were not fully understood by British high command, which helps to explain why, in Richard Holmes's words, 'the staffs at GHQ and First Army went through a curious process of self-deception'.[115] This was the consequence of an attempt to understand the lessons of recent operations and to take account of expert opinion.

Armed 'with the *very extensive* gas and smoke arrangements which have been prepared', Haig now believed decisive results 'are almost certain to be obtained'.[116] It is possible that Haig confused the strategic direction to carry out a vigorous attack with the tactical necessity of achieving a breakthrough; thus he ignored GHQ's hint of a deliberate approach. More likely Haig understood the situation very well, but truly believed that the decisive moment was at hand and shaped his plans accordingly. Letters to Doris show a rising tide of confidence, until three days before the infantry assault, he stated that he was 'pretty confident of some success' and that by October he hoped the BEF 'may be a good distance on the road to Brussels'.[117]

The traditional version of Loos has Haig denied his operational reserve, XI Corps (which he wanted situated close behind First Army's front to be ready to exploit success), by French who, unwilling to devolve authority because of his jealousy of Haig, insisted on holding it further back.[118] Nick Lloyd has transformed our understanding of this crucial issue by showing that the two men held fundamentally different concepts of the battle. The C-in-C anticipated a methodical offensive in which there would be ample time to deploy the reserves when they were needed. French in effect abdicated his role in the planning of the offensive. He was frequently ill and generally displayed lethargy and stupor at a time when dynamism was needed.[119]

Ultimately, GHQ denied Haig flexibility over the timing of the battle. He did have the option of a more limited attack by one division from each of his two corps.[120] In the early hours of 25 September, Haig consulted with Captain Gold, First Army's meteorologist, who 'could not say anything definitely beyond that the wind would probably be stronger just after sunrise [5.30] than later in the day'. Haig thus set Zero hour for 5.50 a.m., with the infantry to go in at 6.30 a.m.[121] A little after 5 a.m. his ADC 'Alan Fletcher lit a cigarette and the smoke drifted in puffs towards the north-east', towards the enemy trenches. This cigarette has been much mythologized. Far from it prompting Haig to order the use of gas, he took another 15 minutes to decide, as the wind died down a short time later. He 'feared the gas simply hang[ing] about *our* trenches!' At around 5.15 a.m. Gough was telephoned to ask whether it was possible to switch to the more limited option. Gough replied, almost certainly correctly, that it was too late to get the message to the troops.[122] Haig was 'quite upset'.[123] Gough's reply effectively left him no choice but to launch the full-blown attack. Just after 5 a.m. Haig had been told by Foulkes that the gas officers would use their initiative and decide not use the gas should the wind be locally unfavourable, a 'fail-safe' mechanism which provided him with a degree of reassurance.[124] But the responsibility of ordering the attack obviously weighed heavily on him. At about 5.15 a.m. Haig gave the order to attack.[125] His diary is not generally an introspective document; however, when he came to revise it some time after the event Haig added a significant sentence to the original handwritten version that baldly recorded the decision to go ahead: 'But what a risk I must run of gas blowing back upon our dense masses of troops!'[126]

The Battle of Loos

In the early hours of 25 September Rawlinson was transfixed by the sight of the gradual emergence of 'a huge cloud of white and yellow gas [that] rose from our trenches to a height between 200 and 300 feet and floated quietly away towards the enemy lines'.[127] The infantry attack went in at 6.30 a.m., and the results were mixed. Taking a bird's eye view of the battle from left to right, 2nd Division on the flank had little success. Here, the British gas was a failure, and in places it blew back on the advancing troops. The fail-safe measures did not work – gas officers allowed themselves to be browbeaten by overzealous superiors into releasing the gas.[128] However the other five divisions – 9th (Scottish), 7th, 1st, 15th (Scottish) and 47th (London) – were much more successful, taking the German first line and [129] in some places, getting to the second line. The advance was by no means uniform, but overall the reports reaching Haig that morning were positive. 15th Division captured the first two German positions, the village of Loos and a crucial tactical feature, Hill 70. It is unclear whether 15th Division actually broke through.[130] But Haig *believed* that there was an opportunity for a major breakthrough – that if the operational reserves were thrown in, victory was his for the seizing.[131] Haig ordered forward his only immediate reserves, two brigades of 3rd Cavalry Division, in accordance with evolving doctrine for mobile forces. At 7 a.m., and again at 8.45 a.m. Haig urged the C-in-C to place XI Corps under his command. At 9.30 a.m. French acceded to this request to the extent of ordering forward 21st and 24th Divisions 'as soon as the situation requires and permits'. These formations only passed under First Army's command once they arrived on the battlefield. It was not until late afternoon that 21st and 24th Divisions were in a position to begin to move to contact, and Haig postponed the attack of XI Corps until the morning of 26 September.[132]

Later in the day reports of German reserves coming into the line reached Haig.[133] But he was still determined to commit XI Corps to battle, to exploit the First Army's success. Such opportunities for success came but rarely. However, in his optimism Haig overlooked the fact that XI Corps would have to fight through strong German positions, recently reinforced, without the benefit of a substantial artillery bombardment or gas. He appears to have assumed that the previous day's fighting had done the defenders sufficient damage to create the conditions for success. Just as earlier Major-General Briggs had visited the front and ascertained for himself that conditions were not suitable for his 3rd Cavalry Division to advance, Haig could and should have done likewise. This was a wholly avoidable error with dreadful consequences.

XI Corps' attack on 26 September was a disaster. Thanks to the long approach march, the troops were tired before they went into action. A combination of poor staff work, inexperience (21st and 24th Divisions were both Kitchener formations, recently arrived in France, fighting in their first battle), strong German resistance and bad luck led to the attack being repulsed and some of the attackers routed. Haig's frustration is evident in his reaction to a report that 21st and 24th Divisions were 'running away in great disorder': if it was found to be untrue, the sender of the message should be court-martialled 'for sending in an alarmist report'.[134] The battle continued with attack and counterattack until 28

September but any chance of a comprehensive victory had long vanished. The French attacks in Champagne and Artois had also failed, and Joffre temporarily halted the offensive. It was renewed with a limited attack by the British on 13–14 October.[135] In spite of some careful preparations, the attack on the Hohenzollern Redoubt failed. The official historian later described it as nothing but a 'useless slaughter of infantry'. The 46th (North Midland) Division suffered especially badly, and Haig ungenerously and unfairly ascribed the failure in part to the incompetence of the divisional commander Major-General the Hon. E.J. Montagu-Stuart-Wortley and his troops.[136]

The Fall of Sir John French

Shortly after Loos there occurred one of the most embarrassing incidents in Haig's career. The King spent 28 October inspecting troops, mounted on Haig's chestnut mare. Haig had been typically meticulous in his preparations for his Royal guest. Lieutenant 'Geordie' Black, his ADC, had the day before 'tried her with cheering men and children waving flags', and had experienced no problems. All went well until George V reached 1st Wing RFC. The mare was startled by a loud cheer, reared up, threw her rider, and fell on the prostrate monarch. 'I was standing a short distance away', recalled the Prince of Wales, 'when I heard someone shout, "Oh, my God!". I shall never forget the sight of the horse getting up, leaving my father lying still on the ground. For a few terrifying seconds I thought he was dead'. Cries of pain mingled with 'indignant rage' reassured him. 'It was a most unfortunate accident' a mortified Haig confided to his diary; but it did not affect his relationship with his Sovereign.[137] On the contrary: George V was to prove a staunch supporter in the last act of Sir John French's tenure as Commander-in-Chief.

In his public dispatch of 2 November, French clumsily tried to shift the blame for the reserves fiasco at Loos to First Army. Not only Haig but First Army staff were angered by the dispatch, and a covering article in *The Times* written by French's ally Repington. 'Both are full of studied inaccuracies,' Gerry Thompson wrote to his wife. 'Fortunately remaining evidence – in the form of telegrams, letters etc – are in very safe hands.' Other senior figures in the army, such as Rawlinson and Cavan, the commander of the Guards Division, also blamed French for the problem with the reserves. When Haig attempted to put his side of the story an unseemly dispute began. Doris and Lord Stamfordham, the King's principal private secretary, sent Haig's rebuttal of French's dispatch to George V. All this added to the impression in London that it was time for French to go.[138]

Writers have tended to focus on Haig's role in French's downfall, leading to the impression that the C-in-C was 'assassinated' by a devious and disloyal subordinate who then stepped into his place. Personal ambition of course played a part in Haig's manoeuvres, but he also acted because his professionalism was offended by the drift at the top of the BEF.[139] Significantly, French had also alienated other powerful figures: Kitchener, Robertson, and the King. By himself, Haig was incapable of bringing French down; indeed, he may not even have been the main wielder of the dagger.

Haig received a letter from Asquith on 10 December appointing him as Commander-in-Chief; he formally took over nine days later.[140] Major changes had also taken place in London. Robertson became CIGS in November. He had insisted on having much greater power than his predecessor, advising the Cabinet directly, rather than through the Secretary of State for War, and Kitchener's role was diminished as a consequence. Robertson and Haig were to be formidable partners in command.

For the most part, the army were pleased with the changes; Haig was widely seen as French's natural successor. Some officers had decided long before that Haig would do a better job.[141] A few were more dubious. Repington was no friend of the new C-in-C, but his point that Haig was a superb staff officer rather than a commander had some force. 'The changes in command should be a good thing on the whole,' one officer thought. 'You will have Robertson in London, a trained soldier, and Haig here, who is undoubtedly a strong man and a good soldier. He is very determined but does not always realise the limitations of his men and has lost thousands of lives by this. But one learns war by war, and he has probably learned his lesson'.[142] The year ahead would test the validity of these views.

The new Commander-in-Chief firmly believed that it was entirely possible to fight and win a breakthrough battle on the Western Front. He was convinced that at Loos a 'great opportunity [was] missed . . . all we wanted was some Reserves at hand to reap the fruits of victory and open the road for our Cavalry to gallop through!' French was 'solely to blame' for the mishandling of the reserves.[143] Haig believed that the battles of 1915 had in any case exhausted the Germans, and he was optimistic about the future.[144]

Underpinning this confidence was the beginning of the awakening of faith that was to be so important to him as C-in-C. During the fighting at Loos, Haig, on finding Gough 'downhearted', reminded him that 'we shall win "not by might, not by power but by My Spirit, saith the Lord of Hosts" '.[145] Gough, too, was a man of faith. But in this there was nothing unusual. Religion thoroughly permeated the late Victorian upper classes. Churchgoing, prayer, and knowledge of the Bible were the norm, and indeed Christianity of various types was an important influence throughout society. Other pious senior generals included Cavan, Plumer and Horne. Some have seen Haig's faith as an aberration. It was not.[146]

Although he worshipped for much of his adult life in Anglican churches, Haig was by upbringing a Presbyterian, a member of the Church of Scotland. His Church taught that 'all human endeavours are as dust without the Divine inspiration and will'. One of the signs of being among the Elect was success in one's enterprises. Appointment as C-in-C in December 1915 convinced Haig that he was chosen by God to carry out His work – not as an 'unthinking tool of Divine Providence', but as an individual using his God-given talents. It was natural for Haig to give thanks to God when he was successful, and as by extension, the achievements of his army were God's doing, to give credit to his soldiers.[147] A week after assuming command as C-in-C, Haig wrote to Doris that 'all seem to expect success as the result of my arrival, and somehow give me the idea that I am "meant to win" by some Superior Power. As you know, while doing my utmost, I feel one's best can go but a short way without help from above'.[148]

5

Commander-in-Chief

Before the war, 'few people in England knew anything about Sir Douglas Haig', a journalist remarked in February 1916. Now, as Commander-in-Chief, he was a household name.[1] 'Tall, broad shouldered and handsome', blue-eyed and impressively moustachioed, with a determined 'Fifeshire chin', Haig looked every inch a general from his red-banded peaked cap to his highly polished boots. He walked, wrote a French journalist, with an 'alert, quick and very firm step . . . What struck one at once in Sir Douglas Haig, in his face, in his bearing . . . is his decision, which one feels is well considered and based on precision'. He radiated confidence, calmness and imperturbability.[2]

Haig's responsibilities were huge. He was answerable to the government for the operations, discipline, training, logistics and welfare of the largest British army in history. Not surprisingly, a formidable amount of paperwork passed across Haig's desk. In today's terms he was an Army Group Commander, responsible for conducting operations; a Theatre commander with a huge political and administrative burden; and a National Contingent Commander, the senior British soldier in the coalition forces on the Western Front. Today his responsibilities might be split between two or even three individuals. Arguably, as C-in-C he simply had too much to do, but Haig was not keen to give up any of his responsibilities.

To command a great army in war can be a crushing burden, but Charteris maintained that Haig 'was fully conscious of, but in no way depressed by, the magnitude of the task that confronted him'.[3] He had a number of coping mechanisms. Foremost was faith in his own abilities, allied, as we have seen, to a conviction that he had a divine calling. Earthly as well as heavenly factors contributed to his confidence. *Field Service Regulations*, he sincerely believed, gave a sound doctrinal underpinning to decision-making. He had implicit faith in his principal staff, and had the confidence of Kitchener, Asquith and the King.

His family proved a great solace. Haig's regular letters to his wife are testimony to the strength of their marriage and the role that her love and support played in keeping up his morale. Clearly, he doted on his children, and the regular periods of leave enabled him to see them far more often than was the case with an ordinary soldier. 'It was so nice being with Daddy for a fortnight,' wrote his daughter Xandra in 1917. 'I hope the war will soon end, and that he will be able to stay with us'. Haig had been at home in London for a number of difficult meetings, and it is easy to imagine the release of tension when he got home at night and saw his family.[4]

Haig liked having familiar faces about him. Colonel Ryan, after a spell commanding a Casualty Clearing Station, returned to GHQ in September 1916. Alongside his formal job of medical officer, Ryan had a clearly understood role of simply being there for Haig. Ryan admired Haig, telling a new ADC, 'What a big man he is and how human. "He's all right if you only treat him as a man and not as a bloody Field Marshal"'. Ryan and Secrett would sometimes conspire if Haig was late to bed or neglected his exercises, and senior officers would stand amazed as the C-in-C meekly accepted Ryan's scolding.[5]

Another favourite was Captain George Black, who commanded Haig's personal escort troop of 17th Lancers. Haig's fondness for Black became well-known. After nearly three years in this role, Haig finally allowed him to join the Tank Corps. With sad inevitability Black was killed. Haig was badly upset at his death, repeating, 'Poor lad, poor lad' when he heard the news. He opened his heart to Black's mother: 'When things were very critical his brightness and cheery talk made one, for the moment, forget the war'.[6]

The most unlikely member of Haig's entourage was his private secretary, Sir Philip Sassoon MP, a millionaire Jewish aesthete memorably described as being like 'an exotic bird of paradise'. Sassoon, a distant relative of the poet Siegfried, had, like Haig, been a member of the Bullingdon Club and was a keen polo-player. He amused and soothed

Haig and provided a valuable link with politicians, Buckingham Palace and journalists. Although their affection was mutual and genuine, Sassoon's mask slipped sometimes, as when in the privacy of his diary he criticised Haig's behaviour, opinions and, particularly cuttingly, the decor of the Haig family home in Kingston.[7]

Haig's taciturnity could make it hard work for others. His manner was courteous but formal. Although he enjoyed listening to sparkling conversation (George Bernard Shaw was 'An interesting man of original views. A great talker!'), even his old friend John Vaughan could find lunch with the Chief punctuated by long silences. Charteris left an amusing description of the nervousness of senior officers waiting to be admitted to the presence, remarking on the 'the large number of matches used to light cigarettes'. But opinions changed as people got to know the C-in-C. The 24-year old Prince of Wales confided to his mistress that after a pleasant dinner with Haig that 'he didn't frighten me as much as he used to!!'[8] Similarly Major Ivor Hedley, 17th Lancers, newly joined as Haig's ADC, found that after riding with the great man his 'terror somewhat abated'. Haig tried to put him at his ease by asking questions about the regiment and his time at university, before delivering the conversation-stopping 'I always think it's a fine clean life a Soldier's – not like a Politician's or even a Parson's. We Soldiers can at least always afford to be honest'. Four days later Hedley rode with Haig again and 'felt tongue tied . . . Am told everyone feels like that sometimes but it is an awful feeling'. As he grew to know Haig better, Hedley, like so many others who worked closely with him, became devoted to his boss.[9] Another ADC mused when Haig turned down his request to return to the front that

If he was a music-hall general and made a habit of thoroughly damning his entourage occasionally I shouldn't hesitate to insist on going: but he is such a very humane person that I feel, for once in my life, that the best I can do is to suppress my own inclinations.[10]

Haig had carefully structured his time. During a typical day, after a short run or walk, he would breakfast at 8.30 a.m. The morning was taken up with paperwork and consultations with his staff and senior figures. Haig disliked using the telephone, leaving that to his staff, and, although a master of military detail, he preferred to allow his staff to draft papers, sending back for redrafting any presented for his signature that did not meet his standards. Some mornings Haig had meetings with a bewildering range of visitors. At 1.00 p.m. he would give his visitors lunch, which rarely lasted longer than thirty minutes, or have a roadside picnic *en route* to visiting a headquarters or unit. He spent most afternoons on such visits. He was briefed about the unit before arrival – 10/Northumberland Fusiliers was originally composed of men from north-east England, but now about 40% were from Bradford and Leeds, one briefing note from 1916 read – and questioned the people he met, senior and junior, and jotting his impressions in his diary.[11] This was Haig's way of keeping in touch with his army.

J. Jellen, a clerk at V Corps headquarters, recorded that Haig arrived unexpectedly and addressed the only officer present, a young and nervous man, with 'What are you'? Later in the war Jellen now promoted to sergeant-major, was introduced to Haig and had the same treatment. This, he realised, was Haig's 'method of gauging the character of the person . . . If he did not react favourably', he 'had no use for him'. Following this alarming preliminary, Haig asked Jellen about discontent in the ranks over lack of leave.[12] Maxse wrote an account of a visit to XVIII Corps HQ when Haig was in a less intimidating mood. Perhaps he toned things down with more junior ranks, as Maxse found him 'crack[ing] suitable jokes with the humbler members of my staff including all the NCOS and clerks . . . D.H. did his part excellently well and produced a very good impression on all'.[13]

On the way home from visits, Haig would often rendezvous with his horses and ride for exercise, or sometimes walk back to GHQ. In the evening there would be guests for dinner at 8 p.m., but after about an hour, he would slip away for more work. Sometimes he would be joined by an important visitor for further discussion, or talk with his CoS. After writing up his diary, he went to bed at 10.45 p.m. 'There were only rare occasions', Charteris wrote, 'when this routine of the Commander-in-Chief's day was broken even by a minute'.[14]

Haig's Army

The BEF of 1916 was very different from the army of 1914, and a major part of Haig's job in the first half of 1916 was preparing this force for battle. Between January and July 17 divisions arrived, and the number of guns grew from 324 to 716; by the end of the year the BEF had reached 53 divisions. The bulk of his army on the eve of the Somme consisted of wartime volunteers, men who had been civilians at the outbreak of war and had responded to Lord Kitchener's call to arms in 1914–15. The Indian infantry left the Western Front in 1915. There was a remnant of the old force, but even the ranks of nominally 'Regular' units contained few professional soldiers. Likewise, the many pre-war Territorial battalions that had come out in 1915 had suffered heavy losses. Many of the Kitchener and Territorial units had names that smacked of civic pride and the volunteering impulse of 1914, such as 11/South Wales Borderers (2nd Gwent) and 22/Royal Fusiliers (Kensington). Such battalions had enthusiasm and high morale, but few if any officers and NCOs with pre-war experience.

Haig's command resembled the 'National Army' he had envisaged a decade earlier, although that force would have undergone at least the rudiments of training in peacetime, under the command of officers from the public schools. Before the war Haig had foreseen the principal attributes of these civilian soldiers: 'Discipline, physical courage and hardihood' and that there would be 'little scope for exercise of much tactical judgment in the most junior ranks'. The National Army 'must be capable of taking part in great offensive operations with hope of decisive success *before we are financially exhausted*'.[15] Haig's words of 1906 presciently described the state of his army, and its task, in 1916.

Like a series of Russian dolls, the BEF was a coalition force composed mainly of troops from the British Isles but with significant Dominion formations, and which in turn fitted into the wider coalition. Like Britain, the Dominions had responded to the outbreak of war with mass volunteering. Attempts by modern nationalist writers to argue that the war was not the concern of Canada, South Africa, Australia or New Zealand are ahistorical. In 1914 the peoples of these places regarded themselves as in some sense British,[16] and in any case their national security was bound up with Britain's fate. Dominion forces were to prove highly effective, and in time the Canadian and Australian Corps and the New Zealand Division emerged as something more than components of the BEF whose soldiers had distinctive accents. By 1918 Monash, Currie and Russell, the commanders of the Australian and Canadian Corps and the New Zealand Division were commanders of proto-national armies. Although he admired and supported all three men, it took time for Haig to adjust to this new reality. After a series of disputes in 1918 over Currie's determination to keep their divisions together in a Corps, Haig complained that some Canadians saw themselves as 'allies rather than fellow citizens in the Empire!'[17] However, his attitude to the evolution of Dominion military nationalism was pragmatic. Dominion soldiers were among the best he commanded, and their prowess on the battlefield earned his respect.

One of Haig's urgent tasks on becoming C-in-C was to establish his authority. The senior ranks of the army were a small, relatively homogenous group, and Haig had just emerged from the pack. As a full general, he was the same rank as Army commanders such as Rawlinson.[18] Very early on he made clear that 'I had no "friends" when it came to military promotion, and I would not tolerate a "job" being done'. 'Friends' and 'job' had very specific meanings in the army of the time, and this was a statement of intent: that Haig would only allow promotion on merit. He promptly showed that he was serious by vetoing Winston Churchill's appointment to the brigade he had been promised by French.[19] Haig largely stuck to his principles. There was certainly no cavalry mafia dominating the upper reaches of the BEF, and although he brought on the careers of officers of whom he thought highly – Charteris, Butler, Hubert Gough and Horne are the most obvious ones – friendship had nothing to do with it. Arthur Blair, his Staff College pal, did not prosper, and he moved his friend John Vaughan from a divisional command into an uncongenial administrative post, taking the trouble to break the bad news in person.[20] Haig also worked with men with whom he had sometimes tense relations, such as Allenby and Rawlinson.

Haig's knowledge of the pre-war officer corps was second to none, and although the process of appointments is not entirely clear, he seems to have listened to recommendations from trusted subordinates. He was certainly keen to bring on talent. Some highly competent men benefited from his patronage, such as Byng (elevated to command Third Army in 1917) and John Monash. Haig thought little of Birdwood as a general, and his promotion to command Fifth Army in 1918 may have owed something to Haig's desire to promote Monash to command the Australian Corps. Haig's choice of 'Tim' Harington to be Plumer's CoS, was inspired. Another beneficiary was Lieutenant-General Travers

Clarke, a 'young and energetic' man according to Horne, who had begun the war a mere major and worked with Haig at I Corps. Clarke replaced R.C. Maxwell as QMG in late 1917 after the latter was forced out – much against Haig's will, as Maxwell was a fine logistician. Haig stood by Travers Clark 'through thick and thin' in spite of opposition to 'his ruthless methods' as QMG.[21]

But there is some substance to Haig's reputation as a bad picker of subordinates and a reluctant sacker. His protégé Hubert Gough was overpromoted. Haig fought the removal of both Charteris and Kiggell, even though their ultimate replacements, Edgar Cox and Herbert Lawrence, were much superior. The C-in-C's influence could also work in the opposite direction, as when he blocked a recommendation that Major-General Nugent be given a corps, or when he sacked Lieutenant-General Keir from VI Corps on Allenby's recommendation in 1916.[22]

Surprisingly, in some ways Haig's authority was quite limited. He did not have a free hand in hiring and firing. Butler was his first choice as CoS at GHQ, but he was deemed too junior by the War Office, and Kiggell was posted in instead. When Haig attempted to elevate Richard Haking to command First Army, albeit temporarily (probably to prevent Henry Wilson being wished on him as an Army commander) the move was firmly blocked in London.[23] In early 1916 Haig had to build a relationship with his subordinates, Army commanders who were roughly his peers. One method was to hold regular Army Commanders' conferences to develop 'mutual understanding'; they would also help him impose his authority. A more brutal way was to sack them, or at least threaten to. Plumer, a potential rival as C-in-C, came close to being 'degummed' in February 1916 over supposed inefficiency, but Haig gave him a second chance. Plumer responded with marked loyalty to Haig thereafter, and Haig grew to admire 'the old man's' talents.[24]

Did Haig rule by fear, brooking no criticism? The Plumer incident gives some credence to the argument that Haig's forbidding character discouraged subordinates from discussion because they were scared of him. But it must be said that most of the sources for this view comes from individuals who had reasons to portray Haig in a poor light.[25] If Army Commanders really were frightened of him, presumably they would have obeyed him to the letter in planning and fighting battles – which, as we shall see, was not always the case. Unlike Sir John French, as C-in-C Haig retained his authority within the army. He did not create a situation among his senior subordinates where an heir apparent was hungrily waiting in the wings.

Haig's visits to his Army Commanders gave an opportunity for discussion outside the confines of the formal conferences. There were some tensions, but the picture of Haig-as-ogre is overdrawn. He certainly disliked face-to-face argument and being criticised, and was intolerant of waffle in discussion, but his mind was far from closed. From personal experience Charteris wrote that Haig made decisions after carrying out a detailed examination of the relevant factors. He was always prepared to revise his judgments if new facts emerged, and would accept different opinions from those he trusted, even if they rarely affected his final decision. He had a 'queer blend of confidence in [his] *judgment* [but] *diffidence* in claim to knowledge' which 'made him very (unusually so) open to new ideas'.[26]

Associated with the idea of rule by fear is that of a 'command vacuum'. In line with pre-war thinking, Haig's concept of command in line was for him to set broad non-prescriptive objectives, but it is sometimes said that his subordinates were afraid to take decisive action. Some have argued, whatever the theory, that Haig was prone to intervene, leading to paralysis of command.[27] This, too, contains some truth, but as we shall see, it does not show the complete picture.

GHQ staff have also come in for much criticism. Kiggell is seen as a nonentity. In fact he was an accomplished staff officer, although he was an administrator rather than a hands-on operational Chief of Staff, and he was too self-effacing to be an effective counterpoint to Haig.[28] Brigadier-General John 'Tavish' Davidson, Director of Military Operations at GHQ was also an effective staff officer but tended to be marginalised in the planning process. Charteris, Haig's head of Intelligence, was a weak link, a 'flatulent windbag' according to one of his enemies.[29] Some of Charteris's assessments of enemy morale and manpower 'bordered on wishful thinking' although the idea that he deliberately fed Haig information that he thought the C-in-C wanted to hear is untrue. Charteris shared Haig's optimism rather than being the cause of it.[30] A staff officer claimed that he heard Haig admit that he knew Charteris embellished intelligence, but that he was correct more frequently than he was wrong. If this was true, it does not reflect well on Haig's judgment.[31] In short, too often, Haig believed what he wanted to believe about the Germans, and this was his most serious defect as a commander.

Haig and His Soldiers

For most of Haig's period of command, GHQ was located in the small town of Montreuil, with the C-in-C in a nearby chateau. Most staff officers rarely saw Haig, and his appearance in the town would cause them to cluster at windows to 'catch a glimpse' of him.[32] Juicy quotations like this have led to the belief that Haig spent most of his time isolated in his chateau, but this was not really the case. He spent most afternoons visiting different parts of his army, and during major battles moved to an Advanced Headquarters to be nearer the front. In 1918, Haig gained more flexibility by commanding from a headquarters train.

By comparison with Montgomery in the Second World War, Haig was a much more remote figure to the men he commanded. This was partly because of the different circumstances – Haig lacked the radios, aircraft and jeeps that Monty used to get around his army, which was much smaller than Haig's – but also to different personalities. Haig would have regarded Monty's style as vulgar, and the common soldiers of 1914–18 would have been bemused by it. In a deferential age, they expected their officers to behave as aloof gentlemen. Haig's means of imposing his personality on the army was mostly limited to parades and published orders, although, as an ADC noted, Haig 'talks to any odd man in the road: all being a means to the end, to keep in touch with the spirit of his troops'.[33]

Haig was moved by the sufferings of his men. 'Why waste your time painting me?' he burst out to William Orpen. 'Go and paint the men. They're the fellows that are saving the world, and they're getting killed every day'.[34] Sergeant Secrett, Haig's valet, gave a very interesting perspective on Haig's relationship with the ordinary soldier. Haig frowned on 'familiarity', but, whilst 'preserving his dignity, he managed to convey to the Tommy the fact that he respected him'. Like many Regular officers, he admired the wartime volunteers and conscripts but felt most at home with soldiers of the pre-war professional army. Given Haig's paternalistic relations with his men as a regimental officer, Secrett's portrait rings true, and needs to be set alongside familiar stories of Haig's slightly comic attempts at speaking to Other Ranks.[35]

Charteris argued that Haig was respected by his men but failed to gain 'their personal affection'. 'I hope the Army will get to know him [Haig] more' wrote an infantry officer in late 1917, 'because I am sure that this will be a good thing' – and this after Haig had been C-in-C for nearly two years![36] During the war, criticism of Haig from the ranks was very limited: 'to them, he was a figure so remote in rank and personality as to be almost unimaginable' although the average private would have known who Haig was, if only from reading newspapers.[37] References to Haig or any other general in the letters and diaries of ordinary soldiers are sparse. 'Paraded with Company and inspected by Sir D Haig and marched past him' is a typical diary entry.[38]

Secrett was probably right, that Haig did inspire affection in those common soldiers that met him. Most soldiers never met Haig and probably had no strong feelings either way. Written in an elderly hand in the margin of Charteris's biography of Haig held in the library of RMA Sandhurst is a comment apparently by a Great War veteran: Haig 'was known as Duggy [to the army] but with no enthusiasm. He was too remote – but that was not his fault. The show was too big'.[39]

'The question of morale', Brigadier-General Davidson stated, 'carried great weight' with Haig. He firmly believed in the importance of moral factors in war. At bottom, Haig believed that British and Dominion troops, notwithstanding the casualties and the 'strain, both mental and physical . . . would have a greater staying power' than the Germans or French.[40] Davidson was referring to autumn 1917: Haig was concerned but not overly worried by the mutiny at Etaples base camp in September 1917.[41] Davidson's comments were of broader application. Despite this view, GHQ did not create a central organisation devoted to morale. The reasons were related partly to Haig's belief in character and the inherent superiority of the British 'race', but also confidence in regimental officers and the vast bureaucracy of paternalism that he headed. The most junior officer was trained to place the welfare of their men first and foremost, and soldiers' morale was sustained by baths, canteens, YMCA huts, organised sport, even trips to the seaside.[42] Although it ran counter to Haig's personal moral code, he reluctantly endorsed the use of licensed brothels by his troops; it was 'a matter which concerns vitally the health and fighting efficiency of soldiers [in France]'. This was the lesser evil; venereal disease hospitalised a division's worth of soldiers every day, and at least the prostitutes in a brothel could be regularly medically examined.[43]

Trust in medical facilities plays an important role in maintaining soldiers' morale, and effective medical services, returning as many wounded as possible to action as soon as possible, was an essential part of Haig's attritional strategy. Typically, Haig took a close interest in medical matters and proved very supportive of his senior medical staff as they carried out radical changes in response to the lessons learned in the first years of the war. The importance of such institutional 'top cover' to military reformers should not be underestimated.[44] Haig was influenced by his friendship with Colonel Mickey Ryan, his Medical Officer at the beginning of the war, who commanded a Casualty Clearing Station in 1915–16. It was Ryan who seems to have persuaded Haig of the value of treating as many men as close to the front as possible – 'If the men are allowed to go to the Base we never see them again!', and in 1916 'forward treatment' became general across the BEF.[45] In medical matters Haig proved considerably more enlightened than two of his contemporaries, generals Sir Ian Hamilton and Sir John Nixon, commanders at Gallipoli and in Mesopotamia respectively, whose ignoring of their senior medical people had 'horrific consequences'.[46]

There was also a darker side to the picture. Haig placed faith in discipline and coercion – including, notoriously, executions. Part of the purpose of military discipline was to condition men to obey orders, to turn them from individuals into part of an effective unit – or mere cogs in the military machine. Haig, along with senior officers of his generation, set great store by outward show. But when the C-in-C was displeased that men of 16th (Irish) Division were too slow in saluting his car, this was not merely an example of mindless 'bull'.[47] Clean kit and saluting were thought to be the outward signs of an inward discipline that would pull men through the hideous experience of the battlefield. Soldiers who lacked this discipline were unlikely to be able to stand the strain.

British military discipline ranged from petty annoyances to savage injustices. Some of the worse aspects of the disciplinary system were mitigated at regimental level by sympathetic officers and NCOs. But they could only do so much. Haig was a keen supporter of Field Punishment No.1, which involved, among other things, tying the offender to a post, wagon wheel or similar object for up to two hours a day for a strictly limited period. Haig supported it on pragmatic grounds, although he recommended that men should not be tied with their arms outstretched (which led to the nickname 'crucifixion'). F.P. No.1, he argued in a submission to the War Office, offered a punishment that fell short of imprisonment, whereby men escaped from the trenches; and that more

> of those men whose moral fibre requires bracing by the daily fear of adequate punishment would give way in moments of stress, and the recourse to the death penalty would be more frequent.[48]

Military executions remain a hugely emotive issue. 346 soldiers were shot, 266 for desertion; 37 were executed for murder, an offence that carried the death penalty in civilian life. Roughly 90% of the 3,080 death sentences passed were commuted, a percentage that may have been deliberate, so the executions were an example of 'decimation' in its original sense. Many of the unlucky tenth were strictly guilty as charged, and nearly a third were repeat offenders, but some were shell-shocked, or were denied a trial that would be seen as fair by modern standards. And some were executed for reasons of discipline, not justice. Today this seems shocking, but, as Australian historian Peter Stanley has pithily observed, 'we do not have to control a vast citizen army and win a war'.[49] Haig was typical of his time in believing that the deterrent value of the death penalty played an essential role in keeping men in the line, of preventing them from giving way to natural fear and running away. The number of executions increased at times of major battles, and the state of morale and discipline of an offender's unit or formation had a bearing on whether or not he was shot.[50]

Soldiers convicted at a court martial of a capital offence had their cases passed up the chain of command for recommendations at various levels, and these could have an important impact on the outcome. The issue of life or death ultimately rested with the C-in-C, who could either confirm or commute the sentence. The sheer volume of cases means that Haig was probably advised by a specialist officer. Haig made his attitude clear as early as September 1914, when he recommended confirmation of a sentence: 'I am of the opinion that it is necessary to make an example to prevent cowardice in the face of the enemy as far as possible'.[51]

Usually Haig merely wrote 'Confirmed', with his signature and the date, on the paperwork of the 255 soldiers and three officers he condemned to death.[52] The exception he made for Pte. A Earp (1/5 Royal Warwicks) unwittingly reveals a great deal about Haig's attitudes. Earp deserted during the build-up to 1 July 1916, 'unnerved by the enemy's counter-barrage'. The court martial recommended clemency and his divisional and corps commanders concurred. Gough, his Army commander, did not. Neither did Haig, who wrote on the proceedings 'How can we ever win if this plea is allowed'? and rapped the knuckles of the generals who had wanted the sentence commuted. Earp was executed on 22 July, just before his division went into action. The timing has been interpreted as due to 'the army's determination to impose its authority'. It is likely that Earp had shell-shock and was executed precisely because of his condition – that is the implication of Haig's comment. To commute the sentence would legitimise shell-shock and risk a flood of similar cases as soldiers saw a way out of the trenches. In autumn 1916 Pte. Harry Farr (1st West Yorks) was court-martialled for cowardice. His nerves were 'destroyed', Farr's Officer Commanding wrote, and his 'behaviour under fire' was 'likely to cause a panic'. Haig obviously agreed. He confirmed the sentence. Farr was shot at dawn on 16 October 1916.[53]

Haig took a similarly ruthless line with Lieutenant E.S. Poole (11th West Yorks), a shell-shocked officer condemned to death for deserting in October 1916. Although his brigade commander asked for clemency, Plumer, his Army Commander, disagreed. Haig wrote about the case in his diary (an indication of how strongly he felt about it). 'After careful consideration, I confirmed the proceedings . . . Such a crime is more serious in the case of an officer than of a man, and also it is highly important that all ranks should realise that the law is the same for an officer as a private'.[54]

The fact that Australian soldiers could not be executed caused Haig some anguish. Compared to British and other Dominion troops, Australian rates of absence and desertion were very high. In early 1918 Haig pointedly compared them with the Canadians, who were 'really fine disciplined troops now and so smart and clean'. No less than 9.0

Australians per thousand were in military prisons; the figures for other Dominion troops and British troops were 1.6 and 1.0 per thousand respectively. 'That is to say that nearly one Australian in every hundred men is in prison. This is greatly due to the fact that the Australian government refuses to allow capital punishment to be awarded to any Australian'. Without the threat of the supreme penalty, GHQ argued, 'we really have no hold over these men', and senior Australian officers wanted their government to change the rules.[55] The Australians, however, were the exception that proved the rule. Although lacking what the British Regular officers considered essential discipline (at the other extreme from desertion, Australians were notoriously slack in saluting), time and again Australian divisions proved to be highly effective on the battlefield. Perhaps this suggests that a slight relaxation of discipline in the rest of the BEF would have done no harm.

Rankers' attitudes to the death penalty were ambiguous. Some resented it or thought it damaged morale, but others had little sympathy for individual offenders. Overall, it almost certainly did have a deterrent effect, but one should not run away with the idea that Haig's men were only kept in the trenches by fear of punishment. The BEF's solidity rested on the consent of the khaki masses, and a range of factors – social conditioning, officer–man relations, group cohesion, pride in regiment, patriotism – contributed to it.[56]

Most importantly of all, most British soldiers believed that they had a stake in their home country. The army contained a disproportionate number of middle-class men, especially after the introduction of conscription in 1916. Junior clerks and professional men were many rungs apart on the ladder of prosperity, but both feared that their world would be shattered if Britain was defeated by Germany. The bulk of the army was drawn from the working classes. While in civilian life many lived in appalling poverty, there was a feeling that this was still better than the conditions their parents and grandparents had known. They were right. Many things had improved the lives of those at the bottom of society in the years before the First World War. Some, like cheaper food brought about by free trade, were the results of economic and political forces. Others like the introduction of Old Age Pensions were the consequences of the action of governments. Yet others – improved conditions in individual industries, for instance – were the result of workers' campaigning. Even the poorest people felt they had something to lose. Just glancing at the ruined villages on the Western Front, or hearing the pitiful tales of Belgian refugees in England, was enough to convince soldiers that the war was worth fighting to defeat the Germans on the far side of the Channel. They didn't want to see the same things happening at home.[57] Men from the Dominions had similar feelings. For most, Britain was still 'home', even if they had never set eyes on the place before joining the army. The security of Australia and New Zealand rested on the shield of the Royal Navy. Hard-nosed calculation jostled with patriotism in men's motives for fighting. Douglas Haig may not have fully understood why British and Dominion soldiers were so resilient, but his instinctive belief in their 'staying power' was correct.

Behind the Lines

'I have not got an Army in France really,' Haig wrote in March 1916 ' but a collection of divisions untrained for the Field. [The actual fighting Army will be evolved from them]'.[58] Heavy casualties and a massive expansion in the size of the army meant that men with military experience were spread thinly, especially in Territorial and Kitchener battalions. The result, as Haig noted ruefully during Loos, was that the army lacked 'junior officers with some tactical knowledge and training' to take the right decisions at the right time.[59] The same was true of NCOs. Ideally, the BEF should have been left to complete its training before being committed to battle, but in the strategic circumstances of 1916 that was a non-starter. Instead, the BEF had to go through the hideously costly business of on-the-job training while fighting an immensely tough, well-trained and well-prepared enemy. Effective training was a victim of the rapid and massive expansion of the army in early 1916. At that time GHQ had a *laissez faire* attitude to training, and did not ensure a uniform approach in the various schools of instruction being set up by formations at various levels.[60] This failure to take a lead, and spread best practice throughout the BEF, was a major mistake, despite Haig's keen interest in training. A typical diary entry concerns his visit to 25th Division: 'I impressed on all the need for *thoroughness* in military training'.[61]

Haig continued to see the broad principles of *FSR* as underpinning the BEF's efforts, and they did indeed provide experienced officers with a sound framework for decision-making.[62] But a semi-trained citizen army really needed a doctrinal cook-book, a prescriptive manual containing some easy to follow 'recipes' giving precise tactical guidance. May 1916 saw GHQ take a tentative step in this direction with the issue of *SS109 Training of Divisions for Offensive Action*, but much more needed to be done to address the problem of the lack of common doctrine and organisation across the BEF.[63]

Trench raiding was regarded as an important form of training.[64] Whereas in 1915, raids tended to have a local, tactical purpose, under Haig's regime they became part of an attritional strategy directed by GHQ. How useful they were is controversial, but the view of one astute observer is probably fair: 'Raids were frequently useful, and sometimes imperatively necessary; but the British raided too often.'[65] Criticism has tended to focus on whether or not raiding encouraged 'offensive spirit', but its positive side, of allowing soldiers to gain combat experience and develop fighting skills was more significant, especially in the run-up to the Somme.[66]

> The more I see of war, the more I realise how it all depends on administration and transportation . . . It takes little skill or imagination to see *where* you would like your army to be and *when;* it takes much more knowledge and hard work to know where you can place your forces and whether you can maintain them there.[67]

All the evidence suggests that Haig would have agreed with Field-Marshal Wavell, a senor commander in the Second World War who cut his teeth on the Western Front. Britain had never before created an organisation of the size and complexity of the army of the First World War. At its peak the BEF had to feed 2,700,000 men. It had nearly 50,000 motor vehicles and over 400,000 horses and mules, and in May to October 1918 an average 1,800 trains a week carried 400,000 tons. To keep one division in the field for one day required 'nearly 200 tons dead weight' of supplies, and Haig's army consisted of more than 60 divisions. Front-line troops were supported by a network of depots, hospitals, docks, canals, railways, repair shops, instructional schools, baths, canteens, recreational facilities and many other rear-area services.[68] As Haig fully realised, getting the logistics right was the foundation of everything else.

Significantly, on his first full day in office, Haig saw his Adjutant-General and Quartermaster-General, who dealt with personnel matters and logistics respectively (what the army called 'administration') before he visited the G Branch, which handled operations and intelligence. This signalled that, unlike his predecessor, he would take a close interest in administration.[69] A snapshot of his correspondence in April 1916 is instructive. Letters in his name were sent about, among other things, the elevation of the 9.2 inch howitzer, the inclusion of cooks in the war establishment of units, the formation of a labour corps, motor ambulance convoys, and Stokes mortars.

Q/1538/46, dated 22 April from G.O.C.-in-C to W.O. in reply to W.O. letter 77/6/4620 (A.3) dated 1/4/16 saying that a chest as a component part of the equipment of a Machine-gun is unnecessary. The chest will be regarded as a packing case and will be returned to England on arrival of the gun at its destination.

This was typical of the sort of paperwork that passed across his desk. Haig would not have gone deeply into or made decisions about every single matter – that is what his staff was for, and he gave his A and Q staff powerful institutional backing. He was not a micromanager, but he devoted a disproportionate amount of his time in 1916 to logistics, as there were major challenges that needed to be addressed.[70] He tended to engage with issues until he was content that challenges had been overcome, after which he stood back. Railways often cropped up in his diary in early 1917, but in March references dropped off because problems started to be resolved.

Nevertheless, Haig made two major logistic mistakes in 1916. First, he failed to address the organisational divide between operations and administrative staff: a consequence of *FSR II*, for which he was responsible, which was still causing problems in 1918. The split may have contributed to his second mistake, which was to underestimate the strain that the Somme offensive would place on the transport system, which, under the strain of moving men and materiel, came close to disintegration. Even if there had been a major breakthrough on the Somme, the logistic system could not have supported it.[71]

It was David Lloyd George, the Secretary of State for War, who

provided a way out of the problem, when in August 1916 he sent a
civilian railway expert to the Western Front. Sir Eric Geddes thoroughly
overhauled the BEF's transport network, and thus created the conditions
for eventual operational success.[72] Haig's single most important
contribution to logistics was to support Geddes in his work. Although he
was initially unsure, he very quickly came to appreciate Geddes's
qualities. The admiration was mutual and long-lasting. The arrival of a
civilian with temporary military rank, and his admission to Haig's inner
circle, caused some jealousy among the military. Haig's response was to
smooth over the problems – in October, he persuaded his QMG,
Maxwell, not to resign over a demarcation dispute with Geddes – but
without budging on the need to put 'men of *practical* experience' in key
posts 'of a civilian nature'; men such as Henry Maybury, a prominent
civil engineer who became Director of Roads in October 1917. To use
soldiers 'merely because they are generals and colonels, would be to
ensure failure!'[73]

Logistics posed major challenges to the BEF throughout the war. A
major reorganisation of motor transport over the winter of 1917,
complemented by a parallel investment in broad-gauge railways was
critical in allowing the BEF to weather the storm of the German
offensives in 1918, and then to carry the battle to the enemy. Road stone
(for repair of highways) was given virtually the same priority as
ammunition. It comes as no surprise to find Haig visiting a stone quarry,
noting much detailed information about this unglamorous but crucial
item in his diary; nor that he was one of the 'patron saints' of military
police, who had a vital role in traffic control.[74]

In his *Final Dispatch*, Haig paid tribute to his logisticians.

> The greatest testimony to the efficiency of these services is the rapidity of
> our advances, which otherwise would have been impossible. Their work
> was unostentatious, but its effect was far reaching.[75]

The support he gave them was not the least of Haig's contributions as
Commander-in-Chief.

The army that fought on the Somme was the most technologically
advanced in British history. Haig has often been depicted as an
antediluvian cavalryman, all at sea in a high-technology war, but this is

very wide of the mark. If he had a fault, it lay not ignoring innovations but expecting too much from untried weapons, as his attitude to gas at Loos and tanks on the Somme showed. The canard that in 1915 he said that 'the machine-gun was a much overrated weapon, and two per battalion were more than sufficient' was exploded as long ago as 1980 – not that that has stopped writers trotting it out to the present day. Yet again a much-quoted damning verdict on Haig is based on a single, dubious source: a hostile witness, this time Brigadier-General Baker-Carr. The facts are rather different. In 1909 Haig, in supporting some progressive views on the weapon at a high-level military conference, said that 'I have taken a good deal of interest in machine-guns', an interest that dates back at least to 1898 (see page 31). At about the time when Baker-Carr places the notorious remark, Haig was actually reporting to GHQ that 'at least four Machine-guns are required with each Infantry battalion' and telling his nephew, serving near Ypres, 'train your machine-guns, it will repay you'. There is simply no credible evidence that Haig ever thought them 'overrated' or wanted to limit their numbers. Machine-guns proliferated and machine-gunners prospered during Haig's tenure as C-in-C. Later on in the war he was enthusiastic about the introduction of massed machine-gun barrage fire.[76]

If any technology was cutting edge in the Great War, it was air power. Haig had been interested in the military employment of aircraft since at least 1911, and as I Corps and First Army commander had used them to good effect. As C-in-C he became the single most important backer of the Royal Flying Corps, for instance backing Trenchard against attempts by other parts of the army to hijack part of the air service.[77] Along with most other senior officers, Haig knew how critical aircraft were to the effective use of artillery and to intelligence gathering, and he was a diligent reader and annotator of RFC HQ's daily reports.

As in so many other spheres, Haig relied heavily on a specialist that he trusted, in this case Hugh Trenchard, who, as a major-general, was what today would be described as his Air Component Commander and had considerable latitude. They had much in common. Both were inarticulate in speech, had powerful personalities and shared the strategic vision of 'attacking the enemy'. Trenchard was the implementer and interpreter rather than the originator of the RFC's offensive strategy. His vision of 'relentless and incessant offensive' was set out in his September

1916 paper, *Future Policy in the Air*, which Haig approved without much argument. This meant RFC fighter aircraft ranging over enemy lines, to prevent German aircraft from reconnoitring and accurately directing fire onto British positions and to help protect the vulnerable British artillery-observation and ground-attack aeroplanes. Trenchard also saw this strategy as giving the British moral ascendancy – German morale would be affected by constantly having to operate under observation and attack from the RFC. Recent research suggests that his views were not misplaced.[78] The offensive strategy had critics at the time and subsequently. It was undoubtedly costly in pilots' lives and machines. Both Haig and Trenchard thought the price was worth paying. 'The air service . . . has done and is doing invaluable work,' Haig wrote in mid-September 1916, 'and has secured practically complete mastery over the Germans.'[79]

Trenchard proved himself inflexible in many ways; even if the strategy was sound, sometimes the tactics were not.[80] Here was the drawback of the freedom that Haig gave him. Not for the only time in his career, Haig was at fault for failing to 'grip' a subordinate: his loyalty blurred his judgment. But by 1918 Trenchard's single-mindedness and drive had contributed mightily to the creation of an extremely effective tactical air force. Trenchard responded to Haig's backing with life-long support for his boss. 'Haig made me all I rose to in France,' he recorded in his unpublished memoirs.[81] Haig's relationship with John Salmond, Trenchard's successor in 1918, was not as close, but was also effective. Haig deserved his place among pioneers of air power.

The Politics of War

High-level command is as much about politics as operations. Whether dealing with the government at home, with allies, or their subordinates, high commanders have to deploy a range of political skills to survive, let alone to thrive. Haig's political abilities have often been underrated, but he rose to lead the BEF in 1915 and held the post until 1919, in spite of the arrival of a hostile Prime Minister and seeing close allies replaced by sceptics in the critical posts of CIGS and Secretary of State for War. In part his longevity can be put down to external factors, such as the support of the press and the Unionists (Conservatives) in the coalition, but his own political skills cannot be dismissed.

Haig's ideal was that the government should give him the men and resources and then stand back and let him get on with the war. The period when reality came nearest to this model was 1916, when there was a fragile political consensus over the Somme. Asquith adopted very much a hands-off approach, and discontent about Haig's methods and the heavy losses in France was muted. Haig affected a lofty disdain for the whole murky business, and he certainly lacked Henry Wilson's enthusiasm for politics. But that did not stop him playing the game if he needed to. In October 1916 Ivor Maxse passed on the information from his brother Leo, the editor of the *National Review,* that F.E. Smith (the Attorney General) was conspiring to get Haig sacked. Maxse asked whether Leo should start a press campaign in favour of Haig. Haig replied that he would not get involved, but should Leo Maxse 'chose to come to France and go round the Army and see whether F.E. Smith's statements were true or false he was free to do so in the ordinary way'.[82] Clearly, Haig was not adverse to others working on his behalf. For two years Lord Derby carried out this role, first as Undersecretary and later Secretary of State for War. At first Haig was impressed. 'He has done wonders to get us men . . . We want an honest Englishman like him as Prime Minister at this time'.[83] The Field Marshal became disillusioned with Derby; Haig's lack of generosity towards colleagues who gave him loyal support was one of his less endearing traits.

It was a remarkable achievement for Britain to wage two total wars in the twentieth century and emerge with parliamentary democracy not only intact but enhanced. Waging total war meant that many freedoms were temporarily restricted and government took unprecedented powers – and the military was given greater political power and influence than it had in time of peace. In Germany the military effectively seized control of the government. By contrast, Britain ended the war with the civilian government firmly in control. Douglas Haig played a major role in this outcome. Unlike Sir John French, he did not see it as his or the army's place to 'make and unmake governments'.[84]

Too much has been made of Haig's royal connections. Being friendly with King George V did Haig's career no harm at all, but the King's influence on army appointments was not unlimited, and, in any case Haig had been closer to George's father, Edward VII. Smith-Dorrien was extremely friendly with King George, but this did nothing to save his career. Haig was but one of a number of senior officers who during the war was invited to correspond with the Monarch, either directly or through his private secretaries; others included French, Smith-Dorrien, Gough, Rawlinson and Robertson. Smith-Dorrien sent instalments of his journal to the Palace, while Doris forwarded extracts from Haig's diaries.'[U]se your own judgement,' Haig told her, 'send him of course whatever *you think necessary*'. That Haig should give this important political task to his wife, with minimum supervision, says a great deal about their relationship. Only when he became C-in-C did the King invite him to write directly to him.[85]

One of Haig's least favourite parts of his job was dealing with the press.[86] In the Boer War he had become aware of the political significance of the press and its power as an instrument of mass communication. Since he 'loathed interviews', he delegated most of his dealings with the press, except for the most significant figures, to Charteris and Sassoon.[87] This arm's-length approach allowed him to play the press with a degree of deniability. However, he got off on the wrong foot with the reporters accredited to GHQ. One of them, Philip Gibbs, wrote that Haig showed a 'complete misunderstanding of our purpose and our work' by saying 'You want to get hold of little stories of heroism, and so forth, and to write them up in a bright way to make good reading for Mary Ann in the kitchen, and the man in the street'. The journalists' reaction rapidly disabused him of this notion. But from this low point, relations improved to such an extent that, at the end of the war, there was a ceremony in the highly symbolic setting of the Hohenzollern Bridge in occupied Cologne at which Haig thanked the press with the words 'Gentlemen, you have played the game like men!' He then gave each man a handshake, and a small Union Jack. (Rather ungratefully, the reporters 'thought this was too much like a cracker off a Christmas tree'.[88])

Nothing illustrates the point that the C-in-C could not devote his full attention to fighting battles better than his dealings with the press during the Somme. He tried to avoid meeting Colonel Repington, military correspondent of *The Times*. In the end a disgruntled Haig did meet Repington, who, despite their mutual dislike, was an important supporter. Even more critical was the visit of Lord Northcliffe on 21 July; although Haig had to be persuaded that meeting him was a good idea, the two men got on well, and a mutually beneficial relationship developed. Philip Sassoon recognised the importance of the meeting, which 'to my mind will prove as good as a victory . . . one must do all one can to direct Press opinion in the right channel'. Sassoon's reaction to Northcliffe's article reflected Haig's own contemptuous attitudes to popular journalism: 'apparently the British Public have much more confidence in him [Haig] now they know at what time he has his breakfast!' But, as Haig was to discover, Northcliffe could be a fickle friend and dangerous enemy.[89]

Haig and Religion

Shortly after he became C-in-C, one Sunday morning, Haig encountered a man who was to play an important role in his life. 'I attended the Scotch Church,' he wrote in his diary for 9 January 1916. 'The clergyman . . . is most earnest and impressive, quite after the old covenanting style'. He was the Reverend George Duncan, a 32-year-old recently ordained into the Church of Scotland. The two men developed a close relationship, Duncan becoming the spiritual equivalent of Mickey Ryan. Like Ryan, whatever his formal title, Duncan had a special responsibility to Haig. When Duncan proposed leaving for a different post, his superior was horrified, likening him to Aaron, who held up Moses' hands. This was a telling comparison: in the Biblical story, as long as Moses' arms were raised, the Israelites were victorious in battle (Exodus 17).[90]

Duncan's services became a highlight of Haig's week, offering him a brief period of spiritual refreshment. He appreciated that Duncan 'preaches a fine manly Christianity always', and regularly commented on his sermons in his diary. After the war Haig candidly told Duncan that 'It was very difficult to keep going all the time of the long War . . . I can truly say that you were a great help to me . . . in putting things into proper perspective on the Sundays'.[91] Part of Duncan's appeal was probably a sense of coming home to the church of his childhood, especially since Haig had grown rather weary of insipid Anglican sermons. Charteris recorded 'a regular Scottish Sunday' in 1917 when he and Haig dissected the sermon, just as he had as a child in Scotland. Haig's faith, and his attachment to the Church of Scotland, endured until his death.[92]

On occasions Duncan did deliver sermons that he thought appropriate for Haig – once realising that a sermon 'aglow with confident hope' would have been better than the one he actually delivered. But it is too crude, and impugns Duncan's integrity, to argue that he simply preached messages that Haig wanted to hear. Duncan never heard Haig speak of himself as God's instrument, but was sure such beliefs were held 'in all humility, not out of egotism or wishful thinking, but with a sober grasp of the situation as he saw it'.[93]

Also unsustainable is the idea that his sense of destiny 'absolved Haig from examining his methods of command'.[94] Apart from the fact that Haig underwent a personal learning process throughout the war, Duncan himself was no tub-thumping fundamentalist; he was a sophisticated liberal academic theologian who went on to an extremely distinguished post-war career. He categorically denied that Haig was a 'religious fanatic' or that 'spiritual conceit' had clouded Haig's military judgement:

> With some men, no doubt, belief in a divine 'call' leads easily to fanaticism. But Haig was no fanatic. There was about him a mental balance which was associated not a little with his stern sense of duty; and like other devout men down the ages he heard in the call of duty the voice of God. He takes his place with those heroic figures (like Moses and Joshua in the Scripture records, or like Cromwell and Lincoln in the story of the nations) who in some critical hour of history begin by recognising the need for action in the situation which confronts them, and then, in a spirit of obedience and faith in God, find themselves braced to meet it with courage and resolution, and in so doing draw strength from unseen sources.[95]

Like many of his generals, Haig saw religion and morale as closely linked, and chaplains had an important role to play in sustaining fighting spirit. Very early in his tenure as C-in-C Haig told the Deputy Chaplain General, Bishop L.H. Gwynne, that 'A good chaplain is as valuable as a good general'. Randall Davidson, the Archbishop of Canterbury, visited GHQ in May 1916 and was told by Haig 'that the Chaplains should preach to [the troops] about the objects of Great Britain in carrying on this war. We have no selfish motive, but are fighting for the good of humanity'. Haig had been irritated by squabbles between High and Low Church padres, and he insisted that they 'must cease quarrelling amongst themselves. In the Field we cannot tolerate any narrow sectarian ideas. We must all be united.'[96]

In January, at an Army Commanders' conference, Haig had ordered that the role of padres, up to that time restricted to religious duties and acting as welfare officers behind the lines, was to be expanded: they could now minister in the trenches. During Davidson's visit in May the C-in-C was particularly keen to emphasise the importance of this change. Although the Archbishop 'pressed Haig for criticism about the work of the chaplains' he 'could not elicit anything except laudation'. The C-in-C enthused about 'the fine young type of Padre now at work in all parts of the line'. By the end of June, Haig was singing the praises of 'the Parsons' to the King, giving them a large share of the credit for the 'great spirits' of the troops.[97] He continued to believe that chaplains had an essential part to play. In a speech to generals in autumn 1917, he said 'he believed in the power of prayer' and praised the 'magnificent work' of the padres which 'had kept up the morale of the troops'.[98]

Haig and Strategy

Haig's strategic aim was simple, although difficult to achieve: to take the offensive and inflict a crushing defeat on the German army, to force Germany to accept the victors' terms, and to deter it from military adventures for the foreseeable future. Britain's security would be secured by neutralising the German fleet, the evacuation of Belgium and, crucially, the restoration of the balance of power in Europe. For Haig, the logic of this position was obvious. Although measures must be taken to safeguard Britain's position in the Middle East and Asia, every sinew must be strained to defeat the Germans in the main theatre, the Western Front. Haig had been worried by the growth of German power for some years, and believed the war was being fought over nothing less than 'the existence of England as a free nation'. He was absolutely correct in identifying the German threat as being of the first magnitude.[99] But he was not seeking a 'total' victory such as the overthrow of the Imperial regime in Berlin. A chastened Germany would be enough; a ruined Germany would destabilise Europe.[100]

For all that, his strategic vision had distinct limitations. Kitchener and Robertson shared Haig's belief in the need for a decisive victory in the field, but, unlike them, and the government, Haig had the luxury of concentrating solely on the Western Front. Haig's constant demands for every man and gun to be sent to France were unrealistic. His disillusionment with Robertson during 1917 was bound up with his view that the CIGS was too ready to divert resources away from France. This was utterly unfair. Britain was fighting a global war, and defence of the Middle East and India was critical to survival as a great Imperial power. At one level Haig, who before the war had been much concerned with imperial defence, realised this: in March 1918 he called for 'immediate action in Persia' to stall the German threat to India and Afghanistan.[101] Usually Haig was too focused on the Western Front to raise his eyes to the hills.

When it came to Britain's allies, Haig's record was mixed but generally positive. The anti-German powers came together not out of friendship but because of a common threat. All had their own interests, which they were perfectly willing to pursue at the expense of their coalition partners. Linguistic problems were overcome rather more easily than cultural prejudices about states which had been natural enemies for years. Yet the advantages of fighting in coalition vastly outweighed the negatives. Jointly, the anti-German coalition possessed formidable power. Severally, its members faced at best stalemate, more likely defeat.[102]

Once constructed, like buildings, coalitions need to be kept in good repair by constant maintenance. In some ways Haig was a good citizen of the coalition, but his single-mindedness led him to undervalue the importance of the other fronts in a multi-front war. He certainly underestimated the significance of Russia.[103] In mid-July 1916 the question of sending guns and ammunition to Russia arose, not for the first time. Haig dug in his heels, arguing that 'the most patriotic and the wisest policy is to provide all that we require ourselves before we give to others'.[104] It was frustrating that the BEF might be denied munitions at a time when it seemed a victory on the Somme was near. The government had to take the wider view that it was essential to keep Russia in the war.

Italy also got short shrift. In December 1916 Haig successfully fought against 200 guns being lent to the Italians – he feared, with good reason, that he would not get them back, at least not in time use them in the new campaigning season. At the same meeting he argued that 'it was a waste of power to send guns and munitions to Russia until it was certain that she was able to use them'. Instead he requested that the Belgians 'be given the heavy guns which had been promised them'.[105] This brief exchange unwittingly revealed a great deal about Douglas Haig's weaknesses as a coalition commander. He downplayed the importance of Italy (as he did consistently) and had effectively written off Russia as an ally, even though the collapse of the Eastern Front would (and in 1918, did) put the Allies at a huge disadvantage. But, with an eye on his forthcoming Flanders offensive, at the December 1916 meeting Haig was keen that the Belgians should receive guns (although not from the BEF).[106]

The question of the Salonika campaign cropped up in a conference in June 1916, as it did with monotonous regularity at Anglo-French summits throughout the war. To Haig, Salonika was a French folly that made no strategic sense, particularly given that he was about to launch an offensive to relieve the attacks on the French army at Verdun. 'All our resources in men and ammunition should therefore be sent to the decisive points, viz., France, and not wasted against Bulgars in the Balkans'. In purely military terms Haig was correct, but he could not – or perhaps would not – see that, as the Salonika campaign was sustained largely for reasons of French domestic politics, Britain had to acquiesce for reasons of coalition harmony.[107]

And yet criticism of Haig as a coalition commander should not go too far. However much he might privately (or semi-publicly) complain about his Allies, the British army could not go it alone, and Haig never lost sight of this. He was keenly aware of the coalition dimension to his job. For the Somme, Joffre was the *de facto* overall commander on the Western Front, given the role of directing the offensive. We should judge Haig on his actions rather than his words, and essentially he was a loyal and co-operative ally. He could be an awkward partner; he could be petty and bear grudges; but on the things that really mattered, he was co-operative. Kiggell was once described as 'cordially disliking and mistrusting the French, yet honestly trying to do them justice'. Much the same could be said of Kiggell's boss.[108]

Preparing the Somme

Allied strategy for the coming year had been decided at a conference at Chantilly on 6 December 1915; Haig, not yet C-in-C, was absent. The British, Russians and Italians accepted Joffre's plan for synchronised attacks to overwhelm the Germans. In a major rationalisation of the machinery of command, Joffre was made the effective director of the Allied effort.[109]

One of Haig's primary tasks on assuming command was to decide what part the BEF would play in this strategy. Lord Kitchener's instructions to him on becoming C-in-C stressed that Haig's 'governing policy' should be to 'achieve . . . the closest co-operation of French and British as a united army'. However, Kitchener continued, 'I wish you distinctly to understand that your command is an independent one, and that you will in no case come under the orders of any Allied General further than the necessary co-operation with our Allies above referred to'.[110] Haig had to negotiate with Joffre knowing that he did not have complete freedom, but the BEF had to be committed to a major battle during 1916 in support of the French.

'Strategically, there is no doubt,' Charteris noted, that Flanders was

> the best place for us to attack. It strikes direct at the main railway communications of all the German armies. The Germans could not even make good their retreat. A victory, however great, on the Somme would still let them get back to the Meuse.[111]

Haig viewed the coast of Belgium as 'an objective of great political and naval as well as military importance'. He took clearance of the littoral with the utmost seriousness, discussing joint operations with Rear-Admiral Bacon and Lieutenant-General Hunter-Weston (the latter having experience of commanding 29th Division in the amphibious landings at Gallipoli) and pressed Plumer on the question of operations at Ypres.[112] There is no doubt that if he could have ignored the French he would have fought around Ypres in 1916. As the defences in the Salient were far less developed than they would later become it is conceivable that the BEF would have done rather better in a 'Third Ypres' fought in 1916 than it did during the real-life Somme.[113] The problem was that 'the time of execution must depend on General Joffre's plan for the general offensive in the spring'.[114]

The true pattern of Haig's relationship with the French was established at the end of December, when Joffre proposed an Anglo-French offensive in the Somme area, and asked for the British to take over a portion of front held by his Tenth Army.[115] Haig agreed, only to receive another, more ambitious request. On 20 January he and Joffre agreed to a preliminary British 'wearing-out' fight on the Somme on or around 20 April, to be followed by a British offensive on the Flanders coast and a French attack further south.[116] A few days later Joffre raised the bar with the suggestion that the BEF mount an additional attritional battle elsewhere in May. This was difficult for Haig. It was becoming clear that that it was politically unacceptable for the army to be used in this way. Perhaps Joffre, himself under domestic political pressure, was testing the new C-in-C to see how much he could get away with. Haig demurred at the suggestion, fearing such battles 'will appear . . . as 'failures', thereby affecting our "credit" in the world, which is of vital importance as money in England is becoming scarcer'.

Wearing out the enemy and then launching the main attack was in accordance with Haig's military thinking, but he wanted a properly co-ordinated, continuous effort 'by all the allies'; Joffre's plan smacked of dumping the job no one wanted on the new boy. On 14 February Haig and Joffre agreed to attack on the Somme at the beginning of July. Although the idea of preliminary offensives in April and May was discarded, Haig agreed to a limited attack in the Ypres–La Bassée sector one or two weeks before the main effort on the Somme.[117]

Robertson's appointment as CIGS signalled the primacy of the Western Front and was a tacit admission of the bankruptcy of the alternatives: Gallipoli, Mesopotamia and Salonika.[118] During the first period of the war the General Staff had been marginalised in the making of strategy by the dominance of Kitchener and Lieutenant-Colonel Maurice Hankey, who acted as secretary to the inner cabinet.[119] 'Wullie' Robertson, a working-class ex-ranker who had clawed his way to the top by sheer talent, changed that. He possessed a powerful mind and a blunt, dogged personality and had refused to take the post unless he was to be the sole source of military advice to the government, thus clipping Kitchener's wings. Robertson's partnership with Haig was never one of equals – Robertson always saw Haig as the senior man, and Haig was privately condescending about Robertson, calling him 'the iron ration' – but it dominated British strategy for the next two years and more.

The War Council was reluctant to acknowledge the primacy of the front in France and Belgium. A War Committee meeting on 13 January produced only provisional acceptance of significant Franco-British offensives in the West, leaving the door open for further 'Eastern' operations. It seems that it was a combination of Kitchener and Balfour who tipped the balance. At a meeting on 21 January 1916 Kitchener assured Balfour that what was proposed was 'of an essentially different character' to battles such as Loos, involving exhaustion of the enemy reserves rather than a breakthrough attempt. This 'heavy and continuous pressure', hopefully combined with Russian offensives, would 'bring the Central Powers to terms by the end of the year'.[120]

Kitchener and Robertson both believed that that war could only be won on the Western Front, through attrition, and that participation in a combined offensive with the French was essential to keep the coalition alive. Neither man was optimistic about the possibility of achieving a successful breakthrough.[121] Douglas Haig had a rather different view.

The Chantilly concept of a co-ordinated Allied strategy unravelled with alarming speed in February. The German offensive at Verdun launched on 21 February 1916 decisively derailed the Allies' existing plans.[122] Erich von Falkenhayn, *de facto* commander of the German army, probably intended a limited attritional offensive to inflict such losses that the French would be forced to negotiate a peace favourable to Germany.[123] Joffre's response was to rush troops to Verdun. The battle developed a momentum of its own. On 25 February Haig met Kitchener to discuss the British response. Verdun had taken Haig by surprise, and now he argued, in the case of French success, for an attack by Third Army, or, in the case of catastrophe, for an attack alongside the French. If however, a 'stalemate' ensued, the burden of takng the war to the enemy would pass to the BEF. The French should be asked to take over line from the British, who would launch a major offensive 'on the front from Ypres to Armentières', unless the French were able to participate in the planned combined offensive on the Somme.[124] They were, but Verdun severely reduced their committment. By default, the British took the lead in the Battle of the Somme.

Understandably, the French pressed Haig to attack to help them at Verdun. This would have been playing into to the enemy's hands, as the Germans hoped for a premature offensive by the inexperienced BEF.[125] Haig needed the maximum possible time to train his raw troops and allow as much supporting technology of 'machine warfare' as possible to be deployed. If the battle was delayed into August, then more heavy guns would be available, and perhaps the first tanks too.[126] Haig therefore steadfastly refused pleas and demands for premature action, giving Georges Clemenceau, a senior French politican, a realistic assessement in early May that the BEF needed 'much careful training before we could attack with hope of success'.[127]

Armed with a letter from Haig requesting formal permission for a major offensive, Robertson went to the War Committee on 7 April. Kitchener, having been won over by Robertson, supported the request, arguing that Haig would be continuing the pattern of present operations but on a greater scale. Robertson stressed that Haig 'would not do any foolish thing'. At length, the War Cabinet gave its assent, but political approval of what became the Somme offensive was fragile and contingent on events.[128]

The suspicion is that Haig misled Robertson, Kitchener and the War Committee by implying (or stating) that the battle would be a larger and more intensified version of existing operations, rather than an attempt at a breakthrough.[129] While it is impossible to know precisely what Haig said to Robertson and Kitchener, and one should never forget his inarticulacy, it is unlikely that he deliberately deceived them. In late March, for instance, Kitchener warned Haig 'to beware of the French, and to husband the strength of the Army in France'.[130] Kitchener's comments about husbanding concerned his worries about French pressure for a premature offensive, not Haig's methods of attack.[131]

Haig told Robertson in late May that, while he intended to wear out the enemy 'by raids and every means', he explicitly stated that he would 'be ready to support the French by a resolute attack'. Haig went further, referring to preparations to 'exploit a success on the lines of 1806'. This referred to the deep cavalry pursuit after Napoleon's destruction of the Prussian army at Jena-Auerstadt. The reference should have been obvious to Robertson, a cavalryman and former Staff College commandant. In the same letter Haig wrote about the difficulties of advancing beyond the 'Pozières ridge' and the possibility of establishing 'favourable positions' for a 1917 spring campaign. This letter reflects the ambiguities in the planning for the Somme. Haig prepared for both a limited attritional offensive and to take advantage of opportunities in a more ambitious operation.[132] Around the same time Haig expressed very similar views to Rawlinson and Lord Bertie, the British Ambassador in Paris. Haig prepared the ground at home by briefing the press at GHQ in late May in stark terms. The British people had to learn 'patience, self-sacrifice and confidence' in ultimate victory. 'The aim for which the war is being waged is the destruction of German militarism. Three years of war and the loss of one-tenth of the manhood of the nation is not too great a price to pay in so great a cause'.[133]

The planning for the Somme was rife with ambiguities. Joffre's view shifted as Verdun wore on: now it was seen as a way of indirectly helping the struggle at Verdun through attrition and, by pinning German forces to the Western Front, perhaps aiding the Russians. By May 1916 Haig too was less optimistic about what the forthcoming battle could achieve. Indeed, for a brief period when it seemed that no French troops would be available for the Somme, Haig thought about giving priority to an attack in Flanders.[134] The idea of a preliminary offensive was quietly dropped. As the date of the battle grew near Haig still hoped it might still bring about a breakthrough, but accepted it might turn out to be an attritional slog. 'We do not expect any great advance', wrote Charteris on 30 June,

> or any great place of arms to fall. We are fighting primarily to wear down the German armies and the German nation, to interfere with their plans, gain some valuable position and generally to prepare for the great decisive offensive which must come sooner or later, if not this year or even next year . . . It is always well to disclaim great hopes before an attack.[135]

An inter-Allied conference on 26 May proved the crunch time for setting the date of the battle. Haig thoroughly investigated the pros and cons of holding out for an attack on 15 August, when the BEF's preparations would be well advanced, but 'came to the conclusion that we *must* march to the support of the French'. Robertson agreed.[136] Haig did float the idea of 15 August, which produced a predictable explosion from Joffre, but, his point being made, settled on early July.[137] Ultimately, the BEF fought on the Somme because of the demands of coalition warfare. The French, the senior partners, set the agenda, and the British had to fall in with it.

The Plans for the Somme

In the run-up to the battle there were lengthy negotiations about objectives between Haig and Joffre. The initial idea of the British attacking in support of the efforts of French Sixth Army astride the River Somme went by the board. While the French intended a limited, attritional battle, Joffre indicated to Haig that the offensive could be decisive.[138] A fortnight before the battle began Haig outlined his plans at a conference with his Army Commanders:

> As regards the objective of the Fourth Army attack, it was, *Firstly*, to gain the line of the Pozières heights, organise good observation posts, and consolidate a strong position. Then, secondly, (a) If enemy's defence broke down, occupy enemy's third line (on line Flers–Miraumont) push detachment of Cavalry to hold Bapaume and work Northwards with bulk of Cavalry and other arms so as to widen the breach in enemy's line, and capture the enemy's forces in the re-entrant south of Arras. The hill at Monchy le Preux (5 miles South-east of Arras) with intermediate points between it and Bapaume, seems a suitable line for the Cavalry to hold as a flank guard for covering the operations of the other arms.
>
> (b) *If enemy's defence is strong* and fighting continues for many days, as soon as Pozières heights are gained, the position should be consolidated, and improved, while arrangements will be made to start an attack on the Second Army front.[139]

This plan was certainly ambitious. Its context was reports by intelligence agents of substantial German forces leaving the Western Front in response to the Russian Brusilov offensive, which had begun on 4 June.[140] But it was not simply a 'haroosh' attack: bursting through, smashing the German trenches and reopening mobile warfare all in one day. Rather, Haig anticipated a battle that would unfold in stages, possibly over a prolonged period. In that sense it was 'step-by-step' attack. Haig was clear that '[t]he length of each bound forward by the Infantry depends on the area which has been prepared by the Artillery'.

Pushing through the German front lines and then occupying the German Second Position on the key high ground of the Pozières ridge was the first stage, and what occurred next depended on the state of the enemy and other factors. Haig envisaged putting a 'Plan B' into operation if

German resistance proved particularly tough, switching the offensive to Second Army's front at Ypres, but logistic problems and Joffre's insistence on the priority of the Somme made this option impractical.

If, however, the attack broke through German resistance in the First and Second Positions on the first day of the battle cavalry would be committed in a more ambitious role, as the British offensive would move into a mobile phase. After the capture of Bapaume (10 miles away), possibly by cavalry dashing to surprise the defenders, mounted forces would be pushed out to form a defensive flank. There would then be an attempt to destroy German forces south of Arras.[141] This was a significantly less ambitious concept than operations on the scale of an 1806-style pursuit. So Haig prepared for either a modest or major success. Hoping for a major triumph, perhaps he expected something rather less dramatic, hence he planned for various degrees of success.

What happened at Loos suggested that limiting the advance to the first position acted as a disincentive for troops and commanders to take advantage of initial success while the enemy was shaken. Developing the ideas that had emerged in 1915, Haig designed all-arms groups of 'cavalry and mobile troops' that would 'bite' into the enemy line and then enlarge the breach prior to exploitation. 'The keynote is co-operation with the other arms,' he directed in training instructions for cavalry he wrote in March 1916.

> When a break in [the Enemy's] line is made, cavalry and mobile troops must be at hand to advance at once to make a bridgehead (until relieved by infantry) beyond the gap with the object of checking hostile reserves which Enemy might rush up, and so give time for our own divisions to deploy. At the same time our mounted troops must cooperate with our main attacking force in widening the gap both by
> (a) Operating offensively in rear, of that part of the Enemy's defences which may still be holding out as well as
> (b) By extending the flank of the 'bridgehead' as a protection to our attacking Forces' outer flank.[142]

To this end, on 3 March 1916 Haig disbanded the two Cavalry Corps, instead devolving the cavalry divisions to the four Armies and the newly-formed Reserve Corps.[143]

Hubert Gough was a key figure in this emerging tactical concept. He was appointed in April to command the Reserve Corps, which became Reserve Army in June. Exactly what Haig intended Gough's force to do at the beginning of the forthcoming battle is not easy to divine. '[T]he area in which the Reserve Corps [sic] may be employed,' noted Kiggell on 4 June, 'must be dependent on events, and cannot be foreseen.' For that reason Haig was opposed to using some of its artillery to support XIII and XV Corps' battle if it hampered the ability of Reserve Army to act as a unified formation.[144] At one point Haig was thinking of placing these corps under Gough, apparently under Rawlinson's overall command.[145] Part of Gough's job specification was to train the cavalry in the new methods. '[H]e is to spread the "doctrine",' Haig noted, 'and get cavalry officers to believe in the power of their arm when acting in co-operation with guns and infantry'.[146] 'Opportunities to use cavalry, supported by guns, machine-guns etc., and infantry,' Haig informed Rawlinson in April, 'should be sought for, both during the early stages of the attack and subsequently.'[147] Although the evidence is scanty, some heroic detective work by Stephen Badsey has produced the persuasive argument that Reserve Army was to act as a sort of conveyor belt to exploit Fourth Army's success, with 25th Division in the lead, at least two cavalry divisions behind, to be followed by II Corps' infantry.[148]

This was a bold, imaginative response to the problems identified in 1915, firmly grounded in the practice of earlier years, and anticipating many of the post-1918 developments in mobile warfare. But it was also extremely ambitious, and the staff work and traffic-control issues alone would have severely taxed the inexperienced BEF.[149] As it happened, 'Gough's Mobile Army' was the victim of a fundamental disagreement between Haig and Rawlinson about how the battle of the Somme should be fought.

Rawlinson's plan aimed for limited advances to capture the high ground followed by a pause to break up the inevitable German counterattacks. He rightly suspected that Haig would disapprove of his scheme, but seems to have misunderstood what Haig the C-in-C wanted to achieve, writing that 'It is clear that D.H. would like us to do the whole thing in one rush'.[150] The eventual plan that emerged was an unhappy compromise between two fundamentally different concepts of operations. The men also wrangled over the length of the preliminary bombardment, with Haig eventually deciding on a prolonged period. Evidently Rawlinson had little faith in Haig's plan and paid lip service to the C-in-C's concept while working quietly to subvert it.

In mid-June Gough's Army was effectively reduced to a cavalry force, as II Corps was placed in GHQ reserve, and Rawlinson persuaded Haig that Reserve Army should come under Fourth Army's command rather than GHQ's.[151] Haig took the decision in order to ease command-and-control problems: 'once a break is effected, a Commander and Staff is necessary to take charge on the spot', and it made more sense for Gough to be under the immediate operational commander than GHQ. Perhaps Haig had the unfortunate precedent of the reserves at Loos in mind.

Haig clearly hoped that these decisions would facilitate the transition from trench fighting to mobile warfare, but actually they gave Rawlinson the opportunity to block the more ambitious part of Haig's plans.[152] Two of Gough's cavalry divisions were deployed five miles back on the central axis of Fourth Army's advance, but they were only to be committed to action 'if the Enemy's resistance breaks down'. Moreover, the 'Cavalry of the Reserve Army will remain in their places of assembly until . . . [the reserve infantry divisions of III and X Corps] have moved forward and cleared the line of advance for the Cavalry'; in other words, the horsemen should not get in the way of anyone else. Later Rawlinson tried to cover his tracks by claiming that Haig intended Gough and the cavalry only to be used 'should we be successful all along the line in gaining the whole of the objectives allotted for the first day'.[153] The gulf between the thinking of the Commander-in-Chief and his principal operational commander could not have been starker.

All this raises the question of whether 'Rawly' was really the right man to conduct the battle. Haig knew from the Davies incident in aftermath of Neuve Chapelle that Rawlinson was ruthless and devious (see page 110), and he was clearly aware that the Fourth Army commander was out of sympathy with his vision of the battle. As late as 27 June Haig had to make clear what he expected Rawlinson to do. The main reason why Haig kept faith with Rawlinson was that he viewed him as the best man for the job. In December 1915 Haig had recommended Rawlinson for promotion knowing that he was 'not a sincere man' but believing 'he has brains and experience'.[154] Six months later, Haig had not changed his mind.

On the eve of battle, Haig jotted in his diary that:

With God's help, I feel hopeful for tomorrow. The men are in splendid spirits: several have said that they have never before been so instructed and informed of the nature of the operation before them. The wire has never been so well cut, nor the artillery preparation so thorough. I have seen personally all the Corps Commanders and one and all are full of confidence.[155]

The following day, 1 July 1916, would show that this confidence was horribly misplaced.

6

Attrition

The First of July 1916, the First Day on the Somme, is the most notorious day in British military history. After a seven-day bombardment, at 7.30 a.m. 14 British and 6 French infantry divisions went into battle. Third Army's diversionary attack at Gommecourt was repulsed. In the northern sector of Fourth Army there was almost complete failure. South of the Roman road that bisected the battlefield XV Corps took Mametz, XIII Corps captured all of its objectives, and French Sixth Army made major gains. The dreadful 'butcher's bill' for the BEF was 57,470, of which 19,240 were killed or died of wounds.

Haig spent the morning of 1 July at his Advanced HQ. At noon, a time of death and blood on the battlefield, Haig calmly picked up his pen and wrote a letter to Lord Esher.[1] After some lines about press matters, he discussed the progress of the attack. It had, Haig wrote

> progressed well. I have great hopes of getting some measure of success . . .
> The wire has been more thoroughly cut than ever before, and also the
> Artillery bombardment has been methodical and continuous . . . Forgive
> a disjointed letter, but a battle is going on and telegrams keep coming in
> at every moment.

This letter is eloquent testimony to the impotence of the high commander on the Western Front. Although it may seem incongruous, or even obscene, for the general in command of a great army to be catching up with his routine paperwork in the middle of a terrible battle, in truth it was as sensible a use of Haig's time as any. Given the lack of communications, Haig did not know what was going on and was unable to affect the events on the battlefield. Because he noted the exact time on his letter we have an idea of how much he knew about the true situation four-and-a-half hours after the infantry went over the top. As he mentioned that the French were 'already talking about the Rhine', perhaps he was aware of the success of French Sixth Army. As his diary shows, the reports he received from the front line were incomplete, often false and almost invariably too rosy. Comments appear in his diary such as 'Reports up to 8 a.m. most satisfactory. Our troops had everywhere crossed the enemy's front trenches'.[2]

Haig was also in a state of ignorance about events on the southern part of Fourth Army's front, where there was the opportunity for major gains. The advance of XIII Corps was achieved at a high cost in casualties, but, as a relieved Rawlinson noted in his diary, they had 'taken all the objectives allotted to them'.[3] The French on their flank had done spectacularly well, with very light losses. Now was the time for Fourth Army to push on in this sector. It did not happen. The evidence is overwhelming that Rawlinson spurned the real possibility of achieving a breakthrough on the British southern flank.

Rawlinson had badly misjudged the strength of the German defences in the south, and so the objectives of XIII Corps had been limited to the First Position. It is possible that had the Second Position been an objective it could have been taken as well – although, given the heavy casualties and exhaustion of the assault divisions, the reserve formations (two brigades of 17th (Northern) Division for XV Corps, 9th (Scottish) Division for XIII Corps) would have had to have been committed. Actually, these troops remained in reserve. The situation in the early afternoon cried out for Gough's Reserve Army to fight its way onto the Second Position. The Germans had few forces to stop a determined push on from their newly captured First Position. The Second Position was weakly defended, and could probably have been overrun on 2 July, with the tantalising prospect of seizing High Wood and Delville Wood, which in reality took months to capture at the cost of thousands of lives. It is even conceivable that Gough's force could have penetrated the German Third Position, which was extremely sketchy at this stage.

In the real world Rawlinson ignored Haig's clearly expressed concept of operations. He paid no attention to Gough, who with the nucleus of his Reserve Army staff simply hung aimlessly about Fourth Army HQ with no orders and nothing to do. Rawlinson does not seem even to have briefed Gough on the situation and, worst of all, at midday issued an order that Reserve Army was to stand down. At 12.15 he wrote in his diary: 'there is of course no hope of getting cavalry through today'.[4] It is possible that that afternoon Congreve, XIII Corps commander, after carrying out a personal reconnaissance, telephoned Rawlinson for permission to advance, only to be turned down.[5] That evening Rawlinson seems to have been glad to assign Gough the northernmost two corps of Fourth Army as a separate Army command, but, as these were holding a stretch of line, it signalled the final demise of Haig's original Reserve Army concept.

Why did Rawlinson refuse to advance? The logistic problems of moving Reserve Army into battle perhaps provide a partial explanation, but that does not account for the failure to use local reserves – and even a modest advance would have taken some valuable ground and helped French XX Corps. Most likely Rawlinson had made up his mind long before the battle. In a classic example of cognitive dissonance he refused to believe optimistic reports.

Haig was little more than a bystander while his plans were being wrecked by his principal subordinate. Haig arrived at Querrieu, Rawlinson's HQ, 'after lunch'. Haig did not intervene to rescind the order for Reserve Army to stand down, if indeed he knew of it. He requested, but did not order, Fourth Army to continue to attack on 2 July to gain ground that would leave his divisions well placed to attack the Second Position. At 5 p.m. Haig was still optimistic about a breakthrough, ordering two divisions of II Corps forward 'as the Fourth Army was putting through its Reserve' with orders that they were not to be used up in the wearing-out battle.[6] Two hours later Rawlinson, presumably as a result of Haig's prodding, ordered that the attack should go on 'under corps arrangements as early as possible compatible with adequate previous artillery preparations'.[7]

Even the official historian discreetly suggested that a breakthrough, even if it failed to inflict a major defeat on the Germans, would have forced the defenders

to retire on a broad front and take up a new position, which could not be made as strong as the one abandoned . . . Against any new enemy position taken up in the field after his expulsion from the Somme defences the offensive could be repeated with still better chances of success.[8]

So the evidence strongly suggests Haig's plan to seize the German Second Position on the first day of the battle was achievable, at least on the southern sector. This does not absolve Douglas Haig from the mistakes he committed in planning and preparing the Somme, errors that had terrible consequences for tens of thousands of soldiers and their families. It does however severely undermine the arguments of his critics. Far from being an egregious folly, a romantic throwback to the days of Napoleon, Haig's plan to use a cavalry-based all-arms force to exploit success and fight its way forward was a sensible response to the tactical situation. If employed, in all likelihood it would have brought at least modest success, and an advance of one to three miles would have taken the BEF past German strongpoints like Thiepval that on this plane of reality took months of fighting to capture.[9]

This is not to argue that, if Rawlinson had committed the mobile reserves, Haig's ambitious breakthrough plan would have succeeded in full. Apart from anything else, the BEF's logistic system was incapable of sustaining a major advance (see p. 149). It might have led to the battle Haig dreamed of (a mobile, or at least semi-open, affair in the Arras area), and how the BEF would have fared in this is anyone's guess. But even an advance of twenty or so miles ending in a resumption of static warfare would have been a major political victory that enhanced Britain's standing in the coalition and might, just might, have undermined German confidence sufficiently to have brought about an offer of a compromise peace on terms acceptable to the Allies. While Haig has often been accused of blindly adhering to a doctrine of breakthrough, on the first day on the Somme it was Rawlinson's rigid refusal to countenance anything but a limited bite-and-hold approach that was disastrous.

Here is not the place for a detailed analysis of the reasons for the BEF's failure and success,[10] but we can identify elements for which Haig was personally responsible. On the evening before his men went over the top, Haig told Doris that 'I feel that everything possible for us to do to achieve success has been done'.[11] These words reflected the huge efforts put into preparing the army for battle – and, as Commander-in-Chief, Haig deserved a share of the credit for any success and ultimate responsibility for any failures. His operational plan was sound in principle, but far too ambitious in practice given the state of training and inexperience of his army. The fact that he failed to impose his will on Rawlinson, who busied himself in sabotaging Haig's concept of operations, was critically important. While Haig made his views on tactics clear to his Army commanders, the actual methods used by brigades and battalions were decided by local commanders. The idea that the infantry uniformly advanced slowly in lines has been shown to be false.[12]

The stark discrepancy on 1 July 1916 between the BEF's huge losses for scant gains and the light casualties and impressive advances of the French inevitably poses the question of whether, had Haig followed French methods, the result would have been different. Foch's methods involving 'Lots of artillery, few infantry' have been lauded. Haig's and Joffre's belief that if the German line was placed under enough strain it would give way, let alone Haig's attempt to break through and reopen mobile warfare, have been decried. Foch saw the war as not 'a single decisive clash, but as a succession of operations geared to destroying the fighting capacity of the enemy army'.[13] Actually, Haig had a very similar concept, but he combined this with belief that the dominance of the defensive was temporary and it did not completely preclude ambitious manoeuvre.

On 1 July 1916 French methods were undoubtedly superior: 1915 had been their 'Somme', their period of learning. Judging whether Haig was foolish to adopt a different approach in the end comes down to whether one believes that slow attrition was the only possible course in summer 1916, or whether there were opportunities for mobile warfare. Haig was very clear that they existed. On 27 June he told Rawlinson that

> it is better to prepare to advance beyond the Enemy's last line of trenches, because we are then in a position to take advantage of any breakdown in the Enemy's defence. Where there is a stubborn resistance put up the matter settles itself! On the other hand if no preparations for an advance are made till next morning, we might lose a golden opportunity.[14]

He proved prescient: on both 1 and 14 July such 'golden opportunities' were indeed thrown away when the enemy defence collapsed without Fourth Army being in a position to take advantage. Such advances even if only of a mile or so, would in the context of the Somme have had important tactical, operational and even strategic consequences. This does not excuse Haig's over-optimistic pre-battle planning or his overestimation of the impact of attrition on the Germans, which might open the door to sustained advances, or his failure to pay more attention to French methods. But it does suggest that Haig was right to plan for manoeuvre.

Foch's methods were underpinned by the effective use of a potent force of artillery. In mid-1916 the Royal Artillery, lacking training and experience, lagged far behind their French counterparts. Haig was clearly aware both of the importance of artillery and of the BEF's problems in this department. '[T]he utmost and most skilful development of artillery fire is essential to any tactical success', Kiggell wrote to Robertson at Haig's request, a month before the battle, 'but want of trained personnel remains and will remain a severe handicap'; GHQ wanted more gunner officers sent from other theatres.[15] But Haig was to make a bad situation worse. As Major-General J.F.N. 'Curly' Birch, Artillery Advisor at GHQ later reflected, 'Poor Haig – as he was always inclined to – spread his guns'.[16] In theory, Haig understood very well the need to concentrate artillery fire.[17] This insight deserted him when planning the Somme. The sector to be attacked was too wide for the number of guns the BEF could bring to bear. Haig made things worse by directing that a greater depth of trench, an average of 2,500 yards, should be included in the bombardment plan. Birch told Haig that 'he was "stretching" his artillery too much'.[18] Unfortunately, Haig simply overruled him. The result was that the weight of shell was dispersed, not concentrated. Too few guns were given too much to do.[19] It was a ghastly error on Haig's part, perhaps prompted by a misreading of the lessons of Loos and/or Verdun.[20]

After 1 July

The question is often asked why Haig did not simply call off the battle of the Somme at the end of the disastrous first day. Lurking behind it is the notion that Haig should have been shocked by the size of the casualty list into abandoning the battle. One does not reach the command of a great army without being mentally robust, although Haig's comment in his diary on the day after the battle 'total casualties are estimated at over 40,000 to date. This cannot be considered severe in view of the numbers engaged, and the length of front attacked . . .' sounds suspiciously like an attempt to convince himself, especially after his visit earlier that day to two casualty clearing stations.[21]

Great battles cannot simply be turned on and off like a light switch. It appeared that British troops were cut off behind German lines, and they could not be abandoned. Haig did not know how bad the situation was on the ground, and in any case his Plan B had been for a long-drawn-out attritional battle, and the Germans had also clearly suffered. But the over-riding reason was coalition politics. As Robertson said in August, 'we were under a mutual obligation to go on, and . . . we could not tell Paris that we had had enough and meant to stop'.[22] On 3 July Joffre reacted furiously when Haig refused to renew the offensive north of the Bapaume road, as the French general wanted, and instead insisted on attacking in the south.[23] One can imagine Joffre's reaction if Haig had calmly announced that he was suspending the BEF's role in the battle, even though French soldiers were still fighting at Verdun. The other allies would also have been offended if the British had simply ditched the Chantilly agreement. Simply calling off the battle of the Somme because the first day went badly was not an option. In fact, Haig soon received information that the achievements of BEF had boosted its reputation with the French public and politicians.[24]

Haig's men also gained some grudging German admirers. Clumsy preparations had told the Germans where the battle was to be fought, but Falkenhayn deliberately kept his Second Army, the guardians of the Somme front, comparatively weak, intending to absorb the British blow and then to counterattack around Arras with Sixth Army, which was therefore kept strong.[25] All the attention paid in the Anglophone world to British casualties of 1 July have obscured the damage done to the German army in the first days of the battle, which for them began a full week earlier, with the British bombardment. An aura of crisis hung over German high command. The loss of guns was particularly serious. The sheer force of the Allied assault derailed Falkenhayn's plans. Instead he was forced to send sizeable reinforcements to Second Army to help them cling on. Fifth Army at Verdun was ordered to go 'strictly on the defensive' on 12 July.[26] However clumsy the British offensive, it had wrested the initiative from the Germans and was inflicting punishing casualties on them. Allied strategy was working.

On the second day on the Somme, 2 July 1916, Haig and Rawlinson continued to act at cross-purposes. At a midday meeting Haig made his priorities clear to Rawlinson: to build upon the gains in the south. Operations in the northern sector were to be kept strictly limited, not least because of ammunition shortages. In Haig's view the Germans were 'shaken' and had 'few reserves in hand'. Haig's strategy was to take pressure off Verdun by 'Press[ing] him [the enemy] hard with the least possible delay', in the area where real gains were achievable. Even at this early stage, Haig was suggesting an assault on the Bazentin–Longueval ridge, some 2,000 yards away and therefore 'well within reach of our guns', but deferred to Rawlinson's judgment.[27]

While there were some gains on the right on 2 July, Rawlinson again failed to make the most of the opportunities. Although the need to consult with the French and worries about advancing into a vulnerable salient played a role, at bottom Rawlinson was reluctant to depart from his self-written script. Haig was optimistic but frustrated by the lack of effort in the south and urged Rawlinson on. As late as 4 July Haig visited XIII, XV and III Corps HQs to urge 'them to press their advance, because by delaying, the enemy was given more time to strengthen his second line'.[28]

There were definite echoes here of the 1915 battles, of Haig fearing that subordinates were letting opportunities slip by failing to drive hard enough. By 8 July Haig was resigned to the fact that the opportunity for surprise had vanished. This did not dent his optimism, for he felt the crisis of the battle could well arrive in two weeks as the wearing-out fight went on. 'In the meantime', he told Doris, 'we must be patient and determined'.[29] Haig's confidence was based on the intelligence he was receiving, which indicated that the Germans were running short of reserves, and that the morale of their front-line soldiers was deteriorating.[30]

With battle raging on the Somme front, it made sense to carry out minor actions on other sectors of the front to confuse the enemy, to contribute to the wearing-down battle by denying respite to troops sent from the Somme, and to tie down troops. In the most optimistic scenario, they might even cause German resistance to crack. Such was the genesis of the disastrous Fromelles battle of 19–20 July.[31]

The plan for Fromelles was produced by the greatest enthusiast for the battle, Richard Haking, commander of XI Corps in Monro's First Army. Haig and GHQ had severe doubts about the operation. Although Haig would not allow Haking to attempt to take Aubers Ridge, ultimately, true to the man-on-the-spot philosophy, the C-in-C left it up to Monro to sanction the operation. Haig sent Monro 'mixed messages'; all things being equal he wanted the attack to be launched, but he deferred to his subordinate's judgment on whether 'conditions are favourable'. Monro genuinely had 'perfect liberty' to call off the offensive, but he took what was under the circumstances the easy option.[32]

The attack went ahead. Two inexperienced divisions, 61st and 5th Australian, attacked and suffered horrific casualties: 1,550 British and 5,500 Australian. In 2008 the battle was given added poignancy by the discovery of a previously unknown mass grave.

Haig's response to the news shows him at his insensitive worst:

> The reality of the fighting and shelling seems to have been greater than many had expected! So the experience must have been of value to all, and the enterprise has certainly had the effect of obliging the enemy to retain reserves in that area. Besides, by merely bombarding the enemy's front on similar lines again, we will compel him to mass troops to oppose a possible attack.[33]

One would have to be an optimist indeed to discern any positive benefit from Fromelles for the troops that took part. However, the battle did not damage Haking's reputation in Haig's eyes. Within a matter of weeks he was recommending him to take temporary command of First Army on Monro's departure for India.[34]

The strategic idea was sensible, however bungled the execution of the attack. For many years the received wisdom was that it had little or no effect, but recently it has been argued that it pinned six German divisions to XI Corps sector for up to nine weeks. If this is the case, Fromelles was a strategic success.[35] But there were no more major diversionary offensives while the Somme was in progress.

Following Haig's conference with Joffre and Foch (whom Joffre shortly was to task with co-ordinating the battle) on 3 July, Fourth Army issued orders to attack the German Second Position between Longueval and Bazentin le Petit. In preparation for the assault, Rawlinson was to capture a good jumping-off position for the attack. Gough's Reserve Army would play a secondary role in fixing German forces on its front.[36] Fourth Army thus did begin to build up force on the right, but it was a case of too little, too late. By 4 July the Germans had occupied Mametz Wood, which had earlier been there for the taking by the British. Every German soldier that reached the area marked the gradual closing of the window of opportunity.

It took until 14 July to mount the concerted assault Haig wanted. Instead, the British launched a series of uncoordinated 'penny-packet' attacks, often with inadequate artillery support, that were costly in casualties and often unsuccessful. From 3 July, in the run-up to the 14th, elements of Fourth Army fought in 46 actions, a reflection of the perceived need to keep hammering away at an enemy perceived as rocking back on his heels, to deny him the time and space to regroup. When Haig told Doris that 'The battle is being fought out on lines which suit us. That is to say the enemy puts his reserves straight into the Battle on arrival, to attack us, thereby suffering big losses,'[37] he was not entirely wrong. The German policy of immediate counterattack certainly helped to magnify their casualties. It is as well to be reminded that for the Germans this barren period and the successful 14 July attack were of a piece, for they were aware that the Allies had gained the initiative and the German army was 'being kept constantly off balance'. But British casualties were also very high: some 25,000 in this period.[38]

Joffre later criticised the BEF on the grounds that by August its attacks had 'little by little' degenerated 'into a series of disconnected actions, both costly and unprofitable'.[39] He favoured building up strength for the next major push, even if it meant conducting operations at a lower tempo in the meantime. Joffre saw Haig as too concerned with straightening the line, mounting local attacks to eliminate outposts, perhaps at the cost of delaying the main operation.[40] The fault was primarily Rawlinson's, but Haig was ultimately responsible, both for failing to rein in his subordinate and also for his policy of keeping up constant attacks on the enemy.

Haig was well aware of Rawlinson's merits and weaknesses, but chose not to enforce his will on the Fourth Army commander. In part this reflected the limitations on Haig's authority; but it was also in keeping with the army's command philosophy (see p. 26). Charteris put his finger on Haig's dilemma: how to make up for the inexperience of subordinates while avoiding 'cramping the[ir] initiative'.[41] During the Somme fighting, once GHQ had issued the broad objectives Haig generally advised, cajoled and hinted to Rawlinson, but rarely gave him orders. This was the worst of all worlds. Haig was clearly uncomfortable with this situation, not because he shied away from debate with the supposedly 'quicker thinking and more articulate' Rawlinson,[42] but rather there was a clash between his urge to intervene and his belief that the 'man-on-the-spot' doctrine was correct. This can only have been reinforced by his experiences in 1914 and 1915, of opportunities missed and of chafing under French's ineffectual attempts at remote control. Haig was much happier in 1918, when he was able to command much more in the way he preferred, because his subordinates and their staffs were more experienced and competent.

On the Somme Haig commanded by issuing broad orders, which would result in plans being formulated by corps and armies, which were then criticised by Haig and GHQ until a synthesis emerged – the idea that Haig did not allow debate does not square with the facts. Once an operation was in progress Haig would visit his Army and sometimes Corps commanders for discussions, or hold more formal conferences with subordinates. He would also make his views known through Kiggell, his Chief of Staff, either by telephone or telegram. On occasion, he would issue tactical advice, for instance aiming a memorandum on matters such as avoiding crowding in trenches, at brigade and battalion commanders.[43]

The planning of the attack of 14 July shows the way the system worked. Rawlinson and Congreve submitted a plan that envisaged an assault on a two-corps front. To gain surprise the troops would assemble at night and attack at dawn after a mere five-minute bombardment. Initially, Haig thought the plan was too complicated, and the capture of Trones and Mametz Woods were essential preconditions for the attack.[44] Although at a meeting on 11 July, when Haig told him that the plan was 'unsound', Rawlinson 'at once, in the most broad-minded way, said he would change it', that afternoon Rawlinson phoned Kiggell to say 'he still thought his old plan the best' – a fine example of consent and evade. There were further exchanges that day, and on the 12th Haig discussed the latest iteration of Fourth Army's plan with his key advisers at GHQ. He posed four questions which cut to the chase and shows Haig's staff training coming to the fore:

1. Can we take the position in the manner proposed?
2. Can we hold it after capture?
3. What will be the results in case of a failure?
4. What are the advantages, or otherwise, of proceeding methodically, viz. extending our front and sapping forward to take the position by assault?

The conclusion was favourable. Thus, after debate involving Haig and GHQ staff, Rawlinson and Fourth Army staff, and Horne and Congreve of XV and XIII Corps respectively, a plan had been agreed: basically Rawlinson's original, but, at Haig's insistence, 18th Division was given the preliminary objective of capturing Trones Wood, and 1st Division was to form a defensive flank; and Rawlinson was directed to put more emphasis on counter-battery fire. The story of the planning for Bazentin ridge undermines the view that subordinates were afraid to argue with Haig.

Rawlinson's plan indeed was bolder than Haig's, not only in the concept of a night assembly and dawn attack but in his use of cavalry (he had probably become aware of Haig's displeasure at his behaviour on 1 July): 'far reaching results' were obtainable 'especially if I can get the cavalry through and catch the guns and break up their commands'. Possibly he recognised that a sufficient 'bite' would carry Fourth Army through the enemy Second and Third positions. Rawlinson deliberately kept control of two of the cavalry divisions, devolving the 2nd Indian Cavalry Division to XIII Corps for immediate exploitation of infantry success. Unfortunately, this decision effectively excluded the other divisions from action, since releasing them only after the breakthrough had occurred was worse than useless: their move to the front needed to be well advanced while the attack was going on. Strangely Haig, by contrast, had a more conservative and cautious approach, worrying that the cavalry would be committed prematurely.[45]

The attack began at dawn on 14 July, and about 6,000 yards of the German Second Position were in British hands by mid-morning. The gunners were much more effective than on 1 July – they achieved a much greater concentration of fire power by massing guns on a relatively narrow front and did not disperse their fire over too great a depth of target.[46] Rawlinson's attack had demonstrated how formidably effective the step-by-step approach could be. The opportunity beckoned for the cavalry to apply Haig's all-arms concept to turn it into something more ambitious.

At 10.55 a.m. a telegram was wired to Lady Haig summarising events and stating 'hope to get cavalry through'.[47] A cavalry force (the Secunderabad Brigade of two regiments plus supporting troops) was on the British front line by 7 a.m. That they did not advance until the evening was the result of the friction of war. Initially placed under XIII Corps, the cavalry's opportunity beckoned on XV Corps' front, and it took until 6 p.m. for authority to command the cavalry pass from one formation to the other. This episode does not show the cumbersome British chain of command on the Somme in a good light, or say much about the willingness of commanders to use their initiative.

When the advance finally got under way, a combination of a mounted charge supported by the cavalry's machine-guns, followed by dismounted action supported by two infantry battalions, took part of High Wood. The mounted cavalry suffered only eight fatalities and less than 100 wounded while inflicting heavier losses on the Germans and capturing 38 prisoners. This modest success strongly suggests that Haig's cavalry concept was effective, and could have reaped dividends if used on a wider scale. There were more German defenders in the area than there had been on 1 July and defences were more advanced than a fortnight earlier. Still, the opportunity was real enough for cavalry to move ahead and seize ground until relieved. If the cavalry followed by infantry had advanced a mile, this would have taken Fourth Army clear of High Wood (which was to take an appalling toll of infantry until cleared in September) and onto the Third Position. Delville Wood, also the scene of a bitter and protracted struggle, would have been outflanked and could have been taken from the rear. This would not have led to a complete breakthrough, but it would have spared at least some of the agony of attritional fighting that engulfed Fourth Army from mid-July onwards.

Haig declared that 14 July was 'The best day we have had this war'.[48] The day not only validated Haig's all-arms concept but demonstrated that his doubts about the capabilities of the British citizen volunteer army were misplaced. It also showed the importance of using artillery correctly, concentrating firepower and weaving the batteries into the embryo all-arms weapons system. Sadly, the next couple of months were to show that these lessons had been imperfectly understood, as British generals failed to stick to the winning formula of Bazentin ridge. This too was ultimately the Commander-in-Chief's responsibility, as he failed to impose a uniform doctrine. If his suggestions had the force of orders, he failed to enforce them.

The Practicalities of Command

During the Somme there had been a great deal of tactical experimentation at unit level. Numerous 'lessons learned' reports were written and issued, for instance by Fourth and Reserve Armies, and informal networks existed by which, for example, Lord Loch, a staff officer in VI Corps near Arras, received reports from friends on the Somme.[49] The Canadian Corps was particularly active at the end of 1916 in analysing and applying lessons.[50] Although GHQ did try to capture recent experiences (S.S. 119, 'Preliminary Notes on the Tactical Lessons of the Recent Operations' was issued in July for example) what was missing was a central authority to collect and codify this material, to turn it into tactical doctrine and then disseminate and enforce it throughout the BEF.

Haig returned time and again to the problems of co-ordinating the operations of different formations.[51] This was in part a matter of staff work, ensuring that troops were at the right place at the right time, but also of liaison between headquarters. On occasion, Haig himself took a hand.[52] He had a clear grasp of some of the underlying problems of command. Visiting the headquarters of II Corps in mid-August, He spoke to the highly competent team of Claud Jacob and his chief of staff, Haig's friend Philip Howell:

[As] Information from Divisions frequently reaches H.Q.s of Corps, Armies and GHQ very slowly . . . I desired Jacob to see that inter-communication between subordinate units in a Division and Divisional HQ was efficiently kept up. I further pointed out that staff officers must be able to explain the plans of their general, as well as to see that the actual orders are carried out. I have noticed lately that in many Divisions, the Staff does not circulate sufficiently amongst the Brigades and Battalions when operations are in progress . . .[53]

The major target for Haig's ire was, however, Henry Rawlinson, who intermittently came in for a prodding. Unhappy with Fourth Army's attempts to link up with troops cut off in Guillemont, on 8 August Haig had Kiggell phone Rawlinson to demand greater efforts: '[t]he Chief . . . is not satisfied that Commanders have a proper grip of the situation'.[54] Things came to a head in late August when Haig first lectured Rawlinson in person and then wrote what has become known as the 'boys' own guide on how to command an army'.[55] He laid down that attacks should not be carried out on over-narrow fronts, and that sufficient weight of force should be used. Frustrated with Rawlinson's abdication of command, Haig stated that while in battle, 'subordinates on the spot must act on their own initiative', in the preparation period 'close supervision is not only possible, but is their duty' to help ensure success, as far as that was possible:

It appears to the Commander-in-Chief that some misconception exists in the Army as to the object and the limitations of the principle of the initiative of subordinates, and it is essential that this misconception should be corrected at once . . .[56]

This was sensible advice. It would take no particular time to act upon, providing Rawlinson had sufficient flexibility of mind.

From the vantage point of GHQ, Haig could see the growing accomplishment of his army. The heady optimism of earlier in the month had ebbed, but incidents such as the defeat of '5th Brandenburg Division, the crack corps of Germany' at Delville Wood, allied to interrogation of prisoners of war and analysis of captured documents, seemed to suggest that, by plugging away, the BEF was winning the battle of attrition. Some of his senior commanders shared this optimism.[57] Conversely, Haig could be hard on troops and commanders who fell short. He was incensed by 23rd Division's inability to hold Contalmaison after capturing it on 7 July, and by the failure of 38th

(Welsh) Division to capture Mametz Wood: 'such incidents are unworthy of the traditions of our Army . . . Victory is not won by half hearted performances'.[58]

These comments were terribly unfair on the troops involved. 23rd Division's attack was all too typical of the uncoordinated and poorly supported assaults of this time. 1st Worcesters hung on to Contalmaison until they ran out of bombs and ammunition.[59] All that can be said in mitigation of Haig's remarks is that he was unaware of the true situation, a victim of the fog of war that enveloped the high commander.

Haig's comments on 38th Division were also unfair, but a note in his diary querying the competence of the divisional commander, Major-General Ivor Philipps got somewhere near the truth. Philipps, a 'dugout' retired officer, was a political appointee in a 'division begotten in Welsh parish politics'. Lloyd George took a keen personal interest. At Horne's instigation, Philipps was sacked, and, following a second assault Horne reported that 38th Division had a state of training too poor to allow them to undertake further offensive operations. Haig assented to this conclusion, in spite of the fact that the Division captured the Wood on 11 July. Over the following months it became an effective formation.[60]

Haig showed a rather different side to his character in the case of Lieutenant G.N. Kirkwood RAMC, the Regimental Medical Officer (RMO) of 11th Border Regiment. On 9 July this battalion, which had lost 516 men out of 850 on the 1st, was ordered to find 100 men to take part in a trench raid. As the news seeped out, many soldiers opted to avoid duty legitimately by reporting sick to the RMO. Kirkwood was ordered to give an opinion on the state of the unit, and bravely reported that it was not fit for active service as a consequence of the traumatic events of 1 July. The raid took place and duly failed. Kirkwood found himself in deep trouble with Gough, his Army Commander, who demanded his dismissal from the service as 'a source of danger'. Kirkwood, however, was defended by Sir Arthur Sloggett, Director General of Medical Services. Haig sided with his DGMS:

The Commander-in-Chief . . . considers that this medical officer ought not to have been asked the question which he was called upon to answer – for though it is the duty of a Regimental Medical Officer to inspect individual cases, it is most improper to require him to give a general opinion on the physical fitness of 100 men in the circumstances set out in this correspondence.

Haig placed the blame on the acting battalion CO (whose nerve, it later transpired, was 'absolutely broken' as a result of previous fighting at Hill 60) and the brigade commander. It is significant that Haig chose to back Sloggett rather than Gough, another instance of the faith Haig placed in his specialists.[61]

The Long Slog

The two weeks following the attack on Bazentin ridge saw Fourth Army get bogged down in a series of brutal, slow-moving attritional battles. The high hopes of 14 July had vanished, and instead a grim struggle for places like Delville Wood and High Wood devoured infantry. Haig's plans outlined on 16 July have a distinctly limited feel:

1. Consolidate the Longueval–Bazentin le Petit position so as to make it absolutely safe against counter attack.
2. Establish our right flank in Ginchy and Guillemont.
3. Take Pozières village.

Pozières was captured by 1st Australian Division on 23 July, as Reserve Army began to take on a larger share of the fighting. By the end of July Haig, informed by accurate intelligence of German movements, realised that the enemy forces had recovered their poise and were not going to collapse under the weight of British attacks. Instead, on 2 August he ordered 'careful and methodical preparation' of attacks. Commanders were to practice 'economy of men and material' so that a sufficient reserve remained for the 'crisis of the fight' in late September. The aim was to achieve a reasonable jumping-off point for a major attack in September.[62] Haig's instructions have been criticised as being contradictory and muddled.[63] While there is some validity in this, the larger point is that this document reflects the difficulties of balancing a number of demands, all jostling for priority. The BEF thus fought a series of costly 'line-straightening' operations – for in 1916 the straighter the start line, the more accurate the artillery barrage was likely to be, and the fewer complicated manoeuvres the infantry were called upon to carry out, the better.

Haig was concerned that north of Longueval the British had pushed ahead of the French, and was keen to bring the French line forward. In the area from Longueval to Pozières, attacks should be limited to minor efforts to gain 'observation points to improve our position, but no big attack Northward is to be undertaken at present'.[64] In spite of the ferocity of the fighting and the lack of progress, Haig's optimism was fundamentally undimmed. Hearing in mid-August that tanks would not be available until the beginning of September, he expressed disappointment, as he expected 'decisive results' from using these new weapons 'at an early date'.[65]

Stitching together a combined Franco-British offensive proved to be a difficult task. Haig and Foch hammered out an agreement for a combined attack but, whatever the intentions, the armies ended up attacking separately. While the French went ahead on 7 August, the British could only attack a day later. A tense meeting between Haig and Joffre on 11 August starkly exposed the differences in strategic thinking between the two men. The French commander favoured large-scale operations involving both Allied armies on a wide front. This was also Haig's ultimate aim, but in the meantime, he thought it essential that Fourth Army continue to fight for positions in the south like Guillemont and Ginchy to help the French to get forward.[66] He had to fend off Joffre's demands for the BEF to carry out a major attack before Haig believed his forces were ready.[67] This was a difficult balancing act, since Haig acknowledged that Joffre had the overall strategic direction of the battle, but had to assert his independence. In effect Joffre could request, and Haig would do his best to agree, but he was not prepared to let Joffre dictate to him.

The compromise decision was an Anglo-French offensive in the Guillemont–Maurepas area. Bedevilled by bad weather, the attack achieved little, and a further major combined operation was delayed until 3 September. Until then the British reverted to smaller attacks. By mid-September the British had gained a reasonable start line for a new 'big push' but the human cost was terribly high.

The British had no monopoly on suffering. Allied artillery, aided by control of the skies, dominated the battlefield. One German junior officer spoke for many when he wrote of the 'shells that flattened everything, dominated everything and destroyed everything'. By contrast, the

Germans were short of artillery and ammunition. This ordeal took lives and broke nerves.[68] One indirect victim was Falkenhayn, replaced at the end of August by the team of General Paul von Hindenburg and General Erich Ludendorff, which abandoned the doctrine of holding ground at all costs and counterattacking enemy lodgements. Instead, there was a move towards a more flexible policy of defence-in-depth, and from late September the creation of the *Siegfried Stellung* (the Hindenburg Line to the British) about 15–20 miles to the rear.

Foch directed a fresh Allied offensive in September, with the French attacking on the 12th and the BEF joining in three days later. Preliminary skirmishing over plans once again took place between Haig and Rawlinson. Haig saw the forthcoming operations as having a decisive character. Reserve and Fourth Armies were to break through the German Third Position between Flers and Courcelette. Then the newly reformed Cavalry Corps, with two divisions in the lead, was to pass through the lead formations and capture Bapaume as the first stage in rolling up the German defences.[69] Predictably enough, Rawlinson wanted a limited operation. Haig won the argument.

Haig's optimism was based on the view that 'the enemy seemed to have exhausted his Reserves' and 'the crisis of the battle' was at hand.[70] GHQ was encouraged by Falkenhayn's dismissal, and by intelligence assessments that pointed to a crisis of morale on the home front as well as poor morale among front-line units, and by the belief that Germany's supply of reinforcements for the Somme was not keeping pace with the demand.[71] Haig's cavalryman's antennae started to twitch, as he foresaw work for horsemen in a pursuit. The seriousness with which Haig regarded the possibility of a decisive breakthrough can be judged by the fact that he provided more cavalry for 15 September – five divisions – than for 1 July. Perhaps believing that his 'all-arms' message was now understood, he did not allocate infantry units to Kavanagh's Cavalry Corps. '[I]f so,' as David Kenyon drily comments, 'he was to be disappointed'. Rawlinson paid lip service to the importance of the cavalry but was afraid that precipitate action by Kavanagh would hamper the action of the other arms, especially the artillery. Fourth Army thus issued orders that the cavalry were not to be committed until the infantry had advanced 2½ miles and (to rub salt into the cavalry's wounds) the guns had been moved forward to the newly captured position. Stern instructions forbade the cavalry from clogging up the routes to the battlefront. Curiously, thereafter he was hopeful of getting the cavalry into action, although one would have thought that he would have realised that it would be – literally and metaphorically – very late in the day. Short of telling Haig to his face that he didn't want the cavalry cluttering up the battlefield, Rawlinson could not have made his views on the mounted arm in the main battle clearer.[72]

Tanks, not horses, are the reason why the Battle of Flers-Courelette is remembered while so many other Western Front actions have slipped into oblivion. Just as Haig had enthusiastically embraced the potential of gas in 1915, he welcomed the chance to use the tank – although he did not, as at Loos, place this piece of untried technology at the centre of his plan. As we have seen, tanks were not available, as Haig had hoped, for the beginning of the battle in July, but he hoped that they would materially aid the offensive being prepared for mid-September. 'I hope and think they will add very greatly to the prospects of success and to the extent of it', he wrote on 22 August. Some writers, applying 20/20 hindsight, have criticised his decision to use tanks on 15 September as revealing the secret of their existence prematurely, before the BEF had enough of the armoured beasts to attack on a grand scale. Such claims do not stand serious scrutiny. Haig himself argued against the 'folly' of failing 'to use every means at my disposal in what is likely to be the crowning effort of this year'. And, once the tanks had reached France, it is highly unlikely that their existence could have remained secret for very long in any case.[73]

15 September proved to be another disappointment for Haig. The messages reaching him in the morning seemed to promise success, with the tanks living up to expectation. At 10.15 a.m. he noted '14th Division has apparently got the third objective and a Tank has been seen marching through the "High Street of Flers, followed by large numbers of infantry cheering."'! This incident was the basis of a famous report in the press that 'A tank is walking up the High Street of Flers with the British Army cheering behind'. 'Certainly some of the Tanks have done marvels,' Haig recorded, more than a trifle optimistically, 'and have enabled our attack to progress at a surprisingly fast pace.'[74] In practice, the tanks, in any case slow and unreliable, were the cause of catastrophic losses for the infantry in some sectors, as 'tank lanes' (gaps) had been left in the barrage. Back in

August, after witnessing an 'encouraging' demonstration of tanks, Haig
had astutely noted 'we require to clear our ideas as to the tactical
handling of these machines'.[75] Perhaps significantly, Rawlinson was less
impressed by tanks, and in reality, this process of integration of armour
into the emerging weapons system was far from complete when the
battle began.[76]

Gradually, bad news began to reach Haig. Alarmed by the lack of
progress on the right, Haig arrived at Fourth Army HQ at Querrieu
shortly after 2 p.m. to urge Rawlinson to push forward that night to Les
Boeufs and Gueudecourt. He 'impressed' on Rawlinson the importance
of this advance, but without apparently giving a direct order. Haig,
having picked up some tactical intelligence from aerial reconnaisance,
told Rawlinson to pass it on to his corps commanders and 'direct them
to send out patrols (if that had not already been done) to probe the
situation'. While it might have been reasonable for the C-in-C personally
to ensure that the latest intelligence reached corps commanders, it was
not for him to spell out the very basics of their jobs. Haig also visited
Gough's HQ to tell Reserve Army CoS Neill Malcolm what Fourth Army
were doing. Either this was interfering or it was an attempt to ensure co-
ordination between the Armies.

By the end of 15 September the British had pushed forward about
2,500 yards, and 1,000 yards further than that in the Flers sector. The
territory gained 'was about twice that gained on 1 July and at about half
the cost in casualties'; the German Third Position had been captured on
a 4,500 yard front.[77] The defenders had undoubtedly, in the words of the
official historian 'been dealt a severe blow', but it was equally true that
the assault 'fell far short of the desired achievement'. Tanks had not fully
lived up to their initial promise.[78] The weight of shells delivered in the
preliminary bombardment had been an improvement on 1 July, but
inferior to 14 July. Briefly there had seemed to be the possibility of a
breakthrough in the Flers sector, where, if fresh troops had been to hand,
a further advance might have been achievable. The situation seems
tailor-made for Haig's original all-arms concept, or even cavalry alone.
But this is ultimately fruitless speculation, since the dispositions of troops
as a consequence of Rawlinson's plan effectively neutered the cavalry.

Haig and the Politicians

Against this background of heavy losses and meagre gains, disquiet began to mount among the politicians at home, but, thanks in large part to Robertson's efforts, there was no serious challenge to Haig's authority. Asquith was supportive. On a visit to GHQ in September the PM told Haig that 'he and the Government are well pleased with the way the operations have been conducted here, and he is anxious to help me in every way possible'. Asquith's visit caused Haig some amusement: 'The PM seemed to like our old Brandy . . . [after dinner] his legs were unsteady, but his head was quite clear, and he was able to read a map and discuss the situation with me. Indeed he was most charming and quite alert in mind.'[79] However, Haig was not complacent. Both Robertson and the King warned him that French and other sacked generals were making trouble for him at home. Churchill, out of office but not without influence, had a critical paper, 'Variants of the Offensive', circulated to the Cabinet in early August. But as Robertson, watching Haig's back, informed him it had little effect. 'Winston's head is gone from taking drugs,' Haig retorted.[80] It was in October that Haig learned from Leo Maxse of F.E. Smith's machinations at home (see p. 153).

All this was small beer compared to the Lloyd George affair in September. On Kitchener's death in June, the dynamic, charismatic Welsh Radical Liberal had succeeded as Secretary of State for War. He was highly effective in mobilising the nation for total war, but shrank from the logical outcome: a war of attrition on the Western Front. Although Haig had disapproved of Lloyd George's politics since before the war, initially he had been well disposed to his new political master. 'LG was very pleasant,' Haig noted after they met in August. 'He assured me that he had "no intention of meddling" and that his sole object was to help'.[81] What poisoned Haig's mind was what he saw as Lloyd George's underhand behaviour. Passionately opposed to the dreadful losses in France, on a visit in September 1916 Lloyd George asked French generals for their opinions of British generalship. 'I would not have believed that a British Minister could have been so ungentlemanly as to go to a foreigner and put such questions regarding his own subordinates,' wrote Haig.[82] Things got worse in 1917.

The Autumn Battles

The battle of Morval (25 September 1916) was a striking example of how well a limited approach could work. This time, the creeping barrage was continuous. And since the tanks were placed in reserve, there was no need for tank lanes. The attack, on a single enemy trench system significantly weaker than the position assaulted on the 15th, was aided by a much more powerful artillery bombardment. The infantry, too, showed that they were able to apply the lessons of previous fighting. Because the battle had been planned as a limited affair from the beginning, the cavalry were allotted a peripheral role. However Horne of XV Corps, who seems to have been one of the few commanders to understand Haig's all-arms concept (he was a protégé of Haig, and – perhaps significantly – a horse artilleryman by background) did use a small force of cavalry, which was all that was available, to seize tactical objectives.[83]

At the same time as Morval, Reserve Army finally captured two German positions that had held out doggedly for weeks: Mouquet Farm and, more importantly, Thiepval. Haig's optimism was given a boost, and he began planning for more extensive operations. This was a chimera. It was getting late in the season, and the opportunities for breakthrough had almost certainly vanished. RFC reconnaissance showed that the Germans were feverishly constructing new defensive lines in their rear.[84] These developments greatly complicated the BEF's tasks. The additional defences called for a series of bite-and-hold operations that, even if the mobile element was added to exploit success, were beyond the capability of the BEF to mount in sufficient time to push out into open country.

This seems to have eluded Haig. Believing that German reserves were exhausted, even before Morval he planned for ambitious operations involving Third Army, writing of the need to 'run risks' in striking against 'the enemy's communications'.[85] On 29 September GHQ issued orders for Third Army, Reserve Army and Fourth Armies to advance. Rawlinson was to carry the Le Transloy Line in the initial phase of a push towards Cambrai, some 20 miles distant.[86] It did not happen. Fourth and Reserve Armies struggled on in October through worsening weather and increasingly unrewarding actions. Although displaying an increasing level of tactical skill and inflicting significant losses on the enemy, British troops were taking heavy losses for the most miserly of territorial gains.

Why did Haig persist in this unrewarding offensive? Certainly he believed that the battle of attrition was working in the Allies' favour, the skill of his army was improving, and simply grinding down the Germans was in itself a valid military objective.[87] Another factor was his over-estimation of what was physically possible for the troops amid the rain and mud of a Somme autumn, and yet another was the military situation of the Allies on other fronts. But perhaps most significant was the pressure that the French high command was bringing to bear on Haig. GHQ's direction to attack the Le Transloy Line on 5 November caused Cavan, GOC XIV Corps, to write to Rawlinson that the assault was all but impossible. Haig noted this in his diary with some sympathy – he had a high regard for 'Fatty' Cavan as a general – but followed it with the pertinent comment '[t]he question is how not to leave the French left in the air!'[88] Haig swiftly organised a meeting with Rawlinson and Foch. The attack went ahead.

Similarly, in late October Joffre wrote to Haig with asking him to undertake more ambitious operations. Haig rebutted the insinuation that he was reducing the BEF's effort:

> Meanwhile to the utmost extent of the means at my disposal, and so far as weather conditions render possible, I will continue to co-operate with you in exploiting to the full the successes already gained. But I must remind you that it lies with me to judge what I can undertake and when I can undertake it.[89]

In other words, he reasserted that he was the independent commander of the army of a sovereign state, not a mere subordinate of Joffre's. French high command could legitimately give strategic direction, but he would not be told where, when or how his army would fight. There was time for one last major effort on the Somme before the battle was closed down for the winter. Fifth Army (as Gough's command had been renamed) launched the Battle of the Ancre on 13 November. This was always intended to be a limited affair, and by the dismal standards of the latter part of the Somme was a modest success, which strengthened Haig's hand at an inter-Allied conference going on at that time. Beaumont Hamel (another 1 July objective) was captured, as was Beaucourt. A second phase took some more ground, inevitably at heavy cost, and the battle petered out in minor but savage fighting. On 18 November the Ancre fighting, and the Battle of the Somme as a whole, came to an end.

Summing up the Somme, and Douglas Haig's part in it, is a controversial business. Haig himself had no doubt how he wanted the battle to be understood and remembered. His dispatch of 23 December 1916 was uncompromisingly entitled 'The Opening of the Wearing-Out Battle', and he downplayed his hopes of achieving a decisive victory to the point of invisibility. Instead Haig argued that the 'main objects' for which the battle had been fought had been attained: 'Verdun had been relieved; the main German forces had been held on the Western front; and the enemy's strength had been very considerably worn down'.[90] Haig chose not to remember that the Somme clearly failed to achieve one of his objectives; open warfare was as far away as ever.

The Somme did bring about some tangible results. The Allied offensive indeed tipped the balance in favour of the French at Verdun where the battle had become stalemated. It put paid to a key plank in Falkenhayn's strategy, a counteroffensive to destroy what was left of the Allied armies after they had been shattered by their own relief offensives.[91] In February–March 1917 the Germans cut their losses and pulled back up to 20 miles to the Hindenburg Line, which undeniably gave them tactical advantages. But was also a tacit admission of defeat. Hindenburg and Ludendorff were not prepared to stand and undergo another attritional struggle on the Somme. There is plenty of evidence that the German army suffered severely on the Somme (incurring by most estimates higher losses than the 370,000 sustained at Verdun, perhaps as many as 600,000). It was still a formidable enemy, but its overall quality had declined as a result of the battle.[92]

At the beginning of 1916 German high command judged Britain's strengths as its financial power and the Royal Navy. The army's morale was thought to be high but its usefulness on the battlefield suspect.[93] On the Somme the British had shown they were fighting the war not just with ships and cash, but with soldiers, vast numbers of them. Haig well understood the wider ramifications. The Germans were 'shaken', and Germany's 'friends' and 'doubting neutrals' were 'impressed', and 'England's strength and determination' was demonstrated to the world.[94]

Although the BEF's tactical and operational performance had often been amateurish and clumsy, it improved over time, and did enormous damage to the German forces. From the very beginning of the battle German soldiers at all levels had been impressed and shocked by the power of the Royal Artillery. Crown Prince Rupprecht of Bavaria, who in September took command of a 'Group of Armies' that covered the Somme, reported that the overwhelming superiority of enemy artillery, the sheer quality of shells at their disposal, and the Allies' domination of the air had wreaked havoc on the battlefield. Trenches were smashed, communications were cut, and men were reduced to lying 'in shell-holes, without barriers or shelters'.[95] The German forces on the Somme were, by the end, utterly worn out.

Ludendorff retrospectively articulated the problem of the German senior military leadership at the end of 1916. It had to

> bear in mind that the enemy's great superiority in men and material would be even more painfully felt in 1917 than in 1916. They had to face the danger that 'Somme fighting' would soon break out at various points on our fronts, and that even our troops would not be able to withstand such attacks indefinitely, especially if the enemy gave us no time for rest and for the accumulation of material.[96]

This analysis led to the decision to pull back to the Hindenburg Line, and to implement the 'Hindenburg Programme' of mobilisation for total war. The way in which the Programme was developed significantly weakened support for the war among the German population by 1918. The Somme also prompted the decision to win the war at sea. In 1917 Germany sought to win the war by using U-boats to cut the 'Atlantic lifeline' through sinking the merchant shipping that kept Britain supplied with food, munitions and other essential supplies. This was a calculated gamble, for the move to 'unrestricted' submarine warfare involved attacking neutral shipping, a move that was highly likely to add the United States to the coalition arrayed against Germany. And this is exactly what did happen – a by-product of the failed attempt to starve the British out of the war. This major shift in the strategic balance in favour of the Allies was an indirect consequence of the Battle of the Somme.

Could Haig claim any credit? The answer is a qualified 'yes'. Attrition had both military and broader political objectives. The attention that Charteris paid to political as well as military intelligence gives some indication of the importance that Haig attached to this. Hammering away at the German army on the Somme did not produce a crisis of the magnitude that Haig hoped for, but it did nonetheless weaken it. It also had an impact on the minds of the German politico-military leadership that helped to deflect them onto paths that proved ultimately disastrous for their cause.

Haig was not much given to self-criticism and introspection, but in late 1916, for a moment, the mask slipped. Haig thanked Major-General Oliver Nugent, the commander of 36th (Ulster) Division, for his Division's outstanding performance on 1 July, adding 'I always think with regret that we failed to give you all the support we ought to have done'. Gratified – for he and Haig were not close – Nugent responded by suggesting 'that perhaps we had all been rather optimistic as to what it was possible to do'. Haig's reply was unusually candid: 'Well, we were all learning.'[97]

Judged by his performance as (in modern terms) a National Contingent Commander, Haig emerges with more credit. He was in an exceptionally difficult position *vis-à-vis* the French, and his attempts to maintain harmony within the coalition while upholding British interests must be entered on the plus side of the ledger. During the Somme Haig was fortunate to have Robertson in London defending him against the politicians. He also benefited from the consensus in favour of the battle, however fragile, which shielded him to a large extent from political interference and criticisms. Things changed shortly after the battle ended. Lloyd George supplanted Asquith as Prime Minister in December 1916, and this rather reshaped relations between the 'brass hats' and the politicians, the 'frocks', in 1917.[98]

And yet, if Haig's most ambitious plans were never really on the cards, more limited success was certainly possible, had things turned out a little differently. Germany was under huge strain in July to September 1916, fighting simultaneously at Verdun, on the Somme and on the Eastern Front. If Rumania had entered the war in late June instead of procrastinating until the end of August this might have tipped the Central Powers over the edge. Given that Haig's attritional strategy was aimed at breaking German morale, it is interesting that there is some evidence that in September 1916 the confidence of the German middle classes appeared to waver.[99] One is left with the intriguing possibility – although it is no more than that – that, had the Allies done a little better on the Somme, the Germans might have offered to make peace on terms that the Allies could accept.

On the Somme, the BEF did the best it could in grinding down the Germans. To accept huge losses for little tangible gain stuck in the throats of many, during the war and ever since. And the losses were appalling: 419,654 British casualties, approximately 128,000 of them fatalities. There were another 204,000 or so French, pushing the Allied total to nearly 624,000.[100] One fatality was 20-year-old Charles Tompson from Watford, killed in the ranks of the Queen Victoria Rifles at Gommecourt on 1 July. Many rungs further up society's ladder, the losses of the Guards Division in September had caused 'very long faces at Windsor [Castle]'. Downing Street was also in mourning, for Raymond Asquith, the Prime Minister's son, was amongst the dead. Grand house, suburban villa, and terraced cottage were united by bereavement and mourning that terrible summer.[101]

Even before the battle, Haig was aware of potential manpower problems, and at the end of the fighting set out his requirements to the War Office, confessing that 'the lack of men seems so great and the time before fighting recommences so short': one million men were needed for 1917.[102] Haig undoubtedly deserves a large share of the blame for the profligacy of British operations, but the inescapable problem was that the political imperative was to attack, and keep on attacking under conditions that Haig knew would be difficult. The sheer inexperience of his 'de-skilled' army, the need to work out how to adapt to fighting at a time when the conduct of warfare was undergoing radical changes, and the toughness of the German army – all these factors pointed to heavy casualties whatever the Commander-in-Chief did.

For all that, Haig's strategy contributed to an Allied success on the Somme. The term victory is simply inappropriate for an affair that in the end was aimed at inflicting maximum damage on the enemy. The apprenticeship of the British army on the Somme made it a much more formidable military machine, and its morale was intact in spite of its ordeal. And the German army had suffered grievously. Haig's argument was, in effect, that the Somme had not resulted in a decisive victory because the German army had not yet suffered enough pain from attrition.[103] 'The Somme battle of 1916 won the war', Esher assured Haig in 1918.[104] Esher's view was exaggerated but it was not entirely wrong. The Somme, or something very like it, was an essential stepping-stone to victory.

New Battles

1916 ended well for Haig. As a mark of his respect, and as a slap in the face to Lloyd George, the King made him a field marshal. Haig looked forward to 1917 with confidence, believing the campaigns of the new year could be decisive. His plans were blown off course in the first half of 1917, as the BEF had to fight an unwanted battle at Arras at the behest of a new French Commander-in-Chief, after Haig had fought a fierce and unexpected battle with his own government.

When the Somme campaign was halted in November 1916 he fully intended to renew the battle before long: 'All resources will be concentrated as far as possible towards the most complete preparations for active operations early next year on [the Arras–Somme] front'.[1] This 'Somme Plus' was intended to be a preliminary to shifting British forces to Flanders and launching a major offensive to capture the Belgian coast, so as to counter the U-boat menace. The Atlantic lifeline was Britain's centre of gravity: the thing which, if attacked successfully, would cause maximum damage to its war effort. If the supplies of vital materials carried in merchant ships could be halted by the action of German submarines, it would matter little how well or badly the army was doing on the Western Front – Britain would be forced to make peace. An operation to capture the Belgian coast by land would not necessarily end the threat, but it would be an important step in that direction. On 1 January Robertson wrote anxiously to Haig asking whether, 'in view of the great importance which the War Cabinet attach . . . to the capture of Ostend and Zeebrugge' new French plans would scupper operations in Belgium.[2] Joffre had been kicked upstairs in December 1916 and replaced by a new man with new plans, General Robert Nivelle. Nivelle, who had come to prominence through conducting small-scale, well-planned and well-executed attacks at Verdun, had his first meeting with Haig on 20 December 1916. Straight away, Nivelle indicated that he would not be bound by the plans agreed with Joffre at the Chantilly conference in November. He sought a decisive battle. Nivelle, 'a most straightforward and soldierly man', was 'confident of breaking through the Enemy's front now that the Enemy's morale is weakened,' Haig noted, 'but the blow must be struck by surprise and go through in 24 hours'.[3]

Nivelle's successes at Verdun had been based on the techniques of massed artillery fire covering the advance of the infantry, who were set limited objectives.[4] These methods worked because they aimed at maximising firepower by minimising the ground to be covered. But Nivelle was looking to use them to open the door for a hugely ambitious offensive. His objective was the 'destruction of enemy main forces on the western front', envisaging a 'prolonged battle' to break the enemy front and 'defeat' the German reserves, followed by exploitation. The French would land the main blow in Champagne, while British and French forces pinned German divisions in the Arras–Somme area. Specifically, the BEF was to 'pierce' the enemy positions, take the Hindenburg Line in the rear, and advance in the direction of Valenciennes–Louvain, and ultimately to Mons, Tournai and Courtrai. Further north, British Second Army was to exploit German weakness in Flanders and push forward.[5] Haig agreed to Nivelle's plans, knowing it meant that he had to abandon his own, at least in the short term.

At an inter-Allied conference in Rome in January 1917 the new Prime Minister unveiled his strategic vision to transfer forces to the Italian front for a combined British-French-Italian offensive against Austria-Hungary. Rebuffed in Rome but still eager to avoid another major British offensive in France, Lloyd George eventually embraced Nivelle's plan. It had a major attraction – the French would do the bulk of the fighting and therefore take most of the casualties. Lloyd George, no slouch at eloquence himself, was impressed by Nivelle's articulate command of English (learned from a British mother) – very different from Haig's verbal hesitancy. 'Nivelle has proved himself to be a Man at Verdun,' Lloyd George told Frances Stevenson, his secretary and mistress, 'and when you get a Man against one who has not proved himself, why, you back the Man!'[6]

Nivelle, in Duff Cooper's dry phrase, 'proved the first and last person capable of persuading Lloyd George that victory could be won on the western front'.[7] At this stage the Prime Minister and the C-in-C were in agreement, Haig believing that Nivelle's offensive had 'every prospect of gaining the fruits of victory'.[8] Robertson was less sure. Nivelle, he told Esher, had been too boastful during his visit to London, claiming success was guaranteed.[9]

As Haig considered Nivelle's plan, he grew more cautious. He would not commit the BEF 'to an indefinite continuation' of the battle, reminding Nivelle of the Frenchman's claim that he would be able to gauge within 24 to 48 hours whether 'your decisive attack had succeeded or should be abandoned'. If the latter, Haig would hold Nivelle to his promise that French troops would take over British-held line to enable Haig to launch his offensive on Flanders.[10] Nivelle's private response was to accuse Haig of having the Belgian coast on the brain and failing to see the '[western] front as a whole'.[11] Formally, he replied that, although he was not prepared to go as far as Haig wanted, 'you will find me ready to give all possible help'. Haig had to be content with that. If Nivelle's plan worked, the Belgian offensive would be stillborn, so he had to hope that the French operations went so well that the Flanders coast would be freed indirectly.[12]

Before the battle Robertson grumbled that 'As usual, the French wish us to take over a great deal more line and at the same time prepare for a big offensive'.[13] The issues were thrashed out in a meeting on 15 January at 10 Downing Street. The tone for the day was set when, in a meeting with Haig, Lloyd George unfavourably contrasted the competence of the BEF with that of the French army. Haig's retort included some comments on the lack of 'discipline and thoroughness' of French infantry.[14]

Haig attended a meeting of the War Committee the next day, where they were told that the BEF had to take over more line from the French. Haig would get two additional divisions, not the five he requested, with the offensive beginning not later than 1 April (Haig had argued for 1 May).[15] Unimpressed, Haig thought these 'conclusions were hastily considered by the War Committee'.[16]

Among the factors that worried Haig was the poor condition of the French railway system. Nivelle and Lloyd George suspected, probably unfairly, that it suited Haig to use the transport situation to delay the beginning of the battle. The Prime Minister began stealthily to conspire to subordinate the British C-in-C to Nivelle.[17]

Nivelle was receptive to Lloyd George's overtures. Back in December General Jean de Vallières, the senior French liaison officer at GHQ, had given Nivelle a very downbeat assessment of the Joffre–Haig relationship, stressing Haig's skill at 'sliding out of things'.[18] More generally, Nivelle was influenced by his anti-British chief of staff Colonel Audemard d'Alençon.[19] After three months of working with Haig, Nivelle had concluded that he was 'a man of indifferent brain, of narrow vision, of suspicious mind and very difficult to get on with'.[20]

Haig knew that, as the junior coalition partner, the British had to 'support our Allies, and so probably play a less glorious part than they are likely to do'. Playing a secondary role did not appeal, but he was prepared to do so for 'the general good and with our eyes fully open to the consequences'.[21] Thus was born the Arras offensive. It was a battle that Haig considered a distraction from his main priority for 1917, clearing the Belgian coast. What is more, it was a battle fought under the shadow of one of the most serious civil–military clashes of the war.

Politicians Against Generals

Haig spent the morning of 1 February 1917 as usual, at GHQ receiving visitors. They included a group of French politician-journalists, who 'seemed very pleased at my receiving them'. After lunch Haig departed to see a demonstration of 'flame projectors'.[22] It had been, in short, a fairly routine day, but unknowingly, Haig had triggered a crisis that might have led to him being replaced as C-in-C. Two weeks later, accounts of Haig's interview appeared in the French press. On the following day, a translation appeared in *The Times* accompanied by an editorial robustly supportive of Haig, and a crisis in civil–military relations ensued.[23]

The interview quoted Haig at length and verbatim. There is no doubt that it reflected Haig's views, but whether this was truly a verbatim account is much less certain. Whatever the truth, from a politician's point of view, Haig gave a dangerous hostage to fortune in declaring that 1917 would see 'the decision of the war on the field of battle'. Although Haig qualified this by saying that that it did not mean that peace would come in 1917, such caveats tend to be forgotten. Worse, coming so soon after the Prime Minister's attempt to move the point of main effort to Italy, Haig's trenchant comments on the primacy of the Western Front could be read as none-too-subtle criticism of Lloyd George. At best, Haig's comments were tactless. At worst they could be seen as a calculated challenge to Lloyd George's authority by an over-mighty general backed by the Northcliffe press.[24]

The truth was much more prosaic. Haig was generally very reluctant to speak to foreign journalists, but was persuaded to do so by Esher and the Foreign Office. He does not seem to have regarded his talk with the French journalists as a formal interview at all. When the storm broke Haig noted in his diary that he occasionally had conversations with journalists, at which he would 'merely talk platitudes and state my confidence' in Allied victory, but it seems that on this occasion he became carried away.[25] The journalists' copy was sent for censorship to Charteris, who was at home on leave and, by his own admission, spent barely ten minutes on the job. Probably concerned only with the impact on French opinion, Charteris ignored the political ramifications in Britain, or indeed the effect of over-literal translation into English, which made Haig appear 'boasting and vainglorious'.[26] French reaction was very positive.

In London Haig received strong support from Northcliffe – the Hon. Neville Lytton of GHQ's press staff thought that without the newspaper baron's support Haig's position would have been untenable – and also from Lord Derby. The Secretary of State for War argued that Lloyd George should not read too much into the affair, while warning of the political reality that Haig had some powerful political allies and, if Haig received a censure, he might resign: 'a state of affairs which I know you will deplore, and which I do not think the country will consider justified by this indiscretion.'[27]

Balfour and Bonar Law acted as moderating influences on an incandescent Lloyd George, and in the House of Commons, Law backed Haig's version of events. Publicly, the crisis had abated, but it had long-term consequences. Conceivably it was the final straw for Lloyd George and led to the Calais conspiracy (see below); it certainly reinforced his suspicion of Haig. The affair left an impression in political circles, however unfair, that Haig's staff was incompetent. Derby told Lloyd George that Haig had 'been badly let down by Charteris'.[28] The whole question of GHQ staff was to return with a vengeance at the end of the year. As a clash between Haig and Lloyd George, the interview affair was a mere curtain-raiser for what was to follow.

Haig arrived at Calais on 26 February for what promised to be a straightforward if high-level conference on transport. Discussions on logistics lasted for a short time before Lloyd George suggested that they be left to technical experts, while the others looked at wider issues. At Lloyd George's prompting, Nivelle brought up the question of how the BEF was to be used in the forthcoming battle. The French commander was unhappy at Haig's proposal to attack Vimy Ridge. Haig stoutly defended, on solid tactical grounds, why this key position had to be taken and made clear that there was a wider issue at stake; as an independent commander, he would loyally adhere to Nivelle's strategy, but 'in the matter of tactics I alone could decide'. It was the same argument he had had with Joffre in 1916. Lloyd George hurriedly disclaimed any knowledge of 'strategy and tactics', but said that he wanted to be clear about delineation of responsibilities. Before dinner, he asked innocently, could the French draw up proposals for a command system?[29]

When Robertson saw the paper he 'bellowed' "Get 'Aig". In Haig's pithy summary, the French proposed

> to organise a British CGS and Staff at Beauvais (French GQG) with what they called a 'Quartermaster General'. The CGS to report to the War Committee at home. The C-in-C would apparently only administer the discipline [and look after reinforcements].[30]

Far from being drawn up in pre-prandial haste, the French proposals were part of a prearranged plot to break Haig's grip by placing the BEF under French command. Senior French generals and politicians had been contemplating such a move since the end of 1916. The French liaison officer at the War Office, Bertier de Sauvigny, had met Hankey and Lloyd George on 15 February and discussed placing the BEF under French command, sacking Haig if necessary. Possibly significantly, this was the same day that Haig's 'interview' appeared in The Times.[31] Nivelle was complicit in this plot, but Haig did not suspect this. General Lyautey, whom Haig trusted, was aware of the conspiracy, as was Joffre, although neither necessarily approved of it.[32] The War Cabinet had met on 24 February, but neither Robertson nor Derby were invited. In their absence, the view prevailed that French generalship and staff work were 'immeasurably superior' to that of the British, and Haig should be subordinated to Nivelle. The Cabinet authorised Lloyd George to 'ensure unity of command both in the preparatory stages of and during the operations'.[33]

For Haig, it was 'an intrigue of the worst description'.[34] Robertson and Haig confronted Lloyd George and there were angry exchanges. The Prime Minister conveyed the War Cabinet's decisions, although he disingenuously said that the French demands were 'excessive'.[35] The generals' outrage was fuelled, and their position strengthened, by Hankey's admission that the War Cabinet had not given the Prime Minster 'full authority' for his actions. Haig, Robertson and Kiggell 'agreed we would rather be tried by Court Martial than betray the Army by agreeing to its being placed under the French. Robertson agreed that we must resign rather than be partners in this transaction.'[36]

Robertson spent the night consulting with Major-General Frederick Maurice (his assistant), preparing the ground for a counterattack. Before turning in, Hankey drafted a compromise document.[37] Haig's one major contribution was an unhelpful note ruling out any middle course.

With Hankey's invaluable help a compromise gradually emerged. Gone was the proposal to permanently subordinate the BEF to the French Army and to sideline Haig into a mere administrative role. Now Haig was to 'conform his plans of operations' to Nivelle's scheme. Crucially, Haig was given the right to appeal to London. Haig would come under Nivelle's strategic orders for the battle itself, but was given considerable freedom in operations. This was how his relationship with Joffre had worked. Once the battle was over – and at this stage Haig estimated that it would last for two weeks – the arrangements would lapse. To make his views clear, on Haig's copy of the agreement he noted 'Signed by me as a correct statement, but not as approving the arrangement'.[38]

On the French side, Nivelle and Briand accused Haig of dragging his feet in implementing the Calais agreement. Haig was genuinely concerned about the intelligence picture that was emerging. By shortening the length of front to be defended, the withdrawal to the Hindenburg Line freed up about a dozen divisions that could be deployed elsewhere. The Germans carried out a sophisticated deception operation that led GHQ to fear that an offensive was planned around Ypres, directed at the Channel ports. If Haig had been forced to commit his reserves to support Nivelle's offensive, it could make the BEF's position highly vulnerable in the event of such a German attack. Moreover, he pointed out that Nivelle could find himself landing 'a blow in the air', as part of the German line that was to be attacked had now been evacuated.[39]

By querying the continued relevance of Nivelle's plan, Haig showed a firm grasp of operational realities that the French commander patently lacked. Nivelle responded by asking Lloyd George to sack Haig. As rumours to this effect quickly began to circulate in France, Nivelle seems to have been as indiscreet on this matter as he was with the details of the offensive.[40]

Robertson carefully prepared the ground for a fresh conference by mobilising supporters at home.[41] Haig also worked behind the scenes. He wrote to the King that, while he did not wish to resign, he realised that he might have lost the confidence of the War Cabinet, and 'I leave myself in Your Majesty's hands to decide what is best for me to do at this juncture. Haig's letter was calculated to play on George V's fears of the consequences of the Calais business. Stamfordham entreated Haig not to resign, which would be 'disastrous to his [i.e. the King's] Army'. The King was angry at being kept in the dark, and feared that Lloyd George wanted a republic. If Haig and Derby resigned, George V was worried that the government would fall but that the subsequent general election would see Lloyd George return to Downing Street with his power immensely enhanced.[42]

Lloyd George certainly considered forcing Haig's resignation, but first consulted Hankey. Lloyd George, Hankey noted in his diary, 'is always trying to get me to say Haig is no use, but I refuse to do so'.[43] He made a compelling case that Haig's dismissal would damage the government, as it would give Lloyd George's enemies an issue on which to marshal their forces. Even if Haig was removed as C-in-C, Hankey recommend that he should be appointed to another 'high military command'.[44]

This was not advice that Lloyd George wanted to hear, but it became increasingly clear he was becoming isolated. The King on 12 March took him to task over the affair. Lloyd George responded hotly, the King being 'rather upset' by his Prime Minister's 'outburst'.[45] The Prime Minister bowed to the formidable group of Haig's supporters. An Anglo-French conference was held in London beginning on 12 March, where the Calais agreement was substantially revised in Haig's favour. Lloyd George, at the direction of the Cabinet and through what must have been the most clenched of teeth, announced that the War Cabinet had 'full confidence' in Haig, who was 'regarded with admiration in England'[46] – although clearly not in all parts of Wales.

Haig signed the Agreement, but insisted on noting on the document:

> I agree with the above on the understanding that while I am fully determined to carry out the Calais Agreement in spirit and letter, the British Army and its CinC will be regarded by General Nivelle as Allies and not as subordinates, except during the particular operations which he explained at the Calais Conference. Further, while I also accept the Agreement respecting the functions of the British Mission at French HQ, it should be understood that these functions may he subject to modifications as experience shows to be necessary.[47]

Unity of command on the Western Front was highly desirable, but the Calais coup would not have brought it about. Simply placing the BEF under the French army would have been an abdication by the Cabinet of British national interests. French aspirations to gain greater control over the BEF coincided with Lloyd George's desire to marginalise Haig. But both overplayed their hands. Their scheme was never going to be acceptable to British high command, or the King, or much of the Cabinet, and in practical terms the idea of placing the BEF directly under the commander of the French army was deeply flawed. Ferdinand Foch was successful as supreme allied commander in 1918 not least because he was seen as being above the national armies. If Nivelle had attempted direct command of the BEF, it would have undermined the cohesion of the coalition or even destroyed it.

One reason why Haig was so opposed to the Nivelle scheme was that he believed that he had established an effective working relationship with Joffre in 1916. Joffre, in his view, had overstepped the mark on occasions, but this was followed by apologies, and reconciliation. Nivelle, on the other hand, aroused the British C-in-C's resentment and undermined the basis of the relationship by his imperious treatment of Haig,[48] even though Haig did not realise the depth of Nivelle's involvement in the conspiracy.

Sassoon's summary of the results of the London Conference reveals something of the mistrust at GHQ: 'everyone – the King, LlG [sic], Curzon etc – all patted D.H. on the back and told him what a fine fellow he was – but with that exception matters remained very much as Calais had left them and the future may be full of difficulties'.[49]

Why Lloyd George, a consummate politician, took such a high-risk approach is something of a mystery. At the 15 February meeting Lloyd George and Hankey stressed that Haig's prestige at home precluded his simple subordination to Nivelle. Small wonder that Hankey's reaction on seeing the French paper at Calais was that it 'took my breath away'.[50] The simplest answer is that Lloyd George overestimated his political strength and was defeated in the clash with the military.[51] Frances Stevenson noted that 'I fear that D [i.e. Lloyd George] will have to be very careful in future as to his backings of the French against the English'. Not the least important consequence was that having expended so much political capital on supporting Nivelle, after the French general fell from grace, Lloyd George was less able to influence the decision-making process over Passchendaele, just a few months later.[52] Conversely, Haig emerged from the crisis with his authority enhanced. A different sort of man might have been tempted, like Sir John French before him, to work to replace the government. Much as he disliked and disagreed with Lloyd George, Haig recognised civilian authority.

Throughout the crisis, Robertson rather than Haig led the counter-offensive, tirelessly deploying the full range of his formidable political skills. Symbolically, after the scheme was unveiled at Calais, Robertson spent the night working on a response, while Haig went to sleep. With a weaker or less supportive CIGS, Haig's position would have been much more precarious. Similarly, he benefited from the support of Derby, who had been offended at being shut out of the decision-making process by Lloyd George. The Calais crisis shows how powerful and effective the triumvirate of Haig, Robertson and Derby could be. It makes Haig's behaviour seem ruthless and ungrateful when he discarded both men once their influence was on the wane.

As the date of Nivelle's offensive grew closer, his personal position became less secure. At conference of senior politicians and generals at Compiègne on 6 April, Nivelle was discredited but left in power, about to begin an offensive in which few had any faith. He was suffering from the strain of command. He had burst into tears after the London conference in March, wracked by guilt that his actions had imperilled the coalition.[53] The implications for the coalition had the offensive been cancelled would have been profound, as the British were due to attack at Arras only three days after Compiègne, and the battle would have become largely redundant.[54]

Planning for Arras

While these high-level machinations were going on the army in France prepared for the campaigns ahead. We have seen that there was a good deal of tactical experimentation during the Somme, and some attempt to capture 'lessons', but no central authority to disseminate best practice. By the autumn of 1916 Haig and GHQ were aware that its *laissez faire* attitude to training would no longer suffice.[55] Richard Butler seems to have overseen the production of a new manual, SS135 *Instructions for the Training of Divisions for Offensive Action*, which appeared in December 1916 and incorporated the lessons of the Somme. So when senior officers asked GHQ to establish a training organisation to ensure a uniform approach they were pushing at an open door. At the end of January 1917 Haig authorised the creation of a Training Directorate (or Branch), and he almost certainly personally chose the new director, Brigadier-General Arthur Solly-Flood, the commander of Third Army School at Auxi-le-Château; he definitely gave him full backing once in post. Solly-Flood was a cavalryman (4th Dragoon Guards) who had worked under Haig a decade before in the Directorate of Military Training and may have contributed to *FSR*. As 35 Brigade commander he had earned a reputation as an innovative and effective trainer. Solly-Flood was to prove an outstandingly successful appointment.

The new organisation consisted of two sections. One handled the writing of tactical doctrine, issued as manuals, while the other oversaw training. Below GHQ, each Army and Corps had a staff officer to supervise training, answerable to Solly-Flood's Directorate. This meant that not only would doctrine be produced centrally, but also that his organisation would have the power to ensure formations trained according to its precepts.

Haig visited Auxi-le-Château on 2 February and saw Solly-Flood put an infantry company through its paces in demonstrating a new tactical organisation 'which had for object the full co-operation of all infantry weapons in the attack'. He took careful notes of the exercise and was pleased with what he saw. The platoon consisted of four sections, three specialised (one each dedicated to bombs (i.e. hand grenades), rifle grenades, and Lewis guns) and a rifle and bayonet section, which gave the platoon commander greater flexibility and firepower. Typically he took the trouble to find out about the company commander – an ex-sergeant of the 7th Dragoon Guards – and his CSM, who had been wounded twice at the beginning of the war. That evening, Solly-Flood dined with Haig, doubtless to discuss the day's events. Interestingly, Haig seems to have put forward his views on the organisation of Lewis Guns, which Solly-Flood politely ignored – a fact which says much about their relationship. The C-in-C met Rawlinson and Major-General A.A. Montgomery Fourth Army CoS on the following day, and discussed Solly-Flood's work. Haig told them

> The average officer now does not know enough of tactical principles to enable him to adapt a particular formation to suit the particular task confronting him. So I decided that normal attack formation was to be laid down and practised. This can be dispensed with in years to come when our officers become more educated in military principles![56]

With these words Haig admitted that he had been wrong in 1916. If tactics were to become standardised throughout the army, the existing situation needed to be rationalised. This called for a powerful Training Directorate headed by a man with Haig's personal backing.

Under Solly-Flood the training system was thoroughly overhauled and standardised, and much sensible doctrine produced. He was probably responsible for writing two key manuals that appeared in February-March 1917, SS143 *Instructions for the Training of Platoons for Offensive Action*, and SS144, *The Normal Formation for the Attack*. These two manuals, updated periodically, were to form the basis for the BEF's infantry training and tactics until the end of the war.[57] The new doctrine incorporated the BEF's hard-won experience of the Somme fighting, and was heavily influenced by French models. It put British infantry tactics onto a sound footing by providing a simple tactical 'cook book' and was equivalent of the celebrated 1918 German 'storm trooper's manual', but issued some eleven months earlier. Solly-Flood had a vital role in the BEF's learning process. Haig learned from his own mistakes and responded to a challenge by taking decisive action in appointing and then sustaining the right man to sort it out. As a modern historian has argued Haig 'recognised the need to intervene wherever it was needed . . . Throughout 1917 he took a critical and direct interest in the tactical preparations and training of his armies.'[58]

The BEF's first major action of 1917 saw Fifth Army attack over terrain familiar from 1916, in the Ancre valley. In January and February 1917 it pushed five miles up the Ancre valley on a four-mile front. The Germans, planning a major withdrawal, were forced into a premature retreat in this sector.[59] Although Haig's plans had not come fully to fruition, it was an encouraging start to the campaigning season. It was followed, on the night of 22 February by a major surprise, when the Germans began a systematic retreat. The Allies cautiously followed them over country devastated by fighting or by a deliberate scorched-earth policy carried out by the retreating troops. By 28 March the Germans were back to the Hindenburg Line.

The German retreat presented the BEF with the challenge of conducting a type of mobile warfare of the sort it had not experienced since late 1914. Infantrymen, gunners, staff officers, commanders and logisticians had, for a short period, to grapple with open warfare. Once they arrived in front of the new position they were faced with another challenge. Learning from the Somme, the Germans had replaced the linear defence based on conventional trenches with 'elastic' defence-in-depth. Attackers would need to fight through a lightly-held outpost zone, intended to canalize them, before reaching the 'battle zone' of mutually supporting strong-points, backed by further rearward defences. Disorganised by these defences, assault troops would be faced by *Eingreif* (counterattack) divisions to push back enemy attackers. Coming to terms with these new German tactics would be a major problem for the BEF in 1917.[60]

GHQ's plan for the Battle of Arras 1917 allocated a leading part to a man who had been little more than a supporting actor in 1916. General Sir

Edmund Allenby's Third Army was to attack in the Arras sector, to capture 'the high ground about Monchy le Preux' – and then, driving forward, to outflank the enemy defences to the south of Arras. On Allenby's flank First Army (now commanded by Horne) was to assault the formidable Vimy Ridge. Allenby and Haig were not close (see p. 25), but Allenby's response to GHQ's instructions indicated that their relationship would be very different from Rawlinson's with Haig in 1916. No doubt keen to make the best of his first attempt to conduct a major offensive as an Army Commander, Allenby, after a short (48-hour) bombardment,

> hoped to be able to be able to break through all the organised German defensive system on Zero day on his front of attack . . . and to be able to exploit these successes at once with the Cavalry Corps and his Army reserves and 3 divisions in G.H.Q. reserve.[61]

An 'Appreciation' produced by Third Army included such telling phrases as the 'beginning of open warfare', and 'Artillery as well as infantry must shake off the habits of trench warfare'. To aid their progress corps cavalry and infantry were to move ahead of the main body, up to two miles, to seize key tactical points.[62]

This approach was more to Haig's taste than Rawlinson's caution, and since the artillery situation was far healthier than on the Somme nine months earlier there was scope for optimism. Overall the BEF now had 1,157 'heavies', and at the beginning of the battle of Arras the density of heavy guns was about three times greater than at the equivalent stage of the Somme: 963 guns, or one per 21 yards, as opposed to 455, or one per 57 yards.[63] But Haig did not like the idea of a 48-hour bombardment. In this he was supported by Horne, Rawlinson and Gough. Their will prevailed, and the artillery was in action for five days before the attack.[64]

Allenby's proposal to use corps mounted troops and infantry to press ahead was along the lines of Haig's own thinking. While the new German defence-in-depth doctrine might have made a straightforward breakthrough more difficult to achieve, the defences were less dense, which actually gave more scope for mounted operations like Haig's cavalry-based all-arms concept.[65]

Haig's comments on Third Army's plan give an insight into his tactical thinking in early 1917. He pointed out that what Allenby was proposing was more ambitious than anything that had been achieved so far, but in the light of weakening enemy morale it was worth trying. Nevertheless, Haig urged caution, as German resistance would not be even along the front, and this posed the risk of isolated British parties pushing ahead and getting cut off. His solution was consistent with the way his thinking had been evolving since 1915, seeking to enlarge a 'break-in' into something bigger:

> Their [the advancing troops'] object must be to push on just far enough to enable the breach they have made to be utilized for action against the flank and rear of the strong points still holding out. All must combine in overcoming these strongpoints quickly (while holding off counterattacks from troops further in rear) and thus enable the general front to be re-established as quickly as possible.

Haig was obviously alarmed by Allenby's airy dismissal of trench warfare, pointing out that it was essential to entrench against counterattacks and artillery fire when the advance came to an end on the first day. In short, while the two generals were in broad agreement on the plan, Haig took the more cautious and realistic view.[66]

Arras

The retreat to the Hindenburg Line complicated the planning for the Allied offensives. The blows might land 'in the air', so GHQ, in consultation with the Armies, considered a range of options. On 12 March it was decided to go ahead with the assault, due to begin on 8 April (it was eventually put back a day).[67] If the attacks of First and Third Armies were successful, reserves (from Fifth Army) and cavalry would be used for exploitation. Should the Arras attack run into difficulties, which in mid-March Haig seemed to consider most likely, Second Army would get priority for an attack at Ypres.[68] There were some modifications to the plans, as the Bapaume salient was disappearing.[69]

Still, nervousness remained at GHQ about the intentions of the Germans. Nivelle had been disastrously indiscreet in talking about his plans, and Haig believed (correctly) that the enemy were probably aware of Nivelle's plan. Looking back to the battle of the Frontiers in 1914, Haig feared that the Germans might once again try to draw the attackers on to a strong position, defeat the initial assault and then counterattack with devastating effect. Haig therefore decreed that the BEF should advance with caution, feeling out the German positions, and not launch the main attack until all the preparations were complete.[70] Both Horne and Allenby were ordered to be ready at 24 hours notice to launch attacks ranging from 'minor' to – somewhat inconsistently – a 'general assault' to disrupt a withdrawal.[71]

Douglas Haig approached the Battle of Arras with a sober view of the task ahead. Looking for signs of domestic disquiet among the enemy, he argued that, while a collapse might occur in Austria because of food shortages, 'we cannot expect to defeat the German and Prussian peoples except by force of arms'.[72] Two days before the attack Haig toured Army and Corps Headquarters. He found the general mood optimistic. Horne was 'well satisfied' with preparations for the assault on Vimy Ridge and 'confident of success', and all of Allenby's corps commanders were similarly positive, although the 'general opinion in 3rd Army is that the Enemy will put up a fight and will only retire when forced to do so'.[73] Intelligence reports indicated that the Germans were likely to be caught in two minds: whether to fight on the front line, as on the Somme, or to be more flexible and pull back if pressurised to positions in the rear but in reach of their guns.[74] What happened on the next day showed that this was a fairly accurate prediction,

Easter Monday, 9 April 1917 was the BEF's most successful day since the beginning of trench warfare. Lieutenant-General Sir Julian Byng's Canadian Corps (First Army) stormed Vimy Ridge. Third Army made deep inroads into German territory, with 9th (Scottish) Division advancing 3½ miles and another Kitchener division, the 12th, capturing enemy guns in Battery Valley. The First Day at Arras was in stark contrast to the First Day on the Somme, some nine months before, and demonstrated the huge strides that the BEF had made in tactical proficiency – and incidentally shored up Haig's position at home. Failure, Horne thought, would have unleashed 'a pack of jackals' on the C-in-C. Understandably Haig was in triumphant mood:

Your Majesty will be pleased to hear that I found the troops everywhere in the most splendid spirits . . . the fact that the Army was *advancing* made everyone happy! . . . Our success is already the largest obtained on this front in *one* day.[75]

The successes were real enough and demonstrated the BEF's ability to deliver a highly effective set-piece attack. True, the results were disappointing on some sectors. But more, much more, seemed temptingly within reach. Third Army's plan had envisaged the Cavalry Corps getting into the battle at the end of the first day of the fighting. The Cavalry was actually in position beyond the old German front line by 4 p.m. on 9 April, only to be sent back four hours later; the infantry had done well, but not well enough to get all the way through the German defences. To make things worse, again an opportunity to use mounted troops cropped up where there were none within easy reach. Allenby asked Haig on the afternoon of 9 April to send a cavalry brigade to support XVII Corps, where no mounted support had originally been allocated. In an episode horribly reminiscent of 14 July 1916, creaky command arrangements meant that by the time the brigade moved the moment had passed. By contrast, the action of the Northamptonshire Yeomanry in pushing ahead and seizing the bridges at Fampoux showed what could be achieved by small numbers of cavalry pushed well forward and able to take on targets of opportunity.[76]

On 10 April things still seemed to look rosy from the perspective of High Command. Allenby urged his forces on, believing that Third Army could build on the success of the previous day to rip open the German front. At 10.30 a.m. Haig met Allenby and Horne, and 'urged on Allenby the importance of keeping the Enemy on the move during the next 24 hours, before he can bring up Reserves to meet our advance'. That afternoon Haig received disturbing indications that things were not going as well as he had been led to believe. Visiting the HQ of Cavalry Corps, General Kavanagh, still kicking his heels in reserve, told Haig that the infantry were still struggling to get forward, and the key village of Monchy-le-Preux was not yet in British hands.[77]

Third Army was finding it very difficult to capitalise on its early success. The band of German defences was simply too wide for their initial impetus to carry the attackers straight through, and troops and com-manders were not finding it easy to adjust to semi-open warfare.

Lieutenant-General Haldane of VI Corps explained to Haig on 11 April that

> [h]is difficulty was to get the Commanders of Divisions to go forward, and take control of the operations. They had been accustomed to sit behind trenches and command by the aid of telegraph. Now their wires in the open soon get [sic] broken, and they lost connection with their Brigades who were fighting.

Later that day a worried Kavanagh, still waiting to get his Cavalry Corps into action, told Haig that the Germans had counterattacked after a British cavalry brigade had passed through the advancing infantry. Pushed back, British infantry and dismounted cavalry were now defending Monchy village. This proved to be a shelltrap, and the defenders lost very heavily.[78]

Fundamentally, Allenby misunderstood what was happening on the battlefield. A telegram he sent to his Corps commanders at 7.40 p.m. on the 10th sums up his tragic misconception: 'The A[rmy] C[ommander] wishes all troops to understand that Third Army is now pursuing a defeated enemy and that risks must be freely taken'. German strong-points were to be by-passed so as not to delay the advance.[79] The weather was poor – the 9 April battle had been fought in a snowstorm – and this denied Allenby the benefits of aerial reconnaissance. German reinforcements arrived on the scene just as British troops were growing tired and their attacks becoming sluggish. Highly effective work by the BEF's gunners had been a critical element on 9 April. When the infantry pushed forward to take on the rearward German defences on the 11th, not untypically the 'barrage was ragged and frequently short'. 'Attack by 3rd Division on GUEMAPPE failed on account of machine-gun fire' – this was an all too typical report.[80] Part of the problem was that guns were still struggling forward over the shattered ground.[81]

Battering against the German defences got Third Army nowhere. With hard news slow to reach him, Haig remained upbeat on 11 April. That evening the cold reality started to become clear when he spoke to Kavanagh and McCracken (GOC 15th (Scottish) Division) who were gloomy. Perhaps Haig was also was affected by the sight of 'a number of Cavalrymen marching back on foot having had their horses killed'.[82]

Not all the news that reached Haig on 12 April was bad. He was encouraged by the news of the capture of 'the Pimple', a small outcrop on Vimy Ridge, by a Canadian brigade commanded, he noted approvingly, by Edward Hilliam, a former sergeant major in the 17th Lancers. But overall the initiative was shifting away from the British. Visiting Third Army HQ, Haig spoke to Major-General Louis Bols, Allenby's Chief of Staff. The strengthening German resistance meant

> Our advance must therefore be more methodical than was permissible on Monday night and Tuesday after the victory. Then *great risks* might have been made without danger because Enemy had been surprised and had no reserves on the spot! Now we must try and substitute shells as far as possible for Infantry . . .

Eminently sensible, this assessment paralleled Haig's decision to move towards a more methodical approach on the Somme in early August 1916. But Allenby continued with ill-prepared and costly attacks. It has been suggested that Haig failed to convey his meaning to Allenby. Certainly, there was a history of mutual non-comprehension. But given that Haig initially spoke to Bols rather than Allenby, and was accompanied by Kiggell – who, whatever his faults, was not incoherent – this is unlikely. Third Army's orders for 12 April 'differed markedly' from those of the 11th, being more limited in scope.[83] Most likely Allenby, who was inexperienced in command at this level, gradually lost control of the battle.

Haig began to suspect that things were not as they should be as early as the afternoon of 13 April. Visiting the three divisional headquarters, Haig and Kiggell found that 'the nature of the orders which had reached them . . . differed in some cases in essentials from those which had been issued from Army HQ'. There was little that was methodical about the attacks over the next few days, and doubts about Allenby's control of the battle began to creep into Haig's mind.[84] These doubts were crystallised by the extraordinary happenings of 15 April. The same three divisional commanders whom Haig had visited on the 13th, Wilkinson of the 50th, de Lisle of the 29th and Robertson of the 17th, held a meeting also attended by Lord Loch from VI Corps. In effect, there was a motion of no confidence in Allenby's handling of the battle, tacitly supported at corps level. The mutineers' 'resolution', it seems, was made direct to Haig, and it almost certainly influenced his decision to suspend operations for a week.[85]

For major-generals to protest like this was a potentially career-limiting act. For them to get away with it was a shattering blow to Allenby's authority and credibility. Having on 14 April issued orders for more operations, Allenby on the following day discovered that Haig had ordered a pause to regroup. The C-in-C intended to take personal charge of drawing up a new plan.

To the south of Third Army, Fifth Army opened a new front at Bullecourt on 10–11 April. While this further turned the screw on the Germans, Gough's generalship was poor and the attack mishandled, especially the use of artillery and tanks. 4th Australian Division took heavy losses, which added to growing disenchantment with British generalship.[86] Like all battles, Arras gained momentum of its own, but its primary purpose was to support the French offensive on the Chemin des Dames. This began on 16 April, and on that day Haig conferred with Horne, Allenby and Gough and decided on a co-ordinated attack on 20 April, although this was eventually delayed until the 23rd.

With a note of resignation, Haig interpreted the unwillingness of the French to give him much information about their offensive as 'a bad sign'. He was right. Although by Western Front standards the Nivelle Offensive was a modest success in terms of ground gained, it had fallen catastrophically short of the French C-in-C's grandiose goals. 'It is a pity that Nivelle was so very optimistic as regards breaking the enemy's line,' Haig noted, without apparently recalling his enthusiasm for Nivelle's methods in the far away days of December 1916.[87] Nivelle's failure to deliver on his extravagant promises triggered serious indiscipline in many French units, although Haig was unaware of the mutinies until early June.

Haig regarded the success achieved so far at Arras as a vindication of GHQ's attritional strategy. In a private conversation with Repington at Bavincourt, Haig's Advanced HQ during Arras, he urged the journalist 'to show the connection between the Somme and Arras, and how necessary it was to wear out the German Armies in the field before doing anything else'.[88] Haig was worried by hints from Paris and London that offensive operations should be suspended until the arrival of the Americans and revival of the Russians. This was something that Haig judged was unlikely to occur until the spring of 1918, and he impressed on Robertson the need for patience and 'hard fighting'. To halt would be to discourage the BEF and give the Germans time to recover 'and to seize the initiative either in this theatre or in another'.[89]

The Second Battle of the Scarpe, the attack of 23 April, clawed about a mile of ground from the enemy. While not up to the standard set by 9 April, it compared very favourably with much of the Somme fighting. At a meeting with Nivelle on 24 April Haig made clear that the U-boat threat meant that his priority remained the clearance of the Belgian coast. This could be done either by means of an offensive in Flanders, or indirectly by continuing the Arras fighting. The BEF would make maximum efforts to break the Hindenburg Line, but continued French resistance was imperative. Haig candidly told Nivelle that he feared that the British army would become exhausted in fighting to support the Chemin des Dames offensive, but the government in Paris would halt French operations leaving the BEF too weak to attack in the north. Nivelle, with a degree of sincerity it is difficult to determine, hastened to reassure Haig that he would not halt the offensive, and neither would his government, and the men thrashed out plans for future operations.[90]

Within two days of the meeting with Nivelle Haig learned from Painlevé, the French War Minister, that Nivelle was likely to be replaced by Pétain. Haig argued for Nivelle's retention, urging that this was no time to make such an important change (privately he opted for Nivelle on the grounds of 'the devil you know'[91]). Haig had no illusions about what the future held. He was officially notified of Pétain's elevation on 29 April, writing to Robertson on the same day that the French commander referred to his methods as '"Aggressive/Defensive", and doubtless in his mind he figures the British Army doing the aggressive work, while the French Army squats on the defensive!' Under the new conditions there was no point in attempting to take Cambrai.[92]

On 30 April Haig briefed Horne, Gough and Allenby on the new facts of strategic life: that the arrival of Pétain would probably mean the French moving over to the defensive and waiting for the arrival of the Americans, whatever the promises of the French government.[93] Haig thought, wrongly, that 'French troops themselves are believed to be in good heart'. Against this background, Haig intended to push 'steadily forward to a good defensive line' by the middle of May and then 'consolidate it' and wait on events before deciding on future operations. 'In the meantime' the Germans had be fooled into believing that the BEF was undertaking a 'methodical offensive' similar to the Somme in 1916.[94]

Nivelle's professional demise occurred in slow motion.[95] Pétain was appointed to the Paris-based post of Chief of Staff to the War Ministry on 29 April, which led to an uneasy double-act with Nivelle, with the latter's influence in obvious decline. All this led to further difficulties and confusion for Haig. Who was really pulling the strings at GQG? In a farcical episode Kiggell sent a letter to Nivelle with the instruction that, if he had been sacked by the time it arrived, 'it should be handed to whoever *is* C-in-C'.[96] At a conference on 4 May a joint statement was signed by Haig and Robertson for the British and Nivelle and Pétain for the French. It bore Pétain's fingerprints, with its dismissal of attempts at a breakthrough and its insistence on 'limited objectives'.[97] This was also something of a victory for Robertson's concept of operations. The CIGS had earlier written to Haig castigating Nivelle's 'very silly theory'. None too subtly, he went on implicitly to criticise Haig's continued belief that a breakthrough could be achieved:

> To my mind no war has ever differed so much from previous wars as does the present one, and it is futile, to put it mildly, hanging on to old theories when facts show them to be wrong. At one time audacity and determination to push on regardless of loss were the predominating factors, but that was before the days of machine-guns and other modern armament . . .[98]

Haig agreed – up to a point. His assessment was that the Germans had been weakened, but not sufficiently for the 'decisive blow' in which he maintained faith. Nivelle's problems, Haig believed, stemmed from a misjudgement of the 'guiding principles' from 'time immemorial' of the structured battle, 'and the remedy now is to return to wearing-down methods for a further period, the duration of which cannot yet be calculated'.[99]

An attack on 3 May gained little ground at heavy cost but it brought the curtain down on the main part of the Battle of Arras. Small-scale but bloody local actions spluttered on, as part of the wearing-out process, throughout May. Allenby, normally ultra-loyal whatever his private feelings, gave tongue to his misgivings about the demands these attacks were making on his men. He was also frustrated with Gough, who had talked Haig into agreeing a compromise start time for the night attack of 3 May that proved to be highly unfortunate.[100] At a conference on 7 May Haig laid down the law to his Army commanders: they 'must realize that in the general interest they have to carry on with tired troops and 'cut their coats' accordingly'.[101]

Arras proved to be the end of Allenby's career on the Western Front. He was shunted off to the Middle East. This was not merely an act of malice by Haig against a rival. Allenby's credibility as a commander had been badly damaged.[102] It is a rich irony that his removal to Palestine, which Allenby rightly saw as a demotion, gave him the opportunity to make his name. Palestine was very different from the cramped confines of the Arras sector. Using a judicious mixture of Western Front techniques and the methods of open warfare, Allenby pulled off a series of brilliant victories over the Turks, earning an enduring reputation as a master of mobile warfare.[103] By sacking him, Haig, had unwittingly done Allenby an enormous favour.

Arras was the product of coalition warfare, a battle demanded by the French, the senior partners, and one that Haig was initially reluctant to fight. It had some utility, according to Haig's plans, as a wearing-out battle before the main offensive in Flanders. In this way it served the same purpose as the preliminary offensives demanded by Joffre the year before. Given the extraordinarily high costs of Arras, it is as well that Haig resisted Joffre's wishes.

Arras certainly benefited Haig in political terms. 'I cannot tell you what an excellent effect Haig's victories have had,' Derby wrote to Sassoon. 'They have given satisfaction to everybody . . .' The battles vindicated the line that Derby had been holding in Cabinet, that 'given a free hand there is nothing he and his troops cannot do'. In short, Haig had 'complete ascendency'.[104]

Perhaps Haig let the battle go on too long. Certainly he pushed his troops hard, as Allenby's protests reveal. Haig's motives in fighting on were partly to achieve a good line on which to halt and consolidate, hence his satisfaction at the capture of the Chemical Works at Roeux on 11–12 May.[105] He also wanted to inflict maximum damage on the enemy before launching the offensive in Flanders, which he hoped would have decisive consequences. Judging whether he allowed the battle to drag on is further complicated by the turmoil in the French army. Haig did not find out about the French mutinies until 2 June, but, unwittingly, the BEF aided the beleaguered GQG by attacking at a time when the French wanted the Germans to focus anywhere but on their front. On balance, continuing to fight on to the end of May probably was the right thing to do.

Arras sent mixed messages about the battlefield efficiency of the BEF. The initial assault demonstrated a high degree of competence in a limited, set-piece attack. British 13 Brigade, serving under the Canadian Corps on Vimy Ridge, listed four factors in their success on 9 April: 'perfect steadiness' of the troops 'despite being under a barrage'; 'the initiative and dash of Company and Platoon Commanders'; 'the intensity and accuracy of the barrage put up by the Canadian [and British] artillery' and 'previous practice over the taped course, which all Commanders state was of immense assistance'.[106] But after 9 April the BEF's deficiencies in semi-open fighting became all too apparent. 34th Division's frank assessment of the operations of 28–29 April mentioned problems adjusting to the new circumstances, including 'The rapidity in [sic] which plans had to be made, reconnaissances carried out and orders issued' and 'the weakness of the artillery barrage owing possibly to lack of time for reconnaissance and casualties to materiel and personnel'.[107] 34th Division, and the BEF as a whole, still had much to learn.

The question remains whether Arras was worth the vast cost in blood and treasure. While the seizure of Vimy Ridge was a magnificent feat of arms by the Anglo-Canadian forces, it was not in any way 'decisive' or a 'turning point' in the war, as it is often claimed.[108] Vimy Ridge proved an invaluable defensive position in the bitter fighting during the German offensive of March 1918. But, overall, the huge effort expended at Arras might have been better employed around Ypres, where the capture of Observatory Ridge would have been of more immediate value than Vimy.

With Arras out of the way, Haig could now turn his attention to Flanders. For the time being the French army was damaged as an offensive instrument, and Pétain, who had finally replaced Nivelle on 15 May, devoted the rest of 1917 to repairing it. The BEF would have to shoulder the burden of the Allied offensive.

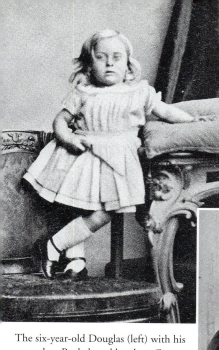

The infant Douglas Haig glares furiously at the camera. He has not yet undergone 'breeching', that is being put into trousers, which marked the transition from infancy to boyhood. He had to be bribed into posing for the picture by being allowed to hold his toy pistol. (See p.11) *National Library of Scotland*

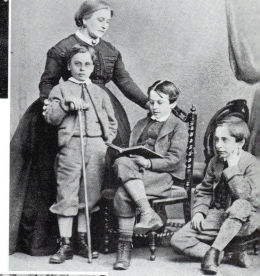

The six-year-old Douglas (left) with his mother, Rachel, and brothers George (centre) and John, nicknamed Bee (right). Douglas was Rachel's favourite child, and she was the dominant figure in his young life. *National Library of Scotland*

Although a Scot, Haig was sent to an English public school, Clifton College near Bristol. In this 1877 photograph of the school football team he is at extreme left, back row. The values inculcated at public schools were an important influence on the officer corps of the late-Victorian army. *National Library of Scotland*

A group of undergraduates at Brasenose College, Oxford: Haig is third from right, back row. He left without taking a degree, having through illness failed to complete the residence requirements. At Oxford Haig first acquired the habit of keeping a diary. *National Library of Scotland*

Douglas Haig as a subaltern in the 7th (Queen's Own) Hussars, *c.* 1885. Haig was a conscientious regimental officer, who made a success of the position of Adjutant. This was the first of the many demanding administrative positions he held over the next two decades. *National Library of Scotland*

Haig (seated in chair) and his polo team in India. Haig was an accomplished player, achieving success with both the 7th Hussars and 17th Lancers. Contemporaries saw equestrian sports as training for war, developing an eye for ground, teamwork and initiative.

National Library of Scotland

On campaign in the Second Boer War, *c.* 1900. In South Africa Haig gained valuable practical experience of staff work and command, both in conventional campaigning and counter-insurgency. He also worked with a number of soldiers who, as senior officers, were later to serve under his command on the Western Front.

National Library of Scotland

Royal connections: Haig (left) with King George V and Princess Mary, 1913. At the time Haig was commanding Britain's only permanent Army Corps at Aldershot. He had been a part of the Royal circle since the days of King Edward VII, a decade and more before. *National Library of Scotland*

Liberal statesman Lord Haldane (right) with Haig in early 1914. Haldane and Haig had a highly effective partnership in reforming the British army and held each other in the highest regard. During the Great War Haldane was hounded out of office for allegedly holding pro-German views. *Getty Images*

As commander of I Corps, Haig (far left) talks to Major-General Monro (second from left) of 1st Division, *c.* August 1914. Haig's Chief of Staff, Brigadier-General Johnnie Gough VC (second from right) confers with Brigadier-General Perceval (far right), senior artilleryman of 2nd Division. Gough was killed by a sniper in early 1915. His brother, Hubert, later commanded Fifth Army under Haig. *Imperial War Museum*

An artist's impression of the Battle of Loos, September 1915. Men of Haig's First Army advance, their gas helmets rolled up on their heads. In the background is the pair of pithead gear towers nicknamed 'Tower Bridge'. The dispute between Haig and French over the battle was the catalyst for the change of commander of the BEF. *Mary Evans/Rue des Archives/Tallandier*

Field-Marshal Sir John French, later the Earl of Ypres. Haig's career was closely intertwined with French's from before the Boer War until 1915. Even before the First World War Haig had begun to doubt French's fitness for high command, and French's behaviour in 1915 sealed his fate by alienating the King, Kitchener and Robertson as well. *Getty Images*

An Indian cavalry regiment, the Deccan Horse, in Carnoy Valley on the Somme, July 1916. Haig never lost his faith in the usefulness of cavalry on the battlefield, and the successful charge of this regiment and the 7th Dragoon Guards near High Wood on 14 July 1916 offers some evidence that he was not entirely misguided. *Imperial War Museum*

The planning for Third Ypres (or Passchendaele), 1917, as depicted by a contemporary artist. Haig is seated on the left, next to Horne of First Army. Standing, left to right, are Gough (Fifth Army), Rawlinson (Fourth Army) and Plumer (Second Army). Gough was initially given the lead role in the offensive, to be replaced by Plumer in August.

Archive Images/Alamy

The reality of war: the shell-shattered, rain-sodden battleground of Passchendaele. The battle has come to symbolise all that was terrible about the campaigns on the Western Front, and became a principal charge against Haig when his reputation came under attack in the 1930s. *Imperial War Museum*

A significant feature of Haig's work as Commander-in-Chief involved dealing with allies. Here he is pictured (second from left) with the Frenchmen Pétain (far left) and Foch (second from right), and Pershing (far right) of the United States. His relations with all three men were strained on occasions, but Haig was fundamentally a good citizen of the coalition. *Getty Images*

Accompanied by an escort from his old regiment, the 17th Lancers, Haig inspects a detachment of Canadian troops in 1918. He had a high opinion of the fighting qualities of Dominion troops. In some ways the BEF was a coalition force, containing semi-independent formations from the Empire. *Getty Images*

Savouring the moment of victory at 11.00 a.m. on 11 November 1918 in Cambrai, Haig (front centre) is flanked by Plumer (front left) and Rawlinson (front right). On the step behind, from left, are Byng, Birdwood and Horne. Behind these Army Commanders are an assortment of senior staff officers.

Imperial War Museum

Back home in 1919: Haig with his wife, Dorothy ('Doris'), and his daughters, Victoria and Alexandra. His son, known by his courtesy title of Dawyck, was born the year before. Doris and the children gave Haig a bedrock of emotional support that was invaluable in helping him cope with the pressures of high command.
Illustrated London News Ltd/Mary Evans

Douglas Haig addressing the General Assembly of the Church of Scotland, 29 May 1919, as depicted in a painting by the artist Robert Hope. Haig's Christian faith was not unusual among senior officers. Reviving during the First World War, it undoubtedly played a role in maintaining his personal morale. *Gary Doak/Alamy*

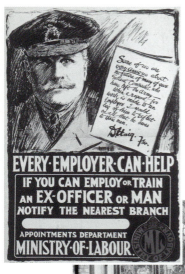

After the First World War Haig emerged as a vocal advocate for ex-servicemen. The use of his image in this poster of *c.* 1919 indicates just how famous and popular he was at this period. His work with war veterans, especially in the British Legion, was to increase his popularity during the 1920s. *Imperial War Museum*

Haig's body lay in state, in a flag-draped coffin topped by his plumed ceremonial cocked hat, in a London church, St Columba's, for two days after his death on 29 January 1928. One of those filing past to pay their respects has a crutch – he is almost certainly a disabled ex-serviceman. *Getty Images*

A.F. Hardman's statue of Haig in Whitehall has been controversial since its unveiling in 1937. Pro-Haig veterans criticised the stylised horse and the fact that the Field Marshal is bare-headed. His reputation had declined so far by 1998 that the *Express* called for it to be torn down, as it said commemorating Haig was an insult to the dead of the war. *Getty Images*

8

False Dawns

For the British, 1917 is dominated by one battle. 'Passchendaele' proved a mighty and lasting blow to Haig's post-war reputation. It was, wrote Lloyd George, 'one of the greatest disasters of the War'. General Sir Ian Hamilton, the commander at Gallipoli, agreed. 'Passchendaele was the most damnable battle in history and should never have been fought'.[1] The Third Battle of Ypres – Passchendaele – is central to an assessment of Haig's generalship. Mere mention of it conjures up images of blind attrition, of men struggling forward in glutinous mud, of futile death. Yet the preliminary operation at Messines was an outstanding success. The middle phase of Third Ypres brought the enemy to the verge of defeat, and at the end of the year the battle of Cambrai briefly offered a tantalising vision of a return to mobile warfare. So for the British Empire 1917 was not just the year of 'Passion Dale', of men sacrificed on a hellish battlefield.[2] It was also a year of false dawns.

In 1917 the rationale for an offensive in Flanders was just as compelling as in the previous year (see p. 160), and the situation at sea gave it added urgency. The capture of the Belgian coast would help combat the menace of German submarines which was threatening Britain's very ability to go on fighting. A relatively modest advance of about seven miles in front of Ypres would drive the Germans from the half-moon of high ground that faced the city. The vital communications junction of Roulers was only twelve miles from Ypres, and its seizure would put the coast within striking distance and place German logistics in Flanders in jeopardy, and might even force German withdrawal from the area. A Flanders offensive offered a big prize.

Tasked in 1916 to produce a plan, Rawlinson had advocated a 'stepping stones' approach, taking one objective to ease the way to the next. In early March 1916 GHQ built on Rawlinson's plan to produce an advance in six phases.[3] In November Plumer of Second Army was put in charge of planning. His initial draft was deemed too cautious by the C-in-C, but his revised plan, delivered at the end of January 1917, bore the hallmarks of the methodical process which would prove highly successful later in the year. The capture of the high ground around Ypres by two armies would lead to a gradual push out of the Salient; then an advance would begin from Nieuport (on the coast), and an amphibious force would land in the German rear at Middelkerke.[4]

In the end, the plan actually put into operation at the end of July 1917 differed in significant ways from Rawlinson's and Plumer's proposals. As Andrew Wiest has argued, 'a series of General Staff reports and tactical debates altered the nature of Third Ypres'. First in the field were Kiggell and Davidson, the head of GHQ Operations Branch. Then, on 14 February came a report by two GHQ staff officers. Plumer and Rawlinson were also consulted. It is clear from the documents that these men had thought through the various problems and were not simply behaving as nodding dogs. Although a preliminary limited offensive was mounted to capture Messines Ridge, Pilckem and Observatory Ridges were supposed to fall in the initial rush of a main attack by a single Army that aimed at a breakthrough. In rejecting a step-by-step approach involving two Armies, Haig 'acted on the advice of Rawlinson, Plumer and members of his own staff at GHQ'.[5]

Messines Ridge was to be the scene of a separate operation in June 1917. Captured during First Ypres, this stretch of German-held high ground dominated the southern flank of the Ypres Salient. On the surface, it seems odd that Haig decided to launch the Messines operation before the main attack; it seems to flatly contradict his previous insistence on simultaneous attacks in the Ypres salient. The answer seems to lie with the changed circumstances. In early 1917 Haig had envisaged the Germans being severely weakened by Nivelle's all-out offensive.[6] On 7 May he announced that the Allied objective was now 'to wear down and exhaust the enemy's resistance'; with this achieved, the British would then strike 'the main blow' from Ypres towards the Belgian coast. Lacking the troops to continue the Arras campaign at maximum force and also concentrate in Flanders, First, Third and Fifth Armies would 'simulate a continuance' of the Arras battle, mounting attacks on 'strictly limited' objectives, well past the time when the Messines operation would be carried out. It was hoped to fool the enemy into regarding the preparations opposite Messines as an attempt to draw German reserves from the main effort.[7]

Rapidly, the plan unravelled. Faced with widespread mutinies in the French army Pétain was unable to fulfil the promises of offensive action in the short term; by late April German intelligence had already picked up that there was going to be a substantial British attack in the area, and it proved beyond the resources of the BEF to keep Arras going as a plausible battle into June.

Haig's concept for the Flanders operation sought to use a step-by-step approach to open the way for mobility:

> as the wearing-down process continues, advanced guards and cavalry will be able to progress for much longer distances profiting by the enemy's demoralization until a real decision is reached.[8]

Rawlinson's ignoring of this process on the Somme, and Plumer's caution perhaps explains why Haig turned to Gough to carry out the attack.

Messines gives us some interesting insights into Haig's methods of command. Having been presented with Second Army's plan, he took pains to investigate both the broad principles and fine detail. There is a fine line between a commander taking an intelligent interest in the plans of subordinates and unwarranted interference that stifles initiative. During Messines, Haig was just on the side of the angels. The centrepiece of Plumer's plan was the detonation of 19 mines (tunnels packed with high explosive) under the German positions culminating in chambers packed with high explosive. Haig proposed blowing the mines before the main attack to make the Germans show their hand prematurely. Plumer and Harington, his CoS, held out against this – and won the argument.[9]

More controversial was the fact that Haig introduced the idea of an advance towards Courtrai and Roulers. While this can be interpreted as spectacularly missing the point of a limited advance, echoing Plumer's rather puzzled response, a close reading of the documents shows that

Haig was actually engaging in contingency planning in case the Messines operation triggered a major German collapse. Similarly, Haig was concerned that Plumer should prepare to take advantage of possible chaos by seizing the Passchendaele Ridge.[10] The failures to exploit success in earlier battles had made a deep impression.

Haig's confidence soared as the day of battle neared. Addressing his Army commanders on 5 June, he observed that, '[i]f, during the next few weeks, failure to stop the steady, determined, never-wearying advance of our Armies is added to a realisation of the failure of the submarine campaign, the possibility of the collapse of Germany before next winter becomes appreciably greater'.[11]

Visiting Second Army HQ at Cassel on 6 June, shaking hands with the main staff officers and wishing them luck, Haig was struck by their confidence. He congratulated Plumer on Second Army's preparations, which were methodical and meticulous.[12] Artillery fire was so effective that the Germans lost about half of their guns even before the infantry attack began. At 3.10 a.m. on 7 June the mines were detonated, wrenching off the crest of the ridge. Nine divisions then moved to the attack, and Messines Ridge passed back under British control for the first time since November 1914.

That afternoon, Haig visited Plumer to offer his congratulations. He was still hoping for immediate exploitation on the back of the advance. Previously, Plumer had asked Haig for three days to redeploy artillery in preparation for a follow-up to the initial attack. Plumer repeated his request on 8 June. Haig promptly turned the operation over to Gough. The Fifth Army commander then studied the options before reporting to GHQ on 14 June in favour of abandoning the idea of a further preliminary attack, fearing that success would simply result in 'a very exposed and difficult salient'.[13]

Reading between the lines of his diary of 8 June, it seems that Haig was displeased at Plumer's insistence on 'further methodical preparation' for an attack. He feared that the opportunities for exploitation while the Germans were reeling would slip away, as in earlier battles, and it is difficult not to read into the decision Haig's anger at Plumer's apparent ignoring of previous express instructions concerning the use of advanced guards. Arguably Plumer made a mistake in not making more active preparations for immediate exploitation on the lines suggested by Haig.

This error was compounded by Haig, who turned to Gough, only to be given an even less welcome answer at a time when it was too late to do anything but acquiesce. Thus the Germans were allowed time to recover when they were at a point of maximum vulnerability. Plumer should have been allowed his three days to prepare to for a follow-up attack. Logistically it was impossible to segue from the Battle of Messines into the main attack around Ypres without an operational pause of some weeks.[14]

Preparing the Third Battle of Ypres

Seven days after the Messines action had begun, Haig laid out his objectives at an Army commanders' conference. It is sometimes suggested that Haig was unclear in his own mind what the forthcoming offensive was supposed to achieve. In truth, as at the Somme a year earlier, he had dual objectives: 'wearing out the Enemy' and 'securing the Belgian Coast and connecting with the Dutch frontier'. To achieve both these aims he envisaged three phases: capturing the Passchendaele Ridge; moving on Roulers; and an amphibious landing combined with an attack along the coast from Nieuport. 'If effectives, or guns inadequate it may be necessary to call a halt after No 1 is gained.'[15]

If this was Haig's 'big picture', the fine detail was filled in through a prolonged series of exchanges between Fifth Army and GHQ. The intention was to produce clarity, but in reality what emerged was confusion. It might be called a comedy of errors but for the fact that the outcome was so tragic. At bottom was a fundamental flaw in Haig's methods of command. Instead of 'gripping' Gough, giving him his intent and leaving Fifth Army to fill in the details, Haig made suggestions and gave advice but did not give an unambiguous directive. Haig's operational concept was essentially sound. While he certainly believed that a breakthrough was possible, he realised that the best way of achieving it, in line with his operational thinking that had developed over the previous couple of years, might be to proceed one step at a time, to wear out and grind down enemy forces. Unfortunately, Gough 'was not subtle enough to understand the dual nature of the offensive'.[16] Putting Gough in charge of what became the Third Battle of Ypres was a bad and costly decision.

Kiggell spelt out that German positions in the Ypres area were based on the principle of defence-in-depth, and thus a limited advance was appropriate. Haig, when he put Gough in charge of the abortive follow-on offensive after Messines, stressed the importance of Fifth Army 'secur[ing] its right flank' by taking the high ground. Nonetheless, Gough dropped the idea of a preliminary operation along these lines and rejected the planning that had already taken place. Instead he presented a scheme with distant objectives.[17] Davidson sent him a memorandum from GHQ, which surely reflected Haig's views, advocating a series of deliberate attacks of a maximum of 3,000 yards at two- to three-day intervals, which would smash up German reserves and give the enemy no time to recover. It linked together 'steps' to bring about a breakthrough.[18]

Gough's reaction was to come up with a very different concept of operations from GHQ's. Haig, deferring to the man on the spot, backed Gough's approach but nonetheless had some reservations. At a lunch meeting with Gough on 28 June, Haig urged 'that the advance north should be limited until our right flank has really been secured on this ridge'.[19] Haig gave Gough a number of extremely sensible suggestions – but they were no more than that. Advice can be ignored; orders should be obeyed. Gough chose to ignore Haig's counsel, which was never translated into firm orders. This amounted to a dreadful abdication of command responsibility on Haig's part.

While GHQ and Fifth Army were conducting their dialogue of the deaf, Haig also had to argue his case in London. For two weeks in June, he had to defend his plans in Whitehall and Westminster. At stake was the fundamental issue of whether the government would permit the British army to mount the major offensive in Flanders that Haig planned. Constitutionally, His Majesty's Government had every right to forbid it. Lloyd George and his colleagues chose not to do so. After the war Lloyd George would claim that Haig had kept the government in the dark about the preparations for 'Passchendaele' until June 1917. This is simply untrue. Not for nothing did he earn the nickname 'Lliar George'.[20]

If there was a dominant feeling in the War Cabinet that June, it was unease about the military prospects for the future and cynicism about advice it had received from the military. The result was a review to be conducted by War Policy Committee of Lloyd George, Lord Curzon, Lord Milner and J.C. Smuts, with the ubiquitous Hankey as secretary.

'There is trouble in the land' Robertson reported to Haig.[21] As far as GHQ's strategy was concerned, he was right.

The Third Battle of Ypres was not inevitable. One alternative strategy was to carry out what Lloyd George described as 'Pétain tactics': short, sharp blows against the Germans on different parts of the front as part of a 'process of wearing down the enemy'.[22] Another was to wait for the arrival of masses of American troops, which realistically would mean 1918. Naturally, Haig rejected this; 'There is no time like the present,' he urged Derby.[23] Yet another was to make the main Allied offensive on the Italian front, which the British could support with guns and gunners from the Western Front. When Robertson put forward this plan, Haig's reply was utterly predictable: ' Send to France every possible man . . . airoplane [sic] . . . [and] gun.[24]

In a cogently argued document sent to the CIGS Haig set out his beliefs of what his Flanders offensive could achieve. He was careful to factor in French support and made an astute link between the Eastern and Western Fronts. At present the Russians were still fixing a considerable body of German troops on their front, but this situation might not go on for ever, given the revolutionary ferment in the country. Prompt action by the British was essential to make the most of this favourable situation. On top of this, he set out his belief that declining morale, strain on the home front and an escalating manpower shortage was bringing the German army to the point of crisis. Haig offered the probability of clearing the Belgian coast in 1917, and that 'Germany may well be forced to conclude peace on our terms before the end of the year'. Robertson was alarmed, not least because he could see how badly Haig's confidence would go down with the Cabinet: 'Don't argue that you can finish the war this year . . . Argue that your plan is the best plan – as it is – and leave them to reject your advice and mine. They dare not do that.'[25]

Did Haig mislead London about the forthcoming battle? Most of Lloyd George's claims were false but they contained a grain of truth. First, in their presentations to the War Cabinet in June Haig followed the advice that Robertson had given him. His language was 'moderate and cautious', as was the CIGS's. Haig made reference to a phased attack that would grind down the enemy and would avoid a 'tremendous offensive involving heavy losses'. Certainly Haig and Robertson were not being wholly candid, but Haig's comments did reflect his intentions; influenced by Messines, he hoped to avoid a repetition of Somme style fighting. In his memoirs Lloyd George penned a dramatic scene in which Haig used his hands to 'sweep' across a map to point to the ultimate objective of the Flanders offensive: the German frontier. If this actually happened, it is difficult to see how Lloyd George could claim that the War Cabinet was misled as to the nature of the forthcoming battle. Alternatively, he could simply have made up the whole episode.[26]

A further charge is that Haig and Robertson misled the War Cabinet as to the likely scale of French support for the Flanders offensive by failing to pass on what they knew about the mutinies in the French army. It is true that the military men were backward in coming forward with their intelligence on the state of the French army, and offered what turned out to be exaggerated estimates of the size of its contribution to the battle. Pétain had offered General Anthoine's six-division-strong French First Army to serve under Haig's orders, and it seems that the British C-in-C remained hopeful that Pétain would be able to deliver on his earlier promises of substantial offensives. In any case the War Policy Committee came to its own (realistic) conclusions about the likelihood of the scale of French support, so the generals' views seem to have made little influence.[27]

Haig was in two minds about the French Army. He firmly believed that the BEF was capable of winning a great victory, with or without major French support.[28] The idea that he had to fight Passchendaele to keep the pressure off the French army recovering from mutiny is not wholly convincing. Senior French commanders were opposed to the battle, wanting instead limited battles.[29] However it is clear that Haig did not fully trust the French army. He seems to have been affected by reports such as one from Esher that told of the horrors of *poilus* demanding peace, electing officers, and refusing to salute.[30] Haig thought the best way of preserving it was to keep the Germans away by attacking them. On 19 September, for example, he recorded in his diary 'Pétain's opinion [that] its discipline is so bad that it could not resist a determined German offensive'.[31] Whether Haig's low opinion of the French army was closely related to the facts is a different matter; he believed it to be true, and it was undoubtedly a factor in his thinking.

So was the naval situation. When on 20 June Admiral Jellicoe, the First

Sea Lord, burst out that that was 'no good discussing plans for next Spring – we [i.e. Britain] cannot go on' because of the submarine threat, he was exaggerating, as Haig well understood.[32] Nonetheless, the opinion of the professional head of the Royal Navy could not simply be ignored. There was no single solution to the naval crisis. Only a minority of U-boats were based in the major Belgian ports, as Britain's senior sailors knew, but the occupation of the Flanders coast would bring other important advantages, including neutralising German surface raiders, for '[t]he more the general U-boat threat sucked the [Royal] Navy's light forces out of the Channel, the more vulnerable would the Army's supply lines be to local German attack'.[33] No one believed that clearing the Belgian coast would decide the maritime struggle, but it would be a very useful step in the right direction. It is as wrong to think that concern for the naval position was foremost among Haig's motives for launching the Third Battle of Ypres as it is to underestimate it as a factor.

At the War Cabinet on 21 June Lloyd George made a forceful case against the Flanders offensive, but then said in effect that, if the generals ignored the War Policy Committee's advice, so be it: the politicians would not obstruct the soldiers' plans. By default, through a failure of leadership, Haig had been given the green light.

This was compounded by the War Policy Committee's report, which did not appear until 20 July. It gave Haig the go-ahead for the offensive, but ordered that 'on no account' should the battle go the way of the Somme with 'protracted, costly and indecisive operations'. This was to be avoided by 'a frequent review of the results', and the offensive was to be halted if the casualties outweighed the advantages. Who would do the assessing – Haig, or the War Cabinet? It just was not clear.[34] Haig entered upon his great Flanders offensive aware that political support was shaky and dependant on results. But he was convinced his army could do great things.

After returning from London Haig spent much of his time doing something rather more to his taste, visiting his army. On a visit to 8th Division he witnessed one of Colonel Ronnie Campbell's notorious lectures on bayonet fighting. Haig 'unobtrusively assisted, sharing in the general enjoyment of Colonel Campbell's grim and intensely practical humour'.[35] On 17 July he saw a rehearsal of 73 Brigade's attack against Shrewsbury Forest and Tower Hamlets Ridge. 'It gave me great confidence as to the result of the attack, to talk to the officers and men'. The Corps' senior commanders and staff officers also gave Haig confidence: 'Looking round the faces opposite to me, I felt what fine, hard looking, determined men the war had brought to the front . . .'[36]

Third Ypres

The Flanders offensive exploded into life on 31 July 1917. Postponed for three days at the request of General Anthoine, the opening of the offensive demonstrated how adept the BEF had become at low-level tactics, with effective artillery fire, infantry tactics and all-arms co-operation to the fore. 14th Hampshires fought their way through a chequerboard of German pillboxes, working around these defences to attack from the rear. They reached their third objective but had to pull back about 300 yards to the second, where the troops dug in and inflicted heavy damage on counterattacking German troops. This story was not untypical of Fifth Army units in the centre and left of the attack.[37] German defensive doctrine meant that the front was held lightly: 'The enemy's counter-attacks', reported a divisional commander, 'were so timed as to strike the leading waves about the same time as they reached their objectives, when they were more or less disorganised, and had been unable to consolidate the ground gained'.[38] The British were unable to push on to the ambitious objectives set by Gough and approved, however reluctantly, by Haig.

On the extreme right of Fifth Army, there was a particularly tough fight for the Gheluvelt plateau. 73 Brigade, which Haig had seen in training on 17 July, got as far as a group of pillboxes short of its second objective. Haig's suggestion of preliminary attacks looked more sensible than ever; there was simply insufficient combat power amassed against this position, resulting in the very things that the War Cabinet had feared, attritional fighting and heavy losses (some 33,000 Allied casualties, 27,000 in Fifth Army). Second Army to the south conformed to the modest advances achieved by Gough's right, while in the north, Anthoine's French First Army kept in step with Fifth Army's left. Overall, Fifth Army was 'less than half-way to the first day's objectives' and from 30 to 60 per cent of its 'fighting strength' had been lost. To put it no more strongly, if GHQ's plan had been followed, concentrating on the capture of the Gheluvelt plateau might have led to success on the lines of Messines or

Vimy Ridge. And this would have left the British army in a much more favourable position to attempt the subsequent phases.[39]

Haig was woken by the guns at 4.15 a.m. 'The whole ground was shaking with the terrific bombardment'. He spent the morning of 31 July reading reports on the progress of the attack delivered to him at his Advanced Headquarters in a camouflaged train. In the afternoon he visited the headquarters of XIX and II Corps, responsible for the sector that worried him most, Gough's right.

> Fighting on our right had been most severe. This I had expected. Our Divisions had made good progress and were on top of the ridge which the Menin Road crosses, but had not advanced sufficiently eastwards to have observation into the valleys beyond . . . This was a fine day's work. Gough thinks that he has taken over 5,000 prisoners and 60 guns or more.[40]

His complacent reaction probably reflected what he thought was a reasonable achievement for the first day of battle.

Haig ordered Gough to continue with his 'original plan: to consolidate ground gained, and to improve his position as he may deem necessary for facilitating the next advance: the next advance will be made as soon as possible, but only after adequate bombardment and after dominating the hostile artillery'. Over the next couple of days he continued to point out the importance of the dominating ground on the right to Gough. At last Fifth Army reflected this advice in the orders to renew the attack on 2 August.[41]

The weather then complicated matters. In the afternoon of 31 July the heavens opened. 'The effect upon the shell-tormented battle ground is known only to those who saw it with their own eyes, for it cannot be described in words'.[42] Such sand gets thrown into the engine of the most polished military limousine. For many years the story that there was a regular 'monsoon' in Flanders which was ignored by High Command in its planning has been put forward as an example of GHQ's obtuseness, but it has no foundation in fact. The rain in Flanders during the battle was abnormally heavy.[43] Likewise, a favourite but almost certainly untrue story has Kiggell, on seeing the Ypres battlefield for the first time, tearfully exclaiming, 'Good God, did we send men to fight in that?' This implies that that Haig and GHQ were ignorant of the terrible conditions on the battlefield. This too is untrue.[44] On 1 August, Haig noted 'A terrible day of rain. The ground is like a bog in this low lying country!'.[45] This is why Gough's attack was delayed, eventually until 10 August – but it was not cancelled. The wider dictates of strategy meant that the fighting had to go on.

In the meantime Haig, through Kiggell, sent Gough instructions based on an analysis of German defensive tactics, 'directing him to reduce the length of his next advance to what the men can easily do in the bad state of the ground (say about 2,000 yards). The Enemy will then when he counter attacks be held up by our troops while they are still fresh'. In effect this set out a doctrine of bite-and-hold limited attacks to exhaust and disorganise the enemy: the latest version of the operational methods Haig had advocated since 1915. These were not intended to be an end in themselves but to open the way to mobile warfare: 'reducing the length of our advance may make our progress slow to begin with,' Haig calculated, 'but will pay us later on, I hope, when the Enemy's troops are worn out, and discouraged through failures in counter attacking . . .' Haig, as ever, was keen to note examples of weaknesses in German morale. Robertson was encouraged by the 'sane views' on bite-and-hold at GHQ, even if it was only accepted 'unwillingly'.[46]

Gough's attack of 10 August was another disappointment. The assaulting troops of II Corps were not fresh, and Fifth Army was at fault in failing to provide sufficient artillery fire. By contrast, German gunnery and counterattacks did major damage. Haig's initial reaction was favourable[47] – but his patience with Gough was starting to wear thin. 8th Division and II Corps asked Fifth Army for an operation to capture the objective of the 10th prior to the next major attack. But Gough, mindful of the timetable for the amphibious landing, at that time due to take place on 6 September, stuck to the concept of a broad-front attack and would only agree to a 24-hour postponement of the main operation. Bad weather meant that the assault was actually delayed until 16 August.[48]

In the north of the 16th August attack, there was a solid gain: Langemarck, which gave its name to the whole battle. Here XIV Corps pushed forward up to 1,500 yards. This merely exaggerated the salient on the left of Fifth Army, because of the slow progress on the Gheluvelt Plateau. One of the attacking brigades made 'a net gain of 400 yards'.[49]

Haig was not happy. He was clearly irritated with Gough's failure to deal with the problem on the right. 'It is very difficult in these battles quickly to discover what the real situation is,' Haig had lamented on 16 August, but on the next day, talking to senior commanders, he knew all too well that the latest push had been a failure. He noted that Cavan, whose XIV Corps had obtained the one success of the day, had paid particular attention to minor tactics. Haig was not taken in by Gough's scapegoating of 16th (Irish) and 36th (Ulster) Divisions. As for the Gheluvelt Plateau, Haig discerned that the artillery preparation was incomplete: '3 more days should have been allowed in which, if fine, the artillery would have dominated the Enemy's artillery, and destroyed the concrete defences! After Gough has got at the facts more fully I have arranged to talk the matter over with him'.[50]

Gough's response to the setback on 16 August was to begin a series of small-scale operations to straighten the line before the next major attack began on the 25th. Some ground was seized, but usually at heavy cost. After the war Gough tried to cover his tracks by claiming that Haig had overridden his protests about the difficulty of fighting on under these conditions, but these claims are 'disingenuous'.[51]

Inverness Copse, captured on 22 August, was lost to a German attack on the 24th. According to the official historian, this was the point at which Haig gave up on Fifth Army. Gough's failure to apply GHQ's sensible tactical advice, or even reply to the memorandum until 24 August, probably did him no favours. Plumer, by contrast, replied within five days, endorsing GHQ's thinking.[52] It was also perhaps unfortunate for Gough that the failure of his ambitious approach contrasted with news from the Lens front, where, in a carefully planned limited operation, the Canadian Corps had seized Hill 70 on 15 August. Haig was gratified by the capture of places 'well known to us in September 1915 at the time of the Battle of Loos'.[53]

Gough's methods had failed, and Haig gave Plumer primary responsibility for the battle. There was no question of ending the battle there and then. Haig clearly believed a decisive victory which would lead to peace was still possible. In late August he worried that the Allies would accept compromise peace terms from the Germans. Two months later his view on accepting a compromise peace was even bleaker. The Germans could chose to renew the war at their leisure, and Britain's international prestige and 'self-respect' would suffer catastrophic collapse. If he feared a peace that was too moderate, he also feared one that was too radical. The popular unrest in Europe in 1917, and the collapse of Russia into revolution, made Haig profoundly nervous. Removing the Hohenzollerns, as US President Woodrow Wilson was proposing, 'would be a mistake', Haig thought; it would 'leave Germany at the mercy of Revolutionaries, and that if disorder started in Germany it would spread to France and England'.[54]

And what was the War Cabinet's reaction during the grim August battles? It shrugged its collective shoulders. Britain's senior politicians knew that Haig's armies had made little progress and losses were high. However much Lloyd George might rail against Haig in private – 'We must formulate new plans. Our soldiers have no imagination'[55] – with his Unionist coalition colleagues continuing to support the generals, his hands were tied. At an inter-Allied conference in London Lloyd George tried an indirect approach by returning to his well-rehearsed theme of supporting an offensive in Italy with British guns from the Western Front, which would have had the effect of crippling Haig's offensive. This stratagem got nowhere. Lloyd George did not pursue it with much vigour; his credibility as a warlord was at a low ebb following the Nivelle affair. By default he sanctioned the continuation of the battle. He later admitted that 'the government could have stopped it if they had had the moral courage to do it'; but the generals would then have complained that they were robbed of victory by political interference.[56] Lloyd George suffered with remorse for the rest of his life. Long after he had left office, his savage denunciations in the 1930s of the safely dead Haig were an attempt to expiate his guilt – and shift the blame.

Plumer asked for three weeks to prepare the next stage of the battle. Haig agreed, GHQ pointedly ordered Gough to restrict himself to strictly limited 'methodical and well combined attacks' on key tactical features that would prepare the ground for a future major attack.[57] Plumer and Harington set to work to prepare for the attack with meticulous attention to detail.[58]

While Second Army was preparing, Fifth Army carried out a series of minor operations that were operationally valid but badly handled. Ahead of Gough's attack on Glencorse Wood in early September Haig was insistent that it should only be launched if conditions were favourable.

Alerted by Kiggell that Corps commanders were afraid to speak their mind to Gough, Haig consulted with them and with Gough and ordered that the small attacks should cease.[59] But the pain was not all on one side. Ludendorff described the battle of Langemarck on 16 August as 'another great blow' that landed on the defenders – a sobering reminder that the success of a battle can only be judged by considering both sides of No Man's Land. In August the Germans lost several important positions in the salient. Ludendorff later spoke, in terms that would have gladdened Haig's heart, of some of the Germans defenders 'no longer displaying that firmness' that their commanders expected.[60]

When Haig met his Army Commanders on 21 August, he had a stern message: the battle might last until November, but manpower, especially infantry manpower, was running short. The British army's prodigious expenditure of human life since 1914 was threatening to become a check on future operations. 'Under the circumstances there is no alternative but to throw into the battle, as a fighting man, every single able-bodied man in France who is not directly concerned with the prosecution of operations'. Rear areas were to be combed out and the men retrained as infantry, to be available by October, or the risk would be run that the fighting might have to be halted 'when complete success may be within our grasp'.[61]

Fighting on the Western Front was almost invariably bloody, but on too many occasions the problem had been exacerbated by tactics that led to needless loss of life. Major Valentine Fleming MP, a friend of Winston Churchill, was killed in May 1917, following his orders to the letter in defending Guillemont Farm, an obscure position of little tactical significance.[62] Clearly, Haig was not directly to blame for this, but as the man at the top, he bore ultimate responsibility for the BEF's approach to fighting. He didn't belatedly wake up to the operational consequences of heavy losses in August 1917. Neither was he indifferent to the human cost. But he didn't do enough to minimise losses. Attempts to change the culture and philosophy of command would not have produced a bloodless Passchendaele, but they might have reduced the number of Guillemont Farms, and this would have had a significant cumulative effect.

Plumer outlined his plans to GHQ on 29 August. X and I Anzac Corps were to attack the Gheluvelt Plateau, with II Anzac Corps in reserve.

The attack would be in four phases, with a six days pause between each to allow guns and supplies to be brought forward. Each infantry assault of a maximum 1,500 yards would be conducted under the cover of an artillery barrage, with fresh troops at hand to deal with the inevitable German counterattacks. The advance would be in three bounds, with pauses for mopping up, consolidation and the bringing up of reserves. By restricting the length of each bound the infantry would stay within range of their own artillery and machine-guns. Having taken the objective, they would dig in and smash up the counterattacks.[63] This model would transform the fortunes of the British army in the Third Battle of Ypres.

Haig generally let Plumer get on with preparations for the offensive but was careful to check that all had been done to his satisfaction, in one case ordering artillery plans to be recast. He visited all Second Army's corps and was pleased at what he found. 'In every case I found the officers full of confidence as to the results of the forthcoming attack. Every detail has been gone into most thoroughly, and their troops most carefully trained'. When Haig met Plumer on 18 September, 'I could only wish him success and good luck. The old man was full of good spirits and most confident'.[64] Plumer's confidence was not misplaced.

The main blow in the Battle of the Menin Road was delivered in a surprise attack by four divisions – 41st, 23rd, and 1st and 2nd Australian – on 20 September 1917. Fifth Army guarded the flank. 'The Enemy's counter attacks were numerous and determined,' Haig noted, but 'Second Army reported at 10.20 p.m. all had been destroyed . . .' Aided by fine weather, highly effective infantry tactics, and a crushing weight of artillery, on 20 September 1917 the German tactics based on elastic defences and counterattacks were neutralised. The BEF gained a notable victory, although it was not bought cheaply. The two Armies had sustained 20,000 casualties between them between 20 and 25 September.[65] It has been argued that the success of Menin Road has been exaggerated and that the praise heaped on Plumer was the product of 'the diminishing expectations accompanying the campaign'. Gough had promised much but failed to deliver, whereas Plumer's more modest endeavour lived up to lower expectations.[66] True enough, but Menin Road had a more profound impact on the Germans than the operations of 31 July. On that day German defensive tactics worked successfully. At Menin Road they did not, and the battle heralded a run of British offensives that brought the Germans close to defeat.

At last, at long last, things were happening in the way Haig had envisaged. The success of 20 September was repeated six days later at Polygon Wood. Second Army had spent the intervening time getting guns and supplies some 2,000 yards forward over the shattered ground, with engineers slaving to put down plank roads so that the guns could get in place to herald the new attack. The weather continued to hold. Indeed, in place of rain the infantry had the problem of thick dust thrown up from dry ground by artillery fire.

Hankey, visiting GHQ with Lloyd George, sat next to Haig at dinner on the 25th but found him 'rather preoccupied about tomorrow's attack'.[67] A German attack that afternoon had disrupted preparations for the following day, when it was the turn of 4th and 5th Australian Divisions of I Anzac Corps to swing the axe.[68] Haig spent the morning in a conference at GHQ with Lloyd George and Robertson focused on political and strategic matters; an eloquent comment on the impotence of the high commander when troops went over the top. Hankey was a fascinated observer at the conference:

> All the time . . . messages were coming in from the front. Haig had a great map showing the line we wanted to reach, and it was very interesting the way first one bit was filled in, then another, until by the time we finished . . . the picture was complete except for a small section, where two brigades had been held up [as a result of the enemy attack on the 25th]. In the evening, when we came back to GHQ . . . news came that this bit was also captured, and the whole picture was complete like a jigsaw puzzle.[69]

At the cost of 15,375 BEF casualties, all objectives were taken and heavy damage inflicted on the enemy. Polygon Wood confirmed the message of Menin Road. Massed artillery covering infantry attacks limited to a thousand yards or so was a highly effective counter to the new German defensive tactics.

At 5 p.m. on the 26th Haig, Gough and Plumer met to discuss what would happen next. Since the 20th Haig had identified the possibilities of expanding operations as the bite-and-hold operations took their toll on

the Germans. In his diary on 23 September he explained his belief that
'we shall be able to accomplish things after the next offensive [i.e. 26
September] which we could not dare even to attempt now'.[70] Now, with
the victory of Polygon Wood under his belt, he looked to the point when
enemy demoralisation and the exhaustion of reserves would allow more
than just the 'gain [of] a definite and limited objective line'. Exploitation
was back on the agenda, to achieve 'more decisive results'.

What Haig proposed was firmly in line with his cherished operational
concept: to have fresh troops, including dismounted cavalry, equipped
and ready for mobile action, to seize the initiative after German
counterattacks had been repulsed to hammer the wedge further into the
enemy positions and thus prise them open even further. This was not a
proposal for a wild dash into the enemy rear: 'advances . . . must be
carefully planned and prepared and supported by Artillery', and he
ordered improvement of roads and rail links on the battlefield to
'facilitate the rapid transport of troops'. It might be that conditions were
ripe for the use of cavalry to raid the German communications, but it is
significant that Haig envisaged them in a dismounted role at the
beginning of the operation, and mounted only in the later stages.[71] This
was a more cautious approach than on the Somme and seems to indicate
a further modification of Haig's ideas to suit the circumstances.

Both Gough and Plumer were concerned that to attempt far-reaching
exploitation was not yet feasible, that further bite-and-hold operations
to push further onto the high ground were first necessary. Haig explained
that he was not saying that exploitation would follow the 10 October
attack, but commanders needed to be in a position to do it if necessary.
Moreover he firmly corrected Fifth Army's misapprehension that he was
contemplating 'an advance under approximately open warfare conditions': 'I did not intend this: I mean that arrangements be made to pass
beyond the limited object to exploit a success'.[72]

This view has been pilloried by historians, but it was a wise precaution
that did not affect the limited nature of the next attack. More contentious
was Haig's view, stated at a conference on 2 October. He looked back to
the German failure to capitalise on British weakness and exhaustion three
years earlier, on 31 October 1914, during First Ypres; he would not make
the same mistake, and would concentrate forces in Flanders to attempt
to push the battle to a conclusion (see p. 98).[73]

Second Army prepared to exploit success along the lines ordered by Haig. Before the Battle of Broodseinde, fought on 4 October, a plan was issued for the follow-up operation (then planned for the 10th). A mobile artillery group was organised in each corps, and tanks and Corps Mounted Troops were placed in readiness to move. If the attack of 10 October triggered a 'general withdrawal' by the Germans, reserve brigades would follow them up until they were well clear of Passchendaele Ridge. That day four reserve divisions would be sent forward by train. The Director-General of Transportation, Major-General P.A.M. Nash, committed himself to moving the reserve divisions into place within four hours, provided he was given three hours' warning, ready for them to pick up the pursuit on the following morning. Two divisions of the Cavalry Corps were held 'ready to go forward and exploit any success Reserve Divisions of the two Armies may have achieved'. This was a notably conservative use of cavalry, in line with Haig's own views at this stage of the war.[74]

Broodseinde saw the Plumer formula successfully applied for the third time. This time the four primary assault formations were three Australian divisions and the New Zealanders. German casualties were magnified by the fact that the British attack just pre-empted one of their own, and the barrage crashed down onto positions crammed with *feldgrau*-clad infantry preparing for the assault. Australasian losses were also heavy from the German bombardment, but it was the Allied troops which were able to take advantage. At 6.00 a.m. the infantry attack went in. By midday it was clear that, in the words of Charles Bean, the Australian official historian, 'an overwhelming blow had been struck and both sides knew it'. Ludendorff described Broodseinde as 'extraordinarily severe'.[75]

Straight away the question of exploitation came up. Haig sent Charteris to Plumer, who demurred. Later Plumer havered, but his corps commanders were divided over whether to push on, albeit in a limited fashion, and in the early afternoon Plumer came down decisively against exploitation. Gough, too, toyed with the idea but gave it up. Inevitably, Haig was eager to build on this success. At a meeting with Plumer and Gough at 3 p.m. divergent views on the state of the enemy emerged. 'Plumer stated that in his opinion we had only up to date fought the leading troops of the Enemy's Divisions on his front,' Haig noted, while Charteris believed 'there were few more available Reserves'.[76]

Faced with evidence of German defeat, Haig planned to take advantage of a likely consequence: enemy withdrawal after a further attack. This was not a wildly optimistic assumption. Faced by mounting casualties – 159,000 men by this stage – and a precipitous decline in morale, in mid-October one faction in German high command advocated limited withdrawal to force Haig to redeploy his artillery. Crown Prince Rupprecht, the local Army Group commander, even began to prepare for 'a comprehensive withdrawal' that would have entailed giving up the Channel ports – which, of course, would have fulfilled one of the major British objectives of the campaign at a stroke.[77]

At that point things started to go wrong. Ominously, it had begun to rain on the afternoon of 4 October, and over the next three days the weather worsened. The fine 'Plumer weather' had gone, and it was not to return during this campaigning season. The rain exacerbated the already difficult logistic situation, for the three battles had placed enormous strain on the infrastructure. The Chief Engineer of II Anzac Corps 'was in despair, saying that as the heavy guns went forward in preparation for our next attack, they took his roads with them!'[78] As at Arras earlier in the year, the very success of artillery in bite-and-hold cratered the ground so badly it made it very difficult to get guns, men and equipment forward. This is where the engineers came into their own, but they had an appallingly difficult task to be ready for the next push on 9 October. Haig's eagerness to push on was related to operational tempo: 'The timing of successive operations was crucial: too slow and the enemy recovers; too fast and the assault out-ranges its own artillery support.'[79] Haig got the timing wrong. Artillery support at the Battle of Poelcappelle on 9 October was too weak, insufficient to ensure a repeat of the earlier successes, although German sources pay testimony to the 'crisis in command' produced by this battle and First Passchendaele on 12 October.[80]

Broodseinde, in hindsight, represented the high point of the offensive. After three rapid victories in less than two weeks it is not surprising that Haig decided to carry on attacking. He believed that the capture of Passchendaele Ridge would force the Germans to pull back from the Dixmude area and Houthulst Forest for fear of forces 'being cut off'. There was an element of wishful thinking in this. The intelligence picture that Haig received in October was encouraging, but did not in itself justify continuation of the offensive.[81]. He told Repington in mid-October that 'in Flanders the Huns cannot go back without letting go their hold on the Belgian coast, and therefore here they must fight'. Haig would therefore not be diverted by Pétain's suggestion that Haig should co-operate in operations further south.[82]

Haig's soldier's instinct told him that the enemy was in distress, and what we know from the other side of the hill suggests that he was not totally wrong. This helps to explain Haig's fury when Macdonogh, now Director of Military Intelligence at the War Office, provided a pessimistic assessment. Haig's notorious outburst, when he accused Macdonogh of relying on 'tainted' Roman Catholic sources, was not simply an example of bigotry: it referred to the belief that the Pope, by launching a peace initiative in August 1917, had taken a pro-German stance.[83] It also probably reflected Haig's frustration that a base wallah in London should implicitly question the judgment of the commander in the field.

All three high commanders at Ypres were united in agreeing that the offensive should continue. Although Edmonds wrote that at a conference on 7 October Haig ignored his Army Commanders' advice to shut the battle down, Robin Prior and Trevor Wilson have questioned whether this conference ever took place, and present compelling evidence that Gough and Plumer, army commanders, favoured fighting on. Repington found Plumer 'heart and soul for the Flanders offensive' on 14 October, even although he waxed 'sarcastic about Charteris's optimism'.[84]

Poelcappelle was a great disappointment after the high hopes of Broodseinde. Haig was at least partially aware, through Birch, of the problems of getting enough guns forward over the shattered terrain, which ruled out exploitation. 66th, 49th and 2nd Australian Divisions attacked but made little headway. Haig, obviously seriously mis-informed, stated that night in his diary that 66th Division 'took all objectives'. The commander of this division was Herbert Lawrence, who, years before, had been pipped to command of the 17th Lancers by Haig (see page 53) and rejoined the army on the outbreak of war. Within a few months of Poelcappelle he replaced Kiggell as Haig's Chief of Staff. One wonders whether this fiasco, in which 66th Division suffered 3,119 casualties out of a total for the three attacking divisions of just under 7,000, influenced his behaviour in this vital post.[85]

It was more of the same when the New Zealand Division and 3rd Australian Division took the lead in the First Battle of Passchendaele on 12 October. These formations were commanded by two of the most effective commanders in the BEF, Major-Generals Andrew Russell and John Monash, both of whom Haig admired, but it made little difference. A little ground was captured for heavy losses. The generals bowed to the inevitable. At a conference on 13 October it was decided to impose an operational pause to allow for the logisticians and engineers to undertake critical work and to wait for the weather to improve.[86]

First Passchendaele also signalled the cancellation of the amphibious landing. Serious planning had been carried out, with Haig taking a keen interest.[87] 1st Division had secretly undertaken intensive training for the operation in the so-called 'Hush Camp'. Originally the landing was slated for 8 August, but, as the campaign bogged down, it was progressively postponed. In mid-August Rawlinson was keen to launch a push along the coast with or without the landings. Haig was dubious about separating the two, still holding to the belief that the time to launch both was once the forces around Ypres had reached Roulers. In the end caution prevailed. Haig postponed the dual operation twice, and when Kiggell's letter of 15 October announcing that the landing was now definitely cancelled arrived on Admiral R.H.S. Bacon's desk, the sailor's reaction was disappointment but not, one suspects, surprise.[88]

Reading through the mass of evidence for the later stages of the Third Ypres it is difficult not to be overwhelmed by the sheer horror of it all. Yet the decision to fight on after Broodseinde was not irrational. Simply calling the battle off was no easy matter. The obvious move was to shift the point of main effort from the area fought over since August to another part of the front, or even to open another major offensive elsewhere. This was a method employed with great success a year later but this option was not possible in 1917 because of two critical factors: lack of guns and logistic inflexibility.

In autumn 1917 the BEF had insufficient guns for two concurrent major offensives, or even for one major battle and a sizeable feint.[89] On active service guns wore out, and the appalling conditions in the latter stages of Third Ypres meant that the Royal Artillery struggled to keep even the nominal number of guns available in the field. In June 1917 restrictions were placed on the use of artillery in quiet sectors 'to preserve the lives of the guns'. Three weeks before the opening of Third Ypres 7.7% of 18-pounders, 4.8% of 60-pounders, and no less than 23.1% of the BEF's 6-inch guns were unusable.[90] The Canadian Corps was allocated 227 heavy and medium guns and howitzers for its attack at Passchendaele on 26 October, but the hard fact was that only 139 guns came into action.[91]

The aftermath of Messines demonstrated that moving guns, even to an adjacent battlefield, was a time-consuming business. Shortage of guns and lack of mobility meant that the BEF could land only one major blow at a time, leading to the temptation to exploit any success to its utmost, even though experience showed that pushing on rarely brought dividends. Halting and redeploying would inevitably give the Germans time to recover.

With the impossibility of shifting the axis of attack, in mid-October Haig was faced with three possibilities, none of them attractive. The first was to halt the campaign and establish a line short of the high ground of Passchendaele Ridge. On paper this was possible, but actually it was a fantasy. Harington wrote that he

> personally reconnoitred all the ground under the most appalling conditions and I feel sure that if he had been with me on the Gravenstafel Ridge, the most violent critic of Passchendaele would not have voted for staying there for the winter, or even for any more minutes than necessary.[92]

The second option was to fall back to the Westhoek–Pilckem ridge position closer to Ypres. This was sensible in narrowly military terms but would have meant abandoning territorial gains that had been made at such huge cost.[93] To accept the logic of a battle of pure attrition, that ground was unimportant, and to give up territory so recently captured at such heavy cost, was psychologically and politically impossible.

The final option was to fight on to secure the Passchendaele Ridge and there establish a line on which the BEF could remain for the winter. It would also serve as a jumping-off position for a spring offensive. In October Kiggell was talking about an offensive in April 1918 that would clear the Belgian coast. Fighting on would mean operating in terrible conditions, although there was the lingering hope that as Kiggell put it, 'the Huns are weakening and may give way at any moment'.[94] Haig was convinced that the ridge could be captured. He was right, although the efforts involved were prodigious and the loss of life dreadful. Byng, now commander of Third Army, preparing an offensive at Cambrai, would not be ready until mid-November and thus wanted the Ypres fighting to go on. The wider situation also gave compelling reasons to continue. Rightly or not, Haig was still concerned about the French army, and the Flanders offensive would help to keep the Germans away from the French front. Finally, there was the worry that the Russians (still in the war, but only just) and Italians would be attacked. Third Ypres might detain enemy troops that would otherwise be used elsewhere.[95]

In London, Britain's senior politicians seemed to be congenitally incapable of focussing upon what should have been one of the most important issues on their agenda. A WPC meeting on 24 September discussed Italy, not Flanders. Plumer's three successes did not still criticism in the War Cabinet,[96] and in October operations against the Turks were high on the agenda. Lloyd George was deeply sceptical about the offensive achieving anything, but neither he nor his colleagues issued the order that would have reined in the Field Marshal. In the absence of either a definite political decision either for or against the battle, 'Passchendaele' ground on.

For 'Second Passchendaele', Haig summoned up the Canadian Corps. The Corps commander, Lieutenant-General Arthur Currie, a Canadian-born estate agent and militia officer, had earned Haig's admiration and trust. After a personal reconnaissance, Currie argued against trying to capture Passchendaele Ridge so vociferously that he himself believed that, had he been a British officer, Haig would have had him sent home. As it was Haig bit his lip and instead made an emotional appeal. 'Some day I will tell you why,' he said, as Currie recalled shortly after the war, 'but Passchendaele must be taken'. What exactly Haig meant by this was unclear: his diary is silent on the meeting. Currie reluctantly agreed to take on the task, accurately predicting it would cost some 16,000 casualties. Haig valued the Canadian's methodical approach and told Plumer not to hurry him.[97] After extensive engineering work under the most dangerous and difficult conditions, Currie's men launched four attacks, the last on 10 November. This brought most of Passchendaele Ridge into Allied hands. Finally, Haig called off the battle.

Assessing the pros and cons of Third Ypres is far from straightforward. The Germans clung to parts of the Passchendaele Ridge, comprehensively thwarting Haig's wider ambition: Roulers and the coast, ambitiously marked as objectives on GHQ maps back in the summer, remained as far away as ever.[98] But that does not mean that Haig was wrong to seek these objectives. What he wanted to achieve in autumn 1917 actually occurred a year later. Following the Allied breakout from the Ypres salient on 28 September 1918 the Germans began to retire from the coast, allowing Ostend and Zeebrugge to be captured in rapid succession, and three days after a British naval force had seized Ostend the Germans had evacuated the entire Belgian coastline. The circumstances were certainly very different from a year earlier. In hindsight, it took another six months or so of tactical development before the breakthrough battle once again became possible. But this was not obvious in mid-1917. In opting for the thrusting Gough over the cautious Plumer Haig chose the wrong general to lead off in the battle, although the decision was not inherently unreasonable in the light of Allenby's near-success at the beginning of Arras.

For Haig, Third Ypres was unfinished business. The final position on Passchendaele Ridge was not particularly defensible, but it offered an excellent starting point for a fresh campaign in 1918.[99] Haig made much the same case about the impact of Third Ypres on the German army as he had about the Somme.[100] This is difficult to refute, but similar damage was done to the BEF. Statistically, Passchendaele was not the worst battle for the British in 1917, let alone the war; there was a higher daily loss rate at Arras. But by eating into British manpower reserves the battle eroded Haig's future liberty of action. And Passchendaele dealt a blow to the morale of the army; not a mortal blow, but serious nonetheless. Collectively, the men of Haig's army were pushed close to the abyss; but they did not topple into it.

Let the last word on Passchendaele go to one of Haig's opponents: General Hermann von Kuhl, Chief of Staff to Crown Prince Rupprecht's Army Group. As with any opinions expressed after the event, one must take care in using this as evidence; but it is, nonetheless, a very interesting perspective. Kuhl paid tribute to the BEF's 'courage' and obstinacy in attacking in Flanders, while denying there was any prospect of a breakthrough. However, given the strategic context – Russian and Italian

weakness, the state of the French army, and that the Americans had not
yet arrived in France in force – the BEF was the

> only [Allied] army capable of offensive action . . . If they had broken off
> their offensive, the German army would have seized the initiative and
> attacked the Allies where they were weak. To that end it would have been
> possible to withdraw strong forces from the east . . . For these reasons
> the British had to go on attacking until the onset of winter ruled out a
> German counter-attack . . .
>
> Today [1929], now that we are fully aware about the critical situation
> in which the French army found itself during the summer of 1917, there
> can be absolutely no doubt that through its tenacity, the British army
> bridged the crisis in France. The French army gained time to recover its
> strength, the German reserves were drawn towards Flanders. The
> sacrifices that the British made for the Entente were fully justified.[101]

Cambrai

Scarcely had the fighting around Ypres subsided when another major
attack was launched, in the vicinity of Cambrai. Haig had had his eye on
this area for some time. On 1 May Pulteney's III Corps was tasked with
drawing up a plan for an attack in this sector. In particular, the staff's
attention was drawn to the German salient named after the village of
Flesquières. Seize the ridge line here, and some intriguing possibilities
for unravelling the Hindenburg Line defences became possible. The
Flesquières plan, arrived at GHQ on 19 June. With preparations for Third
Ypres in full swing, it was put to one side.[102]

The idea of a major offensive at Cambrai moved high up the agenda
thanks to two schemes that emerged more or less simultaneously.[103] One
was the brainchild of Brigadier-General H.H. Tudor, head gunner of 9th
(Scottish) Division. By late 1917 some sophisticated techniques were
available to the Royal Artillery, which meant that guns no longer needed
to be pre-registered – that is, to fire ranging shots before a bombardment
– and enemy gun positions could be detected with some accuracy,
making counter-battery fire much more efficient.[104] Tudor recognised
that these developments made it feasible for a major attack to be
launched without sacrificing surprise. He chose the Cambrai area as the

place where a surprise offensive with limited aims could be put into practice. His plan found its way to Third Army HQ, at about the same time as a second and subsequently rather more famous plan.

Lieutenant-Colonel J.F.C. Fuller, chief of staff of the Tank Corps (and subsequently an influential military thinker) was the author of this 'other' Cambrai plan. He proposed a 'tank raid': the use of some 200 tanks, to overrun and destroy German artillery in the Banteux–Ribécourt sector. This was a bold and imaginative proposal, but inherently risky. The plan for the attack that was eventually launched on 20 November was in part an amalgam of both Tudor's and Fuller's concepts, with the substantial addition of a role for cavalry. It was very much a Third Army scheme.

Haig's involvement in the planning for Cambrai followed the pattern of earlier operations. On 18 July 1917 he gave his first thoughts on proposals from Third Army. He made it clear that that a major offensive by Byng's force that summer was unlikely, but he saw the value in going through the motions of preparing an offensive as a deception measure. The C-in-C viewed the sector from Bullecourt to Cherisy as more promising than Havrincourt, but in a sentence typical of his way of doing business he left it to Byng 'to decide the scope of such preparations, having regard to the means at your disposal'.[105]

Operations on Third Army's front reappeared in Haig's in-tray two months later. After he had entertained Byng to lunch on 16 September, the two men discussed the possibility of a new offensive. Haig was encouraging, although the Cambrai operation was effectively contingent on the rate of progress around Ypres.[106]

A month later, as Third Ypres bogged down, the scales tipped in Byng's direction. The timing of Byng's formal request for permission to proceed was good. Haig gave his approval on 13 October, the day after the infantry had clawed their way up the slopes in the First Battle of Passchendaele.[107] Byng was given six infantry divisions, the five-division Cavalry Corps and nine tank battalions, supported by 1,000 guns. Briefing his corps commanders on 26 October, Byng outlined a plan to break through the Hindenburg Line using tanks and infantry, push cavalry through the gap to seize Cambrai, trapping enemy troops between River Sensée and the Canal du Nord, and then exploit the success, driving north-eastward.[108] Surprise was essential, and the key to surprise was secrecy and, not least, the silent registration of the guns.

Byng's plan was very ambitious, and in the discussions between GHQ and Army it became bolder. Essentially, Haig and Byng sought an encirclement of German forces to the east of Cambrai.[109] Haig's stamp was on the revised plan, including the provision of cavalry detachments to support 'infantry advanced guards' so they would not have to wait for the Cavalry Corps to arrive. A particularly interesting idea was the provision of a 'special detachment of all arms lightly equipped' to seize Bourlon Wood and another to capture Marquion.[110]

Bourlon Wood (which sat upon a ridge), rather than Cambrai itself, was made the principal objective on the first day. If the British could capture this high ground they would have observation over some key terrain: the loss of Bourlon 'would probably cause the abandonment by the Germans of their carefully prepared defence systems for a considerable distance to the north of it'.[111] Even if Haig's expectations were a little exaggerated, Bourlon ridge was a piece of ground well worth having. Cambrai, even if captured, would have been difficult to defend and might have caused the British troops (cavalry in the first instance) to be sucked into street fighting. Haig's more limited approach of masking the city by cutting off the exits greatly reduced this risk.

Another limiting factor was Haig's declaration to Byng that he would review the progress of the battle after 48 hours in the light of the arrival of enemy reserves and halt it at that point if the game no longer appeared to be worth the candle. Seemingly Haig recognised that he could not let Cambrai go the same way as Passchendaele. The final Cambrai plan had a distinct family likeness to Haig's previous excursions into operational design. It had a series of phases in which all-arms teams would exploit initial success and widen the penetration (typically Haig recommended – rather than ordered – that the 2,500 yard gap between Marcoing and Masnières should be broadened at an early stage). Cavalry were to seize the crossings over the Saint-Quentin canal ('a truly formidable obstacle for mounted troops') and hold until relieved: the exploitation 'would depend upon the boldness and enterprise with which the cavalry was handled'.[112]

Cambrai was arguably the biggest gamble Haig had ever taken on an offensive. Every previous one had had, from the evidence available to him, a reasonable chance of success. However in launching Cambrai he knew that the BEF simply lacked the resources to sustain a major offensive. At home the bottom of the manpower barrel was being scraped. The heavy defeat of the Italians at Caporetto in October had dealt a near-terminal blow to the Italian army, and Haig was coming under pressure to send forces to Italy. Although he sent Plumer and five divisions, Cambrai offered an opportunity to limit the flow of British troops.[113] Moreover Passchendaele had led to Haig's credibility as a commander draining away; Cambrai offered an opportunity for a top-up.

The final and perhaps most important factor in Haig's decision to fight at Cambrai was his unshakeable optimism, founded on a shrewd appreciation of what his army was capable of doing. Third Ypres had given plenty of indications that the BEF was now tactically highly efficient. The conditions in the Salient at the end of the battle denied the tactical 'weapons-system' a chance to work properly. Over better terrain things might be different.

Beginning at 6.20 a.m. on 20 November 1917 just over 1,000 guns began a thunderous bombardment of the enemy lines, the shock effect on the defenders being magnified by surprise. Six infantry divisions were supported by 476 tanks, including 98 support vehicles. A combination of artillery dominance and the use of tanks *en masse* cracked open the German defences. The success of the day's attacks was recorded by Haig in his diary with 'as much emotion as a laundry list',[114] but the Field-Marshal's deadpan delivery belied the fact that he was stirred by the day's events. Third Army had advanced up to five miles on a six-mile frontage. His plan seemed to be unfolding more or less as intended.

'More or less' – that caveat is important. The 'cavalry gap' between Marcoing and Masnières failed to materialise. 51st (Highland) Division, was held up by the strong defences, including anti-tank guns, at Flesquières village,[115] and this had a knock-on effect on the timetable for the advance. It was too late to attack Bourlon Wood before dark. The fog of battle and general command confusion imposed severe delays on the advance of the cavalry. Some that did get into action proved tactically effective but lacked sufficient numbers to make a difference.

Intriguingly, the action of III Corps cavalry, two troops of Northumberland Hussars, in pushing ahead and co-operating with infantry and tanks in a mixture of mounted and dismounted action, was very successful; this was exactly what Haig had in mind for his all-arms advanced guards. These numbers were small, however; the bulk of the mounted troops, organised into cavalry divisions, were further back and had difficulties getting forward. However the Canadian Fort Garry Horse arrived at the Masnières bridge only to discover that it had been destroyed. Already weakened by a German attempt to detonate it, the bridge had been finished off by a British tank which attempted to cross (and plunged into the canal – happily, the crew survived). The Canadian cavalry were able to find another place to cross, using the lock gates, but yet more time was lost as the short daylight hours of this winter day leached away. Worse, Major-General W.H. Greenly, 2nd Cavalry Division's commander, decided that with daylight fading it was too risky to push any more cavalry over the lock crossing. This was one of a number of questionable decisions by senior cavalry commanders; some cavalrymen on the scene had no doubt that there was a real opportunity for mounted action. Failures of communication and the fog of war (literal fog in this case, which severely reduced visibility and hampered air reconnaissance) meant that higher levels of command were in ignorance of the opportunities.[116]

In the fighting on 21 November Third Army made some more progress. Flesquières village fell after the Germans pulled back. Haig visited the battlefield, standing on some high ground and peering through binoculars towards Bourlon Wood. The wood was attacked that day, but parts remained under German occupation. Nevertheless the impetus of the offensive was starting to diminish. Ominously, German reinforcements arrived, and the British were hit by counterattacks. Having promised to review the situation after 48 hours, Haig had a decision to make.

At some point he picked up a story that at Flesquières on 20 November a lone German officer gathered a handful of men and used an artillery piece to knock out eight or nine tanks. He included the story in his Cambrai dispatch, and thus enshrined a legend, the truth of which is debated by historians to this day. Of more significance to an assessment of Haig as a commander is his next comment: that this incident 'shows the importance of Infantry operating with Tanks at times acting as skirmishers to clear away hostile guns and reconnoitre'.[117] This lesson – the critical importance of infantry–tank co-operation, without which tanks are extremely vulnerable – was to be relearned by commanders at sporadic intervals over the coming decades.

Haig was frustrated by the events of 21 November. The attacks on Bourlon ridge had been 'feeble and ill-coordinated'.[118] He was annoyed to find when visiting IV Corps that its commander, Lieutenant-General Charles Woollcombe, was 'out walking', and thought that 'Divisional Commanders should be closer up so as to take a grip of the battle'. Perhaps the most revealing comment concerned his meeting with Major-General R.L. 'Gobby Chops' Mullens, commander of 1st Cavalry Division, who told Haig of his disappointment that his division had been sent back from the front line. The cavalry was under Woollcoombe's command, and Haig fought down his inclination to send them back.

In the evening of 21 November, at about 9. p.m., Haig decided to carry on with the battle. As the official history states, GHQ, believed 'on somewhat slender evidence' that the Germans were 'showing a disposition to retire'. Bourlon Wood's dominating position meant that Third Army's positions were effectively untenable if it was not captured, and Byng would have to withdraw to Flesquières ridge. The three untouched divisions of V Corps were available, and Robertson had delayed the dispatch of 2nd and 47th Divisions to Italy. Haig peremptorily ended III Corps attacks, reducing the original ambitious operation to a straightforward assault on the formidable Bourlon ridge. The Germans only had to hold on there for reinforcements to arrive and allow them to mount a major counterstroke.[119] *Déjà vu*: British troops attacking uphill against a heavily defended ridge.

Although the prosecution case seems cut-and-dried, there were some compelling reasons why Haig should continue the battle. Bourlon ridge was a considerable prize in itself. In the intricate chess game of trench warfare, taking a piece of ground could bring important tactical advantages. With the ridge controlled by the British Third Army could bring accurate artillery fire on the Hindenburg Line, perhaps even forcing a withdrawal from this sector. And artillery could also be used to good effect against Cambrai, jeopardising a major railhead, vital for keeping German forces in supply.[120] Ending such a disappointing year with a success would strengthen Britain's position and, more parochially, quieten demands to send troops to Italy. Not incidentally, it would also shore up Haig's own position at home. Pulling the plug on the offensive would have left Haig vulnerable to the charge of conducting yet another pointless attack that achieved very little. Byng and his Chief of Staff,

Louis Vaughan, thought it worth pressing on, as Byng made clear to Haig in the afternoon of 21 November.[121] Bryn Hammond gets it right: however flawed the decision, '[b]ased on the evidence before him at the time, it seems entirely understandable that Haig chose to continue'.[122]

In the short term Haig's decision seemed to be vindicated. In the course of 23 November 40th Division aided by tanks seized Bourlon Wood. Crucially, Bourlon and other important villages remained in German possession, which left the British position vulnerable. Haig, acutely aware of his shortage of infantry, ordered Byng to use dismounted cavalry 'in any numbers' to hold Bourlon Wood. This was a significant development in view of Haig's aspirations. On 24 November the Cavalry Corps was ordered to take over all operations to the north when breakthrough occurred.[123]

Unfortunately for Haig's plans, the Germans did not treat the capture of Bourlon Wood as the end of the matter. The British were rapidly forced to turn from attackers to defenders as the Germans threw in one counterattack after another. Echoing the dilemma of Passchendaele, if Bourlon could not be securely held, Haig could continue to go forward or fall back, because consolidating a line dominated by Bourlon Wood would have been nonsensical. At some stage Haig had to make a choice one way or the other, if only because he lacked the reserves to carry on indefinitely. That bitter decision came in stages, the first one on 27 November.

Haig arrived at Havrincourt at mid-morning on 26 November to join a meeting between Byng, Woollcombe and other high-ranking officers to discuss the following day's attack. The meeting had been going on for some time already, and Major-General G.P.T. Feilding had argued forcefully against the role his Guards Division had been allocated. Kiggell contacted Byng and passed on Haig's views: not only that the Bourlon position should be secured on the 27th but the need for Byng to take personal control of the operation. Even at this late stage Haig stressed the need to take advantage of any 'favourable opportunities . . . for local exploitation of success . . . especially mounted troops' and to follow up any German withdrawal. This was contingency planning rather than anything else.[124] Haig had effectively reduced Byng's liberty to make decisions, and he had to overrule Feilding. The Guardsman responded 'We shall do our best, sir, but you ask a lot of us'.[125]

Predictably, the attacks of 27 November made little impact. Byng realised that the sands had run out, that 'the resources at the disposal of the [Third] Army do not permit of the offensive being continued any longer'.[126] Byng ordered Third Army onto the defensive. Haig rubber-stamped Byng's instructions but he fulminated in his diary that 'the situation is most favourable for us'. Only the lack of two more fresh divisions prevented the army from breaking through.[127] This was self-deception, pure and simple.

Third Army's initial success created a pronounced salient of some four miles on a front of nine miles. The classic response of a defender to such a bulge is to attempt to pinch it off by striking the flanks. That is exactly what the Germans did on the morning of 30 November, and the blow landed with shattering force. The attackers, using some of the methods, such as stormtroop tactics, that were to cause such problems the following spring, advanced up to three miles. They even captured some ground beyond the British front line of 20 November before the situation was stabilised. Further north the Germans had a harder task, but this successful defence only made the overall salient even more precarious.

The British had been badly surprised, not because there were no indications of a threat, but because, when presented with the pieces of jigsaw, they had failed to put them together to make a coherent intelligence picture. 55th Division issued an 'Urgent Operations Priority' order on 28 November warning of an attack. GHQ intelligence largely discounted the possibility of a major (although not a smaller) German assault. However, Byng and his staff were the worst culprits, paying little attention to the warnings from their subordinate formations.[128]

Haig shielded Byng from criticism. Called upon to provide a statement for the House of Commons, he leaned heavily on a report telephoned to GHQ by Byng, which stated categorically that the German attack had been 'in no sense a surprise' (which was contradicted by evidence from GHQ) and that he 'attributed the reasons for the . . . [German] success to one cause and one alone, namely, lack of training on the part of junior officers and N.C.O.s and men'. At Derby's prompting, Haig instigated a court of enquiry into the German attack, and that came to similar conclusions.[129] Byng and his chief of staff Vaughan were not called to testify at the enquiry.

The German offensive came to a halt on 2 December, leaving the Bourlon salient, six miles by six miles, looking more vulnerable than ever. The same day Haig formally suspended the offensive, and spent some time talking over with Kiggell whether to order Third Army to abandon the salient altogether. Haig had arrived at a bleakly realistic analysis:

> although Bourlon is itself a strong position, the Salient will be costly to hold. Moreover its main value is for offence. Now we have not sufficient Reserves to take the offensive on a large scale. Also, with the fact of Russia entering negotiations for peace before us, it is possible that Germany may start a big offensive on this front [in 1918]. We ought therefore to make our front as strong as possible and avoid having weak points. The Marcoing salient is a source of weakness and will be a constant anxiety in my opinion.

Haig and Byng met on 3 December, and Byng confirmed that 'the rear line was very strong and quite suitable' Haig gave the go-ahead for the withdrawal to take place.[130] Quietly slipping away on the night of 4–5 December, Third Army fell back about three miles to a new position which included Flesquières and part of the Hindenburg Line.

Cambrai was a drawn battle. Roughly 45,000 casualties were lost on each side, and the ground each army gained was just about equivalent. For the British, however, it felt like a defeat. The initial euphoria at the achievements of 20 November gave way to bitter disappointment.[131] This did more damage to Haig's reputation than even the losses and struggles at Ypres. When the news of the initial breakthrough had reached England, church bells were rung, for the first time in the war, to celebrate a great victory. Briefly, Haig reaped the political benefit at home.[132] This soon changed.

Haig faced the music. In a report to the CIGS on Christmas Eve he said

> all blame for the mishap of November 30th must rest on my shoulders. It was I who decided on the 22nd that the BOURLON position should be attacked and occupied . . . [This] increased our front and threw extra work on our troops. As events on the 30th show, many of the men were very

tired and unable to resist the enemy's blow, as I believe they could have done had they been fresher.[133]

It could have been worse for Haig. A high-level War Office committee supported his conduct of operations and his conclusions about the reverse of 30 November. General Smuts was then commissioned by the War Cabinet to look at the German counter-offensive, and he too exonerated the high command.[134] However, Haig was damaged. J.C. Wedgwood, an MP who had turned against him much earlier, made an outspoken attack in the House of Commons, demanding a change of command to ensure that the soldiers of the BEF had 'the best possible generalship'. The Northcliffe press 'opened up its guns upon Robertson and Haig'.[135] The journalist Lovat Fraser, who had been appalled by Haig's strategy for some time, published an article in the *Daily Mail* on 21 January 1918 ('one sided and unjust', Horne thought), which was so damning that, ironically, it had the short-term effect of strengthening Haig's position. Northcliffe was offended when, on a visit to GHQ, Haig had been less than riveted by his guest's conversation. Although relations between the two men never entirely broke down, Haig had lost a powerful ally.[136] He began 1918 less secure in his post than at any time since he had become Commander-in-Chief two years before.

Discussing future plans at an Army Commanders conference at Doullens on 7 December, Haig reflected on the meeting at Doullens, exactly six months earlier:

> I . . . issued orders for the offensive against Messines etc. We expected at that time help from Russia, Italy and France! In reality the British Army has had to bear the brunt of it all. I added that we might well be proud of the achievements of the armies this year and I thanked them one and all for their help and support.[137]

After the false dawns of Messines and Cambrai, and the long agony of Passchendaele, an even more testing year lay ahead.

Backs to the Wall

The prospects for Haig's third year as C-in-C were the gloomiest he had ever known. 'The year 1917 closed in an atmosphere of depression,' an officer of 51st (Highland) Division wrote. 'Most Divisions on the Western Front had been engaged continuously in offensive operations . . . all were exhausted, and . . . weak[ened]'.[1] The defeat of Russia in 1917 handed the strategic initiative to the Germans, and Haig, his generals and the BEF as a whole were forced to grapple with the unfamiliar challenge of preparing to defend against a major offensive. Cambrai had been a serious blow to Haig's prestige. 'There is no doubt it has created a great feeling in this country,' Derby bluntly told him.[2]

Over the winter of 1917–18 Haig lost members of his inner circle. Derby had turned decisively against Charteris in March 1917 (see p. 204). On the same day that an editorial attacking Haig's subordinates appeared in Northcliffe's *The Times*, Derby, who was under pressure from the Prime Minister, wrote Haig a frank letter, spelling out the danger that Charteris posed to the C-in-C.[3] After Cambrai, Charteris's credibility as Haig's intelligence chief was shot to pieces, a symbol of GHQ's failures over the last two years, of raised hopes and crushing disappointments. Charteris's eventual replacement was Brigadier-General Edgar Cox, who brought a breath of fresh air to GHQ intelligence. Haig fought to keep Charteris and also Kiggell, who was removed on health grounds.[4] Kiggell was undoubtedly tired, but few, least of all Haig, doubted that he was a political sacrifice. His replacement was Bertie Lawrence, who injected a very different dynamic into GHQ. In December 1917 Lawrence was moved from 66th Division to replace Charteris, and was rapidly elevated to become Haig's Chief of Staff. 'Lorenzo' was very much his own man and had no desire to carry on in the army after the war, therefore he was not beholden to Haig or anyone else. Although they had some history, Haig and Lawrence made a good team.[5]

At the beginning of 1918, it was obvious that Germany had achieved an immensely powerful geostrategic position, having carved out a vast empire in the east ripe for economic exploitation. The shrewdest move that OHL (*Oberste Heeresleitung* – the German equivalent of GHQ) could have made would have been to have swapped the battlefield for the conference table, to bank its winnings in the East and negotiate an end to the war in the West. Skilful diplomacy backed by territorial concessions might well have fractured the anti-German coalition. Some key figures such as Robertson certainly feared this as a possibility, and that any peace would prove a mere truce, and war would begin again at some point in the future with the British at a major disadvantage.[6]

In January 1918 Haig was involved in discussions in London about future strategy. During a convivial lunch, Lord Derby wagered the Prime Minister '100 cigars to 100 cigarettes that war would be over by next new year'. Lloyd George was not convinced. Haig then gave his views, that 'the *internal* state of Germany' would force Berlin to make peace by the autumn. He also highlighted the dangers to Germany if it did attempt a major offensive. 'Germany having only one million men as Reserves for this year's fighting, I doubted whether they would risk them in an attempt to "break through." If they did, it would be a gambler's throw.' Haig believed that there was a power struggle between the civilians and military in Germany, and, should the generals win, 'they would certainly attack and try and deliver a knockout blow against the western front, probably against France'.[7] In this postprandial conversation Haig was more right than wrong. His political intelligence was out of date. The 'silent dictatorship' of Hindenburg and Ludendorff already had a grip on power, and the eventual attack was aimed at the BEF not the French. Both armies had to be defeated before American troops arrived in sufficient numbers to overwhelm the German forces. More importantly, Haig had accurately identified the irrationality of German grand strategy in 1918. It was militarism gone mad. German High Command demanded total victory in the west at all costs, but did not know what total victory would look like – it was a gambler's throw indeed.[8]

At a War Cabinet meeting on 7 January Haig stated that 'the coming four months would be the critical period' and proposed a bold move: continuing the Flanders attack to rob the Germans of the initiative. Unfortunately, presumably as a result of his inarticulacy, Haig left the Cabinet with the idea that he did not believe that the Germans would mount an offensive on a truly large scale but rather carry out limited attacks along the lines of Cambrai.[9]

In principle, a 'Fourth Ypres' was an attractive proposition. Having captured most of Passchendaele Ridge, it would take a relatively modest advance to break out onto the plain, and Roulers remained tantalisingly just outside the BEF's reach. A spoiling attack to pre-empt the Germans also had its attractions – again, on paper. How feasible all this was in practice was another matter. Morale in the BEF was not at its highest; although the army was far from demoralised the troops were very tired. And the logistic infrastructure in the salient had taken a tremendous hammering, which posed major problems. Moreover, whatever the military practicalities, the political backing simply was not there. It was rumoured that Lloyd George tried to hamstring Haig, holding reinforcements for the BEF back in Britain.[10]

Part of the German strategy for 1918 was to carry out a deception plan. Some elements worked better than others. The Allies did not fall for the attempt to persuade them through a series of rumours that found their way to London that the major offensive would take place in the Balkans or Italy.[11] Allied intelligence tracked the massive build up of troops in France and picked up many various signals that a major offensive was brewing in the West.[12] What was not clear was where and when the blow would land. German intelligence agents did their job well in spreading disinformation that presented their Allied counterparts with a bewildering array of more or less plausible possibilities. When Derby warned Haig on 5 March of an attack 'within a very short time' on Fifth Army's front, Cox and his staff were also picking up signals that indicated threats to other parts of the line – although not, crucially, south of Saint-Quentin. The Germans were able to mask their preparations by, for example, constantly swapping wireless codes, while bad weather reduced the possibility of aerial reconnaissance.[13]

Nonetheless Haig made one important and sound decision. As early as the turn of the year, he had recognised that 'Arras to St Quentin is the most vulnerable point of the British front'.[14] Realising that he could not be strong everywhere, he decided that it was in the sector of the southernmost Army, Gough's Fifth, that he could most afford to give ground. Giving Gough 12 divisions to hold a 42-mile front was risky. Strengthening Fifth Army at the expense of the forces defending Arras and Artois would have been an unwarranted gamble; weakening Plumer's command, guarding Ypres and the shortest route to the Channel ports, would have verged on the suicidal. Although the critical communications centre of Amiens was to Gough's rear, it might be possible to retreat and slow the German advance. The further north, the more dangerous it was to retreat and uncover communication centres, roads and railway lines and (above all) the routes to the Channel ports should everything go disastrously wrong. 'Of course, I am uneasy', Haig told an officer asking about Fifth Army's front, 'but where else can I afford to bend without risk of losing the war?'[15]

There were also real dangers in the south. In late January Wilson carried out a map exercise at the Supreme War Council (SWC, see p. 262) of a major attack on the point where the French and British met. Haig was present for part of this map exercise and showed signs of boredom and irritation: Wilson's insistence that the 'enemy' team wear their caps back to front to signify that they were playing Germans probably did not help. Even worse was the fact that, earlier, the SWC had recommended that Haig take over more line from the French, based on a wargame.[16] In fact Haig did not need telling that an attack there could split the Allied forces in two. The BEF would be likely to fall back towards the coast while Pétain would instinctively cover Paris. As it was, Haig held his reserves to the north of Fifth Army in the knowledge that Pétain had ordered French Third Army to aid Gough if he was attacked.

On the eve of the German offensive GHQ were fairly certain that the attack would come in the Cambrai–Saint-Quentin area, although it failed to predict that there would be a major effort in the south of the sector.[17] Prudently keeping his reserves in a roughly central position, Haig hedged his bets against getting things badly wrong. Confused by the deception plan, GHQ made a wrong call and took a risk. Events were to demonstrate that the BEF got away with it – just.

In the absence of unity of command, a good relationship between commanders is imperative, so everything hinged on how well the two national C-in-Cs got on. Haig's personal alliance with Pétain served as a substitute for a proper inter-Allied command organisation. Haig found Pétain a distinct improvement on his garrulous predecessor Nivelle. Dealing with Pétain in September 1917 he gave him high praise: 'straightforward' and 'businesslike'. In spite of their differences over strategy, Haig and Pétain had much to push them together. Both distrusted the ambitious Foch, and both set their faces against unity of command.[18] For one to serve under the other was unthinkable and unworkable. Haig was deeply scarred by the Nivelle affair. In November 1917 Brigadier-General G.S. Clive, a senior liaison officer with the French spoke to Haig and

> broached the subject of an Allied C in C, but found that Nivelle's experiment is still much too fresh in DH's and Kiggell's mind to allow them to look at it quietly.[19]

To have another general, probably Foch, appointed over both Pétain and Haig also united both commanders in opposition.

At the end of 1917 leading players in both Britain and France were determined to force the issue of unity of command. Lloyd George's motives went far beyond maximising military efficiency. The PM 'has conceived an ingenious device for depriving Robertson of his power' wrote Frances Stevenson. By setting up an Inter-Allied Military Council with responsibility for deciding strategy, with Henry Wilson as the senior British representative, Robertson would be circumvented.[20] Haig's freedom of action would also be greatly constrained, and the thrust of Allied strategy would most likely be for action away from the Western Front combined with 'a wait for the Americans' policy .

Even before the formation of the SWC at the Rapallo conference in November 1917, Haig had laid out his response to unity of command. He endorsed a paper Pétain had written which attacked the idea, touching upon one of the central issues. Military coalitions run more smoothly when there is one dominating nation that ultimately calls the shots and can act as a military framework for its allies. For states of roughly equal power things are far more difficult.[21]

In a blatant attempt to destabilise Haig, in October 1917 Lloyd George had asked for 'independent' (i.e. anti-Haig) advice from Sir John (now

Lord) French and Henry Wilson. Both men came out against a continuation of Haig's Western Front strategy and called for an inter-allied council of some sort.[22] The SWC threatened to give rival generals authority over him.

Lloyd George had his way. The Italian disaster at Caporetto in October made obvious the gaping hole in Allied strategy: the inability to co-ordinate military action across different armies and fronts.[23] The French, British and Italian governments agreed to the formation of the Supreme War Council, with Permanent Military Representatives based at Versailles. As the general staffs of each army retained their powers, friction between the two bodies was almost guaranteed, especially since Lloyd George appointed Henry Wilson to Versailles. This gave the PM the opportunity of dividing and ruling. Lloyd George 'now had a constitutional military adviser able and willing to give him the advice he wanted'.[24]

In spite of Haig being forced to take over more line, the Haig–Pétain mutual admiration society remained strong.[25] This allowed them to form a powerful combination against the SWC's Executive War Board, a body, chaired by Foch and with Wilson as a member, which was tasked to bring about and then control an Allied general reserve across all the fronts. This would sharply reduce the power of the C-in-C. Pétain put it bluntly to Repington: 'he did not mean to allow Foch and Co. to interfere with his reserves'.[26]

The two Commanders-in-Chief co-ordinated their counter-offensive.[27] Haig deployed an array of arguments, ranging from the legal (it would be unconstitutional for him to receive orders from a foreign general) to the practical (he did not have the divisions to spare without disrupting his defensive plans).[28] Shrewdly, Haig enlisted the support of Georges Clemenceau, who became French Prime Minister in November 1917, who was alarmed when Haig told him he was contemplating resignation, and passed on the news to President Poincaré. Foch's aspirations to control the reserves were slapped down. At the SWC on 14 March it was agreed that the creation of the allied reserve would be delayed. In the meantime, Haig and Pétain would arrange the matter between themselves.[29]

Just seven days after the SWC's decision the Allies were plunged in to a crisis which showed how badly unity of command was needed. Milner described Haig's 'obdurate' stance as 'desperately stupid'. It was also a clear case of the generals defying political authority.[30] But what was on offer was a badly flawed concept. For a committee to complicate the C-in-C's job by controlling the reserves was a military nonsense. Clive believed that the present arrangements would work: 'Haig was quite prepared to . . . [physically] be beside Pétain when the pinch came'.[31] In fact, when the pinch did come, Allied command arrangements, and the Haig–Pétain relationship, rapidly came to the point of crisis.

An important by-product of the battle over the SWC was the political demise of Robertson. As CIGS, Robertson dug in his heels over the question of his authority *vis-à-vis* the Supreme War Council. The Prime Minster offered him two unpalatable alternatives: to keep his job but with diminished powers, or to go to Versailles as the British representative. In the end, Robertson walked the plank and was succeeded as CIGS by Henry Wilson. Haig did nothing to save him.[32] From September 1917 the Haig–Robertson alliance was visibly fracturing. Haig grew disillusioned with Robertson because he had 'not resolutely adhered to the policy of "concentration on the Western Front". He . . . has allowed all kinds of resources to be diverted to distant theatres at the bidding of his political masters'. Moreover, Wullie's increasing pessimism on the chances of victory caused Haig alarm. Haig myopically saw Robertson's broad strategic grasp, a major asset to the Allies, as a weakness. This view, and his abandoning of Robertson as 'the trade-off for [his] survival' as C-in-C, did not do Haig credit.[33]

Now Lloyd George had a CIGS more to his taste, the time was ripe for confrontation with Haig. Some on the Right, such as *Morning Post* editor H.A. Gwynne, wanted to see Robertson replace Lloyd George. It didn't happen. The Conservatives would not break with Lloyd George. After his earlier performance as Prime Minister, the return to No. 10 of the only other possible political ally of the generals, Asquith, had no credibility. Significantly neither Robertson nor Haig had any intention of behaving unconstitutionally. Fundamental to Haig's view of civil–military relations was his belief that, ultimately, soldiers had to obey the orders of the government; he told Robertson that it was his '*duty* to go to Versailles', if so ordered.[34]

Temperamentally, Haig and Wilson were very different. In spite of their mutual dislike, relations between the two were, generally 'quite amicable'. Rawlinson even reported that Haig had told him 'how much

easier he found it' with the new CIGS 'instead of Wullie'.[35] Haig and
Wilson by no means always saw eye to eye over the coming year, but
there was a gradual, if wary, growth of mutual respect.

Waiting for the German Offensive

That Haig approached each of the major offensive battles in which he
commanded with optimism is perhaps understandable. For him to view
the coming German attack with equanimity takes more explaining. In
large part this must be put down to the success of the German deception
operation. Apparently, Haig also thought it necessary to keep up a public
display of confidence in front of the politicians. He had some private
qualms about the state of his army, for instance referring to the Guards
Division as 'our *only* really reliable reserve'.[36] Haig put on a bullish
display to the War Cabinet on 7 January about the prospects of defeating
a German attack.[37] In some ways, this was a consequence of Haig's
frustration at having to deal with what he plainly regarded as ignorant if
well-meaning amateurs. 'I spent yesterday with the War Cabinet' he
wrote to Kiggell. '*All* were particularly friendly, but many stupid
questions were asked. I did my best to answer them'.[38]

In many major intelligence failures, self-deception on the part of the
victims plays a role. At first sight, Haig's diary entry of 2 March 1918
indicates that Haig fell into this trap. After Cox had stated that latest
intelligence indicated an attack was coming against Third and Fifth
Armies, the C-in-C

> told the Army Commanders that I was very pleased at all I had seen on
> the fronts of the three Armies which I had recently visited. Plans were
> sound and thorough, and much work had already been done. *I was
> only afraid that that the Enemy would find our front so very strong that he will
> hesitate to commit his army to the attack with the almost certainty of losing
> very heavily.*[39]

That last sentence has caused outrage and derision among writers, who
have the advantage of knowing what happened three weeks later. The
official record of the meeting is less incendiary. It merely has Haig
thanking the Army commanders for their efforts and 'express[ing] his
satisfaction at what he has seen of the troops and the defences during his

recent tour of the front . . . All officers appear to understand thoroughly the principles of defence'.[40]

To attempt to discover why Haig came to these conclusions we need to know more about his tour of the front. It began on 27 February. Reflecting concerns about where the Germans would attack, he spent the day in Third Army's sector, rather than going south to Fifth Army. Accompanied by Lawrence, he discussed the local situation with various commanders and staff. Haig was clearly impressed by what he saw that day. 'A great deal of work has been done in the area I visited today,' he wrote in his diary, 'and in a week's time all commanders considered that they would be well prepared to meet any attack by the Enemy.'[41]

The next day, 28 February, Haig headed north to First Army's area, again accompanied by Lawrence. His programme was similar to that laid on by Third Army. Haig was most impressed by the Canadians. 'They are really fine disciplined soldiers now and so smart and clean,' he wrote to Lady Haig – unlike, he added, the Australians. Currie explained the defensive scheme. 'It certainly gives me a feeling of confidence in having such reliable troops and such methodical defensive arrangements in this most important area'. On the final day of his tour of inspection, Haig visited Fourth Army (as Second Army had been renamed) and walked around the defences near Messines with General Sir William Birdwood, the acting Army commander. 'A great deal of wiring has been done and the position is already very strong'.[42]

We cannot discount the possibility that Haig was lulled into a false sense of security on this visit. When on 2 March he said 'that I was very pleased at all I had seen on the fronts of the three Armies I had recently visited' he was not being outrageously foolish or naive: he was simply reflecting his experience. Smuts and Hankey came to a similar view during their visit to the front in January.[43] When the battle began, these defences, especially those of Third Army, did prove to be strong. But Haig had not yet visited Fifth Army.

Gough was very aware of the magnitude of the task faced by his Army. The intelligence reaching him all pointed to a major German offensive on Fifth Army's front. He wrote to GHQ on 1 February itemising a depressingly long list of shortages. If these were made good, 'by 15th March the whole of the Battle and Rear Zones could be made into a good defended area'. With this done, he would work on defences defending the crossings over the River Somme.[44]

The Commander-in-Chief inspected Fifth Army over three days, 7–9 March 1918. Haig's diary entries for this period reflect his concern at what he found. He was particularly worried by the southernmost formation, III Corps commanded by his former Deputy Chief of Staff Lieutenant-General Sir Richard Butler, as 'it has a very wide front to defend with three divisions'. Haig feared that the Germans could achieve a major success here and advance along the Oise valley aiming at Paris. When Congreve of VII Corps told Haig that he wished he had a division in Corps reserve, Haig replied, 'And I wish I had one to give you'. 'I fear you will be asked for more troops everywhere,' Gough told him. 'They ask me the same thing every time I see them'.[45] Butler's situation was so obviously dire that Haig released 39th Division from GHQ reserve, and shipped 50th Division from Flanders to Fifth Army's rear, where it remained in GHQ's gift. As he explained to Gough, Humbert's French Third Army would be available to support Fifth Army. Humbert had a Staff, but no troops. 'But they will all come back if needed' Humbert told Gough. 'It is well understood with GQG'.[46] Four French divisions were in striking distance of the British right wing on 21 March.

To recap: Haig was well aware of Fifth Army's weakness and recognised the real danger of a breakthrough on III Corps front. He had to balance that against his concern for his positions further north, worries fuelled by the German deception operation, and the knowledge that Fifth Army had strategic depth that the other Armies lacked. In the end, Haig felt justified in taking a risk in this sector. Even on 19 March Lawrence refused Gough's request to bring 20th and 50th Divisions forward closer to the front line, giving what Gough described as 'an absurd little homily on the mistake of moving reserves prematurely'.[47] With so few reserves, such caution does not appear at all absurd.

Only four days before the attack, on 17 March, Cox demonstrated that Charteris held no monopoly on misleading intelligence briefings. He reported that 'the Enemy's preparations for attack had not developed, and he [Cox] personally thought attack was not so imminent, although we must still expect to be attacked in force at short notice'. Moreover, a German attempt to end the war might lead to an offer of terms of peace, giving France all that it wanted in the West. Haig believed that there was a struggle between military hard-liners and civilian doves in Germany that would decide whether the attack would take place at all.[48]

In the days before the battle GHQ paid more attention on the area where the attack would actually begin. On the 20th, the day before the battle began, German preparations were reported near Bullecourt on Third Army's front, and even more importantly deserters to Fifth Army revealed a build up of trench mortars near Saint-Quentin. Photographic reconnaissance quickly confirmed the truth of this story, and British guns opened fire. Haig 'thought that this should greatly upset the Enemy's intended attack!' Not for the first or last time, he was too sanguine.[49]

The state of the BEF on the eve of battle could certainly have been better. Morale was adequate but not first class. The manpower crisis had forced the reduction of divisions from twelve infantry battalions to nine. Most British troops were not well trained in the new defensive tactics, modelled on the German pattern of Forward, Battle and Rear Zones. Too often the Rear Zone was never constructed, and the Forward Zone was frequently overmanned, rather than held as an outpost. This had disastrous effects on 21 March.[50] Another drawback of the new methods was concisely summarised by an officer: 'Defence-in-depth means forces more scattered and greater difficulty in keeping up communication'.[51]

Operation *Michael*, the German Spring Offensive, launched three armies against the British. The plan was for Otto von Below's Seventeenth Army was to assault Byng's British Third Army. To the south, von der Marwitz's Second Army was up against Byng's right and the left of Fifth Army. Von Hutier's Eighteenth Army was to drive through Gough's left and act as a flank guard, watching for French intervention from the south. The other two armies would wheel north. Crucially, missing was a recognition of the importance of Amiens, a major railway bottleneck. Take Amiens and the BEF's ability to fight could be crippled.

The Battle Begins

Haig received the news that the storm had broken while he was dressing in his room at Montreuil on 21 March. Lawrence came to his room at roughly 8 a.m. 'to tell me that the German attack had begun' – this was shortly after the infantry went in, the German artillery having opened a heavy and intense bombardment of Fifth and Third Army's front at

4.40 a.m. Charteris, now Deputy Inspector-General of Transportation, finding that 'There was nothing to be done at GHQ', headed out to Fifth Army, but could discover little there. The day was foggy, and telephone lines were down. It seemed that the battle was going to plan. 'Our thinly held front line had been driven in, and the enemy was up against our real defensive line, and seemed to be held'.[52]

Charteris's optimism was born of an information vacuum, and it was shared by his boss. Haig's diary for the day contains the entry 'Very severe fighting on the Third and Fifth Army fronts continued well into the evening. Our men seem to be fighting magnificently'. Earlier in the day he had had a worried message from Byng, only for it to be countermanded because Third Army had discovered that the enemy penetration was not as deep as feared at first. Third Army reported that troops had withdrawn, as planned, from the Flesquières salient. This was to the good, Haig thought, as shortening the line allowed a division to be added to the reserve.

News from Gough's front also seemed to be broadly positive. 'From opposite La Fère Northwards to Benay,' Haig noted, 'our III Corps held the battle zone all day and inflicted great losses on the enemy'. Elsewhere on the fronts of the other Corps there had been some tactical withdrawals, but the fight for the Battle Zone went on.

Overall, on the night of 21 March Haig was upbeat.[53] Quite simply, he was unaware of the true picture. Overall, his troops had put up a hard fight. The idea that Fifth Army broke and ran has long been discredited. On three-quarters of the 50-mile front attacked, the Germans had failed to reach their first-day objectives and were still held up in the Battle Zone. But this summary disguises a very mixed picture. On the whole, Third Army held up fairly well, although much of IV Corps were clinging to the rear of the Battle Zone. Byng had deployed three reserve divisions, and had another three up his sleeve. Fifth Army's left had also been fairly successful, with the exception of 16th (Irish) Division which had been driven back across the Battle Zone. 30th and 61st Divisions, opposite Saint-Quentin, had even held most of the Battle Zone.

For Butler's III Corps, things had been very different. Here, too few troops manning underdeveloped defences were spread out over too wide an area, and the Germans had taken maximum advantage. If sufficient reserves had been available it is possible that the rot might have been stopped. During the course of 21 March Gough had been forced to use what reserves he had. They did not amount to much. The three dismounted cavalry divisions had the rifle strength of one infantry division. 20th and 39th Divisions were fed into the battle. The French could not give any immediate help. Humbert arrived at Gough's HQ at about 1 p.m., but told him ruefully that all he had available was the general's pennant flying from the car. GQG had failed to allocate reserves in time. Fresh British divisions from GHQ reserve would take 72 hours to arrive from the north, and so 50th Division was the only reserve that could be committed within 24 hours. Butler and Gough took the only possible decision, to order a retreat to the Crozat canal. During 21 March the BEF had lost some 500 guns and suffered 38,000 casualties. With Fifth Army's right flank in disorder, the situation was critical.

Haig was aware of some of this. He approved Gough's decision to pull back to the canal, which was after all in accordance with the plans worked out before the battle, and asked the French to send reserves to help Gough. He allocated two divisions moving down from Flanders to go to Fifth Army from GHQ reserve. But the true gravity of the situation still eluded GHQ. To Gough's disappointment, Haig had not telephoned him during the day, although Gough spoke to Davidson and Lawrence. Haig remained at GHQ and carried on with at least part of his planned programme for the day. At 11 a.m. he met a party of four generals from Siam, and he hosted a high-level American delegation, including Newton D. Baker, the US Secretary of War, for dinner.

With hindsight, it might seem obvious that Haig should have visited Gough to see the situation in person. But the fifty-plus miles' drive from Montreuil would have put him out of contact for several hours. Staying put, remaining in reach of a telephone, monitoring developments on the fronts of Fifth and Third Armies and watching for developments elsewhere (an attack on another part of the front could not be discounted – Haig took careful note of a German bombardment of the French in Champagne, which might have presaged an attack) was the prudent approach.[54]

GHQ's optimism continued into 22 March. From Montreuil the situation appeared difficult but not yet critical. Morning reports suggested that III Corps' withdrawal to the Crozat canal was 'proceeding satisfactorily' and 'our men are in great spirits'. Gough's news that came through at 8 p.m. was bad: enemy groups had broken through Fifth Army's rear line. Haig agreed with Gough's decision to fall back to the River Somme and defend the bridgehead at Péronne – this had been anticipated before the battle – and asked Pétain for further help. GHQ anticipated a German attack on Arras, and so could not dispatch troops from this sector to the Somme. Charteris's summary was accurate: 'The fighting to-day has gone badly for us.'[55]

Saturday 23 March saw Haig visit Byng and Gough for the first time since the German offensive had begun. Byng was generally contented with the state of his front. Gough was not. According to Gough's account published 13 years later, his conversation with Haig was superficial. The C-in-C, 'calm and cheerful', did not discuss the wider situation, or the role of Third Army, and did little more than offer sympathy: 'Well, Hubert, one can't fight without men.' Haig's diary suggests a more substantial conversation about the current position of Fifth Army and its problems over the previous days. Revealingly, in the typescript version of the diary, Haig inserted a sentence missing from the original: 'I cannot make out why the Fifth Army has gone so far back without making some kind of a stand'.[56] Presumably this indicates Haig's realisation that the situation was far worse than he had believed.

Despite the arrival of French support on III Corps front, by 2 p.m. the Germans (now known to be in larger numbers than previously believed) had crossed the Crozat canal and forced the now badly weakened defenders back about two miles. At dawn on 24 March almost the entire Fifth Army had been pushed back four to six miles.

Haig's action later on the 23rd certainly suggests that the scales had fallen from his eyes. He arranged for Plumer to reduce Second Army's forces in Flanders. 'I shall be glad to see the Divisions thus set free near the Somme! It is most satisfactory to have a Commander of Plumer's temperament at a time of crisis like the present.' Haig's use of the loaded word 'crisis', and his recognition of Plumer's solid virtues (perhaps unconsciously comparing them to Gough's personality) shows that at last GHQ understood the threat posed by the remorseless German assaults on Fifth Army.[57] Although Haig was seriously concerned, he remained calm.

Pétain and Haig met at 4 p.m. on 23 March. So far, although French reserves had arrived more slowly than the British would have liked, the agreement for mutual support had worked well enough. Pétain had sent three divisions to support Gough on the evening of the 21st and, having decided that the weight of the German attack was indeed against the British, he directed more divisions to head for the Somme, although he refused Haig's request for 20 French divisions to assemble near Amiens.[58] At their meeting, Pétain reassured Haig that he

> has arranged to put 2 Armies under General Fayolle on my right, to operate in Somme Valley and keep our two Armies in touch with one another. Pétain is most anxious to do all he can to support me. The basic principle of co-operation is to keep the two Armies in touch. If this is lost and the enemy comes in between us, then probably the British will be rounded up and driven into the sea! This must be prevented even at the cost of abandoning the North flank.

These last two sentences represented the heart of the strategic issue. If the Germans could separate the BEF from the French, both armies could then be defeated in turn. The success of the German attack on the boundary between the two armies threatened to bring about this catastrophe. To prevent this nightmare Haig was even prepared to contemplate the unthinkable and lose touch with the coast.[59] GHQ issued an uncompromising order at 5 p.m.: 'Fifth Army will hold the line of the Somme at all costs . . . It is of the greatest importance that the Fifth Army should effect [actually, maintain] a junction with the French on their right without delay. The Third and Fifth Armies must keep in closest touch in order to secure their junction and must mutually assist each other in maintaining Péronne as a pivot.'[60]

What happened the next day is deeply controversial. For Douglas Haig 24 March 1918 was probably the most traumatic day he had endured since the crisis at the First Battle of Ypres in 1914. During the day the news continued to be bad. The Germans had reached the old 1916 Somme battlefield, which must have been a psychological blow to Haig, and he feared the enemy advancing as far as Amiens. This town was a major choke point on the British rail network. About fifty per cent of the BEF's supplies came in through the ports of Rouen, Dieppe and Le Havre and passed by train through Amiens.[61] Worse was to follow. At a late-night meeting with Pétain it appeared that the French general had reneged on the commitment he had made only the day before. The French army would manoeuvre to cover Paris, and the link with the BEF would be severed. In short, the very thing that Haig feared the most was about to come true.

Even at their meeting on the previous day it is possible that Haig had some doubts that Pétain would deliver on his promises.[62] Pétain certainly had reservations about Haig. A French staff officer's diary for 22 March recorded doubts growing in Pétain's mind. Earlier that day, he had expressed confidence in that the BEF could hold the line of the River Somme but 'towards evening he has become more anxious, seeing that the British are continually looking backwards; and he wonders if they will really be able to hold on the Somme'. The officer recorded in his diary for 23 March his fears, apparently shared by Pétain, that Haig 'is continually thinking of moving northwards to cover his bases . . . it is we who have to stretch out our hand to him, and we are stretching too wide . . .'[63]

Anxieties, mutual suspicion, the resurgence of national interests and, above all, misunderstandings brought the Anglo-French alliance close to disaster when at 11 p.m. on 24 March, Haig and Pétain met at Dury. The account in Haig's contemporary handwritten diary is relatively brief:

> I explained my plans as above and asked him to concentrate a large force near Abbeville astride the Somme to cooperate on my right. He said he expected every moment to be attacked in Champagne, but would give Fayolle all his available troops. . . Situation seems better, but we must expect these great attacks to continue.[64]

At the meeting Pétain gave Haig a copy of an order he had issued at 9 p.m. This stated that the primary task was to maintain the unity of the French armies and 'Secondly, if it is possible, to maintain liaison with the British forces'.[65]

The typescript diary adds a good deal more material and gives the impression that the meeting provoked a crisis. Pétain was 'almost unbalanced and most anxious'. He had issued an order which would

> separate the French from the British right flank, and so allow the enemy to penetrate between the two armies. I at once asked Pétain if he meant

to abandon my right flank. He nodded assent, and added, It is the only thing possible, if the enemy compel the Allies to fall back still further.

Pétain had 'attended a Cabinet meeting in Paris and . . . his orders from his Government are to "*cover Paris at all* costs" '.

On the other hand to keep in touch with the British Army is no longer the basic principle of French strategy . . . So I hurried back to my headquarters at Beaurepaire Château to report the serious change in *French strategy* to the CIGS and Secretary of State for War, and ask them to come to France.[66]

Trying to unravel the mystery is complicated by the fact that we simply do not know when the typescript diary was created. The existing version is certainly post-war, but it is possible that another version was typed shortly after the events it depicts. The most likely explanation is that Haig wanted to claim much of the credit for Foch's appointment as 'generalissimo' or Supreme Allied Commander. Fearing that Pétain was planning break contact with the BEF, Haig claimed to be instrumental in bringing about the Doullens conference of 26 March that proposed Foch's appointment. In his typed diary (but not the manuscript original) he wrote that at about 3 a.m. Lawrence sent a telegram to the CIGS, Henry Wilson, 'requesting him and Lord Milner to come to France at once in order to arrange that General Foch or some other determined general, who would fight, should be given supreme control of the operations in France.' No record survives of this telegram, and Milner (who was shortly to replace Derby as secretary of state for war) and Wilson were already on their way to France at the time the telegram was supposed to have been sent. There are also discrepancies in the written records that make it impossible to confirm Haig's claims about his activities at the Doullens conference.[67]

Tim Travers has argued that Haig altered his diary to conceal the fact that he was considering falling back away from Pétain. Historian Elizabeth Greenhalgh has recently dismissed the idea of a conspiracy, arguing that the two diary versions 'do not contradict each other on the whole . . . The later additions and emendations are expansions'. As she suggests, there is evidence that by 21 April Haig truly believed the version that he had set down in the typescript diary.[68] However, to interpret Haig's motivations in expanding his diary is to enter the world of psychohistory. The simplest explanation is that a tired and stressed man let off steam in his diary, apportioning blame and giving himself the credit he believed he deserved.[69]

By late on 24 March Haig's optimism had vanished. One claim is that there was 'panic' at GHQ, with key staff officers including Lawrence and Davidson 'apparently losing their nerve'.[70] While this is probably going too far, Haig was deeply concerned about the situation around Arras. Meeting Byng on the 24th, he directed him to 'hold on with . . . [Third Army's] left at all costs to the right of First Army near Arras, and if forced to give ground, to do so by throwing back his right on to our old trench system from Arras via Ransart etc along our old defence line'. If the enemy reached as far as Amiens, he aimed to launch a counterstroke to the south, using reserves gained from 'thinning my line in the North'. This was an inevitable response to the tactical situation on Third Army's right flank. While this did run the risk of losing touch with Gough and the French, it was as a means to an end, and was not a signal that Haig intended to abandon his allies.[71]

While there is some evidence that Haig was contemplating falling back on the Channel ports – it would have been a dereliction of duty if he had not – one of the key pieces of evidence, Haig's letter of 25 March sent to Foch's key staff officer Major-General Maxime Weygand, is ambiguous. It asks for 'at least' 20 French divisions 'to operate on the flank of the German movement against the English Army which must fight its way slowly back covering the Channel Ports'.[72] Rather than meaning that Haig intended *heading* for the coast, it is more likely this signalled the intention not to lose contact with it during the retirement.

Haig's suspicions about Pétain were not entirely unfounded. Although Pétain did not contemplate carrying out the sort of withdrawal that Haig feared, he was disenchanted with Haig and clearly recognised the need to protect Paris. Fayolle was ordered 'if possible' to stay in touch with the BEF. In effect Pétain had decided that covering Paris took priority.[73] Greenhalgh makes the plausible suggestion that Haig and Lawrence simply misunderstood Pétain at their meeting on 24 March, and on the long drive back to GHQ, at the end of a long and tiring day (the meeting began at 11 p.m. and they did not get home until 3 a.m.) 'convinced each other that Pétain was indeed intending '"to abandon [Haig's] right flank"'.[74]

The success of Haig's alliance with Pétain in blocking unity of command seemed retrospectively Pyrrhic indeed, as Wilson could not resist pointing out when the two men met on 25 March.[75] One intriguing point that remains unanswerable is whether the mutual support agreement of December 1917 could have been made to work. An earlier generation of historians saw the problem as the result of inevitable national interests that tugged the French towards Paris and the British towards the coast.[76] But if in actuality neither Haig nor Pétain was actively planning to abandon the other, perhaps the crisis could have been averted by clearer communications between GHQ and GQG. Whatever Haig's precise role in his appointment, Foch's new post brought the immediate crisis to an end.

There is no doubt that Haig was still rattled on 25 March; he struck Wilson as 'cowed' when they met at 11 a.m. According to Wilson, when the discussion came round to a generalissimo Haig suggested Pétain but eventually agreed with Wilson's suggestion of Foch. The previous August, Haig had fought against a proposal that Foch become generalissimo, but the objection had been to the principle, rather than to Foch himself. The two of them had worked together in the past, and, crucially, Foch had steered clear of the Nivelle affair in spring 1917 and thus built up credit with Haig. By now, the situation had changed radically. Foch's time had come. At Doullens the following day he was appointed to co-ordinate the Allied forces on the Western Front. The initial proposal had only been for Foch's writ to run around Amiens, but this was changed; Haig claimed the credit for this initiative. When Wilson dropped into GHQ that afternoon, Haig told him that he was 'greatly pleased' with the result of the conference. Wilson thought Haig 'is 10 years younger tonight than he was yesterday afternoon'.[77]

However, Haig seems to have retained his composure in front of more junior members of his staff. Major Ivor Hedley, his ADC, wrote that Haig 'has been simply wonderful. The further the enemy has advanced the more cheerful he has appeared – "Think how much worse it will be for him when we start to drive him back".'[78] The mask of command was firmly in place.

A further meeting at Beauvais on 3 April, which Haig attended, gave

Foch power of 'strategic direction' over British, French and US forces on the Western Front.[79] Foch was a co-ordinator rather than a true military supreme commander and lacked a large multinational staff. Foch had to feel his way, persuading rather than ordering, and exercising tact and sensitivity towards national interests. He took some time to grow into his post, but in the end proved a priceless asset to the Allies. Foch's relationship with Haig was by no means always easy – a saying at GHQ was that Haig had to fight three foes – 'Boche, Foch and Loygeorges [Lloyd George]'[80] – but the partnership between the two men was to be a critical factor in the eventual Allied victory.

All along Haig had feared a major attack against Arras, and on 28 March it came to pass when the Germans launched Operation *Mars*, the second phase of their offensive. It made good strategic sense for the Germans to attack there. British First and Third Armies met in the Arras sector, and it is always difficult to organise command-and-control across formation boundaries. A breakthrough at Arras could shatter the cohesion of the BEF and would place the Anglo-French coalition under strain, as Haig would again have had to look over his shoulder towards the coast.

When he heard the news of *Mars*, Haig ordered three of the divisions *en route* from Plumer and Horne to go to the Arras sector.[81] In fact the crisis was short-lived. Nine German divisions attacked north of the River Scarpe, using the same methods that had brought success against Fifth Army a week earlier, but on 28 March the defenders were more than a match for them. Attacking strong and resolute forces in well-constructed defences (the ones that Haig had praised in early March) in clear weather, the Germans were defeated so comprehensively that Ludendorff abandoned the offensive after only one day. Haig could not know this, of course, and had to anticipate the battle being renewed on the 29th.

From the south the news was mixed. North of the Somme, the British front had solidified, and with the arrival of substantial French forces the impetus of the German attack south of the river was beginning to wear down. Still, on 27 March the Germans took Montdidier from the French, and as a result Foch informed Haig on the afternoon of 28 March that it was impossible to 'extend the French front towards the Somme'. Fifth Army, due for relief, would have to stay put and be reconstituted in place.[82]

The German Spring Offensive had one last spasm of action. Between 29 and 31 March the Germans halted to prepare for a major push towards Amiens. Belatedly the capture of this town had become the focus of the German offensive. Had it been so from the beginning the operation could have inflicted a crippling blow on the Allies by denying them a critical rail centre. On 4 April the attack began, to be stopped on Fifth Army's front at Villers-Bretonneux by Australian troops newly arrived from Flanders. A major attack on Third Army on 5 April got nowhere. The Germans had not succeeded in reaching Amiens, and they called off the offensive.

The German gamble had failed. This was obvious to Ludendorff but not to the Allied commanders. On 5 April Haig discussed with General Asser, the commander of the Lines of Communication area, the 'arrangements for holding succession of lines in the event of the enemy succeeding in capturing Amiens and advancing to Abbeville, with the object of covering Rouen and Havre'.[83] Even though the threat on the Somme had diminished, there were worrying signs of the Germans preparing for an attack in Flanders. Haig's role during Operation *Michael* had been a curious mixture of crisis management and routine. During the bitter fighting for Villers-Bretonneux, for instance, he had had a long meeting with the Military Secretary discussing awards to appear in the 'King's Birthday Gazette'.[84]

Haig was by nature a calm, self-confident man, and his personal crisis of confidence of 24–26 March was the most serious of the entire war. As in August 1914, Douglas Haig was all too aware of the sheer weight of responsibility resting on his shoulders: responsibility for his army, his country and the future of the Empire. Once Foch was in place as Generalissimo Haig quickly recovered his equilibrium. On wider issues Haig emerges reasonably well from Operation *Michael*. While he was wrong to frustrate the unity of command proposals at the turn of the year, his decision to leave Gough's army weak was wholly under-standable. Haig considered the maintenance of the coalition to be imperative, but he was right to consider the British national interest in his decision-making, just as Pétain was right to have the wellbeing of his country at the forefront of his mind. Ultimately national interests, rightly or wrongly, trump coalition solidarity, as in the decision of the commander of a later BEF in 1940 to evacuate from Dunkirk. Things were never so bad in 1918 that this became a serious proposition.

Once Foch had emerged as supreme commander, Haig began to feel his way towards establishing a rapport with him. The framework was already in place. At the Beauvais conference that enhanced Foch's powers, Haig stated 'this new arrangement did not in any way alter my attitude towards Foch, or C-in-C French Army. I had always regarded the latter as being responsible for indicating the general strategical policy and, as far as possible, I tried to fall in with his views'.[85] Foch and Haig had had dealings with each other, on and off, since 1914. The British C-in-C's initial impressions were favourable. After meeting Foch on 29 March Haig recorded that 'Foch has brought great energy to bear on the present situation, and has, instead of permitting French troops *to retire* Southwest from Amiens, insisted on some of them relieving our troops and on covering Amiens at all costs. He and I are quite in agreement as to the general plan of operations.'[86] Over the next few weeks Foch was to disappoint Haig in some of his requests for support, but we can see that the key command relationship that was to flower in the second half of 1918 was already developing. The partnership between Foch and Haig was never smooth, but ultimately it proved highly effective.

In early April 1918 it was by means certain that Haig would survive in command into the second half of the year. The news of the breakthrough on Fifth Army's front had been greeted with horror at home. Repington thought it 'the worst defeat in the history of the Army'.[87] A search for scapegoats was inevitable. One was Hubert Gough. He was relieved as Army commander by Rawlinson at the end of March, but had every reason to believe that he would have further employment on the Western Front. But 'there is no doubt whatever that there is a want of confidence in this country with regard to Gough,' Derby informed Haig, 'and an intense feeling against him'.[88]

Lloyd George told Haig that Gough must go. 'To this I said I could not condemn an officer unheard, and that if LG wishes him suspended he must send me an order to that effect.' He got his wish. The very next day Haig received a telegram from Derby ordering Gough's super-session. Haig's reaction was to wire back accepting the decision and recommending Cavan for the vacant post. Two days later he wrote to Derby offering to resign:

Personally, I have a clear conscience and feel that I have done the best with the means at my disposal, and am prepared to continue to carry on here as long as the government wish me to do so. But, as I have more than once said to you and to others of the government, the moment they feel they would prefer someone else to command in France, I am prepared to place my resignation in your hands. The needs of the State and the wishes of the Government must take first place, and the wishes of the individual must be ignored.[89]

Haig's letter reflected his sense of the weakness of his position. His political standing was diminished, and he had already played the strongest card when the King visited GHQ on 29 March. Haig told George V, who he thought looked as if he had 'been suffering from anxiety and "funk" ', of the problems his Army had faced, making clear Lloyd George's government's share of the blame.[90]

Derby read out Haig's letter at a War Cabinet meeting on 8 April. Lloyd George gathered a small informal committee to discuss, in Hankey's words, 'the desirability of getting rid of Haig'. The conclusion, surprisingly, was to leave Haig in place. Lloyd George was willing 'to take Haig at his word' and allow him to fall on his sword, but Wilson said that 'failing some really outstanding personality, and we have none, I thought we ought to wait for Haig's report'. The Prime Minister had sent Smuts and Hankey had visited the Western Front in January to assess if there was anyone who could replace Haig. Their only suggestion was Claud Jacob of II Corps, but they came down in favour of keeping Haig in place.[91] Now, in April, Hankey similarly claimed that Haig had 'no very obvious successor', gratuitously adding that 'Plumer, in whom the troops are said to have confidence, being about as stupid as Haig himself'.[92] The politicians thought that Haig was a poor general but there was no one better. With that not very ringing endorsement, Douglas Haig was given leave to carry on as Commander-in-Chief of the British Expeditionary Force – for the moment.

The question of his succession would not go away. In May, Doris wrote of rumours at home that he was about to be appointed C-in-C Home Forces. A couple of weeks later Wilson denied the rumour to Haig's face. Haig's reaction was cynical but not far from the truth: 'So no one has been chosen yet!'[93]

Haig had survived one crisis only to be plunged into another. On 9 April 1918 the Germans attacked in Flanders. The fighting that followed, called Operation *Georgette* by the Germans and the Battle of the Lys by the British, had the potential to be catastrophic for the BEF. Running north from the La Bassée canal, the sector assaulted by German Sixth Army on 9 April covered 12 miles to Armentières, south of Ypres. This was dangerously close to the coast, so a relatively short advance could place the Channel ports in peril. A more modest advance could break a vital railway line, which would have had a catastrophic impact on the BEF's ability to supply its divisions. A 'battering train' of guns was sent up from Picardy, so the Royal Artillery was outnumbered in the all-important category of heavy batteries by 230 to 200. Just as Fifth Army had been short of reserves three weeks earlier, the formations directly in the path of the German attack, XI and XV Corps of Horne's First Army, had most of their combat power in the shop window. Two divisions per corps were in the line, with one in reserve, and there was a single division at the disposal of First Army. The day before, Foch had refused Haig's plea for French troops to take over the northern part of the Ypres salient, to enable him to build up a reserve in the area. This was very nearly a costly mistake.[94]

By a quirk of fate, one of the most ferocious assaults of the war fell upon one of the formations least able to withstand it. The Portuguese division was poorly led and discontented and crumpled in the space of two hours. The two British divisions on its flanks, the 40th and 55th, fought hard, and British reinforcements were rushed up to plug the gap, but by the end of the day the Germans had pushed forward 3½ miles – this in an area where there was no strategic depth. The British were now defending an unwieldy salient of 18 miles jutting into their lines.

Having jabbed with the left, on 10 April the Germans unleashed their right. German Fourth Army, 33 divisions strong, assaulted the positions of Hamilton-Gordon's IX Corps north of Armentières. Hamilton-Gordon had only three divisions, and all of them had gone through the mill of the fighting in Picardy – 25th Division had lost over 50 per cent of its strength. The floodgates having finally opened in Britain, infantry replacements were now arriving in sizeable numbers, but many were 19-year-old boys.[95]

Once again the Germans outgunned the British, this time by 240 heavy guns to 105. IX Corps fought hard but was gradually forced back, while German Sixth Army renewed its onslaught south of Armentières. These were desperate times. At 10.50 a.m. First Army ordered the town of Armentières to be evacuated.[96] The city was untenable against a major German attack, but to lose such a key rail junction was a heavy blow. IX Corps' right wing gave up three miles, including part of Messines Ridge. There was little Haig could do apart from, yet again, to ask Foch to send reinforcements, and to juggle his scanty reserves. 'Yesterday we had drawn on Plumer to help Horne,' Haig wrote ruefully, 'Now we are strengthening Plumer by moving reserve Divisions from 1st Army to the left and replacing them from Third Army'. Two cavalry divisions were put into GHQ Reserve, and 33rd and 5th Divisions were sent up to the threatened areas.

That night Foch visited GHQ and in a discussion with Haig said that he had identified the major threat as being in the Somme–Arras area, and he would send Maistre's French Tenth Army to reinforce this sector. For Haig this was partial good news, as it dealt with a potential future threat. However, it did little to relieve the immediate crises, although it allowed 1st Australian Division to be sent north to cover the vital communication centre at Hazebrouck.[97] The following day, 11 April 1918, promised to be critical.

On that day the Germans pushed to within five miles of Hazebrouck. It is difficult to overstate the importance of the town: it was more than simply a collection of buildings, it was the Amiens of the north – a major choke point on the BEF's railway system. 'Almost everything that came in through the three northern ports had to go through Hazebrouck.'[98] Put simply, if Hazebrouck was lost the BEF would find it difficult to fight – quite apart from the fact that the Germans would have driven a wedge between First and Second Army, leaving Plumer's force vulnerable to being cut off and destroyed. It could even have led to the capture of some of the Channel ports, and the eventual collapse of the Anglo-French alliance in mutual recrimination as the British troops were evacuated by sea. Something very like this happened in 1940.

Haig's diary gives a valuable insight into his state of mind on 11 April. He was clearly very anxious, although far from panicking, and calmly set out the strategic problem, perhaps as an exercise in mind-clearing. 'It seems to me that Enemy will do his utmost to exploit his success towards

Hazebroucke [sic] and Calais. So it is very necessary to give Plumer sufficient troops to hold up the enemy's advance . . . [but] my reserves are very few indeed.' That day GHQ's intelligence staff had raised the estimate of German divisions in the Lys battle from 13 to 25. The 'most important thing' was to stay in touch with the French army, so he 'had to be strong' in the sector south of Arras. Only Foch could provide troops, but in reply to Haig's request for a minimum of four French infantry divisions in the Dunkirk area to support the British, he would only offer a cavalry corps, confident that the British could hold on. Haig, as during First Ypres four years earlier, had to 'putty up' using his reserves to fill in gaps in the line.[99]

Strangely, Haig's diary for 11 April does not mention that he issued a 'Special Order of the Day'. This was one of the few attempts he made as a high commander to offer inspirational leadership to his men:

> With our backs to the wall and believing in the justice of our cause each one of us must fight on to the end. The safety of our homes and the Freedom of mankind alike depend upon the conduct of each one of us at this critical moment.[100]

Written from the heart, it was firmly in the tradition of British calls to arms, sitting between Nelson's stirring signal at Trafalgar and Churchill's defiant rhetoric of 1940.[101] Haig's message was undoubtedly directed at himself as well as his troops. The reaction of the ordinary soldier is difficult to judge. It would have had little if any effect on the men actually fighting in front of Hazebrouck. For some soldiers when they did get to read or hear it, Haig's order simply alerted them to how dangerous the situation really was. This was not a universal reaction. '[A]s one who heard it,' a Machine Gun Corps officer wrote many years later, 'I can testify to its effect'.[102]

Haig's message chimed with British propaganda, which had made much of the harsh terms imposed on Bolshevik Russia by the victorious Germans at the peace of Brest-Litovsk only a month before. This had brought home to the British people what a German victory would cost them, and went a long way to stiffening wobbling home front morale. When he wrote that the 'safety of our homes and the Freedom of mankind' were at stake, Haig really believed that this was true, and his fears were widely shared at home and in the army. He scarcely exaggerated.[103]

In desperate fighting, the Germans were stopped short of Hazebrouck. Ludendorff had been disappointed by the lack of progress made by the attackers ever since the beginning of the offensive. The sheer stubbornness and refusal to be beaten of the British troops had made the Germans' advance patchy at best. Ludendorff's conclusion on the attack of 9 April was blunt: the 'result was not satisfactory', but he thought that battering away at the British would eventually force them to give way.[104] He was wrong. As darkness fell on 11 April, Hazebrouck was still held by the British.

The following day Haig visited the headquarters of IV, V and Australian Corps. What he heard cheered him. He was particularly impressed by Brudenell White, Chief of Staff of the Australian Corps, but 'I was greatly struck with the fine spirit of confidence and cheerfulness which existed everywhere . . . It gave me a great feeling of confidence seeing these Commanders and staffs so well after all their trying times, and so confident!' Haig's anxiety levels, which had prompted the 'backs to the wall' order the previous day, perhaps subsided a little. But the view from GHQ on the 12th was still grim. Planning for the worst while hoping for the best, Haig was thinking in terms of Second Army pulling back slowly to the Dunkirk area.[105]

Although neither Haig nor anyone else knew it, the BEF had weathered the crisis of the Battle of the Lys. British, French and Australian reinforcements were arriving – again, just in time. Second Army retreated from Passchendaele Ridge, at first leaving an outpost line and then pulling back altogether. By the end of April the line was back at Ypres itself. In an interesting contrast of responses, Plumer was deeply emotional at ordering the abandonment of Passchendaele, but Haig recorded it matter-of-factly in his diary.[106]

Yet another attempt to break through the Allied positions began on 17 April. Once again the Allies, including by this stage the Belgian army, remained firm. At a conference with Foch at Abbeville on 14 April Haig reiterated his case for reinforcements. Foch's reply was a resounding 'non'. He looked back nostalgically to the resilience and bloody-mindedness of the British Regulars at First Ypres and expected the conscripts and volunteers of 1918 to show the same fortitude.[107]

Standing back from the battle, Foch believed that the Lys battle was all but over. By parsimoniously doling out French divisions as reinforcements, he was able to keep a reserve in case the Germans mounted another offensive elsewhere. His guess about the Lys was wrong but overall he was right. Edmonds's assessment in the official British history was that Foch's obduracy resulted in the deaths of many British soldiers and caused Haig and other senior British commanders much anxiety, but 'in the circumstances one cannot but admire his judgment of the situation and his resistance to the very heavy pressure placed on him'.[108] Unlike some of Edmonds's judgments, this one is eminently fair.

Since early April, the Somme front had been fairly quiet, but on 24 April the Germans attacked towards Amiens. Supported by tanks, the Germans made deep gains around Villers-Bretonneux, 10 miles from Amiens, the world's first tank-against-tank combat taking place in the process. An Australian-British counterattack slammed shut the door to Amiens. On the same day, in Flanders, the Germans captured Mount Kemmel from the French. Again the Allies did enough to prevent the attackers from building on their success.

Ludendorff finally called off the Lys battle on 30 April. The Allies, and principally the British army, had won a victory of immense significance. Most of the key decisions were taken way below the level of GHQ, and the decisive factor was undoubtedly the front-line infantryman. Haig's major role was to allocate reserves, and this, of course, was largely dependent on the forces that Foch was prepared to give him. His other contribution was to hold his nerve. Haig passed the test on both counts. On the first, by juggling the troops available he was just about able to keep the firing line strong enough. On the second, during the battle he opened his heart to the Reverend Duncan: 'I *know* I am sustained in my efforts by that Great Unseen Power, otherwise I could not be standing the strain as I am doing'.[109] By drawing on his mental and spiritual reserves, Haig saw it through. Although he had deep reservations about the way Foch was handling the reserves, and told him so, Haig accepted his decisions and operated within the command set-up rather than kicking against it. Foch was the answer to Haig's despairing demand back in March: he was a determined general, who fought. Foch's decision on reserves, though risky, was correct. British battalions, although savagely depleted and with their men at the point of exhaustion, fought the

Germans to a standstill. Haig had been right to demand that his troops should be relieved. Foch was equally right to say no.

Ludendorff was far from finished. He remained convinced that he had to crush the British army to win the war. Operation *Hagen*, a fresh offensive in Flanders, was to deliver the fatal blow. But first there were to be two sequential battles against the French to reduce their chance of reinforcing the British. On 7 May Haig noted the best guess of Allied intelligence staff: offensives on the Somme, around Arras and near Givenchy within the next week. This was wrong, but just as wrong as the other estimates. The Germans took almost a month in preparing for their next offensive, and this time proved invaluable for the Allied soldiers. An inherently aggressive commander like Haig was not content simply to wait to be attacked. On 17 May he visited Rawlinson, and gave him the outline for an offensive in the Villers-Bretonneux area. Over two months later, this was to take shape as the battle of Amiens.[110]

Rebuilding the Army

In late spring 1918 Haig was painfully aware of how much his army had been damaged. The BEF had taken huge losses during March and April, a total of 301,340 from all causes.[111] Some divisions had been reduced to cadre, others completely reconstituted with battalions brought in from the Middle East. In May he spent much time going around his army, getting a personal 'feel' for the state of his divisions. After visiting V Corps, Haig noted: 'Latest Drafts are young, but men have been well trained. They lack muscle, but have fought well. One officer said they are "like the young Soldiers at Waterloo, and will again save the Empire".'[112]

Even at times of worst battlefield crisis, the administrative side of Haig's position could not be set aside, and among the subjects that vied for his attention was tactical reform. From late 1917 Solly-Flood's successor as DGT, Brigadier-General Charles Bonham-Carter, became aware of criticism of the current platoon organisation from frontline officers. Partly as a manpower saving-measure after the German offensives, and with reduction in numbers of soldiers in a platoon offset by an increase in Lewis guns, in June 1918 GHQ changed the platoon structure from four sections to three on a temporary basis. Haig once again put his personal authority behind the change.[113]

GHQ made another major change to the training regime in July 1918 when Lieutenant-General Sir Ivor Maxse was appointed Inspector-General of Training. Major-General Guy Dawnay, head of Staff Duties at GHQ, seems to have suggested the creation of the Inspectorate, and Haig was quick to respond. It is entirely possible that the idea emerged from discussions between the two. The new organisation reinforced the existing Directorate and reflected its struggles to impose uniformity of training, probably as a result of the turmoil created by the open warfare of early 1918. Maxse may well have been Haig's personal choice, probably on Dawnay's advice.[114] He was under a cloud as a consequence of his corps' performance in the March offensive but was a 'heavy-hitter' with a reputation as an excellent trainer of troops. Before he took up the post, Haig had Maxse to dinner, at which he 'spoke to him' about his task; a measure of how seriously he took Maxse's task.[115] Maxse was a good choice, bringing drive and enthusiasm to the job, building on the good work of Solly-Flood and Bonham-Carter. Maxse summed up his task as 'to interpret G.H.Q. doctrine, as regards training, and to inculcate uniformity in the several Armies in France'; he also had responsibility for overseeing training at home.[116]

Maxse was appointed only four-and-a-half months before the Armistice, which limited his impact on training. Nonetheless one achievement sheds some light on Haig's input. Maxse disliked the three-section platoon, and by September he had won the argument. Haig followed his usual practice of backing his subject-matter expert and putting his personal stamp on the decision to help ensure compliance. A lecture by a senior officer of Maxse's Inspectorate to 3rd Australian Division made this clear: 'the Commander-in-Chief has laid down that every . . . Platoon shall consist of four sections, viz, 2 rifle and 2 Lewis Gun Sections'.[117] The 1918 training saga is a reminder that, behind the headlines, the high-level meetings and strategic decision-making, Haig was engaged with the running and development of the BEF. Ultimately he was the man in charge. While his practice was to devolve authority to experts, in this case Dawnay and Maxse, he took an active interest and gave his subordinates powerful institutional backing, allowing expertise to flourish. Haig moulded his army, playing a major role, both direct and indirect, in its emergence by 1918 as a formidable fighting force.

The Final German Blow

Nonetheless, in the early summer 1918 the BEF was desperately in need of rest and of time for training and to integrate individual replacements from home into their units. An obvious solution was to send British troops to hold quiet stretches of the front in the French sector. Foch had suggested this in mid-April, in order to build up a reserve of fresh French troops. Haig saw the sense of this but the proposal touched a raw nerve. Ever sensitive to the nuances of coalition warfare, he was suspicious that this might lead to 'a permanent "Amalgam"' of British and French forces along the lines of the Nivelle proposals of a year earlier 'by which the British GHQ was to disappear'. Lord Milner, the newly appointed Secretary of State for War, concurred. Fourteen months on, the legacy of the Calais conference threatened the still-fragile unity of command established at Doullens.[118]

What happened next gives a clue to why the Doullens system was made to work. Haig gave Foch the benefit of the doubt, accepting that he was acting in good faith. At a subsequent meeting on 27 April both sides made efforts to be conciliatory, and the French in particular tried hard to recognise British sensitivities.[119] Four tired British divisions of IX Corps were sent off to a quiet French sector, the Chemin des Dames.

Ironically, the very idea that Haig resisted in regard to British troops was the idea that he wished to apply to the Americans. During the first half of 1918 the numbers of US troops arriving in France increased steadily. This transfusion of fresh troops was, in the medium and long term, an enormous advantage to the Allies, but in the short term it posed a difficult problem. The British and French wanted American units to serve under British or French command, or even individual soldiers posted to their units.

General John J. Pershing, Haig's American opposite number, would have none of it. His goal was to create an American field army. Somewhat reluctantly, Pershing allowed US units and formations to serve under French and British command as a temporary measure to gain experience. After a particularly tense meeting in May 1918, in the privacy of his diary, Haig sounded off that he 'thought Pershing was very obstinate, and stupid. He did not seem to realise the urgency of the situation'.[120] Frustration with Pershing was a slow-burning fuse for much of 1918. If Haig recognised his double-standards, they did not seem to worry him.

The atmosphere of guarded co-operation between Foch and Haig finally produced a definitive statement on the problem that had produced the Doullens agreement in the first place. What would happen if a future German attack threatened to divide the Allied armies? At Abbeville on 2 May it was

> agreed that: (1) touch with the French and British Armies must be maintained, and (2) that the Channel Ports must be covered. If, however, circumstances required the CinC to decide between the two objects, then rather than allow the Armies to be separated, a retirement would be made southwards towards the Somme.[121]

Whether this arrangement would have worked if ever put to the test is another matter. That the British would have voluntarily abandoned the Channel ports takes a considerable suspension of disbelief, although GHQ certainly made some preliminary plans.[122] The emerging partnership of Foch and Haig offered the best hope of making unity of command a reality.

Hamilton-Gordon's weary IX Corps, sent to the Chemin des Dames for a rest cure after the Lys, faced the fury of the next German offensive on 27 May. French Sixth Army commander General Duchêne, ineptly ignoring the principles of defence-in-depth, made the attacker's job easy for them. IX Corps fought well, but suffered heavily, and the remnants were caught up in the general rearward movement. The offensive brought Germans dangerously close to Paris. In a neat reversal of fortune, Foch now demanded that Haig provide reserves. At first Haig havered; he was worried that the Germans would attack his front if he weakened it (as, in fact, Ludendorff originally intended). As the crisis grew worse, he complied, sending XXII Corps but formally protesting.[123] Haig's back-covering was less significant than the fact that unity of command was, after a fashion, working.

This was a critical period for Haig's relationship with Foch. The supreme commander behaved in a high-handed fashion that would have been merely rude in normal circumstances but was actively dangerous in the context of a fragile coalition. Foch removed divisions from the

Détachement de l'Armée du Nord (DAN) – the French force in Flanders – without bothering to inform, let alone consult, the British C-in-C. Haig swallowed this, but at a conference on 7 June fired a warning shot, a formal statement that demands to send British divisions to support the French might endanger the BEF. In this case, he would, under the provisions of the Beauvais agreement appeal to his government. Foch took immediate steps to sooth Haig's feelings. This was a turning point. Haig adjusted to his place in the hierarchy, having his letter of authority from the Secretary of State amended to reflect the fact that he no longer had supreme responsibility for the BEF. Foch came to realise how – and, more importantly, how not – to treat the British C-in-C. Mutual confidence grew. This augured well for the months ahead.[124]

At home, the recriminations over the March offensive continued. On 6 May Major-General Sir Frederick Maurice published a scathing attack on Lloyd George in a letter to the press, accusing him of misleading parliament about the strength of the BEF in early 1918. The context was, of course, whether the government bore any responsibility for the weakness of the army at the time of the March offensive. Maurice knew that he was sacrificing his military career, but he firmly believed that he was acting in the interests of the army.[125] His initiative rapidly span out of control, with the government cleverly bringing about a vote in the House of Commons on 9 May. In effect, this was a vote of confidence in the government's handling of the war, which threatened to restore Asquith as Prime Minister if it lost. Lloyd George duly won the vote and thus emerged from the crisis with his authority enhanced.

Haig opposed Maurice's action. 'This is a grave mistake. No one can be both a soldier and a politician at the same time. We soldiers have to do our duty, and keep silent, trusting to Ministers to protect us'. He clearly had some sympathy for Maurice as his reaction to the parliamentary debate indicates: 'Poor Maurice! How terrible to see the House of Commons so easily taken in by a clap trap speech by Lloyd George'.[126] Maurice believed that by firing a shot across Lloyd George's bows he had saved Haig from dismissal. But there is no reason to doubt the sincerity of Haig's belief that in politics there were some lines that soldiers simply should not cross; many other senior soldiers shared this view.[127] If he had taken a different view, British history might have been radically different.

June and July 1918 was dominated by anticipation of when the Germans would attack again. Haig had no doubt that it was a question of 'when' rather than 'if'. Perhaps, he thought, the influenza epidemic was causing the delay?[128] Operation *Gneisenau* on 9 June made some progress against the French in the area of the Matz before it was brought juddering to a halt by a counteroffensive two days later. British troops were not involved. Haig feared that this was a diversionary offensive and the Germans intended to strike against the British next. To pick just one piece of intelligence pointing that way, on the day *Gneisenau* began Cox reported that additional hospital space had been provided by the Germans in the La Bassée area.[129]

GHQ had correctly divined Ludendorff's intentions, but its estimate of the timings was out. Looking at the situation in Flanders, OHL remained worried that it still needed to draw away Allied reserves. On 14 June Ludendorff decreed that another offensive would take place in the Reims area. It would take a month before the Germans were ready to attack.

From late June, Foch and Pétain became steadily more concerned about indications of a major German build-up in Champagne. Sure as night follows day, there would be pressure on Haig to move British divisions to the south – this at a time when there was plenty of intelligence pointing towards attacks on the BEF's front. Sure enough, on 12–13 July, Lawrence, standing in for Haig who was on leave in England, was asked to send eight divisions. Lawrence ordered the two-division XXII Corps to move.[130]

Haig was annoyed that Foch had abandoned the views laid out in a 'Directive' on 1 July, which stated that 'Paris and Abbeville', the port at the mouth of the Somme, must be covered 'before all else'.[131] He asked London for guidance. After consulting members of the War Cabinet, Wilson phoned GHQ in the early hours of 15 July. His reply was about as unhelpful as it could have possibly been, telling Haig to 'exercise . . . [his] judgment' on the matter. Sounding off (at some length) in his diary, Haig wrote that it was 'a case of "heads you win, and tails I lose"! If things go well, the Government take credit to themselves and the Generalissimo: if badly, the Field Marshal will be blamed!'[132]

By the time Haig and Foch had their meeting later that day, the Second Battle of the Marne had already begun. Foch agreed that the

British reserves 'would be in a position *ready to return . . . at once* in case the British front was threatened'. Haig was mollified for the moment but, as the German attack made little progress, GHQ decided that the threat in Flanders outweighed the one on the Marne. On 17 July Lawrence presented a letter to Haig asking for XXII Corps to be sent back north. Coincidentally, a message arrived from Foch. The Allies would counterattack on the following day on the Marne. Haig signed and sent the letter, but informed Foch that XXII Corps could be used for exploitation – although it would leave him dangerously short of troops.[133]

It was all academic. The counteroffensive of 18 July led by French General Charles Mangin on the Marne wrenched the strategic initiative from the Germans. On that very day Ludendorff had held a conference to plan Operation *Hagen,* the offensive in Flanders which was to be launched in early August. *Hagen* never happened. The French and British had survived their greatest crisis of the war. Now they could return to the offensive.

Victory

On the eve of the battles that were to win the war, Haig's army was very different from the one that had fought on the Somme two years before. The remaining volunteers had been topped up by conscripts. Only the Australians retained an all-volunteer force. The BEF was more experienced, from high command down; it had evolved effective procedures for battle and staff work; and its morale was robust. Thanks in no small part to Churchill at the Ministry of Munitions, the British could now fight a rich man's war, with unlimited supplies of materiel. Infantry battalions, lucky to have four Lewis light machine-guns in 1916, now had 30.[1] Guns, shells, tanks, aeroplanes, vehicles – all the things that were in short supply in earlier years were now there in superabundance, and a vast and efficient logistic system meant that they could get to the right place at the right time. What all this portended became clear on 4 July 1918.

Hamel and Amiens

In mid-July Haig visited Esher, and 'explained with his love of G[eneral] S[taff] detail this last attack of the Australians, aided by the American Battalions'. He was talking about the attack at Hamel, near Amiens, on 4 July carried out by 4th Australian Division and four companies from US 33rd Division. Haig had little to do with the preliminaries of the action, apart from becoming involved at the last minute when Pershing objected to his men participating. In just over 90 minutes the village was captured and 1,470 prisoners taken for the losses of fewer than 1,000 men – light by the standards of 1918. Hamel was a model bite-and-hold attack, with exemplary all-arms co-operation. In short order a pamphlet on the lessons of the battle was distributed to the rest of the army.[2] Although small-scale, Hamel was a highly significant action. Greatly expanded, Hamel methods underpinned the next major battle fought a month later.

Rawlinson, now keenly aware of German weakness, asked Haig to sanction a further limited advance on his front. Haig said no, as he did not believe it was sustainable, but he did give Rawlinson permission to 'study the problem and prepare a plan'.[3] Haig did see the possibilities of an offensive in the Amiens area, which would push the Germans back from vulnerable railway lines. At this time he was still expecting the Germans to reignite the Flanders battle, but by 23 July it was clear that the Marne counteroffensive had been a major success. Haig gave Rawlinson the go-ahead to carry out serious planning for an Amiens offensive. Even at this late stage he made Fourth Army's operation contingent on Mangin's success.[4] Two days earlier Rawlinson had held a planning conference with Lieutenant-General Sir John Monash, now commander of the Australian Corps, and Currie, and on 16 July he asked for the Canadian Corps. To his 'surprise and delight', he found that Haig had already decided to bring the Canadians and Australians together.[5]

Preparations rapidly gathered momentum. On 25 July Foch and Haig agreed to the attack taking place *as soon as possible*. Foch's directive indicated that the Allied offensives would seize the initiative and clear key railways lines to prepare the way for future operations. General Marie-Eugène Debeney, commander of French First Army, advised that the attack should be limited. This advice was rejected by Foch, who ordered something much more ambitious, in keeping with Haig's vision: 'the offensive will be pushed as far as Roye', which was about 25 miles south-east of Amiens. Haig in turn overruled Rawlinson, who did not want French assistance, and was rewarded on 28 July when Debeney and his army were placed under his command. Naturally, Haig was 'pleased that Foch should have entrusted me with the direction of these operations'.[6] It was a mark of the way that the relationship between the two men had developed since March.

Haig and Foch deliberately kept the British government in the dark about the impending attack. Neither the Prime Minister nor the Chief of the Imperial General Staff 'knew anything about it until zero hour'.[7] Disingenuously, Haig told the CIGS that 'nothing startling happened at the meeting' on the 25th.[8] Secrecy was paramount, and the fewer people in London who knew about the operation the better. But Haig also seems to have feared that if the government had advance notice of a major new offensive it would interfere, on the principle of 'no more Passchendaeles'. This was not the way civil–military relations should be handled in a democracy, but mutual trust was at a low ebb.

The ambition being shown by Foch and Haig contrasted sharply with the prevailing gloom in London. In a document dated 25 July 1918 Wilson concluded that there was little chance of breaking the stalemate in France before mid-1919, but prospects in other theatres were better. When a copy of 'British Military Policy 1918–1919' landed on Haig's desk, in disgust he scrawled on the cover 'Words! Words! Words! Lots of words! And little else'.[9]

On the eve of the BEF resuming the offensive, Haig turned to practical matters. He was concerned at the lack of uniformity of tactical methods within the divisions, despite the improvements in doctrine and training over the last eighteen months. He ordered corps commanders to ensure that correct procedures as laid down by GHQ were followed, and charged the Army commanders with checking up on the corps. Haig was convinced that a new phase of warfare was imminent. 'Army Commanders must do their utmost to get troops out of the influence of *Trench* methods'. The key was low-level training of leaders, at battalion and below. 'This is really a "platoon commanders' war".'[10] His message fell on receptive ears. 'Everyone is "nuts" on training now'a'days,' wrote an officer tasked with writing doctrine at GHQ.[11]

Brudenell White, then CoS to the Australian Corps, had carried out the initial planning back in May on Rawlinson's instructions, and the outline plan was given to Haig on 6 June.[12] Rawlinson, in keeping with his bite-and-hold philosophy, planned for a limited advance of six miles, up to the Outer Amiens Defence Line, on a ten-mile front. This was an old French defensive position dating from 1916, now taken into use by the Germans. It seemed to be a fairly formidable obstacle, and beyond it lay the old Somme battlefield, which would be extremely difficult ground for an attacker. Fourth Army thus planned to get to the Defence Line, halt and dig in. Except for the ambition of the bite, this was similar to Rawlinson's approach in 1916. But there were important differences between Amiens and the Somme battles. In August 1918 the defenders were weaker in numbers and morale, and their positions were significantly more difficult to defend; furthermore, their problems were exacerbated by the fact that the Allies achieved surprise. The BEF of August 1918 was a vastly more sophisticated and proficient instrument of war that it had been two years earlier, and Fourth Army had deliberately drawn upon the lessons of recent operations. Also, Haig was at last able to lay down the law on the use of cavalry, and Rawlinson, perhaps reluctantly, fully integrated them into his operational design.[13]

As a Fourth Army staff officer wrote, 'The essence of the whole plan was secrecy'. Secrecy is the midwife of surprise. An elaborate and successful deception plan concealed the arrival of the Canadians on the Amiens front. If the Germans had identified that the most powerful and freshest formation in the BEF's order of battle had appeared in the area, it would have been the strongest possible indicator that a major attack was about to take place. And on this occasion, there was no preliminary artillery bombardment. At zero hour the barrage crashed down, and the advance began.[14]

Another innovation was that the Cavalry Corps was to be involved from the outset, with brigades due to pass through the assaulting infantry and press on, accompanied by Whippet tanks. Their objective was 'to secure the line of the outer Amiens defences, and hold it until relieved by the infantry of the Canadian Corps'.[15] Critically, the problems that had bedevilled previous cavalry operations were at least partially overcome by devoting time to training with the infantry and devolving control of the mounted troops to a local level, and by having them advance according to a timetable.[16]

Rawlinson, of course, had long practice of debating his plans with Haig, but he now discovered that Foch's involvement gave him another, unpredictable, factor to take into account. Foch was worried that the post-Marne advance would get bogged down, and so asked Haig to change the date from 10 to 8 August, to engage German reserves. Haig, to Rawlinson's dismay, agreed. Then, as a result of a Haig–Foch conference on 3 August, Rawlinson had to field another fast ball. Foch had been so encouraged by the Marne that he wanted Amiens to be more ambitious. Consequently Haig extended the advance to Ham, a full 15 miles further than Roye, on the far bank of the River Somme.[17] Haig has been heavily criticised for this decision, for it seems that he had learned nothing from previous years of the dangers of over-ambitious objectives.[18] Perhaps there is more to this matter than meets the eye. GHQ's operation order of 29 July to Fourth and French First Armies directed that 'the enemy . . . will be attacked with the utmost vigour and driven back in the direction of HAM'; to achieve this Rawlinson was to 'press the enemy in the direction of Chaulnes'. Debeney, in similar language, was ordered to 'press the enemy in the direction of ROYE'. The version issued on 5 August stated that the two Armies must 'push forward in the general direction of the line ROYE–CHAULNES *with the least possible delay*, thrusting the enemy back with determination in the general direction of Ham, and so facilitating the operations of the French from the front Noyon–Montdidier'. In other words, apart from an exhortation to advance as speedily as possible, and also some details on the use of cavalry, the two operations orders are effectively identical.[19]

Seemingly, Haig was paying lip service to Foch's demands for the sake of harmony within the alliance.[20] GHQ's revised Operation Order of 5 August certainly smacks of tokenism. If this is so, it would certainly help explain Rawlinson's lack of reaction: he did not protest against the new objectives, even in the privacy of his diary. The objectives were so distant, existing artillery arrangements did not need to be disturbed – as Haig surely knew.[21] A likely explanation of the new order combines this political motive with Haig's feeling that, based on Rawlinson's previous form, he needed to be prodded to take advantage of opportunities. Haig 'thought that the Fourth Army orders aimed too much at getting a *final* objective on the old Amiens defence line, and stopping counter-attacks on it. This is not far enough, in my opinion, if we start by surprising the enemy!' Once the Outer Amiens Defence Line had been captured, 'at once reserves must be pushed on to capture the line Chaulnes–Roye . . . I said that the Cavalry must keep in touch with the battle and be prepared to pass through *anywhere* between the river Somme and the Roye–Amiens road.'[22] The key phrase here is 'surprising the enemy'. He wanted to ensure that, in the case of initial success, his operational concept of using mobile troops to expand upon initial success would not fail through lack of ambition. His delighted reaction to the actual achievements of the cavalry on 8 August perhaps adds weight to the idea that Haig regarded the extended objectives as an ideal rather than anything else.[23]

Haig set up his Advanced HQ for the battle in a train at Wiry-au-Mont station. He had a busy day on 7 August. In the morning he hosted the King, who 'looked well and very cheery. So different to his frame of mind on the occasion of his last visit in March'. Colonel S.S. Butler, of the Intelligence staff at GHQ, recalled that after briefing him that morning Haig,

> sitting, as usual, at his roll top desk . . . pulled out a drawer, from which he took a bunch of white heather, and handed me a piece of it saying 'Good luck to me! Good luck to us all and here's a piece for you. It was sent me by my wife this morning![24]

Haig then spent the afternoon touring headquarters and talking to some of the key players. According to Rawlinson, everything was going as planned, and there was no indication that the Germans were aware of what was about to hit them. This was no doubt a relief, because a German attack against III Corps on 6 August had captured some ground, meaning that Butler's troops would have to regain their start line before they could carry out their designated task on 8 August. Butler was ordered to regard the battle as having already commenced for III Corps; its role was vital in covering the flank of the Australian Corps' attack. But it seemed that the German attack was a local initiative. The secrecy surrounding the offensive was intact.

From Fourth Army HQ Haig went to visit the Canadian Corps. Currie reassured Haig that all was ready, 'although it had been a hustle'. The real moment of danger had been on the previous day, when it would have been impossible to respond to a German bombardment of the Canadian area. The C-in-C placed a great deal of trust in the Canadians and their commander, but he could not resist tweaking Currie's tail by reminding him of the huge battle that the BEF had fought without Canadian help earlier in the year.[25] Over the next four months the Canadian Corps was to more than make up for its absence in the spring.

The attack began at 4.20 a.m. on 8 August 1918 and achieved complete surprise. British III Corps attacked along the Chipilly Spur, guarding the flank of the spearhead formations, the Australian and Canadian Corps, with French First Army on the southern flank. By the end of the day Fourth Army had advanced a maximum of eight miles, the longest single advance achieved on the Western Front in one day since 1914. Fourth Army suffered losses of 9,000, and the Germans lost about 27,000 men (including 12,000 prisoners) and 450 guns. A map prepared for Crown Prince Rupprecht's Army Group, dated 8 a.m. on 8 August, shows that German intelligence still placed the Canadians around Arras.[26] When an intense bombardment suddenly crashed down on the German positions, it came as an utter shock to the defenders.

The BEF's gunners fired 350,000 shells from 700 guns during the battle. Counterbattery fire was particularly significant, as 504 out of 530 German guns had been identified before the attack, and 450 heavy guns set to work pounding the German batteries.[27] To be deprived of artillery support was just too much for the German infantry, already under strength and clinging to defences of miserable weakness. They were unable to resist the attack by the Allied infantry, principally the Australians and Canadians, supported by large numbers of tanks: 552, making this the biggest tank battle of the war.

Amiens signalled the beginning of the 'Hundred Days', the climactic campaign of the war. For Douglas Haig 8 August 1918 was the most satisfying day of his command so far: 'the situation had developed more favourably for us than I, optimist though I am, had dared even to hope'.[28] The success of the cavalry was particularly sweet. At 11.30 a.m. he heard that 1st Cavalry Division had captured Harbonnières, and 3rd Cavalry Division had reached the line Caix–Beaucourt. At last, his operational concept was coming right. Haig was keen to get French cavalry into action, so they could operate ahead of French First Army, but he was disappointed to be met by a series of reasons why they could not get into action until the following day. By contrast, with the command-and-control problems of previous years largely overcome, the British cavalry were sent in to action early enough to take advantage of the chaos among the defenders. The experiment in using cavalry in conjunction with Whippet tanks was not a success, but that said more about the incompatibility of two very different troop types than any failures on the part of the cavalry.

Alongside the infantry, tanks, artillery, aircraft and sundry other troops, the cavalry were integrated into the weapons system that triumphed on 8 August.[29] Haig wrote, correctly, that 'without the rapid advance of the Cavalry the effect of the surprise attack on the 8th would have been much less and very probably the Amiens outer defence line would not have been gained either so soon or so cheaply'.[30] The battle of Amiens not only vindicated the cavalry. It also vindicated the operational concept developed by Douglas Haig.

The C-in-C visited Rawlinson at midday and gave him orders to carry on with the cavalry in the lead. Fourth Army's major thrust would be to the south-east, to help French First Army. Going on to see Debeney, Haig was less impressed, as he had to prod him to take vigorous action. Foch, who had been elevated to a Marshal of France on 6 August, visited Haig at 6 p.m. in jubilant mood and endorsed Haig's future plans. 'Who would have believed this possible even 2 months ago?' Haig wrote to his wife that night. Thinking back a few short months, he added, 'How much easier it is to attack, than to stand and await an enemy's attack! As you well know, I feel that I am only the instrument of that Divine Power who watches over each one of us, so all the Honour must be His.'[31]

Inevitably, things did not turn out quite the way that Haig had hoped. III Corps' advance was more sluggish than had been anticipated. Butler's divisions have received much criticism for this, but, given the difficulties that they faced – not least the 'truly formidable' terrain over which they had to fight – their advance of two miles was not discreditable.[32] It did, however, put paid to Haig's idea of greatly pushing forward Fourth Army's left. And even after three days further fighting, Fourth Army was just short of Chaulnes at nightfall on 11 August. Amiens, after the drama of the first phases of the battle, had begun to conform to a depressingly familiar pattern. The initial rush was difficult to sustain, and, as German resistance intensified, the advance slowed. Haig was faced with an important and difficult decision. Should he continue the battle, hoping to wring every last drop of advantage out of it? Or should he cut his losses before it decayed into debilitating attrition?

Foch had no doubts, informing Haig on 10 August that he wanted the BEF to push straight ahead and capture the crossings over the Somme. Sounding like the Haig of earlier years, the Generalissimo was convinced that the Germans were showing signs of demoralisation. The Haig of August 1918 was not so sure. 'I pointed out the difficulty of the undertaking unless the enemy is quite demoralised.' Instead he proposed expanding the offensive by First Army attacking Aubers and bringing

Third Army into the battle towards Bapaume. In the end Haig agreed to continue to push on the River Somme.[33]

Later that day Haig spoke to Currie, Rawlinson and Major-General T.S. Lambert of 32nd Division. Lambert in particular stressed the difficulties of pushing forward over difficult ground against increasing resistance. Rawlinson was also starting to worry about the immediate future. According to Edmonds, Rawlinson was 'almost insubordinate' when Haig told him that Foch had directed a further advance: 'Are you commanding the British Army or is Maréchal Foch?'.[34] Since neither Haig nor Rawlinson mentions meeting each other in their diary entries for 10 August, there must be a question-mark over this story.[35] Whatever the truth, by nightfall Haig's doubts about Fourth Army simply pushing on towards the Somme had been reinforced by the views of some of his subordinates. Moreover the idea of a major offensive further north was crystallising in his mind.

The next day, 11 August 1918, was the turning point. In the morning Haig met Byng and told him to be ready to attack towards Bapaume as soon as he could be reinforced. After an impromptu tour of the battlefield on horseback, Haig met Rawlinson, who asked for an operational pause, and it seems the C-in-C gave at least implicit approval. In truth, Haig needed little persuading by this point. At a meeting with his corps commanders that afternoon, Rawlinson ordered that operations be confined to local attacks. Late in the morning of 11 August Montgomery, Rawlinson's Chief of Staff, phoned Davidson at GHQ to tell him that 'German resistance is stiffening' and recommended a pause and then renewing the offensive on 14 August. As Montgomery wrote shortly after the war, while Fourth Army's 'troops had performed wonders . . . it was realised that, in the stress of modern battle . . . there are limits to human endurance'.[36] Foch, too, was having second thoughts. Late that night he arrived at Haig's train for a discussion. Although Foch believed that success should still 'be exploited for all it is worth', they agreed to limit Fourth Army's objectives, and bring Third Army in the north and French Tenth Army in the south into action.[37]

Haig visited Fourth Army HQ on the 12th and briefed Rawlinson, Debeney and Byng. Fourth Army's next attack was timed for 15 August, the earliest it could be ready. This decision has been described as 'ridiculous', as a new attack was highly unlikely to succeed.[38] However in ordering a new push Haig was being a coalition good citizen. Foch had told Haig on 2 August to expect a pause after three days of fighting, but to '[r]enew the attack as soon as you can and you may force him [the enemy] over the Somme'. On the 11th Foch had been adamant that the attack on Fourth and French First Army's front should go on. National commanders within a coalition constantly have to make decisions whether to put the wider good or national interests first. It is no light matter to defy a supreme commander, and such fights have to be chosen very carefully. On this occasion Haig bowed to Foch's demands. A reinforced Third Army was due to mount its offensive five days after Fourth Army renewed its attack. Byng was to smash through the enemy positions and then advance north towards Arras and east towards Bapaume and then Péronne, thus outflanking the Germans on Fourth Army's front.[39] If nothing else, Rawlinson's attack would probably fix the Germans on his front.

Currie, the Canadian Corps commander, had other ideas. He complained to Rawlinson about the task his men had been set, giving him some aerial photographs that showed how difficult the obstacle was. On 14 August Rawlinson took the photos and a letter from Currie to Haig, and the alacrity with which he agreed to postpone the operation indicates the C-in-C's doubts about the enterprise.[40] It was a classic case of the higher commander deferring to the wishes of the men on the spot. Next came a painful scene with Foch on the 15th, when Haig 'spoke to Foch quite straightly, and let him understand that I was responsible for the handling of the British forces'. Foch realised that Haig was not going to move on this one and decided not to provoke a crisis by insisting. His price was the removal of French First Army from Haig's control.[41]

Foch was probably mollified by the fact that on Byng's front the German Seventeenth Army had begun a local withdrawal on 14 August. Third Army followed up, and on the 15th Haig directed Byng to harass the Germans as much as possible, sending the Cavalry Corps to act as advanced guards and for possible exploitation. First Army had already been ordered to be ready to take advantage of Third Army's advance by attacking in the Arras area, and Fourth Army's left was to move once advances to the north had slackened the tension on their front.[42] Seemingly, Haig was having doubts about Byng's caution, and this was to be a major theme over the weeks to come.[43]

Back in 1915 Haig had talked about his ideal of an offensive over a very wide front (see page 121). Now, in 1918, Haig had the men, the guns and the logistic support to make it happen. The Allies had hit upon a highly effective operational technique. Rather than plunging forward until they ran out of steam, as the Germans did in the spring, advances were limited and logistically sustainable. Once resistance stiffened in one sector, the point of attack was switched elsewhere. The German army was always on the back foot, never able to initiate. It was ground down and driven backwards until it was brought to defeat.

Third Army attacked on 21 August, with its objectives lying across some very familiar ground – basically the 1916 Somme and 1917 Arras battlefields. Beyond that was the Hindenburg Line. In some ways, the Battle of Albert was a reprise of Amiens. A very high premium indeed was placed on achieving on surprise, although Third Army relied on security rather than deception to achieve it. But there were also significant differences. Byng had fewer guns, a smaller numerical advantage and far fewer tanks (156, as opposed to over 500) than Fourth Army at Amiens. And while Rawlinson had spearheaded his assault with the elite Australian and Canadian Corps, Third Army had to make do, in the main, with a mixture of British Territorial, New Army and Regular divisions, although such designations were fairly nominal by that stage of the war. On paper, only two divisions stood out from the crowd: the Guards Division, and the New Zealand Division. In accounts of the battle the word 'boys' keeps cropping up as a description of Third Army's infantry. Battalions had been topped up with teenage conscripts. They had little training in open warfare but were otherwise well-trained, their discipline was good, and they were 'keen'. Byng seems to have believed that they could be nursed through their first battle, and this seems to have contributed to his cautious approach.[44]

Haig reviewed Third Army's plans with Byng on 19 August. Two corps, Harper's IV and Haldane's VI, were to attack eight divisions of German Seventeenth Army. If this attack went well, Shute's V Corps would be committed to battle on the southern flank. An advance of about three miles would take VI and IV Corps through the German forward zone and achieve a good start line for the next phase of the attack, which would continue after a pause. Haig thought Byng's scheme was 'too limited in its scope'. He directed Byng 'to break the Enemy's front, and *gain Bapaume as soon as possible*'. Believing from intelligence reports that the initial attack might meet little resistance, Haig 'request[ed]' Byng to 'carefully consider this possibility' and prepared all-arms advanced guards to take advantage of success. The tone of the message gives a flavour of Haig's semi-hands-on, semi-hands-off approach to command in the Hundred Days.[45]

Byng favoured a cautious approach, Haig an aggressive one. Every indication that Haig was receiving was of an opportunity to smash an enemy in crisis. In the unlikely event that Haig had thought about taking his foot off the accelerator, he had Foch to contend with. On 20 August Foch wrote about the attack, pointedly mentioning that it had been postponed until the 21st and calling for it to be mounted '*with violence* . . . any timidity on their part would hardly be justified in view of the enemy's situation and the moral ascendancy you have gained over him'.[46] This last sentence was preaching to the converted. Haig thought Byng was being distinctly timid. Consenting but evading, Byng seems to have agreed with Haig but then left the plan as it was. Certainly, in spite of Haig's promptings, he made little effort to make use of cavalry.[47]

Third Army achieved a limited success on 21 August. As at Amiens, the BEF's weapons system worked well, with tanks and aircraft contributing to the success. Although the defenders took a considerable toll, all three corps surged over the German forward positions, and by the end of the day the British had pushed up against the main German line, which rested on the Amiens-to-Arras railway. This was a far more formidable obstacle, and with his troops weary (it had been a very hot day) Byng called the advance to a halt to reorganise and bring up his artillery.

During the day Haig had entertained to lunch the Minister of Munitions, Winston Churchill, who had the knack of being on the scene to witness critical moments on the Western Front. Haig was genuinely appreciative of Churchill's efforts. But Churchill, like Henry Wilson and the General Staff in London, was working to a completely different timetable to the one that Haig was now sensing was possible. Churchill's

schemes are all timed for completion in next June! I told him we ought to do our utmost to get a decision this autumn. We are engaged in a 'wearing out battle' and are outlasting the enemy. If we have a period of quiet, he will recover, and the 'wearing out' process must be recommenced.

This was of course the same argument that Haig had used before. The difference was that in August 1918 the reality on the battlefield was matching Haig's predictions.[48]

On reaching Third Army HQ at 4.45 p.m. on 21 August, Haig's conversation with Byng reinforced the ambitious objectives he expected Third Army to achieve. Later, at 10.30 p.m. Lawrence reported Byng's halt order to Haig, and Haig 'expressed the wish that the attack should be resumed at the earliest possible moment'. He seems to have expressed it in unmistakable terms, because Byng spent the following day working with Haldane of VI Corps on a more ambitious plan for Third Army's offensive on 23 August, and then taking it to Lawrence, who gave it the stamp of approval.[49]

In spite of GHQ's pressure, Third Army stayed still on 22 August, although the divisions did easily repulse a counterattack by German Seventeenth Army. Byng seems to have been severely lacking in self-confidence at this stage. His orders late on 21 August verged on the pusillanimous. After a day of preparation VI Corps was to attack to improve its position for future operations. When these operations were to take place was not clear. It is difficult to conceive a set of orders more at odds with Haig's strategy.[50]

At this time Fourth Army's III Corps went back on the offensive, with 18th Division taking Albert. The recapture of this town, the forward base for Fourth Army during the Somme two years before, was symbolic of the turning tide. 'Foch's strategy,' Haig recorded after meeting the Generalissimo, 'is a simple straightforward advance of all troops on the Western Front and to keep the Enemy on the move!' That morning GHQ had ordered Third Army's offensive to resume with 'the utmost determination'.[51] At 11.30 p.m. Haig went further, sending out a long telegram:

I request that Army Commanders will, without delay, bring to the notice of all subordinate leaders the changed conditions under which operations are now being carried on, and the consequent necessity for all ranks to act

with the utmost boldness and resolution in order to get full advantage
from the present favourable situation . . .

To turn the present situation to account, the most resolute offensive
is everywhere desirable. Risks which a month ago would have been
criminal to incur, ought now to be incurred as a duty.

It is no longer necessary to advance in regular lines and step by step.
On the contrary, each division should be given a distant objective which
must be reached independently of its neighbour, and even if one's flank
is thereby exposed for the time being . . .

The situation is most favourable; let each one of us act energetically
and without hesitation push forward to our objective.[52]

Although the telegram was sent to all five Army Commanders and
Kavanagh of the Cavalry Corps, the immediate target was very obviously
Byng.

This telegram encapsulated Haig's belief that conditions on the
battlefront had undergone a fundamental change, that war fighting had
ceased to be abnormal. On the following day Haig sent out further
guidance that specifically referred to the relevant sections of *FSR*, for
instance on advance guards to find points of resistance in the German
depth defences.[53] This 'sound mixture of justified optimism, encouragement and tactical common sense'[54] recognised that the BEF was no
longer up against the German army of the Somme and Passchendaele.
With vigorous action, victory was within its grasp.

The problem was that Haig had said similar things on previous
occasions. As would become transparently obvious, by August 1918
his optimism lacked credibility in some quarters. When Derby, now
Ambassador in Paris, was told by Maurice that German morale was
low, he took notice, because Maurice was not renowned as an optimist:
the comparison with Haig was left dangling in the air.[55] But on the
Western Front Haig retained his authority among his subordinate
commanders, and by imposing his will on Byng, he provided drive and
vision at precisely the right moment. Battlefield conditions *had*
changed. The German army was weaker in morale and numbers than
ever before. The BEF was reaching a peak of skill. The pendulum that
had swung in favour of the defender since 1914 had moved decisively
towards the attacker.

Haig realised this. It was not simply a case of saying something often enough and it will eventually come true. The intelligence briefings from Cox, the news he was receiving from the French front, the ease with which ground was being gained – all of this reinforced his soldier's instinct that the critical time had arrived. It is interesting to see what Haig's orders of 22 and 23 August did, and did not, direct. He was not ordering an unlimited breakthrough. Rather, he envisaged a form of 'soft spot' infiltration, of divisions crumbling the enemy line by attacking at various points, by-passing strongpoints, and by thrusting into rear areas causing the defenders to collapse. Haig's rejection of what he called 'limited objectives' is a little misleading. What he was advocating in effect was *extending* limited objectives rather than rejecting them: being more ambitious in the 'bites' taken out of the enemy positions. Haig's methods were to widen the front of attack by bringing neighbouring Armies into the battle. In short, his operational ideas had evolved another stage. Now the BEF had the materiel and the logistic infrastructure to fight on the sort of broad front that Haig had envisaged in 1915.[56] That is not to say that Haig had completely given up hope of mounting deeper operations, as his plans for the Cavalry Corps reveal.

John Terraine, Haig's doughtiest defender, argued that if Haig had taken command of the BEF in 1918 there could be no doubt about his status as a 'great captain'. But the previous years of Haig's command cannot simply be excluded from the balance sheet; in 1915–17 Haig made mistakes which had bloody consequences, and they must be taken into account. But in August 1918 he got it right. The proof came the very next day, 23 August 1918, a day perhaps even more remarkable than the first phase of the Battle of Amiens, a fortnight earlier. Third Army pushed forward on a front of 11 miles, penetrating from 2,000 to 4,000 yards into the enemy positions and taking 5,000 prisoners. For the German commanders there were worrying signs of lack of will to fight among the infantry, with machine-guns and artillery putting up the bulk of the resistance.[57] On its southern flank Rawlinson's Fourth Army advanced a maximum of three miles. Byng had won a major victory. But for the C-in-C's prodding of Byng, success on this scale would not have happened.

Amiens has been described as 'The day we won the war'.[58] Hyperbole aside, there is an excellent case that the blow struck on the 8 August 1918 did indeed mark the beginning of the end on the Western Front. In some ways, the Battle of Albert was even more significant. Like Messines, Amiens was an unrepeatable 'one-off', with the BEF assembling both Dominion corps to fight side-by-side, achieving such a measure of surprise, massing an unprecedented (and subsequently unequalled) number of tanks, and attacking enemy forces in especially weak positions. Albert showed that such optimum conditions were not essential for success. Standard British divisions with weaker artillery and armoured support could win dramatic victories as well. Very quickly troops and commanders learned the new methods and techniques necessary to meet the challenges of semi-open warfare, showing a high degree of initiative and the ability to improvise. This was a commentary on both armies. The maturing of the BEF coincided with a precipitate fall in German morale, discipline and skill.[59] While the German army was not yet at its last gasp, and the BEF's weapons system could and did fail, in late August 1918 the view from Advanced GHQ was bright.

Byng and Rawlinson kept up the pressure on the Albert front on 24 and 25 August, advancing another three miles, and on the 26th Horne's First Army broadened the offensive by attacking around Arras. Haig personally briefed Currie on 24 August in the presence of Horne. It is unlikely this reflected a lack of faith in Horne, rather, it showed Haig's recognition of the importance (and semi-detached status) of Currie and the Canadian Corps, the most powerful formation in the BEF.[60] Haig tasked the Canadian Corps with breaking the Drocourt–Quéant (D-Q) Line and reaching the line of the Canal du Nord, and it was then to 'sweep down behind the Hindenburg Line' where it would fall on the right flank of the forces opposing Third Army.[61] In essence, having pushed the Germans hard in the south, Haig wanted to unbalance them by switching the point of attack to the north. Accordingly, on 25 August he turned down Rawlinson's request for reinforcements, saying 'the decisive point was the Arras–Cambrai road'. Haig hoped that First Army would open the way to an even greater advance to Marquion, on the far bank of the Canal du Nord, the location of an important logistic depot. He planned for a major collapse by the Germans on this front, so he wanted most of the cavalry concentrated in a single corps under one commander 'in the hope of achieving strategical results when a favourable situation arrives'.[62]

Plainly, Haig hoped that this would be created by Currie. The Cavalry

Corps reinforced by motorised infantry (4 (Guards) Brigade in buses) and 'extra machine-gun batteries in motors', was to pass through the Canadians once they had reached the Canal du Nord and press on to Bourlon Wood to cut off the retreating Germans.[63] In the event, the Canadians took two separate major operations to cross the Canal du Nord. Haig was too optimistic – although it was sensible to plan for substantial success given recent experience. He was not alone in having excessive confidence. Currie, too, underestimated the level of resistance the Canadian Corps would face. Horne told Haig that Currie was 'a little "sticky"', but, judging from the ambition of Currie's plan – which featured a night attack and deep pushes into the enemy rear, very much on the lines of Haig's 22 August directive – this was not the case. Probably Horne's comment was prompted by the latent tension between the Army commander and his talented subordinate. Haig shrugged his shoulders. He had spoken to Burstall, the commander of 2nd Canadian Division, and was sure that the attack would be on the right lines 'whatever Currie might feel!'[64]

When the blow landed, the timing was perfect. The impetus of Third Army's attack was running down as its troops came up against the Hindenburg Line and the old Somme battlefield, so the sudden eruption of the Canadian attack (the Battle of the Scarpe), which gained some three miles in the Arras sector, gave a decisive push to an already nervous OHL. Ludendorff ordered a major retirement on a wide front, to a maximum depth of 10 miles, which was carried out on the night of 26/27 August. The new German position was forward of the main Hindenburg Line. Ludendorff's decision gave the Allies some cheap gains – all the ground wrested from the British on the Lys at huge cost in April was given up, for example – and it was a clear admission of the scale of the German defeat. Perhaps the speed with which Haig's call to arms of 22 August was vindicated surprised even him.

Dashing off a letter to Doris, he declared the Scarpe was 'the greatest victory which a British Army has ever achieved'.[65] The Canadian Corps' advance was indeed a formidable achievement, but by the 28th the D-Q Line was still beyond reach. Faced with strengthening resistance and growing losses, it was clear that Currie would need to mount another offensive to crack open these powerful defences. Further south, the two days of 27–29 August saw Fourth Army pushed forward as much as six miles. Monash's Australian Corps, which included the British 32nd Division, advanced up to the banks of the River Somme around Péronne, and French First Army moved up in parallel. Third Army joined in the general advance but did not make such spectacular progress, although Bapaume fell to the New Zealand Division on the 29th.

By 29 August Haig seems to have realised that his optimism had been premature, and at least one more phase of fighting was needed before the German front disintegrated. It is a measure of his confidence in Currie that he expected that Byng's and Rawlinson's divisions to mark time in front of strong German defences, pinning the enemy in place 'by vigorous action', while the Canadians broke through the D-Q Line. This would allow Kavanagh's Cavalry Corps to leapfrog the Canadians and move south-east, to cut the communications of the enemy forces opposite Third and Fourth Armies. This was a bold manoeuvre in the classical tradition of generalship, which, if it worked, would break the logjam by forcing the Germans into retreat. However, the use of cavalry in this manner was something that had not yet been achieved under conditions of trench warfare.[66]

In earlier years, British battles had often been marked by two characteristics: a slow tempo of operations, and a 'top-down' approach to command. Both factors had changed by August 1918. Staff work had improved, thanks to the emergence of a meritocracy of staff officers with much practical experience, the increasing willingness of higher commanders to let their subordinates take key decisions, the achievement of surprise whenever possible, and doctrinal recognition of the need to plan two battles ahead. These factors and others had enabled formations and units to speed up the rate at which they could plan and execute operations.[67] Over a period of four days in the late summer of 1918 the Australian Corps was to show how much had changed by giving a masterclass in the rapid planning and fighting of a battle.

Monash had been 'sorely perplexed' to receive cautious orders from Rawlinson on 25 August. He was convinced that his Australians, although hard worked since 8 August, could do more. Exploiting the loophole in Fourth Army orders which spoke of the need to remain in contact with the enemy, on 29 August Monash briefed his divisional commanders on a plan to use two brigades to cross the Somme and seize Mont-Saint-Quentin, the key to Péronne, and then the city itself.

This was a daring plan that pushed his troops to the limit, and Monash and his commanders, in Peter Stanley's words 'barely kept up with a fast-moving battle'. But it worked: 2nd Australian Division's capture of Mont-Saint-Quentin was, to Rawlinson, 'a magnificent performance'. Péronne was captured by the evening of 2 September, and III Corps was able to move up in support.[68] The shock waves from this battle were far-reaching.[69] The Australians drove a wedge into the line along the Somme that Ludendorff had hoped to hold over the winter. Now, faced with a firm jumping-off point for Allied attacks, the position was virtually untenable.

Two names have been conspicuously absent from this account: Henry Rawlinson and Douglas Haig. When Rawlinson was told about it, he thought it 'over-bold to attempt with so weak a force', although he unenthusiastically sanctioned the attack.[70] Haig does not seem to have known about the attack until after it had taken place – or, if he did, he didn't mention it in his diary, probably because he was concentrating on the assault on the D-Q Line. The lack of involvement of the Commander-in-Chief and the Army commander in planning such a major attack says much about the devolution of command during the Hundred Days.

Haig's immediate reaction to the news of Mont-Saint-Quentin was a practical one, to order that III Corps be reinforced to support the Australian advance. The news was undoubtedly in his mind when later that day he told a visitor, Admiral Sir Roger Keyes, that he doubted that the Germans could even hold the Hindenburg Line for very long, and they would be forced to retreat to the Meuse. One view sees Haig as in 'a tenser, less confident mood' than a week earlier, but his buoyant comment to Keyes, which he repeated to Plumer on the following day, casts doubt on this. In fact Haig's discussion with Keyes revolved around an amphibious landing on the Belgian coast in the event of the Germans evacuating the area.[71] Lord Derby, who visited GHQ at this time, was 'impressed' by the sense of realism he found there: there was no 'unwarranted optimism' but nonetheless 'their tails are well up and [they] anticipate further successes'.[72]

There seemed to be two major, interconnecting strands in Haig's mind at this time. First, in the not too distant future, manpower would become a major challenge. The Adjutant-General had explained that the

61 infantry divisions currently on the Western Front would be reduced in the spring to 42 'active' divisions, ten of them from the Dominions.[73] At the same time, Pershing was threatening to exacerbate the problem by asking for the five American divisions training with the BEF to be removed from Haig's command.[74] Realistically Haig had no choice but to agree. 'I trust that events may justify your decision to withdraw the American troops from the British battle front at the present moment', Haig glacially informed Pershing, 'for I make no doubt but that the arrival in this battle of a few strong and vigorous American Divisions, when the enemy's units are thoroughly worn out, would lead to the most decisive results'. Eventually Pershing compromised and left the US 27th and 30th Divisions under British command.[75]

The second strand in Haig's thinking was to be ready for the climactic battle that he was convinced was about to occur. Manpower shortages threatened to undermine the BEF's operational capability just at the time when it mattered most. At the end of August he noted the Adjutant-General's prediction the army could afford losses of 50,000 men over the next month without having to 'reduce any Divisions'.[76] Undoubtedly Haig was paying the price for the profligacy with lives in earlier battles, and he belatedly began to insist on conserving his army's strength. Lawrence was despatched to First Army to tell Currie and Horne that 'I have no wish to attack the Quéant–Drocourt line, if they are in any doubt about taking it'. Haig was well aware of the importance of the Canadian Corps, probably his most precious asset in terms of combat effectiveness and sheer size. Now Haig's strategy was 'to wear out the enemy by continually attacking him, and so to prevent him from settling into a strong position', looking to the 'decisive moment' when Pershing's Americans began their major offensive. 'The British Army must still be able to attack then, and to have the means of exploiting the victory and making it decisive'. For that reason Haig turned down Lawrence's suggestion to use a cavalry division to exploit the successes on the Somme. He wanted to keep a large force of cavalry in being to use at the optimum moment, which was close but not yet.[77] So, far from losing confidence, Haig was convinced that the final phase of the structured battle recognised by British doctrine was close.

Lloyd George, Henry Wilson and the War Cabinet were also deeply concerned about manpower, but Haig thought they were 'quite unconscious of what had happened' on the Western Front.[78] Indeed, it is remarkable how little sense Wilson and the politicians had of the Allied victories almost until the end of the war. A sharp reminder of this political reality arrived in the shape of a telegram from the CIGS on 1 September:

> Just a word of caution in regard to incurring heavy losses in attacks on Hindenburg Line as opposed to losses when driving the enemy back to that line. I do not mean to say that you have incurred such losses, but I know the War Cabinet would become anxious if we received heavy punishment in attacking the Hindenburg Line WITHOUT SUCCESS.

Haig was incandescent. He read this as an unofficial warning that the War Cabinet would gladly 'take credit for every success' but blame him in the event of a defeat, or heavy losses 'in which case I can hope for no mercy!' 'What a wretched lot!' Haig replied to Wilson. 'And how well they mean to support me!! What confidence!'[79]

Lloyd George may have had little confidence in Haig, but the British C-in-C had risen steadily in Foch's esteem and was exerting real influence on the Generalissimo's strategy. Foch had agreed to Pershing's pet scheme to assault the Saint-Mihiel sector and then advance on Mars-la-Tour. Ultimately Pershing wanted to advance on Metz and even beyond. To Haig, this made no strategic sense. The Americans would be advancing east, away from the critical area where the British and French were pushing back the enemy. Far better, he reasoned, for the US forces to thrust north-west towards the key railway junction of Mézières. With the main British and French force striking broadly in an easterly direction, this would create a convergent offensive, with the Germans facing threats from several fronts. Haig spelled out his ideas in a letter to Foch on 27 August and was pleased at the response.[80] His suggestion

> appears to have been decisive in altering Foch's entire concept of the Allied offensive. It is surely more than coincidence that, from this point on, with the slogan *Tout le monde à la bataille!* ('Everyone into battle!') Foch began to think in terms of a series of violent and interrelated hammer blows with more lethal intentions than merely eliminating salients or freeing railways.[81]

A currently fashionable view sees Haig as the 'accidental victor' in 1918, marginalised by his superior, Foch. It is more accurate to see the two as being partners – not equal partners, as is often the case within a coalition, but it was a partnership nonetheless.

Foch's regard for Haig was undoubtedly related to the BEF's success rate. On 4 September Foch spoke to Haig of '"la grande bataille" won by us . . . and thought that it would produce a great effect on the enemy's plans'.[82] He was referring to the breaking of the Drocourt–Quéant Line by the Canadians supported by British XVII Corps. Haig had visited various Canadian headquarters on the 2nd, and had been impressed by reports of German prisoners' low morale and their refusal to obey their officers. 'Discipline in the German army seemed to have gone,' he noted. 'If this is true, then the end cannot now be far off, I think.'[83]

For the second time in less than a month, the two Dominion Corps had had major successes. Like the seizure of Mont-Saint-Quentin, the piercing of the Drocourt–Quéant Line by the Canadian Corps had immediate strategic repercussions. Over the night of 2/3 September, the Germans began a major retreat back to the Hindenburg Line and the Canal du Nord. Opposite Third and First Armies, German Seventeenth Army melted away into the night before the Allies realised what was happening. To the south, German Second Army was to pull back to the Hindenburg Line on the next night, with Eighteenth and Ninth Armies following suit in turn, and, to the north, Fourth and Sixth Armies were to give up ground between Lens and Ypres. In short, all the ground won at such great cost in the offensives of March and April was abandoned. GHQ's pursuit orders were in line with Haig's desire to conserve strength for the climactic battle: 'press the enemy with advanced guards with the object of driving in the enemy's rearguards and outposts, and ascertaining his dispositions. No deliberate operations on a large scale will be undertaken for the present'.[84]

What was not immediately clear to GHQ was where the Germans intended to end their retreat. Haig suspected on good military grounds that the enemy would hold the Hindenburg Line for a short period but would then 'seek for rest and peace behind the Meuse and the Namur defences, in order to refit his shattered divisions'.[85] Hindenburg indeed suggested falling back 45 miles to a line between Antwerp and the Meuse but Ludendorff refused to contemplate it. Lieutenant-Colonel Wetzell, a key adviser at OHL, was sacked by Ludendorff for seeking 'to keep his master on the right path'. Thus, as GHQ was aware by about 6 September, the BEF would have to mount a major operation against the Hindenburg Line.[86]

During 1917 the BEF had learned the hard way just how formidable the Hindenburg Line was as a defensive position. In September 1918 there were reasons to be more optimistic about the chances of an attack succeeding. Surprise had returned to the battlefield, and GHQ set in train a deception operation to fool the Germans that the next major blow would be on First Army's front.[87] Responding to Haig's request to his Army commanders to share their opinions on future operations, Julian Byng wrote that, with the Germans in their current state of dis-organisation and low morale, it was important to attack quickly before they had time to recover by sheltering behind the Hindenburg Line.[88]

Byng, who seems to have recovered from his wobbles of a few weeks before, was thinking on very much the same lines as the Commander-in-Chief. 'In my opinion it is much less costly in lives to press the enemy after a victorious battle than to give him time to recover and organise afresh his defence of a position,' Haig had commented in reference to Wilson's telegram of 1 September.[89] Horne and Rawlinson also wanted to push on quickly, in spite of the formidable nature of the German positions their armies faced.[90] As First, Third and Fourth Armies closed up to the German defences, the scene was set for the their greatest test yet.

These operations formed part of a Grand Offensive ordered by Foch in a directive of 3 September. The British, with the French left in support, were to drive in the direction of Cambrai and Saint-Quentin; Pétain's central French armies would attack over the Aisne; and the Americans would attack at Saint-Mihiel and then redeploy and strike towards Mézières with the French Fourth Army. Haig noted with a degree of justifiable satisfaction that the Directive 'did not affect the task of the British'; Foch had effectively adopted the plan he had suggested a week or two earlier. After the conference on 4 September Foch and Haig went for a walk together. Foch spoke of his difficulties with Pershing. Haig might have been forgiven for reflecting on his own greater collegiality as coalition commander. Overall, Foch was 'most hopeful, and thinks the German is nearing the end'.[91]

Five days later the scope of the Grand Offensive was extended yet further. After a series of meetings with King Albert of the Belgians, Haig and Plumer, Foch formed an Army Group that included the Belgian army, French Sixth Army, and Plumer's Second Army. This '*Groupe d'Armées des Flandres*' (GAF) would be commanded by King Albert with a French officer, General Degoutte, as Chief of Staff. Haig therefore no longer had operational control over Second Army. He was content with this in the short term, although he declined to throw three cavalry divisions into the bargain,[92] but this extended loan was to cause a serious clash with Foch.

Not surprisingly, given his keen interest in Flanders over the years, Haig had already discussed with Plumer the possibility of co-operating with the Belgians and joint operations with the Royal Navy. The prospect of retaking Passchendaele Ridge and breaking out onto the plain beyond was extremely enticing. In a curious echo of debates in 1917, on 5 September Plumer proposed a limited operation to retake Messines. Haig brushed this aside: he was thinking on an altogether grander scale. The Belgians had taken part in little major fighting since 1914, and plainly Haig had some doubts about whether they would be of much use in an offensive. Plumer was ordered to stiffen the Belgian army with two British divisions on their right flank, and attack and capture some horribly familiar ground: 'the CLERKEN– PASSCHENDAELE ridge, and if possible the high ground around GHELUVELT'. When the rest of the Grand Offensive unfolded, Haig verbally informed Plumer that he should 'be prepared to move a Division by sea to Ostend and occupy Bruges with left on the Dutch frontier, and connecting with Anglo-Belgian Army on the line Thourout–Roulers'.[93] Plumer remained cautious about the prospects of success, telling Lawrence on 13 September that he doubted that he would be able to advance towards Menin and Courtrai unless the German defenders suffered a major collapse.[94]

All the evidence points to the fact that in mid-September 1918 Douglas Haig was utterly convinced that, after many false starts, the crisis of the battle had arrived, and the war could be won this year, or at least by the summer of 1919.[95] He dropped heavy hints to the King that the Prince of Wales ought to be present '[i]n view of the events which are taking place in France, and the possibility that greater events may take place in the

near future'.[96] He refused Rawlinson's plea to release 6th Division from
GHQ Reserve, which was to be held back until the great combined
offensive began. Haig held discussions with Maxse, Inspector-General of
Training, and Kavanagh on training infantry divisions to co-operate with
the Cavalry Corps in the pursuit.[97] Having done as much as he could to
prepare the field army for the battle to come, on 10 September Haig set
out for London to try to persuade the politicians.

At his meeting with Milner Haig was in the position of a gambler
heaping everything on the table. Now was the time to take risks:

> Within the last four weeks we had captured 77,000 prisoners and nearly
> 800 guns! There has never been such a victory in the annals of Britain,
> and its effects are not yet apparent . . . The discipline of the German Army
> is quickly going, and the German Officer is no longer what he was. It
> seems to me to be the beginning of the end. From these and other facts I
> draw the conclusion that the enemy's Troops will not await our attacks
> in even the strongest positions.

Because of these newly favourable conditions, mobile troops retained in
the UK for home defence should be sent to France, and all available men
should be sent to the army, even those earmarked for the Royal Navy or
to work in munitions. The War Cabinet's assumption that the war-
winning offensive would not begin until 1 July 1919 was simply wrong,
Haig argued, and all units should be brought up to strength by 1 April.[98]

If the government were to do what Haig asked and then the offensive
got bogged down, this reallocation of manpower would place the
national war effort in jeopardy. Churchill, Minister of Munitions, had
had a taste of the passion of Haig's advocacy on a visit to GHQ on 8
September, and he had fought a number of battles to prevent the
conscription of skilled workers which had a disproportionately large
impact on war production. Something similar was probably in Milner's
mind. At the end of the meeting he made noises that Haig took as
signifying assent, but this was not the end of the matter. Milner had no
great regard for Haig as a general, but recognised that there was no one
better to replace him.[99]

The two men met again in France on 21 September, and two days
later Milner told Henry Wilson that Haig was being 'ridiculously

optimistic' and that he feared that 'he may embark on another Paschendal [sic]'. Milner 'warned Haig that if he knocked his present army about there was no other to replace it'. When in France Milner had seen a number of senior officers. 'Manpower is the trouble, and Douglas Haig and Foch and Du Cane can't understand it'.[100] On the contrary, in September 1918 Haig was painfully aware of the shortage of manpower, and was seeking victory before the supply ran out. Like Foch, he believed 'that the greatest economy in man-power would be complete victory'.[101]

Breaking the Hindenburg Line

12 September 1918 was a landmark in American military history: the day when Pershing's army fought its first major battle. For this reason, the successful attack at Saint-Mihiel is justly famous. But a far tougher battle of much greater strategic significance also began that day. This was British Third Army's action later dubbed the 'Battle of Havrincourt', which marked the beginning of the difficult stretch of fighting conducted by Third and Fourth Armies to force their way through the outer defences of the Hindenburg Line. Third Army inched its way forward for two weeks. Haig was not displeased with Third Army's efforts, noting that, unlike on the fronts of First and Fourth Armies the enemy had fought hard.[102] V Corps' attack on 18 September was timed to support the opening of the Battle of Epéhy, Fourth Army's attack on the outworks of the Hindenburg defences. Haig regarded this battle as of critical importance. His optimism was such that he ordered 'Kavanagh with Cavalry Corps and a Brigade of Infantry in Busses [sic] etc will be ready to pursue'.[103] The battle was a major success. The 'flash-to-bang' time between ordering and launching the offensive was extremely short, pointing to a high level of efficiency among staffs at every level from GHQ downwards. And, although the Australian Corps made the most ground in the centre, the tired III Corps did well in fighting through the outer defences of the Bellicourt tunnel, the sector thought by the Germans to be the most vulnerable and therefore the one with the strongest defences.[104] The effects of the battles of Havrincourt and Epéhy were considerable. Byng thought Havrincourt was the most significant thing that he had achieved with Third Army, as the Germans were 'well beaten, and the heart was out of the enemy afterwards'.[105] Divisions on the flanks of these attacks were able to push forward and establish, by

26 September, good start-lines for what Haig firmly believed would be the decisive blow against the Hindenburg Line.

When the news of the Battle of Epéhy reached London, the penny finally dropped with Henry Wilson about the magnitude of the BEF's successes in France. He sent a brief note to Haig: 'Well done! you must be a famous general!' Haig's reply was characteristic:

> Very many thanks for your kind little note of yesterday. – No, certainly not! I am not, nor am I likely to be a "*famous* general". For that must we not have pandered to Repington and the gutter Press? But we have a surprisingly large number of *very capable* generals. Thanks to these gentlemen, and to their "sound military knowledge built up of study and practice until it has become an instinct", and to a steady adherence to the principles of our FSR Part I are our successes to be chiefly attributed.[106]

Effective higher commanders and sound doctrine – Haig had accurately identified two of the key factors in the BEF's success.

On the day before the Grand Offensive began, Haig wrote to Esher in a positive mood. 'The month beginning 8th August was certainly a very remarkable period, and I doubt whether a British army has ever gained such a series of great successes . . . I am full of confidence, and even with our small number of mounted troops I expect the Enemy will be driven back pretty quickly, because his "moral" is already much shaken'.[107] Haig was well aware that the battle was not going to be a pushover, that the enemy had strong defences and a number of reserves. The Grand Offensive was to be sequential rather than simultaneous, and Haig hoped that his forces would benefit from attacking after the Franco-American assault in the Meuse-Argonne, especially if there was a lapse of a few days in which the Germans might redeploy their reserves.[108]

Byng's optimism seems to have drained away again. At a meeting on 25 September Haig gained the distinct impression that Byng and Vaughan, his CoS, were worried and wanted 'me to wait and do nothing for some days, so as to allow the other attacks to have an effect and cause enemy to withdraw some of his reserves from before us'. They were out of luck. That day the precise dates of the offensives were promulgated. Haig was able to tell them that the Franco-American attack would go in on 26 September, followed by British First and Third

Armies on the 27th, the GAF on the 28th, and Fourth Army on 29 September.[109]

With the first British forces not going into action until the second day of the offensive, Haig was able to spend 26 September visiting various parts of his armies. He met both Rawlinson and Byng at Fourth Army HQ and found the mood of the two Army commanders sharply contrasted, the former confident and the latter still pessimistic. When he reached the joint HQ of the Australian and II US Corps (Major-General George W. Read, the American corps commander, had wisely accepted Australian tutelage for his first major battle) Monash insisted that he address a conference of senior officers. Today Monash is an Australian nationalist icon and Haig is, if possible, even more of a bogeyman in Australia than he is in Britain. But this small incident is evidence of the dangers of reading modern attitudes back into the First World War. Haig went in to the meeting, shook hands and gave a short pep talk, telling them that 'the biggest battle of the War had started this morning'.[110]

Going on to IX Corps HQ, Haig spoke to Lieutenant-General Sir Walter Braithwaite. IX Corps had only recently joined Fourth Army, and Braithwaite himself had only become the commander on 13 September. As Hamilton's CoS at Gallipoli, 'Braithwaite and his staff achieved an unenviable reputation for arrogance and incompetence'. However he had done well as GOC 62nd Division in 1917, and he was admired by Haig, who recommended him for promotion. Haig was clearly impressed by Braithwaite's preparations. 'In one sector his men have to cross the [Saint-Quentin] canal: for this every conceivable device has been provided, including life protecting jackets from the Channel leave steamers'.[111] Braithwaite and his corps would rise further in Haig's esteem after their attack on 29 September 1918.

First Army's task on 27 September was to protect Third Army's left flank by crossing the (dry) Canal du Nord and capturing Bourlon Ridge. Inevitably, Horne delegated the task to the Canadian Corps. It was a formidable obstacle. Crossing the Canal itself was only one challenge, with three trench systems also to be fought through. Backed by 594 heavy guns and howitzers and supported by 56th (London) Division, by the end of the day the five-division Canadian Corps (including British 11th Division) had reached or exceeded its objectives. Third Army's advance was patchier, but it had fewer heavy artillery pieces (425) than

First Army, and the worse-performing corps, Harper's IV, still managed an advance of over a mile. Even so, 27 September 1918 was not Third Army's finest hour. A better performance by Byng and his staff in co-ordinating the attacks might well have yielded better results.[112]

Haig was reasonably satisfied with the progress of the day and the magnitude of First Army's achievements encouraged him to plan for decisive success. On the afternoon of 27 September he visited Horne's HQ and outlined his vision for the use of Kavanagh's Cavalry Corps. 'First Army should continue to form a defensive flank on right bank of Scheldt while the Cavalry Corps passed beyond and took (if possible) Valenciennes and (if Plumer and Belgians are successful) moves down river towards Ghent'.[113] Haig believed the main defensive line was broken and the pursuit phase could begin.

The Cavalry Corps was by this stage a shadow of its former self. There was a paradox here. In many ways, the increased mobility of the fighting had brought mounted troops back into its own. To pick just one example, during the operations on the Selle on 16–18 October a squadron of 1/1 Northumberland Hussars was attached to 50th Division. The yeomen did invaluable work as 'Forward Observation Posts, Special Patrols, Mounted Orderlies, and Escorts to Prisoners of War'.[114] Haig's dire warnings in the past of the consequences of cutting the cavalry were now being amply justified, not that that was much compensation. In early September 2nd Cavalry Division was broken up to provide squadron-sized divisional cavalry units. That left the Cavalry Corps with just two divisions, which, even when reinforced with an infantry brigade in buses (see above), was still very weak. At that time Allenby had four mounted divisions and seven infantry divisions with his army in Palestine; cavalry was thus a much larger proportion of his total force than it was of Haig's – and it is not surprising to find that mounted troops played a much more significant role in Palestine than on the Western Front.[115]

Nonetheless, Haig continued to plan to use the Cavalry Corps as a strategic asset directly answerable to him. Once Fourth Army had cracked open the German defences, the Cavalry Corps was to exploit towards Le Cateau, attack the flanks and rear of the German forces opposing Third and First Armies, and sever the enemy communications in the Valenciennes area.[116] This was a lot to expect of two cavalry divisions. Nonetheless Haig took it deadly seriously. He spent a precious day with the Cavalry Corps on 17 September on a tactical exercise he had ordered, covering the pursuit following the crumbling of enemy resistance. This was followed by a conference that analysed the lessons of the day, and then Haig wrote a memorandum on the scheme.[117] Haig's belief that the horsed cavalryman still had a place on the modern battlefield had been handsomely vindicated in 1918, and massed cavalry might well have had some effect on a particular area. However in actively planning to use the Cavalry Corps in a strategic pursuit he seems to have lost his sense of proportion. Haig's plans might just have been achievable by the five-division Corps of earlier years, but it was simply asking too much of the formation in its present shrunken state.

The news reaching Advanced GHQ on 28 September added to Haig's sense of impending success. By this stage advances of several miles a day had become routine, but the GAF's advance of six miles on the Ypres sector must have been startling to any Passchendaele veteran. The attack took place across muddy, cratered ground – no change there – but by 30 September the entire horseshoe of high ground overlooking Ypres was at long last held by the Allies. As one infantry officer put it, 'The dismal belt of land devastated by four years of war lies behind'.[118]

It only remained for Fourth Army to enter the battle on the following day. On the 28th Haig visited Byng, who was more optimistic, observing 'that the enemy on his front shows signs of "cracking"'. Then the C-in-C visited Read, the US II Corps commander, and tried to jolly him along. The Australian Corps, with Read's corps under command, was expected to play the major role in Fourth Army's attack on the Hindenburg Line. The Saint-Quentin canal was such an obviously strong position, impassable to tanks, that the sector where the canal disappeared into the Bellicourt tunnel was chosen for the main attack. Naturally, the Germans identified the threat and made sure that the tunnel area was heavily defended. Earlier Haig had seen Monash who was 'in what he called "a state of despair"'. Some reports had come back that American troops had captured some German positions, while aerial reconnaissance said that they were still held by the Germans. The attack due on the next day ran the risk of killing the Americans, if indeed they were there. Haig's advice was ruthless: 'it was not a serious matter, and he should attack tomorrow morning in force as arranged'; in other words the success of the operation outweighed the lives of the American infantry. This callous view was the only possible one for Haig, as Commander-in-Chief, to take.[119]

Fourth Army punched through the Hindenburg Line in the Saint-Quentin sector in a day. During August the British had captured a detailed plan of the Hindenburg defences, but the critical factor in the victory was the intervention of Braithwaite of IX Corps. Much to Monash's annoyance, Rawlinson accepted Braithwaite's plan to use 46th (North Midland) Division to assault directly across the canal; as we have seen, on 26 September Haig had been impressed by their preparations.[120] While the Americans and Australians struggled through the dense German defences at the Bellicourt tunnel Braithwaite's gambit broke the deadlock. 137 Brigade, a formation of Staffordshire Territorials, crossed the canal using life belts, canvas boats or the masonry blown into the canal by the bombardment. Some crossed dryshod by a small bridge that was captured intact by a daring *coup de main*. 46th Division's achievement was particularly admired at GHQ. 'Not much to be learned tactically from this attack,' ran a post-war assessment, 'but it is a good example of what can be done by good organization, fine leadership, and the fighting spirit'.[121] Defences were surprisingly shallow in this sector, and 46th Division's assault unhinged the German position. A three-mile-deep gash had been ripped in the Hindenburg Line.

Haig's immediate action was to consult with Kavanagh about the 'great opportunity offering [sic] for the Cavalry'.[122] He was to be disappointed, partly because of the sluggish advance of French First Army on the right of IX Corps, which left Braithwaite's troops in a vulnerable salient. The Cavalry Corps remained in reserve and was formally ordered back to billets on 2 October.[123] Instead there was hard infantry fighting as the Germans were gradually pushed out of what remained of the Hindenburg position.

Haig did not give up hope of getting the Cavalry Corps into action, giving orders for it to be in position to exploit success once the last part of the Hindenburg defences, the Beaurevoir Line, was captured. Once key objectives had fallen, and 5 Cavalry Brigade (attached to IX Corps) had pushed beyond the town of Beaurevoir, the Cavalry Corps was to set off on its independent mission. Briefly, at 8 a.m. on 3 October, it seemed as if Kavanagh's moment was about to arrive. Major-General G.F. Boyd called for 5 Cavalry Brigade to come up in support of his 46th Division as the Germans were 'in disorderly retreat'. 5 Cavalry Brigade's commander was the C-in-C's cousin Neil Haig. Sadly, Brigadier-General Haig was not destined to bring about Field-Marshal Haig's heart's desire. As the cavalry arrived in the front line, it was dismounted and used as infantry.[124]

After the Canal du Nord Currie had driven his Canadians hard, his determination to push on despite the heavy cost recalling Haig's own. In five exhausting and bloody days from 27 September to 1 October they forced the Germans back towards Cambrai and attracted sizeable enemy reserves to the Canadian sector.[125] Third Army, too, continued to advance, Byng's left wing forcing the Saint-Quentin Canal on 29 and 30 September and then slowly edging towards Cambrai. Fourth Army's progress further south compelled the Canal's defenders to retire to the Beaurevoir Line on 5 October, and at last Third Army was able to cross the waterway on its entire frontage.[126]

Operations on the Western Front might have been reaching a climax, but this fact still eluded some key figures in London. Replying to Winston Churchill on 3 October, Haig politely wrote that he had 'read the memorandum you enclose with great interest, and I hope everything will be done to maintain this Army at full strength in order to beat the enemy as soon as possible'. Actually, Haig had scrawled against a paragraph calling for conservation of resources 'for the decisive struggles of 1920', 'What rubbish: Who will last till 1920. Only America??'[127] Few in London seemed to have realised that the BEF was winning truly outstanding victories. Even at this late stage there were rumours that Haig would be sacked and replaced by Allenby.[128]

The critical sectors were on the front of British First, Third and Fourth Armies. In the north the GAF, after its electrifying sprinter's start, had encountered an enemy far more difficult to overcome than the hapless defenders of Passchendaele Ridge: logistics. Mud and Belgian inexperience had created logistic chaos, and the advance had ground to a halt. 'What very valuable days are being lost!' Haig complained. 'All this is the result of inexperience and ignorance of the needs of a modern attacking force'.[129] Certainly the logistic performance of the GAF compared very poorly with the herculean efforts of the BEF's supply and transport troops further south. American and French forces in the Meuse-

Argonne were also struggling to make much impression, again because of inexperience. Brigadier-General Charlie Grant, a liaison officer with Foch, arrived at GHQ on 5 October with the latest gossip, which Haig recorded in his diary with an air of grim satisfaction. Grant said that the Generalissimo's staff were 'terribly disappointed' with the Americans. Despite weak opposition, Pershing's forces were unable to advance because their logistics had collapsed. Poor American staff work was to blame. And, worse, Pershing was stubbornly refusing to send any of what Haig called his 'fine divisions' to another sector, where they might produce decisive results.[130]

The snarl-ups in Flanders and the Argonne meant that Haig held the future of the Allied offensive in his palm. The bulk of what German reserves remained were located opposite Byng, Rawlinson and French First Army.[131] When Haig consulted Byng and Rawlinson on 1 October, he found that their confidence matched his own. 'Both consider that enemy has suffered very much, and that it is merely a question of our continuing our pressure to ensure his breaking.' At this meeting the three men agreed that Haig would step back a little from the conduct of the offensive. 'They agreed that no further orders from me were necessary, and both would be able to carry on without difficulty.' This arm's-length approach was very much in keeping with Haig's ideal of command. In an increasingly fluid situation, such devolution of command was very sensible, and, as all three men recognised, the strategy for both Third and Fourth Armies was simple – keep driving ahead until the German army disintegrated.[132]

Developments over the next few days reinforced this view. On the night of 1/2 October the Germans, reacting to advances on their flanks, fell back on a 17-mile front from Armentières to Lens. Over the next few days Fifth Army (reconstituted under Birdwood in May) cautiously followed up, occupying places with names familiar from 1915 – Aubers Ridge, Fromelles and Loos. The character of the fighting was now very different from 1915, with divisions deploying special Advanced Guard battalions and batteries to pursue the enemy. Talking to two divisional commanders in Third Army, Haig gathered that morale among the ranks was good: 'They feel that the Bosch [sic] is gradually cracking.'[133]

They were indeed. Momentous events occurred in Germany in the first week of October. Hindenburg on 2 October told the German Crown

Council that the German army could no longer win a military victory. Allied forces were relentlessly grinding down the German armies. Hindenburg and Ludendorff wanted an armistice to bring the fighting to an end – or else the German army would disintegrate.[134] Faced with defeat, the German government resigned on 3 October, and the politically liberal Prince Max of Baden took up the unenviable post of Chancellor. Acting quickly to salvage what it could from the disaster, the new government put out peace feelers to President Wilson. It wanted an end to the war based on the Fourteen Points – an idealistic and vague programme put forward in very different circumstances by Wilson in early 1918, which was not fully supported by Britain or France. The United States was formally an 'Associated Power', not an Ally; and Wilson's independent stance seemed to offer the Germans a way to divide her enemies and achieve a more moderate peace.

Haig visited Foch on 6 October, to find he had a newspaper spread out in front of him giving details of the peace note. '"Here," said Foch, "here is the immediate result of the British piercing the Hindenburg Line. The enemy has asked for an armistice"'. Characteristically, Haig's reaction to the news was not to rest on his laurels but to explain his plans for his next offensive by Third and Fourth Armies, and to declare 'that with 3 fresh American Divisions it would be possible to reach Valenciennes in 48 hours!' Foch, no doubt wearily, explained – again – that Pershing was refusing to relinquish control of any of his divisions.[135]

Throughout the war, Haig had preached the necessity of continually hammering away at the enemy, denying them time to recover from one blow before another landed. Accordingly, while Fourth Army gathered its strength after its recent exertions – on 6 October Haig sent Lawrence to tell Rawlinson not to attack until all preparations were complete – GHQ put together a plan for the next phase. This document gives a good insight into how Haig saw the situation, now that Fourth Army was clear of the trenches and operating over terrain that appeared to be open and cavalry-friendly, and the other Armies were also either into open country or about to get there. It depicted the Germans as having suffered heavy casualties and running out of reserves, using those that they had to plug gaps in the line. The front-line soldier was 'dispirited'. Enemy forces opposite Fourth and the right of Third Armies were particularly vulnerable. 'The Field-Marshal Commanding-in-Chief [therefore] intends to strike the enemy a vigorous blow, and exploit success with mounted troops before a new defensive position can be organized.' Byng (whose Army had done little fighting since 2 October) and Rawlinson were to take the lead, with First Army joining in as a flank guard. The Cavalry Corps was then to exploit.[136]

The attack of 8 October, the second Battle of Cambrai, was another major success, with one exception. Although 'every effort' was made to get the cavalry into action to attack enemy communications, 'only a few patrols got much further than the infantry front line'. Cavalry units got involved in the fighting, and suffered a number of casualties, but they were unable to exploit the infantry's success. That aside, 8 October was another victory to add to the BEF's already impressive roll. Some 8,000 Germans went into the bag that day, and under the impact of another body blow, OHL ordered a general retreat to the River Selle. Cambrai was quietly abandoned by the Germans during the night of 8/9 October.[137] When the three British Armies and French First Army moved forward on 9 October, they found themselves opposed by rearguards alone.

9 October was a momentous day for the Cavalry Corps: the first opportunity for the use of mounted troops *en masse* since the beginning of the Battle of Amiens, a month and a day earlier. It was also to be the last. The cavalry undoubtedly extended the reach of the army by moving about twice as far as the infantry were capable of (eight as opposed to four miles) and gave the attackers more stamina, for mounted troops were able to continue to advance after the infantry had reached the point of exhaustion. This enabled more effective harassment of the retreating Germans.[138] Cavalry reached Le Cateau, last seen by retreating British troops of Smith-Dorrien's II Corps in August 1914. Although the Cavalry Corps' achievements on 9 October fell well short of Haig's grandiose vision of its use in a strategic 'breakthrough' role, it did vindicate his cherished operational concept. Held close to the front, and committed in a timely fashion, cavalry was able to extend and widen the infantry's 'bite'.[139]

After the success of 8–9 October the British Armies advanced to the River Selle. Here enemy resistance increased, and there was a pause to allow supplies to catch up and troops to prepare for the next set-piece offensive. Looking ahead, Haig could see advantages in continuing north-eastwards 'between the Scheldt and Sambre' so his Armies could eventually link up with the GAF. Foch would not agree to a drastic shift in the axis of British thrust, but he did order the reinforcement of French First Army on Rawlinson's right 'with all available French resources, including tanks'.[140] No one at GHQ could know it, but the fighting on the Western Front had just over a month to run.

Wars are won and lost both on the front line and around the conference table, and reputations are often made and marred in the post-war battle of the memoirs. In mid-October Haig had two glimpses of the non-military struggles ahead. The first came with what he called 'a clumsy wire', a factually inaccurate telegram of congratulation from Lloyd George. He contrived to insult the BEF by implying that the British Prime Minister was ignorant of everything that that had happened from 8 August until the end of September, and offended Haig by a scarcely-veiled reference to his subordination to Foch.[141] This was a preview of Lloyd George's post-war campaign of denigration against Britain's generals, especially Haig.

The second was a discussion on 10 October with Foch about possible terms for an armistice with Germany. Foch showed Haig a paper he had drawn up, advocating a complete German evacuation, not only of French and Belgian territory but also Alsace-Lorraine. The withdrawing Germans were to leave their war-making materiel behind, and the Allies would take control of the Rhineland and have three bridgeheads across the Rhine itself. Haig remarked,

> the only difference between his (Foch's) conditions and a 'general surrender' is that the German Army is allowed to march back with its rifles, and officers with their swords. He is evidently of opinion that the enemy is so desirous of peace that he will agree to any terms of this nature which we impose.

At this stage, Haig remained intensely optimistic. That evening he reassured Lawrence, whose morale had been dented by struggling through his tasks while suffering from a cold:

> [T]he enemy has not the means, nor the will-power, to launch an attack strong enough to affect even our front line troops. We have got the

enemy down, in fact he is a beaten Army, and my plan is to go on hitting him as hard as we possibly can, till he begs for mercy.[142]

In this mood, Haig awaited the next stage of the BEF's operations.

First to move was Plumer's Second Army in Flanders. The GAF had finally untangled its logistics and on 14 October resumed the offensive. In theory, Plumer's role was to protect the flank of the Belgians, but the French (who were supposed to be the lead element of the GAF's advance) proved sluggish, which incurred Foch's ire. Plumer interpreted his orders liberally and drove on over the Lys, eventually taking Courtrai on the 19th. This helped trigger a German retreat to the south, on Fifth Army's front. With the military position growing worse almost by the hour, the German leadership desperately hoped to pull off a diplomatic coup to avert complete defeat. Orders were given to hold on to the Belgian coast, and the major industrial centres of Lille, Roubaix and Tourcoing – these would be useful bargaining chips in negotiations to end the war. But on 14 October President Wilson effectively rejected German overtures of 5 October. With that hope dashed, Ludendorff ordered the evacuation of these areas, suddenly no longer militarily tenable.[143] The German decision to abandon the coast meant that Britain had achieved one of the principal aims for which it had gone to war in the first place. On battlefront and diplomatic front alike, the Germans were losing badly. On 17 October Lille fell to Birdwood's Fifth Army. For Birdwood, the 'scenes of delight and enthusiasm were indescribable', with the people of Lille, 'free for the first time in four years . . . to give expression to their emotions'. English-speaking readers all too often forget that the Allies were fighting a war of liberation in 1918.[144]

Rawlinson's attack on the Selle position on 17 October was another success. Using II US Corps, XIII Corps (Morland) and IX Corps (Braithwaite), by nightfall Fourth Army was across the river. But the fighting was tougher than expected.[145] Surprise had been sacrificed by a preliminary bombardment, and the Germans were present in greater strength than anticipated. On the surface, GHQ was pleased with the day's activities, issuing an operations order for the next phase of the campaign. Byng, Horne and Rawlinson, in co-operation with French First Army were to prepare for 'a general attack' towards the Sambre canal, and the Armies were to inform GHQ when they were ready to attack.[146]

Privately, the fierceness of the German resistance rang alarm bells. That evening, Lawrence and Haig talked about the shape an armistice should take – the C-in-C had been summoned to London to give his views to the War Cabinet. In Lawrence's view, 'it should not be too exacting because it is in the interests of Great Britain to end the war this year'. It is possible, although not certain, that the news of the fighting on the Selle reinforced Lawrence's pessimism, and this in turn influenced Haig. At first sight there seems to be a huge gulf between Haig's upbeat diary entry of 17 October – 'Fourth Army met with considerable opposition but made good progress' – and the pessimistic advice he presented in London on the 19th.[147]

While he miscalculated both Allied and German strength and resilience, Haig's views were based on acute awareness of the challenges (especially logistic problems) faced by the BEF and a conviction that the British armies were carrying out a disproportionate share of the fighting. He was also receiving gloomy intelligence briefings that the Germans were holding back the 1920 class of conscripts, and these might provide the German army with a timely injection of manpower.[148] Haig was well aware of the possibly damaging consequences to British national interests if the war dragged on. He had suspicions of French motives and ambitions, and knew that American power and influence would inexorably increase if the war lasted into 1919. Above all, Haig dreaded the consequences of political instability. He was influenced by the arguments of Sydney Clive, his intelligence chief (Cox had accidentally drowned in August), that Prince Max's government could be brought down by a harsh armistice, and 'The militarists would return to Power, and begin a life and death struggle'.[149]

Alternatively, authority could collapse in Germany, leading to Bolshevik revolution that might spread beyond its borders. Like many others of the British elite, Haig genuinely feared revolution. In July 1917 he had told the Archbishop of York there should be 'a great Imperial church to which all honest citizens of the Empire could belong . . . Church and State must advance together, and hold together against those forces of revolution which threaten to destroy the State.'[150] Back in January 1918 Haig had bluntly told the King, 'Few of us feel that the "democratising of Germany" is worth the loss of an Englishman!' and that forcing out the Hohenzollerns 'is likely to result in anarchy just as was the case in Russia. This might prove a serious evil for the rest of Europe.' Ten months later his prophecy seemed to be coming true, and supporting Max's government offered a chance of averting the worst. Henry Wilson shared Haig's fears. 'We have 2 dangers facing us,' Wilson told Esher. '1. Bolshevism. 2. My Cousin.[151] I am not fully persuaded that they are not one and indivisible'.[152]

In October Haig was winning the military victory he believed would curb German aggression, even if it was not as decisive as he would have liked. So what might appear to be an abrupt change of heart in October 1918 was in fact broadly in line with his long-held views. Haig told the War Cabinet that only the British army was capable of fighting effectively, and the German army was not yet 'so beaten that . . . [Germany] will accept whatever terms the Allies may offer'. He recommended to the War Cabinet that the Germans should be offered relatively moderate terms, including the evacuation of Belgium (thus fulfilling a primary British war aim), occupied France and Alsace-Lorraine. In a later addition to the diary that undoubtedly reflected his views at the time, Haig commented that the BEF 'alone might bring the enemy to his knees. But why expend more British lives – and for what?'[153]

Haig's views were moderate in comparison with the opinions of Henry Wilson and Foch, but they were not 'lenient', nor was he advocating a 'compromise peace'. In the words of a modern historian

> Haig's terms gave adequate security, but were insufficient to ensure fulfilment of Britain's war aims, even though the members of the cabinet believed Haig's provisions included as much as the Allies could reasonably ask for.[154]

After the initial success on the 17th, over the next two days Fourth Army pushed forward in a steady but unspectacular fashion. First and Third Armies swung into action on 20 October, getting across the Selle in a daring night attack. In accordance with what had become standard operating procedure across the BEF, Byng then put attacks on hold while the guns were moved forward. 23 and 24 October saw Byng's and Rawlinson's Armies fight side by side and drive the Germans back six miles in the direction of the River Sambre. To the north Haig's forces were also tasting success, as Fifth and First Armies advanced over ground recently abandoned by the Germans as they fell back to the so-called 'Hermann Position' along the line of the Schelde. Plumer's Second Army, now in touch with Birdwood's Fifth, had more problems. Plumer managed to get one corps forward to the Schelde on 20 October. Getting the guns forward proved difficult, and so in the meantime the attack slowed down, with the rest of Second Army echeloned back. Apart from that, all five British Armies were now in line, but Haig only controlled four of them. Ascribing to Foch devious political motives for keeping Plumer under the command of the King of the Belgians, in late October Haig carried out a wearying argument with the Generalissimo demanding that Second Army be returned to his command. The exchanges were bad-tempered and stand in stark contrast to the previous co-operative spirit. Foch's refusal to return Second Army struck 'at the very foundation of my position' as the BEF's commander, Haig argued.[155] Grudgingly, Foch released Second Army on 4 November.

Everywhere they looked in this first week of November, the German leadership surveyed a bleak scene. On 23 October President Wilson had publicly snuffed out the faint hope of a lenient deal being struck with the Americans, that ignored the British and French. Ludendorff had resigned on the 26th and had been replaced by his long-term rival General Groener. On 1 November US First Army (a Second Army had recently been formed) finally broke clear of the German defences in the Meuse-Argonne and on the 3rd severed the crucial Metz–Lille railway line. Turkey had dropped out of the war at the end of October. Vittorio Veneto, a major victory by Allied forces in Italy in which British divisions played a major role (and Italian Tenth Army was commanded by Cavan), had broken the resolve of the Austrians, and an armistice came into effect on 4 November. By that stage the Austro-Hungarian Empire had all but disintegrated, and revolution had broken out on the German home front.

As late as the Senlis conference 25 October Haig repeated to Foch his views that the German army, although much of it was 'badly beaten', was not sufficiently crushed so that the Allies could impose any terms they liked, and therefore recommended offering relatively moderate peace terms. President Wilson's representative, Colonel Edward House, reported that Haig feared 'prolonging the war . . . and exasperating

German national feeling, with very doubtful results'. In the privacy of his diary Haig was intensely suspicious of French motives. As a war nears its end, coalition partners begin to jostle for position, and 1918 was no exception. Haig was worried that behind Foch and Pétain's argument that the Allies should seize 'the left bank of the Rhine with bridgeheads' was an attempt to dominate 'the Palatinate' (i.e. the Rhineland).[156]

Whatever qualms Haig may have had about the strength of enemy resistance, there was no sign of it in GHQ's orders for the Battle of the Sambre: 'The Fourth, Third and First Armies will be prepared to resume the offensive on or after the 3rd November with a view to breaking the enemy's resistance south of the Condé canal and advancing in the general direction Avesnes-Maubeuge-Mons.' French First Army would also attack, and there would be a preliminary offensive by British First Army against Valenciennes.[157]

After a period out of the line, the Canadian Corps returned to the offensive, seizing Valenciennes in a two-day battle on 1–2 November. Supported by XXII Corps and the left-hand division of Third Army, the Canadians attacked with the support of 'a deluge of shrapnel, machine-gun bullets, [and] high explosive shells, of an intensity the like of which has never been approached . . . Prisoners, stupefied and demoralized, surrendered freely' to the attacking infantry.[158] Defeated, the Germans abandoned the line of the Schelde, with First Army in pursuit.

And yet, amazingly, even now the German high command hoped to save something from the ruins. This wasn't entirely self-delusion, as the positions that British Fourth and Third and French First Armies were gearing up to assault were quite strong in some places, especially along the Sambre-Oise Canal. It made no difference. Although the fighting was fierce in some sectors, IX Corps got across the canal, while further north Landrecies, the scene of Haig's uncharacteristic wobble in August 1914, was captured by 25th Division. On Third Army's front the most remarkable feat was the New Zealand Division's storming of the walled town of Le Quesnoy using scaling ladders. Some 10,000 German prisoners passed into British POW cages, while Debeney's army also took a number.[159]

It was the end. The Battle of the Sambre dispelled any lingering illusions among the German leadership. The war had to be ended before the German army collapsed.

The great victory of 4 November revived Haig's optimism. As recently as 1 November he had thought that, although the disintegration of Germany's allies might mean an armistice could be imposed on 'stiff terms . . . the determined fight put up by the enemy today shows that the German Army is not yet *demoralised*'. After the Sambre something of the old Haig reappeared. He offered the Cavalry Corps to Byng 'in view of the enemy's opposition being so slight'. (Byng politely declined, on account of the logistic difficulties it would create. So did Rawlinson that afternoon, on the same grounds. Perhaps they colluded.) On the 6th Second and Fifth Armies were ordered to prepare to push across the Schelde – '(if the enemy remained!)', Haig added – and then he would unleash the Cavalry Corps. This scheme strongly suggests that Haig's period of uncertainty was over, and that once again he believed the German army was on the point of defeat. He was right. The crossing of the Schelde was scheduled for the following Monday, which would fall on 11 November, 1918.

Haig's premonition that the Germans would not stay around to be attacked proved correct, and Second Army crossed the Schelde on the 9th. From that point on it was a case of trying to keep up with the enemy falling back in great haste to the Antwerp-Meuse position. In fact across almost the entire Allied front the German retreat was turning into a rout, and on 9 November Foch sent a telegram to Haig, Pershing and Pétain in which he ordered, 'I appeal to the energy and initiative of the Commanders-in-Chief . . . to make the results obtained decisive'. Characteristically, Haig wrote 'Quite unnecessary!' on the bottom of his copy,[160] and his diary for 9 November vividly captures the unfolding situation as seen from GHQ:

3 p.m.	Second Army reports		"No opposition on 40th Division front".
2 p.m.	Fifth	,, ,,	"Enemy offering no opposition".
1.30 p.m.	First	,, ,,	"Advance continued on whole Army front without opposition".
"	Fourth	,, ,,	"Enemy retreating rapidly on whole of Army front followed by our Cavalry patrols".

All Corps Commanders are anxious for more Cavalry as advanced guards
of all arms are being organised to keep touch with the retreating enemy.

And then, on 11 November, it was over. In the morning the news arrived
at GHQ that the armistice negotiations, which had been going on for a
couple of days, had come to an end. The fighting would stop at 11 a.m.
Just before then, the Canadians entered Mons, the lead troops halting
just a few yards from where the 4th Dragoon Guards had launched the
BEF's first action of the war back in August 1914.

At 11 a.m. Haig was in Cambrai conferring with his five Army
commanders and Kavanagh. First, the arrangements for sending Second
and Fourth Armies up to the German frontier as the British contribution
to the Allied army of occupation were sorted out. Then Haig raised the
problem of how to keep his vast citizen army busy, now the fighting was
over: 'It is as much the *duty* of all Officers to keep their men amused as
it is to train them for war.' This was the authentic voice of the pre-war
Regular officer. With business out of the way, it was time to savour the
moment of victory, which was captured in a group photograph.

Haig and his team posed on the steps of the Mairie. He stands in front
of the group, immaculately dressed and holding a swagger stick,
glaring past the camera. On either side and slightly behind Haig stand
Plumer and Rawlinson, who are looking directly at the camera. On the
step behind them are Byng, Birdwood and Horne, their positions
perhaps reflecting a hierarchy within the Army commanders, and at the
rear are a group of staff officers. Captured for posterity, this is the top
team of the army that has just won the greatest series of victories in
British military history.

The generals could not keep up the pose of conquering heroes for
long. Plumer, Haig recorded, 'whom I told to "go off and be cinema'ed"
went off most obediently and stood before the camera trying to look his
best, while Byng and others near him were chaffing the old man and
trying to make him laugh'. But the last reflection in Haig's diary on that
historic day was a sober one. He had heard that the Kaiser had gone into
exile in the Netherlands:

If the war had gone against us no doubt our King would have had to go,
and probably our Army would have become insubordinate like the

German Army! cf, John Bunyan's remark on seeing a man on his way to
be hanged, "But for the Grace of God, John Bunyan would have been in
that man's place!"[161]

On 12 November it was said in England that the Kaiser was only in
Holland because 'he wished to give himself up to Haig, but his own
soldiers turned him back'.[162] This was only a rumour, but it reflected a
view that it would have been a fitting end for the arch-enemy to have
surrendered to the man who had just led the armies of the Empire to
victory.

Accidental Victor?

If Haig had been removed from command at any time from the end of
1917 to the summer of 1918, the instant verdict would have been that he
had been a failure as Commander-in-Chief of the BEF. Suppose that
under a new commander, such as Plumer, events had followed roughly
the same course as happened in reality. Haig's successor would
undoubtedly have garnered the plaudits for victory, but the more
thoughtful would have wondered how much credit Haig deserved, both
for creating the army that won in 1918 and for weakening the German
army. Of course Haig *was* in command of the victorious BEF in
November 1918, but that question – how much credit did he deserve for
the victory? – continues to nag away.

  Historian John Terraine had no doubts that Haig's conduct of
operations in 1918 and his attritional campaigns of previous years
contributed mightily to victory. His interpretation follows Haig's own,
laid out in his *Final Dispatch* of 1919. More recently Tim Travers came to
a very different conclusion. Travers saw Haig as largely irrelevant to the
victory, arguing that, by the Hundred Days, Haig's power was curtailed
by the appointment of Foch as generalissimo, Lawrence as his Chief of
Staff, and Henry Wilson as CIGS. The impact of the German spring
offensives on the rigid, hierarchical, British command system was to
shatter it: 'an increasingly mobile style of warfare dictated a centralized
command structure until the Armistice', with lower-level commanders
taking key decisions. It 'appears that Haig and his GHQ . . . did not have
a critical influence on the victory in the last 100 days of the war. In fact
it can be argued that in the second half of 1918, Haig and the senior staff

at GHQ lost power to the army commanders, and retained only a symbolic form of leadership.'[163]

It is difficult to reconcile the view that Haig was a largely symbolic leader in the Hundred Days with the evidence presented in this chapter. Foch's activities as supreme commander were undoubtedly of huge significance, but Haig was Foch's *de facto* principal subordinate, meeting him some sixty times between April and November 1918, and had a major influence on strategy.[164] Having realised early in August that there was a real possibility (although not a certainty) of winning the war in 1918, Haig's drive and pressure on his Army commanders, especially Byng, helped to ensure that the BEF continued to seize the moment. His was almost a lone voice, recognising that the German army was suffering badly from the combined efforts of the Allied armies. In the midst of the victories of August to November 1918 there was deep pessimism among other British decision-makers. 'Haig alone had realised how drastic was the disconnection between conception in London and reality in France . . . For this he deserves more praise than he has yet received.'[165] However, Haig's optimism in previous years undermined his credibility when he repeated the same mantra in 1918.

Not the least of Haig's roles in the Hundred Days was as a coalition commander. There are plenty of examples of friction – between Haig and Foch, and Haig and Pershing, for instance – but ultimately Haig played an important role in keeping the coalition on an even keel and bringing about victory. For it was a *coalition* victory. The figures for captures of prisoners and guns give a sense of the immense importance of the forces of the British Empire in the defeat of Germany on the Western Front. But the efforts of the French, in particular, were far from negligible. Michael Neiberg has argued persuasively that the picture of a 'worn-out' French army in 1918 is misleading, at least during Second Marne. Later on, as Robert Doughty has shown, the French 'were on their last legs in the final two months of the war'; their fine performances from March to September 1918 meant that 'French soldiers had little left to give'.[166] Haig's dyspeptic view that the BEF was doing all the major fighting in 1918 should not be taken at face value, but neither should his ungenerous comments about the effectiveness of his Allies be allowed to detract from the significance of his role in making the coalition work.

Haig's role was subtly different in the Hundred Days than in earlier campaigns. At last he was able to behave as the sort of 'arms-length' C-in-C that was his ideal: setting broad objectives, but devolving responsibility for detailed planning and execution to subordinates. There were two basic reasons for this change. First, his senior subordinates at Army and Corps level, and their staffs, were displaying an impressive level of competence by August 1918, a competence founded on hard-won experience. As Haig had told Henry Wilson on 20 September 1918, the BEF had 'a surprisingly large number of *very capable* generals' (see page 319). Second, the BEF had developed into a highly complex, multi-faceted force in which the generalist had increasingly been replaced by the specialist. Haig was well aware of this: indeed he had presided over the transformation of the army, promoted the development of speciali-sation, and championed many 'subject-matter experts' such as Geddes, Solly-Flood and Trenchard. Haig's performance as a general improved as the army matured. He was, in sum, doing fewer things better, and saw less need to intervene.

On this basis Prior and Wilson, although they retain their scepticism about Haig's generalship, judge his performance in the Hundred Days as much improved. Haig was still prone to intervene, sometimes at unhelpful moments, but more often, as in the case of his prodding of Byng in mid-August, to good effect. Haig has been rightly criticised for failing to grip his Army commanders on the Somme in 1916, but tighter control of subordinate formations in the very different circumstances of 1918 would have been utterly inappropriate. Haig and GHQ's Operations staff played a vital part in the Grand Offensive of 26–29 September by sequencing the offensives, a job for which it was better suited than carrying out planning in detail for subsidiary formations. Similarly, the Adjutant-General's (A) and Quartermaster Generals (Q) branches of GHQ kept the BEF in supply under very difficult circumstances.[167] Faced with such evidence, the idea that Haig was a mere onlooker during the Hundred Days, an accidental victor, is impossible to sustain.

The First World War was in many ways a total war, but, unlike the Second World War, it did not end with Germany being forced to surrender unconditionally. The fact that the Allies did not dictate terms in Berlin, hold victory parades in major cities and herd the entire German army into prisoner-of-war camps enabled its politicians to proclaim that

Germany had not truly lost the war. Even the Social Democratic party leader Friedrich Ebert, who had spent his career in opposition to the Kaiser's regime, welcomed homecoming troops with the words 'No enemy has overcome you!' This inability to face the unpalatable truth left a poisonous legacy for the new Weimar republic in the form of the 'stab-in-the back' myth.[168] The ultimate beneficiary was Adolf Hitler. Arguably, if the French had been allowed to impose stiffer armistice terms, or if the Allies had simply fought on for several more weeks, the faces of the German population would have been rubbed in the brutal reality of military defeat; the idea of an undefeated army betrayed would never have taken hold. This is a powerful and ultimately unanswerable case – the German army might well have collapsed completely, but we can never know for sure.

Judged in hindsight, then, Haig's advocacy of a relatively moderate peace can be seen as deeply flawed. But other factors must be put into the equation. Haig's opinion on the armistice terms carried much less weight than Foch's. His favoured terms were tough, not weak, and moderate only in comparison to some of the other views being put forward. Under Haig's plan the Germans would have been forced back to their pre-1914 frontier (minus Alsace-Lorraine), and this would have placed the Allies in a strong position if the fighting had to be renewed. But that was exactly what Haig hoped to avoid. His concerns about forcing the Germans into a corner, with all that might mean in terms of a prolonged and bloody fight, not to mention the added risk of communist revolution, were reasonable, given his essentially conservative views and the partial and unreliable intelligence he was receiving. Haig's friend Eric Geddes wrote shortly after the armistice: 'Had we known how bad things were in Germany we might have got stiffer terms; however, it is easy to be wise after the event.'[169] Just as Lloyd George was in most ways the consummate total warrior, but he shied away from the reality of the battlefield, Haig fought a total war to achieve an aim which, if not 'limited', fell well short of unconditional surrender. For all his reputation as a 'butcher', Haig was not as ruthless as some of his Second World War counterparts.

Veterans' Champion – and
Potential Dictator?

'What are we to do with him [?] He can't settle down to a life of domestic inactivity he will go mad – on the other hand what job is there for him?'[1] Philip Sassoon's concern for Haig was premature. In retirement Haig confounded these fears by carving out a career as the leading champion of ex-servicemen in Britain and the Empire. He became a hugely influential figure, his role in defending the war veteran adrift in a hostile and uncaring land, which was manifestly not 'fit for heroes', earning him a level of popularity that far exceeded anything he had known during the war. Politicians were wary of tangling with him. Some worried that Haig was a potential dictator. When he died in 1928 the crowds that turned out for his funeral were larger than those who paid their respects to another twentieth-century icon, Diana, Princess of Wales, in 1997.[2] Within a few years of his death Haig's reputation came under sustained attack, and it virtually collapsed altogether.

The aftermath

This was far in the future on 11 November 1918. With the Armistice came some relief from the strain of high command. A visitor to GHQ in December thought Haig 'seemed a different man, with a load of care and responsibility lifted from him'.[3] With great satisfaction, on 16 December Haig noted in his diary 'I crossed the Rhine', and in a ceremony in Cologne (see p 154) he gave a 'short address'. He said, 'I sincerely hope that in our time of victory we may not lose our heads, as the Germans lost theirs after 1870 – with the result that we are here'.[4]

It was a touch of humility from a victorious general at the moment of triumph. Haig does seem to have remained remarkably level-headed despite the adulation. Returning home to Kingston on 19 December, he was very touched by the tremendous reception from the ordinary folk, which showed 'how the people of England realise what has been accomplished by the Army and myself. This more than compensates me for the difficulties put in my way and the coldness towards me by the Prime Minister.'[5]

In December the idea of a peerage was floated, but Haig refused to accept a title or a grant of money until adequate provision had been made for his officers and soldiers. In taking this stand he made himself unpopular with various members of the establishment, because his refusal meant that the whole process of awarding honours was held up. There was no danger of adulation from Lloyd George, who asked Haig to come to London for a victory parade. He 'was to be in the fifth carriage along with General Henry Wilson. I felt that this was more of an insult than I could put up with, even from the PM'.[6]

With the Germans beaten, the British army started to implode. This was not the result of revolutionary impulses. Rather, the civilians-in-uniform who filled the ranks considered they had joined up to do a job; the job had been completed, and they wanted to go home. Strikes, riots, refusal to obey orders and simple apathy rotted the army from within. Haig had foreseen this 'general relaxation of the bonds of discipline' as far back as October 1917, but was nonetheless alarmed by some of its manifestations. He reacted to a major mutiny at Calais base in January 1919 by surrounding the camp with loyal troops. Haig wanted to impose the death penalty on three ringleaders, but Churchill disagreed, and with bad grace, Haig took his advice. It is as well he did. A heavy-handed approach could have sent a containable situation out of control.[7] One of the problems was the complicated demobilisation scheme, which did not stick to the principle of 'first in, first out'. In 1917 Haig had argued that soldiers would see the plan as unfair, and this would cause disciplinary problems, and he repeated his criticisms when demobilisation was under way. Winston Churchill, the new Secretary of State for War, told the Cabinet in February 1919 that 'It is surprising that the Commander-in-Chief's prescient warnings were utterly ignored'. Haig feared the state of the army would affect the outcome of the peace settlement.

'Demobilisation Orders and counter orders' would lead to the Army melting away, leaving the British 'at the mercy of the Germans as regards enforcing certain terms of the Peace'.[8]

Churchill gripped the situation decisively, producing a new scheme of demobilisation in short order. Haig admired his handling of the issue: 'he has not only courage, but foresight and a knowledge of Statesmanship. All of these qualities most of his colleagues seem to have lacked so lamentably throughout this war.'[9]

Although Haig was not part of the British team that negotiated the Treaty of Versailles, he was involved in the preliminary discussions about the peace terms. At a conference with Foch and Pershing on 26 January, he argued that Germany should be broken up into separate states, as a 'great block of 70 to 80 million Germans in the centre of Europe must produce trouble in the future'. Foch shared these views, and Clemenceau toyed with the idea of a separate Rhineland at the least. In spite of this convergence of views, Haig was highly suspicious of French aims and motives, believing that they 'steal away as many of the plums as they can lay their hands on'.[10] Haig wanted the peace to be concluded as soon as possible. In theory, hostilities could have begun again if a final settlement could not be reached, but Haig knew the BEF now 'consisted only of fragments of Divisions', and whether or not the army would fight 'willingly or not must depend on the reason for recommencing hostilities'. Fears of revolution had not abated. At a meeting with Milner and Wilson on 19 February, he urged that arrangements be put into place for feeding Germany immediately. With Germany 'on the verge of famine', he feared the breakdown of law and order, which would force Allied intervention and the increase the likelihood of Bolshevism spreading to France and Britain. 'There is therefore every reason for feeding Germany'.[11]

The military terms of the peace treaty were a source of much argument between the Allies. It was agreed that Foch would head a high-level military committee to discuss the matter. Haig wished that he and Henry Wilson would 'speak with one voice', and that is largely what happened, the CIGS producing a paper at a meeting on 17 February that met with Haig's approval.[12] Haig watched the formal negotiations in Paris from a distance, apparently glad not to be involved. 'What fun you and the "frocks" seem to be having in Paris!' he wrote to Henry Wilson in March 1919. 'I expect . . . you will be as glad as I am to leave "la belle France" with all its mud and not a little intrigue!' Watching the internal situation in Germany, Haig grew concerned. 'The wretched German government is between the Devil and the Deep Sea, I mean the Bolshiviki [sic] and the Peace Conference,' he wrote to Wilson. It was so enfeebled that it could not keep 'internal order'. '[S]ign *something soon!*' Haig pleaded.[13] The Treaty of Versailles was finally signed on 28 June 1919.

'There is no more difficult or distasteful work which a soldier can be called upon to undertake than the maintaining of order against civil disturbance or rebellion.'[14] Haig was talking about the 17th Lancers' service in Ireland, but he could equally have been referring to his own time as a Commander-in-Chief Home Forces in the turbulent aftermath of the Great War. Trade Union membership rocketed from 4.1 million in 1914 to 8.3 million in 1920, and British workers made use of this industrial muscle: 5 million working days were lost in 1919.[15] For two-and-a-half years, until mid-1921, there seemed to be a real possibility of revolution in Britain.[16] However exaggerated these fears, Haig and other senior figures took them very seriously. Churchill's appointment to the position of a soldier of Haig's experience and reputation was wise, but also shows how worried he was about the domestic situation. Taking up the post on 15 April, Haig was faced with a strike-ridden country wracked with social unrest.

Intelligence of a very different sort from that which Charteris had analysed now reached Haig's desk. Leeds tramworkers, for example, had been awarded a 4/- pay rise when they had asked for 12/-, and this caused 'general dissatisfaction', while the Comrades of the Great War, a veterans' association, helped the authorities during the railway strike of September–October 1919 and were denounced as blacklegs by Trade Unions.[17]

Haig's report on this strike gives valuable insights into his approach in this period. When the strike began, contingency plans, previously prepared with other government departments, were actioned. Troops were moved to guard 'vulnerable points', such as power stations, having up to that stage kept as low a profile as possible. Haig reinforced particular areas as the need arose and, fearing a general strike in October, he suggested a massive reinforcement from the continent, but the strike was called off. The strike refused to boil. There was no 'sabotage or violence', and troops did not 'come into collision with the strikers', but the military response had been on a large scale: 23,000 troops were actually used, backed up by 86 infantry battalions and six cavalry regiments. Plainly Haig was uncomfortable with the army's prominent role, much preferring the traditional primacy of the police. Since the police were overstretched, he therefore called for the formation of a 'Citizen Guard' to supplement them.[18] This suggestion inadvertently gave ammunition to those who suspected that Haig had undemocratic political ambitions.

Reflections on the War

Haig emerged from the war a celebrity. In faraway Argentina in November 1918 a British expatriate organised a football team, Club Atlético Douglas Haig', which still thrives today, as their 'Douglas Mania' website shows. 'Douglas' became one of the 50 most popular boys' Christian names for the only time in the century in the interwar period. Some parents went further in the naming of their children. Douglas Haig Greaves, born 4 April 1917, grew up to be an RAF night fighter ace and survived the Second World War, and Douglas Haig Diggens of the Royal Norfolks died as a prisoner on a Japanese hellship in 1944, aged 26.[19]

'Welcome Home – Sir Douglas Haig among his "Ain Folk"' was the headline in *The Scotsman* that heralded his tour of Scotland in May 1919. It became a triumphal progress. He was feted wherever he went, receiving the freedom of five burghs, including Glasgow, Edinburgh and Dundee.[20] Haig was clearly delighted at his reception from his fellow Scots. 'Their affectionate welcome makes up for a great deal of my worries in France,' he wrote to Esher, 'and is worth all the empty titles and honours which the P.M. may bestow on me. The crowds at Dundee were *quite extraordinary,* and I fancy the reception there must have surprised their member [of parliament, Winston Churchill].' Haig gave a speech at the Church of Scotland's General Assembly, in which he returned to a wartime theme (see page 330), issuing a plea for a 'united National Church' in Britain followed by a 'great Imperial Church', because 'The one means by which peace could be made permanent was to develop throughout the whole world the spirit of brotherhood born of the war'[21]. His audience's reaction is uncertain. Haig's idealism perhaps may surprise a modern reader.

The most significant event of Haig's tour of the land of his birth was his visit to the University of St Andrews. The students had elected him Rector of the University at a difficult time in October 1916, an act that seems to have reassured him as to his popular support at home. Now, 31 months later, on 14 May 1919 he was at last installed in the post. In private, he was self-deprecating – 'what a business it all is,' he wrote to Sassoon, 'but I suppose it will please the lads'. In his address Haig demonstrated his passionate faith in the Empire as a force for good, a profound respect and admiration for the ordinary soldier, and a firm belief in the values of the Edwardian officer. All three factors were to influence the rôle he created for himself in the last nine years of his life.[22]

As the huge British Army of 1918 was dismantled, the future of the Territorial Force came into question. Haig, on his installation as a Freeman of the City of London, called for 'a strong Citizen Army on Territorial Lines'. This would ensure that the problems of 1914–16 would not be repeated: that the future citizen soldier would not be 'a willing, patriotic but militarily ignorant volunteer'. Instead, he would be 'a trained man'.[23] The importance that Haig attached to the Territorials was symbolised by his acceptance of the Honorary Colonelcy of the London Scottish, a commitment only slightly undermined by his comment that 'I presume that the duties of Hon. Colonel are not very exacting!'[24] The renamed Territorial Army was reconstituted in 1921, but the reality in the interwar period fell well short of Haig's ideal. Not until a new threat emerged in the late 1930s did it receive a new lease of life.

At an obscure ceremony in 1925 Haig made a remark which has become one of the most notorious of his career. He said that armies 'would find just as much use for . . . the well-bred horse . . . as they had ever done in the past'. The sentence has been used time and again and as evidence of his stupidity and military Luddism.[25] As always, however, context is everything, and to understand why Haig made this remark it is necessary to give a lengthy extract from the speech, and delve into the background.

Some enthusiasts to-day talked about the probability of horses becoming extinct and prophesied that the aeroplane, the tank, and the motor-car would supersede the horse in future wars. But history had always shown that great inventions somehow or other cured themselves; they always produced antidotes, and he believed that the value of the horse, and the opportunity for the horse in the future were likely to be as great as ever. How could infantry, piled up with all their equipment, take advantage of a decisive moment created by fire from machine-guns at a range of 5,000 to 6,000 yards? It was by utilizing light mounted troops and mounted artillery that advantage could be taken of these modern weapons. He was all for using aeroplanes and tanks, but they were only accessories to the man and the horse, and he felt sure that as time went on they would find just as much use for the horse – the well-bred horse – as they had ever done in the past.[26]

The occasion of the speech was an award by the Royal College of Veterinary Surgeons. As the President of the College made clear in his introductory comments, one of the reasons why Haig was being honoured was his appreciation of 'the value of the Royal Army Veterinary Corps during the Great War'. Haig's reply warmly praised the wartime work of the RAVC under the Director of Veterinary Services, Major-General Sir John Moore. Advances in horsemastership had led to a drastic decline in military horse mortality between the South African War and the First World War. It is in the context of veterinary science that Haig's comment about the 'well-bred horse' was made; he was expressing an appreciation of improvements in horse-breeding.

In spite of the increasing mechanisation of the Army during the First World War, in 1925 it was difficult to conceive of an army that would not rely on large numbers of horses for transport. Shortly after the Armistice, out of 394,443 horses and mules in the BEF, only 25,414 belonged to the Cavalry Corps.[27] However the main thrust of Haig's comments was clearly directed at rebutting those who asserted that horsed cavalry had no future on the battlefield. In arguing otherwise Haig proved to be a poor prophet, but at the time this was by no means obvious. Cavalry had had an important role in Allenby's 1918 campaign in Palestine and at the Battle of Warsaw in 1920. Both campaigns were fought in conditions very different from the Western Front. In a 1927 study the CIGS invited him to write, Haig supported the army's retention of substantial numbers of cavalry because '[we] don't know where we shall have to fight next' – perhaps Afghanistan. 'The only thing we can say for certain is that the next war will NOT be like the last in Flanders.'[28]

'The most valuable acquisition which modern inventions have conferred on Cavalry is Machine Guns,' Haig declared in 1927. 'The equipment of Cavalry with Anti-Tank weapons, Armoured cars and Tankettes of their own is a vital necessity.'[29] The 1929 cavalry doctrine manual reflected Haig's views: 'Cavalry is the arm of opportunity,' it stated, and the use of superior fire could create conditions for a mounted attack.[30] Although the description of tanks, aircraft and motor vehicles as 'auxiliaries' on the battlefield is excessive, what seems at first sight to be an example of a military dinosaur engaging in the worst sort of reactionary diatribe is, on examination, nothing of the sort. In the context in which they were put forward, Haig's views were solidly founded on recent operational experience, moderately conservative in some ways, mildly progressive in others, and generally unexceptional. It is worth remembering that, though cavalry had mostly disappeared from Western armies by 1939, it still retained a significant role on the decisive Eastern Front in the Second World War.

The first use of this recondite speech to the veterinary surgeons to attack Haig seems to stem from the military writer Basil Liddell Hart in 1959, when he cited the 'well-bred horse' passage but gave no indication of the context. Liddell Hart – who had moved from credulous adulation of Haig and high command during the war to become a fierce critic – was a vain man, determined to portray himself as a prophet of modern warfare who struggled against the forces of military reaction. He didn't scruple to doctor the evidence by omitting the sentence about using mounted troops in combination with machine guns – thus removing inconvenient evidence of the cautiously progressive nature of Haig's views on cavalry.[31]

In retirement Haig kept a fatherly eye on the 17th Lancers, and behind the scenes pressed for the amalgamation rather than disbandment of surplus cavalry regiments. He put his authority behind the creation of the new 'vulgar fraction', the 17th/21st Lancers, making clear to the regiment's CO that it must be made to work. The Field-Marshal was invited to a training exercise in 1925, and Bob-tail – his favourite horse, which he had passed to the 17th on his retirement – was made ready. Regimental officers can be a little nervous about a great man breathing down their necks, but this time they need not have worried. It rained so hard that Haig, with Foch and Cavan, spent all day in a shepherd's hut, being served tea by the shepherd's wife.[32]

An Ex-Serviceman's Leader Emerges

Haig's concern for ex-servicemen had deep roots. While travelling over the old Somme battlefield in March 1917 he had ruminated on the men who had fought in the battle: 'I have not the time to put down all the thoughts which rush into my mind when I think of all those fine fellows who either have given their lives for their country, or have been maimed in its service. Later on I hope we may have a Prime Minister and a Government who will do them justice'.[33] A little later he showed his interest in veterans' issues by becoming the first life member of the Comrades of the Great War, a conservative body formed in 1917 in response to the creation of two radical, left-wing ex-servicemen's groups, the National Association of Discharged Sailors and Soldiers, and the National Federation of Discharged and Demobilised Sailors and Soldiers.[34] On his death, 11 years later, Haig was the President of the British Legion, a conservative, supposedly non-political organisation created through the difficult process of uniting the various groups.

Haig and the Legion leadership helped to tame the major ex-service organisations in Britain; the Legion had none of the political power and radicalism of some continental veterans' groups. Haig's innate social and political conservatism was no doubt a factor in his decision to get involved in veterans' affairs, but it was not the primary reason. In speech after speech, he spoke of his admiration and gratitude to the men who had served under him in France and Flanders. How could he, he reflected in a speech in Chester in July 1919, repay the efforts of the men he had commanded? He

> could at least do his best to see that those who came back from the war, and above all those who had suffered in the course of it, were fairly and justly treated. That he intended to do to the best of his ability.[35]

He does not seem to have acted from a sense of guilt. He had thoroughly absorbed the paternalistic ethos of the Victorian army officer, which in his case was underpinned by Christian compassion. His work with ex-servicemen was a natural extension of the credo of *noblesse oblige* that had governed his professional career.

He did not have to do all this. At one of the many lunches in Haig's honour a speaker remarked that not all military commanders 'had been so solicitous for the welfare of the officers and men who fought under them'.[36] He was one of the relatively few senior officers who took concern for the welfare of ex-servicemen to such lengths, although he certainly found it a strain. When visiting Haig, Micky Ryan found that he often toiled late into the night answering letters from distressed ex-servicemen – working himself to death, in the medical man's opinion. 'I think that they rather prefer to get a letter in one's own handwriting,' Haig said. 'The personal touch, I think, counts for something, and I can do so little for them.'[37]

Problems with pensions and the like had come to Haig's attention through his dealings with the Disabled Officers Fund during the war. Even before he left France, he was corresponding with the Minister of Pensions when payments to disabled officers were delayed: 'The Field-Marshal is very insistent upon something being done immediately'.[38] Once he returned to Britain in April, his concern became public knowledge. At a high-profile speech at the Mansion House in June 1919, he expressed his concern for

the future of all those splendid young men, officers and other ranks alike, lately under my command . . . I feel it my duty to use such influence as I possess to urge upon all . . . to do all they can to open the gates of civil employment to the many thousands of young men who are now seeking for employment.[39]

The point at which Haig decisively emerged as the champion of the war veteran came in July 1919, when he gave evidence to the Parliamentary Select Committee on Pensions. He handed in a written statement in which he stated that in the summer of 1918 he had been 'appalled' at 'the methods of the State to provide for the disabled . . . I hold strongly that is the duty of the State to provide for those who suffered in the great war.' He lambasted the lack of a proper 'chain of responsibility' that left some officers 'penniless . . . The War Office should

not discharge the man until the Ministry of Pensions can take him over.'
Then he turned his fire on the Medical Boards, claiming that some
Boards 'lacked all sympathy and generosity . . . and treat every wretched
individual who appears before them as a malingerer'. He cited the case
of an officer suffering from TB, whose family was in poverty. He had
not been notified of the 'children's allowance'. 'However,' Haig went
on with a sarcasm that must have made the listeners wince, 'his little boy
has just died, probably from starvation, so this would save the
Government £24 a year'. He showed scant sympathy for concerns of
Trade Unionists, 'indignantly' criticising their 'hostility' in preventing
disabled men from obtaining skilled work without having undergone a
full apprenticeship. Haig concluded his evidence by demanding to know
how the country was supposed to celebrate Peace – the official victory
parade was to be held shortly – when this lamentable state of affairs
existed which might 'pauperize' a man 'who has risked his life on the
field of battle. You want to be generous . . . and just.'[40]

Haig's anger belied his reputation as an unemotional, reserved man,
and his passion on the subject, allied to his huge prestige, made a great
impression on the members of the Select Committee. By early August
1919 Haig believed that he had won a significant victory over the
government on pensions and therefore could receive the honours the
country wished to offer him. He accepted an earldom, a grant of
£100,000, and in 1921 was presented with the ancestral home of the Haig
family, Bemersyde House.

Throughout 1919 Haig returned to the same key themes in his public
utterances: justice for ex-servicemen in the form of work and pensions;
recreation of the wartime spirit of comradeship and co-operation; the
necessity for rival veterans' organisations to come together; and the need
for ex-servicemen to avoid political activity. Implicit was the promise
that Haig himself would act in their interests, although he stated (and
undoubtedly believed) that he would not undertake a 'political
campaign'.[41] This was a straightforward relocation into peace of the
wartime attitudes of paternalism: that officers would act vigorously on
the behalf of the ranks providing that they offered loyalty and obedience
– but officers were well aware that failures of paternalism could lead to
soldiers taking direct action.

This was not a perspective that all politicians found easy to understand. At a meeting in Newcastle in July 1919 Edward Shortt, the Liberal Home Secretary in Lloyd George's coalition government, spoke after Haig and undermined his message, saying that he hoped that the Field Marshal's advice would be ignored, as 'if they wanted anything they would get it through politics far better than through any other way'. As Chief Secretary for Ireland in 1918 and Home Secretary during the 1919 police strike, Shortt had seen individuals taking extra-parliamentary action, and encouraging ex-servicemen to become involved in conventional politics was, for him, a preferable option. Shortt's comments were greeted by cries from the audience of 'no!', while Haig seems to have sat through the speech tight-lipped. Safely on home ground at the 17th Lancers Old Comrades dinner in October 1919, Haig expressed the hope that all veterans' bodies would follow his old regiment's lead in steering clear of politics.[42]

Although he made clear that he would be an outspoken champion of the interests of war veterans, Haig set out in unambiguous language the parameters within which he would be operating. By stressing the non-political (by which he meant non-party) nature of his approach, he served notice that he did not have any personal political ambitions – unlike Henry Wilson, who after his retirement from the army did move into party politics, only to be assassinated in 1922. Rather fancifully, Wilson has been described as a 'lost dictator'.[43] Haig's prestige was such that he was a much more credible candidate to lead a military party in politics if he had so chosen.

While his blunt interventions certainly ruffled the feathers of some in government and organised labour, Haig always held to his conception of himself as a non-political figure who simply spoke out to say what he believed was true, no matter who might find the truth unpalatable. Thus he condemned both employers who took advantage of veterans and also the practice of 'ca' canny' – the deliberate limitation of output by workers – saying that, although it might be thought to increase work for veterans, it was 'fatal . . . to the interests of ex-Servicemen'. As he bluntly put it, 'if any of the supporters of the government thought that he was a nuisance, they should think of these [ex-service] men'.[44]

Haig aspired to lead a united ex-servicemen's movement from very early on. In 1918 his military secretary, Major Ruggles-Brise, represented Haig on a War Office committee that explored ways of bringing the various groups together.[45] His motives were a mixture of ambition, desire for social control and concern that divisions would reduce the influence of veterans. Haig did not 'found' the British Legion, but he was 'a commanding figure', and his advocacy of unity 'carried great weight' among ex-servicemen immediately after the war.[46]

By mid-1919 there were a number of bodies working for ex-officers, and Haig successfully helped them come together into one Officers' Association (OA). 'My ultimate aim,' he wrote 'is to form One Association to include all who have served in H.M.s service, regardless of their rank or present position. I hope that the meeting . . . [of 26 August] may be the beginning of the "Ex-Officer branch" of that Great Association'.[47]

In February 1920 GHQ Home Forces was due to be abolished. At the end of January *The Times* reported that Haig had not been offered a new post but that 'It can definitely be stated that it is not the Field-Marshal's intention to retire permanently from the force in which he has rendered such signal service'. Although the War Office and the Government gave Haig glowing thanks, they did not offer him another job. On 1 February 1920 Douglas Haig retired as a field marshal from the Army he had joined 36 years previously as a Sandhurst gentleman cadet.[48]

Rawlinson, Plumer, Allenby and Byng found post-war careers in high positions – commander-in-chief, high commissioner, governor-general in various parts of the Empire. Such posts did not come Haig's way, despite rumours that circulated shortly after the war of his appointment as Viceroy of India. It was not a snub to appoint Haig to the Home Forces post, but to abolish this position in January 1920 without offering him any further employment most certainly was. He was unlikely to receive preferment from Downing Street as long as Lloyd George remained Prime Minister. In 1926, when Lloyd George had been out of office for four years, George V proposed Haig as Viceroy, but the then Prime Minister, Stanley Baldwin, preferred the future Lord Halifax.[49] It is unlikely that Haig would have accepted such an offer, or any earlier ones, because it would have distracted him from the cause to which he dedicated the last years of his life, the welfare of ex-servicemen.[50]

Haig's retirement coincided with the launch of the Officers' Association. Haig played his part, and the appeal for funds was hugely successful, £637,000 being donated by the end of the year. The very success of the OA's appeal damaged the Comrades of the Great War, which, faced with rapidly-emptying coffers, had been about to launch one of their own. Haig was offered the Presidency of the Comrades but refused, instead urging the Comrades to work towards unity; this helped propel the Comrades towards accepting the need for a united movement.[51] By contrast, Haig was happy to accept the Presidency of the Welsh Legion, created when several ex-service groups in the Principality amalgamated.[52] From August 1920 there were a series of 'unity conferences' from which the British Legion gradually emerged.[53] Haig steered clear of these discussions but spoke in favour of unity at various gatherings of veterans.[54] His message to the war veterans of Cambridge University said:

> Ex-servicemen have now the chance of becoming a great power in the land, a great influence for good, reaching to all corners of the Empire. The spirit of comradeship born of common service . . . the remembrance of dangers shared and victory won together, are loads which should know no class distinctions, no differences of birth or occupation. They should knit together in a lasting fellowship . . . I ask them all to join 'The Empire Guild of Warriors'![55]

Haig exercised particular influence on the Officers' Association, some of whose leaders were reluctant to share their funds with the other organisations. In a private letter Haig wrote:

> I am really anxious about trouble of a serious kind [i.e. industrial unrest] in the coming winter. Hence I am doing all I can to induce all ex-servicemen's societies to unite with the Officers Association. This at any rate will be a steadying element . . . Indeed all are anxious to unite except the 'Association' of ex-soldiers and sailors: that is a very revolutionary society.[56]

On 8 August 1920 Haig published a letter that proclaimed that the nation had a 'debt of honour to find employment for the fighting man'. Haig's appeals on the anniversary of the outbreak of war and around Armistice Day were to become annual events. His appeals did have a modest effect in increasing employment for ex-servicemen, but Haig's wider ambitions in this area were to be disappointed.[57]

The climax to the protracted negotiations between veterans' organisations came in May 1921. It was agreed that the 'British Legion' should formerly come into being on 1 July of that year. Haig was not present, as he was returning by sea from South Africa, but he was elected as President, defeating the only other candidate by 658 votes to 49. The Legion was to be the main focus of Haig's activities until his death, seven years later.

Within a few months of the formal beginning of the British Legion, it acquired a symbol that came to stand not merely for the organisation, but more generally for remembrance. The red Flanders poppy had already achieved iconic status, thanks in part to John McCrae's 1915 poem 'In Flanders Fields', and in August 1921 it was suggested that paper poppies be sold on Armistice Day to raise funds for the Legion. Rather hesitantly, the Legion authorities agreed.

The first Poppy Day appeal was a huge success. In the words of one journalist, London became a 'scarlet city'. Haig and Doris drove to the poppy distribution centre in London, their car bedecked with the paper flowers that were rapidly plucked and sold. Haig autographed copies of a pamphlet, *Remembrance Day – Poppy Day*, that were sold for sizeable sums. In all, £106,000 was raised. A factory where disabled war veterans produced poppies was set up. By 1926 200 such men were manufacturing 25 million poppies a year. On Armistice Day 1921 Haig commented that he hoped that Poppy Day might become a regular event at which 'the Glorious Dead' would be remembered. Poppy Day has now been a fixture in the British calendar for nearly 90 years. The artificial poppy, which until recently bore the title 'Haig Fund', became an instant tradition.[58]

As National President, Haig was the public face of the British Legion, making speeches, inspecting parades, generally keeping the Legion in the public eye. He was a regular at the annual conference. Generally he steered clear of detailed administration of the help for veterans that was the Legion's core business, but he also worked behind the scenes. At the 1927 annual conference the Chairman, T.F. Lister, observed that Haig 'had preserved his proud record of 100 per cent attendance at meetings of the Benevolent Committee'.[59] Haig's dedication to the welfare of ex-servicemen, and the British Legion in particular, was widely recognised. At the first annual conference in 1922 Haig's appearance on the platform was greeted by 'a spontaneous and enthusiastic ovation' indicating that 'Legionaires [sic] whole-heartedly appreciate the splendid work he had done on behalf of all'.[60] Three years later Prince Arthur of Connaught, paying tribute to Haig, claimed that he had 'even excelled his great record as Commander-in-Chief of the B.E.F. by his untiring effort on behalf of the rank and file of ex-service men'.[61]

In the 1920s the conference was held at Whitsun, with a parade on Whit Sunday. The military overtones were clear. Haig, resplendent in top hat, wing collar and medals, inspected lines of bemedalled men in civilian attire but with a soldierly bearing.[62] The parade at the Cenotaph on Whit Sunday 1927 was broadcast for the first time by the fledgling BBC. As a journalist commented, this means that 'war veterans all over the country could imagine themselves with their comrades at the shrine of the Glorious Dead'. Haig and the Duke of Connaught inspected the assembled legionaires on Horse Guards Parade and then led the march down Whitehall.[63]

A British Mussolini?

The image of the hugely popular Field Marshal commanding a peacetime 'army' of veterans just as he had led them in war alarmed some on the Left, who feared the Legion would be used as a paramilitary force for strike-breaking and the suppression of disturbances. Left-wing critics labelled the Legion as, variously, Haig's 'White Guard' (a reference to the Russian Civil War), 'Anti-Bolshie' and 'Fascisti'. The left-wing *Daily Herald* ran a campaign against what it plainly saw as an embryo fascist movement, with a ready-made British Mussolini.[64] Some of Haig's public pronouncements stoked the fears of the Left. To its critics, the Legion might seem to fit the bill of the Citizen Guards he had called for in 1919 (see page 344). In 1926 he publicly stated that, by incorporating veterans' groups with 'Bolshevik' tendencies into the Legion, Britain had been 'saved . . . from bloodshed'.[65] Similarly, Haig referred to the General Strike of May 1926 in apocalyptic terms:

the country had been through a grievous experience such as he hoped would never be repeated. By this upheaval the strength and existence of the Legion were severely tested. It emerged, he was glad to say, with its good name enhanced, not only by its *strict impartiality,* but also by this firmness in adhering to these ideals. There was no doubt that the Legion, by *supporting the cause of law and order, saved the country from bloodshed and attempted revolution.*[66]

Haig was obviously unconscious of the contradiction in his speech, of claiming that the Legion had been simultaneously impartial and upholding the *status quo.* Clearly, he held the not uncommon belief that holding conservative views was the same as being 'non-political'. In reality, although the General Strike was far from being a revolutionary movement, the Legion in the midst of it had published an appeal that 'called upon all ex-servicemen who saved the country in the war, to come forward once more and offer their services in any way that may be needed by the authorities'. This appeal was controversial and divisive, particularly among Legion branches in working-class areas. As a former leading light of the Comrades of the Great War, Colonel George Crosfield, a leading Legion figure, could hardly be accused of being a closet left-winger, but in 1927 he tactfully tried to get Haig to tone down his rhetoric. Many Legion members were Labour supporters, he warned, and if the themes of Empire and duty were laid on too thickly without stressing that responsibility affects all classes, it would encourage talk of 'Haig's White Guard'.[67] For all that, Haig retained his popularity in the Legion, during his lifetime, and even more so after his death.

Like many others in the 1920s, Haig admired Benito Mussolini. Fascism at this time had a wide appeal to those disillusioned with the state of democratic Britain. Haig met the Italian dictator on a visit to Italy in February 1926. 'What a man!' he was quoted as saying. 'He really is exceptional'.[68] Like many of Mussolini's other British admirers, most famously Winston Churchill, Haig downplayed the violence in the Fascist regime, respecting a strong leader and the corporate state. Haig was worried by developments in post-war politics: the threat of Bolshevism, industrial militancy and the threat to the Empire. Writing at a time of increased industrial militancy – the General Strike was only a couple of months away – Haig declared 'We want someone like that at home at the present time'. But it would be as misleading to label Haig as fundamentally anti-democratic as it would be to tar Churchill with the same brush. As Alex Danchev has commented, 'Nearly everyone . . . flirted with Mussolini in the 1920s'.[69]

It was not only the political Left that was worried by the British Legion's political activities. Born of frustration at the lack of progress in getting favourable legislation passed in parliament, there was an attempt in 1926 by some branches to amend the Legion's constitution. In the words of one Resolution, this would have allowed the 'use of the whole force of the Legion . . . to oppose every Parliamentary Candidate who has voted against the Pensions Policy of the Legion'. The attempt failed, but the Conservative government found the prospect of the Legion taking an overtly party political role distinctly unappealing. The Minister of Pensions, Major G.C. Tryon, was concerned about the Legion's campaign of 'worrying M.P.s in their own constituencies' in an attempt to improve the lot of the ex-serviceman. Haig received a letter from the cabinet committee, in which he was urged 'in the interests of the British Legion, to invite those responsible to exercise restraint'. Haig hastened to reassure the government that the Legion's constitution would not change, and that he felt the 'strength of the organisation' was opposed to such politicisation. Haig's reaction, that he did not want the Legion to behave as a conventional political pressure group, says much about his essential conservatism and his limited vision of his role.[70] Although he took his seat in the Lords and attended some debates, he does not seem to have spoken in the chamber. Fears that he would turn the British Legion into some sort of far-Right paramilitary militia were unfounded.

Haig's post-war efforts on behalf of ex-servicemen brought him a degree of genuine popularity that he had lacked during the war. The army's code of Other Ranks offering deference in exchange for the paternal leadership of officers was replicated in the British Legion, an organisation that similarly laid great store on duty, patriotism and loyalty. Haig was effectively beyond criticism; but, the feelings of many Legion members went beyond mere loyalty. The general public, too, shared the Legion's admiration for his work on behalf of ex-servicemen.

Shortly after Haig's death, the Legion published a piece of doggerel by J.F. McMilan (sic) that depicted Haig as a comrade of the PBI. Two lines read:

He was known as 'Haig, Field Marshal', but up in the old Front line
When he passed that way, you could hear men say, 'Why he's a pal o'
mine'.

This vision of Haig the wartime commander was 'sheer fantasy'. The
author was projecting back to the war years the very different image of
Haig, the British Legion President, who had become in some sense a
comrade of the rank and file. On Haig's death T.F. Lister commented
that the Legion had 'lost a President but gained a Patron Saint'. Bitterness
followed in the decade to come, when Haig's reputation as a commander
and a man came under attack.[71]

Haig regarded himself as having responsibility for ex-soldiers of the
Dominions as well as in Britain. He was influential in the formation of
the British Empire Services League, which was inaugurated at a
conference in Cape Town that he attended in March 1921. The BESL
was intended to bring together the ex-servicemen's organisations across
the Empire. It was clearly seen by Haig as complementing the work of
the Legion in Britain, and he became Grand President. Haig and Doris
then undertook a triumphant tour of South Africa, revisiting some of his
old Boer War battlefields.

The Haigs visited Newfoundland in July 1924, and the following year
they once again crossed the Atlantic to tour Canada; 10,000 people
turned out to see Haig lay the corner stone of a cenotaph in Toronto. In
Canada his speeches had the theme of unity of Empire and ex-
servicemen. He put his immense prestige and authority behind the
creation of a unified ex-serviceman's body, the Canadian Legion.
Privately, Haig was scathing about the lack of leadership given to the
divided Canadian veterans by Currie and Byng (now Governor-General),
seeing them as frightened of gripping the problem.[72] In Canada Doris
taught him to dance. On one occasion, tired of being offered only elderly
ladies as dancing partners, he 'seized the prettiest girl on the boat and
hung on to her for rest of the dance, refusing to give her up'.[73] During a
round of golf in Jasper National Park Haig's game was disturbed by two
bears that appeared on the course to fight over a ball. 'From the
comparative security of the first tee,' *Time* magazine reported, 'the Earl
and his party gazed down upon the struggle, resolutely determining to
play with no bears.'[74]

In November 1925 Haig addressed a dinner presided over by the Canadian High Commissioner. He spoke about the deep impression his visit to Canada had made, and about his vision of a united, self-sufficient empire.[75] With hindsight, we know that this concept of empire was doomed. Haig, however, died before this was evident.

Life was hard for the many veterans of the British army domiciled in the newly independent Irish Free State. They suffered economic discrimination, and sometimes physical intimidation and, unlike their counterparts in the UK, they did not even have the compensation of a sympathetic population. In a state dominated by a narrative of revolutionary struggle against colonial masters, there was no place for such an embarrassing reminder of the degree of Catholic Irish support for the British war effort. Haig's call in 1927 to remember the response of 'thousands of Irishmen to the Empire's call for men' in 1914 caused little stir in the UK, and he publicly regretted 'the inadequate response' to the appeal.[76]

Mourning and Commemoration

Armistice Day, 11 November 1920, was a time for national mourning and reflection. It was marked in London by a major military procession. It might have been one of the displays of pageantry and might of Empire except that, in place of the cheering crowds of the Lord Mayor's Show, the onlookers were subdued. The centre of attention was a gun carriage on which reposed a coffin draped with the union flag. Alongside marched the pall-bearers, high-ranking military officers, Douglas Haig among them. They were followed by ordinary sailors, soldiers and airmen, and behind them ex-servicemen, now in civilian clothes. The Unknown Warrior was on his way to burial in Westminster Abbey.

In the years immediately following the War Britain was in a kind of communal daze at the magnitude of the slaughter – one million British Empire dead, three-quarters from the British Isles. The 1920s and 1930s witnessed the birth of a secular religion of collective commemoration of the dead that may have helped the bereaved to bear their terrible burden by grieving with others. The Unknown Warrior, exhumed from a grave in France or Flanders and interred with great ceremony on Armistice Day, 11 November 1920, allowed the bereaved to hope – to believe with absolute conviction in some cases – that it was their husband, son or brother who was buried in Westminster Abbey.[77]

The Cenotaph in Whitehall, along with local and regimental war memorials across the country, was unveiled with appropriate solemnity and ceremony. These memorials were substitutes for graves, as the dead lay under Imperial War Graves Commission headstones in cemeteries overseas, inaccessible to the vast majority of their families – if indeed they had a named grave. Many youngsters were regularly taken to the local war memorial to see the name of their dead father carved there. The two-minutes silence, instituted in 1919 and observed on 11 November, was a time when people reflected, not on the dead of the Great War in the abstract, but on individuals: absent fathers, brothers and sons.[78]

Armistice Day was the pinnacle of remembrance of the dead of the Great War, but it was one of a large number of rituals and ceremonies aimed in part at helping the bereaved to cope with their loss. In the last decade of his life Haig played an important role in many of these ceremonies of remembrance. He accepted this role, although it was certainly wearing, as one of his duties towards his demobilised army. He hated public speaking, and many of his speeches and writings (such as forewords to regimental histories) were drafted for him by Lieutenant-Colonel J.H. Boraston, his private secretary, and Colonel George Crosfield.[79]

Ceremonies took various forms, but the unveiling of the Household Cavalry memorial in Zandvoorde near Ypres on 4 May 1925 may stand for them all. Following a trumpet fanfare, a clergyman recited the Lord's Prayer. Then Haig made a short, dignified speech in which he paid tribute to the valour and achievements of the Household Cavalrymen in October 1914. As appropriate for a ceremony on Allied soil, he made reference to the bonds between the dead of Britain, Belgium and France. He then performed the act of unveiling, and the clergyman said the words of dedication. The ceremony concluded with the Last Post, two minutes silence, and the national anthems of Britain and Belgium. Later, there was a ceremonial lunch and, later still, a dinner.[80]

Rather different was Haig's visit to Swansea in July 1922. After being made a freeman of the City and reviewing 4,000 ex-servicemen, he laid the foundation stone for the city memorial. For this ceremony he was accompanied by Mrs Gertrude Fewings, the widow of a soldier in the 14th (Swansea) Battalion, Welch Regiment. Mrs Fewings, the mother of five children, had been selected when her name was drawn out of a hat by the mayor, and a reporter crassly congratulated her on her luck in being selected. "Is it luck, I wonder?" Mrs Fewings replied.[81]

Haig was inundated with invitations to unveil memorials and could not accept them all. In 1927 he declined the chance to open the Menin Gate, the enormous and impressive memorial to the Missing of the Ypres Salient. Instead, Plumer performed the ceremony – a highly appropriate choice, which may have influenced Haig's decision, given his regard for the 'old man'.[82] Some ceremonies Haig used to pay tribute to particular specialised groups. These reflected his wide interests and his awareness of the complexity of modern army, and also had the beneficial effect of inclusivity. At the unveiling of the memorial to the 3,719 dead of the London and North-Western Railway Company in October 1921 he quoted some impressive statistics about contribution of railways to the BEF in 1918.[83]

Unveilings of memorials were times of heightened emotion, and some grieving people found the events difficult to bear. Haig unveiled the cenotaph in Glasgow in June 1924, and in 'the one minute's silence that was observed . . . many women fainted. Pathetic scenes were witnessed when wreaths were being laid on the memorial'; some 60 incidents of 'fainting and hysteria' were reported.[84] Yet there seems to have been little enmity to Haig in person at such emotionally charged events. Later generations might be surprised to find that in June 1925 Haig opened the Newfoundland Memorial Park at Beaumont Hamel. This place was where the 1st Newfoundland Regiment attacked on 1 July 1916, taking horrific casualties for no gains whatsoever. Today the Newfoundland Park is much visited by parties of British schoolchildren, most of whom are told (one suspects) by their teachers about the incompetence and callousness of Douglas Haig. That Haig was invited to perform the opening ceremony by the government of Newfoundland speaks volumes about attitudes towards the war and Haig in the mid-1920s.[85]

The whole business of memorialisation was an important part of Haig's activities. It has been argued that speeches that attended the ceremonies of commemoration often attempted to 'understand and interpret the wishes and ideals of the dead' and 'apply them to the post-war world' so that their deaths would continue to have meaning.[86] Such

speeches were not politically neutral. In Haig's speeches there was a
heavy emphasis on the needs of ex-servicemen, on sacrifice, comradeship, patriotism and duty, on the glories of the efforts of regiments during
the war and the consolation of relatives. When unveiling the memorial
to the Cameronians (Scottish Rifles) he said that comfort for the bereaved
could be found in the 'proud story' of the regiment from Mons to the
Armistice 'and in the thought that those who fought and died . . . did not
sacrifice themselves in vain'.[87] There was little on the need to end war.
Rather, he urged that in a future war Britain should never again be as
unprepared as it was in 1914.[88] Haig died shortly before the reaction
against the war had properly begun. Thus he was able to talk of the glory
of war, and of the righteousness of the Great War, in ways that would in
a very short time become deeply unfashionable in a shallowly pacifist
society.

The Battle of the Memoirs

In public Haig said little about the conduct of the war. In June 1919,
however, he defended the decision to offer the Germans an armistice in
November 1918. He acknowledged that after the crushing victory of the
Sambre on 4 November the BEF could have pushed on (although he
hinted at logistic difficulties in doing so), but this would have been at the
cost of 'further loss of life, the destruction of property, and expenditure
of money'. He did not think that the military results would have been
commensurate with the sacrifices, and he was loath to 'spen[d] men's
lives in pursuit of the shadow, when the substance of victory was already
achieved'. He also publicly reflected on Ludendorff's *Memoirs*. He said
that the most striking passage concerned 'the mental distress and
hopelessness of outlook that overcame' Ludendorff when he realised
that 'the great German army had broken to pieces in his hand. That was
an experience that I never had to contemplate . . . [the BEF] would never
break in my hand'.[89] However Haig was not tempted to follow his
former opponent's example of going into print.

   If journalism constitutes the first draft of history, then memoirs form
the second, an important source for historians in the absence of access to
archives. In the two decades following the war, the battle of the memoirs
began, as participants such as Churchill, Lloyd George and Gough strove
to put their stamp on the emerging history of the conflict. Haig,

however, told Foch that he was not 'going to write a book on the war, that it was too soon to tell the truth!'[90]

If Haig had written his memoirs, they would undoubtedly have been commercially very successful. Haig reportedly told the King that he had been offered £100,000 for his memoirs, to which George V replied that if that was so, his would be worth a million![91] Haig's attitude stemmed from a wish to avoid public controversy, for to 'tell the truth' would be to wash dirty linen in public, and he hated to appear as 'an Advertiser', as he once put it.[92] These opinions can only have been reinforced by the uproar caused by the publication of Lord French's tendentious account of his command in France, which further damaged his reputation.

That is not to say that Haig was indifferent to the state of his reputation. Indeed, in his *Final Dispatch* of 21 March 1919, he set out to shape the terms within which the debate would be conducted. It contained a carefully constructed and powerful interpretation of the BEF's operations, designed to pre-empt obvious criticisms. He argued that the fighting on the Western Front from 1914 to 1918 formed 'a single continuous campaign'. The length of the war was the product of factors such as Britain's need to build an army and a war economy from scratch, and thus the inability of the Allies to field their full strength simultaneously; the vicissitudes of coalition warfare; and the impossibility, in the circumstances of approximately equal forces and the absence of flanks to turn, of avoiding a lengthy attritional 'struggle for supremacy'.

The casualties, although heavy, were consequently 'no larger than were to be expected'. The policy of constant offensives was the right one, not least because 'the object of all war is victory, and a purely defensive attitude can never bring about a successful decision'. His strategy of 'ceaseless attrition' was based on the fundamental principles of war, and the battles of 1916 and 1917, which appeared to be 'indecisive', were an essential part of the process of wearing out the enemy. 'If the whole of the operations of the present war are regarded in proper perspective, the victories of the summer and autumn of 1918 will be seen to be directly dependent upon the two years of stubborn fighting that preceded them.'[93]

This case for the defence was skilfully argued and compelling. Much of it has withstood nearly nine decades of criticism. The main weakness lies in the fact that Haig imposed a degree of coherence on events that other evidence, notably his diary, reveals was absent during the years 1916 to 1918. At various times he believed that both the Somme and Third Ypres, for example, would bring decisive success. In the short term, Haig's *Final Dispatch* had relatively little impact on views on the war. Forty years later John Terraine put these arguments at the centre of his controversial and hugely influential rehabilitation of Haig's reputation. More recent historians have been more critical, but in the early twenty-first century a modified version of Haig's 1919 thesis continues to have a major influence on serious debate on the Western Front. One does not have to accept Terraine's argument that Haig was a 'Great Captain', or ignore the extent of Haig's *ex post facto* rationalisation, to recognise the validity of much of the case set out in the *Final Dispatch*.[94]

After the publication of the *Final Dispatch*, Haig chose indirect ways of protecting his reputation, especially against Lloyd George. Sometimes this took the form of private correspondence (and, we can imagine, conversations) with influential people. Thus in August 1919 Haig responded to Lloyd George's speech in Parliament about the war by writing to John St Loe Strachey, the editor of *The Spectator*. Haig argued that 1917 had been the 'most critical period of the war . . . and it was only the continuous attacks of the British Army' that saved the day.[95] In 1920 Haig had Kiggell and Lawrence prepare a 'Memorandum on Operations on the Western Front, 1916–18'. Copies were sent to, among others, the King and Edmonds, the official historian.[96]

Haig also encouraged (although he may not have initiated) the writing of a book that defended him and attacked Lloyd George. 'There is great need for enlightenment. Indeed the current estimate of the part played by the British Army in 1916–1918 is very incorrect,' Haig complained in 1921 to Boraston, 'and I hope your book will completely change it.'[97] Some attacks on Haig's wartime generalship appeared in print in the early 1920s. 'Where Haig went wrong – vast and useless waste of life in the Great War' was the title of one newspaper piece by his old foe Lovat Fraser.[98] Boraston's *Sir Douglas Haig's Command*, co-written with G.A.B. Dewar, appeared in time for the general election in November 1922, in the hope of embarrassing Lloyd George, who had in fact already fallen from power by that time. Boraston and Dewar's book just helped to stoke the furnace – Haig's critics, it claimed, knew as much about military matters as they did about 'the Basque language' – but while Haig was alive, although many reserved judgment on his wartime career, criticism was generally kept within bounds.[99]

Like many other officers, Haig helped Edmonds with the compilation of the multi-volume official history, commenting on drafts and lending a copy of the typescript of his diary. Edmonds was not uncritical of Haig and GHQ in the volumes of the official history. However his criticism tended to be implicit rather than direct, or buried in footnotes – although there are plenty of exceptions to this rule. Haig saw little to disagree with in the drafts that he read, and he approved of Edmonds's discretion in writing: 'I congratulate you on the way in which you have told the story so accurately and yet without attaching blame to anyone'.[100]

Rather more surprisingly, Haig also assisted Winston Churchill in the writing of his history of the war, *The World Crisis*.[101] Churchill included some passages that were highly critical of generalship on the Western Front. Churchill sought expert military advice and Haig proved willing to offer it, sending Churchill extracts from his diaries and commenting on drafts, and Churchill was persuaded to amend his text in some ways. Churchill frankly stated to Haig in November 1926 that he remained 'a convinced and outspoken opponent to our offensive policy at Loos, on the Somme and at Passchendaele' but it is plain that Churchill also admired the victories of the Hundred Days. He admitted privately that his 'subsequent study of the war has led me to think a good deal better of Haig than I did at the time. It is absolutely certain there was no one who could have taken his place'.[102]

Undoubtedly it was in Haig's interest that a bestselling, widely-read and very influential book should to some degree reflect his interpretations, but *The World Crisis* also contained some trenchant criticism of High Command. Although he thought Churchill's views on the Somme and Passchendaele were 'most mischievous', Haig was willing to accept at least some criticism. Unfortunately for Haig's reputation, it is Churchill's criticism of British generalship, rather than his generally positive account of 1918, that is remembered today. In a rare example of the self-analysis that was so noticeably absent from his diary Haig wrote to Churchill

In order to enjoy reading your writings it is not, I find, necessary to agree

with *all* the opinions which you express. And as for criticisms of what I did
or did not do, no one knows as well as I do how far short of the ideal my
own conduct both of the 1st Corps and 1st Army was, as well as of the
B.E.F. when C in C. But I do take credit for this, that it was due to the
decisions which I took in August and September 1918 that the war ended
in Nov . . .[103]

During the early 1920s Haig and Doris carried out the huge task of
typing up and adding to his wartime diary, which he intended to be 'his
personal account of the war' to be published after his death.[104] Naturally,
he wished it to be as complete a record as possible. According to Lady
Haig, there was another reason for Haig's diligence in working on his
diary: it 'was a great godsend to him because it bridged over the difficult
days when his work for the British army was at an end'.[105]

In 1928 a great flood of 'disillusioned' war literature appeared, such
as Siegfried Sassoon's *Memoirs of a Fox-Hunting Man* and Remarque's *All
Quiet on the Western Front*. This opened a new phase of writing about the
war, in which Haig's reputation came under increasingly bitter attack as
the country flirted with pacifism.

Haig did not live to see this happen. His last public act took place on
Saturday, 28 January 1928, when he was guest of honour at a Cub and
Scout rally in Richmond, Surrey. Haig shook hands with each of the boys
– fittingly, they were the sons of British Legion members, the troop being
attached to the Legion Poppy Factory – and then he gave a short speech.
It was full of familiar sentiments: '. . . be courageous . . . Always play the
game. Try to realise what public spirit means . . .'. During his speech
Haig stopped for a moment, 'looking,' Lady Haig remembered, 'deadly
pale', but recovered to finish his peroration. On the night of Sunday, 29
January 1928, while staying with Henrietta and Willie Jameson at their
home, Douglas, First Earl Haig, the 29th Laird of Bemersyde, had a fatal
heart attack. He was 66 years old.[106]

Haig's death came as a shock to the nation and Empire. He had
seemed to be in reasonable health, although just before his death he had
been kicked in the face by a horse while out hunting. Doris had little
doubt about what had killed her husband: the sheer strain of wartime
command had worn out his heart.[107] Mickey Ryan had been concerned
at the punishing peacetime schedule that Haig had imposed on himself.

The press picked up on this. 'Field Marshal a War Victim: death caused by the strain,' ran one headline. 'For a moment,' a columnist wrote, 'it seemed if the war had come back and presented us with another stunning casualty.' The extent of the public's mourning for Earl Haig was remarkable, far greater than occurred after the death of any other British Great War general.[108]

The British do state occasions well, and Haig's funeral was no exception. Haig's body was taken to the church of St Columba, which he attended when in London, where for two days tens of thousands of mourners shuffled, heads bowed, past his coffin. Vast crowds lined the streets on 3 February as the coffin was moved to Westminster Abbey on the gun carriage that had borne the Unknown Warrior in 1920. The King's three sons walked behind. Thus Haig's body was accompanied by two future kings, Edward VIII and George VI. His pall-bearers included two Marshals of France, Foch and Pétain. The funeral service was broadcast live on the BBC, one of the earliest occasions when the nation as a whole was able to participate in a national event via the wireless. On the following Sunday cities, towns and villages throughout the land held remembrance services. Even football matches were affected: on Saturday 4 February many a kick-off was delayed by an act of commemoration.

St Paul's, Wren's great cathedral, was considered as Haig's final resting place, where he would have lain close by Wellington and Nelson, the premier military heroes of the 'Great War' of the previous century. But Haig had asked to be buried at home. The coffin was sent north by rail, where another huge crowd waited in Edinburgh, late at night and in bad weather, to pay their respects. Haig lay in state in St Giles' cathedral, while many more filed past his coffin. The final journey of Douglas Haig was to his beloved Borders, where he was interred in the grounds of Dryburgh Abbey, near Bemersyde. Here he was interred beneath a headstone of the standard Imperial War Graves Commission pattern. The old soldier was dead, his battles long past; but the war of words over his career was about to escalate. In this new conflict Haig's military reputation was to be a major casualty.[109]

Haig the Soldier: An Assessment

Shortly after Haig's death Lieutenant-General Sir Gerald Ellison, who had worked with him on army reform before the First World War, claimed that the late Field Marshal 'combined in quite an unusual degree great administrative capacity with innate powers of command'.[1] The first part of this statement, about Haig the staff officer, is relatively uncontentious. Ellison's view of Haig the commander is anything but.

From the time he entered the army until the time he took I Corps to war in 1914, Douglas Haig barely put a foot wrong. He acquired a balanced ticket of regimental soldiering; operational experience that included both command and staff work; had attended Staff College; and done some formidably demanding staff jobs that put him at the centre of army reform. With a deserved reputation as a high flyer, Haig was an exceptionally dedicated professional in an army that was gradually modernising. Recognising the gravity of the threat posed by Imperial Germany, he was determined to prepare the army for the clash that he believed was inevitable.

Haig added to his standing by his fine performance as a defensive general in October–November 1914, and by his hugely important work in transforming the BEF from a small Regular army to 1918's mass war-winning force. His achievements cannot properly be understood without taking into account his work as an administrator and army reformer. Nonetheless, like it or not, his reputation rests on his performance as a battlefield commander. His generalship on the offensive in 1915–17 remains deeply controversial. Haig strove for a breakthrough without achieving one, but combined this with attrition of the enemy forces which in the end proved to be highly significant. Back on the defensive in 1918, once his sagging morale had recovered, his performance was sound. Then, when the Allies passed onto the offensive in August, he had his best spell as an attacking general; many of the circumstances that had handicapped him in 1915–1917 had changed, and he made a mighty contribution to the Allied victory of November 1918.

Haig's argument in his *Final Despatch* of 1919 was fundamentally correct, in spite of the many caveats that historians want to add (see pp. 363–4). The previous battles had worn down the German army, and this allowed the Allies to deliver the *coup de grâce* during the Hundred Days of August–November 1918. In terms of scale, this was the greatest victory in British military history – and yet the reputation of Haig, the commander of the BEF at this crucial period, remains toxic. It is time to examine the charge sheet against him.

Optimism and Technology

Haig was frequently too optimistic. As he himself effectively admitted, he was a glass half-full rather than a glass half-empty man. Although it is unfair to blame Charteris for feeding Haig intelligence that he thought his boss wanted to hear – both men were optimistic – it is undoubtedly true that Cox was a great improvement as the BEF's intelligence chief. Haig's performance also improved when Lawrence replaced Kiggell as his Chief-of-Staff. Although Kiggell had his merits, he was too self-effacing to be a good foil to Haig. Lawrence was a much more robust character.

There were also at various times apparently sound reasons for optimism. Post-battle analysis of the fighting in 1915 identified problems that, if fixed, promised success next time. But the Germans as well as the BEF were learning, and at the next battle they presented the attackers with different challenges to overcome. Looking to the preparations for the Somme in 1916 we can see the mistakes with awful clarity, but they were not evident to Haig and GHQ at the time. Haig personally bears a large share of the responsibility for the disaster of 1 July, but, as we have seen, the system as a whole (which, for example, failed to accurately assess the success in cutting the German wire) and individuals (notably Henry Rawlinson, who sabotaged Haig's operational design) were also culpable. Likewise Haig deserves censure for the Third Battle of Ypres in 1917 – not so much for his optimism, but for neglecting to curb that of his subordinate, Hubert Gough, by failing to insist during the planning stage that Fifth Army employ the sensible 'stepping stones' method of achieving a breakthrough. Haig's decision to continue the offensive in bad weather after Broodseinde (4 October 1917) was in retrospect, a mistake, but it was understandable in the context of Plumer having just achieved his third remarkable victory in a fortnight.

Successful generals, especially in the First World War, were men with ruthless determination to impose their will on the enemy, who could bear the human cost of their decisions and shoulder a crushing burden of responsibility. In Haig's case, this could on occasions translate into overconfidence, with damaging consequences. Some commanders have had the opposite problem, like Union general George B. McClellan in the American Civil War. President Abraham Lincoln wrote perceptively of 'the Young Napoleon' that he

> had the capacity to make arrangements properly for a great conflict, but as the hour for action approached he became nervous and oppressed with the responsibility and hesitated to meet the crisis.[2]

Haig was a very different sort of man and general, and his willingness 'to meet the crisis' was a huge asset to the Allies. McClellan's timid and pusillanimous conduct as commander of the Army of the Potomac arguably threw away the chance to defeat the Confederacy in 1862. Tellingly, it took the emergence of a very different Union general, Ulysses S. Grant, a man with many Haig-like characteristics, to defeat the Confederate armies in Virginia by waging a series of brutal but effective attritional battles in 1864–65.[3]

Haig's reputation as 'a technophobe with little appreciation of anything that didn't eat hay'[4] rests heavily on post-1918 criticisms by his enemies, which some historians have unwisely followed. We have already seen how Baker-Carr and Liddell Hart successfully tarred Haig as a reactionary on machine-guns and cavalry respectively. By contrast, Trenchard, for much of the war Haig's senior commander of the most technologically advanced arm, the Royal Flying Corps, defended his old chief's reputation to the end of his long life. Another detractor was J.F.C. Fuller, a first-class military intellectual and author of many influential books, who served on the staff of the Tank Corps in 1917–18.

Fuller was a passionate advocate of tanks, which, if provided in sufficient numbers and used in innovative ways, he believed were war-winners. He saw Haig as a barrier to progress. On 2 February 1918 he wrote about Haig and senior generals, who had just witnessed a demonstration of tanks:

> They reminded me of the heathen gods assembled to watch the entry of the new Christian Era. They felt it was better than their own epoch and left determined to destroy it, for it was beyond them, they could never play their part in it. The army is full of vested interests which fight for existence again [sic] what is considered an innovation.[5]

This was a complete misreading of Haig's views on technology and innovation. Haig's diary entry for that day shows that he was impressed by the 'very great development' that had taken place in tank design over the previous year, and his official papers, and his actions, demonstrate that he was keenly aware of the tank's importance. But he had to take into account the well-being of the whole BEF, not just one part of it.[6] Fuller's visionary 'Plan 1919', was not practical politics, not least because it revolved around an 'untested weapon', the Medium D tank. Fuller was inclined to wave away practical difficulties.[7] Haig could not, and the idea that the medium D could have been the centrepiece of a major offensive was unrealistic. The idea that Plan 1919 might have led to a 'swift and resounding military victory', as Fuller's biographer suggested, is wholly unrealistic.[8]

In fact the most potent criticism of Haig's attitude to technology was that he was rather too keen on it. One instance of this had elements of farce, when Haig was taken in by a charlatan who claimed to have invented a death ray, only to be sadly disillusioned.[9] At Loos in September 1915, when he based his plan of attack on the use of poison gas, and at the debut of the tank at Flers-Courcelette almost exactly a year later, Haig expected far too much of untried and unreliable new weapons. Yet these problems need to be weighed in the balance against the fact that Haig, a man born into mid-Victorian Britain, enthusiastically embraced the technology of a new generation and provided powerful institutional backing for tanks, aircraft, advanced artillery techniques and the like. The first aircraft only flew in 1903, but in 1909 Haig was commenting favourably on their military potential. Five years after that, Haig emerged as an influential advocate of air power.

Haig's Learning Process

Central to current argument on the British army in the First World War is the debate on the 'learning curve', better described as the 'learning process'. In recent years the impressive extent to which the BEF learned and applied lessons has been well documented by historians, but what is less clear is the nature of Haig's personal learning process, and his contribution to that of the BEF.

Certain themes were constant in Haig's thinking. He remained committed to the notion that cavalry were usable on the battlefield at two levels: as a strategic / operational tool (broadly, the use of the Cavalry Corps in a semi-independent role) and at a tactical level (the use of cavalry units on the battlefield integrated into an all-arms plan). Closely linked to the latter was the operational concept articulated in 1915 of using all-arms advance guards to broaden and deepen the initial 'bite'. We have seen how Haig's ideas on these matters evolved over time, as he tried to learn from experience. There is also evidence of continuity. For example, his idea of using infantry transported in buses to accompany the cavalry surfaced at the time of Loos in 1915 and reappeared during the Hundred Days in 1918.

Some examples of learning and applying lessons were negative, that is trying something that did not work. Poison gas, the centrepiece of Haig's plans for Loos, never had such prominence again, although he remained keen to integrate chemical weapons into the BEF's weapons system. After Aubers Ridge in 1915 he abandoned the idea of hurricane artillery bombardments, although these were to reappear in late 1917. Other examples were positive. By introducing regular conferences with his Army commanders when he became C-in-C, Haig established an important means of exchanging information and views and team-building, avoiding the remoteness that had characterised the latter stages of Sir John French's time at GHQ.

The core of the case against Haig can be summed up in one word: casualties. Battles on the Western Front were invariably bloody, and some of his decisions were undoubtedly poor and helped to swell the casualty lists. However, his scope for keeping casualties low was limited.

It just wasn't that sort of war. Haig's strategy recognised that Germany was the main enemy, that the Western Front was the main theatre, and victory required that the Allies mass men and resources in France and Flanders to fight the German army there. Political imperatives, not least that of coalition warfare, dictated offensive action. The idea that Haig eschewed an obviously better approach to operations by ignoring 'step-by-step' operations in favour of breakthrough has been discussed – and discounted – above. During the Somme, and arguably until the end of the war, the BEF was incapable of conducting any sort of offensive operations that were economical in human lives.

Attrition was the key: wearing down the enemy's army by destroying its manpower and breaking its morale. Haig never deviated from that basic understanding. From early in the war he identified some of the factors that were to prove the keys to victory in 1918: the need to fight on a broad front; the necessity of having artillery in abundance, especially heavy guns; the desirability of shifting the main point of attack from sector to sector. Haig may have pinpointed what was necessary, but until the middle of 1918 the tools were simply not available. There was insufficient artillery to attack on a very wide front. As a result, in 1917 a huge amount of effort was spent in moving heavy guns from sector to sector. There was nothing wrong with his idea in 1916 of opening a second front at Ypres if the Somme offensive slowed – in theory: switching from sector to sector was to be an important facet of operational success in the Hundred Days of 1918. But in mid-1916 it was beyond the capabilities of the British army's transport and logistic system. Haig had to learn the logistic art of the possible.

Morale lay at the heart of Haig's style of generalship. If attrition was designed in large part to grind down the enemy's morale, the largely unspoken assumption was that the British soldier's morale would hold up, despite the enormous losses. He continually underestimated the morale of the German army, seizing upon local and temporary examples of low spirits and extrapolating from them that the enemy army's willingness to fight was about to collapse. Likewise, Haig read too much into intelligence suggesting poor morale on the German home front. He did not factor any decline in British morale into his plans. And yet there are some other important factors that need to be properly considered. The fact is that the British army's morale and discipline did remain substantially intact through out the war, while in 1918 that of the German army suffered a crisis that severely degraded its ability to fight effectively. That is not to argue that British morale remained at a constantly high level – it did not – but when it mattered Haig's troops proved to have depths of stamina and resolve that saw them through. Haig understood the importance of the paternalism of the officer corps in maintaining morale. He took a calculated risk in his offensive strategy, that the BEF's morale would survive, while German morale would crumble. On both counts, he was eventually proved right.

An obvious plank on which to build the case that Haig failed to learn from his experience is his consistent pursuit of the breakthrough. From 1915 to the end of the war, it could be argued, he planned operations designed to rupture the enemy front, reopen mobile warfare, and achieve ambitious goals, whether it be the capture of territory or the destruction of German forces. The fact that time after time he failed to attain these objectives did not deter him from trying again. Loos, the Somme, Passchendaele, Cambrai – there was a steady pattern of ambitious planning followed by disillusionment.

There is some truth in this, but only some. Haig did not plan exclusively for breakthrough. In the planning for the Somme and Third Ypres, for example, he fully recognised that it might take a period of fighting to capture key objectives and wear out the enemy before the breakthrough came. In the latter case he cautioned against Gough's extreme ideas of achieving a breakthrough, adding some sensible advice about what should be done first. Haig has been heavily criticised for planning for success. But had he *failed* to plan for success, he would have been guilty of neglecting his duty. Sound military planning encompasses a range of contingencies. Haig always bore in mind the truth that trench warfare was a temporary phase brought about by unusual tactical conditions that would at some point revert to a more 'normal' state. He can fairly be criticised for being taken in by false dawns, but it is unjust to take him to task for carrying out contingency planning.

Indeed, Haig's continued belief that the mobile battlefield would reassert itself was a great strength. His constant battle to prevent his resources of mounted forces draining away, although only partially successful, did ensure that the BEF had a bare minimum of cavalry that proved indispensable in 1918. His refusal to abandon his belief that the deadlock could be broken and military victory was possible was an invaluable counterbalance to the gloomy assessments in other quarters in 1917–18. When in the summer of 1918 Henry Wilson was thinking of victory in 1919 or 1920, Haig correctly recognised that the German army could be defeated by the end of the year. Haig undoubtedly deserved criticism for his earlier unwarranted optimism, but he has received much less credit than he deserves for the positive impact of his confidence in victory in 1918. In large part this was Haig's own fault, having cried wolf so often in the past.

A much more convincing line of attack than an obsession with the breakthrough is that Haig, despite understanding how a multi-formation battle should be fought, failed to bring about 'joined-up' operations. This was especially true of the Somme, but it also applied to the early stages of Third Ypres. Haig's comments to Rawlinson during the Somme show that he knew perfectly well that a battle of that size should be properly co-ordinated, and yet liaison was often poor between Fourth and Reserve Armies, and even between corps and divisions within Armies. Haig was at fault for offering advice rather than giving firm orders, just as he did during the planning stages of Third Ypres. Advice, no matter how good, is useless if it is not acted upon. In short, Haig lacked grip. The picture of the dysfunctional pre-war army to be found in some accounts is greatly overdrawn, but in this case the critics have a point: the army itself as well as the individual was at fault. The command culture was consensual, with the judgment of the man on the spot accorded much respect. Such a system had many advantages, but in this case it had a downside. Haig proved incapable of breaking out of the cultural cage and start giving orders rather than merely offering suggestions.

Matters did improve over time. In the conditions of the Hundred Days in 1918, when operations could be widely separated in time and space, GHQ played a critical role in sequencing offensives. Haig's comment to Wilson in September 1918 that 'we have a surprisingly large number of *very capable* generals' is significant. During the Hundred Days Haig's subordinates needed less supervision than in previous campaigns, and his direct interventions grew fewer. As in so many other matters, a mixture of hard-won experience and the promotion of competent officers allowed the BEF to improve its performance.

Haig and Best Practice

War is a collaborative activity. As Commander-in-Chief, Haig presided over an organisation that examined its own performance in a way that became increasingly sophisticated as time progressed. This complicates the task of assessing Haig himself, since it is difficult to disentangle his personal learning process from that of the wider BEF. One of his underrated but important roles was to nurture best practice. This could take the form of simple acquiescence, of not interfering when things were going well, but he often took a proactive role. He took determined action to influence the BEF's training and tactics – two matters at the very heart of the learning curve. He also had a role in the significant artillery reorganisation carried out by Major-General J.F.N Birch, the senior gunner at GHQ, in November 1916. 'Curly' Birch's initiative was taken to address the problem that the Somme fighting had underlined: Haig needed a field artillery reserve. This would save wear and tear on the divisional batteries, and build in a welcome degree of flexibility. This was Birch's initiative, but Haig provided important 'top cover'.[10] To this example could be added Haig's staunch support of Eric Geddes, whose root-and-branch reorganisation of the BEF's transport system in the winter of 1916–17 was of vital importance, and his encouragement of air power, machine-guns and tanks.

One of the most impressive actions on the Somme was the capture of Thiepval on 26 September 1916 by Major-General Ivor Maxse's 18th (Eastern) Division. Maxse had a deserved reputation as one of the best trainers in the British army, and the rigorous preparation of the division undoubtedly contributed to 18th Division's success on 1 July 1916, when as part of XIII Corps it had taken all its objectives. Both commander and division were singled out as highly effective and subsequently picked to carry out various tough assignments. 18th Division was moved to II Corps, commanded by Claud Jacob with Haig's protégé Philip Howell as his Chief of Staff, a combination that was gaining a deserved reputation for competence. 18th Division was given time to bed in before the attack at Thiepval. Both Haig and Gough stood back from the planning process, making little effort to intervene; the obvious inference is that they trusted their subordinates. Carefully planned, prepared and executed, the attack finally delivered Thiepval, an objective on 1 July, into British hands. General Palat, a future French official historian, saw Thiepval as 'the end of the British army's apprenticeship'.[11]

Haig was impressed. He visited II Corps HQ on the afternoon of 27 September and then went on to personally congratulate Maxse. Referring to the disaster at Étreux in 1914, for which he held Maxse partly responsible, Haig wrote that '[i]n view of what he has done with his Division, I think his misdeeds as a Brigadier at the beginning of the war should be forgotten'. Maxse published an account of the action, which also contains a good deal of material on doctrine and lessons learned, and it seems to have been quite widely disseminated. It confirmed the importance of *FSR*, which would have appealed to Haig. For Maxse, rewards came quickly. At the beginning of January 1917 he was promoted to lieutenant-general and knighted; more important was his appointment to command XVIII Corps later that month, which was a true mark of Haig's approbation. The Thiepval episode shows Haig encouraging and promoting best practice. It was an important part of his role as C-in-C.

Haig's battles in 1916–17 – the Somme, Arras, Third Ypres – played a vital role in eviscerating the enemy, and in the Hundred Days the BEF led the way in defeating the Imperial German army in the field. Yet this was not the most significant thing that Haig achieved. In 1940 the novelist John Buchan, who had served at GHQ, wrote a pen-picture of the Commander-in-Chief. Although Buchan liked Haig and regarded him as a 'highly competent professional soldier,' he argued that soldiering was 'a closed technique'. Changes therefore came 'by the sheer pressure of events after much tragic trial and error. Haig was as slow to learn as any of his colleagues and he made grave mistakes. But he did learn'.[12] Buchan's masterclass in damning with faint praise was grossly unfair. Haig did indeed make 'grave mistakes', but his record in learning and innovation was commendable. Reviewing recent work, a leading American historian, Andrew Wiest, has argued that 'Haig remains central to the story of the transformation of the BEF'.[13] He is right. Haig was not peripheral to the process. He was essential to it. Transforming the British army on the Western Front was one of his greatest achievements.

Haig's Legacy

Strangely, in spite of his successes on and off the battlefield, Haig's immediate legacy for the post-1918 British army was limited. The army was a different organisation after the post-Boer War reforms, it is true, although the army that went to war in 1939 had many of the problems, faults and bad habits of its ancestor. As Haig and most other soldiers believed, the huge army of the Western Front had been an aberration never likely to recur. In the 1920s another war on the scale of 1914–1918 seemed a remote prospect. In any case, the army was doing other things, having switched from waging a world war to fighting small wars without pausing for breath. With troops heavily committed to conflicts in Ireland, Afghanistan, Palestine, Egypt, Mesopotamia and sundry other outposts of Empire, the experience of the Western Front did not seem very relevant to the here and now. Practical soldiers, including Haig himself, were focused on the very different challenges of brushfire wars and insurgencies. It was not until 1932 that an official report on the lessons of the First World War was issued. Even then, few imagined that another world war would begin by the end of the decade.

Conversely, Haig had a major influence on the British army that fought the Second World War. This was not because of his beloved cavalry. In the mid-1920s cavalry did seem to have a place in order of battle in the British army, but by 1939 things had moved on. The process of mechanising the cavalry had moved far more swiftly than had seemed possible 15 years earlier, and on the outbreak of Hitler's war it was all but complete. Even so, Haig's influence on British politicians and generals in the Second World War was powerful, pervasive – and negative. Put simply, there was a general feeling of 'no more Passchendaeles'. Britain would never – Britain *could* never – fight another campaign in the style of the Western Front from 1915 to 1918. Government and people would not stand for it. Fate decreed that for the British army, the Second World War followed a very different path from the First. Britain was able to avoid heavy attritional fighting on the pattern of 1915–18, although this was largely through good luck. There was plenty of bloody combat for the Poor Bloody Infantry up at the sharp end, at places like Alamein, Kohima, Normandy and Cassino, and loss rates sometimes equalled or exceeded those of 1914–18. But there were fewer men involved for shorter periods of time, and so overall British casualties were much lower.

The generals of the Second World War had mostly been junior officers in the First. Reaction against Haig led some, in the desert in

1941–2, to try almost anything to avoid attrition. This attempt at manoeuvre warfare failed time after time against a skilful enemy. It was not until Bernard Montgomery took over as Eighth Army commander in August 1942, and introduced a modified, updated version of the attritional methods of 1918, that success returned to British arms. Neither Haig, not any other First World War commander, received any credit for this. Instead Montgomery presented himself as a sort of anti-Haig, a general who delivered victory at an acceptable cost in British Empire lives. He was prepared to incur heavy losses, but only if he felt that the objective was truly worth it. In place of the piecemeal attacks that too often characterised Western Front battles, Montgomery amassed overwhelming combat power and landed 'colossal cracks' on the enemy. And of course Montgomery portrayed himself as 'Monty', a People's General for a people's war, with an informal style of leadership radically different from Haig's. Montgomery and many other generals avoided any suggestion of 'chateau generalship' by being seen close to the front line (advances in radio technology made it possible for them to leave headquarters and still practise command – something that was nearly impossible for Haig). They dressed informally and behaved towards their troops like politicians electioneering. The rejection of Haig by the generation of high commanders that followed him seemed complete. It has coloured perceptions of Haig to this day.[14]

Haig was a man of his era. He was a Victorian, yet all too often he is judged by the standards of later times. His virtues and values are not held in high regard by modern society, while a reserved, austere personality like Haig's is out of fashion in the confessional celebrity culture of today. His style of leading his army was made obsolete seventy years ago by the 'People's Generals', in the Second World War. Above all, Haig's strategy, like those of other Great War generals of all nationalities, implicitly accepted that there would be very heavy losses among his own troops. To the casualty-intolerant twenty-first century, this is callous disregard for human life. All this points to an obvious conclusion: Douglas Haig was not a modern man, and he should not be judged as if he was. Just like any other historical figure, whether Julius Caesar, King Henry VIII, or the Duke of Wellington, he should be examined in the context of his own times, his own society, his own culture. 'The past is a foreign country: they do things differently there'.[15]

With the centenary of 1914 rapidly approaching, it is high time to stop regarding the First World War as current affairs and Douglas Haig as our contemporary. Both the war and the man need to be placed in the historical context in which they belong. Only if this is done can Haig's true historical significance be properly assessed. His mistakes were outweighed by four achievements. *First*, before 1914 Haig took a leading part in reforming the army and preparing it for a major war. *Second*, between 1916 and 1918 he played a major role in transforming the BEF into a war-winning army, and *third*, Haig's generalship was a vital component in the Allied victory. *Fourth*, extending his military paternalism into civilian life, Haig's post-war leadership of ex-servicemen provided a crucial element of political and social stability in dangerously volatile times.

Douglas Haig might not have been the greatest military figure Britain has ever produced, but he was one of the most significant – and one of the most successful.

Afterword

The reception of the hardback edition of *The Chief* was highly gratifying. Given the controversial subject matter, it perhaps shows that there is a greater degree of open-mindedness towards the military history of the First World War than was the case a few years ago. In that sense, one of my principal objectives in writing *The Chief* has gone some way to being achieved: I wanted Douglas Haig to be discussed as an historical figure like another. It remains to be seen, however, how he will be treated in the media extravaganza that will undoubtedly accompany the centenary of the Great War which as I write this, is just over two years away.

Since the book went to press some important new books relevant to the study of Douglas Haig have appeared. Among others, David Stevenson's *With Our Backs to the Wall* (Allen Lane, 2011) is a magisterial book which provides important context for the last year of the war, as well as some incisive insights; the title is of course taken from Haig's famous order of the day of 11 April 1918. Elizabeth Greenhalgh's *Foch in Command : The Forging of a First World War General* (Cambridge University Press, 2011) is a stimulating study that intersects with Haig's story at some key places; and Jonathan Boff's forthcoming *Winning and Losing on the Western Front: British Third Army and the Defeat of Germany, 1918* (Cambridge University Press, 2012), apart from being an excellent study of one of Haig's Armies in the Hundred Days, provides a valuable comparative element, looking at both sides of No Mans' Land.

Every author knows the strange affliction which sometimes makes you write 'left' instead of 'right', and the accompanying fog before the eyes which means that you don't spot the mistake until the finished book is in your hand. I have taken the opportunity to correct some typos and minor mistakes in the text that managed to slip through the original editorial process. It did not prove possible to correct three of them in the main body of the book, so they are mentioned here. As my PhD student Mr Stuart Mitchell pointed out, on p.185 I was mistaken in saying that the raid that the 11th Borders were ordered to carry out actually went ahead. In reality, it was subverted by the battalion's NCOs, and was eventually cancelled by an officer. Also on p.367 I inadvertently mislaid several sons of King George V, who had five male offspring, not three. On p.335, I followed previous historians in stating that the photograph of Haig and his top team on 11 November 1918 was taken at the Mairie in Cambrai. In fact, Mr Michael Orr, who has walked the ground, tells me that it was actually taken on the steps of a late-Victorian bourgeois house in central Cambrai. Finally, in the footnotes I make reference to Badsey (2008). This book was inadvertently omitted from the bibliography, and the full reference reads: Stephen Badsey, *Doctrine and Reform in the British Cavalry 1880–1918* (Aldershot: Ashgate, 2008).

Belatedly, I can offer thanks to three people who did pre-university work experience with me and helped with the research, but were unaccountably omitted from the acknowledgements in the hardback: my godson, Michael Bird; Isaac Harland; and James Mabbett. It was a pleasure to work with all three of them. I also forgot to mention Lord Snooty, who proved invaluable at various times during the writing of the book. I would also like to thank Liz Somers of Aurum for her exemplary work on publicity. Finally, I would like to thank a number of historians whose opinions on the First World War are worth listening to, who, unprompted, privately said or wrote some very kind things about my scholarship.

Completing this book took place against the background of a particularly challenging set of circumstances, and I'd like to reiterate my thanks to my family and friends for their love and support. At Birmingham, I could not ask for a better set of colleagues than my fellow military historians, to which Dr Jonathan Boff has been a recent and very welcome addition. Having embraced twenty-first century communications technology, I can be followed on Twitter @ProfGSheffield, and my website is garysheffield-historian.com.

Wantage
Holy Week 2012

Sources and Select Bibliography

NB: All books published in London unless stated. Where a subsequent edition has been used, the date of the original publication is shown in square brackets. Books and articles are cited in the endnotes by a short title, which is given at the beginning of the entry in the bibliography.

PRIMARY SOURCES

Unpublished
Australian War Memorial
AWM 34
AWM 45
AWM 51

Bodleian Library, Oxford
Asquith papers

Bovington Tank Museum
Fuller papers
Lindsay papers

Cambridge University Library
University archives

Churchill College, Cambridge
Cavan papers
Churchill papers
Duff Cooper papers
Esher papers
Hankey papers
Rawlinson papers

Houghton Hall
Sassoon papers

Imperial War Museum
Butler papers   PP/MCR/107
Boraston papers   71/13/1–3
Fletcher papers   96/7/1
French papers   75/46/6
Hedley papers   96/7/1
Horne papers
Loch papers   71/12/4
Maxse papers   69/53/8
Price-Davies papers   77/78/1
Thompson papers   69/73/1
Wedgwood papers   PP/MCR/104
Wilson papers

Joint Services Command and Staff College Library
Montgomery-Massingberd papers
Miscellaneous documents

Liddell Hart Centre for Military Archives, King's College London
Clive papers
Grant papers
Edmonds papers
Howell papers
Maurice papers
Montgomery-Massingberd papers

Liverpool Record Office
Derby papers

National Archives (formerly Public Record Office)
CAB 23
CAB 24
CAB 42
CAB 45
CAB 63
WO 32
WO 95
WO 158
WO 256 (Haig papers including Typescript Diary)

National Army Museum
Ellison papers
Rawlinson papers

National Library of Scotland
Curle papers
Haig Papers
Lawrence papers

NB: The Haig papers are being recatalogued, but are currently listed in NLS guide as Acc.3155. For simplicity, in the footnotes, references are to Haig Papers (HP) followed by the box and (if appropriate) piece number, e.g. HP/322a. The Manuscript diary is in HP/96 and 97; the typescript diary in HP/98 to 136; Haig's letters to Henrietta in HP/6b; Haig's wartime letters to Lady Haig in HP/141 to 153.

Parliamentary Archive
Lloyd George papers
Strachey papers

Privately held
Ryan papers
Royal Archives, Windsor Castle

Scott Polar Research Institute, Cambridge
Scott–Haig correspondence

Published
Cavalry Training 1907
Cavalry Training 1929
Field Service Regulations, Part II, 1909
Parliamentary Debates
Royal Commission on the War in South Africa (HMSO, 1903)

Newspapers and Magazines
British Legion Journal
Current History
Daily Mirror
New York Times
The Scotsman
Sunday Pictorial
The Times
Time

Collections of Documents
Beach (2010)   Jim Beach (ed.), *The Military Papers of Lieutenant-Colonel Sir Cuthbert Headlam 1910–1942* (Stroud: The History Press for the ARS, 2010).
Beckett (1993)   Ian F.W. Beckett, *The Judgement of History: Sir Horace Smith-Dorrien, Lord French and '1914'* (Tom Donovan, 1993)
Beddington   Edward Beddington, *My Life* (privately published, 1960).
Bickersteth   John Bickersteth (ed.) *The Bickersteth Diaries 1914–18* (London: Leo Cooper, 1998 [1995])
Blake   Robert Blake (ed.), *The Private Papers of Douglas Haig 1914–1919* (Eyre and Spottiswoode, 1952)
Boraston   J.H. Boraston (ed.) *Sir Douglas Haig's Despatches* (J.M. Dent, 1979 [1919])
Brett   Maurice V. Brett, *Journals and Letters of Reginald, Viscount Esher* (Ivor Nicolson & Watson, 4 vols, 1934, 1938)
Briscoe   Diana Briscoe (ed.), *The Diary of a World War I Cavalry Officer* (Tunbridge Wells, Costello, 1985)

Coates   Tim Coates, *The World War I Collection: Gallipoli and the Early Battles, 1914–15* (HMSO, 2001)

Craster   J.M. Craster, *Fifteen Rounds A Minute: The Grenadiers At War, August to December 1914* (Macmillan, 1976)

DeGroot (1997)   Gerard J. DeGroot, *The Reverend George S. Duncan at GHQ, 1916–1918* in Alan J. Guy et al., *Military Miscellany* I (Stroud: Sutton Publishing for ARS, 1997)

Dutton (2001)   David Dutton (ed.) *Paris 1918: The War Diary of the British Ambassador, the 17th Earl of Derby* (Liverpool: Liverpool UP, 2001)

Gilbert   Martin Gilbert (ed.) *Winston S Churchill: Volume V, Companion Documents, Part 1 (1924–29)* (Heinemann, 1979)

Godfrey   Rupert Godfrey (ed.) *Letters from a Prince* (Little, Brown, 1998).

Gordon Lennox   Lady Algernon Gordon Lennox (ed.) *The Diary of Lord Bertie of Thame, 1914–1918* 2 vols (Hodder & Stoughton, 1924).

Jeffery (1985)   Keith Jeffery (ed.), *The Military Correspondence of Field Marshal Sir Henry Wilson 1918–1922* (Bodley Head for the ARS, 1985)

McNaughton   A.G.L. McNaughton, 'The Capture of Valenciennes'.

NB: This was a lecture originally given in 1933 and printed in about 1940 by the Canadian authorities with four other of his articles. In libraries, it is probably listed under the title of the first article, 'The Development of Artillery in the Great War'.

Maurice, N.   Nancy Maurice (ed.) *The Maurice Case* (Leo Cooper, 1972)

Morris (1999)   A.J.A. Morris (ed.), *The Letters of Lieutenant-Colonel Charles à Court Repington* (Stroud: Sutton for ARS, 1999)

Perry   Nicholas Perry, *Major-General Oliver Nugent and the Ulster Division 1915–1918* (Stroud: Sutton for ARS, 2007)

Repington (1920)   Charles à Court Repington, *The First World War* 2 vols (Constable, 1920) [Repington's diary]

Richter (1997)   Donald C. Richter (ed.), *Lionel Sotheby's Great War* (Athens OH: Ohio UP, 1997)

Riddell   Lord Riddell, *Lord Riddell's War Diary 1914–1918* (Ivor Nicolson & Watson, c. 1933)

Robbins (2009)   Simon Robbins (ed.) *The First World War Letters of General Lord Horne* (Stroud: History Press for ARS, 2009)

Roynon   Gavin Roynon (ed.) *Massacre of the Innocents: The Crofton Diaries 1914–1915* (Stroud: Sutton, 2004)

Scott   Douglas Scott, *Douglas Haig: The Preparatory Prologue 1861–1914* (Barnsley: Pen and Sword, 2006)

Seymour   Charles Seymour (ed.) *The Intimate Papers of Colonel House,* 4 vols (Ernest Benn, 1928).

Sheffield and Bourne (2005)   Gary Sheffield and John Bourne (eds), *Douglas Haig: War Diaries and Letters 1914–1918* (Weidenfeld & Nicolson, 2005)

Statistics   *Statistics of the Military Effort of the British Empire During the Great War 1914–1920* (HMSO, 1922)

Taylor   A.J.P. Taylor (ed.) *Lloyd George: A Diary by Frances Stevenson* (Hutchinson, 1971)

Terraine (1984)   John Terraine, *The Road to Passchendaele* (Leo Cooper, 1984 [1977])

Terraine (2000)   John Terraine (ed.) *General Jack's Diary* (Cassell, 2000 [1964])

Wessels (2000)   André Wessels (ed.), *Lord Roberts and the War in South Africa 1899–1902* (Stroud: Sutton Publishing for ARS, 2000)

Wilson (1970)   Trevor Wilson (ed.) *The Political Diaries of C.P. Scott 1911–1928* (Collins, 1970)

Woodward (1989)   David R. Woodward, *The Military Correspondence of Field-Marshal Sir William Robertson, Chief of the Imperial General Staff December 1915–February 1918* (Bodley Head for ARS, 1989)

Memoirs, contemporary and near-contemporary material

Adye   John Adye, *Soldiers and Others I have Known* (Jenkins, 1925)

Amery (1953)   L.S. Amery, *My Political Life* Vol. II (Hutchinson, 1953)

Anderson   J.H. Anderson, *The Campaign of Jena 1806* (Hugh Rees, 1913)

Arthur   Sir George Arthur, *Lord Haig* (Heinemann, 1928)

Askwith   Lord Askwith, 'Haig at Oxford', *The Oxford Magazine* 23 Feb. 1928.

Atkinson (1927)   C.T. Atkinson, *The Seventh Division 1914–1918* (London: John Murray, 1927)

Atkinson (1952)   C.T. Atkinson, *The Royal Hampshire Regiment,* II, *1914–1918* (Glasgow: UP, 1952)

Baden-Powell   Lord Baden-Powell, *Lessons from the Varsity of Life* (1933) at www.pinetreeweb.com/bp-vars.htm

Baker-Carr   C.D. Baker-Carr, *From Chauffeur to Brigadier* (Ernest Benn, 1930)

Barrow (1942)   Sir George Barrow, *The Fire of Life* (Hutchinson, 1942)

Bell   G.K.A. Bell, *Randall Davidson, Archbishop of Canterbury*, vol. I (Oxford: OUP, 1935)

Bewsher   F.W. Bewsher, *The History of the 51st (Highland) Divisions 1914–1918* (Edinburgh and London: Blackwood, 1921)

Birdwood   Lord Birdwood, *Khaki and Gown* (Ward Lock, 1941)

Boraston and Bax   J.H. Boraston and Cyril E.O. Bax, *The Eighth Division 1914–1918* (Medici Society, 1926)

Brunker   H.M.E. Brunker, *Story of the Jena Campaign, 1806* (Forster Groom, 1913)

Buchan   John Buchan, *Memory Hold-The-Door* (Hodder and Stoughton, 1940)

Charteris (1931)   John Charteris, *At GHQ* (Cassell, 1931)

Churchill   Winston S. Churchill, *The World Crisis*, 2 vols (Odhams, 1938 [5 vols 1923–31]),

Coop   J.O. Coop, *The Story of the 55th (West Lancashire) Division* (Liverpool: 'Daily Post' Printers, 1919)

Croft   [Henry Page] Lord Croft, *My Life of Strife* (Hutchinson, n.d. *c.* 1948)

Dewar and Boraston   George A.B. Dewar, assisted by J.H. Boraston, *Sir Douglas Haig's Command 1915–1918*, 2 vols (Constable, 1922)

Dudley Ward   C.H. Dudley Ward, *The Fifty Sixth Division 1914–1918* (John Murray, 1921)

Duncan   G.S. Duncan, *Douglas Haig As I Knew Him* (Allen & Unwin 1966)

Dunn   J.C. Dunn, *The War the Infantry Knew* (London: Jane's, 1987 [1938])

Elton   O. Elton, *C.E. Montague, A Memoir* (Chatto & Windus, 1929)

Falls   Cyril Falls, *The History of the 36th (Ulster) Division* (Belfast: M'Caw, Stevenson & Orr, 1922)

French, J.   Viscount French of Ypres, *1914* (Constable, 1919)

Fuller   J.F.C. Fuller, *Generalship: Its Diseases and Their Cure. A Study of*

the Personal Factor in Command (Harrisburg, PA: Military Service Publishing, 1936)

Gale   Richard Gale, *Call to Arms* (London: Hutchinson, 1968)

Gibbs   Philip Gibbs, *Realities of War* (Heinemann, 1920)

Godley   Alexander Godley, *Life of an Irish Soldier* (John Murray, 1939)

Gough (1931)   Hubert Gough, *The Fifth Army* (Hodder and Stoughton, 1931)

Gough (1954)   Hubert Gough, *Soldiering On* (Arthur Barker, 1954)

Greaves   Sir George Greaves, *Memoirs of General Sir George Richards Greaves* (John Murray, 1924)

'G.S.O.'   [Sir Frank Fox], *GHQ (Montreuil-Sur-Mer)* (Philip Allan, 1920)

Haig (1907)   Douglas Haig, *Cavalry Studies* (Hugh Rees, 1907)

Haig (1919)   Sir Douglas Haig, *A Rectorial Address Delivered to the Students of the University of St Andrews, 14th May 1919* (St Andrews: Henderson, 1919)

Haig, Lady   The Countess Haig, *The Man I Knew* (Edinburgh and London: Moray Press, 1936)

Harington (1940)   Sir Charles Harington, *Tim Harington Looks Back* (John Murray, 1940)

Head   Charles O. Head, *No Great Shakes: An Autobiography* (Robert Hale, 1943)

Heavy Gunner   'A Heavy Gunner Looks Back', in *Twenty Years After*, vol. I (George Newnes, *c.* 1938)

Huguet   V. Huguet, *Britain and the War: A French Indictment* (Cassell, 1928)

Joffre   Joseph Joffre, *The Memoirs of Marshal Joffre*, 2 vols (Geoffrey Bles, 1932)

Keith-Falconer   Adrian Keith-Falconer, *The Oxfordshire Hussars in the Great War (1914–1918)* (London: John Murray, 1927)

Kincaid-Smith   M. Kincaid-Smith, *The 25th Division in France and Flanders* (Harrison, *c.* 1919)

Lloyd George   David Lloyd George, *War Memoirs* (Odhams, n.d., 2-vol. ed.)

Ludendorff   Erich Ludendorff, *My War Memories 1914–18*, 2 vols (Uckfield; Naval and Military Press, 2005 [1919])

Lytton   Neville Lytton, *The Press and the General Staff* (Collins, 1921)

MacMunn   Sir George MacMunn, *Behind the Scenes in Many Wars* (John Murray, 1930)

Maydon   J.G. Maydon, *French's Cavalry Campaign* (Pearson, 1901)

Monash   Sir John Monash, *The Australian Victories in France in 1918* (Hutchinson, 1920)

Montgomery   A.A. Montgomery, *The Story of the Fourth Army in the Battles of the Hundred Days* (Hodder and Stoughton, 1920)

Murray-Philipson   Nina Murray-Philipson, *Colonel Standfast: The Memoirs of W.A. Tilney 1868–1947* (Norwich: Michael Russell, 2001)

Needham   E.J. Needham, *The First Three Months* (Aldershot: Gale & Polden, n.d.)

Pagan   A.W. Pagan, *Infantry* (Aldershot: Gale & Polden, 1951)

Repington (1919)   Charles à Court Repington, *Vestigia* (Constable, 1919)

Sandilands   H.R. Sandilands, *The 23rd Division 1914–1919* (Edinburgh: Blackwood, 1925)

Secrett   Thomas Secrett, *Twenty-Five Years with Earl Haig* (Jarrolds, 1929)

Slim   William Slim, *Defeat into Victory* (Cassell, 1956)

Sparrow   W. Shaw Sparrow, *The Fifth Army in March 1918* (Lane, 1921)

Spears (1939)   Edward Spears, *Prelude to Victory* (London: Cape, 1939)

Spears (2000)   Edward Spears, *Liaison 1914* (Cassell, 2000 [1930])

Sykes   Sir Frederick Sykes, *From Many Angles: An Autobiography* (Harrap, 1942)

Vaughan   John Vaughan, *Cavalry and Sporting Memories* (Bala Press, 1954)

Willcocks   Sir John Willcocks, *With the Indians in France* (Constable, 1920)

Windsor   The Duke of Windsor, *A King's Story* (London, Reprint Society, 1953 [1951])

Wood   Sir Evelyn Wood, *Winnowed Memories* (Cassell, 1918)

Wylly   H.C. Wylly, *A Short History of the Cameronians (Scottish Rifles)* (Aldershot: Gale & Polden, 1924)

Wynne (1934)   G.C. Wynne, 'The Other Side of the Hill: No. 12 The Night Attack at Landrecies: 25th August 1914', *AQ*, 28, 34 (1934)

SECONDARY SOURCES

Official Histories

(AOH)   C.E.W. Bean (ed.) *Official History of Australia in the War of 1914–1918* (12 vols, 1920–42)

Volumes are referred to in the notes by year and volume e.g. AOH 1917 IV. All volumes referred to in this book were written by Bean.

(OH)   J.E. Edmonds (ed.) *Military Operations, France and Belgium,* (14 vols, 1922–48)

Volumes are referred to in the notes by year and volume e.g. OH 1914 I. OH 1915 I was co-written by Edmonds and G.C. Wynne; OH 1916 II was written by Wilfred Miles; OH 1917 I by Cyril Falls; OH 1917 III by Miles; OH 1918 V co-written by Edmonds and R. Maxwell-Hyslop. All other volumes were written by Edmonds.

Books

Adam Smith   Janet Adam Smith, *John Buchan* (Rupert Hart-Davis, 1965)

Andrew   Christopher Andrew, *Secret Service: The Making of the British Intelligence Community* (William Heinemann, 1985)

Anglesey (1986)   The Marquess of Anglesey, *A History of the British Cavalry* Vol. 4 *1899–1913* (Leo Cooper, 1986)

Anglesey (1997)   The Marquess of Anglesey, *A History of the British Cavalry*, vol. 8 *The Western Front 1915–1918* (Leo Cooper, 1997)

Ascoli   David Ascoli, *The Mons Star* (Harrap, 1981)

Ash   Eric A. Ash, *Sir Frederick Sykes and the Air Revolution 1912–1918* (Routledge, 1999)

Ash B.   Bernard Ash, *The Lost Dictator* (Cassell, 1968)

Ashworth   Tony Ashworth, *Trench Warfare 1914–1918* (Macmillan, 1980)

Astore and Showalter   William J. Astore and Dennis E. Showalter, *Hindenburg: Icon of German Militarism* (Dulles VA: Potomac Books, 2005)

Babington   Anthony Babington, *For the Sake of Example* (Leo Cooper, 1983)

Barr (2005)   Niall Barr, *The Lion and the Poppy: British Veterans, Politics and Society, 1921–1939* (Westport CT: Praeger, 2005)

Barrow (1931)   Sir George Barrow, *The Life of General Sir Charles Carmichael Monro* (Hutchinson, 1931)

Baynes   John Baynes, *Far From a Donkey: The Life of General Sir Ivor Maxse* (Brassey's, 1995)

Beckett (1989)   Ian F.W. Beckett, *Johnnie Gough V.C.* (Tom Donovan, 1989)

Beckett (2003)   Ian F.W. Beckett, *The Victorians at War* (Hambledon, 2003)

Beckett (2004)   Ian F.W. Beckett, *Ypres The First Battle, 1914* (Pearson, 2004)

Beckett and Corvi   Ian F.W. Beckett and Steven J. Corvi, *Haig's Generals* (Barnsley: Pen & Sword, 2006)

Beckett and Simpson   Ian F.W. Beckett and Keith Simpson, *A Nation in Arms* (Manchester: Manchester UP, 1985)

Bell   P.M.H. Bell, *France and Britain 1900–1940: Entente & Estrangement* (Longman, 1996)

Bessel   Richard Bessel, *Germany after the First World War* (Oxford: Clarendon, 1995 [1993])

Best   Geoffrey Best, *Churchill and War* (Hambledon, 2005)

Boemeke, Chickering and Förster (1999)   Manfred F. Boemeke, Roger Chickering and Stig Förster (eds), *Anticipating Total War* (Cambridge: Cambridge UP, 1999)

Bond (1999)   Brian Bond *et al.*, *'Look To Your Front': Studies in the First World War* (Staplehurst: Spellmount, 1999)

Bond and Cave (1999)   Brian Bond and Nigel Cave (eds), *Douglas Haig: A Reappraisal 70 Years On* (Leo Cooper, 1999)

Bourne (1989)   J.M. Bourne, *Britain and the Great War 1914–1918* (Edward Arnold, 1989)

Bourne (2001)   J.M Bourne, *Who's Who in World War One* (Routledge, 2001)

Bristow   Adrian Bristow, *A Serious Disappointment* (Leo Cooper, 1995)

Brown   Ian Malcolm Brown, *British Logistics on the Western Front 1914–1919* (Westport CT and London: Praeger, 1998)

Callwell (1927)   C.E. Callwell, *Field Marshal Sir Henry Wilson: His Life and Diaries*, 2 vols (Cassell, 1927)

Cannadine (1994)   David Cannadine, *Aspects of Aristocracy* (New Haven and London: Yale UP, 1994)

Cannadine (2000)   David Cannadine, *Class in Britain* (Penguin, 2000 [1998])

Cassar (1977)   George H. Cassar, *Kitchener: Architect of Victory* (Kimber, 1977)

Cassar (1985)   George H. Cassar, *The Tragedy of Sir John French* (Cranbury NJ: Associated University Presses, 1985)

Cassar (2004)   George Cassar, *Kitchener's War – British Strategy from 1914 to 1916* (Washington DC: Potomac Books, 2004)

Cave and Sheldon   Nigel Cave and Jack Sheldon, *Le Cateau* (Pen and Sword, 2008)

Chandler and Beckett   David Chandler and Ian Beckett (eds), *The Oxford Illustrated History of the British Army* (Oxford: Oxford UP, 1994)

Charteris (1929)   John Charteris, *Field-Marshal Earl Haig* (Cassell, 1929)

Clark   Alan Clark, *The Donkeys* (Hutchinson, 1961)

Clifford   Colin Clifford, *The Asquiths* (London: John Murray, 2002)

Cobb   Paul Cobb, *Fromelles 1916* (Stroud: Tempus, 2007)

Colley   Linda Colley, *Britons: Forging the Nation 1707–1837* (Pimlico, 1994 [1992]).

Connelly   Mark Connelly, *We Can Take It! Britain and the Memory of the Second World War* (Longman/Pearson, 2004)

Cook (1999)   Tim Cook, *No Place to Hide: The Canadian Corps and Gas Warfare in the First World War* (Vancouver: UBC Press, 1999)

Cook (2007)   Tim Cook, *At the Sharp End: Canadians Fighting the Great War 1914–1916* (Toronto: Viking Canada, 2007)

Cook (2008)   Tim Cook, *Shock Troops: Canadians Fighting the Great War 1917–1918* (Toronto: Viking Canada, 2008)

Corfield   Robin S. Corfield, *Don't Forget Me, Cobber: The Battle of Fromelles* (Carlton, Vic.: Miegunyah Press, 2009 [2000])

Cornish   Paul Cornish, *Machine Guns and the Great War* (Barnsley: Pen & Sword, 2009)

Corrigan   Gordon Corrigan, *Loos: The Unwanted Battle* (Stroud: Spellmount, 2006)

Cruttwell   C.R.M.F. Cruttwell, *A History of the Great War* (Oxford: Clarendon Press, 1936)

Dallas and Gill   Gloden Dallas and Douglas Gill, *The Unknown Army: Mutinies in the British Army in World War I* (Verso, 1985)

Danchev   Alex Danchev, *Alchemist of War: The Life of Basil Liddell Hart* (Weidenfeld & Nicolson, 1998)

Davidson   J. Davidson, *Haig: Master of the Field* (Peter Nevill, 1953)

Dawson   Graham Dawson, *Soldier Heroes: British Adventure, Empire and the Imagining of Masculinities* (Routledge, 1994)

DeGroot (1988)   Gerard J. DeGroot, *Douglas Haig 1861–1928* (Unwin Hyman, 1988).

d'Ombrain   Nicholas d'Ombrain, *War Machinery and High* Policy (Oxford: Oxford UP, 1973)

Doughty   Robert A. Doughty, *Pyrrhic Victory: French Strategy and Operations in the Great War* (Cambridge MA: Belknap Press, 2005)

Doyle   Peter Doyle, *Geology of the Western Front, 1914–1918* (Geologist's Association, 1998)

Duff Cooper   A. Duff Cooper, *Haig*, 2 vols (Faber and Faber, 1935 and 1936)

Duffy   Christopher Duffy, *Through German Eyes: The British on the Somme* (Weidenfeld & Nicolson, 2006)

Dutton   David Dutton, *The Politics of Diplomacy: Britain and France in the Balkans in the First World War* (I.B. Tauris, 1998)

Edmonds   J.E. Edmonds, *A Short History of World War I* (Oxford UP, 1951)

Essame   H. Essame, *The Battle for Europe 1918* (Batsford, 1972)

Evans   Richard J. Evans, *The Coming of the Third Reich* (2003)

Faber   David Faber, *Speaking for England* (Pocket Books, 2007 [2005])

Falls (1939)   Cyril Falls, *Marshal Foch* (London and Glasgow: Blackie, 1939)

Falls (1960)   Cyril Falls, *The First World* War (Longmans, 1960)

Farndale   Sir Martin Farndale, *History of the Royal Regiment of Artillery*, vol. I *Western Front, 1914–18* (Royal Artillery Institution, 1986)

Farrar-Hockley (1967)   Anthony Farrar-Hockley, *Death of an Army* (Arthur Barker, 1967)

Farrar-Hockley (1975)   Anthony Farrar-Hockley, *Goughie* (Hart-Davis, McGibbon, 1975)

Foley (2005) Robert T. Foley, *German Strategy and the Path to Verdun* (Cambridge: Cambridge UP, 2005)

Fraser (1973) Peter Fraser, *Lord Esher: A Political Biography* (Hart-Davis, McGibbon, 1973)

Freedman *et al.* Lawrence Freedman, Paul Hayes and Robert O'Neill (eds), *War, Strategy and International Politics* (Oxford: Clarendon Press, 1992)

French (1995) David French, *The Strategy of the Lloyd George Coalition 1916–1918* (Oxford: Clarendon Press, 1995)

French (2000a) David French, *Raising Churchill's Army* (Oxford: Oxford UP, 2000)

French and Holden Reid (2002) David French and Brian Holden Reid (eds), *The British General Staff: Reform and Innovation, 1890–1939* (Cass, 2002)

French, G Gerald French, *The Life of Field-Marshal Sir John French* (Cassell, 1931)

Fuller, J.G. J.G. Fuller, *Troop Morale and Popular Culture* (Oxford: Clarendon Press, 1990)

Gaffney Angela Gaffney, *Aftermath: Remembering the Great War in Wales* (Cardiff: University of Wales Press, 1998)

Gardner (2003) Nikolas Gardner, *Trial by Fire. Command and the British Expeditionary Force in 1914* (Praeger, 2003),

Gilbert Martin Gilbert, *World in Torment: Winston S. Churchill 1917–1922* (Mandarin, 1990 [1975])

Gooch (1974) John Gooch, *The Plans of War: The General Staff and British Military Strategy c. 1900–1916* (Routledge, 1974)

Gooch (1981) John Gooch, *The Prospect of War* (Cass, 1981)

Green Andrew Green, *Writing the Great War: Sir James Edmonds and the Official Histories 1915–1948* (Cass, 2003)

Greenhalgh (2005) Elizabeth Greenhalgh, *Victory Through Coalition: Britain and France During the First World War* (Cambridge: Cambridge UP, 2005)

Gregory Adrian Gregory, *The Last Great War: British Society and The First World War* (Cambridge: Cambridge UP, 2008)

Griffith (1992) Paddy Griffith, *Battle Tactics of the Western Front* (New Haven CT and London: Yale UP, 1994)

Griffith (1996)   Paddy Griffith (ed.), *British Fighting Methods in the Great War* (Cass, 1996)

Griffiths   Richard Griffiths, *Marshal Pétain* (Constable, 1994 [1970])

Grigg   John Grigg, *Lloyd George: War Leader* (Penguin, 2002)

Hammond (2008)   Bryn Hammond, *Cambrai 1917: The Myth of the First Great Tank Battle* (Weidenfeld & Nicolson, 2008)

Harington (1935)   Charles Harington, *Plumer of Messines* (John Murray, 1935)

Harris (1995)   J.P. Harris, *Men, Ideas and Tanks* (Manchester: Manchester UP, 1995)

Harris (2008)   J.P. Harris, *Douglas Haig and the First World War* (Cambridge: Cambridge UP, 2008)

Harris and Barr   J.P. Harris with Niall Barr, *Amiens to the Armistice* (Brassey's 1998)

Harrison   Mark Harrison, *The Medical War: British Military Medicine in the First World War* (Oxford: Oxford UP, 2010)

Hart, S   Stephen Hart, *Montgomery and 'Colossal Cracks': The 21st Army Group in Northwest Europe, 1944–45* (Westport CT: Praeger, 2000).

Hart   Peter Hart, *The Somme* (Weidenfeld & Nicolson, 2005)

Høiback   H. Høiback, *Command and Control in Military Crisis: Devious Decisions* (Cass, 2003),

Holden Reid (1987)   Brian Holden Reid, *J.F.C. Fuller: Military Thinker* (Macmillan, 1987)

Holmes (1981)   Richard Holmes, *The Little Field Marshal: Sir John French* (Cape, 1981)

Hooton   E.R. Hooton, *War Over the Trenches: Air Power and the Western Front Campaigns 1916–1918* (Hersham, Midland, 2010).

Hughes   Colin Hughes, *Mametz: Lloyd George's 'Welsh Army' at the Battle of the Somme* (Gliddon Books, 1990)

Hughes (1999)   Matthew Hughes, *Allenby and British Strategy in the Middle East 1917–1919* (Cass, 1999)

Hughes and Seligmann   Matthew Hughes and Matthew Seligmann (eds), *Leadership in Conflict 1914–1918* (Leo Cooper, 2000)

Hull   Isabel V. Hull, *Absolute Destruction: Military Culture and the Practices of War in Imperial Germany* (Ithaca NY: Cornell UP, 2005)

Jackson   Stanley Jackson, *The Sassoons* (Heinemann, 1989 [1968])

James   Lawrence James, *Imperial Warrior: The Life and Times of Field-Marshal Viscount Allenby 1861–1936* (Weidenfeld & Nicolson, 1993)

Jeffery (1984)   Keith Jeffery, *The British Army and the Crisis of Empire 1918–22* (Manchester: Manchester UP, 1984)

Jeffery (2006)   Keith Jeffery, *Field Marshal Sir Henry Wilson* (Oxford: Oxford UP, 2006)

Judd and Surridge   Denis Judd and Keith Surridge, *The Boer War* (Murray, 2002)

King   Alex King, *Memorials of the Great War in Britain* (Oxford: Berg, 1998)

Kramer   Alan Kramer, *Dynamic of Destruction: Culture and Mass Killing in the First World War* (Oxford: Oxford UP, 2007)

Lee, J. (2009)   John Lee, *The Gas Attacks Ypres 1915* (Pen & Sword, 2009)

Lee, R.   Roger Lee, *The Battle of Fromelles 1916* (Canberra: Army History Unit, 2010)

Lellenberg   Jon Lellenberg, Daniel Stashower and Charles Foley (eds), *Arthur Conan Doyle – A Life in Letters* (HarperPress, 2007)

Liddell Hart   B.H. Liddell Hart, *The Tanks*, 2 vols (Cassell, 1959)

Liddle (1997)   Peter H. Liddle, (ed.) *Passchendaele in Perspective: The Third Battle of Ypres* (Barnsley: Pen & Sword, 1997)

Lloyd, D.   David W. Lloyd, *Battlefield Tourism: Pilgrimage and the Commemoration of the Great War in Britain, Australia and Canada, 1919–1939* (Oxford: Berg, 1998)

Lloyd (2006)   Nick Lloyd, *Loos 1915* (Stroud: Tempus, 2006)

Lowry   Bullit Lowry, *Armistice 1918* (Kent, OH and London: Kent State UP, 1996)

Lupfer   Timothy T. Lupfer, *The Dynamics of Doctrine* Leavenworth Paper No. 4 (Fort Leavenworth KS, Combat Studies Institute, US Army Command and General Staff College, 1981)

McCarthy (1993)   Chris McCarthy, *The Somme: The Day-by-Day Account* (Arms and Armour, 1993)

MacDonald   Alan MacDonald, *Pro Patria Mori: The 56th (1st London) Division at Gommecourt, 1st July 1916* (Liskeard: Exposure Press, 2006)

Macmillan   Margaret Macmillan, *Peacemakers* (John Murray, 2003 [2001])

McMullin   Ross McMullin, *Pompey Elliott* (Melbourne: Scribe, 2002)

McPherson   James M. McPherson, *Tried By War: Abraham Lincoln as Commander in Chief* (New York: Penguin, 2009 [2008]

Marble   Sanders Marble, '*The Infantry Cannot Do With a Gun Less*': *The Place Of Artillery in the BEF 1914–18* (Gutenberg-e books, 2001)

Maurice (1928)   Frederick Maurice, *The Life of Lord Rawlinson of Trent* (Cassell, 1928)

Mead   Gary Mead, *The Good Soldier: The Biography of Douglas Haig* (Atlantic, 2007)

Messenger (2005)   Charles Messenger, *Call to Arms: The British Army 1914–18* (Weidenfeld and Nicolson, 2005)

Messenger (2008)   Charles Messenger, *The Day We Won the War* (Weidenfeld and Nicolson, 2008)

Middlebrook (1971)   Martin Middlebrook, *The First Day on the Somme* (Allen Lane, 1971)

Middlebrook (1978)   Martin Middlebrook, *The Kaiser's Battle* (Allen Lane, 1978)

Middlebrook M & M.   Martin and Mary Middlebrook, *The Somme Battlefields* (Penguin, 1991)

Millman (2001)   Brock Millman, *Pessimism and British War Policy 1916–18* (Cass, 2001)

Neiberg (2003)   Michael S. Neiberg, *Foch: Supreme Allied Commander in the Great War* (Dulles VA: Brassey's, 2003)

Neiberg (2008)   Michael S. Neiberg, *The Second Battle of the Marne* (Bloomington IN: Indiana UP, 2008)

Neillands   Robin Neillands, *The Death of Glory* (John Murray, 2006)

Neilson (1984)   Keith Neilson, *Strategy and Supply: The Anglo-Russian Alliance 1914–17* (Allen & Unwin, 1984)

Oram   Gerard Christopher Oram, *Military Executions in World War I* (Basingstoke: Palgrave, 2003)

Palazzo   Albert Palazzo, *Seeking Victory on the Western Front* (Lincoln NB and London: University of Nebraska Press, 2000)

Palmer   Alan Palmer, *The Salient: Ypres, 1914–18* (Constable, 2007)

Passingham (1998)   Ian Passingham, *Pillars of Fire: The Battle of Messines Ridge June 1917* (Stroud: Sutton, 1998)

Passingham (2008)   Ian Passingham, *The German Offensives of 1918* (Barnsley: Pen & Sword, 2008)

Pedersen (1992)   P.A. Pedersen, *Monash as Military Commander* (Melbourne, Melbourne UP, 1992)

Philpott (1996)   William Philpott, *Anglo-French Relations and Strategy on the Western Front, 1914–18* (Basingstoke, Macmillan, 1996)

Philpott (2009)   William Philpott, *Bloody Victory: The Sacrifice on the Somme and the Making of the Twentieth Century* (Little, Brown, 2009)

Pollock (2001)   John Pollock, *Kitchener* (Constable, 2001)

Prior (1983)   Robin Prior, *Churchill's World Crisis as History* (Croom Helm, 1983)

Prior (2009)   Robin Prior, *Gallipoli – The End of the Myth* (New Haven CT and London: Yale UP, 2009)

Prior and Wilson (1992)   Robin Prior and Trevor Wilson, *Command on the Western Front* (Oxford: Blackwell, 1992)

Prior and Wilson (1996)   Robin Prior and Trevor Wilson, *Passchendaele: The Untold Story* (New Haven CT and London: Yale UP, 1996)

Prior and Wilson (2005)   Robin Prior and Trevor Wilson, *The Somme* (New Haven CT and London: Yale UP 2005)

Pugh (2006)   Martin Pugh, *Hurrah for the Blackshirts!: Fascists and Fascism in Britain Between the Wars* (Pimlico, 2006 [2005])

Pugh (2008)   Martin Pugh, *'We Danced All Night': A Social History of Britain Between the Wars'* (Bodley Head, 2008)

Pugsley   Christopher Pugsley, *The Anzac Experience* (Auckland: Reed, 2004)

Putkowski and Sykes   Julian Putkowski and Julian Sykes, *Shot at Dawn* (Barnsley: Wharncliffe, 1989)

Rawling   Bill Rawling, *Surviving Trench Warfare* (Toronto: University of Toronto Press, 1992)

Reese   Peter Reese, *The Flying Cowboy* (Stroud: Tempus, 2006)

Reid   Walter Reid, *Douglas Haig: Architect of Victory* (Edinburgh: Birlinn, 2006)

Richter (1992)   Donald Richter, *Chemical Soldiers* (Lawrence KS: University Press of Kansas, 1992)

Robbins (2005)   Simon Robbins, *British Generalship on the Western Front 1914–18* (Abingdon: Cass, 2005)

Robbins (2010)   Simon Robbins, *British Generalship during the Great War: The Military Career of Sir Henry Horne (1861–1929)* (Farnham: Ashgate, 2010)

Rose   Kenneth Rose, *King George V* (Macmillan, 1984 [1983])

Roskill   Stephen Roskill, *Hankey: Man of Secrets*, vol. I (Collins: 1970)

Rothstein   Andrew Rothstein, *The Soldiers' Strikes of 1919* (Journeyman, 1985 [1980])

Samuels   Martin Samuels, *Command or Control? Command, Training and Tactics in the British and German Armies, 1888–1918* (Cass, 1995)

Schreiber   Shane Schreiber, *Shock Army of the British Empire: The Canadian Corps In The Last 100 Days Of The Great War* (Westport CT: Praeger, 1997)

Sheffield (1997)   G.D. Sheffield (ed.), *Leadership and Command: The Anglo-American Military Experience since 1861* (Brassey's, 1997)

Sheffield (2000)   G.D. Sheffield, *Leadership in the Trenches: Officer–Man Relations, Morale and Discipline in the British Army in the Era of the Great War* (Macmillan, 2000).

Sheffield (2001)   Gary Sheffield, *Forgotten Victory: The First World War – Myths and Realities* (Headline, 2001)

Sheffield (2004)   Gary Sheffield, *The Somme* (London: Cassell, 2004 [2003])

Sheffield and Todman   Gary Sheffield and Dan Todman (eds), *Command and Control on the Western Front: The British Army's Experience 1914–18* (Staplehurst: Spellmount, 2004)

Sheldon (2005)   Jack Sheldon, *The German Army on the Somme* (Barnsley: Pen & Sword, 2005)

Sheldon (2007)   Jack Sheldon, *The German Army at Passchendaele* (Barnsley: Pen & Sword, 2007)

Sibley   David Sibley, *The British Working Class and Enthusiasm for War, 1914–1916* (Abingdon: Cass, 2005)

Simkins (1988)   Peter Simkins, *Kitchener's Army* (Manchester: Manchester UP, 1988)

Simkins (1991)   Peter Simkins, *World War I 1914–1918: The Western Front* (Godalming: CLB Publishing, 1991)

Simpson (1995)   Andy Simpson, *The Evolution of Victory* (Tom Donovan, 1995)

Simpson (2006)   Andy Simpson, *Directing Operations: British Corps Command on the Western Front 1914–18* (Stroud: Spellmount, 2006)

Sinclair   Joseph Sinclair, *Arteries of War* (Shrewsbury: Airlife, 1992)

Sixsmith   E.K.G. Sixsmith, *Douglas Haig* (Weidenfeld and Nicolson, 1976)

Smout   T.C. Smout, *A Century of the Scottish People 1830–1950* (Collins, 1986)

Snape (2005)   Michael Snape, *God and the British Soldier* (Abingdon: Routledge, 2005)

Snape (2008)   Michael Snape, *The Royal Army Chaplains' Department 1796–1953* (Woodbridge: Boydell, 2008)

Spiers (1980)   Edward M. Spiers, *Haldane: an Army Reformer* (Edinburgh, Edinburgh UP, 1980)

Spiers (1986)   Edward M. Spiers, *Chemical Warfare* (Macmillan, 1986)

Spiers (1992)   Edward M. Spiers, *The Late Victorian Army 1868–1902* (Manchester: Manchester UP, 1992)

Spiers (1998a)   Edward M. Spiers (ed.), *Sudan: The Reconquest Reappraised* (Cass, 1998)

Stanley (2009)   Peter Stanley, *Men of Mont St Quentin: Between Victory and Death* (Carlton North, Vic.: Scribe, 2009)

Stanley (2010)   Peter Stanley, *Bad Characters: Sex, Crime, Mutiny, Murder and the Australian Imperial Force* (Millers Point, NSW: Pier 9, 2010)

Stansky   Peter Stansky, *Sassoon: The Worlds of Philip and Sybil* (New Haven and London: Yale UP, 2003)

Steel and Hart   Nigel Steel and Peter Hart, *Passchendaele: The Sacrificial Ground* (Cassell, 2000)

Stephenson   David Stephenson, *1914–1918: The History of the First World War* (Allen Lane, 2004)

Stephenson, S.   Scott Stephenson, *The Final Battle: Soldiers of the Western Front and the German Revolution of 1918* (Cambridge: Cambridge UP 2009)

Strachan (1997)   Hew Strachan, *The Politics of the British Army* (Oxford: Clarendon Press, 1997)

Strachan (2001)   *To Arms* (Oxford: Oxford UP, 2001)

Suttie   Andrew Suttie, *Rewriting the First World War: Lloyd George, Politics and Strategy 1914–18* (Basingstoke: Palgrave, 2005)

Swettenham   John Swettenham, *To Seize the Victory: The Canadian Corps in World War I* (Toronto: Ryerson, 1965)

Taylor, J.   James W. Taylor, *The 2nd Royal Irish Rifles in the Great War* (Dublin: Four Courts Press, 2005)

Terraine (1963)   John Terraine, *Douglas Haig: The Educated Soldier* (Hutchinson, 1963)

Terraine (1980)   John Terraine, *The Smoke and the Fire: Myths and Anti-Myths of War 1861–1945* (Sidgwick & Jackson, 1980)

Terraine (1986)   John Terraine, *To Win a War: 1918 the Year of Victory* (Macmillan, 1986 [1978])

Terraine (1991)   John Terraine, *Mons: The Retreat to Victory* (Leo Cooper, 1991 [1960])

Thompson   J. Lee Thompson, *Northcliffe: Press Baron in Politics 1865–1922* (Murray, 2000)

Todman (2005)   Dan Todman, *The Great War: Myth and Memory* (Hambledon and London, 2005)

Travers (1987)   Tim Travers, *The Killing Ground: The British Army, the Western Front and the Emergence of Modern Warfare 1900–1918* (Unwin-Hyman, 1987)

Travers (1992)   Tim Travers, *How the War Was Won: Command and Technology in the British Army on the Western Front 1917–1918* (Routledge, 1992)

Trewin   Ion Trewin, *Alan Clark: The Biography* (Weidenfeld & Nicolson, 2009)

Trythall   Anthony John Trythall, *'Boney' Fuller: Soldier, Strategist and Writer* (Baltimore MD: Nautical and Aviation Publishing Company of America, 1989 [1977])

Turner   John Turner, *British Politics and the Great War* (Newhaven, CT, Yale UP, 1992)

Tyng   Sewell Tyng, *The Campaign of the Marne* (Yardley PA: Westholme, 2007 [1935])

Walker   Jonathan Walker, *The Blood Tub: General Gough and the Battle of Bullecourt, 1917* (Staplehurst: Spellmount, 1998)

Warner   Philip Warner, *Field Marshal Earl Haig* (Bodley Head, 1991)

Watson   Alexander Watson, *Enduring the Great War: Combat, Morale and Collapse in the German and British Armies, 1914–1918* (Cambridge: Cambridge UP 2008)

Wiest (1995)   Andrew A. Wiest, *Passchendaele and the Royal Navy* (Westport CT: Greenwood, 1995)

Wiest (2005)   Andrew A. Wiest, *Haig: The Evolution of a Commander* (Dulles VA, Brassey's, 2005)

Williams, J.   Jeffery Williams, *Byng of Vimy* (Leo Cooper, 1992 [1983])

Williamson   Samuel R. Williamson Jr, *The Politics of Grand Strategy* (Ashfield Press, 1990 [1969]), p. 363

Wilson (1986)   Trevor Wilson, *The Myriad Faces of War* (Cambridge: Polity, 1986)

Winter, D.   Denis Winter, *Haig's Command: A Reassessment* (Viking, 1991)

Winter, J (2006)   Jay Winter, *Remembering War: The Great War Between Memory and History in the Twentieth Century* (New Haven and London: Yale UP, 2006)

Woodward (1998)   David R. Woodward, *Field Marshal Sir William Robertson* (Westport CT and London: Praeger, 1998)

Woollcombe   Robert Woollcombe, *The First Tank Battle: Cambrai 1917* (Barker, 1967)

Wootton   Graham Wootton, *The Official History of the British Legion* (Macdonald and Evans, 1956)

Wynne   G.C. Wynne, *If Germany Attacks* (Faber and Faber, 1940)

Yockelson   Mitchell A. Yockelson, *Borrowed Soldiers: Americans Under British Command, 1918* (Norman OK: University of Oklahoma Press, 2008)

Zabecki   David T. Zabecki, *The German 1918 Offensives* (Abingdon: Routledge, 2006)

Articles

Anglim   S.J. Anglim, 'Haig's Cadetship – A Reassessment', *BAR* (1992)

Badsey (1996)   Stephen Badsey, 'Cavalry and the Development of the Breakthrough Doctrine' in Griffith (1996)

Badsey (1999)   Stephen Badsey, 'Haig and the Press', in Bond and Cave

Badsey (2006)   Stephen Badsey, 'The Politics of High Command: Rank, Authority, and Power During The Battle of the Somme 1916', unpublished paper (2006)

Badsey (2006a)   Stephen Badsey, 'Could the Battle of the Somme Have Been Won'? (Unpublished paper, 2006)

Barr (2004)   Niall Barr, 'Command in the Transition from Mobile to Static Warfare, August 1914 to March 1915' in Sheffield and Todman

Barr and Sheffield   Niall Barr and Gary Sheffield, 'Douglas Haig, the Common Soldier, and the British Legion' in Bond and Cave

Beckett (1985)   Ian F.W. Beckett, 'The Territorial Force' in Beckett and Simpson

Beckett (1999)   Ian F.W. Beckett, 'Hubert Gough, Ian Malcolm and Command on the Western Front' in Bond (1999)

Beckett (ODNB1)   Ian F.W. Beckett, 'Greaves, Sir George Richards', *ODNB*.

Beckett (2000)   Ian F.W. Beckett, 'King George V and his Generals', in Hughes and Seligmann

Boff   Jonathan Boff, 'Combined Arms during the Hundred Days Campaign, August–November 1918', *WiH*, 17,4, 2010

Bond (1997)   Brian Bond, 'Passchendaele: Verdicts, Past and Present' in Liddle (1997)

Bourne (1997)   J.M. Bourne, 'British Generals in the First World War' in Sheffield (1997)

Bourne (1999)   J.M. Bourne, 'Haig and the Historians' in Bond and Cave.

Bourne (2006)   John Bourne, 'Charles Monro' in Beckett and Corvi

Bryant   P. Bryant, 'The Recall of Sir John French' 3 parts, *ST!*, nos. 22, 23, and 24 (1988)

Buckley   Suzann Buckley, 'The Failure to Resolve the Problem of Venereal Disease among the Troops in Britain During World War I', in Brian Bond and Ian Roy (eds) *War and Society: A Yearbook of Military History*, vol. 2 (Croom Helm, 1977)

Bushaway (2004)   Bob Bushaway, 'Haig and the Cavalry', *JCFWWS*, 1, 1 (2004)

Cave (1999)   Nigel Cave, 'Haig and Religion', in Bond and Cave (1999)

DeGroot (1986)   Gerard J. DeGroot, 'Educated Soldier or Cavalry Officer?: Contradictions in the Pre-1914 Career of Douglas Haig', *W&S* 4 (1986)

Echevarria   Antulio J. Echevarria II, 'Combining Firepower and Versatility: Remaking the "Arm of Decision" before the Great War', *JRUSI* (2002)

Farr   Martin Farr, '"Squiff", "Lliar George" and "The McKennae": The Unpersuasive Politics of Personality in the Asquith Coalition, 1915–1916' in Richard Toye and Julie Gottlieb, *Making Reputations* (I.B. Tauris, 2005)

Foley (2007)   Robert T. Foley, 'The Other Side of the Wire: The German Army in 1917', in Peter Dennis and Jeffrey Grey, *1917: Tactics, Training and Technology* (Canberra: Australian History Military Publications, 2007)

French (1986)   David French, 'Official but not History'? Sir James Edmonds and the Official History of the Great War', *JRUSI*, 131, 1, (1986)

French (1988)   David French, 'The Meaning of Attrition, 1914–1916', *EHR* 103,407 (1988)

French (1992)   David French, "Who Knew What and When? The French Army Mutinies and the British Decision to Launch the Third Battle of Ypres" in Freedman *et al.*

French (1996)   David French, 'Failures of Intelligence: The Retreat to the Hindenburg Line and the March 1918 Offensive' in Michael Dockrill and David French (eds), *Strategy and Intelligence: British Policy During the First World War* (Hambledon, 1996)

French (2000)   David French, 'The Strategy of Unlimited Warfare? Kitchener, Robertson, and Haig', in Roger Chickering and Stig Forster (eds), *Great War, Total War: Combat and Mobilization on the Western Front, 1914–1918* (Cambridge: Cambridge UP, 2000)

Gardner (2006)   Nikolas Gardner, 'Julian Byng' in Beckett and Corvi.

Gillings   Ken Gillings, 'The Utilisation of Artillery Fire During the Battle of Spioenkop and the Introduction of Indirect Fire', *JSAHR* 87, 350, (2009)

Goulter   Christina J.M. Goulter, 'The Royal Naval Air Service: A Very Modern Force', in Sebastian Cox and Peter Gray, *Air Power History: Turning Points from Kitty Hawk to Kosovo* (Cass, 2002)

Greenhalgh (2004)   Elizabeth Greenhalgh, 'Myth and Memory: Sir Douglas Haig and the Imposition of Unified Command in March 1918', *JMilH* 68 (2004)

Grieves (1999)   Keith Grieves, 'The Transportation Mission to GHQ, 1916', in Bond and Cave

Hagenlucke   Heinz Hagenlucke, 'The German High Command' in Liddle (1997)

Hammond (1995)   Bryn Hammond, 'General Harper and the Failure of 51st (Highland) Division at Cambrai, 20 November 1917' *Imperial War Museum Review* No. 10 (1995)

Harris and Marble   Paul Harris and Sanders Marble, 'The "Step by Step" Approach: British Military Thought and Operational Method on the Western Front, 1915–1917', *WiH* 15, 1 (2008)

Holden Reid (1992)   Brian Holden Reid, *War Studies at the Staff College 1890–1930* (Camberley, SCSI Occasional Paper 1, 1992)

Howard (1986)   Michael Howard, 'Men Against Fire: The Doctrine of the Offensive in 1914' in Peter Paret (ed.) *Makers of Modern Strategy from Machiavelli to the Nuclear Age* (Oxford, Clarendon Press, 1986)

Howard (1997)   Michael Howard, 'Leadership in the British Army in the Second World War', in Sheffield (1997)

Hughes (2006)   Matthew Hughes, 'Edmund Allenby' in Beckett and Corvi

Hussey (1991)   'Saving Johnny French: Haig's Loan in 1899', *AQ* 121 (3), (1991)

Hussey (1994)   John Hussey, 'A Hard Day at First Ypres – The Allied Generals and their Problems: 31 October 1914', *BAR*, 107 (1994)

Hussey (1994a)   John Hussey, 'Kiggell: A Second Opinion', *AQ*, 124 (4) (1994)

Hussey (1995)   John Hussey, 'Douglas Haig, Adjutant: Recollections of Veterans of the 7th Hussars', *JSAHR* (1995)

Hussey (1996)   John Hussey, '"A Very Substantial Grievance" said the Secretary of State: Douglas Haig's Examination Troubles, 1893', *JSAHR* LXXIV, 299 (1996)

Hussey (1996a)   John Hussey, 'Commentary' on 'Landrecies 25/26 August 1914', *ST!* 46 (1996)

Hussey (1996b)   John Hussey, 'Of the Indian Rope Trick, the Paranormal, and Captain Shearer's Ray: Sidelights on Douglas Haig', *BAR* 112 (1996)

Hussey (1997)   John Hussey, '"Uncle" Harper at Cambrai: A Reconsideration', *BAR* 117 (1997)

Hussey (1997a)   John Hussey, 'The Flanders Battleground and the Weather in 1917' in Liddle (1997)

Hussey (1999)   John Hussey, 'Portrait of a Commander-in-Chief', in Bond (1999)

Jellen   J. Jellen, 'A Clerk in the First World War'. *JRUSI*, 105 (Aug. 1960)

Jones   Simon Jones, 'Under a Green Sea: The British Responses to Gas Warfare', 2 parts, *The Great War* 1, 4, (1989)

Jordan   David Jordan, 'Battle for the Skies: Sir Hugh Trenchard as Commander of the Royal Flying Corps' in Hughes and Seligmann

Lee (1999)   John Lee, 'Some Lessons of the Somme: The British Infantry in 1917' in Bond (1999)

Lloyd (2007)   Nick Lloyd, '"With Faith and without Fear": Sir Douglas Haig's Command of First Army During 1915', *JMilH*, 71 (2007).

McCarthy (2004)   Chris McCarthy, 'Queen of the Battlefield: The Development of Command Organisation and Tactics in the British Infantry Battalion During the Great War' in Sheffield and Todman

Meyer   Jessica Meyer, 'Gladder to be going out than afraid': Shellshock and heroic masculinity in Britain, 1914–1919', in Jenny Macleod and Pierre Purseigle (eds) *Uncovered Fields: Perspectives in First World War Studies* (Leiden: Brill, 2004)

Moreman   Timothy Moreman, 'Lord Kitchener, the General Staff and the Army in India, 1904' in French and Holden Reid (2002)

Neilson (1997)   Keith Neilson, 'For Diplomatic, Economic, Strategy and Telegraphic Reasons: British Imperial Defence, The Middle East and India, 1914–1918' in Keith Neilson and Greg Kennedy, *Far Flung Lines* (Cass, 1997)

Philips (2003)   Gervase Phillips, 'Douglas Haig and the Development of Twentieth-Century Cavalry', *Archives* 28, 109 (2003)

Philpott (1999)   William Philpott, 'Squaring the Circle: The Higher Co-ordination of the Entente in the Winter of 1916', *EHR* (1999)

Philpott (2000)   William Philpott, 'Marshal Ferdinand Foch and Allied Victory', in Hughes and Seligmann

Pugsley (2007)   Christopher Pugsley, 'Haig and his Dominion Commanders: The Evolution of Professional Citizen Armies on the

Western Front', in John Crawford and Ian McGibbon, *New Zealand's Great War: New Zealand, the Allies and the First World War* (Auckland: Exsile, 2007)

Senior Mike Senior, 'Fromelles, 19/20 July 1916 – A Success After All?', *ST!* No.83 (2008)

Sheffield (2000a) Gary Sheffield, 'Reflections on the Experience of British Generalship in the Two World Wars' in John Bourne, Peter Liddle and Ian Whitehead (eds) *The Great World War 1915*, vol. I (HarperCollins, 2000)

Sheffield (2004) Gary Sheffield, 'John Terraine as a Military Historian', *JRUSI* 149, 2, 2004

Sheffield (2005) Gary Sheffield, 'Not the Same as Friendship: The British Empire and Coalition Warfare in the Era of the First World War' in Peter Dennis and Jeffrey Grey (eds) *Entangling Alliances: Coalition Warfare in the Twentieth Century* (Canberra: Australian Military History Publications, 2005)

Sheffield (2007) Gary Sheffield, 'Vimy Ridge and the Battle of Arras: A British Perspective' in Geoffrey Hayes, Andrew Iarocci and Mike Bechthold, *Vimy Ridge: A Canadian Reassessment* (Waterloo, Ont: Wilfrid Laurier UP, 2007)

Sheffield and Badsey Gary Sheffield and Stephen Badsey, 'Misdating of a Document in the Haig Papers', *JSAHR* 82, 330, (2004)

Sheffield and Jordan Gary Sheffield and David Jordan, 'Douglas Haig and Airpower', in Peter W. Gray and Sebastian Cox, (eds) *Air Power Leadership: Theory and Practice* (HMSO, 2002)

Simkins (1999) Peter Simkins, 'Somme Reprise: Reflections on the Fighting for Albert and Bapaume, August 1918' in Bond (1999)

Simkins (1999a) Peter Simkins, 'Haig and his Army Commanders' in Bond and Cave

Simkins (2004) Peter Simkins, '"The Black Man", "The Brat" and Londoners on the Somme: Some Reflections of the Capture of Thiepval, September 1916', *JCFWWS* 1, 2, (2004)

Simpson (2004) Andy Simpson, 'British Corps Command on the Western Front 1914–1918' in Sheffield & Todman

Simpson (2008) Andy Simpson, 'Lancelot Kiggell and Herbert Lawrence', in David Zabecki (ed.) *Chief of Staff* vol.1 (Annapolis, MD, Naval Institute Press, 2008)

Snape (2010)   Michael Snape (ed.) 'Archbishop Davidson's visit to the Western Front, May 1916', *A Lambeth Miscellany*, Church of England Record Society, (Woodbridge: Boydell, 2010)

Spiers (1994)   Edward M. Spiers, 'The Late Victorian Army 1868–1914' in Chandler and Beckett (1994)

Spiers (1998)   Edward M. Spiers, *Wars of Intervention: A Case Study – The Reconquest of the Sudan 1899*, Occasional Paper, No. 32 (Camberley: Strategic and Combat Studies Institute, 1998)

Strachan (1998)   Hew Strachan, 'The Battle of the Somme and British Strategy', *JSS* 21, 1 (1998)

Till   Geoffrey Till, 'Passchendaele: The Maritime Dimension', in Liddle (1997)

Todman (2003)   Dan Todman, '"Sans peur et sans reproche": The Retirement, Death and Mourning of Sir Douglas Haig, 1918–1928', *JMilH* 67 (2003).

Todman (2004)   Dan Todman, 'The Grand Lamasery Revisited: General Headquarters on the Western Front, 1914–18', in Sheffield and Todman

Travers (1994)   Tim Travers, 'The Army and the Challenge of War 1914–18' in Chandler and Beckett

Werth   German Werth, 'Flanders 1917 and the German Soldier', in Liddle (1997)

Wessely   Simon Wessely, 'The Life and Death of Private Harry Farr', *JRUSI,* (Oct. 2006)

Whitmarsh   Andrew Whitmarsh, 'British Army Manoeuvres and the Development of Military Aviation, 1910–913', *WiH* 14, 3 (2007)

Wiest (1997)   Andrew A. Wiest, 'Haig, Gough, and Passchendaele' in Sheffield (1997)

Williams, R.   Rhodri Williams, 'Lord Kitchener and the Battle of Loos: French Politics and British Strategy in the Summer of 1915' in Freedman *et al.*

Winter J (2009)   Jay Winter , 'Approaching the History of the Great War: A User's Guide' in Jay Winter (ed.) *The Legacy of the Great War – Ninety Years On* (Columbia and London: University of Missouri Press, 2009)

Wise (1999)   S.F. Wise, 'The Black Day of the German Army:

Australians and Canadians at Amiens, August 1918' in Peter Dennis
and Jeffrey Grey (eds), *1918: Defining Victory* (Canberra: Army
History Unit, 1999)

Theses and dissertations

Beach (2004)   James Beach, 'British Intelligence and the German
Army, 1918', Ph.D., University College London, 2004

Cook M.N.   M.N. Cook, 'Evaluating the Learning Curve: The 38th
(Welsh) Division on the Western Front 1916–1918', M. Phil.,
University of Birmingham, 2005

Geddes   Alistair Geddes, 'Solly-Flood, GHQ, and Tactical Training in
the BEF, 1916–1918', M.A., University of Birmingham, 2007

Higgens   Simon Higgens, 'How was Richard Haldane able to Reform
the British Army? An historical assessment using a contemporary
change management model', M. Phil., University of Birmingham,
2010

Kenyon   David Kenyon, 'British Cavalry on the Western Front
1916–18' Ph.D., Cranfield University, 2008

Molineux   Dave Molineux, 'The Effect of Platoon Structure on
Tactical Development in the BEF: June to November 1918', M.A.,
University of Birmingham, 2009

Mythen   J.S. Mythen, 'The Revolution in British Battle Tactics July
1916–June 1917: The Spring and Summer Offensives During 1917'.
M. Phil., Pembroke College, Cambridge, 2001

Notes

PREFACE

1 Edward to Fletcher, 8 July 1917, Fletcher papers, 99/55/1, IWM.
2 For controversies over the dating of the diary, see Sheffield and Bourne, pp. 7–9.

INTRODUCTION

1 *Scotsman*, 29 May 1919, p.7. Nero Claudius Drusus Germanicus (38 BC–9 BC), stepson of the Emperor Augustus and brother of the Emperor Tiberius, won significant victories over German tribes.
2 *Scotsman*, 21 July 1919, p. 4.
3 Todman (2005) pp. 91-94; Bond (2002), pp. 45-49; Lloyd George II, p. 2073–76.
4 Sheffield (2004).
5 Sheffield and Badsey, pp. 179–81.
6 DeGroot (1986).
7 Bourne (1999), p. 9.
8 Winter, J. (2009), p. 12.

CHAPTER 1: APPRENTICESHIP

1 'A. M'I.', *Scotsman*, 30 Oct 1918, p. 6.
2 For Haig's early years, in general, see DeGroot (1988) and Mead (2007).
3 W. Stafford to Duff Cooper, 28 May 1933, DUFC 5/2, DCP.
4 A.V. Dicey, quoted in Cannadine (2000), p. 96.
5 Quoted in Robbins (2010), p. 5.
6 Rachel to Haig, 20 July 1877, quoted in DeGroot (1988), p. 10; Mead, pp. 21, 413.
7 John Haig, notes, *c.* 1930, HP/322 a.
8 'Bee' to Lady Haig, 16 Feb. 1930, HP/322a.
9 Janet Haig to Haig, n.d. but *c.*1920, HP/346b.
10 Rachel Haig to John Haig, 9 June 1875, HP/3a.
11 Haig, Lady, p. 10.
12 John Haig, notes, *c.*1930, HP/322a.

13 Haig to John Haig, 5 June 1875, HP/3a.
14 H. Warren to Haig , 11 Jan. 1922, H. Whately to Lady Haig, 5 Feb. 1929, both in HP/324a.
15 Haig (1919), p. 16.
16 Dawson, p. 1.
17 Meyer, pp. 196–7.
18 Beckett (2003), pp. 76–8.
19 James Bryce, quoted in Colley, p. 413.
20 Cannadine (1994), chapter 1.
21 Smout, pp. 32, 34.
22 For Haig at Oxford, see Mead, pp. 35–46, and Askwith, p. 347.
23 Rachel to John Haig, 9 June 1875, HP/3a.
24 Lady Haig to John Haig, 11 Feb. 1930, HP/322a.
25 Duff Cooper (1935), p. 20.
26 L. Marshall to Lady Haig, 9 Oct. 1929, HP/324 a.
27 Scott, p. 13.
28 *New York Times*, 13 June 1913.
29 DHD, 18, 19 Jan. 1883, HP/1a.
30 'Tribute from Mr Miller (Bullingdon)', n.d., HP324a; Askwith, p. 347.
31 Askwith, p. 347.
32 Mead, p. 35.
33 Winter, D., p.32. For a rebuttal, see Beckett (2003), p. 75.
34 Scott, pp. 6–7.
35 French, G., pp. 51–2; Faber p. 21.
36 Anglim, p. 13.
37 Barrow (1931), p. 20.
38 Anglim, p. 13; Haig, Lady (1936), p. 21.
39 Edmonds to Duff Cooper, 1 May 1935, DUFC 5, DCP.
40 Gough (1954), pp. 29–30. Another future Corps commander recalled his time at Sandhurst as 'happy and uneventful': Godley, p. 10.
41 Sixsmith, p. 4; Birdwood, p. 28.
42 Spiers (1992), pp. 99–100; Sheffield (2000), p. 7.
43 Hussey (1995), p. 124. The following is indebted to this article.
44 Repington (1919), p. 74.
45 Vaughan, p. 3.
46 For a selection, see Scott, pp. 25–33.
47 Sheffield (2000), chapter 1.
48 Vaughan, p. 62; Griffiths to Lady Haig, 15 Jan. 1929, HP/324a. Lady Haig annotated this with the words 'delightful letter'.
49 Teale to Haig, 25 Jul. 1903, HP/326a.
50 DHD, 9 Sept 1892, HP/1a; Vaughan, p. 10.
51 H.J. Harrison to Lady Haig, 17 Apr. 1937, HP/324a. This letter was used by DeGroot (1988) to support his portrait of Haig as a 'martinet', but Lady Haig rather liked it: Lady Haig to Harrison, 30 June 1937, HP/324a. Hussey (1995) casts doubt on the veracity of this ex-soldier's evidence.

52 Teale to Haig, 25 Jul. 1903, HP/326a.

53 Scott, p. 30; DHD, 3 Jan. 1892, HP/1; Haig's Foreword to Greaves (1924), p. v. See also Beckett (ODNB1).

54 DHD, 14 Aug. 1892 HP/1.

55 Haig to Henrietta, 1 Sept. 1892, HP/6b (all letters to Henrietta Jameson are in this file).

56 Reid to Haig, 5 Apr. 1894, HP/6e.

57 This paragraph is based on Hussey (1996). He speculates that Henrietta's 'over-zealous lobbying', combined with Buller's desire to give a place to a member of his own regiment, may have contributed to the decision to debar Haig from Staff College on medical grounds. Both suggestions are plausible. For the original of Haig's draft memorandum on the subject, see HP/6e.

58 *Report on the French Cavalry Manoeuvres in Touraine – September 1893*, HP/68.

59 For details of the visit, see Haig's letters and diaries in Scott, pp. 45–51. Haig's *Notes on German Cavalry* are in HP/74.

60 Wood to Haig, 1 Jul. 1895, HP/6g; Haig to Wood, 7 July 1895 in Scott, p. 53; Haig to Henrietta, 4 Jul 1895, HP/6b. Although Wood's regard for Haig is not in doubt, it is possible that his comment about Haig's conversation was delivered tongue in cheek. At one dinner Wood was reported as describing Haig as 'One of the best we've got, but dull!' Given its provenance, it is possible that the story is apocryphal; French, G., p. 40.

61 Travers (1987), pp. xxi, 3–36.

62 Scott, pp. 59–60.

63 Roberts to Kitchener, 4 May 1901, in Wessels (2000), p. 177; Badsey (2006), pp. 15–16; Maurice (1928), pp.16–17; Pollock, (2001), p. 114.

64 The comment was made to me by a fellow postgraduate, the late Rae Russell, *c.* 1989. Traces of the patron/protégé relationship can be found in the British armed forces in the early twenty-first century. Individual officers are recognised by peers and superiors (and the academics that teach them!) as 'going places'. Their trajectory is based on a combination of talent, having 'ticked the right boxes' in terms of jobs done, and having caught the eye of influential superiors.

65 Richard Haking (Hampshire Regiment) was the corps commander; William 'Bill' Furse (Royal Artillery) and Thompson 'Tommy' Capper (East Lancashire Regiment) the divisional commanders.

66 DeGroot (1988), p. 48; Barrow (1942), p. 45.

67 This comment could be read as double-edged, but the tone was typical of the jocular approach used throughout: Haig's friend Blair is described finishing the same race 'with a concertinaed hat'. *The Staff College Drag Hunt 1895–6*, pp. 66, 68 (privately published, copy in HP/54).

68 Mrs C. Henderson [sister-in-law of Col Henderson] to Lady Haig 4 Feb.1929, HP/339b.

69 Edmonds to Haig, 26 Oct. 1903, HP/326a; Haig to Edmonds, 31 Aug. 1911, in Scott, p. 61. Strictly speaking, Henderson's prediction was never fulfilled, as he was talking about the C-in-C of the army, a post abolished in 1904.

70 Holden Reid (1992), pp. 8–9.

71 Travers (1987), p. 98.

72 Travers (1994), pp. 218–19.

73 Samuels, pp. 49–53.

74 Badsey (2006), pp. 21–2.

75 'Strategy II', HP/20. It has been suggested that this (and other) material said to date from Haig's time at Staff College was actually compiled at a later date (letter from John Hussey, 7 June 1996, held in NLS); but the point remains valid, that one should not assume that Haig's notes necessarily reflected his own opinions.

76 Haig to Whatley, 24 Nov. 1927, HP/324a.

77 See two studies aimed at officers: Brunker; Anderson.

78 Slim, p. 296.

79 Echevarria, p. 89.

80 DHD 23 Jan. 1898, HP/1j.

81 Spiers (1998), pp. 10–14. For the campaign generally, see Spiers (1998a).

82 DHD 15 Feb. 1898, HP/1j; Haig to Henrietta, 17 Feb. 1898, HP/3b.

83 Haig to Wood, 15 Mar. 1898, HP/6g.

84 Haig to Henrietta, 1 Apr. 1898, HP/6b.

85 Maurice (1928), p. 31.

86 DeGroot (1988), p. 77.

87 Spiers (1998), pp. 16–17.

88 Haig to Henrietta, 29 May 1898, HP/6b.

89 DHD, 21 Mar. 1898, HP/1j.

90 Haig to Wood, 26 Mar. 1898, HP/6g; DeGroot (1988), p. 58.

91 Haig to Wood, 26 Mar. 1898, HP/6g.

92 DHD, 19, 20 Jan. 1898, HP/6b.

93 Haig to Henrietta, 1 Apr. 1898, HP/6b.

94 DHD, 5 Apr. 1898, HP/1j.

95 Haig to Henrietta, 12 Apr. 1898, HP/6b.

96 Haig to Wood, 29 Apr. 1898, HP/6g.

97 Haig to Wood, 29 Apr. 1898, HP/6g; DeGroot (1988), pp. 62–3.

98 Haig to Wood, 29 Apr. 1898, HP/6g; Haig to Henrietta, 5 June 1898, HP/6b; DeGroot (1988), p. 63.

99 Pollock (2001), p. 149; Cassar, (1977), p. 178.

100 DHD, 12 Apr. 1898, HP/1j.

101 DHD, 1 Sept. 1898, HP/1k.

102 Eliot Cohen, cited in Spiers (1998), p. 9.

103 DHD, 2 Sept. 1898, HP/1k.

104 Quoted in Duff Cooper I, pp. 62–3.

105 DHD, 2 Sept. 1898, HP/1k.

106 Haig to Henrietta, 15 Sept. 1898, HP/6b.

107 Haig to Henrietta, 6 Sept. 1898, HP/6b; Haig to Wood, 7 September 1898 HP/69.

108 DeGroot (1988), p. 68.

109 Duff Cooper I, p. 65.

CHAPTER 2: RISING STAR

1 Haig to Henrietta, 16 May 1899; Hussey (1991).
2 DHD 19 Oct. 1899, HP/38b (all 1899 diary entries are in this file).
3 DHD 20 Oct. 1899.
4 DHD 21 Oct. 1899; Haig to Henrietta, 26 Oct. 1899.
5 DHD 31 Oct. 1899.
6 Telegram in Scott, p. 139.
7 DHD 2 Nov. 1899.
8 See Gillings.
9 'Notes', Nov. 1899, HP/38c.
10 Haig to Henrietta, 15, 26 Nov. 1899.
11 The best study is Badsey (2008).
12 Sir Garnett Wolseley, *Soldier's Pocket Book* quoted in Philips (2003), p. 148.
13 DHD 23 Nov. 1899.
14 DHD 21 Nov., 4 Dec. 1899.
15 Quoted in Judd and Surridge, p. 126.
16 Quoted in Duff Cooper (1935) I, p. 77.
17 Maydon, pp. 42, 108.
18 Haig to Henrietta, 12 Dec. 1899; DHD 11, 23 Dec. 1899.
19 Maydon, pp. 95–6.
20 Haig to Lonsdale Hale, 2 Mar. 1900, in Scott, p. 164.
21 Haig to Lonsdale Hale, 2 Mar. 1900, in Scott, p. 166.
22 Robbins (2010), p. 35.
23 Haig to Lonsdale Hale, 2 Mar. 1900, in Scott, p. 167.
24 Haig to Henrietta, 22 Feb. 1900; Laycock to LH, 1929 in Scott, pp. 163–4.
25 Haig to Henrietta, 14 May 1900.
26 Haig to Hale, 2 Mar. 1900.
27 Haig to Henrietta, 14 May 1900.
28 Holmes (1981), pp. 98, 99.
29 Haig to Henrietta, 16 Mar. 1900.
30 Anglesey (1986), p. 146.
31 See especially Badsey (2008), pp. 90–91, 109–10.
32 Haig to Henrietta, 7, 14 Apr. 1900.
33 'Notes on the Transvaal', quoted in DeGroot (1988), p. 73.
34 Haig to Henrietta, 17 June 1900.
35 Haig to Henrietta, 3 July 1900.
36 Haig to Henrietta, 30 Nov. 1900.
37 Haig to Henrietta, 17 Sept.1900.
38 HP/36.
39 R.T. Gardner to Lady Haig, 23 June 1929, HP/334c.
40 Haig to Henrietta, 29 Oct. 1900.
41 Haig to Henrietta, 15 July 1900.
42 See e.g. Boemeke, Chickering and Förster (1999).
43 Scott, p. 182.
44 Haig to Henrietta, 30 Oct., 18, 26 December 1900.

45 Haig to Henrietta, 20 Jan. 1901.

46 Haig to Henrietta, 18 Dec. 1901.

47 Haig to Henrietta, 10 Mar., 8 July 1901.

48 Haig to Henrietta, 23 Mar., 3 Apr 1901.

49 Haig to Henrietta, 11 Apr. 1901.

50 Holmes (1981), p. 113; Haig to Henrietta, 11 Apr. 1901.

51 Haig to Henrietta, 4 May 1901.

52 Haig to Henrietta, 25 Aug. 1901.

53 Anglesey (1986), p. 230.

54 Haig to Henrietta, 22 Sept. 1901; Anglesey (1986), p. 231.

55 Haig to Henrietta, 30 Sept. 1901.

56 Haig to Henrietta, 30 Mar., 5 June 1902.

57 Haig to Henrietta, 17 Sept. 1902.

58 Hamilton to Roberts, 8 Feb. 1902, in Wessels (2000), p. 232.

59 Maydon had judged Lawrence to be 'the best intelligence officer of the campaign';
    Maydon, p. 42.

60 Murray-Philipson, p. 117.

61 Lawrence to Haig, 12 July 1903, in Scott, p. 222.

62 Murray-Philipson, pp. 117–18.

63 Murray-Philipson, pp. 118–19.

64 Murray-Philipson, p. 119; Scott, p. 222; Head, p. 90; Haig, Lady (1936), p. 31–2.

65 Echevarria, pp. 84–91.

66 HP/2b; Badsey (2008), p. 149.

67 Haig's evidence to *Royal Commission on the War in South Africa,*, vol. II, (HMSO,
    1903), p. 403.

68 Badsey (2008), p. 183.

69 Childers, *War and the Arme Blanche* quoted in Badsey (2008), p. 221.

70 Haig (1907) pp. 8–9; Bushaway (2004), p. 11.

71 Badsey (2008), p. 211.

72 *Cavalry Training 1907*, p. 187; Badsey (2008), p. 209; Phillips (2003), p. 155.

73 Badsey (2008), pp. 177, 179.

74 'Notes on operations', 8 Dec. 1903, HP/40c.

75 Baden-Powell, chapter. IX; Barrow (1942), pp. 104–5.

76 Haig to Henrietta, 1 Sept. 1904.

77 Scott, pp. 240–1.

78 Philpott (2009), p. 66.

79 e.g. Haig to Henrietta, 21 Sept. 1905.

80 Sheffield and Bourne, pp. 11–12; DHD 4 Oct. 1903, in Scott, p. 227; Lee (1927), p.
    364; Duff Cooper (1935) I, p. 104; Edmonds to Swinton, 21 Mar.1950, Edmonds
    papers, II/5/18a, LHCMA.

81 Esher to Haig, 7 Oct. 1904, in Brett II, pp. 68–70.

82 Haig to Esher, 2 Mar. 1903, in Brett, II, p. 51.

83 Esher to Edward VII, 18 Mar. 1903, in Brett I, p. 391. The King was of course
    already well aware of Haig.

84 Esher to M.V. Brett (his son), 9 Aug. 1905, in Bret, II, p. 97; d'Ombrain, pp. 51, 143.

85 Haig to Henrietta, 11 Jan. 1906; Ellison, 'Notes on Certain Letters . . .' 11 Sept.
    1928, HP/40q; Haig to Esher, 15 Mar. 1906, and Kitchener to Esher, 11 Jan. 1906,
    in Brett II, pp. 143, 151.

86 Haig to Kiggell, 27 Apr. 1909, Kiggell 1/2 KP; Haig to Ellison, 11 Sept. 1906, Ellison
    papers, 8704-35-460, NAM. Haig therefore recommend reforming the nation's
    financial system accordingly (I am grateful to Simon Higgens for this reference).

87 Charteris (1929), p. 61.

88 Spiers (1994), p. 211; Haldane to Esher, 8 Sept. 1906, quoted in Spiers (1980), p.
    150; Spiers (1980), p. 150. For the process of reform, see Higgens.

89 Haig to Henrietta, 13 Dec. 1905; Haig to Ellison, 14 Sept. 1910, HP/40q.

90 Haldane did not prepare the expeditionary force specifically for war in Europe;
    nonetheless it was available when it was needed for that role.

91 Ellison, 'Notes on Certain Letters . . .', 11 Sept. 1928, HP/40q.

92 Palazzo, pp. 10–20 (he prefers the word 'ethos' to 'doctrine').

93 Haig, paper on 'National Defence 20 May 1906', HP/40p; d'Ombrain, p. 146;
    Spiers (1980), pp. 88–9, 104, 159; Beckett (1985), pp. 129, 152. The Yeomanry
    became part of the TF, while the Militia was transformed into the Special
    Reserve.

94 Haig to Kiggell, 24 Apr. 1909, Kiggell 1/1, KP; Moreman, p. 66.

95 Haig to Kiggell, 13 July 1911, Kiggell 1/9, Kiggell Papers, LHCMA.

96 Moreman, p. 74; McMunn , p. 84.

97 Ryan's memoir, RP.

98 See the Haig-Scott correspondence at the Scott Polar Research Institute,
    Cambridge.

99 Sykes, p. 105; Ash, p. 198.

100 Haig to Kiggell, 25 May 1911, Kiggell 1/1, KP; Reese, p. 205.

101 Whitmarsh, pp. 335–8.

102 Sheffield and Jordan, p. 268.

103 Beckett (1989), pp. 155–9.

104 'Notes by . . . J.E. Gough on Home Rule', in Beckett (1986), p. 35.

105 DHD 25 Mar. 1914 in Beckett (1986), p. 199; Beckett (1989), p. 164.

106 DHD 21 Mar. 1914; Haig to J. Gough, 21 Mar. 1914; 'Memorandum by Lord
    Stamfordham, 13 Apr. 1914'. All in Beckett (1986), pp. 199, 201–2, 246.

107 Beckett (1986), pp. 20–2; Anglesey (1996), pp. 46–7.

108 Haig to Howell, 27 Mar. 1914, in Beckett (1986), pp. 293–4.

109 Badsey (2008), p. 203; DHTsD 13 Aug. 1914 (for a discussion of the authenticity of
    this document, see Sheffield and Bourne, p. 58).

110 'Memorandum by Lord Stamfordham, 13 Apr. 1914', in Beckett (1896), p. 246;
    Haig to Rothschild, 13 October 1916, HP/214a.

111 Charteris (1929), pp. 32, 59, 60, 64, 68; Hussey (1996b), p. 80. After the end of 1908
    he no longer commented on spiritualism in his diary. Henrietta continued to
    correspond with Haig on the subject as late as 1916. It seems he ignored her; Cave
    (1999), p. 249; Snape (2005), p. 62.

112 Charteris (1929), pp. 60, 65, 68.

113 MacMunn pp. 85–6.

114 Terraine (1963), p. 53.
115 Quoted in Philpott (2009), p. 66.
116 Beckett (1999), p. 10.
117 Bourne (1997), pp. 110–11.

CHAPTER 3 CORPS COMMANDER

1 DHTsD, Aug. 1914. What follows seems to be the most plausible version of events. For a fuller discussion, see Sheffield and Bourne, pp. 5–7.
2 Haig, paper on 'National Defence' 20 May 1906, HP/40p.
3 DHTsD 13 Aug. 1914.
4 DHMsD 17 Aug. 1914; Charteris (1931), pp. 10–11.
5 DHMsD 20 Aug. 1914; Charteris (1931), p. 13.
6 OH 1914 I, pp. 59, 72.
7 OH 1914 I, p. 83.
8 DHMsD 23 Aug. 1914.
9 DHMsD 23 Aug. 1914. There is a small mystery here: some historians (e.g. Strachan (2001), p. 221) state that French ignored the views of Macdonogh, his Director of Military Intelligence and believed that only two German corps were within striking distance. However, Haig's Ms diary clearly states that French himself gave the figure of three corps, a figure confirmed by French's diary.
10 DHTsD 23 Aug. 1914; Strachan (2001), p. 220; Tyng, p. 123.
11 Charteris, (1929), p. 89.
12 DHMsD 23 Aug. 1914; OH 1914 I, p. 73.
13 OH 1914 I, pp. 60-1, 86.
14 DHMsD 23 Aug. 1914.
15 Reproduced in Duff Cooper (1935), pp. 144–5.
16 Simpson (2006), p. 42.
17 French to Kitchener, telegram F.23, 23 Aug. 1914, 12.20 p.m.,75/46/6, FP quotation from; French's dispatch, 7 Sept. 1914 in Coates, p. 281.
18 DHMsD 23 Aug. 1914.
19 DHMsD 23 Aug. 1914.
20 Secrett, pp. 79–81.
21 OH 1914 I, pp. 97–8.
22 Beckett (1989), p. 181.
23 Charteris (1929), pp. 91–2; Arthur, p. 62.
24 DHTsD 24 Aug. 1914; Charteris, 1931 (29 August 1914), p. 161.
25 Beckett (1993), p. 17.
26 French to Kitchener, telegram F.28, 24 Aug. 1914, 75/46/6, FP.
27 French diary, 24 Aug. 1914, FP.
28 French, pp.65–6; Beckett (1993), p. 17.
29 OH I 1914, p. 99.
30 Haig to Smith-Dorrien, 18 Dec. 1919, CAB 45/129. Charteris (1931), p. 16, letter of 29 August 1914, corroborates that Haig was informed that Smith-Dorrien had asked for a day's rest for his troops.

31 DHMsD 24 Aug. 1914 (emphasis in original). Possibly Haig in his diary entry has compressed events, as it seems that the decision to send I Corps east of the Forest of Mormal was not finally made until Haig sent a note, via Charteris, across the town of Bavai at about 6 p.m.
32 Charteris (1929), pp. 91–2. Haig's writings are silent on this.
33 Charteris (1931), p. 17 (29 Aug. 1914); Ryan's account of 1914, RP.
34 Ascoli, p. 93; Charteris (1931), pp. 19–20; Ryan's account of 1914, RP; DHMsD 25 Aug. 1914; 'Action at Landrecies', 25–26 August 1914, and 'Action at Landrecies' and 'First Army Corps' operations . . . to 5th September', both in WO 95/588.
35 Orders of 26 August 1914 in WO 256/1.
36 OH 1914 I, pp. 139–40.
37 DHMsD 27 August. Possibly significantly, in the Ts diary Haig softened his language.
38 OH 1914 I, p. 135.
39 Holmes (1981), p. 222; French diary, 26 Aug. 1914, FP.
40 DHMsD and DHTsD 26 Aug. 1914.
41 Wynne (1934), pp. 247–54. Hussey (1996a), p. 16, suggests that the fighting was possibly more serious than usually thought.
42 French diary 26 Aug. 1914; Price-Davies to wife, 3 Sept. 1914, Price-Davies papers, 77/78/1, IWM.
43 C-in-C's War Diary, 26 August 1914, WO95/1.
44 DHTsD 27 Aug. 1914.
45 On the following day French wrote, after receiving news of Haig's successful retreat, that matters no longer seemed so dark. French diary, 26, 27 Aug. 1914, direct quote from Holmes (1981) p. 222.
46 Terraine (1991), p. 142.
47 OH 1914 I, pp. 141–2; French diary 26 Aug.1914, FP.
48 It has been recently argued the true figure was about 5,000 (Cave and Sheldon, p. 9;), but this was not clear at the time.
49 OH 1914 I, p. 141; Terraine (1993), p. 142.
50 OH 1914 I, p. 201.
51 Actually the rearguard of I Corps had been overwhelmed, but Haig did not discover this until the 27th.
52 OH 1914 I, p. 201.
53 Terraine (1963), pp. 87–88.
54 Holmes (1981), pp. 223–4.
55 Gardner, (2003), pp. 14, 48–9. Beckett (1989), p. 181, also uses Edmonds as a key source. According to Edmonds, there was also a long-standing rivalry between Gough, Haig's Chief of Staff, and George Forestier-Walker, Gough's opposite number at II Corps.
56 Ryan to wife, 29 Aug. 1914, RP; Haig to Lady Haig, 26 Sept. 1914.
57 Tyng, pp. 149–51.
58 Huguet, pp. 73–4; Spears (2000), p. 258.
59 Haig to Murray, 29 Aug. 1914, 7 a.m., WO 256/1; DHMsD 29 Aug. 1914.
60 Simpson (2006), p. 7.

61 DHMsD 29 Aug. 1914.

62 Quoted in Spears (2000), pp. 255–8 (quote from p. 256).

63 'First Army Corps . . . to 5th September', p. 16, WO95/588.

64 Spears (2000), pp. 265–6.

65 OH 1914 I, p. 253; see also Strachan (2001), p. 245.

66 Haig's annotations (24 Sept) to Maxse's report of 27 Aug. 1914, WO95/588.

67 DHMsD 5 Sept. 1914.

68 DHMsD 6 Sept. 1914; OH 1914 I, pp. 297–8.

69 DHMsD 7 Sept. 1914; OH 1914 I, p. 310.

70 DHMsD 8 Sept. 1914; OH 1914 I, p. 286.

71 DHMsD 9 Sept. 1914.

72 Ascoli, p. 160.

73 DHMsD 10 Sept 1914.

74 OH 1914 I, pp. 367, 465.

75 W.D. Bird, quoted in Taylor, J., p. 39.

76 DHMsD 14 Sept. 1914.

77 DHTsD 14 Sept. 1914; narratives in WO95/588.

78 Haig to Lady Haig, 19 Sept. 1914.

79 OH 1914 I, pp. 416, 465–6; entries for 12–13 Sept. 1914, WO 95/1.

80 OH 1914 I, p. 570.

81 DHMsD 16 Sept. 1914.

82 DHMsD 20, 23 Sept. 1914.

83 DHMsD 27, 28 Sept. 1914; Haig to Lady Haig, 21, 23 Sept. 1914.

84 Haig to Lady Haig, 4, 6 Oct. 1914.

85 'Notes on . . . Employment of Aviators . . .' and 'Memorandum on . . . Tactics' 28 Sept. 1914, both in WO 95/588.

86 Haig to Wigram, 22 Sept. 1914, RA PS/GV/Q 2521/V/126. Davies returned to France later in the war as a divisional commander, but he never fully recovered from the strain of the 1914 campaign. In May 1918 he took his own life in a London nursing home.

87 WO 95/588. It seems that Haig was unfair towards Towsey. The OH does not criticise him, and he commanded a brigade later in the war.

88 Howard (1986); Travers (1987) chapter 2.

89 DHMsD 16 Oct. 1914.

90 Cassar (1985), p. 162. For the La Bassée fighting, see Beckett (2004).

91 DHMsD 21 Nov. 1914.

92 Edmonds to Duff Cooper, 1 May 1935, Duff Cooper papers, DC 5/3 CCC.

93 Beckett (2004), pp. 118–19.

94 Farrar-Hockley (1967). p. 131; DHMsD 26 Oct. 1914.

95 OH 1914 II, p. 279; Cassar (1985), p. 169.

96 Farrar-Hockley (1967), pp. 147–8.

97 OH 1914 II, p. 304.

98 WO 95/588, WD 30 Oct. 1914; Palmer, p. 78.

99 Beckett (2004), p. 130.

100 Hussey (1994), p. 77.

101 Barrow (1931), p. 44.

102 French to Kitchener, 31 Oct. 1914, 75/46/5, FP.

103 Hussey (1994), pp. 83–4.

104 Beckett, (1989), p. 193.

105 Rice to Edmonds, 6 Nov. 1922, WO 95/588.

106 WO 95/588, WD 31 Oct. 1914.

107 This version differs slightly from the one in Haig's Ms diary, when he says that he found out about the Worcesters' action in the course of his ride to the front (see below). As this fuller version of events, written when Haig had had time to collect his thoughts, largely agrees with other witnesses, this is probably an occasion when the later typescript diary is more accurate than the immediate hand-written version. Haig had a great deal on his mind on the night of 31 October 1914. See Charteris (1931), p. 53; Hussey (1994), pp. 75–89.

108 DeGroot (1988), pp. 165–6; Winter (1991), pp. 36–7; Gardner (2003), pp. 220–1.

109 Beckett (2004), p. 140.

110 DHTsD 31 Oct. 1914.

111 Hussey (1994), p. 85.

112 FitzClarence was killed on 11 November 1914, and Haig did not learn of the critical role he played in the counterattack of 31 October until August 1915 – which is an interesting commentary on the state of battlefield communications. It is pleasing to record that Haig ordered that sworn statements about FitzClarence's leadership be retrospectively placed in I Corps war diary: see WO 95/588.

113 DHMsD 31 Oct. 1914, Beckett (1989) pp. 193–4.

114 DHMsD 1 Nov. 1914.

115 WO 95/589, WD 11 Nov. 1914; OH 1914 II, pp. 419–45.

116 DHMsD and DHTsD 11 Nov. 1914.

117 Arthur, p. 76.

118 French's Dispatch 8 Oct. 1914, in Coates, p. 297.

119 French to Kitchener, telegram F.150, 15 Sept. 1914, 75/46/6, FP.

120 DHMsD 24 Nov. 1914 (Haig also dined with George V in France on 4 December); see also Wigram to Haig, 20 Nov. 1914, WO 256/2. Gardner (2003), p. 228 makes rather too much of all this.

121 Home diary, 11 Nov.1914, in Briscoe, p. 38.

122 Cassar (1985), p. 178.

123 Wilson to Foch, 5 Jul. 1916, in Jeffrey (2006), p. 168.

124 See Craster, pp. 122, 145; Cavan to wife, 9 Nov. 1914, CAVN 1/1, CP.

125 Haig to Wood, 6 Nov. 1914, in Wood, p. 388; Haig to Lady Haig, 13 Nov. 1914. For evidence of his practical concern for relieving his men see DHTsD 5 Nov. 1914.

126 Needham, pp. 104, 105. 'The 48th' refers to the battalion's pre-1881 designation.

127 Haig to Kiggell, 4 Oct. 1914, 1/36, KP.

128 FSR 1909, p. 107.

129 OH 1917 II, p. 297.

130 Palmer, p. 280.

131 London Gazette, 8 Sept. 1914, in WO 256/2.

132 DHMsD 25 Dec. 1915.

Chapter 4: Grappling with Trench Warfare

1 Lloyd (2007); Harris (2008). See Trewin, pp.152–89, for the writing of *The Donkeys*.
2 Willcocks, p.216.
3 Memo from Robertson, 3 Oct. 1915, WO 95/2.
4 For more detail, see Sheffield (2001), pp. 91–110. I owe the phrase 'rich man's war' to Dr. John Bourne.
5 DHMsD 2 Apr., 14 Dec. 1915; Harrison, p. 37.
6 Thompson to wife, 1 June 1915, TP.
7 DHMsD 20, 28 Jan. 1915; Murray-Philipson, pp. 129–31, 172.
8 Kitchener to French, 2 Jan. 1915, 75/46/5, FP.
9 Cassar (2004), pp.178–9.
10 French diary, 31 Mar. 1915, FP, direct quote from Holmes (1981) p. 285.
11 French (1988), pp.392–3.
12 DHMsD 22 Jan. 1915. See also Haig to Rothschild, 23 Jan. 1915, HP/214a.
13 OH 1915 I, p. 70; DHMsD 23 Feb. 1915.
14 Wynne (1939), p. 31.
15 DHMsD 2 Feb. 1915.
16 Prior and Wilson (1992), p. 26.
17 Haig, 'Memo' 28 Feb. 1915, WO 158/181; DHMsD 28 Feb., 1 Mar 1915. On the previous day Robertson had written to Haig warning of limited supplies of ammunition: 27 Feb. 1915, in WO 158/181.
18 Charteris (1931) 3 March 1915.
19 DHMsD 15 Feb. 1915.
20 DHMsD 23 Feb.1915.
21 Willcocks, p. 232; DHMsD 2 Mar. 1915; 'Notes at Conference on 5/3/15', WO 95/2.
22 Prior and Wilson (1992), pp. 28, 31–2.
23 DHMsD 6 Feb. 1915; RD, 8 Feb. 1915, RWLN 1/1, RwP.
24 Haig, 'Special Order', 9 Mar. 1915, WO 95/2.
25 Richter (1997), p. 86.
26 Trenchard's autobiographical notes, quoted in Jordan, pp. 71–2.
27 DHMsD, 25 Feb. 1915; see also 22 Feb.1915.
28 'First Army weekly report of operations', [10 Mar. 1915] WO 95/2.
29 'Remarks on . . . IV Corps . . . 10 March 1915', WO 158/373.
30 OH 1915 I, p. 130.
31 'Note on . . . Artillery at Neuve Chapelle', WO 158/374.
32 'First Army weekly report of operations', [11 Mar. 1915] WO 95/2; OH 1915 I, p. 130.
33 Atkinson (1927), p. 149.
34 OH 1915 I, pp. 139–41.
35 OH 1915 I, p. 143; First Army weekly report of operations', [12 Mar. 1915] WO 95/2.
36 OH 1915 I, p. 143.
37 Huguet, p. 178.
38 'First Army weekly report of operations', [10 Mar. 1915] WO 95/2; DHMsD 11 Mar. 1915; Haig to Kiggell, 2 Apr. 1915, KIGGELL 1/38, KP.

39 DHMsD 16–17 Mar. 1915. Horne's letter to his wife on 4 July 1915 indicates that the affair became more widely known: Robbins (2009), p. 123.

40 RD, 10 Mar. 1915, RWLN 1/1, RwP.

41 'General Staff Note on the Situation 14.3.15', WO 158/17. See also French diary, 10 Mar. 1915, FP.

42 Du Cane, 'Tactical Notes on Neuve Chapelle', WO 158/374; Barr (2004), pp. 34, 35.

43 Willcocks, pp. 202, 216, 229–30. Willcocks was writing c. 1918. By this time he was a bitter man, angry at being sacked by Haig in September 1915.

44 DHMsD 4 Mar. 1915.

45 DHMSD 4, 16 Mar, 3 Apr. 1915; quote is from Haig to Kiggell, 2 Apr. 1915, KIGGELL 1/38, KP. There were three preliminary naval bombardments before the amphibious landings took place on 25 April 1915. For a recent study highly critical of the naval operation, see Prior (2009).

46 Haig to Kiggell, 1 July 1915, KIGGELL 1/39, KP.

47 DHMsD 17 Oct. 1915; Haig to Oliver Haig, 24 June 1915, HP/334d.

48 DHMsD 13 Feb. 30 Apr. 1915. For a recent account of Second Ypres, see Lee (2009).

49 DHMsD 11 Apr. 1915.

50 Memo from Butler, 13 Apr.1915, WO 158/183.

51 OH 1915 II, pp.7–8; DHMsD 27 Apr. 1915.

52 'Notes on Conference' 30 Apr. 1915, WO 158/183.

53 'First Army Operational Order', 6 May 1915, WO 95/2.

54 RD, 19 Mar. 1915, RWLN 1/1, RwP. For an example of Haig's 'hands-on' approach, see his annotations to 'Notes on Schemes Submitted by Corps' n.d. but c. April 1915, WO 95/155.

55 See, e.g., DHMsD 22 and 25 April 1915.

56 'Paper B', Annex to Memo from Butler, 13 Apr. 1915; Notes on Conference, issued by Butler, 30 Apr. 1915, Haig to Robertson, 8 Apr. 1915; all documents in WO 158/183.

57 'Paper B', Annex to Memo from Butler, 13 Apr. 1915, WO 158/183.

58 First Army Operational Order, 6 May 1915, WO 95/2.

59 Paper B', Annex to Memo from Butler, 13 Apr.1915; Haig to Robertson, 5 May 1915, both documents in WO 158/183.

60 Memo from Robertson, 7 Apr. 1915, WO 158/153.

61 DHMsD 30 Apr. 1915.

62 RD 8 Apr., 6 May 1915, RWLN 1/1, RwP. See also Horne to wife, 8 May 1915 in Robbins (2009).

63 Note by Butler, Dec. 1915, WO 95/155.

64 Pagan, p.17.

65 DHMsD 9 May 1915; Haig to Lady Haig, 9 May 1915. For accounts of the battle see OH 1915 II, pp. 17–43, and Bristow.

66 DHMsD 9 May 1915; Neillands, p. 140.

67 OH 1915 II, p. 40.

68 'Notes of Conference . . . 7 p.m. 9th May', WO95/155.

69 'Situation at Daybreak, 10 May 1915'; see also memo by Butler to subordinate formations, 10 May 1915, both in WO 95/155.

70 'First Army Special Order', 10 May 1915, WO 95/155.

71 Haig to GHQ, 11, 13 May 1915; Robertson to Haig, 11, 14 May 1915, all in WO 95/155.

72 Robertson to Haig, 12 , 14 May 1915, WO 95/155.

73 OH 1915 II, pp. 46–77.

74 Monro to First Army and Gough to I Corps, both 14 May 1915, WO 95/155.

75 Robertson to Haig , 14 May 1915, WO 95/55.

76 OH 1915 II, pp. 66–68; DHMsD 15, 16 May 1915.

77 OH II 1915, p. 68; DHMsD 17 May 1915; Haig to Lady Haig, 17 May 1915.

78 OH 1915 II, pp. 69–71.

79 Haig to Lady Haig, 20, 22 May 1915; OH 1915 II, pp. 77–9.

80 French to Kitchener, 17 May 1915, 75/46/7, FP direct quote from Read p. 209. A week later, Lord Esher explained to French that the New Armies were to be held back as a reserve: Esher to Kitchener, 23 May 1915, ESHR 4/5, EP.

81 Harris and Marble, p.19. They use 'bite-and-hold' to refer to 'relatively brief operations designed to seize vital ground', and 'step-by-step' to refer to 'more sustained offensives' involving 'deliberate attacks'.

82 My ideas on this issue have been informed by discussing it with and reading unpublished papers by Rob Thompson and Peter Simkins, and by discussing it with Stephen Badsey.

83 Rawlinson to Wigram, 25 Mar. 1915, Rawlinson Papers, NAM, 5201/33/17.

84 C.P. Scott, diary, 1 Oct. 1915, in Wilson (1970), p. 139.

85 Esher to Haig, 21 Jan. 1916, ESHR 4–6, EP.

86 Badsey (2008), pp. 255, 256.

87 Harris and Marble state they have chosen to ignore the logistic implications of a step-by-step strategy (p. 24). In fact, logistics are absolutely crucial to the argument.

88 DHMsD 11 Apr. 1915.

89 'General Principles for the Attack'; 'Communication between Cavalry and Artillery', 24 Sept. 1915, both in WO 95/158; Kenyon, pp. 28–30.

90 This was a return to the principles enunciated in *Cavalry Training 1912*. Badsey (2008), p. 257; Badsey to Sheffield, e-mail, 12 Oct. 2008.

91 Haig to Asquith, 25 Jun. 1915, Asquith Papers, 14, fol. 70, Bodleian Library; DHMsD, 8, 22, 30 July 1915 and 'Memorandum on . . . attack on a twenty-five mile front,' HP/101.

92 DHMsD 12, 24 Dec. 1914, 25 June 1915.

93 Strachan (1997), pp.127–31.

94 Haig to Wigram, 27 May 1915, RAs, RA PS/GV/Q 2521/V/129; DHMsD 26 May 1915, 14 July 1915.

95 Thompson to wife, 8 June 1915, TP; Haig to Wigram, 18 June 1915, Royal Archives/RAPS/PSO/GV/C/Q/2521/129.

96 'Conference 22 June', and Haig to GHQ, 23 June 1915, both in WO 95/157; DHMsD 22 June 1915.

97 Haig to Lady Haig, 23 June 1915; Haig to Wigram 27 June 1915, RAs, RA/PS/GV/Q 2521/V/133.

426 THE CHIEF

98 The conclusion that the British drew from this meeting on 19–20 June was that 'to
    have a reasonable chance of success' an offensive would have to be launched 'on a
    continuous front of twenty-five miles' by 36 divisions, with 1,150 heavy guns and
    howitzers in support. Troops and guns on this scale would not be available until
    spring 1916. OH 1915 II, pp. 115-18.

99 Lloyd (2006), p. 36.

100 GHQ to Haig, OAM 582, 22 July 1915, and Haig to GHQ, 23 July 1915, WO
    95/157; DHMsD 21 July 1915.

101 'Report of a Meeting between . . . Sir John French and General Foch, 27 July 1915';
    French to Joffre, 29 July 1915; Joffre to French, 5 Aug. 1915, all in WO 97/157.

102 To be fair to Joffre, this phrase can be read as referring to the general operational
    plan rather than the tactical situation on the ground.

103 DHMsD 2 and 7 Aug. 1915.

104 Joffre to French, 12 Aug. 1915, WO 95/157; Joffre, II, p. 357; Williams, R., pp. 117–
    32; Lloyd, (2006), p. 41–4; DHTsD 19 August 1915.

105 Maurice to Haig 22 Aug. 1915; GHQ to Haig, 23 Aug., WO 95/157.

106 Butler to Corps Commanders, 13 Aug. 1915; Haig to GHQ, 14 Aug. 1915, WO
    95/157; Palazzo, p.56.

107 Butler to Corps Commanders, 13 Aug. 1915; Haig to GHQ, 14 Aug. 1915, WO
    95/157; Palazzo, p. 56; '. . . Conference . . . Monday, 6 September 1915', WO
    95/158.

108 Spiers (1986), pp.13, 31–33; Cook (1999), p. 217.

109 Haig to Lady Haig, 24 Apr. 1915; DHMsD 23, 24, 26 Apr., 2 May 1915.

110 DHMsD 1 May 1915; Haig's marginal notes on IV Corps proposals, 22 Aug. 1915,
    WO 95/58; Palazzo, p. 45.

111 DHMsD 21 July, 2, 15 Aug. 1915; Palazzo, pp. 46, 65–6.

112 Jones I, p. 131–2.

113 Richter (1992), pp. 16–17, 22–23, 36; Palazzo, pp. 46–7, 57–8; Jones I, p. 132; Gough
    (1931), p. 101. Haig's enthusiasm for gas exceeded that of some of his subordinates,
    and there was some friction between Haig and Foulkes: Lloyd (2006), pp. 59–61.

114 DHMsD 16 Sept.1915; Palazzo, p. 64.

115 DHMsD 16 Sept.1915; Palazzo, p. 6; Jones I, p. 132, II, p. 16; Holmes (1981), p. 300.

116 Haig to Robertson, 16 Sept.1915, WO 95/158 (emphasis in original); Lloyd (2006),
    p. 54.

117 Haig to Lady Haig, 15, 24 August, 22 September 1915.

118 Cruttwell, p.166. For a discussion of this episode, including other issues not
    examined here, see Bryant.

119 Lloyd (2006), pp. 54, 65–6; Wilson diary, 13 Sept. 1915, WP; Haig to Lady Haig, 16
    Sept. 1915.

120 GHQ to Haig, 18 Sept. 1915, WO 95/158; DHMsD 24 Sept. 1915.

121 DHMsD 25 Sept.1915.

122 Richter (1992), p. 49.

123 Charteris (1931), p. 114.

124 Richter (1992), p. 87. Lloyd (2006), p. 126, sees Foulkes's assurance as the principal
    factor in Haig's decision to attack.

125 Exact timings are difficult to establish. A telephone message was received at GHQ, apparently at 5.00 a.m., stating that Zero hour was at 5.50 a.m. 75/46/5, FP.

126 DHTsD 25 Sept. 1915.

127 Rawlinson agreed with Haig's decision: Rawlinson to Derby, 29 Sept. 1915, 27/20, DP.

128 Richter (1992), p. 88.

129 9th and 15th Divisions were New Army formations, and the 47th was a Territorial division.

130 Griffith (1994), p. 53; Prior and Wilson (1992), p. 126; Corrigan, p. 86.

131 DHMsD 25 Sept. 1915.

132 Corrigan, pp. 84–5, provides a useful chronology.

133 DHMsD 25 Sept. 1915.

134 DHMsD 26 Sept.1915.

135 'Notes on Conference . . . 5 Oct. 1915', WO 95/159.

136 OH 1915 II, p. 388; Haig to Bonham-Carter, 24 Nov. 1915, Asquith papers, 28, fol. 273, Bodleian Library; Asquith to J.C. Wedgwood, Wedgwood Papers.

137 DHMsD 28 Oct. 1915; Windsor, p. 117.

138 Thompson to wife, 3, 4 Nov. 1915, TP; Rawlinson to Derby, 29 Oct, 27 Nov. 1915, 27/20, DP; Memoir 6–7, CAVN/1, Cavan papers, CCC.

139 Cassar (1985), p. 286.

140 DHMsD 10, 19 Dec. 1915.

141 Crofton diary, 4 June 1915, in Roynon, p. 262.

142 Repington to Bonar Law, 16 Nov. 1915, in Morris (1999), p. 239; Charles Grant to Rosebery, 28 Dec. 1915, Grant papers LHCMA.

143 Haig to L de Rothschild, 18 Oct. 1915 (see also Haig to J. Haig, 5 Oct. 1915, both HP/214a); Haig to Howell, 2 Nov. 1915, Howell Papers, 6/2/149, LHCMA.

144 Haig to Lady Haig, 18 Oct.1915.

145 DHMsD 3 Oct. 1915.

146 Snape (2005), pp. 59–72.

147 Cave (1998), p. 13; Cave (1999), p. 253.

148 Haig to Lady Haig, 27 Dec. 1915, HP/143.

Chapter 5: Commander-In-Chief

1 *Current History* (New York: Feb. 1916), p. 949.

2 Jellen p. 368; Esher to Sassoon, 5 Aug. 1916, Box 9, EP; *Scotsman,* 24 Aug. 1916, p. 5; Thompson to wife, 22 Dec. 1915, TP.

3 Charteris (1929), p. 181.

4 Xandra to Esher, 3 Feb. 1917, ESHR, EP.

5 Diary, 24 Jan. 1918, Hedley papers; Charteris (1929), p. 205.

6 Sassoon diary, 24 Aug. 1918, Box 23, SP; diary entry undated but *c.* Sept. 1917, Bickersteth, p. 209; Haig to Mrs Black, 23 Sept. 1918, HP/324a.

7 Blake, p. 30; Haig to Sassoon, 7 Mar. 1919, Box 13, Sassoon diary 5 May 1918, Box 23, both SP; Jackson, pp. 164–5; Stansky, p. 75.

8 Edward to Freda Dudley-Ward 9 Oct. 1918, in Godfrey, p. 88.

9 DHMsD 1 Feb. 1917; Vaughan, p. 191; Charteris (1929), p. 197; Diary, 21, 25 Jan., 4 Apr. 1918, Hedley papers.
10 Thompson to wife, 17 Oct. 1915, TP.
11 'Units of 68th Inf Bde', TP.
12 Jellen, p. 368.
13 Baynes (1995), p. 171.
14 Charteris (1929), pp. 205–6; Hussey (1999), pp. 16–18.
15 Paper on 'National Defence', 20 May 1906, HP/40p.
16 Francophone Canadians and the Boers were a partial exception.
17 DHMsD 5 May 1918.
18 Robbins (2010), p. 1; Middlebrook (1971), p. 69.
19 DHMsD 14 Dec. 1915.
20 Badsey (2006), p. 16; Vaughan, pp. 191–2.
21 Horne to wife 29 Jan. 1918 in Robbins (2009), p. 241; Essame pp. 25–6.
22 Perry, p. 99; DHMsD 8 Aug. 1916.
23 DHMsD 3 Aug. 1916; Badsey (2006), pp. 32–3.
24 DHMsD 18 Feb. 1916.
25 See the sources cited by Robbins (2005), pp. 118–19.
26 Quoted in Hussey (1999), p. 14. See also Simkins (1999), pp. 95–6; Charteris (1929), pp. 207, 212.
27 See Travers (1987), e.g. p. 110.
28 Hussey (1994a); Simpson (2008), pp. 199–203.
29 Headlam to wife, 27 Oct. 1916, in Beach (2010), p. 145.
30 Bourne (2001), p.,57; Beach (2004) passim.
31 Beddington, p. 89.
32 'G.S.O.' p. 37.
33 Thompson to wife, 15 Jan. 1916, TP.
34 Haig to J. Haig, 12 Jan. 1915, quoted in Warner, p. 12; Terraine (1963), p. 487.
35 Secrett, pp. 66, 116–7, 152–3, 188; Charteris (1929), p. 387–8.
36 Lellenberg (2007), p. 638.
37 Warner p. 85; Howard (1997), pp. 119–20.
38 Quoted in Sheffield and Barr, p. 227.
39 Secrett, 114; Sheffield and Barr, p. 226.
40 Davidson, pp. 64–5.
41 DHMsD 12 Sept. 1917; Dallas and Gill, pp. 73–6, exaggerates the impact of the mutiny.
42 Sheffield (2000), pp. 80–91, 137–40; Fuller J.G., pp. 81–113.
43 Haig to WO, 4 June 1918, WO 32/5597; Buckley, p. 81. Attempts to control VD in the BEF were only partially successful: Harrison, pp. 155–69.
44 Harrison, pp. 34–5, 65, 75, 298.
45 DHMsD 14 Dec. 1915. Harrison, pp. 34–5 does not name the MO who spoke to Haig.
46 Harrison, pp. 298–99.
47 Kiggell to Major-General Hickey, 19 Mar. 1916, KIGGELL 4/14, KP.
48 WO32/5460, quoted in Messenger (2005), p. 372.

49 Oram, p. 9; Stanley (2010), p. 172.

50 Sheffield (2000) *passim*; Oram, especially pp. 3, 15; Peaty, p. 211. 346 men were executed for all reasons, including 37 for murder, a crime that also carried the death penalty in civilian life. These figures exclude Indians.

51 Oram, pp. 55, 100; Babington, p. 7.

52 See e.g. the 'Proceedings' of the court martial on Pte. A. Longshaw, WO71/525.

53 WO71/485,509; Oram, pp. 62, 64, 143; Wessely, p .62.

54 DHMsD 6 Dec. 1916; Putkowski and Sykes, pp. 158–9.

55 Haig to Lady Haig, 28 Feb.1918; DHMsD 3 Mar. 1918; Stanley (2010), p. 174.

56 Sheffield (2000), especially p. 65.

57 Gregory, pp. 244, 281; Sibley, pp. 65, 68.

58 DHMsD 29 Mar. 1916, words in brackets are from DHTsD.

59 Haig to Lady Haig, 14 Oct. 1915.

60 Robbins (2005), p. 94.

61 DHMsD 24, 31 Mar. 1916.

62 Barr (2004), p. 14; Simpson (2004), p. 99.

63 Geddes, pp. 11–12.

64 Despatch, 19 May 1916, in Boraston, p. 4.

65 Falls, *36th Division*, p. 71.

66 Ashworth, p. 196; Griffith (1994), pp. 61–2.

67 Wavell, quoted in Sinclair, p. 1.

68 Simkins (1988), p. xiv; Boraston (1979), pp. 335–40.

69 Brown, pp. 46, 80, 112.

70 WO 95/29; Brown, p. 110.

71 Brown, p. 104, 187–8; Grieves (1999), p. 64.

72 Brown, pp. 142–51; Grieves (1999).

73 Haig to Esher, 6 Sept. 1916, ESHR 4/7, EP; DHMsD 7, 27, 30 Oct. 1916.

74 DHMsD 19 Sept. 1917; Sheffield (1994), p. 76. I am indebted to my colleague Rob Thompson for his advice on logistics.

75 Boraston (1979), p. 306.

76 Baker-Carr, pp. 87–9; 'Conference of General Staff Officers' Jan. 1909', p. 68, RA 33 CON, JSCSCL; Terraine (1980), pp.134–41; Haig to GHQ, 15 Apr. 1915, box 2, Lindsay Papers, BTM; Haig to Oliver Haig, 6 Nov. 1914, HP/334d; Cornish, p. 101. In his letter of April 1915 Haig reported adversely on Baker-Carr's proposal to reorganise machine-guns, as did Smith-Dorrien, which perhaps prompted Baker-Carr's belated revenge.

77 See Sheffield and Jordan, pp. 273–81; Hooton, pp. 84, 91–3, 109.

78 Duffy, pp. 315–16.

79 Haig to Henderson, 10 Sept. 1916, KIGGELL 4/43, KP.

80 Jordan, pp. 79–80; Goulter, p. 52.

81 Quoted in Sheffield and Jordan, p. 282.

82 DHMsD, 16 Oct. 1916.

83 Haig to Esher, 4 Apr. 1916, ESHR 4/6, EP.

84 Maurice, pp. 132, 206; Strachan (1997), pp. 135, 142.

85 Beckett (2000); Haig to Lady Haig, 28 Apr. 1915; Rose, p. 193.

86 This section is indebted to Badsey (1999).

87 See Sassoon's correspondence with Robinson of *The Times*, Northcliffe and Wickham Steed in Box 15, SP.

88 Gibbs (1920), p. 24; Lytton, pp. 65, 219; Badsey (1999), p. 184.

89 Sassoon to Esher, 24 July, 11 Aug., ESHR , EP; Badsey (1999), p. 185; Thompson, p. 255.

90 Simms to Duncan, 4 Aug. 1917, in DeGroot (1997), pp. 378–9.

91 DHMsD 4 Feb. 1917; Haig to Duncan, 31 Jan. 1921, in DeGroot (1997), p. 409.

92 Duncan diary, 22 July 1917, in DeGroot (1997), p. 368; Charteris (1931), p. 219 (29 Apr. 1917).

93 Duncan diary, 25 Feb. 1917, in DeGroot (1997), p. 325.

94 DeGroot (1997), p. 273.

95 Duncan (1966), pp. 26, 125.

96 Cave (1999) p. 243; DHMsD 30 Mar. 1916.

97 Snape (2008), p. 219; Snape (2010), p. 34; Bell, p. 219; Haig to King George V, in Sheffield and Bourne, p. 193.

98 Bickersteth diaries, 2 Oct. 1917 in Bickersteth, p. 142.

99 See Sheffield (2001), p. 40.

100 Millman (2001), p. 12; Gooch (1981), pp. 128–9, 133–4; French (2000), pp. 283–4, 291, 294–5.

101 Neilson (1997), pp. 103–23; DHMsD 13 Mar. 1918.

102 Sheffield (2005); Bell, pp. 15–22, 63–4, 92–112.

103 Neilson (1984), p. 311.

104 Haig to von Donop, 18 July 1916, KIGGELL 4/30, KP.

105 DHMsD 15 Dec. 1916.

106 DHMsD 15 Dec. 1916, 4 Sept, 7, 10 Nov. 1917.

107 DHMsD 9 June 1916; Dutton, pp. 186, 188.

108 Diary, 17 Apr. 1917, G.S. Clive papers II/3, LHCMA.

109 Philpott (1999), especially pp. 892–3; 'Paper by the General Staff . . . 16th December 1915'; Memo . . . Chantilly, 6th December 1915'; both in OH 1916 I, Appendices, pp. 2, 6–27.

110 'Instructions' in *OH 1916* I, Appendices, p. 40.

111 Charteris (1931) (26 Jan. 1916), p. 132. It was also the area where the British logistic infrastructure was most developed.

112 DHMsD 26 Dec. 1915, 14 Jan, 25 Feb. 1916. On 4 Feb. 1916 Haig also instructed Rawlinson to consider operations around Ypres. OH 1916 I, pp. 31–2.

113 OH 1916 I, p. 33.

114 DHMsD 26 Dec.1915.

115 DHMsD 29 Dec. 1915; OH 1916 I, pp. 26–7.

116 Philpott (2009), p. 78.

117 DHMsD 28, 31 Jan. 1916; Haig to Joffre, 21 Feb. 1916, WO158/14.

118 Millman, (2001), p. 21.

119 Gooch (1974) chapter 10, especially pp. 299, 309, 311, 326–9.

120 Balfour, note, 25 Jan. 1916, CAB 42/7/12.

121 Cassar (2004), pp. 265–6; Bourne (1989), pp. 146–8; Harris and Marble.

122 Cassar (2004), p. 269.

123 Herwig, pp.179–82, 196–7; Foley (2005), pp. 187–8, 206.

124 Haig to Robertson, 19 Feb. 1916, in Blake, p. 130; DHMsD 25 Feb. 1916.

125 Foley (2005), pp.157–9, 192–3, 239–41.

126 For context, see Strachan (1998); diary entry not dated but *c.* September 1917 in Bickersteth, p. 209; pp. 83–7.

127 DHMsD 4 May 1916.

128 DHMsD 3, 7 Apr. 1916; Minutes, War Committee, 7 April 1916, CAB 42/12/5; Hankey diary, 2 May 1916, HNKY 1, HyP.

129 Cassar (2004), p. 273; Woodward (1998), p. 42.

130 DHMsD 29 Mar. 1916.

131 This is not the impression given by Cassar (2004), p. 272, which omits to give the context of the quotation.

132 Haig to Robertson 29 May 1916 in Woodward (1989), p. 54.

133 DHMsD 29 May 1916; Haig to Bertie, 5 June 1916, HP/214c; 'Memo On Policy for Press', appx to DHTsD 26 May 1916. See also Haig to Esher, 2 June 1916, ESHR 4/6, EP.

134 GHQ to Rawlinson, 27 May 1916, in OH 1916 I, appx 12, pp. 84–5; DHMsD 27 May 1916.

135 Charteris (1931), p. 151.

136 DHMsD 25 May 1916.

137 DHMsD 26 May 1916.

138 Philpott (2009), pp.109–11, 118, 122.

139 DHMsD 15 June 1916. See also Haig to Joffre, 26 June 1916, WO 158/14.

140 Beach (2004), pp. 160–1. I am very grateful to Dr Beach for making a copy of his seminal work available to me.

141 DHMsD 18 June 1916.

142 DHMsD 24 Mar. 1916.

143 Badsey (2008), p. 270.

144 Kiggell to Gough, 4 June 1916, AWM 45/34/2.

145 RD, 6 May 1916, RWLN 1/5, RwP.

146 DHMsD 9 Apr. 1916.

147 Badsey (1996), p. 153; Haig to Rawlinson, 12 Apr. 1916, OH 1916 I, appx 9, p. 75.

148 Badsey (1996), p. 154.

149 Gough (1931), p. 138; Badsey (1996), pp. 154–5.

150 RD, 3, 4, 14 Apr. 1916, RWLN 1/5, RwP; DHMsD 5 Apr. 1916.

151 Badsey (1996), p. 155; Memo from Kiggell, 21 June 1916, AWM/34/3.

152 RD, 21 June, RWLN 1/5, RwP.

153 'Fourth Army Memo . . .' 28 June 1916, in OH 1916 I, appx. 20, p. 150; Rawlinson's note, 18 July 1916, 27/5, DP.

154 DHMsD 12 Dec. 1915, 27 June 1916.

155 DHMsD 30 June 1916. Rawlinson also commented on the pre-battle confidence of corps commanders in a note of 18 July 1916, 27/5, DP.

CHAPTER 6: ATTRITION

1 Haig to Esher, 1 Jul. 1916, ESHR , EP.
2 DHMsD 1 July 1916.
3 RD, 1 July 1916, RWLN 1/5, RwP.
4 Gough (1931), p. 137; RD, 1 July 1916, RWLN 1/5, RwP.
5 Middlebrook (1971), p. 213. I have been unable to find any other evidence to support this suggestion.
6 'Decisions of C-in-C, 5 p.m., 1/7/16', AWM 45/34/3; DHMsD 1 July 1916.
7 OH 1916 II, p. 3.
8 OH 1916 I, p. vii.
9 Badsey (2006a); OH 1916 I, p. vii.
10 For analysis, see Sheffield (2001), pp. 135–40.
11 Haig to Lady Haig, 30 June 1916.
12 DHMsD 15 June 1916; Sheffield (2001), pp. 138–9; Prior and Wilson (2005), pp. 112–18.
13 Philpott (2009), pp. 98, 128.
14 DHMsD 27 June 1916.
15 Kiggell to Robertson (?), 3 June 1916, KIGGELL 4/19, KP.
16 Birch to Edmonds, 8 July 1930, CAB 45/132.
17 DHMsD 15 June 1916; Haig to Joffre, 25 Apr. 1916, WO 158/14.
18 OH 1916 I, p. 251.
19 Prior and Wilson (1992), pp. 166–70.
20 Hunter-Weston quoted in Repington (1920), I, p. 267 (8 July 1916); Hart (2005), p. 65.
21 DHMsD 2 July 1916.
22 Repington (1920) I p.298 (4 Aug. 1916).
23 DHMsD 3 July 1916; 'Note of interview . . . 3 July 1916.' WO 158/14.
24 Esher to Haig, 4 Jul. 1916, ESHR 4–6, EP.
25 Foley (2005), pp. 249–52.
26 Duffy, p. 171; Foley (2005), pp. 251, 254; Sheffield (2004), p. 68.
27 Note of interview . . . 2 July 1916', AWM 45/34/3; Kiggell to Rawlinson, 2 July 1916, AWM 45/34/3.
28 DHMsD 4 July 1916.
29 DHMsD 8 July 1916; Haig to Lady Haig, 8 July 1916.
30 Beach, 'British Intelligence', p. 167.
31 The best modern account of Fromelles is Lee, R. Also see Cobb; Corfield.
32 McMullin, p. 20; Bourne (2006), pp. 132–6; OH 1916 II, p. 134.
33 DHMsD 20 July 1916.
34 DHMsD 3 Aug. 1916.
35 Senior.
36 'Note of arrangement . . . with Gough, 3 and 4 July 1916', AWM 45.34/3; OH 1916 II, p. 19.
37 Haig to Lady Haig, 10 July 1916.
38 Duffy, p. 173; Prior and Wilson (1992), p. 187.
39 Joffre, II, p. 477.

40 Sheffield, (2004), p. 76.

41 Charteris (1931), p. 159 (29 July 1916).

42 Samuels, pp. 52–3.

43 Butler to Armies, 13 August 1916, JSCSCL.

44 DHMsD 10, 11 July 1916.

45 Anglesey (1997), pp. 45–8; DHMsD 13 July 1916.

46 Prior and Wilson (1992), pp. 191–2; Duffy, p. 177.

47 Sassoon to Lady Haig, 14 July 1916, HP/144.

48 Haig to Lady Haig, 14 July 1916.

49 See correspondence in 4/2, Loch papers, 71/2/4, IWM.

50 See Rawling, chapters 3 and 4, and Pugsley (2004), pp. 176–81.

51 See e.g. DHMsD 17, 21 July 1916.

52 DHMsD 21 July 1916.

53 DHMsD 14 Aug.1916.

54 Kiggell telephone conversation with Rawlinson, 8 Aug.1916, AWM 45/34/1.
    Rawlinson criticised the infantry's 'want of go' at Guillemont: RD, 8 Aug. 1916,
    RWLN 1/5, RwP.

55 RD, 22 Aug. 1916, RWLN 1/5, RwP. The phrase is Prior and Wilson's: (2005), p.
    168.

56 Haig to Rawlinson, 24 Aug. 1916, quoted in Prior and Wilson (2005), p. 168.

57 DHMsD 28 July 1916; Beach, pp. 167–9; Horne to wife 18 Aug. 1916 in Robbins
    (2009), p. 185.

58 Kiggell to Rawlinson, 9 July 1916, AWM 45/34.

59 Sandilands, p. 73.

60 Dunn, p.440; Horne diary, 9 July 1916, Horne Papers, IWM; Hughes, *passim;* Cook
    M.N., *passim.*

61 The relevant papers are in WO 32/17700. Many thanks to Stuart Mitchell for
    bringing them to my attention.

62 2 August 1916, in OH 1916 II, Appendix 13.

63 Prior and Wilson (2005), pp. 159–60.

64 DHMsD 30 July 1916.

65 DHMsD 11 Aug 1916.

66 DHMsD 11 Aug. 1916.

67 DHMsD 23 Aug. 1916.

68 Quoted in Sheldon (2005), p. 250.

69 GHQ memo, 19 Aug. 1916; GHQ memo 31 Aug. 1916, both in WO 158/235;
    DHMsD 29 Aug. 1916.

70 DHMsD 9 Sept. 1916.

71 Beach, pp. 172–5.

72 'Fourth Army Instruction in the event of a general advance', 13 Sept. 1916, in OH
    1916 II, Appendices, pp. 70–1; Kenyon, pp. 72–4; RD, 14 Sept. 1916, RWLN 1/5,
    RwP.

73 Haig to Robertson, 22 Aug. 1916, WO 158/21; Harris, chapters 1 and 2 (for Haig,
    see pp. 54–7, 62–3); Sheffield (2001), pp. 146–7.

74 DHMsD 15 September 1916.

75 DHMsD 26 Aug. 1916.

76 RD, 2 Sept. 1916, RWLN 1/5, RwP.

77 Peter Simkins in McCarthy, p.10.

78 Rawlinson, 'Notes on Operations between 14 September and 8 October 1916', 27/5, DP.

79 DHMsD 6 Sept. 1916; Haig to Lady Haig, 8 Sept. 1916.

80 DHMsD 7, 8 Aug. 1916; Churchill, II, pp. 1084–9.

81 Haig to Ellison, 14 Sept. 1910, HP/40q; DHMsD 12 Aug. 1916.

82 DHMsD 17 Sept. 1917.

83 Kenyon, p. 83.

84 Sheffield (2004), p. 136.

85 DHMsD 24 Sept. 1916.

86 OH 1916 II, pp. 427–8.

87 Haig to King George V, 5 October 1916, in Sheffield and Bourne, pp. 236–7. See also Haig to St Loe Strachey, 1 Nov. 1916, STR/8, PA, where Haig argues for the significance of the increased number of German divisions on the Somme front.

88 DHMsD 4 Nov. 1916.

89 DHMsD 23 Oct. 1916.

90 Boraston (1919), p. 51.

91 Foley (2005), pp. 236–7, 246.

92 Prior and Wilson (2005), p.301, give a much lower figure of 230,000. However, this is based on a controversial source, and the tentative conclusions of an international workshop attended by the author on 'The Unthinkable: The Military Dead of the Great War', held in July 2008, were that at present it is impossible to accept these figures at face value. Prior and Wilson's case (pp. 301–2) that Haig's strategy degraded the BEF much faster than the BEF wore out the Germans is based on these figures. The opposite has been argued, that the British-led operations on the Somme, at least until the end of August wore out 'the German army far more effectively than German action at Verdun wore down the French' (Foley (2005), p. 257).

93 Foley (2005) p.185.

94 DHMsD 'note' appended to 1 Aug. 1916.

95 Quoted in Kramer, p. 215.

96 Ludendorff, I, p. 307.

97 Nugent to wife, 20 Dec. 1916, in Perry, p. 126.

98 The reference is to the frock coats worn by politicians.

99 This related to the decline in the purchase of war loans. Stephenson, p. 223; Strachan (2001), p. 913.

100 Middlebrook, M. & M., pp. 353–4.

101 MacDonald, p. iv; Repington (1920) I, p. 345 (27 Sept. 1916); Clifford, pp. 367–71.

102 Esher to Haig, 11 Mar. 1916, ESHR 4/6, CCC; Haig to WO, 21/11/16, WO158/22.

103 Millman (2001) p.28.

104 Esher to Haig, 15 Sept. 1918, Box 9, SP.

CHAPTER 7: NEW BATTLES

1   Kiggell to Armies, OAD 211, 17 Nov. 1916, AWM 51–2.

2   Robertson to Haig, 1 Jan. 1917, in OH 1917 I, appx. 5, p. 9.

3   DHMsD 20 Dec. 1916.

4   Doughty, pp. 324–5.

5   Nivelle's directive, 4 Apr 1917, WO 256/17; Nivelle to Haig, 21 Dec. 1916, and Haig
    to Nivelle, OAD 262, 6 Jan. 1917, in OH 1917 I, Appendices 2 & 7, pp. 4–6, 13–15;
    Terraine (1963), p. 252.

6   Woodward (1998), p. 84; French (1995), pp. 52–3; Stevenson diary 15 Jan. 1917 in
    Taylor, p. 139.

7   Duff Cooper II, p. 32.

8   DHMsD 7 Feb. 1917.

9   Robertson to Esher 6 Feb. 1917, ESHR, EP.

10 Haig to Nivelle, 6 Jan. 1917, in Blake, pp. 190–1.

11 Spears (1939), pp. 65, 67.

12 DHMsD 13 Jan. 1917.

13 Robertson to Wigram, 12 Jan. 1917, in Woodward (1989), p. 141.

14 DHMsD 15 Jan. 1917; Stevenson diary 15 Jan. 1917 in Taylor, p. 138.

15 OH 1917 I p.45; 'London Convention of 16 Jan. 1917' in OH 1917 I, appx. 8, p. 16.

16 DHMsD 16 Jan. 1917.

17 French (1995), pp. 55–6.

18 Greenhalgh (2005), pp. 138–9.

19 DMsD16 Feb. 1917.

20 Wilson diary 13 March 1917, cited in Jeffrey (2006), p. 188.

21 Haig to Esher, 8 Feb.1917, ESHR , EP. Haig expressed similar sentiments to
    Maurice: DHMsD 7 Feb. 1917.

22 DHMsD 1 Feb. 1917.

23 This account is indebted to Badsey (1999), pp. 186–8.

24 The Times, 15 Feb. 1917, p. 9; Badsey (1999), pp. 187–8.

25 DHMsD 15, 18 Feb. 1917.

26 Charteris (1931), pp. 192–3; Lytton, pp. 64–9.

27 Derby to LG, 19 Feb.1917, Parlimentary Archives, LG-F-14-4-20 LGP.

28 Derby to LG, 20 Feb. 1917, Parlimentary Archives, LG-F-14-4-21. LGP.

29 DHMsD 26 Feb. 1917.

30 Spears (1939), p. 143; DHMsD 26 Feb. 1917. Words in brackets are from DHTsD.

31 Spears (1939), pp. 540, 546.

32 Greenhalgh (2005), pp. 142, 148; Suttie, p. 106.

33 War Cabinet (79) 24 Feb. 1917 CAB 23/1; 'Memorandum . . .'4 Mar. 1917, quoted in
    Woodward (1998), pp. 146–7.

34 Haig to Esher, 4 Mar. 1917, ESHR 4/7, EP.

35 The MS reads 'absurd'.

36 DHMsD 26 Feb. 1917.

37 Hankey diary 26 Feb. 1917, HNKY/1 HyP.

38 OH 1917 I, p. 57.

39 French (1996), pp. 79–84; Cabinet Paper G.T. 114, 7 March 1917, CAB 24/7.

40 Woodward (1998), p. 151; Bertie diary, 10 Mar. 1917 in Gordon Lennox II, p. 114.

41 Woodward (1998), p. 150; Robertson to Haig, 2 March 1917, in Woodward (1989), p. 156.

42 DHMsD 11 Mar. 1917.

43 Hankey diary 16 Jan. 1917, HNKY/1 HyP.

44 Memo by Hankey, 7 Mar. 1917, CAB 63/19.

45 Woodward (1998), p. 152; Stevenson diary 16 Mar. 1917, in Taylor, p. 148.

46 Wilson (1986), p. 445.

47 Quoted in Terraine (1963), p. 275.

48 Balfour to Cambon, 9 Mar. 1917, Parlimentary Archives, LG-F-23, LGP.

49 Sassoon to Esher, n.d. but *c.* 16 March 1917, ESHR , EP.

50 Hankey diary, 26 Feb. 1917, HNKY/1, HyP.

51 Bourne (1989), p. 151.

52 Stevenson diary, 12 May 1917, in Taylor, p. 157; Suttie, p. 99.

53 Greenhalgh (2005), p. 146, suggests that this, and other evidence, indicates that 'Nivelle seems to have realised that he had been used' and that the 'initiative [behind the Calais conspiracy] had always come from London – not from Nivelle'.

54 Grigg, p. 86.

55 Unless otherwise stated, what follows comes from two postgraduate dissertations to which I am indebted: Geddes, and Mythen.

56 DHMsD 2, 3 Feb. 1917.

57 Geddes, pp. 34–5; Lee (1999).

58 Pugsley (2007), p. 295.

59 Kiggell to Armies, OAD 258, 2 Jan. 1917, AWM 51–2; Edmonds, p. 215; Falls (1960), p. 252.

60 See Lupfer; Wynne.

61 'Record of Army Commanders conference . . .' 27 Jan. 1917, OAD 291/22, 3 Feb. 1917, AWM 51–2.

62 'Third Army Appreciation' 7 Feb. 1917, OH 1917 I, appx. 14, p. 47.

63 OH 1917 I, p. 11; Sheffield (2001), p. 162.

64 Record of Army Commanders conference . . .' 27 Jan. 1917, OAD 291/22, 3 Feb. 1917; Kiggell to Third Army, 12 Feb. 1917, OAD 314; both in AWM 51–2.

65 Kenyon, p. 42.

66 Kiggell to Third Army, OAD 314, 12 Feb. 1917, AWM 51–2. Haig and Kiggell had previously discussed the Appreciation: DHMsD 10 Feb.1917.

67 Haig, 'Review of present situation', 2 Mar. 1917; Kiggell to Armies, OAD 329, 9 Mar. 1917; Note of '. . . conference . . . at GHQ', 12 Mar. 1917; all documents in AWM 51–2.

68 DHMsD 14 Mar. 1917.

69 Kiggell to Armies, OAD 337, 16 Mar. 1917, AWM 51–2.

70 'Note of proceedings of Army Commanders conference . . . 17 Mar. 1917' OAD 291/24, AWM 51–2.

71 Kiggell to Armies, OAD 350, 26 Mar. 1917, AWM 51–2.

72 'Note of proceedings of Army Commanders conference . . . 24 Mar. 1917', OAD 291/25, AWM 51–2.

73 DHMsD 7 April 1917.

74 DHMsD 8 Apr. 1917.

75 Horne to wife, 19 Apr. 1917, in Robbins (2009), p. 211; Haig to the King, 9 Apr. 1917, in Sheffield and Bourne, p. 278.

76 Anglesey (1997), p. 76.

77 DHMsD 10 Apr. 1917. According to James, p.101, on the evening of 10 April, Haig visited XVII Corps HQ, became angry at discovering that cavalry was not in place to exploit what seemed to be a 'widening gap' in the enemy defences, and made a heated telephone call to Allenby to demand an explanation. This is based on post-war correspondence of General Ferguson with the official historians. In his Ms diary for 10 April, Haig mentions a number of visits to the headquarters of formations, but not to XVII Corps; the official history also fails to offer any corroborative evidence. The implication of James's account is that it was Haig that prodded Allenby into committing the cavalry against the latter's will. The evidence does not support this interpretation.

78 DHMsD 11 Apr. 1917.

79 Third Army to Corps, 10 Apr. 1917, WO 95/362, appx. A, File 2.

80 WO 95/362, Appx. AQ file 2, no. 143.

81 OH 1917 I, pp. 258, 261.

82 DHMsD 11 Apr. 1917.

83 James, p. 102; OH 1917 I, p. 280.

84 DH Ms 14 Apr. 1917.

85 Hughes (2006), p. 27; Simkins (1999a). Haig does not mention this incident in his diary. The version in OH 1917 I, p. 378 seems to be bowdlerised.

86 See Walker.

87 DHMsD 16, 17 Apr. 1917.

88 Repington (1920) I, p. 535 (23 Apr. 1917).

89 DHMsD 18 Apr. 1917; Haig to Robertson, OAD 405, 19 Apr. 1917, WO 256/17.

90 'Notes of Meeting . . . 26 Apr. 1927', OAD 415; 'Record of a conference . . . 25th April 1917', both in AWM 51–2; DHMsD 24 Apr. 1917.

91 Charteris (1931), p. 219 (28 April 1917).

92 Haig to Robertson, 29 Apr. 1917, in Blake, p. 22.

93 The USA had declared war on Germany on 6 April 1917.

94 French (1992); 'Report of conference . . . 30 Apr. 1917', OAD 426, AWM 51–2.

95 Esher to Haig, 27 Apr. 1917, LG-F-16, LGP.

96 Kiggell to Wilson, 6 May 1917, WO 158/48.

97 Griffiths (1994), pp. 40–1.

98 Robertson to Haig, 20 April 1917, in Woodward (1989), pp. 178–9.

99 DHMsD 1 May 1917; Haig to War Cabinet, 'The Present Situation and Future Plans', OAD 428/1, 1 May 1917, 27/11, DP.

100 OH 1917 I, pp. 30–33.

101 'Record of . . . Army Commander's conference, 7 May 1917', WO 158/224.

102 Simkins (1999a), p. 84; Hughes (2006), pp. 27–8.

103 Hughes (1999).

104 Derby to Sassoon, 19, 30 Apr. 1917, Box 13, SP.

105 DHMsD 12 May 1917.
106 'Report on operations, 18 Apr. 1917', WO 95/1514.
107 'Summary of War Diary . . . April 1917', WO 95/2433.
108 Sheffield (2007), pp.16–17.

Chapter 8: False Dawns

1 Lloyd George II, p. 1333; Sheffield and Barr, p. 235.
2 Bond (1997), p. 479.
3 'Rawlinson's proposals . . . 27 Feb. 1917', OH 1917 II, Appx III, pp. 402–3; 'Project for Operations . . . 5 Mar. 1916', WO 158/19; Wiest (1997), p. 82. Generally I have followed Wiest (1997), but Prior and Wilson (1996) give a slightly different interpretation of the planning of Third Ypres.
4 Paper of 30 Jan. 1917 WO 158/38; Wiest (1997), pp. 78–9.
5 See documents in WO 158/214 and WO 158/38; DHMsD 5, 10 Feb. 1917; OH 1917 II, pp. 17–19, 25; Prior and Wilson (1996), pp. 45–52; Wiest (1997), pp.79, 80.
6 Kiggell to Plumer, 6 Jan. 1917, OH 1917 II, Appx. V pp. 406–7.
7 'Record of instructions . . . 7th May 1917', OAD 434, AWM 45/33/1.
8 OH 1917 II, p. 27.
9 Kiggell to Plumer, 29 May 1917; 'Summary of . . . a conference . . . 30 May 1917', OAD 464, 31 May 1917, both in AWM 51/53.
10 Kiggell to Second Army, OAD 459, 3 Apr. 1917; Haig's marginal notes on '. . . interview between General Plumer and Lt. Col. Macmullen'; Davidson to Second Army, OAD 458, 24 May 1917, all in AWM 51/53.
11 DHMsD 6 June 1917. Privately, Haig went further – the situation was 'favourable for the Allies', and his army could 'force the Enemy to beg for peace': Haig to Esher, 5 June 1917, ESHR 4/7, EP.
12 DHMsD 6 June 1917.
13 OH 1917 II, p. 89.
14 Brown (1998), p. 164.
15 DHMsD 14 June 1917.
16 Wiest, 'Haig, Gough and Passchendaele', p. 90.
17 Kiggell to Commander Second and Fifth Armies, 24 and 29 May 1917, quoted in Wiest, 'Haig, Gough and Passchendaele', p.81; Malcolm to Corps, 30 June 1917, AWM 51–3; 'Fifth Army Instruction for the Offensive', 27 June 1917, OH 1917 II, Appx. XIII, pp. 431–2.
18 Memo from Davidson, 26 June 1917, WO 158/20.
19 DHMsD 28 June 1917. Much later, in 1944, Gough denied that this meeting had taken place. His denial is unconvincing: see Wiest (1997), pp. 84–5.
20 Suttie, p. 122; Farr.
21 Robertson to Haig, 13 June 1917, in Blake, p. 239.
22 Suttie, Rewriting, p. 130.
23 Haig to Derby, 12 June 1917 in Blake, pp. 237–8.
24 DHMsD 9 June 1917.
25 Robertson to Haig, 13 June 1917, in Blake, p. 239.

26 Suttie, pp. 129–39; Lloyd George II, p. 1277; Terraine (1984), p. 145.

27 Suttie, p. 136.

28 Haig to Robertson, 22 June 1917, in Terraine (1984), p. 168.

29 Greenhalgh, (2005), p. 153.

30 Esher to Haig, 9 June 1917, Box 9, SP. Robertson told Haig that Pétain 'talked like a man without a jot of confidence as to the future': Robertson to Haig, 30 June 1917, in Woodward (1989) p. 198.

31 OH 1917 II, p. 184; DHMsD 19 Sept. 1917.

32 DHTsD 20 June 1917.These words do not appear in the original manuscript version of the diary, only in the later typescript version; they are, however, fully consistent with the original entry. It seems Haig deemed them too secret to go into the original diary, which was of course circulated to various people.

33 Till, p. 77.

34 '. . . Cabinet Committee on War Policy', 25 June 1917, and 'Report of War Policy Committee . . . 10 Aug. 1917 [sic] ' in Terraine (1984), pp. 176, 200; Suttie, p. 135.

35 Boraston and Bax, p. 136.

36 DHMSD 17, 20 July 1917.

37 Atkinson (1952), pp. 229–30.

38 Major-General F.A. Dudgeon in Dudley Ward, p. 161. He was writing of the attack of 16 August, but his comments applied equally to 31 July.

39 OH 1917 II, pp. 153–6, 179; Steel and Hart, pp. 136–7.

40 DHMsD 31 July 1917.

41 'Fifth Army Operation Order . . .' 31 July 1917; GHQ Instructions . . .' 1 Aug. 1917; 'Memorandum on . . . II Corps Front . . .' 1 Aug. 1917; all in OH 1917 II, pp. 445–8.

42 Boraston and Bax, p. 136.

43 Hussey (1997), p. 151. See also Doyle.

44 Bond (1997), pp. 482–3.

45 DHMsD 1 Aug. 1917.

46 Quotations from DHMsD 8 Aug. 1917; also Kiggell to Army Commanders, 7 Aug. 1917, HP/116; DHMsD 3 Aug. 1917; Haig to Lady Haig, 5 Aug. 1917; Repington (1920) II, pp. 30–1, 61 (20 Aug., 30 Sept. 1917).

47 DHMsD 10 Aug. 1917.

48 Wiest (1997), p. 88; OH 1917 II, pp. 189–90.

49 Dudley Ward, pp. 159–60.

50 DHMsD 17 Aug. 1917.

51 Gough (1931), p. 205; Steel and Hart, p. 155.

52 Wiest (1997), pp. 88–90.

53 DHMsD 15 Aug. 1917.

54 DHMsD 28 Aug. 1917, Haig to Robertson, 8 Oct. 1917, quoted in French (2000), p. 293.

55 Diary entry, 6 Aug. 1917, Riddell, p. 263.

56 Lloyd George 31 July 1918, quoted in Grigg, p. 542.

57 Kiggell to Gough, OAD 609, 28 Aug. 1917, AWM 51/53.

58 e.g. Harington to Morland, 4 Sept. 1917, AWM 45/39/4.

59 'Notes of a Conference . . .' OAD 610, 30 Aug. 1917, AWM 51/53; DHMsD 7, 10, 11, 12 Aug. 1917.

60 Ludendorff, II, pp. 479–80.

61 'Haig's notes for Army Commanders' Conference', 21 Aug. 1917, in Terraine (1984), p. 236.

62 Keith-Falconer, pp. 195–207.

63 'Notes of a conference . . .' OAD 610, 30 Aug. 1917, AWM 51–3; OH 1917 II. p. 237–42; 'Second Army Instruction . . .' 29 Aug. 1917', OH 1917 II, Appx. XXIII, pp. 452–56; 'Second Army's Notes on Training . . .' 31 Aug. 1917, OH 1917 II, Appx. XXV, pp. 459–64.

64 DHMsD 17, 18 Sept. 1917.

65 OH 1917 II,. p. 279.

66 Prior and Wilson (1996), p. 123.

67 Hankey diary, 25 Sept. 1917, HNY/3, HyP.

68 Kiggell to Army Commanders, OAD 628, 21 Sept. 1917, AWM 45/33/1.

69 Hankey diary, 26 Sept. 1917, HNY/3, HyP.

70 DHMsD 23 Sept. 1917.

71 'Record of Conference . . .' OAD 639, 28 Sept. 1917, AWM 45/31/1.

72 Haig's marginal note on N Malcolm, 'Problem of exploiting success . . .' 1 Oct. 1917, AWM 51–3.

73 OH 1917 II, p. 297.

74 Harington to Corps, 2 Oct. 1917, AWM 51–3; OH 1917 II, pp. 297–8.

75 AOH 1917 IV, p. 875; Ludendorff II, p. 490.

76 DHMsD 4 Oct. 1917.

77 Hagenlucke, p. 53.

78 Godley, p. 225.

79 Rob Thompson, 'Mud Blood, and Wood: BEF Operational and Combat Logistico-Engineering during the Battle of Third Ypres, 1917' (unpublished paper, 2000) quoted in Sheffield (2001), p. 178.

80 Werth, p. 327.

81 DHMsD 5 Oct. 1917; Beach. p. 225; Repington (1920) II, p. 98 (10 Oct. 1917).

82 Repington (1920) II, p. 101 (15 Oct. 1917). Haig himself is unlikely to have used the term 'Huns'.

83 DHMsD 15 Oct. 1917.

84 Prior and Wilson (1996), pp. 160–1; Repington (1920) II, p. 99 (14 Oct. 1917); DHMsD 15 Oct. 1917.

85 DHMsD 9 Oct. 1917; OH 1917 II, pp. 332, 334.

86 'Record of a Conference . . .', OAD 665, 13 Oct. 1917, AWM 51–3.

87 See e.g. Memo from Col. McMullen, with marginal comments by Haig, 1 May 1917, WO 158/20.

88 Wiest (1995), pp. 154–6, 162, 164–5.

89 OH 1917 II, p. 386.

90 Brown, p. 167.

91 OH 1917 II, p. 348.

92 Harington (1940), pp. 63–4.

93 'Appreciation . . . VIII Corps front November 1917', WO 95/821.

94 Repington (1920) II, pp. 102–3 (15 Oct. 1917).

95 OH 1917 II. pp. 325–6, 345–6.

96 Robertson to Haig, 6 Oct. 1917, Williamson (1989), p. 233.

97 Swettenham, pp. 185–6; OH 1917 II, pp. 346–7; Cook (2008) pp. 31–8.

98 Foley (2007), p. 176.

99 For the continuing importance of the Belgian coast in Haig's thinking, see letter to Strachey, 9 Dec. 1917, Parlimentary Archives, STR-8, Strachey papers.

100 Boraston (1979), pp. 133–5, 319–20.

101 Quoted in Sheldon (2007), pp. 315–16 (emphasis in original).

102 OH 1917 III, pp. 4–5.

103 For the origins of Cambrai, see Hammond (2008), pp. 51–9.

104 Simpson (1995), pp. 105–6.

105 Kiggell to Third Army, OAD 557, 18 July 1917, AWM 51/51.

106 DHMsD 16 Sept. 1917; Hammond (2008), p. 59.

107 Byng to GHQ, 10 Oct. 1917, Kiggell to Byng, OAD 664, 13 Oct. 1917, both in AWM 51/51; DHMsD 15 Oct. 1917.

108 OH 1917 III, p. 17.

109 'Third Army Plan, Operation GY', 13 Nov. 1917, OH 1917 III, Appx.1, p. 306. The 'quadrilateral' refers to a rough square formed on the map by drawing imaginary lines between the Escaut canal, River Sensée, Canal du Nord and the Hindenburg Line.

110 Butler to Byng, OAD 690, 3 Nov. 1917, AWM 51/51.

111 Boraston (1919), p. 159.

112 OH 1917 III, pp. 17–19.

113 Haig to Robertson, 28 Oct. 1917, Parlimentary Archives, LG-F-44, LGP.

114 Woollcombe, p. 69.

115 The allegation that 51st Division's infantry–tank co-operation tactics were faulty has been refuted: Hammond (1995), pp. 90–9; Hussey (1997), pp. 76–91.

116 Kenyon, pp. 172–5.

117 DHMsD 22 Nov. 1917.

118 OH 1917 III, p. 116.

119 OH 1917 III, p. 116.

120 'Note on the Effect of the Advance on the Cambrai Front' by Charteris, 25 Nov. 1917, AWM 51/51.

121 Williams J, pp. 190–1.

122 Hammond (2008), p. 436.

123 OH 1917 III, p. 139.

124 Kiggell to Byng, OAD 713, 25 Nov. 1917, AWM 51/51.

125 DHMsD 26 Nov. 1917; Woollcombe, pp. 168–9.

126 'Third Army Instructions . . . 27 Nov. 1917', OH 1917 III, Appx. 15, p. 372.

127 DHMsD 27 Nov. 1917.

128 OH 1917 III, pp.168–9, 373; Gardner (2006).

129 Byng to GHQ, 18 Dec. 1917, WO 158/54; Dill to CIGS, telegram, OAD 731/1, 18 Dec. 1917; Byng to GHQ, 18 Dec. 1917; Charteris to GHQ 30 Dec. 1917, all in AWM 51/51. See Williams, J., pp. 206–8, for the argument that Byng did not intend to shift the blame to the troops. The court of enquiry also blamed the 'want

of supervision' by 'higher commanders' for failure to enforce defensive doctrine (WO 158/53, p. 11).

130 DHMsD 2, 3, 4 Dec. 1917.

131 Derby to Haig, 17 Dec. 1917, Parlimentary Archives, LG-F-14, LGP.

132 Strachey to Haig, 26 Nov. 1917, STR-8, Strachey papers, Parlimentary Archives.

133 Haig to Robertson, OAD 731/1, 24 Dec. 1917, AWM 51/51.

134 Robertson to Derby, 3 Jan. 1918, AWM 51/51; Robertson to Plumer, 10 Dec. 1917, Woodward 1989, p. 265; Smuts, Memo GT 3198, 3 Jan. 1918, AWM 51/51.

135 100 H.C. Deb. 5 s, 20 Dec. 1917, col. 2251, Strachey to Repington, 26 Jan. 1918, quoted in Thompson, p. 295.

136 Horne to wife, 22 Jan. 1918 in Robbins (2009), p. 240; Badsey (1999), p. 189; Northcliffe to Sassoon, 13 Dec. 1917, Box 15, SP; Thompson, p. 294–7.

137 DHMsD 7 Dec. 1917.

CHAPTER 9: BACKS TO THE WALL

1 Bewsher, p. 262.

2 Derby to Haig, 12 Dec. 1917, 27–2, DP.

3 Derby to Haig, 12 Dec. 1917, 27–2, DP.

4 Derby to Haig, 4 Jan. 1918, 27–2, DP.

5 Simpson (2008), pp. 203–6. I am grateful to Mr Paul Harris, Ph.D. candidate at King's College London, for sharing his research on Lawrence with me.

6 See Millman (2001), pp. 4, 13.

7 DHMsD 9 Jan. 1918. Haig held these views until the eve of the German attack: DHMsD 18 Mar. 1918. For the intelligence background, see Beach, p. 247.

8 See Hull, especially chapter 12.

9 Derby to Haig, 14 Jan. 1918 (not sent), 27/2, DP.

10 For projected infrastructure in the salient, see MGGS Second Army, 'Organization of Army Front . . .' 18 November 1918, 7/15, Montgomery-Massingberd Papers, LHCMA.; Turner p. 297. I owe this reference to Michael LoCicero.

11 French (1996), p. 87.

12 DHMsD 25 Jan. 1918.

13 French (1996), pp. 90–3.

14 Haig's marginal comment on 'Extension of British Front', paper by H.H. Wilson, 1 Jan. 1918, WO 158/58.

15 OH 1918 I, p. 64; Croft, pp. 96–7.

16 Amery (1953), pp. 131, 133, 139; DHMsD 14 Jan. 1918.

17 Beach, pp. 244–5.

18 DHMsD 18 May, 7 Sept. 1917; Griffiths, pp. 54–7.

19 Clive diary, 15 Nov. 1917, Clive II/3, G.S. Clive papers, LHCMA, quoted in Sheffield (2005), p. 49.

20 Stephenson diary 5 Nov. 1917, in Taylor, p. 165.

21 DHMsD 1 Nov. 1917.

22 French (1995), pp. 156–8; Derby to Haig, 29 Oct. 1917, 27–2, DP.

23 French (1995), p. 162.

24 French (1995), p. 164.

25 Griffiths, p. 61.

26 Repington (1920) II, p. 222 (6 Feb.).

27 DHMsD 12 Feb. 1918.

28 *Proceedings of the Army Council, 4 Feb. 1918*, 27/11, DP; Haig to SWC, OAD 770, 2 Mar. 1918, WO 158/48.

29 DHMsD 24 Feb., 2 Mar. 1918; Griffiths, pp. 57–8p.

30 Milner to Lloyd George 14 Mar. 1918, Parlimentary Archives, LG-F-38, LGP.

31 Repington (1920) II p. 222 (6 Feb 1918).

32 Woodward (1998), p. 197–201; Terraine (1963), pp. 404–8.

33 Haig to Lady Haig, 4 Feb.1918; Millman (2001), pp. 121–2; Strachan (1997), p. 138.

34 Strachan (1997), p. 138; DHMsD 11 Feb.1918.

35 Jeffery (1985), p. 21.

36 Haig to Kiggell, 4 Jan. 1918, KIGGELL 1/57, KP.

37 French (1995), p. 223.

38 Haig to Kiggell, 8 Jan. 1918, KIGGELL 1/57, KP.

39 DHMsD 2 Mar. 1918 (emphasis added).

40 'Record of a Conference . . . 2 Mar. 1918', 3 Mar. 1918, AWM 45 32/28.

41 DHMsD 27 Feb. 1918.

42 DHMsD 28 Feb., 1 Mar. 1918; Haig to Lady Haig, 28 Feb. 1918.

43 French (1995), p. 223.

44 Gough to GHQ, 1 Feb. 1918, OH 1918 I, Appx 11, pp. 45–7.

45 Quoted in Farrar-Hockley (1975), pp. 264–5.

46 Quoted in Farrar-Hockley (1975), p. 260.

47 Gough (1954), p. 151.

48 DHMsD 17 Mar. 1918.

49 DHMsD 19, 20 Mar. 1918.

50 Middlebrook (1978), pp. 328–9.

51 Quoted in Sparrow, p. 14.

52 Charteris (1931), p. 291.

53 DHMsD 21 Mar. 1918; Haig to Lady Haig, 21 Mar 1918.

54 DHMsD 21 Mar. 1918.

55 DHMsD 22 Mar. 1918; Haig to Lady Haig, 22 Mar. 1918; Charteris (1931), p. 291.

56 Gough (1931), p. 253; DHMsD and DHTsD 23 Mar. 1918; Haig to Lady Haig, 23 Mar. 1918.

57 DHMsD 23 Mar. 1918.

58 Middlebrook (1978) p.277; 'Procès verbal of conference . . . 23 Mar. 1918', OAD 786, WO 256/28.

59 DHMsD 23 Mar. 1918 (in the TS Haig softened his language but the Ms undoubtedly reflects the alarm he felt at the time).

60 GHQ to Third and Fifth Armies, GHQ Order No. 784, 23 Mar. 1918, OH 1918 I, Appx. 26, p. 142.

61 DHMsD 24 Mar. 1918; Zabecki (2006), pp. 84–6.

62 This is the argument in Griffiths, p. 66, but it is weakened slightly by the fact that he

relies on Blake's edition of Haig's Ts diaries, which reproduces material that does not appear in the original entry for 23 March 1918.

63 Colonel Herbillon quoted in Griffiths, pp. 65–6.
64 DHMsD 24 Mar. 1918.
65 Quoted in OH 1918 I, pp. 48–50.
66 DHTsD 24 Mar. 1918.
67 Greenhalgh (2004), p. 814. See also Haig's correspondence with Pétain and Lawrence on this matter in 1920, HP/216h, 228a and Lawrence papers, Acc. 3678, No.7, NLS.
68 Travers (1992), pp. 66–8 ; Greenhalgh (2004), p. 817. See also Høiback, p. 56.
69 Greenhalgh (2004), pp. 817–18; Høiback, pp. 54–5.
70 Travers (1992), p. 54.
71 DHMsD 24 Mar. 1918; OH 1918 I, p. 427.
72 Travers (1992), p. 66–70; Haig to Weygand, 25 Mar. 1918, WO 256/28.
73 Herbillon diary, 24 Mar. 1918, quoted in Griffiths, pp. 66–7; Doughty, p. 435.
74 The idea of a basic misunderstanding is supported by the evidence of a French officer, Pierre Malleterre; see Greenhalgh (2004), 'Myth and Memory', p. 793.
75 Wilson diary, 25 Mar. 1918, WP.
76 e.g. Griffiths, Pétain, p. 69.
77 Wilson diary, 25, 26 Mar. 1918; Neiberg (2003), pp. 49, 54.
78 I.M. Hedley diary, 4 Apr. 1918, 96/7/1, IWM.
79 The US entered the war in April 1917, and by Spring 1918 American forces were arriving on the Western Front.
80 C. Headlam diary 22 Feb. 1923, in Beach (2010), p. 147.
81 Edmonds, p. 294.
82 Foch's note is reproduced in OH 1918 II, p. 75.
83 DHMsD 5 Apr. 1918.
84 DHMsD 4 Apr. 1918.
85 DHMsD 3 Apr. 1918. The SWC rapidly became irrelevant: Derby diary, 12 July 1918, in Dutton (2001), p. 96.
86 DHMsD 29 Mar. 1918.
87 Repington (1920) II, p. 357 (27 Mar. 1918).
88 Derby to Haig, 4 Apr. 1918, 27/2, DP. Even before the German offensive, Derby had tried to persuade Haig to remove Gough: Derby to Haig, 5 Mar. 1918, 2, DP.
89 Haig to Derby, 6 Apr. 1918, 27/2, DP.
90 DHMsD 29 Mar. 1918.
91 Roskill, (1970), pp. 484–5.
92 Wilson diary, 8 Apr. 1918, WP; Hankey diary, 8 Aug. 1918, HNKY/5, HyP.
93 Haig to Lady Haig, 11 May 1918; DHMsD 20 May 1918.
94 Zabecki, pp. 189, 317; DHMsD 8 Apr. 1918.
95 Kincaid-Smith, pp. 193–4.
96 'First Army Order No.204,' in OH 1918 II, Appx. 6, p. 509.
97 DHMsD 10 Apr. 1918; Foch to Haig, 10 Apr. 1918, OH 1918 II, Appx. 7, p. 509.
98 Zabecki, p. 85.
99 DHMsD 11 Apr. 1918; OH 1918 II, pp. 246–8; Beach, p. 256.

100 OH 1918 II, Appx. 10, p. 512.
101 Connelly, pp. 59–61.
102 Heavy Gunner, p. 12; Gale, p. 44.
103 Sheffield (2001), pp. 32–40.
104 Passingham (2008), p. 94.
105 DHMsD 12 Apr. 1918.
106 Harington (1935), p. 161; DHMsD 13, 26, Apr. 1918. In his orders to withdraw, Harington was at pains to point out that Plumer's decision was 'based solely on the necessity of economising on troops': 'Second Army Op. Order No. 19', 14 Apr. 1918, OH 1918 II, Appx. 11, p. 513.
107 DHMsD 14 Apr. 1918.
108 OH 1918 II, p. 315.
109 Haig to Duncan, 16 Apr. 1918, in DeGroot (1997), p. 403.
110 DHMsD 17 May 1918; RD 17 May 1918, RWLN 1, RwP.
111 *Statistics*, p. 267.
112 DHMsD 8 May 1918.
113 Molineux, pp.10, 13, 36, 39, 57, 62. I am indebted to this important work.
114 Geddes, p. 37.
115 Baynes (1995), pp. 209–10; DHMsD 24 June 1918.
116 'Summary of Opening Remarks by I.G.T.', 23 July 1918, quoted in Geddes, p. 41.
117 Lecture, 30 Oct. 1918, quoted in Molineux, p. 15.
118 DHMsD 19 Apr. 1918.
119 DHMsD 27 Apr. 1918.
120 DHMsD 1 May 1918.
121 DHMsD 2 May 1918.
122 See untitled paper of 11 May 1918, WO 158/20.
123 DHMsD 29, 31 May, 4 June 1918.
124 OH 1918 III, p. 167.
125 Maurice, N., p. 98.
126 Derby to Lloyd George, 10 May 1918, 28/7/7, DP; DHMsD 7 May 1918; Haig to Lady Haig, 11 May 1918.
127 Maurice, N., pp. 132, 206; Strachan (1997), pp. 135, 142.
128 DHMsD 21 June 1918; Derby diary, 1 July 1918, in Dutton (2001), p. 78.
129 DHMsD 9 June 1918.
130 OH 1918 III, pp. 223–5.
131 'General Directive No.4, 1 July 1918', in OH 1918 III, p. 218; Haig to Foch, 14 July 1918, WO 158/29.
132 DHMsD 15 July 1918; Wilson diary, 15 July 1918, WP.
133 DHMsD 17 July 1918; OH 1918 III, pp. 236–7; Wilson diary, 19 July 1918.

CHAPTER 10: VICTORY

1 Best (2005), pp. 80–87; Prior and Wilson (1992), p. 311.
2 Esher journal, 14 July 1918, ESHR 2–21, EP; DHMsD 4 July 1918; SS 218, *Operations By the Australian Corps . . . 4th of July, 1918*, p.10. See also Pedersen (1992), p. 232.

3 '8th August, 1918', lecture by Montgomery-Massingberd (1929), MMP; DHMsD 5
   July 1918.
4 Haig to Lady Haig, 19 July 1918; DHMsD 21, 23 July 1918.
5 Montgomery (1920), p. 18; Bean VI, p. 466; RD, 16 July 1918, RWLN 1, RwP.
6 DHMsD 28 July 1918.
7 Sassoon to Esher, 12 Aug. 1918, ESHR 4–10, EP.
8 DHMsD 24 July 1918; Haig to Wilson, 24 Jul. 1918, HHW 2/7B/3, WP.
9 'British Military Policy 1918–1919', 25 July 1918, OH 1918 IV, appx. V, pp. 527–49.
   See also Wilson diary, 31 July 1918, WP.
10 DHMsD 29 July 1918; Lawrence to Third and Fourth Armies and Cavalry Corps, 6
    July 1918, WO 95/437.
11 Headlam to wife, 2 Aug. 1918, in Beach (2010), p. 210. Boff (2010) confirms that
    standardised doctrine was only patchily applied across the BEF in 1918.
12 RD, 24 May 1918, RWLN 1/11, RwP; Wise (1999), p. 24.
13 '8th August 1918', MMP; Badsey (2008), p. 295.
14 R.M. Luckock, 'Brief account . . . of Battle of Amiens'; C.E.D. Budworth, 'Fourth
    Army Artillery in the Battle of Amiens', 26 Aug. 1918; both in MMP.
15 'Fourth Army General Staff Instructions . . . 4 August 1918', OH 1918 IV, appx. V, p.
    558.
16 Lawrence to Third and Fourth Armies and Cavalry Corps, OAD 99, 6 July 1918,
    WO95/437, appx. 1; '8th August 1918', MMP; Kenyon, p. 246.
17 RD, 28 July 1918, RWLN 1/11, RwP; Messenger (2008), pp. 37–8; OH 1918 IV, pp.
    29–30.
18 See for instance Prior and Wilson (1992), pp. 305–6. Curiously, they neglect to
    mention Foch's role in expanding the attack, giving the erroneous impression that
    the change was entirely at Haig's behest.
19 'GHQ Operation Orders' 29 July, 5 Aug. 1918 [emphasis added], WO 95/437,
    appx. 1.
20 Kenyon, p. 247.
21 RD, 5 Aug. 1918, RWLN 1/11, RwP.
22 DHMsD 5 Aug. 1918. Haig's urgings were reflected in Cavalry Corps' orders:
    Kenyon, p. 247.
23 DHMsD 13 Aug. 1918. Haig pointed out some things that could have been
    improved, but he did not criticise the cavalry for failing to reach Ham.
24 S.S. Butler memoir, PP/MCR/107, IWM.
25 DHMsD 6, 7 Aug. 1918.
26 Wise (1999), pp. 23–4.
27 Budworth, 'Fourth Army Artillery in the Battle of Amiens', 26 Aug. 1918, MMP;
    Prior and Wilson (1992), pp. 313–15.
28 DHTsD 8 Aug. 1918; the Ms diary has a slightly different version.
29 Messenger (2008), p. 230.
30 DHMsD 13 Aug. 1918.
31 DHMsD 8 Aug. 1918; Haig to Lady Haig, 8 Aug. 1918.
32 Wise (1999), 'Australians and Canadians', pp. 16–17; Harris and Barr, pp. 95–7.
33 DHTsD, 10 Aug. 1918. The fuller TS diary entry is to be preferred, as it is supported

by a slightly garbled account in Rawlinson's diary for 10 Aug. 1918, RWLN 1/11; 'GHQ Operation Order, OAD 900/22' 10 Aug. 1918, OH 1918 IV, appx. XIV, p. 580.

34 OH 1918 IV, pp. 135–6.

35 As Prior and Wilson (1992), p. 335, point out. However, in Maurice, p. 229, there is an extract from Rawlinson's diary that fairly closely follows the manuscript version in Churchill College, Cambridge, but has the sentence 'I met D.H. at Currie's headquarters' inserted. The plot thickens . . .

36 Montgomery to Davidson, telephone conversation, 1 Aug. 1918, AWM 5/56; 'Fourth Army Operation Orders' 11 Aug. 1918, OH 1918 IV, appx. XVI, p. 582; Montgomery, p. 63.

37 DHMsD 11 Aug. 1918; 'Maréchal Foch's Instruction of 12th August 1918', OH 1918 IV, appx. XVII, pp. 583–4.

38 Prior and Wilson (1992), p. 334.

39 DHMsD 11, 12 Aug. 1918; Lawrence to Third Army, OAD 907, 13 Aug. 1918, AWM 51/56; Lawrence to Fourth Army, OAD 900/23, 12 Aug. 1918, WO 158/241.

40 RD diary, 14 Aug. 1918, RWLN 1/11, RP; DHMsD 14 Aug. 1918; Haig to Foch, 14 Aug. 1918, OAD 900/25, WO 158/29.

41 DHMsD 15 Aug. 1918; Foch to Haig, 15 Aug. 1918, quoted in OH 1918 IV, p. 170.

42 Lawrence to First Army, 14 Aug. 1918, OAD 907/1, WO 58/191; Lawrence to Third Army, 15 Aug. 1918, WO 158/311.

43 Haig to Wilson, 15 Aug. 1918, HHW 2/7B/5, WP.

44 OH 1918 IV, pp.181 184: Williams J., p. 242; Harris and Barr, p. 122.

45 OH 1918 IV, pp.182–6; DHMsD 19 Aug. 1918; Lawrence to Byng, OAD 907/7, 20 Aug. 1918, AWM 51/56.

46 Quoted in OH 1918 IV, p. 173.

47 'Summary of Operations of Third Army . . . 21st August to 30th September . . .' WO 95/372.

48 DHMsD 21 Aug. 1918.

49 DHMsD 21 Aug. 1918; OH 1918 IV, p. 220.

50 Third Army orders 73/40, 21 Aug. 1918, WO 95/372; OH 1918 IV, p. 196; Harris and Barr, p. 132.

51 DHMsD 22 Aug. 1918; OH 1918 IV, pp. 206–7.

52 Haig's telegram, OAD 911, 22 Aug., 1918, OH 1918 IV, appx. XX, pp. 587–8.

53 Lawrence to Army Commanders *et al.*, OAD 912, 23 Aug. 1918, WO 95/372. See also Palazzo, pp. 23–4.

54 Simkins (1999), pp. 149–50.

55 Derby diary, 23 Aug. 1918, in Dutton (2001), p. 164.

56 See also Harris and Barr, pp. 146–7. My analysis differs from theirs in some important respects.

57 Edmonds, pp. 352–3.

58 Messenger (2008).

59 McCarthy (2004), pp. 188–91; Watson, chapter 6; Stephenson S., pp. 8–11, chapter 1.

60 Schreiber, p. 72.

61 'Future Policy of Operations' 25 Aug. 1918, quoted in Schreiber, p. 83.

62 Lawrence to Byng, OAD 907/12, 24 Aug. 1918, AWM 51/56.

63 DHMsD 25 Aug. 1918.

64 Schreiber, p. 74; DHMsD 25 Aug. 1918.

65 Haig to Lady Haig, 27 Aug. 1918.

66 Lawrence to First, Third, Fourth Armies, OAD 907/16, 29 Aug. 1918 WO 158/241.

67 Simpson, pp. 157, 160, 175; McCarthy (2004), p. 191.

68 Stanley, pp.60–3, 125–6; Monash, pp.166–7; RD, 31 Aug. 1918, RWLN 1/11, RwP.

69 Stanley, pp. 83–4, 171, 252–4, revises previous accounts of the battle in many important ways. He is persuasive that the received wisdom on Mont St Quentin owes much to Monash's myth-making, which inflated Monash's own role in the battle.

70 OH 1918 IV, p. 361; RD, 30 Aug. 1918, RWLN 1/11, RwP.

71 DHMsD 31 Aug. 1918; Harris and Barr, p. 167; Haig to Plumer, 1 Sept. 1918, HP/131.

72 Derby to Balfour, 1 Sept. 1918, in Dutton (2001), p. 181.

73 DHMsD 27 Aug. 1918.

74 Yockelson, p. 92.

75 Haig to Pershing, 27 Aug. 1918, in Sheffield and Bourne, p. 451; Yockelson, p. 94.

76 DHMsD 31 Aug. 1918.

77 DHMsD 31 Aug., 1 Sept. 1918.

78 Haig to Esher, 25 Sept. 1918, ESHR 4–10, EP.

79 DHTsD 1 Sept. 1918 (this passage does not appear in the Ms diary, but it echoes some earlier comments noted by Haig on a 3 August telegram from Wilson and repeats verbatim Haig's comments written on Wilson's telegram); Haig to Wilson, 1 Sept.1918, HHW 2/7B/11, WP.

80 Haig to Foch, 27 Aug. 1918; Foch to Haig, 28 Aug. 1918; 'Record of a meeting . . . 29 Aug. 1918', all in WO 158/29.

81 Simkins (1991), p. 210.

82 DHMsD 4 Sept. 1918.

83 DHMsD 2 Sept. 1918.

84 Lawrence to Armies, OAD 915, 3 Sept. 1918, AWM 51/56.

85 DHMsD 3 Sept. 1918.

86 Edmonds, p. 358; OH 1918 IV, pp. 467–8; Harris and Barr, p. 170.

87 Lawrence to Horne, Kavanagh and others, OAD 917, 7 Sept. 1918, AWM 51/56.

88 Lawrence to Armies, OAD 915/2, 8 Sept. 1918, AWM 51/56; Byng to Lawrence, 9 Sept. 1918, WO 158/311; Williams, J., p. 248.

89 DHMsD 3 Sept. 1918.

90 Horne to Lawrence 11 Sept. 1918, WO 158/311; Rawlinson to Lawrence, 11 Sept 1918, WO 158/191.

91 DHMsD 4 Sept. 1918; Falls (1939), p. 159.

92 DHMsD 9 Sept. 1918.

93 Lawrence to Plumer, OAD 916, 5 Sept. 1918, AWM 51/56; DHMsD 5, 9 Sept. 1918.

94 'Record of a meeting . . . between . . . Plumer and . . . the CGS' 13 Sept. 1918, AWM 51/56.

95 DHMsD 21 Sept. 1918; Sassoon to Esher, 14 Sept. 1914, ESHR 4–10, EP.

96 Haig to Stamfordham, 20 Sept. 1918, in Sheffield and Bourne, pp. 462–3.

97 DHMsD 6, 8 Sept. 1918.

98 DHMsD 10 Dept. 1918.

99 Derby diary, 18 Sept. 1918, in Dutton (2001), p. 210.

100 DHMsD 10, 21 Sept. 1918; Wilson diary, 23 Sept. 1918, WP.

101 Falls (1939), p. 161.

102 DHMsD 15, 18 Sept. 1918.

103 DHMsD 15 Sept. 1918.

104 Harris and Barr, pp. 178–9, 320, for a rebuttal of criticisms of III Corps.

105 Repington (1920) II, p. 525 (17 May 1919).

106 Wilson to Haig, 19 Sept. 1918, in Sheffield and Bourne, p. 462; Haig to Wilson, 20 Sept. 1918, HHW 2/7B/16, WP.

107 Haig to Esher, 25 Sept. 1918, ESHR 4–10, EP.

108 DHMsD 21 Sept. 1918.

109 DHMsD 21 Sept. 1918. See Also Lawrence to Rawlinson, OAD 926/4, 25 Sept. 1918, AWM 51/56. The objectives of the various Armies had already been assigned in a GHQ directive of 22 September, quoted in OH 1918 V, pp. 14–15.

110 DHMsD 26 Sept. 1918.

111 Bourne, (2001), p. 35; DHMsD 26 Sept. 1918.

112 OH 1918 V, pp. 15–29, 36–7, 45; Williams, J., p.250.

113 DHMsD 26 September 1918.

114 50th Division, 'Narrative of Operations 18 Oct. 1918', MMP.

115 Kenyon, p. 264.

116 Lawrence to Fourth Army, OAD 928, 29 Sept. 1918, WO 158/242 .

117 DHMsD 17 Sept. 1918; Kenyon, p. 263; Home diary 16, 18 Sept. 1918, in Briscoe, p. 183.

118 Jack diary, 29 Sept. 1918 in Terraine (2000), p. 274.

119 DHMsD 28 Sept. 1918.

120 'Fourth Army Operation Order 22 Sept. 1918' in OH 1918 V, appx. VI, p. 638.

121 Repington (1920) II, p. 462 (9 Oct. 1918); '137th Brigade . . . Attack at Bellenglise', MMP.

122 DHMsD 29 Sept.1918.

123 OH 1918 V, p. 142.

124 DHMsD Oct. 1918; OH 1918 V, p. 161.

125 Schreiber, pp.104–7.

126 Williams, J., pp. 250–1.

127 Haig to Churchill, 3 Oct. 1918, in Sheffield and Bourne, pp. 468–9. The defaced memo on 'Munitions Policy' is in HP/131.

128 Sassoon to Esher, 2 Oct. 1918; Esher to Hankey, 4 Oct. 1918; both in ESHR 4–10, EP.

129 DHMsD 1 Oct. 1918.

130 DHMsD 5 Oct. 1918.

131 OH 1918 V p. 186.

132 DHMsD 1 Oct. 1918.

133 Coop, pp. 139–40; DHMsD 2 Oct. 1918.

134 Astore and Showalter, p. 69.

135 DHMsD 6 Oct. 1918.

136 Lawrence to Armies, 5 Oct. 1918, in OH 1918 V, pp. 172–3.

137 DHMsD 8 Oct. 1918; 'Canadian Cavalry Brigade Narrative of Operations 8–10 Oct. 1918', MMP; OH 1918 V, pp.195, 197, 211.

138 'Canadian Cavalry Brigade Narrative of Operations 8–10 Oct. 1918', MMP, Kenyon, pp. 276–8.

139 'Operations of 3rd Cavalry Division, 9 Oct. 1918', MMP.

140 Haig to Foch, 9 Oct. 1918, OAD 934, WO 158/29; DHMsD 10 Oct. 1918; Foch's *Directive* 10 Oct. 1918, in OH 1918 V, p. 233.

141 Haig to Lady Haig, 11 Oct. 1918; Terraine, (1986), pp. 200–01.

142 DHMsD 10 Oct. 1918.

143 OH 1918 V, pp.293–4; Ludendorff II, p.741.

144 Birdwood, p. 328.

145 For a flavour of the difficulties, see 'Bridging of the River Selle in connection with the operations of 17th November 1918' [by 50th Div.], 26 Oct. 1918, MMP.

146 OH 1918 V, p. 315.

147 DHMsD 17 Oct. 1917.

148 Beach, pp. 280–1.

149 DHMsD 25 Oct. 1918.

150 DHMsD 22 Jul. 1917, 25 Oct 1918.

151 i.e. President Wilson (they were not actually related).

152 DHMsD 2 Jan. 1918; Wilson to Esher, 9 Nov. 1918, ESHR 4–10, EP; Wilson diary, 15 Oct. 1918, WP. See also Horne to wife 2 Nov. 1918 in Robbins (2009), p. 273.

153 DHTsD 19 Oct. 1918.

154 Lowry, pp. 49, 55–6. See this source more generally for a detailed discussion of the formulation of the armistice terms.

155 DHMsD 24 Oct. 1918; Haig to Foch, 27 Oct. 1918, HP/132.

156 Haig to Foch, 25 Oct. 1918, WO 158/29; House diary, 25 Oct. 1918 in Seymour, IV, p. 115; DHMsD 25 Oct., 1918; Lowry, pp. 67–71.

157 Lawrence to Armies, OAD 948, 29 Oct. 1918, WO 158/311; OH 1918 V, p. 463.

158 McNaughton, p. 37. McNaughton was GOC Canadian Corps Heavy Artillery.

159 DHMsD 4 Nov. 1918.

160 Telegram from Foch, 9 Nov. 1918, WO 158/30.

161 DHMsD 11 Nov. 1918.

162 Bickersteth diary, [12 Nov. 1918] in Bickersteth, p. 296.

163 Terraine (1963), p. 482; Travers (1994), pp. 220, 237; Travers (1992), p. 175.

164 Philpott (2000), pp. 38–53; Neiberg (2003), p. 65.

165 Millman, p. 274.

166 Neiberg (2008), pp. 187–9; Doughty, p. 504.

167 Prior and Wilson (1992), p. 305; Simkins (1999), pp. 94, 97; Todman (2004), pp. 63–4.

168 Bessel, pp. 84–5; Evans, p. 61.

169 Quoted in Sheffield (2001), p. 224.

Chapter 11: Veteran's Champion – and Potential Dictator?

1 Sassoon to Esher, 26 Dec.1918, ESHR 4/0, EP.

2 Todman (2005), p. 73. See also Todman (2003), p. 1088–90.

3 Adye, p. 293.

4 Elton, p. 230.

5 DHMsD 19 Dec. 1918.

6 Note by Haig, 16 Feb. 1919, Box 13, SP.

7 Gilbert (1990), pp. 192–3; Rothstein, pp. 69–75.

8 Haig's report and Churchill's comments are in WO32/5241; Haig to WO, 14 Dec. 1918, HP/220.

9 DHTsD 15 Jan. 1919; Haig to Esher, 20 Jan 1919, EHSR 4-11, EP.

10 DH TsD, 26 Jan. 1919; Macmillan, pp. 181–5.

11 DH TsD 12, 19 Feb. 1919.

12 Haig to Wilson, 14 Feb. 1919, HHW 2/89/17, WP; DHTsD 17, 20, 21 Jan. 1919; Jeffery (2006), p. 235.

13 Haig to Wilson, 21 Mar. 1919, HHW 2/89/21; Haig to Wilson, 8 Apr. 1919, HHW 2/89/25, WP.

14 Haig's speech at 17th Lancers' memorial, 22 May 1922, HP/235a.

15 Pugh (2008), p. 13.

16 Jeffrey (1984), p. 12.

17 'Strike Papers' no.68, 15 Oct. 1919, and no. 69, 16 Oct. 1919, 71/13/2, BP.

18 Haig to WO, 17 Oct. 1919, WO 32/5467; The Times, 17 Oct. 1919, p. 9.

19 Scotsman, 21 July 1919, p. 4; www.douglasmania.com; Todman (2003), p. 1099; The Times, 2 Jan. 2007; www.roll-of-honour.org.uk/Hell_Ships/Kachidoki_Maru/html/d.htm.

20 Scotsman 12 May 1919, p. 6; Haig to Esher, 22 Apr. 1919, ESHR 4-11, EP; The Times, 7 May 1919, p. 7.

21 Haig to Esher, 20 May 1919, ESHR 4-11, EP. See also Haig to Sassoon, 19 May 1919, Box 13, SP; The Times 30 May 1919, p. 9.

22 Haig to Sassoon, 11 May 1919, Box 13, SP; Haig (1919).

23 The Times 13 June 1919, p. 6.

24 Haig to Esher, 17 June 1919, EHSR 4- 11, EP.

25 For an academic example, see A.J. Bacevich, 'Preserving the well-bred horse', in The National Interest (Fall, 1994) ('Haig's . . . silliness'); for a popular example, see http://www.diggerhistory.info/pages-leaders/ww1/haig.htm, accessed 24 April 2007 ('There is little doubt that Haig was an idiot').

26 The Times, 5 June 1925, p. 8.

27 Anglesey (1997), p. 287.

28 'Cavalry Notes', 14 Dec. 1927, HP/346.

29 'Cavalry Notes', 14 Dec. 1927, HP/346.

30 Cavalry Training Volume II (War) 1929, pp. 3, 4.

31 Liddell Hart I, p. 234. Many thanks to Bryn Hammond for his help on this point.

32 ffrench-Blake, pp. 4–5, 20–1.

33 DHMsD, 31 Mar. 1917.

34 Wootton, p. 15; Barr (2005), pp.13, 17.

35 *The Times*, 5 July 1919, p. 9.

36 *The Times*, 18 July 1919, p. 11.

37 Barr (2005), p. 37; Haig to Curle, 7 June 1922, Curle Papers, Acc. 9431, NLS; *The Times*, 14 Jan. 1935, p. 7.

38 Worthington-Evans to Lloyd George, 24 Feb. 1919, Parliamentary Archives, LG-F-16-3-1, LGP; Worthington-Evans to Lloyd George, 25 Feb.,1919, Parlimentary Archives, LG-F-16-3-2, LGP.

39 *The Times*, 13 June 1919, p. 6.

40 *The Times*, 2 July 1919, p. 7.

41 *The Times*, 12 July 1919, p. 9.

42 *The Times*, 9 July1919, p.11, 20 Oct. 1919, p. 14.

43 See Ash, B.

44 *The Times*, 12 July 1919, p. 9, 1 Dec. 1920, p. 9.

45 Barr and Sheffield, p. 229.

46 Wootton, p. 16.

47 Haig to Baird, 29 Aug. 1919, in Barr (2005), p. 17.

48 *The Times*, 29 Jan 1920, p. 12, 2 Feb. 1920, p. 12, 3 Feb. 1920, p. 9. Technically, field marshals remained on the active list.

49 Rose, p. 350.

50 Duff Cooper, (1936), p. 413; Blake, p. 363.

51 Wootton, pp. 14–15; Barr (2005), pp. 17–18.

52 *The Times*, 16 Aug. 1920, p. 12.

53 This account of the formation of the Legion is based upon Wootton, and Barr (2005).

54 For his speech to the Comrades, see *The Times*, 28 Feb. 1919, p. 11.

55 24 Nov. 1920, VC Corr. , XII 21 (3), UAC.

56 Haig to P. Giles, 21 Aug. 1920, VC Corr., XII 21 (1), UAC.

57 *The Times*, 10 Aug. 1920, p. 11, 16 Oct.1920, p. 11, 11 Nov. 1918, p. 15.

58 Wootton, pp. 38–40; Barr (2005), pp. 96–7; *The Times*, 12 Nov. 1921, p. 6.

59 *BLJ*, July 1927, p. 5.

60 *BLJ*, July 1922, p. 6.

61 *BLJ*, July 1925, p. 4.

62 *BLJ*, July 1922, p. 9.

63 *Daily Express* article reproduced in *BLJ* July 1927, p. 11.

64 Wootton, p. 66.

65 *The Times*, 14 Dec. 1926, p. 11.

66 *BLJ*, July 1927, p. 5 (emphasis added).

67 Wootton, p. 90; Crosfield to Haig, 9 Nov. 1927, HP/227j.

68 Pugh (2006), p. 39.

69 Danchev (2005), p.197.

70 Barr (2005), pp. 132–3.

71 Barr and Sheffield, pp. 232–3; Wootton, p. 110.

72 *The Times*, 27 July 1925, p. 11; Haig to Boraston, 11 June 1925, BP.

73 Haig, Lady, p. 309.

74 *Time*, 27 Jul. 1925.

75 *The Times*, 21 Nov. 1925, p. 14.

76 *The Times*, 4 Aug. 1927, p. 11; p. 9; *The Times*, 10 Oct.1927, p .9.

77 Lloyd, D., p. 82.

78 Winter, J. (2006), p. 143.

79 Haig to Boraston, 4 Oct. 1926, BP; Haig to Crosfield, 28 May 1922, HP/227a.

80 *The Times*, 5 May 1924, p. 13.

81 *The Times*, 4 July 1922, p. 8; Gaffney, pp. 38, 104.

82 *The Times*, 23 July 1927, p. 12.

83 *The Times*, 22 Oct. 1921, p. 5.

84 *The Times*, 2 June 1924, p. 7.

85 *The Times*, 8 June 1925, p. 13.

86 King, p. 195.

87 Haig's speech in Wylly, pp. 50–1.

88 *The Times*, 27 Jan. 1922, p .6.

89 *The Times*, 11 June 1919, p. 10, 17 Oct. 1919, p. 9.

90 Haig to Maurice, 11 Jan 1923, Maurice 3/5/142, Maurice papers, LHCMA.

91 Rose, p. 314.

92 Haig to Lady Haig, 23 July 1916.

93 Boraston, pp. 321–7.

94 Sheffield (2004).

95 Haig to Strachey, 11 Aug. 1919, Parlimentary Archives, STR/8/1/7, Strachey papers, HLRO.

96 A copy is in HP/213a.

97 Haig to Boraston, 23 June 1921, 71/13/3, BP.

98 *Sunday Pictorial*, 3 Dec. 1922.

99 Boraston and Dewar I, p. 161; French (1985), p. 958; *Daily Mirror*, 29 Nov. 1922; Todman (2003), p.,1094.

100 French (1986), pp. 58–63; Green, pp. 201–5.

101 What follows is indebted to Prior (1983).

102 Churchill to Haig, 20 Nov. 1926; Churchill to Beaverbrook, 23 Nov. 1926, both in Gilbert (1979), pp. 884–5.

103 Haig to Boraston, 22 Apr. 1927, 71/13/1, BP; Haig to Churchill, 13 Mar. 1927, quoted in prior (1983) p. 263.

104 Blake, p. 13.

105 Haig, Lady, p. 316.

106 *British Legion Journal Earl Haig Memorial Number* (Mar. 1928), p. 284; Haig, Lady, p. 319.

107 Haig, Lady, p. 31.

108 Quoted in Todman (2003), pp. 1086–8, 1103; Duff Cooper (1936), pp. 433–4.

109 Todman (2003), pp. 1084–8.

CHAPTER 12: HAIG THE SOLDIER: AN ASSESSMENT

1 Ellison, 'Notes on Certain Letters . . .', 11 Sept. 1928, HP/40q.

2 Quoted in McPherson, p. 82.

3 The link between Grant and Haig is powerfully made in Terraine (1980), pp. 50–5.

4 Sheffield and Jordan, p. 264.

5 Fuller Journal, 5 Feb. 1918, 'Relative to the . . . Tank Corps . . .' A1980.18, BTM.
   See also Fuller's comments on Haig to WO, 30 Apr. 1918, BTM; Trythall, p. 60.

6 DHMsD 2 Feb. 1918; Haig to WO, 12 June 1918, copy in Fuller Journal, BTM;
   Harris (1995), p. 166. For Haig's interactions with the Tank Corps, and some
   trenchant criticisms of Fuller, see Harris (1995) especially pp. 128–71.

7 Holden Reid (1987), p. 54.

8 Trythall, p. 74.

9 Hussey (1996b).

10 Farndale, p. 349. For context, see Marble, chapter 9.

11 I. Maxse, 'The 18th Division in the Battle of the Ancre', 69/53/8, Maxse papers,
   IWM; Baynes, pp. 149–58; Philpott (2009) p. 377.

12 Buchan, pp. 185–6; Adam Smith, p.198. Buchan's views reflect an interwar school of
   thought that condemned all First World War generals as intellectually limited.

13 Wiest (2005), p. xiv.

14 For an introduction to some of these issues in the British army of the Second World
   War, see French (2000); Hart, S.; Sheffield (2000a).

15 L.P. Hartley, *The Go-Between* (Penguin, 1958 [1953]), p. 7.

Index